CANADIAN

Women

A HISTORY
SECOND EDITION

Alison Prentice
Paula Bourne
Gail Cuthbert Brandt
Beth Light
Wendy Mitchinson
Naomi Black

HARCOURT
BRACE
CANADA

Harcourt Brace & Company, Canada

Toronto Montreal Fort Worth New York Orlando
Philadelphia San Diego London Sydney Tokyo

Canadian Cataloguing in Publication Data

Main entry under title:

Canadian women : a history

2nd ed.
ISBN 0-7747-3293-8

1. Women—Canada—History.   2. Women—Canada—
Social conditions.   I. Prentice, Alison, 1934–

HQ1453.C35 1996   305.4'0971   C95-930075-9

Publisher: Heather McWhinney
Senior Acquisitions Editor: Christopher Carson
Projects Manager: Liz Radojkovic
Editorial Assistant: Martina van de Velde
Director of Publishing Services: Jean Davies
Editorial Manager: Marcel Chiera
Supervising Editor: Semareh Al-Hillal
Production Editor: Laurel Parsons
Production Manager: Sue-Ann Becker
Production Co-ordinator: Sheila Barry
Copy Editor: Riça Night
Cover and Interior Design: Opus House
Typesetting and Assembly: Compeer Typographic Services Limited
Printing and Binding: Best Book Manufacturers, Inc.

Cover Art: Paraskeva Clark, *Parachute Riggers* (1946–47), oil on linen canvas, 101.7 × 81.4 cm. Reproduced with permission of the painter's family (Clive and Mary Clark) as well as The Canadian War Museum in Ottawa. Transparency provided by The Canadian War Museum.

This book was printed in Canada.

1 2 3 4 5   00 99 98 97 96

To Our Mothers: Elizabeth Fletcher Smith,
Lucy O'Neill, Sadie Cuthbert, Margaret Light,
Frances Mitchinson, and Michal Black.

Preface

Our intention in writing a second edition of *Canadian Women: A History* was to update our account and to respond to the wealth of new material and interpretations that historians of women have produced since our work on the first edition was completed in late 1980s. The task proved more challenging than we had expected. While we knew that much exciting research had been done since our original study went to press, we were still astonished at its depth and variety. We have finally had to accept the impossibility of incorporating all of the new material in our updated study. Indeed, the immense range of regional, ethnic, and racial responses to the fact of womanhood in Canada may always elude capture — at least between the covers of one volume. In addition, the task of incorporating the very recent past proved impossible to accomplish by simply "adding on" to section IV. We decided that this section had to be reorganized, not only so that the challenges of the last few years could be explored but also to make it conform to a principle that, from the beginning, had informed the whole work. Each section, therefore, begins with an examination of women's work and material culture and then moves from these explorations to analyses of women's family lives, public culture, and politics.

From the outset, our publisher agreed that this second edition should be accompanied by a companion volume of essays examining important themes and issues in greater depth than we could accomplish in a work of synthesis. *Canadian Women: A Reader* was thus organized to correspond to the four sections of *Canadian Women: A History* and to complement this text.

ACKNOWLEDGEMENTS

It remains to thank the many people who have helped us in the production of this book: Denyse Baillargeon, Gloria Baylis, Mary Bernard, Henry V. Bishop, David Bourne, Larry S. Bourne, Catherine Briggs, Louise Carbet, Carol Cooper, Christine Donald, Elizabeth Fear, Jo-Anne Fiske, Frieda Forman, Jill Given-King, Mona Gleason, Gail Heideman, Maxine Hermolin, Virginia Herrige, Rusa Jeremic, Alyson King, Ruth Kohn, Jeanette Corbiere Lavell, Mary Macdonald, Kay Macpherson, Lorna Marsden, Susan Milne, Jill Oakes, Vered Pittel, Jim Prentice, Caralee Price, Frances Rooney, Lisa Rosenberg, Sylvia Van Kirk, and Beulah Worrell.

Finally, and once more, we thank our friends and families. As before, they have helped us in more ways than they can ever know. We are in their debt.

A NOTE FROM THE PUBLISHER

Thank you for selecting *Canadian Women: A History*, Second Edition, by Alison Prentice, Paula Bourne, Beth Light, Wendy Mitchinson, Gail Cuthbert Brandt, and Naomi Black. The authors and the publisher have devoted considerable time to the careful development of this book. We appreciate your recognition of this effort and accomplishment.

We want to hear what you think about this edition of *Canadian Women: A History*. Please take a few minutes to complete the stamped reply card at the back of the book. Your comments and suggestions will be valuable to us in the preparation of new editions.

Contents

Introduction

When second-wave feminists began to raise questions about the place of women in Canada, the absence of women from analysis became a challenge to historians. There was a growing awareness that the fact of gender made women's lives profoundly different from the lives of men. Women had an identity and a history, both barely represented in the standard studies. In the context of the women's movement and of a general widening of historical inquiry, Canadian women's history flowered. By the mid-1980s, enough work had accumulated that we could write a general history of women in Canada. Now, in the mid-1990s, new work, new perspectives, and new questions make a more nuanced account possible.

Much that we learn from conventional history remains problematic for the history of women. The very language used has often failed to describe women's experience. A particularly basic and complex set of problems surrounds the word "work." To begin with, the generally accepted census definition of "occupation" omitted much unpaid work that women did — housework, childcare, care of the elderly or the sick, and community service. Even less recognized has been the "reproductive" work women do in the family, both in bearing children and in providing emotional stability and support. These omissions have stemmed directly from the failure to treat unpaid work with the same respect as work for pay. In addition, much of women's paid work has gone unrecorded, from taking in sewing or boarders to doing housework or childcare for others. We have tried to uncover and discuss all of these different kinds of work, and to describe at the same time the intricate connections between them and women's involvement in paid employment in different times and places in Canada.

A second set of problems emerged with the generally accepted definitions of culture and politics. By using the term culture anthropologically, our aim has been to move beyond "high culture" to a concept that encompasses ways of thinking and acting, ways of being in the world and seeing the world. We have also attempted to explore the question of whether or not a separate women's culture has existed at different times, or among various groupings, and how such a culture or cultures might have changed over the years. We have had similar questions about women's politics. Officially excluded from the politics of men during much of Canada's history, Canadian women focussed on diverse and sometimes conflicting goals of their own.

Can women therefore be said to have had a politics separate and distinct from that of men?

If accepted definitions of work, culture, and politics have been problematic, so too have been the periods into which Canadian history has traditionally been organized. Is it appropriate, for the purposes of dividing Canadian women's history into meaningful periods, to select constitutional events such as Confederation? Or would events more directly affecting women's lives, such as the advent of the pill, make better markers? Neither alternative seems genuinely satisfactory, yet this was an issue that we had to resolve in the writing of this text. Books, after all, have to be divided into chapters, however seamless the fabric of life may be in the real world. Since events of all kinds influence the lives of human beings, we have tried to construct a chronology that takes into account the interaction of the technological, economic, and social, as well as the political, religious, and cultural, dimensions of women's experience.

After much discussion, we identified three major turning points in the history of women in Canada. The first is the transition from a pre-industrial to an industrial society in the mid-nineteenth century, symbolized for us by the establishment in the 1840s of a cotton mill in the eastern townships of Quebec. The first corporate industrial venture in Canada, it was the beginning of an industry that was to employ large numbers of women. The second turning point we selected is World War I, which saw the achievement of two major goals of the first wave of the women's movement in Canada: prohibition and suffrage. These successes marked the end of an era: the worlds of the pioneer, the gentlewoman, and even the Victorian lady now receded from sight and gave way to those of the "flapper" and the "working girl." The third turning point chosen is the beginning, during World War II, of the massive entry of married women into the paid labour force. Marriage, which previously transformed the lives of most women, now became a less definite transition, as they worked outside the home for a growing portion of their adult lives.

Inevitably, markers are artificial. They are the more so when it comes to the life of an individual woman, or the lives of whole groups, whose participation has been on the edges of the mainstream. What did the advent of factories, the achievement of prohibition and suffrage, or the movement of married women into the paid labour force mean to women living on Canada's more isolated resource frontiers or on Indian reserves? Did such changes affect the lives of black women, of lesbians, or of poor or immigrant women in the same ways as they affected mainstream women? We have tried to be particularly attentive to those women who are most remote from the centres of political or economic power. For women who do not leave written records (and most do not), this has been hard to do. And even the women who did leave records of their lives wrote from inside worlds that were often very different from ours. Their voices are difficult to hear and often difficult to interpret.

Like all historians, we have had to face the fact of our own cultural, political, and personal biases. There is no such thing as a completely "objective" truth independent of the observers' points of view. It is therefore important to describe our shared perspective. First of all, we all consider ourselves feminists. Our feminism is a point of view that has necessarily affected what we have selected as important and how we have interpreted or reinterpreted the past; it is the reason for this book. There are many definitions and, more important, many versions of feminism. But underlying all is the commitment to increasing women's autonomy and collective power in a world where these have generally been less than men's. A feminist perspective recognizes that women's situation and experience are distinctive. Increasingly, it has been demonstrated that a feminist perspective must also recognize the importance of differences among women deriving from differing experiences of race, class, ethnicity, religion, bodily condition, and sexual orientation. Finally, a feminist perspective insists that women should not be judged inferior by male standards or in comparison with men.

This is not to deny the value of all comparisons. How women have fared, compared to men, must obviously be a central question in women's history. Here we enter a difficult terrain — the question of women's status. A fundamental and related issue has been the character and interpretation of the existence of "separate spheres" for women and men in any given time or place. Whether we are considering Canada's hunting-and-gathering communities or its Victorian households and non-domestic workplaces, we have had to make judgements about how separate the so-called "domestic" (or "private") and "public" spheres really were. How did their separation or non-separation affect the degree of authority men and women exercised over their own lives, as well as in their respective communities? Certainly the nature and meaning of "public" and "private" life have shifted in Canada over the years. It seems clear that much of the work of education, as well as a good deal of economic production, at first took place in what we would now call the domestic or private sphere. These activities were only gradually removed from private life with the emergence of a public world from which women were, in theory, largely excluded. How and why this occurred, and with what results — and how the trend began to be modified — are questions that we try to address in this book.

Also intriguing are the other possible influences on women's authority and ability to control their work and their lives. For example, have women been more in command of their situations when their numbers relative to men were great, or when they were relatively scarce and therefore presumably especially valuable? When large numbers of women married at an early age, or when fewer married, and did so later in their lives? In addition, questions of relative power have to be examined in the context of broader social structures and of prevailing ideologies. Have particular groups of women been devalued or empowered at particular times and places?

We take the position that the material structures of people's lives are the most important among the many factors influencing them. Yet we would not limit such influences to the economic, for we are convinced that women's bodies are an important part of the material bases of their lives. In all cultures, the lives of the childbearing portion of the community will be greatly influenced by the fact of that childbearing, and by the ideologies and practices surrounding it. But biology itself is less simple and more variable than we have been led to believe; for instance, biological clocks respond to factors such as climate and food supply, so that the age of puberty can vary widely from one place or time to another. And, as feminists focussing on the experience of women, we also recognize the power of ideas and feelings, of social and political movements, and of identities other than gender in fixing or altering how people react to the conditions they encounter.

When we consider such issues, we return to economic configurations and material culture. An important component of both is technological change. The technology of birth control has had the most dramatic potential to alter women's lives.

But a host of other technologies have been important as well. From the washing machine to the microchip, how have women initiated or responded to technological transformations, and how have new technologies changed women's daily work? Who was better off: the women of earlier centuries who did little or no laundry, or the modern housewife, who washes at home, often daily, or lugs the family wash to the laundromat? Such questions are perhaps, in the end, impossible to answer.

In Canada, moreover, all questions must also be considered in the context of the country's immense size and diversity. Whether we are talking about the impact of technology or the women's movement itself, multiple perspectives are always needed if we are to get the picture right. Yet, despite much diversity, a major theme of Canadian women's history has been the quest for a unified women's voice. Indeed, our enterprise here assumes that, with all its internal variety, there is a distinctly Canadian women's experience that can be identified. Often faced with enormous difficulties, sometimes treated with the most cruel injustice in communities that were for the most part decidedly patriarchal, Canadian women struggled to survive, to contribute, and to make their lives meaningful. We study their lives because women have been integral to Canada's history. What they were and did made all the difference.

PART ONE

The Founding Mothers: Beginnings to the Mid-Nineteenth Century

Aataentsic, according to the Hurons, was the great mother. It was for her that the earth was created, to provide a safe haven when she fell from the sky and gave birth to humanity. Similar creation stories may be found in most indigenous cultures. Ojibwa elders tell of Spirit Woman, who gave birth to all the birds, animals, and fish of the world, while Blackfoot and Wet'suwet'en women speak of Old Woman. A modern rendering of Nuu'chah'nulth legend tells us of Copper Woman, the awe-inspiring figure who created the first man from the not very promising materials at hand. With her humour as well as her strength, Copper Woman inspired her daughters to heroic feats of survival in an environment that was often hostile and was always challenging.[1]

Our knowledge of powerful mythic figures like Aataentsic, Spirit Woman, Old Woman, and Copper Woman is fragmentary. What about our knowledge of Canada's founding women, the women of our early indigenous and colonial cultures? Certainly, even in the remote worlds of Canada's traditional peoples, tracings of women's lives can be discovered; indeed, archeologists, anthropologists, and historians continue to piece these scraps of evidence together into larger studies that are of absorbing interest. Yet complete agreement on the character or meaning of women's lives in traditional societies remains elusive. First, from the earliest records of Canada's past to the transitional years of the mid-nineteenth century is an immensely long time. Second, we are considering a great many different peoples under the heading of "founding cultures." Third, as with all history, new ideas and interpretations continue to challenge older ones.

Consider the aboriginal cultures that Europeans encountered when they first came to the northern parts of North America. In the fifteenth and sixteenth centuries, the rich fisheries of the east and west coasts supported a great number of indigenous societies, some of them very populous, while in the region that was to become Ontario, agriculture sustained as many as 30 000 people. This figure is striking when we realize that the people of New France probably numbered no more than 70 000 by the middle of the eighteenth century. Moreover, by the time of contact with Europeans, the indigenous peoples of what was to become Canada belonged to twelve separate language families and spoke an even larger number of languages.[2]

Students of the early Native peoples have also identified several different major regional economies. The hunting-and-gathering cultures in the north and east differed not only from each other and from the partly agricultural economies of the St. Lawrence River valley, but also from the buffalo-centred cultures on the plains. And

Photo on previous page: Betty Hunter (Stoney Band) of Soutwest Alberta (1910). Source: Provincial Archives of Alberta, Harry Pollard Collection, p. 27.

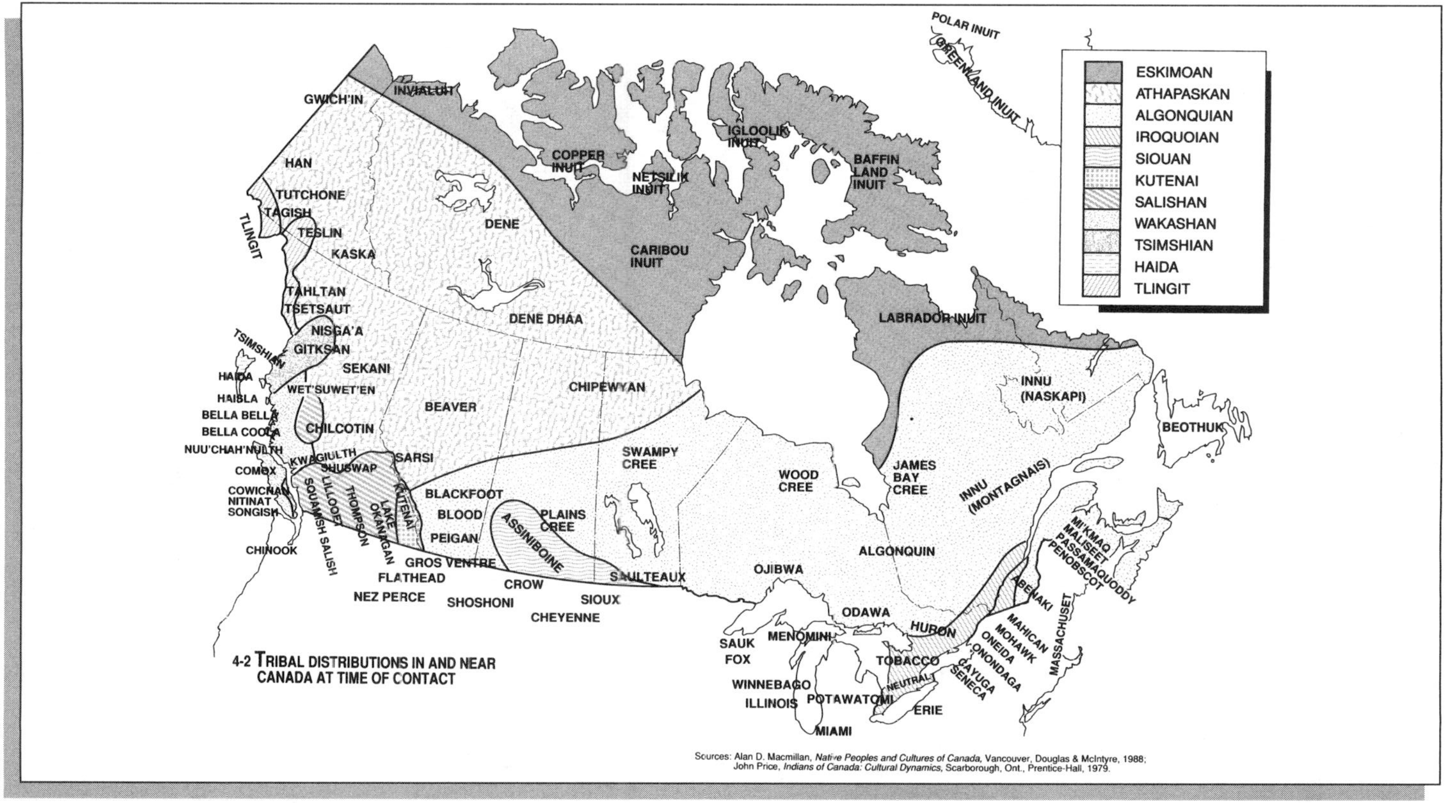

MAP I.1 *Tribal distribution and language groups in and near Canada at time of contact.*

Source: Olive Patricia Dickason, *Canada's First Nations: A History of the Founding Peoples from Earliest Times* (1992). Used by permission of the Canadian Publishers, McClelland & Stewart, Toronto.

these stood in considerable contrast again to the salmon- and whale-based economies of the Pacific west coast. Perhaps the one major factor that aboriginal economies had in common was their very delicate relationships with their various natural environments.[3]

We know that Europeans reached the shores of North America as early as the eleventh century, and Norse legends, as well as the presence of tools for spinning and sewing in a Viking archeological site in Newfoundland, inform us that women were among these early visitors. Gudrid and Freydis, according to the eleventh-century "Vinland" sagas, actually gave birth to children in the New World.[4]

It was not until the sixteenth century, however, that European incursions on Native territory began in earnest. The first arrivals were chiefly fishermen and traders who did not linger. Nevertheless, there is considerable evidence that by the late 1500s the development of trade on the east coast was altering Native economies and, as well, the lives of women. Gradually, as European goods were introduced, women had to adapt to change. Some of the clothing and utensils that they had once manufactured, for example, could now be purchased with furs. Settled communities were forced to move as the trade animals became depleted in any given region. In addition, European diseases were introduced, with drastic effects on the size of populations.[5]

French-speaking European women first began to arrive in North America in the seventeenth century; like the aboriginal women they encountered, they were amazingly diverse. The France from which they sailed was ruled by a monarchy intent on extending its administrative control over a fragmented and fractious realm. From his palace at Versailles, the "Sun King" Louis XIV and his advisers sought to enhance the glory of France by laying claim to much of the North American continent. But mercantilist dreams of prosperous colonies shipping valuable resources to the mother country and importing its manufactured goods could be realized only if this vast territory were populated by French colonists. Steeped in the religious zeal of the Catholic Counter-Reformation, the court at Versailles also viewed colonization as a means of spreading the Catholic faith.[6]

Populating the French colonies was a slow and difficult process. Very soon, New France was embattled on nearly all sides, first by hostile Indians and then by the British, locked as they were in a deadly struggle with the French for empire. Of the French colonies that developed in the northern half of the continent, Acadia had the longest history of French presence, enjoyed the best relations between the French and local Native peoples, but suffered most of the consequences of French–British conflict. Despite prolonged war with the Iroquois throughout much of the seventeenth century, it was the colony of Canada, situated on the banks of the St. Lawrence River, that became the economic and administrative centre of New France. A third major population centre developed in the eighteenth century around the fortress of Louisbourg, located on present-day Cape Breton Island.[7]

In all three colonies, the arrival of French women signalled official intention to create permanent European settlements. The women and men who came to New France brought with them the varying ideals, ambitions, and anxieties of their metropolitan patrons. French merchants sought to transform fish and fur into handsome profits, colonial administrators struggled to reproduce the political and social structures of Bourbon France in the wilderness, and nuns and priests devoted their lives to imposing a particularly austere and mystical brand of French Catholicism on Natives and colonists alike. The resulting cultures reflected all of this, as well as the diverse origins and circumstances of the settlers. The Acadians, for example, were so various in their backgrounds that they found themselves living with women and men who not only spoke different dialects but also had lived in communities ruled by differing laws, customs, and religious traditions in the Old World.[8] The more numerous Canadians hailed from Paris and the surrounding Île de France, as well as from coastal ports; in both colonies, there was initially considerable intermarriage between the French and the indigenous populations. In addition, Canada's first Blacks were brought as slaves to Acadia and the St. Lawrence River valley during this period. Finally, the settlers' experience varied, depending on their social rank and where they lived. Life among the upper classes in Quebec was marked by relative comfort and sophistication, features largely absent from the lives of *habitants* struggling to carve farms from the forest.[9]

Similar variety and a continuing intermingling of peoples characterized the great migrations of the eighteenth and early nineteenth centuries as well. Women came as soldiers' wives and daughters, or as farmers, fisherwomen, and businesswomen, migrating from the British Isles and the American colonies, both before and after the British Conquest of New France; they also came as Loyalists and as post-Loyalist migrants of European, African, and Indian origin, gravitating to British North America before, during, and after the American Revolution. These migrants were uniform neither in their languages, which included Gaelic and German as well as the dominant English, nor in their customs or possessions.

Fixing boundaries for the founding peoples of Canada is as complex a process as attempting to delineate their cultures. Boundaries between indigenous groups were often fluid to begin with, and major shifts occurred in their territories as they relocated in response to the demands of the fur trade, the vagaries of war, the devastations of disease or famine, or their own changing economic or political requirements and agendas. To further complicate the picture, the boundaries established by both the French and their British successors were shortlived. Acadia endured as part of New France only until 1713; the Acadians themselves were finally uprooted in the Great Deportation or Expulsion of 1755–1762, when their British rulers scattered men, women, and children along the coasts of North America and Europe. Despite continuous warfare, New France survived in the St. Lawrence River valley until the British Conquest was completed in 1760; Canada was finally ceded to the British Crown by the Treaty of Paris in 1763. Yet British rule did not bring peace. The American Revolution (1776–1783), the cataclysm that set so many Loyalists on the road north, broke the peace, as did, to a much smaller extent, the eighteenth-century fur trade wars. It was not until the War of 1812 was over and the nineteenth century was well into its second decade that the six colonies of British North America — Newfoundland, Nova Scotia, New Brunswick, Prince Edward Island, and Lower and Upper Canada — began to assume relatively stable boundaries. Even then, Upper and Lower Canada had still to endure the traumatic events of the Rebellions of 1837–1838. Indeed, throughout most of its history British North America, like New France before it, was essentially an armed camp.[10]

Canada's early women therefore lived amid extraordinary conflict and change. War and the effects of war were important factors in their lives. Of equal significance was the mercantile nature of their societies. The Native peoples drew the Europeans into their world; at the same time, they were gradually drawn into the staple economies that the European intruders generated. The quest for furs would eventually become the driving force of many women's lives. Women were also crucial to the inshore fishery and to the economies that subsequently developed around the production of lumber and wheat. In addition, they continued to be active in subsistence hunting and gathering, in farming, in craft production, and in local commerce. Most of the economies in which they participated were family-based. Women and men alike laboured for the subsistence of the family or of larger family groupings, such as clans, or for their improvement; generally, labour was quite sharply divided along the lines of gender.

The problems historians face in analyzing women's roles in such pre-industrial economies are multiple. An outstanding one is to determine what implications the sexual division of labour had for the status of women in any given culture. Were pre-industrial women separate in their work by choice? Did their work give them power, or did it tend to exclude them from authority? How, indeed, do we define "power" and "choice" in these societies? Did women's work help to support a separate, gender-based culture that was different from that of men? If so, how did this cultural identity manifest itself? Equally problematic is the documentation of change and of difference. What was the impact of contact on the roles and status of the aboriginal women who inhabited the regions that were to become Canada? How did the New World affect the lives of European women immigrants to New France and British North America? And what of the many mixed-blood women, who became the women "in between" two cultures?[11] Even within these larger groupings, there are often variations of race, religion, ethnicity, and class, and of urban and rural settings, to be considered in any assessment of how our foremothers lived.

outside?

If the contemporary sources for making these assessments are often mere scraps, it is true that the scraps are sometimes marvellous. Jesuit missionaries writing back to France, fur traders keeping track of what was going on in their trading territories for company officials or friends at home, male travellers of various nationalities writing for a variety of publics — all often had fascinating things to say about women in the New World. But for the lives of indigenous women particularly, historians have to rely almost entirely on the evidence of these men, and such evidence must be treated with great caution, filtered as it was through the eyes of individuals who shared neither the race nor the sex of the people they were describing.[12] Increasingly, some wish to turn to the oral tradition for different perspectives on Native women's history. For European women, the sources are more various, but are still scattered and problematic. Convent women writing the *annales* of their convents are wonderful sources for New France, but their focus is largely, although certainly not exclusively, on the lives of their communities. Notarial records and censuses have proven rich sources for historians of women, as have some groups of family business records. By the eighteenth century, the diaries and letters of laywomen begin to supplement these sources, along with accounts by travellers. But if such records prove exceptionally rich for British North America by the nineteenth century, there is a distinct falling off in the quantitative sources. The superb parish, census, and notarial records of New France were to some extent carried on in Quebec and Lower Canada under British rule, but are not to be found in great profusion elsewhere for the post-Conquest years. The New Brunswick, Nova Scotia, and Upper and Lower Canada censuses of 1851, however, provide a wealth of information for the end of the period covered by Part One. And scattered other local surveys, coupled with what may be gleaned from individual, family, and parish records, as well as the court records and newspapers that are increasingly being examined by historians, help us reconstruct the lives of women, especially in the first half of the nineteenth century.

Altogether, we do well to approach the history of Canadian women in this early period with caution. The temptation to use twentieth-century anthropological findings and extrapolate to firm conclusions about the women of our more remote past is to be avoided. On the other hand, the studies of contemporary anthropologists are valuable guides to the historian trying to understand the beliefs or social configurations that might have influenced women in earlier times. Often it is only with the most imaginative use of fragmentary sources that we are able to construct a picture of those worlds that we, perhaps, have not quite lost.

NOTES

1. Bruce Trigger, *The Children of Aataentsic: A History of the Huron People to 1660* (Montreal and Kingston: McGill-Queen's University Press, 1976), vol. 1, 77; Basil H. Johnston, *Tales the Elders Told: Ojibway Legends* (Toronto: Royal Ontario Museum, 1981), 9–10; Alice B. Kehoe, "Old Woman Had Great Power," *Western Canadian Journal of Anthropology* 6, 3 (November 1976), 68–76; Jo-Anne Fiske, "Gender and Politics in a Carrier Indian Community," University of British Columbia, Ph.D Thesis, 1989, 107–19; Anne Cameron, *Daughters of Copper Woman* (Vancouver: Press Gang, 1981), 26–29; and Christine St. Peter, " 'Woman's Truth' and the Native Tradition: Anne Cameron's *Daughters of Copper Woman*," *Feminist Studies* 15, 3 (Fall 1989), 499–523. Note that the names Wet'suwet'en and Nuu'chah'nulth are preferred by the peoples formerly known as the Carrier and the Nootka, respectively.

2. R. Cole Harris, ed., *Historical Atlas of Canada* (Toronto: University of Toronto Press, 1987), vol. 1, espec. 5–6, and plate 18. See also J. Helm, ed., *Handbook of North American Indians: Subarctic* (Washington: Smithsonian Institution, 1981), vol. 6; and B.G. Trigger, ed., *Handbook of North American Indians: Northeast* (Washington: Smithsonian Institution, 1978), vol. 15.

3. Harris, ed., *Historical Atlas of Canada*, vol. 1, plates 9–13.

4. Jean Johnston, *Wilderness Women: Canada's Forgotten History* (Toronto: Peter Martin Associates, 1973), 1–22.

5. Harris, ed., *Historical Atlas of Canada*, vol. 1, plates 33, 47, 69; Ellice B. Gonzalez, *Changing Economic Roles for Micmac Men and Women: An Ethnohistorical Analysis* (Ottawa: National Museums of Canada, 1981).

6. See W.J. Eccles, *Canada under Louis XIV, 1663–1701* (Toronto: McClelland and Stewart, 1964); and Eccles, *The Canadian Frontier, 1534–1760* (New York: Holt, Rinehart and Winston, 1969).

7. See Andrew Hill Clark, *Acadia: The Geography of Early Nova Scotia to 1760* (Madison: University of Wisconsin Press, 1968); Eccles, *Canadian Frontier*.

8. Naomi Griffiths, "The Acadians," *Dictionary of Canadian Biography* (Toronto: University of Toronto Press, 1979), vol. 4, xvii–xix.

9. See Harris, ed., *Historical Atlas of Canada*, vol. 1, 113–17, and plate 45.

10. See Harris, ed., *Historical Atlas of Canada*, vol. 1, 171–73, and plates 30–32, 46, 54, 68.

11. Sylvia Van Kirk, *"Many Tender Ties": Women in Fur Trade Society, 1670–1870* (Winnipeg: Watson and Dwyer, 1980), chap. 4.

12. See Patricia Kennedy, "Voices in the Shadows," *The Archivist* 20, 1 (January–February 1993), 2–4.

CHAPTER ONE

The First Women

Thanadelthur, an eighteenth-century Chipewyan woman, was referred to by James Knight, the Hudson's Bay Company trader who wrote about her, as "the Slave Woman." Thanadelthur was both a survivor and a peacemaker, and as a result she is one of the few Native women of her period whose individual lives we can document. She and a female companion were captured by Crees, long-standing enemies of the Chipewyan, in 1713. Both managed to escape from their captors, but neither could complete the long journey back to their own band. Narrowly avoiding the death by starvation that was the fate of her friend, Thanadelthur succeeded in making

contact with Hudson's Bay Company traders at York Factory; these traders, in turn, quickly recognized the young Chipewyan's value as a potential link between them and her fur-wealthy people. The eventual result was a peace mission between Cree and Chipewyan, ostensibly led by a Hudson's Bay Company man, but actually the work of Thanadelthur herself, who proved a highly competent go-between. When the mission seemed doomed to failure owing to mounting hostility and fear on both sides, Knight's narrative tells us, it was Thanadelthur whose courage and determination carried the day. By turns, she persuaded both sides to continue the talks, and harangued them until they were finally "forced . . . to ye peace." The trader who accompanied Thanadelthur admired her spirit. It was "Divellish," he reported. If but 50 of her people had the same "Carriage and Resolution," no other Indian tribe would stand a chance in Chipewyan country.

Thanadelthur's life was short. In the few years that remained to her after her arrival at York Factory, she became so valuable to James Knight as an interpreter and envoy that he despaired when, in the bad winter of 1717, she became ill and he was unable to nurse her back to health. "She was one of a Very high Spirit and of the Firmest Resolution that ever I see any Body in my Days," Knight wrote in his log, calling her a person "of very great Courage & forecast." We learn of Thanadelthur's history not from her or chiefly from her own people but, in this account, from the pen of an outsider, and his words are not easy to interpret.[1] Was there a sense in which her position was servile? Or did James Knight see her only as the powerful figure his final description implied: a woman of courage and resolution whose role was so important to his mission that he hardly knew how he would replace her? And what relationship is there between Knight's words and the reality of Thanadelthur's life? A different version of Thanadelthur's story, transmitted orally and written down by the photographer Edward S. Curtis, is somewhat less dramatic, suggesting simply that at some point following her capture by the Cree, the Chipewyan woman followed her Cree husband to the Hudson's Bay Company fort and subsequently led the "White Flesh" to her own people to trade.[2] It is from this version that we learn the woman's name, and its meaning, "marten shake." But in the end, even this version cannot necessarily represent Thanadelthur's own perspective on her story. How did *she* understand her situation as an envoy between three peoples jockeying for position in a world that may once have been the exclusive territory of her own people? What did the events of Thanadelthur's life mean to her?

Although such questions are ultimately impossible to answer, Thanadelthur's story is instructive. First, it suggests something of the power that indigenous women appear to have had when the host peoples of North America first encountered European intruders on their territory. At the same time, it suggests the fragility of that power, especially in periods of conflict and upheaval. Aboriginal women, who may have had considerable authority in their own communities as traders or as interpreters between peoples, were nevertheless vulnerable when men were on the warpath. Secondly, Thanadelthur was on the move. Seasonal migration was normal for hunting-and-gathering groups, but European contact and the fur trade brought new dimensions and additional travelling. Women acting as traders and negotiators, women travelling with their trader husbands, women captives escaping and seeking refuge — countless women might have had tales to tell like Thanadelthur's.

Other Native women would see similar extraordinary changes occurring in their lifetimes. During the pre-contact and early contact years in the eastern Maritime region, for example, whole populations replaced each other. By the time of contact in the fifteenth century, the Mi'kmaq, who had only recently settled in Nova Scotia, had given up the making of pottery and were no longer living in permanent coastal settlements, as their predecessors evidently had done. The large palisaded villages that Cartier saw in his sixteenth-century explorations of the St. Lawrence River valley had been abandoned by the time Champlain came to this region less than a century later. And it was not many years after the beginnings of French settlement in Canada that the Huron, who had once been so numerous north of Lake Ontario, were almost entirely destroyed by disease and war. From an early seventeenth-century population that might have reached 30 000, they were reduced by the 1650s to a scattered few.[3] Yet despite the disruption of their societies, there were survivors — and adapters — and they appear in the records.

The questions that we are bound to ask about aboriginal women are important, but hard to answer. What were women's lives like before the coming of the Europeans? And how did women react to the changes European trade and settlement brought? The groups whose cultures have been studied with such questions in mind include the Mi'kmaq of Nova Scotia; the Innu (Montagnais and Naskapi) of Labrador and Quebec among the eastern Algonquian linguistic groups; and the Huron and the Iroquois of the Great Lakes region among the Iroquoians. Much of our information for these groups dates from the sixteenth and seventeenth centuries, although some is more recent. For the eighteenth and nineteenth centuries, we can also draw on studies of the Chipewyan, Cree, and Wet'suwet'en of the northwest, who were also Algonquian, and of peoples belonging to the Eyak-Athapaskan, Salish, and Haida language groups of the west coast.[4] Useful as well for all periods are various studies not focussed on women or on gender roles specifically, but that nevertheless allude to them in passing. From the work that has been done to date, it is possible to examine women's roles in the economic lives of their communities and, in some cases, to catch glimpses of their status and spiritual power as well in the pre-contact and early contact periods.

NATIVE WOMEN'S WORK

Most historians and anthropologists agree that all North American Native communities organized their work along gender lines. Where they disagree, it is usually about the significance of gendered work roles and the extent to which important economic contributions can be translated into social authority.[5] In general, women in aboriginal communities did work that was compatible with the task of looking after small children. This work did not require "rapt attention," as hunting did; it could be easily interrupted and resumed. It did not place children in danger, and it did not require mothers and children to go very far from home. This applied even when "home" was a movable encampment. Women generally remained close to the camp; men moved farther afield on land or sea to hunt animal food that could not be obtained in any other way.[6]

Within such limits, Native women's work in northern North America varied according to the resources of the region and the group. To many early European observers, some aboriginal women led incredibly hard lives in marginal subsistence economies. This seemed especially true of those groups who depended on hunting and gathering in the northern forests and tundra or who lived in the plateau between the Rocky Mountains and the west coast and lived chiefly on salmon and roots. On the other hand, some observers found Native women in agricultural economies or coastal fishing economies living amid relative ease and plenty.

By the time of European contact, women did most of the planting and harvesting in agricultural communities; but it was the opinion of at least one eighteenth-century British American observer that this work was relaxed and convivial. A white woman who had been taken captive by the Seneca and adopted into the tribe, Mary Jemison seems to have found much to approve of in the lives of Iroquois women.[7] Agricultural work was not only the responsibility of these women but was also under their control. Iroquois and Huron men cleared the land, but the corn, beans, and squash were grown entirely by teams of women organized by leaders chosen by the women themselves. Among the Iroquois, the meat brought home from the hunt went to the wife's household to be distributed by her according to Iroquois rules of hospitality, which dictated that all members of the community as well as all visitors should be fed. The wealth of the community consisted chiefly in its cleared land, but also in the food stored and controlled by the women.[8]

The relative ease with which women's agricultural work was performed depended, no doubt, on a variety of factors, including the climate and the quality of the land, but according to Mary Jemison the labour of Iroquois women was rarely "severe." Even though they had "all the fuel and bread to procure, and the cooking to perform," she noted, their work was "probably not harder" than that of white women who had those articles provided for them. More importantly, "their cares" were neither so numerous nor so great as those of white women. "In the summer season, we planted, tended and harvested the corn, and generally had all our children with us; but had no master to oversee or drive us, so that we could work as leisurely as we pleased."[9]

Jemison's observations cover only the time in which she lived among the Seneca and the particular region where they lived. Captivity narratives, moreover, were sufficiently numerous in Jemison's time to constitute a literary "genre" and so must be treated cautiously as historical evidence.[10] But other evidence suggests that similar working patterns obtained among the agricultural peoples of the lower Great Lakes region generally. Earlier Iroquois and Huron women were also in charge of their communities' farming; and the growing of corn, squash, sunflowers, and beans had been known among the Great Lakes and St. Lawrence valley Iroquoian peoples for at least 1000 years before the arrival of Europeans. Indeed, it is the cultivation of the protein-rich bean that is believed to account for the large Iroquoian populations that the first Europeans encountered.

The Innu were among the non-agricultural hunting-and-gathering peoples encountered by the French of the St. Lawrence River valley. It is apparent that they lived in communities of varying sizes, depending on the season, but probably in social groupings that were smaller than those of the Iroquois or Huron. In wintertime they broke up into hunting bands of one or two families that went into the bush in search of game. As was the case among the Huron and Iroquois, Innu women's work was different from Innu men's; indeed, the Jesuit observers of New France noted that each sex knew the role of the other and that they did not "meddle" with each other's work. Women did participate in the fishing and even, to some extent, in the trapping of small animals, however. They were certainly involved in transporting game, preparing hides, and manufacturing clothing from them. But their main economic role was as gatherers of shellfish and other foods; they generally supplied more than 50 percent of their people's diet by this work. Innu women, like the women of the agricultural Huron and Iroquois, were also in charge of the distribution of the food they gathered as well as of the products of the hunt and fishery.[11]

Among the hardest lives described by early European observers were those of the Chipewyan and Cree women of the northwest. Andrew Graham, who wrote about the Swampy Cree in the late eighteenth century, found that in this community, "all drugery [sic] and domestic duty is performed by the women. They pitch and unpitch the tent, cut fire-wood, dress the victuals. . . . The women also catch fish, hares, fetch all the water used in the tent, knit the snow-shoes, and make the clothes." Graham observed that the women waited on the men when the latter returned from the hunt, and that they worked as hard as ever when pregnant.[12] Alexander Mackenzie, writing in 1802, had similar things to say about Woodland Cree women. He found that they were "in the same subordinate state with those of all other savage tribes," and that they worked extremely hard. "They are . . . subject to every kind of domestic drudgery . . . so that when the duties of maternal care are added, it will appear that the life of these women is an uninterrupted succession of toil and pain. This, indeed, is the sense they entertain of their own situation."[13]

Such statements should be weighed against the observers' background and gender. Although men marvelled at the heavy work performed by Indian women, we must compare their observations to the silence on this subject of European women who wrote about aboriginal peoples. Marie de l'Incarnation of the Ursulines, for example, wrote a great deal about the people she encountered in New France, but she said nothing about the extraordinary labour performed by Native women. Were Graham and Mackenzie comparing the aboriginal women they observed to European women servants or agricultural labourers, or to women of their own more privileged class? Or were they comparing the lives of migratory Indians, both male and female, with the more settled lives of most Europeans? In some cases, they were comparing women's work to that of Native men—who, if they refused to participate in the fur trade in any consistent way, appeared indolent to Europeans, whose major focus happened to be on the trade.[14]

Perhaps Native men viewed women's labour in a different light entirely. Samuel Hearne quoted a Chipewyan chief, Matonabbee: "Women were made for labour," the chief had apparently told him; "one of them can carry, or haul, as much as two men can do." Their work was so important, in fact, that there was "no such thing as travelling any considerable distance, or for any length of time, in this country, without their assistance."[15]

Certainly there is no doubt that the aboriginal women of northern North America worked very hard. Plains women collected food that was essential to communal welfare if the buffalo hunt failed; they also dried, pounded, and mixed berries with fat and buffalo or other meat to make pemmican. They prepared hides and stitched them into carrying bags and tipis. The labour of dressing a single buffalo hide took a minimum of three days, if a woman had no other preoccupations; a tipi made from buffalo skins could require up to 20 hides.[16]

Nearly everywhere, Native women made the moccasins and the leather or woven clothes their people wore, netted the snowshoes that were indispensable to winter travel, and gathered gum and prepared birchbark, spruce, or cedar fibres to make canoes. In many migrant communities, women were the carriers; in nearly all, they pitched the tents and broke camp when travelling. In coastal, riverside, and lakeside communities, women prepared and cured fish and gathered shellfish, as well as berries and plant materials that they dried, coiled, and wove into baskets, fishnets, and various articles of clothing. Similarly, Inuit women were involved in many tasks connected with hunting for — and with preparing food and domestic items from — cariboo, seals, whales, and other mammals; perhaps, if contemporary evidence reflects older traditions, they were also occasionally involved in the hunt itself.[17] The work of aboriginal women, in other words, was essential.

The tasks women performed depended on the characteristics of their environments. The annual Mi'kmaq cycle took the people from the seal fishery on the coast in January to hunting beaver, otter, moose, bears, and cariboo inland in February and March; spring sent them to the river mouths to fish and hunt waterfowl and eggs, while in summer they gathered berries and nuts. In the fall, the people withdrew from the shoreline again to take spawning eels in the rivers and, once again, to hunt the larger animals. The sexual division of labour among the Mi'kmaq, described by an observer in 1612, seems to have meant that the women did nearly everything within this seasonal cycle, while the men focussed exclusively on hunting and warfare.[18]

> The [women] besides the onerous role of bearing and rearing the children, also transport the game from the place where it has fallen; they are the hewers of wood and drawers of water; they make and repair the household utensils; they prepare the food; they skin the game and prepare the hides . . . sew garments . . . catch fish and gather shellfish for food; often they even hunt; they make the canoes . . . set up tents.[19]

Preparing hides and sewing garments among the Mi'kmaq amounted to more than simple tanning and stitchery. Five different techniques of working with dyed porcupine quills were known to them.[20]

Among women everywhere in North America, the care of young children was women's work. Travellers and especially traders with the inland tribes commented on the ease with which mothers gave birth to their children. Andrew Graham noted how few of the symptoms that "afflict the delicate European" were experienced in either pregnancy or parturition by Indian women, "their pains being very light and soon over." Graham went on to give further details about motherhood among the Cree. Women giving birth while travelling, he claimed, simply dropped behind,

Elizabeth Ladds (1837–1922) painted this watercolour of a Mi'kmaq woman and child in dress typical of the period.

Source: *Mi'kmaq Woman and Child*, watercolour by Elizabeth Ladds, c. 1865. History Collection, Nova Scotia Museum, (N-4430), NSM 24.4.4.

brought forth "the little stranger . . . and carrying it on their backs, proceed[ed] to overtake their companions as if nothing had happened." He noted that children were "solely under the direction of the mother . . . being always esteemed the maternal property."[21]

Europeans greatly admired the wooden cradles in which infants were often tied and strapped to their mother's back. Packed in moss and soft deer hides, babies seemed conveniently cared for in these cradles, which were sometimes decorated with beautiful designs. Mothers nursed infants for at least two or three years, and this practice contributed to a relatively low birth rate. Women living in their own communities rarely seem to have had more than three or four children, which must have increased both their mobility and their productivity.[22]

THE QUESTION OF WOMEN'S AUTHORITY

European observers' interest in and admiration for Indian women's control of their children and the apparent ease with which the women bore and cared for children is a clue, perhaps, to a certain unease. What women controlled, men did not; this gave white male observers pause. In addition, white women of their own acquaintance were cast in a somewhat unfavourable light, as comparatively delicate or incompetent. Looking at the cultural and social roles of aboriginal women through the eyes of such European recorders is a complex exercise, one that tells us as much about the observers as about the observed.

There is evidence, both from contemporary anthropology and the historical record, that gathering and hunting economies like those of the Mi'kmaq or Innu, and agricultural economies like those of the Iroquois and Huron, were relatively egalitarian communities in which women enjoyed considerable power in several crucial areas: relative autonomy in sexual life and marriage; some degree of influence in group decision-making;[23] and significant participation in the religious or ceremonial lives of their people. There was essentially no distinction in these societies between the "private" or domestic sphere and "public" life—although, to the extent that decision-making and religious ceremonies were part of the larger communal world, these were in some sense distinct from the immediate purview of the family. Yet women were often involved in both, despite their largely separate and distinct economic roles.

All aboriginal societies appear to have ritually secluded young women at the time of their first menstruation, and to have regarded menstruating women as powerful or even dangerous (as, indeed, did some seventeenth-century Europeans).[24] Marriage customs varied, depending on the tribe or community; gradually, they changed as a result of contact, although it is not always clear how and when. Women among both the Innu and the Iroquois and Huron were evidently as free as men were in their choice of a spouse, although among the latter, mothers often arranged marriages. There was considerable sexual freedom among adolescents, and both young women and young men initiated sexual encounters. Nor did the Iroquois and Huron or the Innu believe that marriage entailed sexual exclusiveness. Persons of either sex had a right to be satisfied with their unions; divorce was apparently easy. This was particularly so because women had control over their children and, in the case of the Iroquois and Huron, exercised control over domestic space. Polygyny, practised among the Innu (as among many west coast groups) provided husbands for women who might otherwise not have had them. Iroquois, Huron, and Innu welcomed children with great delight, and female children were considered a boon.

Prior to and in the early days of contact, a young Innu man generally joined the household and hunting band of his wife, at least temporarily, thus supporting the wife's family in a subsistence economy in which skilled hunters were valuable and added to a family's strength. The unpredictability and difficulty of Innu existence appears to have favoured a subtle and inclusive approach to decision-making, taking the needs and wishes of all group members into consideration before a consensus was reached. Women's role in such decision-making equalled men's, according to seventeenth-century observers. Indeed, Jesuits who came into contact with this group reported that Innu women enjoyed "great power" in their communities. "A man may promise you something," one recounted, "and if he does not keep his promise, he thinks he is sufficiently excused when he tells you his wife did not wish to do it." The Jesuit recorders of Innu life did not approve, and said as much.[25]

Like the Innu, the Iroquois and the Huron were also matrilocal: that is, husbands generally resided with the parents of their wives. In addition, they were matrilineal. To the extent that there were either property or chieftainships to inherit, inheritance was through the female line. Reports about the detailed role of women in Huron or Iroquois government are not consistent; it is true that at tribal councils, only male speakers were usually heard. But it is also true that leading Iroquois women exercised considerable power in selecting chiefs, by bequeathing the names of deceased chiefs related to them. Because they could demand captives to replace male relations who had died, they also sometimes exercised the power of life or death over prisoners. Since the household was central to aboriginal societies, the control that women exercised in the running of the longhouses is also particularly significant. The Iroquois respected the "matrons" or clan mothers who ran the houses they lived in, and this power was reflected in their higher councils. The increase in white settlement, which forced Iroquois men to travel farther and farther afield in the interest of the hunt and diplomacy, placed even greater power in the hands of women. There is also evidence that Iroquois women, in isolated instances, engaged in warfare along with the men. Finally, the changing conditions of colonialism may have led some aboriginal women to take on new or expanded roles. During the smallpox epidemic of 1640, for example, a Huron woman defied tradition and spoke out at an important tribal assembly in order to denounce the Jesuits for spreading disease among the people.[26]

Women's authority was also reflected in the ceremonial and spiritual lives of indigenous peoples. Among the Innu and the Inuit, women as well as men could be shamans or people with special religious powers. In Igloolik in recent times, the people told of a female shaman called Itijjuak, who could not sew, cook, or have children, but who was loved and cared for by her two husbands and others, who brought food, clothing, and children to her. She was a powerful healer in her community.[27] Among the Iroquois, women had a significant role in the management of communal religious ceremonies and festivals and, certainly, control over their own female ceremonial life. Women's dreams and foretellings were considered as important as men's and gave women influence. This was also true of the Ojibwa. Eighteenth-century Ojibwa women were observed conducting a six- or seven-day ceremony designed to assist their men who were away at war, a ceremony that ended when the women divined (correctly, it later turned out) that the warriors had won their battle.[28] In a later period, Blackfoot women were recorded as having similar powers of mediation between the natural and spiritual worlds. Senior medicine women could be central figures in the vital communal ritual of the Sun Dance. In this role, they embodied Elk-Woman and Woman-Who-Married-Morning-Star, the mythical heroines who brought ceremonial dress, the sacred digging stick, and the prairie turnip to the Blackfoot people.[29]

The Roman Catholic priests who first conducted missions among Canada's Native peoples were appalled by such female power, steeped as the missionaries were in a patriarchal tradition. The early priests carried on intense campaigns to change the relations between the sexes, which they clearly felt were disruptive of all "natural" authority. The Jesuits complained about the lack of male control over women and, in the case of the Innu, connected it with their casual attitudes toward authority. The priests preached that wives should obey their husbands, that sexually exclusive monogamy should prevail, and that there should be no divorce. For one thing, they argued, women's sexual permissiveness confused the laws of lineage and inheritance. How could a man know which of his wife's children were his own? At least one Jesuit critic was rebuked for expressing this doubt about Innu mores. "Thou hast no sense," was the Native man's response. "You French people love only your own children; but we love all the children of our tribe."[30]

The zeal of seventeenth-century French missionaries to alter gender relations among the Indians they were attempting to convert was related to the number of formal and informal unions that were occurring between French traders and aboriginal women. The evidence for this is particularly strong among the Acadians, but the practice was likely widespread, especially on the western frontiers of New France. From the Jesuit perspective, it was important that these marriages be "regularized" and that the children be raised according to French and Catholic cultural traditions. Indeed, the government of New France was persuaded to offer financial incentives for Indian girls to be taught French housekeeping skills in order to facilitate such marriages, in the hope that the resulting couples would abandon the forest and settle down to populate the country.[31] The Jesuits made similar efforts to change male/ female relations among the Huron. In both cases, the aim was essentially the same: male control of women's sexuality. The alteration of gender relations in these communities was considered essential if the Native people were to be brought under the control of both the Roman Catholic church and the French state. Hierarchical government could work only when hierarchy permeated the entire culture.[32]

It may be that the mores of the Cree and Chipewyan peoples were very similar to those of the Innu at one time. Certainly these people from the interior were gatherers and hunters, and what we know of Thanadelthur suggests that some Chipewyan and Cree women enjoyed considerable autonomy and power, at least on the edges of their communities. But there is also evidence of greater parental control over marriage among the northwestern tribes, along with evidence that, as fur trade society developed, many marriageable young women lost whatever sexual autonomy their earlier counterparts might have possessed, to become pawns in trading alliances or intertribal rivalries. Among the Chipewyan, women sometimes had no choice at all when it came to a husband; fur traders told stories of seeing Chipewyan men wrestle each other for a wife, who became the possession of the winner. Among the Wet'suwet'en, widows were required to participate in arduous mourning rituals, and a young widow became the virtual slave of her in-laws for a period following the death of her spouse. When communities were at war, captured aboriginal women could also be enslaved by their captors.[33]

The Hudson's Bay Company, unlike the French companies who sent their agents into the woods from the seventeenth century on, was at first reluctant to countenance any intimacy between aboriginal women and its employees. This was not an attitude that could last. It quickly became apparent that a knowledgeable female companion not only fostered trade relations, but was essential to any man who intended to travel great distances or to live for any time in fur trade country. Thus the employees of both the Hudson's Bay and the Northwest companies, like the *coureurs du bois*, not only travelled into Indian country in the course of their work but also married there. Indeed, marriages between Native women and traders "according to the custom of the country" became the rule rather than the exception. Traders developed long-term relationships with aboriginal women, whom they married according to Native customary rites and whom they referred to as their "country" wives. By the nineteenth century, Hudson's Bay Company Chief Factor James Douglas spoke not only of the practical nature of traders' alliances with Native women but also of their psychological value.

If these alliances were important to the traders, they were no less so to the women and their relatives. West coast evidence suggests that marriages conducted with a view to cementing trade alliances were frequent among Native elites. And European traders found that marriages were sometimes initiated by aboriginal women, possibly in league with their families. The story of Alexander Henry's encounter with an Ojibwa woman illustrates the point. Returning from New Year's festivities, Henry found the young woman in question in his rooms. When he asked her to leave, she refused, so Henry went buffalo hunting. We do not know whether or not her family initially instructed this young woman to pursue Alexander Henry. But the fact that her father, an Ojibwa chief, later tried to persuade the trader to marry both of his daughters suggests a strong parental interest in the affair.[34]

When they occurred, such marriage alliances created a reciprocal social bond, which in turn was intended to consolidate economic relations. As a result of their marriages to Indian women, traders were supposed to be drawn into Native kinship circles; in return for access to their women, Indian families expected unhindered access to the trading posts and their provisions. Nor did these families permit their daughters to marry indiscriminately. The Flathead would allow marriages only with traders whom they particularly esteemed, and the evidence generally suggests that, by the end of the eighteenth century, parental consent was essential for unions between Native women and traders. A *voyageur*, recalling his experience, was adamant on the importance of such consent. A man ran the risk of getting his "head broken" if he took an aboriginal girl without her parents' permission. Some bride price was customary; occasionally, large gifts were involved. Among plains people, horses were sometimes given; blankets, guns, or utensils were also typical gifts. It is clear that traders followed Indian custom in these matters. Bride price represented, in essence, a repayment to the daughter's family for their sacrifice of her valuable economic services.[35]

There was no exchange of vows, but there was ritual: for example, a pipe might be smoked. The bride might be lectured by her relatives on her new duties. In some cases the trader visited the home of his bride, and her relatives ceremonially accompanied her to her new home. Similar customs prevailed when aboriginal men and women married within their own communities or chose spouses from neighbouring bands or nations. And intermarriage did take place, perhaps increasingly as European intrusion pushed Native bands from their habitual territories or when warfare resulted in the captivity of women. There is clear evidence of extensive intermarriage, for example, between the Ojibwa and the Cree. Both also intermarried with the Assiniboine, as the former societies moved onto the plains and became involved in the buffalo economy in the eighteenth century.[36]

The special circumstances of women on the west coast add considerable complexity to any discussion of the relative power and autonomy of Native women in pre-contact and early contact societies, for west coast cultures tended to have considerable material property and to be rank-differentiated. Early traders reported three classes: nobility, commoners, and slaves. The Haida of the Queen Charlotte Islands are a case in point. Matrilineal like the Iroquois and the Huron of the Great Lakes, the Haida evidently passed all property through the female line. Older Haida women, like their Tlingit and Tsimshian neighbours, were active traders, often berating men who had given away too much or otherwise failed to trade wisely. The power to trade was likely based, at least in part, on women's roles in domestic and food production and distribution.[37]

However, marriages among the Haida appear to have been arranged by men. The mother might be consulted, but the mother's uncle and the father made the final decision. Moreover, a bride was expected to accept the authority of her husband, and a widow was required to take a new husband selected by her husband's

The ceremonial arrival of a Kwakiutl bride at the home of her husband. Photographed around 1914 by Edward Curtis.

Source: Photo courtesy Garfinkel Publications Inc., Vancouver, B.C.

relatives. Women's subordinate status in marriage was reflected in their limited access to political power. Women could be chiefs, and the number of female chiefs increased after the introduction of European diseases decimated the Haida in the late nineteenth century, but in general chiefs were male, and female participation in political activity was restricted.

Because of menstrual and reproductive taboos, the presence of Haida women was thought dangerous to men who were hunting or fishing, and women were evidently completely excluded from male work of this kind. In the crafts and arts, weaving was the work of women; carving was strictly reserved for men. Yet, despite the fact that the dominant trade role was played by men, trade deals often seem to have required a wife's consent, and women also participated in Haida ceremonial activities. They were involved in the famous feasts known as potlatches that were so important to the wealthy Haida; mothers held potlatches for their daughters at puberty. Women were barred from the more important dances at Haida ceremonies, but they could become shamans.[38]

The behaviour of a west coast Clayoquot woman in connection with the landing of a whale illustrates her importance as a partner, although not necessarily an equal partner, in her husband's work. She was observed coming to her husband's boat and performing certain ritual actions, following which she gave a speech. In her speech she told everyone "that she and her husband had observed strict preparatory rituals for eight moons, had slept in separate beds, and prayed for strength and power." Clearly this woman's actions were vital to the hunt, even as she was excluded from it.[39]

Women seem to have had less authority in the non-matrilineal groups such as the Salish. At the time of contact at least, all important property in this group appears to have been held by men and was passed on from father to son. Women married men chosen by their parents and, upon marriage, went to live in the villages of their husbands. If there was a divorce, the children generally remained with the father. Although, like Native women from a number of other tribes, women did go on quests for guardian spirits, their journeys were not long ones, for — possibly because they were not hunters — their need for spirit helpers was considered to be less than that of men. Community decision-making, in general, belonged to men, and women appear to have been excluded from the governing councils of at least some Salish peoples. In addition, because west coast tribes were ranked societies, some lower-status Native women in the west probably had very little control over their lives. This was of course the case for slaves, who existed among some of the tribes by the time the Europeans arrived. European imperialism brought increased trade and wealth, but it also brought more reason for slavery and polygyny, at least on the west coast. Wives and slaves were pressed into dressing the sea otter pelts that were required in increasing numbers for the coastal fur trade, and this may well have altered the social structure and lowered the status of indigenous women in the Pacific coast region.[40]

Much less is known about the Inuit peoples of the seventeenth, eighteenth, and early nineteenth centuries. The first Europeans to make contact and record their impressions were the people who came to fish on the coasts of what is now Labrador, and the relations between Natives and intruders were poor. When Moravian missionaries came to the area in the mid-eighteenth century, one of their goals was to foster better relations. To this end, the governor over the region was persuaded to

Mikak, the Inuk woman whose visit to London in 1769 was intended to ease Inuk/European relations in eighteenth-century Labrador. The portrait was painted by John Russell.

Source: Photo courtesy Institut und Sammlung fur Völkerkunde der Universität Göttingen. Photo by H. Haase.

send a woman, Mikak, to London, in the hope that she would be impressed with Britain's power and influence her people to stop harassing the fishing fleets. Mikak obliged. What resulted from her mission, we do not know; what is clear from this story is that the governor assumed that Mikak had significant influence among her people.[41]

ABORIGINAL WOMEN'S PERSPECTIVE

How did Native women regard the Europeans, whose patriarchal culture encroached so powerfully on their own? As far as we can tell, the reactions of Native women varied enormously, according to the time and place.

As the Jesuits themselves reported, missionaries did not always succeed in altering the marriage and social patterns of the peoples they had hoped to convert. Innu women regularly ran away from husbands who attempted to impose their Christian will on their wives.[42] And clearly more than one Innu husband came to the conclusion that the Jesuits had no sense. Yet, gradually, the missionaries did begin to influence the lives of those Natives who were attracted more or less permanently to French settlements. In the seventeenth century, at the Amerindian settlement of Sillery, near Quebec, where Native families who had been converted to Christianity were engaged in farming, the land was given to men, who were made "captains" by their benefactors. Charity to families in need was handed out through these newly created chieftains. Unmarried women were strictly controlled, and any wife who disobeyed her husband was beaten. Some aboriginal women met the Jesuits on their own ground, however. Kateri Tekakwitha, an Iroquois orphan who fled to the "praying town" of Kahnawake in the 1670s, was one of many who dedicated themselves to virginity and self-mortification, both spiritually empowering concepts that made sense in an Iroquois cultural framework just as they did in a French Catholic one. Saintly powers were attributed to Tekakwitha soon after her death in 1680 at the young age of 24.[43]

The Jesuits did less well among those Innu who stayed away from French settlements, and among the Huron, whom they attempted to convert in Huronia itself. When the Natives were on their own turf, the system of economic and social dependency that developed at Sillery and other villages that were close to French administrative centres could not be duplicated. The Huron, already agricultural, and with their own complex systems of land use and inheritance, resisted the encroachment of the missionaries. Indeed, it may well have been Huron women who were at the core of the resistance. Any Huron man who adopted Christianity found himself ostracized and ejected from the longhouse by his mother-in-law. Until the 1640s, when the Huron were dispersed by Iroquois incursions, the traditional family-oriented systems of production continued to guarantee to women, along with men, access to the necessities of life.[44] From a material perspective, provided that one was not starving or defeated in battle, there was little temptation for Indian women to adopt the missionaries' culture, which offered so little and in fact threatened so clear a loss of status. But after the dispersal of the Huron, some women of the remaining Huron communities found spiritual satisfaction in Christianity. Khionrea, renamed Thérèse by Marie de l'Incarnation, was eventually captured by the Iroquois and married to a Mohawk. But she retained her new beliefs and by 1653 "was the mistress of the several families of her Iroquois long-house, still praying to her Christian God and leading others publicly in prayer." Cécile Gannendaris, whose story was recorded by the Sisters of the Quebec Hospital, taught the Huron language to Jesuit priests and was an eloquent preacher of Christianity to her own people.[45] The impact of European religion on aboriginal women was ambiguous and variable; but as European trade and settlement increased, so would missionaries' influence.

As trade with Europeans increased in scope and importance in their societies, it was also increasingly difficult for aboriginal women to resist the influence of the white traders. Often, trade altered gender relations for the worse within aboriginal societies. With the introduction of the horse on the plains, men's hunting work was made easier, but the number of hides women had to prepare increased. The more a woman's community depended on trade with Europeans, the less possible it was to maintain independent traditions and customs. If marriage to a trader were a possibility, the temptation for some aboriginal women must have been considerable. Their belief in the interconnectedness of kinship and trade made such relationships not only normal but desirable. The fur traders certainly claimed that Indian women regarded marriage to white men as preferable to marriage within their own tribes. Cree women were reported to consider it an honour to be chosen as a trader's wife. Such perceptions were reinforced by traders' confused notions about both the workload and the status of aboriginal women in their own societies. To European men, the burden of Indian women's work appeared enormous; such women, they felt, could only welcome the relative comfort of life within the trading forts.[46]

When the women married European men and moved into the trading posts, their material circumstances and their leverage with Native and white men alike probably did improve, at least initially. As Nor'Wester George Nelson pointed out, Native women had a particular interest in keeping the peace, and there is no doubt that, for a time, intermarriage between fur traders and Indians did promote better relations between the two groups. Through their marriages, aboriginal women could gain significant power: the power to create or destroy friendly relations by their influence and good offices with both sides.[47]

In general, fur traders' wives did enjoy a life that was physically easier than life in a migratory band. They had the benefit, perhaps illusory, of clothing made from imported textiles, and company servants did some of the heavy work that aboriginal women customarily did—carrying goods and hauling firewood and water. Although domestic tasks were never given over entirely to others by traders' Native wives, they were able to become more sedentary and spend more time on the making of moccasins, snowshoes, and other family goods. Altogether, the material improvement may have seemed very great indeed. The "country" wife's access to European goods, moreover, generally extended to members of her family and band, who had already benefitted from the good trade relations that her marriage helped cement. Finally, there is ample evidence that many fur trade marriages were loving and life-long arrangements, and traders wrote about their Indian and Métis families with great affection and warmth.[48]

But there was a negative side. During the eighteenth century, some traders saw the capture and abuse of a rival's wife as a weapon in the ongoing struggle between different interests for mastery of the trade. Traders' Native wives were also subject to new diseases. They had longer years of childbearing, for fur traders' families, in the early to mid-nineteenth century at least, were large—from eight to twelve children, compared to the four typically born to the average Cree woman. This surely took a physical toll. Childbirth itself appears to have been more difficult for traders' Native wives. Unlike their counterparts in Native society, country wives also had to share the raising of their children with patriarchal husbands, who had European views on discipline and education that were very different from their own. Wives of officers had to face sending children, especially sons, away to boarding schools or to paternal relatives for their education, and often these absent children died.[49]

Finally, changes in the fur trade, coupled with the arrival in the west of missionaries and European wives in the early nineteenth century, brought about a decline in the incidence of traders taking aboriginal spouses. Even before this, traders who wished to return to Europe or to the east had readily engaged in a practice that came to be known as "turning off" their Native wives. At one time such women had been able to return to their Amerindian communities with pride, and they and their children had been welcomed; but this was to be less and less the case, and was probably not an option at all for mixed-blood women. Some wives were turned over to new trader husbands, but others found themselves abandoned and belonging to neither white nor Native worlds.[50]

Such women were probably still better off than those Indian and mixed-blood women who, as European men moved into their territories in greater and greater numbers, found themselves involved in prostitution. The sexual freedom of women in many, if not all, Native tribes was misinterpreted by Europeans. One trader noted that Cree girls were rarely virgins by age 13 or 14; another trader pointed out that "fornication" could hardly be considered a vice among the Indians; according to him, the practice was accepted as "normal."[51] Coupled with the sale of alcohol to Native men and women, prostitution and venereal diseases took their tragic toll. Seventeenth-century accounts of the Nova Scotia Mi'kmaq point to considerable prostitution, drunkenness, and wife-beating. A French traveller saw women who had fallen into "a melancholy so black and profound that they became immersed wholly in a cruel despair." The result, he said, was sometimes suicide.[52]

Yet not all Indian women were victims, nor were their cultures always totally destroyed. Many women and communities wove a careful and resourceful path among the options that were open to them, adapting where possible and surviving as best they could. On the east coast, Mi'kmaq women are examples of those who managed to rescue something of their former lives. Four out of five of their quill-working techniques were lost during the seventeenth century. But by the late eighteenth and early nineteenth centuries, Mi'kmaq craftswomen had developed new techniques for working quills on birchbark, and there was a new flowering of their art, which developed considerable economic importance.[53] It is also probably the case that most Native women who came into intimate contact with white men did so as their tribally sanctioned "country" wives, following the customs of their own peoples, and gaining at least short-term benefits by their actions.

Finally, the vast majority of Indian women, like the Innu, and the Huron before their defeat and dispersal, probably followed a more resistant path, holding on to their cultures and customs and adapting slowly to change. Most of the Huron perished in the Iroquois wars. But by the nineteenth century, Native groups who recognized the damage wrought in their societies by European intrusion retreated where they could, and some at least managed to avoid the tragedies that befell the Beothuk, the Huron, and other decimated groups. In 1838, in a remote part of what was to become the Yukon Territory, a Hudson's Bay Company trader met a 35-year-old "Nahany Chieftainess" whose commanding presence and energy created a lasting impression on him. For perhaps several more generations, women of her region would remain isolated enough to continue their lives relatively untouched by European ways. Certainly by then many aboriginal women clearly understood the threat. In 1850, in the Similkameen and Okanagan areas of the territory that was to become British Columbia, a prophet was travelling through the country urging the Native people to fight white encroachment and to keep their own traditions. They were told to "retain their old customs and not to adopt any of the ways of the white man," because to do this would poison their spirit. The prophet was a woman.[54]

If male observers often referred to the dreariness of Native women's lives, the British feminist Anna Jameson put forward a different opinion when she encountered Amerindian communities in Upper Canada and adjacent regions in the 1830s. Jameson was aware of and called attention to European men's castigations of Amerindian societies for their enslavement and oppression of women. Yet whatever the lot of the Native woman, Jameson pointed out, at least she was not in a *"false* position."

> When we speak of the drudgery of the women, we must note the equal division of labour; there is no class of women privileged to sit still while others work. Every squaw makes the clothing, mats, moccasins, and boils the kettle for her own family. . . . Compare her life with that of a servant-maid of all work, or a factory girl, — I say that the condition of the squaw is gracious in comparison, dignified by domestic feelings, and by equality with all around her. . . . The personal property, as the clothing, mats, cooking and hunting apparatus, all the interior of the wigwam . . . seems to be under the control of the woman. . . . The

corn she raises, and the maple sugar she makes, she can always dispose of as she thinks fit — they are hers.[55]

By all accounts, Indian women worked hard and were strong. Among gatherers and hunters, women supplied a major share of the diet. In all indigenous societies, women's work was essential to the survival of family and band. Should we conclude that Native societies were egalitarian on the whole, at least as far as male/female relations were concerned? Perhaps it is unwise to put our query in these terms. The aboriginal world did not have the concept of individual economic rights. In small gathering-and-hunting bands, where decision-making was often communal, women do seem to have shared power with men. In the Iroquois and Huron agricultural communities, matrons (the leading women in charge of the longhouses) appear to have enjoyed great authority, both in their own realms of production, distribution, and childcare, and in the larger decision-making processes of the group. Among the northwestern and western Native peoples, the situation was more complicated. High-status women could be chieftains, evidently, but many women were relatively powerless.

The history of Indian women continues to be explored; perhaps much of it is permanently lost to us. But where history is lost, legend and story come to our aid. Stories told by contemporary Native and mixed-blood women about the heroines of their mythic past emphasize their ingenuity and practical skills.[56] The Blackfoot tell of "this world's dawn," when the women and the men travelled separately, the women living by their skill near their own buffalo jump in the foothills of Alberta. Two versions of the story agree that it was the men who thought they would benefit by joining up with the women, but that it was the women who chose the husbands they wanted from the group. "Old Man" had been contemptuous of "the leader of the women" in one version; in another, he cheated and tried to get the best woman for himself. In both versions, he ended up an outcast and alone, transformed into a tree; in both versions, women's power is remembered and validated.[57] The stories of Aataentsic and Copper Woman suggest similar legacies of power.

NOTES

1. Sylvia Van Kirk, "Thanadelthur," *The Beaver* (Spring 1974), 40–45.
2. Julia V. Emberley, *Thresholds of Difference: Feminist Critique, Native Women's Writings, Postcolonial Theory* (Toronto: University of Toronto Press, 1993), chap. 4.
3. R. Cole Harris, ed., *Historical Atlas of Canada* (Toronto: University of Toronto Press, 1987), vol. 1, plate 12; Somer Brodribb, "The Traditional Roles of Native Women in Canada and the Impact of Colonization," *Canadian Journal of Native Studies* 4, 1 (1986), 85–103; Karen Anderson, "A Gendered World: Women, Men, and the Political Economy of the Seventeenth Century Huron," in Heather Jon Maroney and Meg Luxton, eds., *Feminism and Political Economy: Women's Work, Women's Struggles* (Toronto: Methuen, 1987), 125. Mi'kmaq is the preferred name for the people formerly known as Micmac.
4. For the distribution of tribal and linguistic groups at the time of contact, see the map on page 7. For more detail on aboriginal peoples prior to and at the time of contact, see Harris, ed., *Historical Atlas of Canada*, vol. 1, plates 2–18, 33–35, and 57–69.

5. See Elisabeth Tooker, "Women in Iroquois Society," in Wendy Mitchinson et al., eds., *Canadian Women: A Reader* (Toronto: Harcourt Brace, 1996), 19–32; and Georges E. Sioui, *For an Amerindian Autohistory* (Montreal and Kingston: McGill-Queen's University Press, 1992), 17.

6. Judith K. Brown, "A Note on the Division of Labour by Sex," *American Anthropologist* 72, 5 (October 1970), 1073–78.

7. Brown, "Note on the Division of Labour," 1076.

8. Judith K. Brown, "Economic Organization and the Position of Women among the Iroquois," *Ethnohistory* 17, 3–4 (Summer/Fall 1970), 151–67; Karen Anderson, "Commodity Exchange and Subordination: Montagnais-Naskapi and Huron Women, 1600–1650," *Signs* 11, 1 (Autumn 1985), 48–62.

9. Brown, "Note on the Division of Labour," 1076. The document is reproduced in James Axtell, ed., *The Indian Peoples of Eastern America: A Documentary History of the Sexes* (New York: Oxford University Press, 1981), 138–39.

10. June Namias, *White Captives: Gender and Ethnicity on the American Frontier* (Chapel Hill: University of North Carolina Press, 1993).

11. Eleanor Leacock and Jacqueline Goodman, "Montagnais Marriage and the Jesuits of the Seventeenth Century: Incidents from the *Relations* of Paul Le Jeune," *Western Canadian Journal of Anthropology* 6, 3 (1976), 77–91; Leacock, "Women in Egalitarian Societies," in Renate Bridenthal and Claudia Koonz, eds., *Becoming Visible: Women in European Society* (Boston: Houghton-Mifflin, 1977), 11–35; Leacock, "Class, Commodity, and the Status of Women," in Ruby Rohrlich-Leavitt, ed., *Women Cross-Culturally: Change and Challenge* (The Hague: Mouton, 1975), 601–16; Leacock, "Montagnais Women and the Jesuit Program for Colonization," in Mona Etienne and Eleanor Leacock, eds., *Women and Colonization: Anthropological Perspectives* (New York: Praeger, 1980), 25–42.

12. Glyndwr Williams, ed., *Andrew Graham's Observations on Hudson's Bay, 1767–91* (London: Hudson's Bay Record Society, 1969), 177–78.

13. W. Kaye Lamb, ed., *The Journals and Letters of Sir Alexander Mackenzie* (Cambridge, U.K.: Published for the Hakluyt Society at Cambridge Press, 1970), 135; Sylvia Van Kirk, *"Many Tender Ties": Women in Fur Trade Society, 1670–1870* (Winnipeg: Watson and Dwyer, 1980), 17–21. Throughout this chapter, except where specifically noted, discussion of women in the fur trade draws on Van Kirk's work.

14. Natalie Zemon Davis, "Iroquois Women, European Women," in Margo Hendricks and Patricia Parker, eds., *Women, "Race," and Writing in the Early Modern Period* (London: Routledge, 1994), 243–58; Elizabeth Vibert, *Traders' Tales: British Fur Traders' Narratives of the Encounter with Plateau Peoples, 1807–1846* (University of Oklahoma Press, 1996).

15. Van Kirk, *"Many Tender Ties,"* 18.

16. Mary Jane Schneider, "Women's Work: An Examination of Women's Roles in Plains Arts and Crafts," and Alan M. Klein, "The Political Economy of Gender: A 19th Century Plains Indian Case Study," both in Patricia Albers and Beatrice Medicine, eds., *The Hidden Half: Studies of Plains Indian Women* (Lanham, N.Y.: University Press of America, 1983), 198, 149; Vibert, *Traders' Tales.*

17. Loraine Littlefield, "Women Traders in the Maritime Fur Trade," in Mitchinson et al., eds., *Canadian Women: A Reader*, 6–19; and Barbara Bodenhorn, " 'I'm Not the Great Hunter, My Wife Is': Inupiat and Anthropological Models of Gender," *Études/ Inuit/Studies* 14, 1–2 (1990), 59–61.

18. Ellice B. Gonzalez, *Changing Economic Roles for Micmac Men and Women: An Ethnohistorical Analysis* (Ottawa: National Museums of Canada, 1981), espec. 15;

Andrew Hill Clark, *Acadia: The Geography of Early Nova Scotia to 1760* (Madison: University of Wisconsin Press, 1968); Virginia P. Miller, "The Decline of Nova Scotia Micmac Population, A.D. 1600–1850," *Culture* 2, 3 (1982), 107–20.

19. Gonzalez, *Changing Economic Roles,* 18.

20. Ruth Holmes Whitehead, *Micmac Quillwork: Micmac Indian Techniques of Porcupine Quill Decoration, 1600–1950* (Halifax: Nova Scotia Museum, 1982).

21. Williams, ed., *Andrew Graham's Observations,* 177.

22. Van Kirk, *"Many Tender Ties,"* 21, 86.

23. Karen Anderson, in her *Chain Her by One Foot: The Subjugation of Women in Seventeenth-Century New France* (London: Routledge, 1991), argues the case for Huron women's power in the political realm prior to and in the early days of contact; Elisabeth Tooker, in "Women in Iroquois Society," and Natalie Zemon Davis, in "Iroquois Women," take a more nuanced view, with Tooker especially seeing little evidence for the argument.

24. Davis, "Iroquois Women," 249.

25. Leacock, "Montagnais Women," 26–27.

26. Davis, "Iroquois Women," 253.

27. Bernard Saladin d'Anglure, "Penser le 'féminin' chamanique, ou le 'tiers sexe' des chamanes inuit," *Recherches amérindiennes au Québec* 18, 2–3 (automne 1988), 24–25.

28. Davis, "Iroquois Women," 248–49; Peter S. Schmalz, *The Ojibwa of Southern Ontario* (Toronto: University of Toronto Press, 1991), 52.

29. Alice B. Kehoe, "The Shackles of Tradition," in Albers and Medicine, eds., *Hidden Half,* 68; Kehoe, "Old Woman Had Great Power," *Western Canadian Journal of Anthropology* 6, 3 (November 1976), 72–74.

30. Leacock, "Montagnais Women"; Leacock and Goodman, "Montagnais Marriage," 80–82.

31. Dickason, *Canada's First Nations,* 169–72.

32. See Anderson, *Chain Her,* for an elaboration of this argument.

33. Van Kirk, *"Many Tender Ties,"* 24–25; Van Kirk, "Toward a Feminist Perspective in Native History," *Occasional Paper* No. 14 (Toronto: Centre for Women's Studies in Education, OISE, 1987), 7.

34. Van Kirk, *"Many Tender Ties,"* espec. chaps. 2 and 4; Margaret Whitehead, " 'A Useful Christian Woman': First Nations' Women and Protestant Missionary Work in British Columbia," *Atlantis* 18, 1–2 (Fall/Winter 1992; Spring/Summer 1993), 153.

35. Van Kirk, *"Many Tender Ties,"* chap. 2; Whitehead, " 'A Useful Christian Woman,' " 162–63 n. 117.

36. Susan R. Sharrock, "Crees, Cree-Assiniboines, and Assiniboines: Interethnic Social Organization on the Far Northern Plains," *Ethnohistory* 12, 2 (Spring 1974), 8.

37. Littlefield, "Women Traders," 173–85.

38. Marjorie Mitchell and Anna Franklin, "When You Don't Know the Language, Listen to the Silence: An Historical Overview of Native Indian Women in B.C.," in Barbara K. Latham and Roberta J. Pazdro, eds., *Not Just Pin Money: Selected Essays on the History of Women's Work in British Columbia* (Victoria: Camosun College, 1984), 17–35.

39. Jan Gould, *Women of British Columbia* (Saanichton: Hancock House, 1975), 13–14.

40. Mitchell and Franklin, "When You Don't," 24.

41. Dickason, *Canada's First Nations,* 226–27. See also William H. Whiteley, "Mikak," *Dictionary of Canadian Biography* (Toronto: University of Toronto Press, 1979), vol. 4, 536–37.

42. Leacock and Goodman, "Montagnais Marriage," 82–88.

43. Cornelius J. Jaenen, *Friend and Foe: Aspects of French–Amerindian Cultural Contact in the Sixteenth and Seventeenth Centuries* (Toronto: McClelland and Stewart, 1976), 76; Nancy Shoemaker, "Kateri Tekakwitha's Tortuous Path to Sainthood," in Nancy Shoemaker, ed., *Negotiators of Change: Historical Perspectives on Native American Women* (New York: Routledge, 1995), 49–71; Henri Béchard, "Tekakwitha," *Dictionary of Canadian Biography* (Toronto: University of Toronto Press, 1966), vol. 1, 635–36.

44. Anderson, "Commodity Exchange," 62.

45. Davis, "Iroquois Women," 254–56.

46. Dickason, *Canada's First Nations*, 169–72.

47. Van Kirk, *"Many Tender Ties,"* 76.

48. Van Kirk, *"Many Tender Ties,"* espec. chap. 4.

49. Van Kirk, *"Many Tender Ties,"* chap. 4; Jennifer S.H. Brown, "Ultimate Respectability: Fur Trade Children in the 'Civilized World,'" *The Beaver* (Winter 1977), 4–10 and (Spring 1978), 48–55.

50. Van Kirk, *"Many Tender Ties,"* chaps. 5–10.

51. Van Kirk, *"Many Tender Ties,"* chap. 1; Mitchell and Franklin, "When You Don't," 25–26.

52. Whitehead, *Micmac Quillwork*, 24.

53. Whitehead, *Micmac Quillwork*, chap. 3.

54. Douglas Sanders, "Indian Women: A Brief History of Their Roles and Rights," *McGill Law Journal* 21, 4 (Winter 1975), 656.

55. Mrs. [Anna] Jameson, *Winter Studies and Summer Rambles in Canada* (London: Saunders and Otley, 1838; reprinted, Toronto: Coles Canadiana Collection, 1972), vol. 3, 305, 308.

56. See Marilyn Ravicz, Diane Battung, and Laura Baker, "Rainbow Women of the Fraser Valley: Lifesongs through the Generations," in Latham and Pazdro, eds., *Not Just Pin Money*, 37–52.

57. Kehoe, "Old Woman," 68; Richard G. Forbis, "The Old Women's Buffalo Jump, Alberta," *National Museum of Canada Bulletin* No. 180, Anthropological Series No. 57 (Ottawa: Department of Northern Affairs and National Resources, 1962), 61.

CHAPTER 2

Women in
New France

On June 25, 1669, just one year after her marriage, a young woman in the advanced stages of pregnancy appeared before the Sovereign Council, the highest judicial body in the colony of Canada. Marie Bourgois had come to charge her husband and father-in-law with denying her the necessities of life. In her moving appeal for support, she reminded the Councillors that she was "a poor woman who had left her father and her mother and her relatives to come to this country."[1] Like Marie Bourgois, many of the women who made the arduous voyage to New France left behind the comforts of family, friends, and familiar surroundings, only to encounter disappoint-

ment and deprivation in a strange and often inhospitable land. Most, however, persevered and took satisfaction in the rerooting of family and society in the New World. Some came from peasant groups, with their superstitions and rowdy rituals, others from bourgeois families of French coastal towns, and others still from the more sophisticated commercial and administrative centres of Paris and Versailles. We have only to think of the nuns, with their mixture of wealthy aristocrats and women with few or no economic resources, to realize the complexities of character and circumstance that marked the lives of French women who came to the New World.

LES PIONNIÈRES

While many of the women who migrated to New France in the seventeenth century were married women or daughters who came with their families, hundreds of single women and widows also tackled the voyage, either alone or in the company of more-distant relations. Some came and went back. Marie Joly, for example, was a Parisian widow who came to Canada with her cousin. In Quebec she contracted a marriage with Antoine Damiens of Rouen, only to return to France and settle in La Rochelle.[2] Many of the single women came with the intention to marry immediately; others came as *engagées* or indentured servants, and had to delay marriage; still others, for whom the religious mission was paramount, came intending to devote their lives to God.

The first married European woman to remain in New France permanently was Marie Rollet, the spouse of the apothecary and farmer Louis Hébert. She established a household in Quebec with her husband in 1617 and lived there with her family until his death, when she joined the farming household of her daughter and son-in-law. This first housewife of New France was on a lower social plane than Hélène Boullé, the 22-year-old gentlewoman who accompanied her husband, the explorer Samuel de Champlain, to Canada in 1620. Hélène Boullé was a wealthy woman: she had been officially married to Champlain at age 12, and by the time she embarked for Quebec her dowry had already paid for the outfitting of one of her husband's earlier expeditions. There must have been a considerable gulf between Madame de Champlain's aristocratic Parisian upbringing and what she found in the New World, but we know little about her except that she had a brother who was in her husband's service and may have given her some companionship during her stay in Canada. She spent four years in the colony, devoting at least some of her time to performing charitable works among the Natives, and then returned to France, eventually to retire to an Ursuline convent that she had founded and endowed.[3]

In sharp contrast to the aristocratic Hélène Boullé, some of the early female colonists were outcasts of French society, recruited from the slums, brothels, and prisons of French ports by unscrupulous representatives of the fur trade monopoly. As part of its contract with the French authorities, the fur trade company was required to send a specified number of settlers each year to New France. However, there was little enthusiasm for this project, since colonists were an unnecessary and expensive investment for those whose primary interest was securing beaver pelts from the aboriginal peoples. Consequently, little attention was paid to the physical or moral qualities of those the company sent out.[4] No doubt it was the initial scarcity of respectable unmarried white women in the colony that led Champlain to favour the establishment of a new "founding race," to be produced as a result of liaisons between French men and Native women. However, the civil and religious authorities in France did not share his enthusiasm, and moved instead to assert more control over the selection of emigrants.

The authorities' efforts to enhance the reputation of the colony and its female inhabitants were greatly aided by women caught up in the zeal of the Counter-Reformation. Inspired by what they read in the *Relations* of the Jesuit missionaries, pious French women soon saw in the New World another and especially fertile field for their spiritual endeavours. These French women were not unique, for similar feelings inspired the Puritans of New England. They were unusual, however, in two important respects. First, a remarkable number of them came to New France independently as single women or as members of female religious societies. Second, the all-female institutions they founded played a vital role in the material, social, and spiritual development of their colony. Similar charitable and social institutions were not created in Britain's American colonies until at least the eighteenth century, and even then few, if any, welfare establishments in those colonies were run by women.[5]

In 1639 an order of nuns called the *Hospitalières* arrived in the vicinity of Quebec. The two sisters who directed Quebec's first medical mission, Marie Grunet and Marie Forrestier, were responding to a need outlined in the 1635 *Relations* of Father Lejeune, and their first thought was for the Native community then living at Sillery, outside the fortress of Quebec. In 1644, the Sillery mission was abandoned as a result of the Iroquois wars; the hospital nuns then moved into the citadel and made the French population the focus of their care. Operating at first in a small wooden structure, the sisters had acquired a larger building by 1658. Boasting eight doors and eight windows, this hospital normally held ten beds, but in times of epidemic could accommodate up to twenty. By 1672 the *Hôtel-Dieu*, as the hospital was called, had expanded to two halls — one for women and one for men — and also included a small chamber for wealthier patients.[6]

The Ursulines also came to Quebec in 1639 expecting to devote themselves to the aboriginal peoples, only to have these expectations crushed when many of their Native charges proved resistant to their "civilizing" mission. The strict discipline of the convent school was alien to homesick Native girls, who, with the aid of their parents, slipped away to the forest. Soon the principal function of the Ursuline convent was to educate the daughters of the French colonists.

Marie (Guyart) de l'Incarnation, the founder of the Quebec Ursuline convent, had nurtured a religious vocation through adolescence, marriage, motherhood, widowhood, and a ten-year business involvement in the mercantile household of her brother-in-law. Her faith eventually led Marie Guyart to enter a convent in Tours, but not before she had learned much in the management of her brother-in-law's business affairs that would be of practical value in her future work in New France. Indeed, the creation of a convent school in Quebec involved far more than an understanding of the management of children. She had to assure the community's finances, which were only partly organized by her patron and chief fundraiser, Mme de la Peltrie; she had to oversee the construction of the first convent and then of a second one when the first was destroyed by fire; and she had to deal with the complicated matter of provisioning her community in the midst of the wars waged between the French and the Iroquois. Held in high regard by the colony's civil authorities, Marie de l'Incarnation was often consulted on matters of public policy. She was also prepared to confront the powerful first bishop of New France, Montmorency de Laval, when it appeared he wanted to change the Ursulines' constitution of 1647.[7] Somehow, while she governed the Quebec Ursulines and ran a boarding school for Amerindian and French girls, this astounding woman also found time to write not only several religious works in Native languages and in French, but also some 12 000 letters to her son and to others in France who were interested in her New World mission.[8]

The lives of the women who founded religious communities in the mission called Ville Marie (Montreal) were no less demanding. In one way these women were even more unusual than the nuns of Quebec, for neither of the two key figures in the women's religious foundations of Montreal were at first members of established orders. Jeanne Mance was a single woman in her mid-thirties when she came to Canada in 1641. She first settled in Quebec, in order to study the organization of the *Hôtel-Dieu* there and to learn the Huron language; only then did she move on to Ville Marie to found its first medical dispensary. As an entrepreneur and organizer, she must have had few equals. Her efforts included three trips back to France to raise money and to search out an order of nuns to staff the new mission, and a major battle with the bishop of Quebec for the right to bring a second nursing order to New France. The hospital nuns of *Saint-Joseph de la Flèche* were installed by permission of the French king against the will of Bishop Laval, who would have preferred to send a detachment of the sisters already established in the hospital at Quebec.[9]

Laval also fought with the *Congrégation de Notre-Dame*, the creation of another laywoman, Marguerite Bourgeoys, who joined Paul de Chomedey de Maisonneuve's Montreal mission as an educator. She eventually felt the need for assistants in her educational work and returned to France to find like-minded women. The result was a secular community, founded in 1671, that was to become the *Congrégation*. The creation of an order of religious women who did not remain behind convent walls, but rather lived and worked in the community, was truly remarkable for this period. The teachers of Bourgeoys's new order came into conflict not only with the bishop of Quebec, but also with the larger church and its rules, because they preferred not to wear distinctive habits, take solemn public vows, or cloister themselves; they argued that their guide and teacher was none other than the Virgin Mary, who had remained in the world without benefit of formal vows or, presumably, distinctive dress. She had nevertheless fulfilled her religious destiny, and so would they.[10]

At first religious communities shared with the fur trading monopoly — the Company of One Hundred Associates — the task of recruiting brides for French soldiers and traders wishing to settle in the New World. It was generally the nuns who took charge of the single women who came to the colony with the intention of marrying, until these *filles à marier* found husbands. When royal officials assumed direct control of the colony in 1663, they became actively involved in promoting the immigration of single women. Between 1643 and 1663, only 230 unmarried female immigrants had made their way to New France; in the next decade, nearly 800 single women, known as the *filles du roi* ("daughters of the king"), arrived. Interested parties like Jean Talon, the intendant of New France during the early years of royal government, wanted to be sure that the young women selected to enjoy the king's bounty were indeed going to be useful immigrants. Talon specified that the women destined for Canada should be in no way "disgraced by nature" or have anything "repulsive about their exterior persons." He also demanded that "they should be healthy and strong for country work, or at least that they have some inclination to work with their hands." Fears were expressed by others that women brought up in cities like Paris might not adapt well to conditions in New France. In fact, on the whole, they adapted well. It has been estimated that only half of all immigrants to New France remained for the rest of their lives, but of the single women who came to be married there, nine out of ten became permanent settlers.[11]

The social origins of the *filles du roi* were diverse. However, more than 30 percent were recruited from the Paris *Hôpital-Général*, an institution that harboured women who had become pregnant out of wedlock, as well as orphans and abandoned children. Two-thirds of these immigrants had not yet attained adulthood before their fathers died, and only one-third were able to sign their own names. Many were clearly young women whose parents or remaining parent could not arrange good marriages for their daughters. Most of the *filles* were of humble origins, with only eight known to have been of noble birth.[12] Three sisters, Françoise, Marie-Madeleine, and Marie- Raclot, not only had good dowries for the time, but were accompanied to New France by their father in 1671. The latter stayed in the colony only long enough to sign the marriage contracts of two of his daughters. Aged 18, 17, and 15 when they came to New France, the Raclot sisters settled in the vicinity of Three Rivers with the husbands they had acquired within a few months of their arrival.[13]

Most of the *filles*, like the inmates of the *Hôpital-Général* and these sisters, came from Paris or from other relatively large centres, and many must have been ill-prepared for the new lives that awaited them. Of those whose ages were recorded, the majority were between 12 and 25, but a significant one in four was older. Their main interest, once in Canada, was reportedly a practical one: to find husbands who had already built houses or cabins on their land. A full 40 percent married within just two months of their arrival, and the fact that some 11 percent entered into more than one marriage contract before going through with the final religious ceremony suggests not only a healthy respect for their own self-interest, but a willingness to take advantage of their major trump card: the scarcity of unmarried women in New France. The women were promised substantial dowries by the king, according to their station, to assist them and their husbands in setting up their households; no doubt these dowries added to their considerable bargaining power. One source values the "king's gift" at between 100 and 500 *livres*, with further disbursements for practical items that would be needed either immediately in the way of clothing or equipment (including 100 sewing needles), or later, in the way of household goods. The Raclot sisters received gifts from the king in addition to the dowry of 1000 *livres* each given by their father. It appears, however, that they were part of a fortunate minority, since only one-third of the women actually received the promised dowry amounts.[14]

At least 770 "daughters of the king" came to New France between 1663 and 1673 to join the approximately 1200 men and women colonists who had arrived earlier. In Montreal by 1681, more than two-thirds of the 161 women immigrants were *filles seules* — women who were neither nuns nor servants and yet had come to the colony alone.[15] After the special push of the 1660s and 1670s and until the 1750s, the French colonies welcomed an average of fewer than 50 new arrivals a year; fewer than one in five of these were women. Altogether, immigrants numbered fewer than 10 000 for the entire French regime. In the eighteenth-century trading and military fortress of Louisbourg, where the immigrants came mostly from the bourgeois and artisan classes, women were never more than one-tenth of the immigrants or one-third of the total population. In New France as a whole, women were also very much a minority at first. But by 1760, of the nearly 70 000 people who made up the total population of New France, the numbers of men and women were finally almost equal.[16]

FAMILY AND WORK

Most of the women who came to New France married. As in comparable English colonies of the period, the rates of marriage and remarriage were very high — in one sample that has been studied, one-third of all widows married again. The story of Anne Le Sont of Three Rivers, while perhaps atypical, is nevertheless instructive. The employer of this middle-aged *engagée* had prevailed upon her to sign a life contract in November 1655, and took her to court when she married Jean Desmarais soon after her arrival. The affair was settled in Anne's favour, but only after a suitable apology for her "insulting words" and on payment of the plaintiff's costs. Perhaps more typical was the case of the young *engagée* Judithe Rigeault, who, when she married a soldier and master tailor named François le Maître, still owed a portion of the five years she had contracted to serve Mme Le Neuf de la Poterie. Once again a court case ensued, and once again the financial obligations of both parties had to be worked out before a settlement could be reached.[17]

Anne Le Sont was much older than the average bride when she married, but this may not have been her first marriage. In general, servants who came out to New France on their own appear to have married in their early twenties.[18] But even this was older than average for girls who were born in the colony in the seventeenth century, for at first the average age at which women married in New France was very young compared to typical marriages in western Europe at this time. Young people were not supposed to marry until puberty, but there is evidence that occasionally girls as young as 12 and 13 embarked on matrimony during the initial period of colonization, when men vastly outnumbered women. Estimates of average age at first marriage have varied depending on the period or region studied. For rural families before 1700, the average was 19.6 for women and 27.3 for men. A different pattern has been uncovered for mid-eighteenth-century Sorel, however. By this time, the numbers of men and women had almost evened out; the average age at first marriage was 22.4 for women, and 26.6 for men. For New France as a whole, the average age for those contracting marriage for the first time has been placed at 22 for women (three years younger than was typical in France itself) and 27 for men. Relatively large groups of people delayed marriage: some 18 percent of men and women did not marry until they were 30 or older; 6 percent were 40 or older.[19]

The royal administration gave explicit encouragement to early marriages in New France. A seventeenth-century statute provided that men marrying at 25 or younger and women marrying by 20 were entitled to a bonus of 20 *livres* from the Crown; a further law imposed fines on the parents of young people who failed to marry by the required age. Colonial authorities publicly regretted young men becoming *coureurs du bois* or fur traders, and persons of either sex remaining celibate. The married state was officially encouraged for both sexes, as was the production of children. The religious authorities also co-operated, as in the case of the *filles du roi*, by dispensing with the requirement that banns be published before a marriage could be celebrated.[20]

Certainly the state's fundamental goal in sponsoring female immigration and rewarding early marriage was to promote population growth. If New France was to survive and prosper, the production of people was considered a vital necessity for obtaining the workers and soldiers essential to mercantilist economics. Individual couples also equated children with wealth. Children were workers, first and foremost for their own families.

For much of the seventeenth century, economic factors and the unequal numbers of men and women probably had most effect on age at marriage and the high rates of marriage and remarriage. They even affected the season of marriage, which, before 1680, was typically early autumn, immediately following the arrival of the ships from France. Later on, when the sexes were more equal in number, January and early

February became the most popular season for weddings. Finally, the relatively low age at which women in New France married and the high rates of remarriage almost certainly helped boost the average number of children per marriage, as did the fact that spouses lived slightly longer than they did in Europe. In eighteenth-century Acadia, for example, four out of five marriages were "complete" in the sense that both spouses survived to the end of the wife's childbearing years. Infant mortality was high in New France — approximately one in four children died before reaching his or her first birthday — but surviving children were probably healthier than they were in the Old World. So were adults. For all these reasons, it is not surprising that women in Canada gave birth to eight or nine children on the average in the early years (seven from 1700 on), and that the average "completed" family was 5.65 children per couple (compared to 4.5 in France at this time). Studies indicate that relatively large families were characteristic of other European colonists in North America in the seventeenth and eighteenth centuries, for good food was generally available and European diseases not so rampant, at least among white populations. Still, the numbers of children born and surviving seem to have been particularly high in New France.[21]

The seasons influenced the rhythms of childbirth in New France. Historians have discovered that conception tended to occur in the winter and spring, and that there were slight differences between Montreal and Quebec in this seasonal timing. The church had an influence as well: there were fewer conceptions during the seasons of Advent and Lent, when the population was expected to focus on religious duties and to refrain from the pleasures of the body.[22] Childbirth was a major social-event. Women gave birth at home, assisted by midwives, and often in the presence of a large group of people — certainly with relatives and perhaps the priest very close at hand. The event frequently took place at the home of the new mother's parents, and was accompanied by important rituals: the baptism, which took place as soon as possible after the birth, and a "*repas de baptême*" or festive meal to repay and thank

TABLE 2.1 *Marriage and Birth Rates, New France, 1681–1760*[a]

	Marriages	Births
1681–1690	9.2	43.3
1691–1700	10.5	53.4
1701–1710	9.1	57.8
1711–1720	10.2	57.5
1721–1730	10.2	55.2
1731–1740	9.4	56.6
1741–1750	10.4	55.9
1751–1760	11.3	59.6

[a] PER 1000 INHABITANTS.

Source: From Jacques Henripin, *Trends and Factors of Fertility in Canada*, 1961 Census Monograph, Cat. No. 99-541 (Ottawa: Minister of Industry, 1968). Reproduced by authority of the Minister of Industry, 1995.

the assistants. A new mother might have women friends stay for a week to help after her child was born; she would usually have her own mother's assistance for at least a month.[23] Unfortunately, childbirth was also dangerous, and the maternal mortality rate was significant; the death rate for women in the childbearing-age category (15 to 49 years) was higher than that for men in the same age classification. When the mother did survive, and her marriage was unbroken by the death of her husband, she was likely to have a child every two to three years. Prolonged breast-feeding reduced the likelihood of more-frequent conceptions. However, there was one social group that deviated from this trend — the nobility. By the eighteenth century, noble-women in Canada were sending 60 to 70 percent of their newborns to a wet nurse, and consequently they experienced shorter intervals between births. The infant mortality rate for the nobility also climbed dramatically as a result of this practice, so that while 73 percent of noble infants survived to 20 years and beyond in the seventeenth century, less than 40 percent of those born between 1735 and 1765 did so.[24]

Children meant work for women, since the labour of childbirth and childrearing was particularly hard in the difficult pioneer conditions that obtained in both town and country in the New World. Yet, as they grew up, many children could eventually lighten a woman's workload. Older children minded younger ones, and girls helped when they were old enough with all the tasks of the household, garden, farm, or workshop that fell to women. These tasks were many, and their value was high. Few households, farms, or businesses could run without the work of women.

Women spent most of their time on the production of food. Soups, stews, roasts, and bread were standard fare and were cooked mostly in open fireplaces.

A depiction by Jean-Claude Dupont of a birthing scene in New France.

Source: Courtesy of Jean-Claude Dupont.

Rural women probably laboured as much at the tasks of butchering, curing, and drying meat, the various tasks of the dairy and the poultry yard, and the growing of vegetables and fruit as they did at the work of preparing the food for the table. In the Lower Richelieu valley by the eighteenth century, women typically grew squash, onions, cabbages, and tobacco in their gardens. Travellers in Acadia commented on the large variety of vegetables that were grown, including "cabbages, beets, onions, carrots, chives, shallots, turnips, and all sorts of salads." Even urban women kept cows and poultry and had vegetable gardens when they could, although most produce and grains were generally purchased from the surrounding countryside.[25]

Women in New France also shared in the work of their husbands. At certain busy times of the year, farm women worked in the fields; artisans' and merchants' wives were frequently skilled assistants to their spouses. Both rural and urban women often kept the accounts and managed the servants or apprentices, if there were any. Owing to the periodic absences of their husbands, soldiers' and traders' wives sometimes had to take complete charge of their households, farms, and businesses. Existing notarial records clearly indicate the extensive responsibilities and legal powers that they assumed in these situations.[26] They also occasionally found that the fur trade or the wars or both had arrived on their very doorsteps. The 14-year-old Madeleine de Verchères was only one of many women who fired a gun, or took over when men were absent, in skirmishes with enemies. Indeed, Madeleine's own mother had defended the fort at Verchères from Iroquois attack in 1690, two years before her daughter was called upon to do so in 1692. In the early days of Acadia, Françoise-Marie Jacquelin de la Tour spent a good part of the first four years of her marriage travelling back and forth between France, New England, and her husband's fort at the mouth of the St. John River, working to defend his precarious position in the Acadian trade. Finally settled in Fort La Tour during one of his absences, she not only took charge of its defence but was forced to witness the execution of nearly all of its men after its capture. Mme de la Tour herself did not survive this defeat by many weeks; she died at Fort La Tour in 1645.[27]

Although not all came to grief in such a traumatic way, most seventeenth-century women of New France probably experienced warfare firsthand. The eighteenth century brought somewhat more peaceful times, as the Iroquois threat declined and New France expanded. It also brought economic development. Few if any women had the time or the facilities for spinning or weaving in seventeenth-century Canada. Except for Native-style clothing made of leather, most wearing apparel and fabrics for bedding and the like had to be imported, and early wills suggest how few clothes even the most prosperous colonists possessed. Despite the scarcity of local materials, clerics and upper-class visitors to the colony commented on women's "idleness," and they urged the authorities to establish a textile industry. The women themselves maintained that more-pressing work took up their time, but as time went on, they began to be involved in the production of spun and woven goods. Acadian women learned many crafts from their Mi'kmaq neighbours; birchbark household utensils and leather moccasins were only a few of the items they adopted as their own. Yet it is important to stress how few farms or communities in the New World were entirely self-sufficient. Goods like needles, metal pots, and farm tools had to be imported, as did fancier items like silk fabrics and dress shoes. The movement of both goods and people was considerable in New France.[28]

Madeleine de Verchères was used as a model of patriotism to inspire Canadian women to enlist in the armed forces during World War II.

Source: AN#56-05-12-139. Photo by William Kent. © Canadian War Museum 1995.

WOMEN'S STATUS

Women worked hard in New France. Some immigrants to the New World, according to seventeenth-century witnesses, longed for the "sweetness" of life in the country of their birth. But others reported that most people were better off in New France than their social equals were in the Old World.[29]

Like the society of France, that of New France was hierarchical, and stratified both by gender and class. A woman's social position was determined first by that of her father, and subsequently by that of her husband. Individual privileges were determined by one's social ranking (*ordre*); and family and group interests, not individual rights, were paramount. Because the colony was fashioned according to the absolutist principles of the seventeenth-century French monarchy, there were no representative institutions or democratic forms of government in the colony. The minority of women who reached the age of majority — set at 25 years — without marrying were deemed to have the same legal status as men in all but one respect: they could not be appointed to public office. There is reason to believe that women's position, both within marriage and outside it, was stronger in New France than would be that of their female descendants in the latter half of the nineteenth century. As in France, the law was harsh in some respects, but it did provide a measure of protection to married women. Women of the upper and middle classes were sometimes able to play influential (if not always "official") roles in trade, political life, and medicine. Finally, the missionary church provided opportunities for religious women, especially those in leadership roles, to organize their own lives.

The women of New France enjoyed relative freedom of choice in marriage. Among rural women in particular, there appears to have been little interference from either parents or clergy in the selection of a partner, although the church was anxious to prevent the marriage of people who were too closely related, and parental permission was officially required.[30] All marriages were subject to the rules laid down in the *Coutume de Paris*. Under this law, married women had a status inferior to that of their husbands and were "severely restricted in their rights and prerogatives." The law clearly regarded the man as the head of the household. Widows usually could not exercise guardianship over their own children. But the same law did afford some important economic protection both to married women and to widows. The spouses were seen to have mutual obligations toward each other. Brides were expected to bring a dowry into marriage, the size of which varied with their social class. Within the colonial elite, parents exerted considerable pressure on their sons to choose a mate who would bring wealth into the family. Because New France was a patriarchal, patrilineal society, a wife adopted her husband's social position: the daughter of a noble family who married a commoner lost her noble status, as did her children, while the daughter of a commoner who married a nobleman became a member of the nobility, and her children were also considered noble.[31]

The "community of property" that came into being at a marriage did impose some restrictions on the husband. Whatever property his wife brought into the marriage, he was to administer with care, and he could not dispose of it without his wife's permission. Furthermore, he was to use whatever property the couple acquired after marriage to support his wife and children. On the death of her husband, the widow could choose to continue the "community" or to renounce it, along with any outstanding debts. By virtue of her dower rights, she was entitled to receive half the income generated by the communal property until her own death.[32]

Because of the complexity of the laws governing matrimony, it is not surprising that a significant proportion of marriages—indeed, as many as 95 percent in some regions of France—involved written contracts. Studies of seventeenth-century Canadian marriages indicate that about 65 percent of marriage partners drew up such contracts, while by the eighteenth century, approximately 80 percent did so.[33] Often signed by dozens of witnesses, these contracts also provide a fascinating glimpse of the social networks surrounding brides and grooms, as well as evidence of their social standing in their communities. Studies of contracts have shown that there was considerable social mobility in New France. Although unions among the wealthier classes were arranged with economic or political interests in mind, they nevertheless crossed boundaries between the landed aristocracy, the merchant class, and the military. A woman could make her way in the world through the right sort of marriage, as could a man.[34]

Considerable information also survives regarding the pensions of older women and widows. If a woman chose to give up her farm or her household to a son or daughter (or another person) in return for her subsistence, the *pension alimentaire* usually contained very specific provisions. The widow Thibeault, who lived in the Richelieu valley in 1760, was to be provided with heat, light, clothing, and house-room, according to the arrangement she made with her family. Her annual allotment of food included 16 *minots* (bushels) of flour, 1/4 *minot* of salt, and 120 pounds of salt pork. Another widow's pension specified that she should be provided with two pairs of French shoes every year.[35] It is hard to know how to interpret these documents. Did such arrangements mean security and comfort for aging widows? Or were they last-ditch attempts to defend women against relatives whose good will could not be counted on? Whatever the answer, at least the notarized pensions of New France did provide a modicum of support to women who otherwise might have had none.

Women played a significant role in the commercial life of New France. The introduction of the textile industry to early eighteenth-century Canada is credited to Agathe de Saint-Père, Madame de Repentigny, of Montreal. Left to manage a family of ten stepsisters and stepbrothers after the death of her mother, Agathe de Saint-Père married Legardeur de Repentigny in 1685 and produced eight children of her own. Children evidently did not take up all her time, however, for Agathe de Saint-Père was heavily involved in the buying and selling of contracts, fur trade licences, and land. Soon Mme de Repentigny was also experimenting with textiles because of continuing shortages in the colony. At first she worked with Native fibres such as bark, cottonweed, and buffalo hair; by 1705, her productions had already caught the king's attention. But it was the sinking of a supply vessel that was the catalyst for her most daring experiment. Mme de Repentigny ransomed nine English weavers who were being held captive by the Native allies of the French, had looms manufactured, engaged apprentices to learn the craft, and turned her home into a workshop to make "linen, drugget, twilled and covert-coating serge." Soon there were more than twenty looms in Montreal, and an independent manufactory had been created.[36]

Agathe de Saint-Père was only one of several women who are known to have been active in the commercial world of New France. Marie-Anne Barbel is another. At first this Quebec housewife must have been much taken up with childbirth and childrearing: she had fourteen children altogether, although only five survived to adulthood. But she must also have been actively involved in the business affairs connected with the store her husband, Jean-Louis Fornel, ran in Quebec between 1723 and 1737. In the late 1730s, Fornel became increasingly involved in entrepreneurial activity and exploration. When he departed in 1743 on a major expedition to explore the Baie des Esquimaux, Fornel left his Quebec business affairs in the hands of his wife. When her husband died two years later, Marie-Anne Barbel did not dissolve the community of property established at her marriage. Instead, she took sole charge. She continued a business partnership with two other entrepreneurs in a fishing concession, fought lawsuits with the government in connection with that concession and another, and traded for furs in Tadoussac. She also bought and sold properties, quarrelled with the Jesuits over a piece of land, and established a brickworks. Not all of her undertakings were successful. The widow Fornel managed to establish only two of her five children in marriages (one of which failed), and she was not among the top-ranking "notables" of New France. On the other hand, this enterprising businesswoman was able to pay off all her debts, and she supported herself, three unmarried children, and the fourth daughter (who had separated from her husband and returned to the family) in relative comfort until her death at age 90. Many similar cases have been recorded of widows being actively involved in the commercial life of New France; perhaps it was this possibility of exercising a considerable degree of autonomy over their own affairs that led upper-class widows, particularly those over the age of 30, to remarry less often and after a longer interval than widowers of the same class.[37]

Women in New France could also play a role in politics — albeit an indirect one, since they were not allowed to hold any public office other than that of midwife. However, as wives and mistresses, or through other relationships, some women did exert considerable influence. Marie-Madeleine Maisonnat, an Acadian woman married to a British officer in Port Royal after its transfer to the British Crown in 1713, was said to have had influence in military circles there, which she used to help her fellow Acadians. And in eighteenth-century Canada, as the French regime was drawing to a close, at least two important government officials were thought to have been under the sway of women. Mme Péan was reputedly the mistress of the powerful intendant François Bigot, attracting him to her salon every evening and thereby becoming the envy of the entire capital. The wife of Governor Vaudreuil became so influential at a certain point that petitioners began to go directly to her rather than to the governor.[38]

Women also played significant business and political roles on a much humbler level. They operated taverns; illegal as well as legal trading operations; and, in one case, a sawmill. Women also protested publicly when things went wrong. One group hurled insults at the governor to express their anger in the 1670s; and in the difficult period just before the fall of Quebec in 1759, women were involved in public demonstrations protesting the food shortages caused by the war with England. The first of these protests occurred in December 1757. Governor Vaudreuil, away from Quebec on business in Montreal, had just ended the distribution of bread, substituting a ration of horsemeat and beef that was to be available at a reduced price. A group of women made their way to the governor's Montreal residence, demanding bread and protesting their repugnance at the idea of eating horsemeat. Vaudreuil responded by arranging for the women to be taken on a tour of the butchery in order to assure themselves that all was in order, but also by threatening to throw the women in jail and hang half of them if they rioted again. Although the ringleaders were to have been arrested, none were, probably because the authorities were more concerned about restive soldiers. In Quebec the following April, continuing food shortages again brought women out into the streets, this time to call on the lieutenant-general of the police. The arrival of ships evidently alleviated the misery for a time; but by the winter of 1758–59, rumours of further rationing of bread produced a final protest. On this occasion, some 400 women marched to the palace of the intendant, demanding redress. Their protest was successful. Wheat was brought to Quebec from Lachine, and the intendant promised an increase in the bread ration.[39]

We do not know whether women participated in the more formally constituted popular assemblies that were occasionally held at the local community level in New France. But their participation in the food riots of the 1750s is significant. When their own interests were at stake, and feeding their households was clearly an important concern, they did not hesitate to move into the streets in an effort to force the government's hand. By doing so, they were following a long tradition of women's street demonstrations in France.

Women also played a vital role in medicine in the colony. Experienced older laywomen were often the leading healers of their communities, and acted as midwives at births. The midwife especially was an important community figure, whose office — sometimes an elective one — was strongly supported and, as time went on, to some extent controlled by the church. By the early 1700s, each territory had an official midwife; by the middle of the century, four midwives in New France were being paid salaries by the French state. Midwives' knowledge was passed on from generation to generation — often, though not always, from mothers to daughters or daughters-in-law. The women who performed this role were by no means impoverished or unskilled. On the contrary, most were educated and respected members of their communities, with above-average wealth.[40]

As nuns, women were actively involved in both the religious life and the secular life of the colony. While the most important male religious orders — the Jesuits and the Sulpicians — remained closed to individuals born in New France, the women's religious orders actively recruited within the local population: by 1690, the majority of nuns were Canadian-born. Interestingly, nearly one out of every five noblewomen who reached age 15 became a nun, compared to just under 4 percent of all *Canadiennes* born before 1739. Convent life was particularly attractive for educated women because it allowed them to exercise their administrative skills, and their work affected a great many people. Quebec's *Hôtel-Dieu*, for example, admitted some 3297 men and 1765 women in the decade between 1689 and 1698 alone. Men probably predominated because they were more susceptible to accidents and military injury, while both sexes suffered from seasonal sickness and from epidemics. Patients of both sexes were usually young, and the hospital's death rate was low. Indeed, from all accounts Quebec's *Hôtel-Dieu* was a far more pleasant place than European hospitals of the same era, or than North American hospitals were later to become.[41]

A study of the financial dealings of the sisters who ran the *Hôpital-Général*, a Quebec almshouse founded in 1701, regarding some property left to the nuns by a generous bishop, shows a group of women deeply aware of their economic interests and prepared to defend them. The battle over the bishop's property lasted fifteen years and did not, in the end, result in a settlement very favourable to the convent. On the other hand, the nuns followed the complexities of the case (a good part of which were unravelled in France) assiduously; they refused to act hastily and defended themselves from accepting financial burdens that might have been insurmountable. They saw their battle, moreover, as a fight for justice and for the rights that were due them. Their efforts show that although they were cloistered, these women had frequent contacts with the outside world and were much involved in the property struggles that were so characteristic of their times. A less happy story is that of the small *Congrégation de Notre-Dame* convent school that the church founded in Louisbourg in 1727. This community was in difficulties from the start: the Quebec bishop, Monseigneur de Saint-Vallier, sent its first teaching sister to Louisbourg against the wishes of both the Crown and the mother superior of her order in Montreal. Marguerite Roy, *Soeur de la Conception*, who managed the school for its first seven years, ran the *Congrégation* into serious debt by tying up two-thirds of her income in payments for the building she bought for her new community.[42]

Most convent managers did better, although financial problems were endemic to all religious orders throughout the history of New France. Convent women made extraordinary efforts to raise money for their communities, however, and some had notable success. Their leaders made frequent fundraising journeys to France; often it was the women themselves who secured the loans or gifts; often it was also women who gave. At a more modest level, there were the efforts of the nuns to support themselves in New France through extra work. In Louisbourg, the teaching sisters made bedding and straw mattresses for the barracks in order to earn much-needed cash;[43] elsewhere, the nuns sold embroidery or raised funds through other crafts.

Not only were convent women involved in managing their communities, they also engaged in the intellectual and spiritual currents of their times. *Mère* Sainte-Hélène of Quebec's *Hôtel-Dieu* corresponded with physicians in France who were willing to send her medical supplies and who were also interested in the medicinal herbs and remedies discovered in New France. Marie Morin is considered to be the first writer born in Canada. Her *annales* of Montreal's *Hôtel-Dieu* are an absorbing account of the nuns' struggles for daily survival in the face of poverty and natural disasters like fires, and of the early years not only of the convent but also of Montreal. The letters and spiritual writings of Marie de l'Incarnation were published by her son in the eighteenth century and circulated widely. Laywomen too were involved in the intellectual currents of their times. The daughter of the explorer Noël Jérémie sent notes about native herbs and medicines to scientists in France, and the Canadian samples she had gathered to the *Jardin des plantes* in Paris.[44]

Although we catch only glimpses of them, there were poor and abused women in New France, particularly in the urban centres of Quebec, Montreal, and Louisbourg; and there were slaves, both Native and black. Domestic servants were frequently forced to accept the sexual advances of the male members of the household in which they were engaged. If they became pregnant, they were likely to lose their employment; in a desperate effort to avoid detection, some resorted to abortion, infanticide, or abandoning their newborn.[45]

In the *annales* of Louisbourg's *Congrégation de Notre-Dame*, we read of a woman and her children who were taken in by the sisters because she had been repeatedly beaten by her husband. In another instance, the parishioners of St-Esprit on Cape Breton Island petitioned the colonial authorities to imprison and then deport a man who regularly beat his wife and children. They appear to have dispensed their own rough justice by giving him a sound thrashing before turning him over to the authorities. However, far too many abused wives were left to their own devices; tragically, some were murdered by their husbands. In an equally tragic although atypical case, a 12-year-old girl married a man who drank heavily and subsequently beat her. Within a year, to save their daughter from further abuse, her parents murdered the man. Because of her young age, the daughter escaped the death penalty but was fined and ordered to watch the execution of her parents.[46]

In addition, there is the fragmentary record of the slave Marie-Joseph-Angélique, who, when threatened with sale, set fire to her owner's house and ran away. Angélique was apprehended and condemned to death; her story survives in history as the first recorded resistance to the cruelty of slavery by a black woman in Canada. Chiefly through the convents, the problems of poverty and abuse were somewhat mitigated in New France. But the concern for the welfare of the population evidently did not extend to those who were slaves. In Louisbourg, for example, black and Native slaves were clearly the most exploited group of women: one black slave named Marie-Louise gave birth to six illegitimate children during the sixteen years she was owned by a local merchant.[47]

It is impossible to speak about the women of New France as a single, undifferentiated entity or to generalize about their position in society. There is no doubt that the founders of convents and the businesswomen of Montreal and Quebec, as members of the upper classes, had more opportunities than others to develop their skills, communicate in the world, and accomplish their goals. Yet these women must have reflected something of their larger communities. They could not have sprung unaided out of a soil that was altogether alien. Their relative wealth compared to that of the majority of women in France, and the leverage created by their small numbers in the early years of the colony's existence, were among the circumstances that helped them survive and sometimes flourish. But theirs was nevertheless a world that officially regarded women as secondary to men in the formal hierarchies of state, church, and family, even as these evolved and changed to meet the challenges of the New World.

EDUCATION AND CULTURE

Originally, the educational mission of the French religious women who came to North America was to teach the aboriginal children. Marie de l'Incarnation of the Ursulines learned two Native languages and translated religious tracts for the use of her pupils and their people, but the results were disappointing. Her subjects resisted acculturation to a way of life that seemed unnatural and alien to them. Some Native girls were assimilated to the extent of marrying French men, but few were willing to stay in the Quebec convent for more than a very short time. Gradually, the Ursulines modified their ambitions, turning their attention to the French girls growing up in the colony.

As in France, the order developed boarding schools chiefly for the daughters of the well-to-do, combining them with day schools for poorer children. By the time of the British Conquest, there were two Ursuline schools, one in Quebec and a second in Three Rivers. The convent in Quebec usually had about twelve boarders at any given time. Since most children attended school for only a year or so, one can argue that the brief but all-enveloping education provided by the sisters affected more girls than would at first seem likely from such a small number. Indeed, there is reason to believe that, if we include the day school, nearly all the girls who lived in Quebec came at least for a time to the Ursulines to be taught.[48]

The other great teaching order of New France was the *Congrégation de Notre-Dame*, founded by Marguerite Bourgeoys in Montreal. The *Congrégation* focussed all its attention at first on the creation of schools for the female children of the poor. The order expanded more rapidly than the Ursulines, founding schools in at least twelve different missions, although not all of them survived. By 1760, the *Congrégation de Notre-Dame* could count a total of seventy sisters in its various convents in New France — twice the number of any other order.[49]

Other religious orders also founded schools for girls, but none achieved the reputation in education of either the *Congrégation* or the Ursulines during the French period. That reputation was based on their success in preparing girls for their first communion (a preparation that involved learning to read and write, and to recite an appropriate catechism) and in teaching girls domestic arts (or, as Marie de l'Incarnation put it, "all sorts of work proper to their sex").[50]

Marguerite Bourgeoys with her Native and French pupils in a painting by Soeur Marie Elmina Lachance.

....

Source: Marguerite Bourgeoys Centre, Congrégation de Notre-Dame, Montreal.

The convent schools of New France in the seventeenth and eighteenth centuries shared with all schools of their time a growing emphasis on regularity and discipline. Because the schools were small and familial, and because pupils stayed for relatively short periods, there was perhaps little of the regimentation and rigidity we associate with educational institutions today. Yet the nuns themselves espoused the "regular" life, and days in school were ordered by the ringing of bells. French nuns, Marie de l'Incarnation included, sometimes found their Canadian pupils almost as undisciplined as the aboriginal ones, and the taming of this wild spirit became a major goal of their schooling. Proper manners, the ability to hold a conversation, delicacy—all were intended results of convent instruction, particularly for Ursuline boarders. The gracious and lively manners of urban *Canadiennes* noted by eighteenth-century travellers may have owed something to this program of social development.

Girls in rural areas, unless their parents could afford to send them to board at a convent school, were less likely to have such an intense training in the social graces, and even Montreal girls were said to be less sophisticated than their Quebec counterparts. Yet rural women were not without formal schooling. In the villages, institutions known as *petites écoles* were run at first by the missionaries and later by parish priests or by lay teachers under the priests' direction. We know that girls were going to such schools by the 1727 ordinance issued by the bishop of Quebec, to the effect that unmarried lay teachers should not teach members of the opposite sex. Indeed, since gender is not specified in the ordinance, young unmarried women may also have been teachers in some parish schools. As in the convents, girls were taught to read, to recite their catechism, and possibly to write. If women were teaching, girls might also have received some instruction in sewing or knitting; the fancier sewing — the embroidery of altar cloths and the like — was probably the monopoly of the convents or of the seamstresses teaching in the larger centres.[51] That the *petites écoles* were not always conducted according to the ideal is suggested by the promulgation of regulations concerning them. In addition to the rule regarding unmarried lay teachers, there were rules instructing priests to make sure that teachers were moral individuals, to supervise what went on in the schools, and to make sure that parents sent their children. There were at least 29 schools of this type by the end of the French regime, a number that may seem very small for a total population of nearly 70 000; but when we recall that most children attended only briefly in order to prepare for first communion, it is possible that this schooling reached a substantial number of girls — at least among those who lived in a region that had such a school.

The people who came to New France were, on the average, more likely to be able to read and write than those who remained in France — probably because so many came from urban centres. There was initially some falling off in literacy in the New World; a study of seventeenth-century Canadian parish registers suggests that there were many people, both male and female, who did not learn to read or write in the early years. But eighteenth-century parish registers from Louisbourg and Three Rivers indicate that more than half the brides married in these communities could sign their names.[52] Although the formal schooling of most women was brief and oriented to religion and domestic learning, some women enjoyed a measure of literary culture in New France; a few may even have been considered "learned." Religious women like Sister Morin and Sister Cuillerier, Morin's successor in writing the *annales* of Montreal's *Hôtel-Dieu*, perhaps had special opportunities — and a special need — for literary culture. But upper-class laywomen were not all that far behind. Elisabeth Bégon, the wife of an eighteenth-century Three Rivers governor, had enough leisure to write at considerable length of the salons that fashionable women attended and of the dances they held; she also wrote about the condition of the St. Lawrence River as the seasons changed, and about her grandchildren. A single letter by Marie-Angélique Hamel regarding the marriage of her son has been preserved; it indicates that even less-elevated women put pen to paper when the occasion required it.[53]

For girls who did not attend school or acquire a literary training, service was probably the dominant form of education. Girls who were put into service were sometimes bound out as young as age 4; their contracts specified that they would stay with their master or mistress until they were married or otherwise provided for. The contracts also provided, somewhat vaguely, that the arrangement was for their well-being and "*bon avancement.*" A study of the contracts of domestics suggests, in fact, that binding girls into service was a way of providing for them when a natural parent was unable to do so. Formal instruction was a major part of a contract only when it was a question of apprenticeship to a trade, such as that of *couturière* or seamstress. In such cases, the person bound was usually a young woman in her late teens or early twenties, the instruction was paid for, and the period of apprenticeship was only one or two years.[54]

All girls, whether they served in the households of others or lived at home with their own families, learned the multiple and time-consuming tasks of house and farm work from the older women with whom they lived. They began to learn from the earliest possible age — gathering eggs, holding yarn, stirring the pot, milking, spinning, and looking after animals and babies — while older women supervised or did other work. Most of their learning was directed toward their becoming competent assistants in the households of their elders, and eventually managers of their own.

Was there a separate "women's culture" in seventeenth- or eighteenth-century New France? Perhaps. The culture of the convent, the separate character of much of women's work, the management of childbirth and of most female education by women — all of these suggest the possibility. On the other hand, there is evidence that the worlds of women and men were in some ways less separate than they would later become, and that even cloistered convent women bustled about "in the world" when they needed to. Then too, the mid-eighteenth century society of Mme Vaudreuil and Mme Bégon was very different from the seventeenth-century society of Marie de l'Incarnation and Marguerite Bourgeoys. The New World community that had been dominated by the fisheries, the fur trade, and the religious mission, and subject to continual warfare, had been replaced by an increasingly secular society based on agriculture and small industries. The existence of official, salaried midwives suggests that even at the intimate level of childbirth, church and state could intrude on the world of women.

Settlements along the St. Lawrence and its tributaries, in Louisbourg, and in Acadia began also to have a sense of permanence as succeeding generations of French inhabitants took root. But the impression of stability was in part deceptive, for the final years of New France were hardly peaceful or static. The Acadians' relatively quiet existence was rudely shattered in 1755, when the British began to force on them the long exodus known as "le Grand Dérangement" or the "Expulsion." Many Acadian women were separated from their families and had their lives permanently disrupted. Some were sent to England; some ended up in France; many were scattered along the shores of the eastern seaboard of North America. A few, remarkably, managed to go into hiding and stay near their homes or to return to Nova Scotia later on.[55] War with the English affected the people of Canada as well, although not so drastically. Still, war meant blockades and food shortages, and ultimately bombardments, raids, and the loss of lives. The presence of troops encouraged prostitution, and the shortage of goods encouraged smuggling. In its last years, Canada as well as Acadia suffered much privation and dislocation.

Throughout the eighteenth century, French-Canadian clerics protested what they perceived as a moral decline. Like the Protestant clergy of New England, they found the world less pure than it had seemed in the early period of religious faith and missionary fervour. Priests no doubt complained about women's low necklines, frivolous dresses, and attendance at dances precisely because the material circumstances of women in eighteenth-century New France were better than those of their seventeenth-century mothers and grandmothers, and such extravagances were now possible. But moral attitudes had possibly shifted. In Montreal, penalties for serious offences like adultery were less severe in the eighteenth century than they had been in the seventeenth.[56]

Increasing numbers of illegitimate or abandoned children also suggest a society in which social controls were not as powerful as they once had been. Indeed, concern for orphans had a great deal to do with the development of a new women's religious community, founded just before the Conquest. The order of the Sisters of Charity (or Grey Nuns, as they came to be called) came into being in the 1740s and received official sanction from the king in 1753. Founded by Marguerite d'Youville, the *Soeurs de la Charité de l'Hôpital-Général* of Montreal had as their original focus the general care of the sick and the poor. But the problem of abandoned infants led to the admission of the hospital's first foundling in 1754, and soon more than twenty babies a year were finding their way to the Grey Nuns' door. The infant death rate at the hostel was extremely high — 80 percent in the first decade — and would eventually match the even higher rates that were typical of similar foundling hospitals in Europe.[57] Evidently the institution was able to do little more than stem the tide of infanticide during difficult times by giving some measure of care and baptism to infants who otherwise would have died even sooner after birth. In New France, as elsewhere in the western world, the presence of foundling hospitals with their high death rates indicated the continuing — or perhaps growing — presence of misery and the inadequacy of institutional efforts to alleviate it.

The founding of the Grey Nuns occurred at a time of growing awareness that the existing religious orders of New France were not attracting recruits. The authorities, some critics believed in 1732, had effectively limited the numbers of women entering convents by insisting more than they had in the past on the payment of large dowries. It was pointed out in support of lower dowries that girls in New France loved liberty too much to be attracted to religious life in large numbers, and that the government need not fear the wholesale abandonment of marriage and childrearing if convent entry were made easier. A genuine social problem existed, moreover, among women who did not find husbands and whose families could not afford the high cost of their entry into the convent. The dowries were finally lowered, although women did not flock into the convents as a result. A population that was more equally balanced as far as gender was concerned may have meant later marriage on average for women than had been typical in the seventeenth century. But most women still married.[58]

The fact that marriage or convent life were their primary choices tells us much about the culture of women in New France. Totally separate or different from men's culture it may not have been. But most women's lives, especially by the eighteenth century, revolved around the demands of family reproduction and production. The majority of women also lived in a world in which both church and state had a good deal to say about how women should live. What we cannot know very well is the extent to which women paid attention. There is evidence that some did not.

The marriages of a woman whose life spanned the years before and after the Conquest tell us something of how ordinary women may have arranged their affairs in mid-eighteenth-century French Canada. Félicité Audet first appears in the records in 1761. A widowed domestic servant with one child, Félicité married Théophile Allaire — himself a widower with one surviving child — in 1761. In the six years they lived together, Félicité and Théophile had three additional children; in 1767, Théophile died and Félicité and her family were left with a farm of 60 *arpents* (acres), 33 of which were still bush; a bed; three chairs; a bureau; and a sideboard. Félicité married once again and had three more children, but this marriage ended in a separation. According to the settlement that was arranged with her third spouse, she kept from this marriage 60 *arpents* of land, a bed, a cow, and a pig. She was also allotted half a *minot* of grain, along with one of the children of this final union. When we last hear of her, Félicité is selling her land in order to buy another farm and a loom, so that she can earn her living.[59]

An eighteenth-century Canadian couple in their Sunday clothes.

....

Source: Collection Gagnon, Bibliothèque de la ville de Montréal.

It is hard to know how typical Audet's three marriages were, but her life was typical in that it focussed on cows and pigs, husbands and children, three chairs and a sideboard, rather than on the church or the state, the governor or the intendant, or even on events in Quebec, Montreal, or Louisbourg. On the other hand, state affairs affected the material conditions of her life, especially if there were shortages because of war. And the church impinged on her life as well. Her children would have been baptized shortly after they were born; she herself may have come to the priest to undergo the traditional purification ritual of "churching" at some point following each birth. Audet no doubt shared the superstitions and beliefs regarding women of her period. Yet there was virtually no persecution for witchcraft in New France, as there had been for several centuries in Europe. People were afraid, perhaps, of aboriginal warriors, of soldiers, and of ghosts and evil spirits; they were also afraid of poverty. But they do not appear to have been afraid of old women.

If the Conquest had any effect on Félicité Audet, we cannot know what it was. We know that, among the elite and governing families of Louisbourg, Montreal, and Quebec, many women were forced to return to France. Others stayed on and wondered how they would cope under the new regime. The lingering of many Scottish and English names in French-Canadian families to this day indicates that some followed the path of Marie-Madeleine Maisonnat: instead of marrying French soldiers, they married English ones. The strength of their culture is suggested in the fact that most of their descendants consider themselves French Canadians, not English Canadians. The vast majority of Acadian and Canadian women probably bided their time and continued as they had always done, coping with the authorities one day and sorting the laundry the next, as they gathered their resources for whatever was to come.

NOTES

1. Silvio Dumas, *Les filles du roi en Nouvelle-France: Étude historique avec répertoire biographique* (Québec: Société historique de Québec, 1972), 114–15.
2. Raymond Douville and Jacques Casanova, *Daily Life in Early Canada*, translated by Carola Congreve (London: George Allen and Unwin, 1968), 27.
3. *Dictionary of Canadian Biography* (Toronto: University of Toronto Press, 1966), vol. 1, 578, 110.
4. D. Owen Carrigan, *Crime and Punishment in Canada: A History* (Toronto: McClelland and Stewart, 1991), 247.
5. Micheline Dumont-Johnson, "Les communautés religieuses et la condition féminine," *Recherches sociographiques* 19, 1 (janvier/avril 1978), 80.
6. François Rousseau, "Hôpital et société en Nouvelle-France: L'Hôtel Dieu de Québec à la fin du XVIIe siècle," *Revue d'histoire de l'Amérique française* 31, 1 (juin 1977), 29–30.
7. Marie-Emmanuel Chabot, "Marie Guyart de l'Incarnation, 1599–1672," in Mary Quayle Innis, ed., *The Clear Spirit: Twenty Canadian Women and Their Times* (Toronto: University of Toronto Press, 1966), 36.
8. Le Collectif Clio, *L'histoire des femmes au Québec depuis quatre siècles* (Montréal: Quinze, 1982), 38; Joyce Marshall, ed., *Word from New France: The Selected Letters of Marie de l'Incarnation* (Toronto: Oxford University Press, 1967); Dom Guy Oury, *Marie de l'Incarnation, 1599–1672*, 2 vols. (Québec: Presses de l'Université Laval, 1973).
9. Le Collectif Clio, *L'histoire des femmes*, 40–41; Soeur Marguerite Jean, "L'état et les communautés religieuses féminines au Québec, 1639–1840," *Studia Canonica* 6, 1 (1972), 166.
10. Le Collectif Clio, *L'histoire des femmes*, 43; Hélène Bernier, ed., *Marguerite Bourgeoys* (Montréal: Fides, 1958).
11. Dumas, *Les filles du roi*, 70 [our translation]; Le Collectif Clio, *L'histoire des femmes*, 48–52.
12. Yves Landry, *Les filles du roi au XVIIIe siècle: Orphelines en France, pionnières au Canada* (Montréal: Leméac, 1992), 258–9. For an abridged discussion of the characteristics of the *filles du roi*, see Landry, "Gender Imbalance, *les filles du roi*, and Choice of Spouse in New France," in Bettina Bradbury, ed., *Canadian Family History. Selected Readings* (Toronto: Copp Clark Pitman, 1992), 14–32.
13. Dumas, *Les filles du roi*, chap. 2; "Les soeurs Raclot," *Nos Ancêtres* 4 (1983).
14. Douville and Casanova, *Daily Life*, 32; Dumas, *Les filles du roi*, 320–21; Landry, *Les filles du roi*, 75–76.
15. Louise Dechêne, *Habitants et marchands de Montréal au XVIIe siècle* (Montréal: Plon, 1974), 45.
16. Jacques Henripin, *La population canadienne au début du XVIIIe siècle*, Institut national d'études démographiques: Travaux et documents, Cahier 22 (Paris: Presses

universitaires de France, 1954); A.J.B. Johnston, *Religion in Life at Louisbourg, 1713–1758* (Montreal and Kingston: McGill-Queen's University Press, 1984), 5.

17. Yves Landry et Jacques Légaré, "Le cycle de vie familiale en Nouvelle-France: méthodologie et application à un échantillon," *Histoire sociale/Social History* 17, 33 (May 1984), 7–20; Isabel Foulché-Delbosc, "Women of Three Rivers: 1651–63," *in* Susan Mann Trofimenkoff and Alison Prentice, eds., *The Neglected Majority: Essays in Canadian Women's History* (Toronto: McClelland and Stewart, 1977), vol. 1, 16–18.

18. Foulché-Delbosc, "Women of Three Rivers," 18.

19. Landry et Légaré, "Le cycle de vie," 11; Alan Greer, *Peasant, Lord, and Merchant: Rural Society in Three Quebec Parishes, 1740–1840* (Toronto: University of Toronto Press, 1985), 51; John Bosher, "The Family in New France," *in* B.M. Gough, ed., *In Search of the Visible Past* (Waterloo: Wilfrid Laurier University Press, 1975), 1–13.

20. See Henripin, *La population canadienne*, 90; P.A. Leclerc, "Le mariage sous le régime français," *Revue d'histoire de l'Amérique française* 13/14 (1959–60), 230–46, 374–406, 525–43; Landry, "Gender Imbalance," 19.

21. Naomi Griffiths, "The Acadians," *Dictionary of Canadian Biography* (Toronto: University of Toronto Press, 1979), vol. 4, xvii–xxxi; Henripin, *La population canadienne*, 49–53; Robert V. Wells, "Quaker Marriage Patterns in Colonial Perspective," *William and Mary Quarterly*, 3rd Series, 24 (July 1972), 41–42; Roderic Beaujot and Kevin McQuillan, *Growth and Dualism: The Demographic Development of Canada* (Toronto: Gage, 1982), 6–9.

22. Hélène Rioux, "Les amours québécoises au XVIIIe siècle," *Histoire* 11 (avril 1979), 71; Beaujot and McQuillan, *Growth and Dualism*, 9.

23. Hélène Laforce, *Histoire de la sage-femme dans la région de Québec* (Québec: Institut québécois de recherche sur la culture, 1985), 30–64.

24. Lorraine Gadoury, *La noblesse de Nouvelle-France: Familles et alliances* (La Salle: Hurtubise HMH, 1992), 120–29, 142–46.

25. Greer, *Peasant, Lord, and Merchant*, chap. 2; Andrew Hill Clark, *Acadia: The Geography of Early Nova Scotia to 1760* (Madison: University of Wisconsin Press, 1968), 165.

26. Josette Brun, "Les femmes d'affaires dans la société coloniale nord-américaine: le cas de l'Île Royale, 1713–1758," Université de Moncton, thèse de maîtrise ès arts, 1994, 103–104.

27. *Dictionary of Canadian Biography*, vol. 3 (1974), 308–13; vol. 1 (1966), 383.

28. Robert-Lionel Séguin, "La canadienne au XVIIe et XVIIIe siècles," *Revue d'histoire de l'Amérique française* 13, 4 (Mars 1960), 492–508; Clark, *Acadia*, 165, 168, 176–77, 377–78, 243; Foulché-Delbosc, "Women of Three Rivers," 25; Griffiths, "The Acadians," xix–xxi; Greer, *Peasant, Lord, and Merchant*, 14.

29. Le Collectif Clio, *L'histoire des femmes*, 23.

30. Greer, *Peasant, Lord, and Merchant*, 49–51; Leclerc, "Le mariage," 375–76.

31. Gadoury, *La noblesse*, 92–103.

32. Yves F. Zoltvany, "Esquisse de la Coutume de Paris," *Revue d'histoire de l'Amérique française* 25, 3 (décembre 1971), 366–83.

33. Landry, "Gender Imbalance," 19.

34. Dechêne, *Habitants et marchands*, 419; Louis Lavallée, "Les archives notariales et l'histoire sociale de la Nouvelle-France," *Revue d'histoire de l'Amérique française* 28, 3 (décembre 1974), 388–89; Johnston, *Religion in Life*, chap. 5; Cameron Nish, *Les bourgeois-gentilshommes de la Nouvelle-France, 1729–1748* (Montréal: Fides, 1968), chap. 10.

35. Greer, *Peasant, Lord, and Merchant*, 34.
36. *Dictionary of Canadian Biography*, vol. 3, 580–81.
37. Liliane Plamondon, "Une femme d'affaires en Nouvelle-France: Marie-Anne Barbel, veuve Fornel," *Revue d'histoire de l'Amérique française* 31, 2 (septembre 1977), 165–86; Josette Brun, "Les femmes d'affaires," 22; Gadoury, *La noblesse*, 81–2.
38. *Dictionary of Canadian Biography*, vol. 3, 421; Douville and Casanova, *Daily Life*, 201; Jan Noel, "New France: Les femmes favorisées," in Allison Prentice and Susan Mann Trofimenkoff, eds., *The Neglected Majority: Essays in Canadian Women's History* (Toronto: McClelland and Stewart, 1985), vol. 2, 25–6.
39. Noel, "Les femmes favorisées," 32; Terence Crowley, "Thunder Gusts: Popular Disturbances in Early French Canada," *Historical Papers/Communications historiques* (1979), 19–20.
40. Laforce, *Histoire de la sage-femme*, 138–200.
41. Gadoury, *La noblesse*, 64–67; Rousseau, "Hôpital et société," 36–47.
42. Micheline D'Allaire, "Les prétensions des religieuses de l'hôpital-général de Québec sur le palais épiscopal de Québec," *Revue d'histoire de l'Amérique française* 23, 1 (juin 1969), 53–67; Johnston, *Religion in Life*, chap. 4.
43. Micheline Dumont-Johnson, "History of the Status of Women in the Province of Quebec," in Royal Commission on the Status of Women in Canada, *Cultural Tradition and Political History of Women in Canada*, Study No. 8 of the RCSW (Ottawa: Information Canada, 1971), 6; Johnston, *Religion in Life*, 96.
44. Antonio Drolet, "Quelques remèdes indigènes à travers la correspondance de Mère Sainte-Hélène," in Yolande Bonenfant et al., *Trois siècles de médecine québécoise*, Cahiers d'histoire No. 22 (Québec: Société historique de Québec, 1972); Soeur Morin, "Annales de l'Hôtel-Dieu de Montréal," *Mémoires de la société historique de Montréal*, vol. 12 (1921); Douville and Casanova, *Daily Life*, 210.
45. Marie-Aimée Cliche, "Unwed Mothers, Families and Society during the French Regime," in Bradbury, ed., *Canadian Family History*, 42–45.
46. A.J.B. Johnston, "Women as Victims in 18th-Century Cape Breton: Violence at Home and in the Street," paper presented to the French Colonial Historical Society, Montreal, May 1992, 20–24; Carrigan, *Crime and Punishment in Canada*, 203, 247.
47. Johnston, *Religion in Life*, 8, 93; Esmerelda Thornhill, "Black Women's Studies in Teaching Related to Women: Help or Hindrance to Universal Sisterhood?" *Fireweed* (Spring 1983), 81; Adrienne Shadd, "300 Years of Black Women in Canadian History: Circa 1700 to 1980," *Tiger Lily* 1, 2 (1987); Johnston, "Women as Victims," 10.
48. Nadia Fahmy-Eid, "L'éducation des filles chez les Ursulines de Québec sous le régime français," in Nadia Fahmy-Eid et Micheline Dumont, eds., *Maîtresses de maison, maîtresses d'école: Femmes, famille et éducation dans l'histoire du Québec* (Montréal: Boréal Express, 1983), espec. 66–67. For English translation, see "The Education of Girls by the Ursulines of Quebec during the French Regime," in Wendy Mitchinson et al., *Canadian Women: A Reader* (Toronto: Harcourt Brace, 1996), 33–49.
49. Johnston, *Religion in Life*, 91. See also Johnston, "Education and Female Literacy at Eighteenth-Century Louisbourg: The Work of the *Soeurs de la Congrégation de Notre Dame*," in J. Donald Wilson, ed., *An Imperfect Past: Education and Society in Canadian History* (Vancouver: Centre for the Study of Curriculum and Instruction, University of British Columbia, 1984).
50. Fahmy-Eid, "L'éducation des filles," 53.

51. Fahmy-Eid, "L'éducation des filles."
52. Johnston, *Religion in Life*, 107; Alan Greer, "The Pattern of Literacy in Quebec, 1745–1899," *Histoire sociale/Social History* 11, 22 (November 1978), 299.
53. Soeur Morin, "Annales"; Ghislaine Légendre, ed., "Relation de Soeur Cuillerier," *Écrits du Canada français* 42 (Montréal 1979); Elisabeth Bégon, *Lettres au cher fils: Correspondance d'Elisabeth Bégon avec son gendre, 1748–1753* (Montréal: Hurtubise, 1972); Douville and Casanova, *Daily Life*, 202–16.
54. Francine Barry, "Familles et domesticité féminine au milieu du 18e siècle," *in* Fahmy-Eid et Dumont, eds., *Maîtresses de maison*, 223–36.
55. See Griffiths, "The Acadians."
56. Andrée Morel, "Réflexions sur la justice criminelle canadienne au 18e siècle," *Revue d'histoire de l'Amérique française* 29, 2 (septembre 1975), 241–53.
57. Peter Gossage, "Foundlings and the Institution: The Case of the Grey Nuns of Montreal," paper presented to the Canadian Historical Association, Winnipeg, 1986.
58. On dowries, see Dechêne, *Habitants et marchands*, 478; Jean, "L'état," 166–68.
59. Greer, *Peasant, Lord, and Merchant*, 25–28, 55–56.

CHAPTER THREE

Carders of Wool, Drawers of Water: Women's Work in British North America

The fall of New France ushered in a century of extraordinary change in North America. While the last decades of the French regime were hardly static, the advent of British government in the French-occupied territories combined with subsequent economic and political events in Europe and in the Thirteen Colonies to the south to produce a century of almost continuous political and military upheaval. One profound effect was a vast movement of peoples. A second was a rapid increase in the number of people of European origin living in the territory that would become Canada. Single men predominated among the first arrivals to the British North American colonies. But if Britain wanted them to remain and her colonies to be settled, it was apparent that women were required. An early comment on the Newfoundland experience by a British naval officer suggests how important women were to permanent settlement. "Soe long as there comes noe women," this gentleman remarked in 1694, the people are not "fixed."[1]

THE NEW MIGRANTS

Men and women from New England gradually began moving to the northeastern regions of British North America after Acadia was transferred to the British Crown in 1713. Not until later in the eighteenth century, however, did families begin making their way from colonies like New York and Pennsylvania to the shores of the St. Lawrence, Lake Ontario, and Lake Erie. This migration, which included Quaker and Mennonite pacifists, preceded the American Revolution (1776–1783) that would eventually result in the birth of the United States of America. The New Englanders came first to Nova Scotia, a province then encompassing much of what is now New Brunswick and Prince Edward Island. Later they and others came to the new British province of Quebec, whose boundaries for most of the late eighteenth century continued to include much of present-day Ontario and vast tracts of the Ohio and Mississippi river valleys to the south and west. Despite the pacifist leanings and religious concerns of some of these American migrants, the chief motivation of most was the quest for new land and new opportunities. Nor were economic motives absent in the vast Loyalist influx into the eastern and northern British colonies that was precipitated by the American Revolution itself. Like the movements that preceded it, this too was largely a migration of families, and included the Abenaki, members of the Iroquois Confederacy (mainly Mohawk), black slaves and former slaves, and migrants of German origin, as well as women and men of Anglo-Celtic backgrounds. These peoples were followed in turn by another generation of American migrants, the "post-Loyalists," whose motives seem to have been overwhelmingly economic. Economic and political upheaval in the British Isles, the Napoleonic wars, and famine in Ireland brought a second great movement of people to British North America, chiefly of English, Irish, and Scottish families. This influx for the most part occurred after the American migration, reaching its peak in the 1830s and 1840s.

Included in all of these movements were female immigrants travelling without families: domestics, schoolmistresses, and businesswomen seeking a living in partnership with other women or alone. Then, in the 1830s, a new group of French *religieuses* seeking to reinvigorate the Roman Catholic mission in the New World began to trickle into French Canada. They, in turn, were followed by Irish and American nuns destined for other parts of British North America.[2]

The first half of the nineteenth century also saw continuing internal migrations, some of which stirred up controversy and concern. During the War of 1812 several thousand slaves, who escaped from Maryland and Virginia when the British occupied Chesapeake Bay, made their way to British "freedom" — only to encounter much hardship and considerable prejudice in their new Nova Scotia and New Brunswick homes, as had other black migrants, both slave and free, before them.[3] Later, many more black refugees made their way to Canada West during the fugitive slave movement via the "underground railroad" and created communities in what was to become southwestern Ontario. Some came with their families, but the circumstances of their migration forced others, including women and mothers with young children, to leave family members behind. This happened to Louisa Pipkins of Yorkville, who was still making inquiries and trying to get her four children out three years after her own escape with her husband in 1853. The Pipkins children were already scattered, living with three different families in North Carolina and Virginia. Some black women went back themselves for their children. A Mrs. Armstrong, disguising herself as a man in order to travel more easily, returned to Kentucky for the seven youngsters she had been forced to leave behind when she had escaped in 1842. She brought out five and arranged with friends for the escape of the other two.[4]

Immigrants and native-born alike often lived in many different places before they settled permanently. Marie-Henriette Lejeune, born in Rochefort of Acadian parents who had been deported to France after the fall of Louisbourg in 1758, became part of an Acadian population that has been described as "constantly expanding and moving." By 1764, she was back in North America and living with her family on the island of Miquelon; but by 1766, the family had once again been forcibly moved to Cape Breton. Returning to Miquelon in 1777, the Lejeune family found themselves once again deported to France. Now 16, Marie-Henriette married another displaced Acadian, a widower with children to raise. By 1786, she was back on Cape Breton, widowed and remarried, this time to a cousin. Her third and last marriage was to a member of the MacDonald Highlanders, a regiment disbanded in 1783. Living with her husband James Ross for a time in Little Bras d'Or on Cape Breton, Marie-Henriette made her final home in the North East Margaree valley. By this time a skilled midwife and healer, she was remembered by her descendants as "Granny Ross."[5]

The Acadians may have travelled more than most of our ancestors, but others moved about as well. Countless Loyalists and other migrants used the Maritime provinces or the old province of Quebec (later known as Lower Canada) as staging grounds for migrations farther west; some black Loyalists in Nova Scotia gave up on the Americas entirely and sought a better life in Sierra Leone, where they nevertheless continued to be known as Nova Scotians.[6] Later, many Maritimers decided that the prospects were better in the eastern United States than at home, and migrant French Canadians began to colonize new parts of British North America or strike out for the towns and factories of New England.

In the early 1800s, Scottish settlers under the leadership of Lord Selkirk planted the Red River colony in a small corner of Rupert's Land, in what would later be the province of Manitoba. Since French-Catholic mixed-blood families settled in the region as well, religious women were not far behind; in 1846, a contingent of Grey Nuns established the first women's religious community in the Canadian West. Another small group of white women helped initiate the pioneer era in what was eventually to become the province of British Columbia. Their voyages by sea from the British Isles were often of six or seven months' duration, rounding Cape Horn and eventually bringing them to the new settlements that were being created in Hudson's Bay Company territory on the west coast.[7]

Who were the women who left the relative comforts of home, and parted from family and friends, for what were often gruelling and extraordinarily long journeys into unknown and inhospitable environments? Did any common themes mark their passage or characterize their lives? One thing these women certainly had in common was the migration experience itself. Sometimes this was an experience the women themselves might not have chosen; many migrated because of political or economic choices made by fathers or husbands, or more remotely by distant landholders, military men, or governors. Loyalist records reveal such forced moves with particular poignancy,[8] but many other women must also have migrated unwillingly. Not all women migrants spent months at sea, for many were overland migrants. Nor did all of them walk for more than 1300 kilometres, as did the women who trekked from York Factory to Red River between 1812 and 1820.[9] But many did have extraordinary experiences as immigrants; and most must have found their lives enormously changed. For those who were refugees or forcibly displaced, their moving was traumatic. Some came with a fair share of the world's goods, but others arrived with very little or with nothing. However they came, they brought traditional skills and knowledge of women's ways and women's work; but they also had to adapt to new ways of doing things in the communities they encountered or founded in British North America.

The story of Sarah McGinnis illustrates both the mobility and the need to adapt. Born in the upper Mohawk River valley to a first-generation family of German immigrants in 1713, Sarah, who had "prevailed upon her parents" to let her live for long periods among the Six Nations Indians, married an Irish fur trader and had produced four children by the time she was widowed at 42. Continuing to operate the family fur trading post, the widow McGinnis was in her sixties when the American Revolution swept away all she possessed and forced her to head north. She watched as her property and goods were sold at public auction, and spent time imprisoned with her family in conditions so bad that her granddaughter ultimately died from the treatment she received. When they escaped, Sarah McGinnis had to abandon a son "who was out of his senses and bound in chains . . . and who was later burnt alive." Then began the long odyssey that would eventually take the widow McGinnis to Canada. During the war, she lived for two protracted periods with the Six Nations, in order to perform important liaison services between the British and their Amerindian allies, and spent brief periods in Niagara and Montreal, in the latter case in great poverty. Her ultimate "settlement" took her first to Carleton Island, then to Ernestown, and finally to Fredericksburgh (all at the eastern end of Lake Ontario), where she died in 1791 at the age of 78.[10]

Most migrants were younger than Sarah McGinnis. Deborah Cottnam was a Nova Scotian who was displaced twice: once to Salem, Massachusetts, when she was only 16, as a result of French/British conflict; and, in her middle age, back again to Nova Scotia as a result of the American revolutionary war. She too did not settle for good in one place. After running an academy in Halifax from 1777 to 1786, this enterprising Loyalist removed herself and her school to Saint John; there she taught for six more years before retiring to Windsor, Nova Scotia, where she died in 1806.[11]

Many were not so successful or so lucky. Rebels not only plundered the house of Filer Dribblee of Long Island, but also turned his wife, Polly, and their five children "naked into the Streets." "Plundered and stripped" two more times before they made their way to New Brunswick, the Dribblee family discovered that a safe arrival in British territory did not mean the end of their troubles. Filer, who had spent six months in prison during the war, succumbed to despair during the first year in Saint John and committed suicide; not long afterward, the widow and her children were burnt out of their log-cabin home twice in one year. In a letter to a brother in England, Polly expressed her gratitude for gifts of clothing that he had sent and recounted some of her trials as a prelude to a request for further aid.

> I assure you, my dear Billy, that many have been the Days since my arrival in this inhospitable Country, that I should have thought myself and Family truly happy could we have "had Potatoes alone—" but this mighty Boon was denied us—! I could have borne these burdens of Loyalty with Fortitude had not my poor Children in doleful accents cried, Mama, why don't you help me and give me Bread?[12]

Polly Dribblee wondered about the value of loyalty to a British Crown whose material assistance, at that stage, had been wholly insufficient; she also worried about the effect the news of her condition would have on her mother, who remained in the United States. At the time of writing (November 1787), she had not had the courage to inform her American relatives of her difficulties.

Frequent moves, insufficient food, and the loss of possessions — or, worse, the loss of family members: these were the lot of many migrants. Others dealt with the vicissitudes of illness and accident. Sarah Sherwood was seven months pregnant when she decided to follow her Loyalist husband into exile. Trekking with two small children and a black slave from her farm in Vermont to the British post of Fort St. Jean on the Richelieu River, Sarah and her family lived first in a barracks, then in a house in the fort, and finally in a blockhouse on North Hero Island for the duration of the American revolutionary war, while her husband performed various services for the British government. Somehow she managed to have her baby, look after her children and the other relatives who followed her north, weave "yards of linsey-woollsey," and keep her family clothed, despite the uncertain conditions of life in wartime. Peace, however, brought another long siege: one after another, everyone in the family had smallpox. The Sherwood family survived and eventually settled in Upper Canada; there Sarah had three more daughters, but lost her husband in a drowning accident when the youngest of this second brood was only 7. The farm was already well established by this time, however, and Sarah Sherwood carried on, ultimately ending her days in Montreal.[13] All Loyalist women suffered the loss of familiar surroundings, communities, and homes; many took on new and unfamiliar roles during the long absences of husbands, fathers, and brothers who were fighting the revolutionary war. Often they endured abuse at the hands of hostile Patriots; a few even lost the support of their parental families, who disagreed with the course taken by sons or sons-in-law. All were forced, at some point, to migrate, frequently under terrible conditions. Some did not make it to the end of their journey.[14]

Nor did migrants' troubles necessarily end with their arrival in British North America. And if it was hard to be Sarah McGinnis, Sarah Sherwood, or Polly Dribblee, how much harder must it have been to be Peggy Qwynn, a black Loyalist who arrived in Nova Scotia, only to be judged by the official recipient of her petition for assistance "not a free woman [who] must be delivered to her owner."[15] Or Phillis George, a black woman who faced not only the problem of feeding her three children despite serious food shortages in Shelburne, Nova Scotia, but ongoing racial violence.

A sketch of a Loyalist camp near Cornwall in 1784. The artist was James Peachey.

Source: National Archives of Canada/C-002001.

In a riot perpetrated by a gang of disbanded soldiers, the George house was overturned and Phillis's husband, David George, was beaten and driven into a swamp. The family retreated to Birchtown, but even there attacks by whites on the black inhabitants continued for more than a month. The Georges were among the black Loyalists of Nova Scotia who eventually sought refuge in Sierra Leone.[16]

Even migrants whose travels were precipitated by causes other than war could suffer privation and loss. The experiences of Catharine Parr Traill and Susanna Moodie, the sisters who were two of Canada's most famous gentlewomen immigrants from the British Isles in the 1830s, were not without their traumas and tragedies. Catharine nearly succumbed to cholera in Montreal before she was able to set out for her homestead near Peterborough, and in the ensuing years lost several homes to fire. Susanna also lost a farmhouse to fire, endured attacks of intermittent fever, and lost a son in a drowning, among what seems to have been a multitude of lesser difficulties. In her famous account of pioneer life, *Roughing It in the Bush*, Susanna portrayed the rigours of backwoods life with particular flair. Commenting somewhat misleadingly on her own lack of the necessary practical skills for backwoods farming, she told a tale of continuous struggle, albeit a struggle laced with humour as well as dogged determination. As a gentlewoman, Moodie felt unprepared for much of the manual work she had to do on her bush farm. She nevertheless persevered, and in the end even admitted to contemplating her own "well-hoed ridge of potatoes" with considerable satisfaction. Moodie was also fortunate in having the knowledge and skill to take up her pen as well as her hoe. She won a government post for her husband by her petitions to the governor and, as an experienced author, was able to supplement the family income considerably through her published writings, in a period when increasing numbers of women were able to earn money through their writing. Finally, as a result of both initiatives, the Moodies were able to leave the hardships of backwoods life behind them. They moved to Belleville, where Susanna and Captain Moodie could more easily pursue work to which they felt better suited.[17]

Not all pioneer stories are as complete as the Moodie story, nor are they all tales of worry and woe. An upper-class woman recorded in her 1789 diary an encounter with one of her domestic servants, who had married a disbanded soldier after the American revolutionary war and settled with him on a farm in the St. Lawrence valley. The former mistress was impressed with what she saw. Already Nancy and her husband had exchanged a small farm for one that was double its size, and now they were in the process of developing their new acreage and raising a fine family of three children. Asked if she was happy, Nancy replied, "Yes, perfectly so." She worked hard, "but it was for herself and the children."

> Her husband took care of the Farm and she of the family, and at their leisure hours she wove Cloth, and he made and mended shoes for their neighbours for which they were well paid, and every year they expected to do better and better.[18]

Also hopeful of bettering their lot were the women who migrated on their own. Many followed relatives who had gone before them, but some women seemed to be entirely independent of close family connections. Sixteen unattached women over 12 years of age were among the 448 Scottish Highlanders who immigrated in 1802 as an organized group to Glengarry, Upper Canada, where they joined other clan members who had reached the area by various routes earlier.[19] Such women immigrants might find their way into the countryside, but more often they would find work in urban centres like Fredericton, Halifax, Montreal, or Toronto, swelling the numbers of single women who were already moving into these communities from rural British North America. By 1851, such centres were reporting disproportionate numbers of young women living in their midst. Most of these women took work as servants in urban households; others followed the path of Deborah Cottnam, establishing themselves as teachers; still others set up dressmaking establishments, shops, or other businesses. Whatever their means of support, these single women too were participating in the extraordinary mobility and change that characterized the lives of British North American women.[20]

Not all adapted easily to the changes in their world. Change was particularly difficult if it brought in its wake a clash of cultures. Molly Brant and her sister-in-law Catharine had to choose, after their migration, between two paths: acculturation to the British way of life in North America or a return to Mohawk ways. In the end, neither choice was clear-cut. Molly always spoke Mohawk and dressed in the Mohawk style, but her daughters all married members of the Upper Canadian elite. Molly Brant saw out her days in Kingston, where three of her daughters had settled. In contrast, Catharine, the daughter of an Irish father and a Mohawk mother, found life uncomfortable in her husband Joseph Brant's lavish establishment in Burlington. Five of her seven children married Mohawks and settled in the Mohawk community at Grand River. When Joseph died, Catharine too returned to Grand River to live.[21]

Native and mixed-blood women suffered increasing hardship as their communities were forced to retreat from the pressure of colonial development. With the coming of white women, the military and fur trade worlds of which they had been so important a part were coming to an end. In the northwest, the Native and mixed-blood women who had married traders did not necessarily fare better than their counterparts in the east, or than those aboriginal women who had remained with their tribal communities in the rapidly changing conditions of the nineteenth century.[22] When white women and missionaries came to fur trade country in the early and mid-nineteenth century, some traders began to feel encumbered by their "country" wives. These men often turned their aboriginal spouses over to others when they retired to eastern British North America or to Britain, or abandoned them. Some, like Sir George Simpson, not only "turned off" their Native wives but also insisted on bringing their new British wives west. Frances Simpson's experience indicates, however, that life in the northwest was not necessarily any happier for white women. Only 18 when she arrived as the new bride of the Hudson's Bay Company governor, Frances valiantly tried to adjust to the new and alien environment of Red River society, but in the end her health failed and she was compelled to return home to England after only a few years.[23]

Despite their own problems and insecurities, women like Frances Simpson constituted a threat to Native and mixed-blood country wives. They represented a world that fur traders increasingly wanted. And when aboriginal wives were abandoned, whole families suffered. The children of mixed marriages might be left with their mothers, sent off to boarding school, or put into trades; few were fully integrated into their fathers' new families.[24] Of course, by no means all country wives or mixed-blood children were abandoned. Many fathers continued to care for their aboriginal offspring; others attempted to move their wives and families into the little European worlds that they were establishing in centres like Red River and Victoria.

This was the experience of Amelia Douglas, the part-Cree wife of Vancouver Island's first governor. A practical woman who had once saved her husband's life, Amelia Douglas was the mother of thirteen children. Nevertheless, first in Fort Vancouver and then in Victoria, she had to endure the insults of the new white settlers, who felt she was beneath them. Amelia Douglas probably found her new world ridiculously artificial as well as unpleasantly prejudiced, but she learned to deal with her new official role with good humour, turning some of the duties connected with it over to her daughters. She also drew on her Native heritage to the end, inviting other Native and mixed-blood men and women into her home, and telling Amerindian legends to her grandchildren. The paths of most mixed-blood women were no doubt far more difficult. They could rarely go back to their mothers' Native bands, but they were not always welcome in white society. Truly women "in between," some were not fully accepted in either world.[25]

The most tragic stories of all were those of the Native women who faced the obliteration of their cultures and, in one case, the virtual wiping out of their people. In the north and west, peoples like the Athapaskans or coastal peoples like the Haida still had some time and sufficient space to maintain their distinctive cultures, but this was not the case in the Atlantic colonies. The Mi'kmaq of Nova Scotia and the Beothuk of Newfoundland had been suffering from economic and social dislocation and enduring the ravages of European-introduced diseases since at least the 1500s. During the late eighteenth and early nineteenth centuries, these groups experienced death by slow starvation. Some of the Mi'kmaq migrated to Newfoundland; others

Five of the daughters of Captain William Henry McNeill and his Kaigani Haida wife, who was known as Mathilda. The photo was taken in the 1870s.

Source: British Columbia Archives and Records Service, 56397.

survived by moving onto reserved lands or developing a tourist trade in crafts that the women managed to preserve or revive. The Beothuk, despite last-ditch efforts on the part of colonial philanthropists to save them, finally dwindled to one woman, Shawandithit. This young Beothuk was taken captive. When she learned to communicate with her captors, she was able to tell them about the final days of her people: how they had hidden from white Newfoundlanders, who seemed to be hunting them even into their last retreat in the interior; how they had watched from the woods as white men returned the body of one of their number to their camp; and how, finally, all but Shawandithit herself had died. The last Beothuk woman succumbed to tuberculosis in 1829.[26]

MARRIAGE AND CHILDBEARING

The majority of women in British North America probably embarked on marriage in their early twenties. The 1851 census for Canada East and West, for example, gave the average age at first marriage for females as 23. In Hamilton in 1851, marriage was considerably delayed. Only 40 percent of the city's women married by the age of 22; of the 25-year-olds, only 60 percent were married. Among those older than 25, the percentage of women who were married gradually rose. Nevertheless, 17 percent of Hamilton's 30-year-old women remained unmarried in 1851.[27]

Late marriage is often correlated with few children, and it may well be that British North American women — especially urban women — were somewhat less fertile than the women of New France. But it is also true that these "pre-industrial" women still produced large families in comparison to average family sizes of later periods. Estimates of the numbers of children born to typical British North American families vary according to the date, the locality, and the data available, but all indicate substantial average birth rates. A study of eighteenth-century Quebec reveals an average figure of more than eight births and an average family size of more than five per "completed family" — that is, children born to women during their years of fertility — while similar figures are given for Peel County, Canada West, in 1851. Mid-nineteenth-century French-Canadian women living in two Prescott County townships also had given birth to an average of more than seven children by the time they reached the end of their childbearing years; English-Canadian mothers in this sample were only slightly less fertile, with an average of about six. Here, age at marriage might have made the difference, for English-Canadian women in these townships tended to marry a few years later than their French-Canadian counterparts. Rural living also clearly made a difference. The average number of children in all of the households in the city of Hamilton when the census was taken in 1851 was fewer than three; where heads of household were in their forties, it was fewer than four. Yet, for all of British North America, the average number of children born to families in 1851 — slightly more than seven — was still remarkably high.[28]

Numbers can tell us only so much. The childbearing stories of Anne Powell and her daughter Mary illustrate the high fertility of early nineteenth-century upper-class women and the stresses that could accompany it. Anne gave birth to nine children, of whom one died in infancy and another died at the age of 9. Her daughter Mary Jarvis had ten deliveries altogether. The first child was stillborn, but all the others lived. After Mary's sixth confinement, a female relative and a friend moved in for a period to provide extra help; Mary also believed herself to be lucky in the competence of her domestic servants. But she was still tired, and she still missed her mother and sister, who were in England. "I was sadly harassed with work," she wrote to her mother. "I have been very sick. . . . My illness was caused I believe by want of rest and too much fatigue before I had quite recovered from my confinement."[29]

Harriet Dobbs, who came to Kingston as a bride in the 1830s, had fewer children and appears to have had a slightly easier time. Although we do not know her age at marriage, we do know that Harriet spent some time at the end of whatever formal education she may have had living at home with her parents in Ireland. In addition to working at the household tasks that absorbed the time of even upper-class young women, Harriet painted every day, an occupation for which she said she had less time after marriage, although she did not abandon it altogether. On marrying her sister-in-law's brother, a young Upper Canadian cleric, Harriet did not immediately acquire her own separate household. She and her husband, Robert Cartwright, eventually occupied a house that had been built for them in Kingston, but claimed only one room of the house as their own. Robert's widowed sister Mary, an uncle Frank, and a doctor who does not appear to have been a relation also lived there. Moreover, the entire household took their meals in another Cartwright family home in Kingston, while Robert and Harriet awaited the arrival of their household effects. Even when these arrived, however, Harriet cheerfully reported that the older sister-in-law, Mary, remained the "mistress" of the household.[30]

Harriet Dobbs Cartwright gave birth to four children, only two of whom survived to adulthood. By the time of the second child's death at the age of 18, she was a widow. She lived for a while with a brother-in-law and his wife, and when he died one presumes that the two sisters-in-law carried on together — if not in the same household, then at least in close companionship. Certainly the widow Cartwright did not fade away. She was able to afford a trip home to visit her family in Dublin; she raised and educated her remaining two children; and she continued to be active in church and charitable circles in Kingston until her death in 1887.

Cartwright was widowed relatively young. All the evidence suggests that there were many other widows like her. The census for Hamilton, Canada West, indicates that nearly one-quarter of the women over 40, and one-third of the women over 50, were widows in 1851.[31] In towns like Hamilton, the large number of women of marriageable age compared to the number of men probably reduced the likelihood of remarriage for many. Furthermore, given the risks of childbirth, many widows who could support themselves perhaps preferred not to remarry. Early widowhood would interrupt the childbearing potential of women, and the decision not to remarry would curtail it. Both may have accounted for Cartwright's having had only four children and, on a larger scale, may help explain the relatively small family sizes in an urban community like Hamilton, with its large number of widows.

Cartwright's household arrangements were also not unusual. All studies of British North American communities indicate that, in most places and times, the majority of households consisted of nuclear families; that is, they were composed of the conjugal couple and their children. In the city of Hamilton and the predominantly rural community of Peel County, for example, the proportions of all households that were "simple" — that is, composed solely of nuclear families — at mid-century were 79.4 and 56.4 percent, respectively. But it is also clear that, over time and as a result of a variety of circumstances, households expanded and contracted. In two places that have been studied, more than one in ten households were "extended" by the presence of relatives in 1851; in Moncton, New Brunswick, nearly one-quarter of all households were "multiple" — that is, contained more than one conjugal couple — in 1851. This high proportion, compared to other British North American localities, is attributed to the press of population resulting from a shipbuilding boom in mid-century Moncton.[32]

The examination of the Hamilton census has shown that the extended families were often headed by young couples, suggesting that many young parents had extra adults on hand at the time when help with first-born and young children would have been most welcome. This was certainly the case for Harriet Dobbs Cartwright, whose widowed sister-in-law, Mary, clearly played a major role in the care of her first child, taking charge of him when Harriet and her husband went on a lengthy trip to the United States. The evidence indicates as well that in some communities it was the more prosperous families that were able to accommodate relatives in their households, if only because they had larger houses and therefore more space.[33] But it is also true that the majority of families may well have been in this "extended" category at one time or another. Studies of less prosperous communities have yielded evidence that it was not always or only the very well-off who shared their households. Among the families living on Campobello Island, New Brunswick, where fishing was the main occupation, 26 percent of all households were extended by the presence of at least one relative in 1851.[34]

Nevertheless, wealthier families probably found it easier to expand when the occasion demanded it. The Jarvis family of Prince Edward Island is a case in point. Large enough, first of all, to accommodate at least three servants, the Jarvis home also became the residence of visiting friends and relatives for various periods during the life of its patriarch, the colony's Chief Justice Edward Jarvis. When his first wife, Maria, died in 1841, Edward's 20-year-old daughter, Mary, took over the running of the household for a while, but at her own marriage she relinquished this task. In 1843, an unmarried aunt was briefly in residence; in the same year Edward married a second wife, Elizabeth Gray. Elizabeth died in childbirth in 1847, leaving several young children of her own in addition to Maria's offspring, who still remained at home. At this point Edward welcomed into his household a second unmarried relation, who evidently continued the domestic management of his household until his death in 1852.[35]

It seems safe to suggest that women who were bearing and raising children and managing households in this period of Canadian history were less likely than is the case today to be working at these tasks single-handed. If they did not have female relatives on hand to help out, a substantial number had servants. A study of early nineteenth-century household service in Montreal and Quebec, for example, shows that 20 percent of Quebec households had at least one servant in 1818. In mid-century Hamilton, about one-quarter of the families had a resident domestic.[36] The continuing prevalence of large families, especially in the countryside, also meant that older daughters were often on hand to help with the housework and the younger children. Frances Stewart, who settled on the Otonabee River near Peterborough with her husband and children in 1833, relied entirely on her daughters when "asthma and weakness" affected her health in 1843. Finally, a woman might have the help of visiting relatives or neighbours. Childbirth in particular brought to a woman's home not only the midwife — or the doctor, in the case of a wealthy or upper-class woman — but also friends, neighbours, mothers, sisters, or cousins. Mary O'Brien, a pioneer wife and mother who was wealthy enough to have permanent assistance in her own home most of the time, was able to help a neighbour give birth in her isolated Upper Canadian community in the 1830s. She also helped the new mother cope with the postpartum depression that followed. Assistance was not always forthcoming, however. Mary O'Brien herself wrote to relatives in England of her own feat of "cheating the doctor" by giving birth attended only by her husband and children on the occasion of at least one of her confinements.[37]

WOMEN'S WORK

Mary O'Brien's support of her neighbour also gives us one of the few recorded examples of the charitable activities that we know pioneer women saw as part of their work as women. By helping one another and the needy, and by attempting to improve the environment for their families, these women were involved from the beginning in community-building. Susanna Moodie wrote of walking miles on a winter day to take food to a woman who had been abandoned by her husband and who, with her children, was starving. Moodie considered her mission of charity both an obligation and a necessity.[38] The charitable tradition was handed down from mother to daughter. Ann Racey, a Loyalist brought to Canada as a small child, settled near what was to become Hamilton, Canada West, and worked among the neighbouring Iroquois; her daughter, Jane O'Reilly, helped nurse the sick in the "plague" or cholera epidemic that struck the province in 1832.[39]

Childbearing, childrearing, and helping other families with these tasks constituted a large part of women's work; the other major part was what women called their "domestic employments." Older women usually managed such work — and, of course, did a great deal of it. In general, however, it was the province of younger women of almost all classes and conditions to perform service tasks in the household and farmyard. Thus, girls and young women did a great deal of the spinning and preparatory work of various kinds, both inside and outside the household. This was true whether they were daughters, domestic servants, or slaves — for slavery continued into the nineteenth century in parts of British North America. Girls and young women also did a lot of "watching" — minding flocks or, even more routinely, younger children.

Frances Stewart's description of her daughters' work is a particularly apt illustration. All three girls were under 16 years of age when Frances outlined their tasks in a letter to a friend. It is worth noting that work like fetching and carrying, or knitting, could begin when a child was as young as 5 or 6.

> Anna Marie is the general overseer of the household concerns, who makes all the preserves and pickles, cakes, etc. She also has the care of Johnny, the third boy, who is now five years old. . . . Ellen mends all the stockings for the little boys and repairs their clothes. She has the care of George in particular who is three; besides this she is manager and caretaker of the poultry. In spring she attends to the sowing and raising of plants and nurseries of young apple trees. Bessie is in charge of Charlie, the infant, she is always busy and can make most of her own underclothes and knits.[40]

Domestic servants were mostly young and, increasingly during the 1800s, more often young women than young men. In early nineteenth-century Montreal and Quebec, some 5 to 8 percent of the population were servants, and two-thirds of them were women. In Hamilton, in 1851, three out of ten girls aged 13 to 16 were servants in the homes of people who were not their relatives; 40 percent of all 17- to 20-year-olds were in domestic service.[41]

Whether they were managers, servants, or slaves, mothers, unmarried aunts, or daughters, the work women did depended to a considerable extent on the occupations of the men of their households. The work of Frances Stewart and her daughters was determined in large part by the fact that they lived on a farm; but not all women lived in the countryside or occupied themselves solely with farm or housework. Eliza Ruggles, a Nova Scotian orphan who was disinherited by her Upper Canadian stepmother when she insisted on marrying a Methodist clergyman in the 1830s, helped her husband with his school for black children. Eventually, their mission to the black community took the couple to the United States and then to Africa. Eliza lost her three children and her husband in the course of this work, and later embarked on a second life as the wife of a Nova Scotian farmer. She gave birth to three more children and lived to tell her seven grandchildren about her missionary days.[42]

Eliza Ruggles's life was unusual, but she was not the only woman who travelled with a missionary husband. Methodist wives accompanied itinerant-preacher husbands on their travels, and, among the Bible Christian and Primitive Methodists, some of these missionary wives were also preachers in their own right. Frances Calloway and her husband William were Bible Christian itinerants in Prince Edward Island between 1846 and 1851; like many English immigrants to British North America, they had trouble getting used to some of the local conditions. In the summertime, their problems included heat and the ubiquitous mosquito. Dealing with the latter difficulty in the home was, evidently, the work of a missionary's wife — but it was a task Frances Calloway performed indifferently. Returning from a prayer meeting with her husband one evening in June 1848, Frances found, according to William's diary, that "a number of insufferable Moschettos had taken possession" of their home. She attempted to put a "Moschetto blind" around the bed, but was not entirely successful. According to her husband's judgement of the matter, she was "not so well skilled in putting them up as the Americans."[43]

The wives and daughters of fur traders were also involved with their husbands' and fathers' work. Thérèse Schindler and Madeleine La Framboise, Métis sisters, accompanied their spouses in the trade; both also became independent traders when widowed.[44] Other wives went to sea with husbands who were mariners. The Englishwoman Frances Hornby Barkley was with her new husband on the voyage of discovery that took them to the Pacific northwest and the coast of what was to become British Columbia in 1787. She journeyed there again with him in the 1790s. Similar voyages were also part of the tradition and practice of Maritime women. Indeed, Maritime women "regularly accompanied" sea captain husbands and fathers on their voyages well into the late nineteenth and early twentieth centuries.[45]

If women like Eliza Ruggles and Frances Calloway, the sisters Schindler and La Framboise, or Frances Barkley travelled in order to play their part, other women worked with their husbands closer to home. Mary Ann Church assisted her husband in a settled ministry. Although not ordained, she preached and helped her husband build up a Universalist congregation in Merrickville, Upper Canada, in the 1830s. The wives and daughters of fishermen also had work connected with their husbands' trade. In the cod fishery on Newfoundland's northeast coast, family workers began to replace the male servants hired by the companies sometime in the eighteenth century; in addition to their own work, women had tasks specific to the fishery.[46] Ephraim Tucker, an American travelling up the coast of Labrador for his health in the summer of 1838, was astonished at how constantly the women worked, noting that they engaged

> in the hard and laborious toils of fishing with as much zeal and activity as the males. When the salmon and trout fishing commences, the women and children employ themselves assiduously in the sport, and are often out night and day while the season of this fishery lasts. At the fish stands, while the cod fishery is in the full tide of operation, the women are seen among the most constant and dextrous in dressing the fish, thrown up by the fishermen. Some of these females will dress two or three thousand fish in a single day.[47]

Women on farms were no less involved in family business. As the women of New France had before them, British North American farm wives and daughters continued taking charge of the poultry and barnyards, and of vegetable and fruit growing, in addition to their household tasks. They were involved in food production

Ojibwa people are shown harvesting wild rice in this nineteenth-century study. The drawing is by Seth Eastman (1808–1875).

Source: Photo courtesy of the Edward E. Ayer Collection, The Newberry Library, Chicago.

The manufacture of straw hats was among the domestic industries that occupied the time of British North American women. After a painting by Cornelius Krieghoff, 1852.

Source: National Archives of Canada/C-11224.

at two levels: tending, growing, and gathering food; and salting, drying, or otherwise preserving it, as well as preparing dairy products such as butter and cheese — all this in addition to cooking meals for large families and for regular farm servants or temporary hired labour. The husbands, brothers, and fathers of farm women were frequently away: off in the lumber shanty, rafting the potash down the river, or taking the wheat to market. At such times women took over all the responsibilities of the farm. The letters of Robert to Eliza Hoyle, of Lacolle, Lower Canada, demonstrate a husband's expectation that his wife should be able to handle everything in the absence of her male partner. In addition to looking after his three offspring from a previous marriage, and her own children, Eliza received detailed instructions from her husband regarding not only the conduct of the farm and the mill, but also the collection of his debts, during Robert's endless sojourns on business in Quebec and Stanstead.[48] Other pioneer diaries and letters tell the same story: a frequently absent husband; wife and children — as well as servants, if there were any — growing vegetables and fruits, looking after animals, and occupying themselves with the production of the family's basic food.

Many women, like the former servant Nancy, or Sarah Sherwood, may also have been occupied in spinning or weaving if they had time left over. Although men eventually dominated professional weaving, women produced the "homespun" flax and wool; some spun and wove for their neighbours as well as for their own families. This work was particularly intense in Lower Canada in the early nineteenth century. The evidence is contradictory about how widespread weaving actually was; but it is clear that in turn-of-the-century Lower Canada, it was chiefly rural women who were the weavers. Lists of equipment, taken from inventories of the household effects of deceased persons, indicate that in the region around Quebec, only 30 percent of households possessed looms. But around 80 percent had spinning wheels. In many families, it would seem, women did all their own spinning, but had their wool and linens woven by others, or went to a neighbour's home to weave.[49]

Whether they bought or wove, most rural women knitted and sewed, manufacturing most or all of their families' clothing. And it was women's subsistence work as well as the production of goods for sale — spun wool, woven goods, butter, cheese, and the like — that made possible the accumulation of capital in many farm families.[50] Mary Morris Bradley of New Brunswick left the following description of her subsistence labour after nine months of marriage to her first husband in 1790. "I had the privilege of two cows' milk," she reported.

> One my husband brought home, and the other my father gave me; so that by an exchange of milk with my mother, I made plenty of cheese and butter for our use. We raised potatoes sufficient for the family, and for fatting our pork; so that with these necessaries of life, milk and butter, potatoes and pork, with but little bread, we lived; excepting particular occasions, I made little use of tea and sugar.[51]

The reminiscences of this New Brunswick housewife also demonstrate the ~~way in which British North American women's work in the home could make the difference to a family's survival~~. In the first year of their marriage, Bradley's husband got into debt over a lumber transaction, with the result that he had "no way to earn anything in the winter." Undaunted, Mary turned to her loom.

> Just at this critical time, it occurred to me, I will commence the business of weaving. Accordingly, I set up my loom, and notified the neighbours, and I soon had plenty of work. I took my pay in such trade as was suitable for our family's use, which made payment easy for my customers. I soon got into the way of helping ourselves greatly. My labor was hard; but I was favoured with a good constitution, and I felt much encouraged and truly thankful for such a providential opening.[52]

Providential or not, Mary Bradley's weaving evidently saved the day. By 1805, the Bradleys were able to move into Saint John. Here Mary and her husband kept a grocery store and rented out part of their house, eventually paying off the mortgage and enjoying the "great blessing" of owning "a comfortable home."

~~Plain and fancy sewing provided another avenue of remunerative work that could be done in one's own household or in the homes of other women on a rotating basis~~. By the middle of the nineteenth-century, sewing had replaced weaving as a major source of income. "Seamstress" is in fact one of the few employments that emerges clearly on mid-nineteenth-century census returns as a woman's occupation. In Canada East and West, 553 women were listed as seamstresses in the census of 1851.[53] Far more women than these 553 were undoubtedly making their livings this way as the fashion trade expanded in British North America. Townswomen of the period not only wanted dresses, shawls, and cloaks, but also produced an increasing demand for corsets, hats, and gloves. The hat industry alone created substantial employment for women. Mrs. Willard of Belleville, Upper Canada, placed an ad for her millinery business in the *Kingston Chronicle* in 1827; Mrs. Caffrey of Brockville advertised her "inexpensive silk, straw and leg horn bonnets" in her local paper in 1832. At about the same time, Mrs. Claris began her dressmaking career in York. These businesswomen were plying their trades in their households, as women had for generations. An examination of eighteenth-century Nova Scotia civil litigation records has revealed women traders, innkeepers, retailers, and others who earned their livings in business; while many of these litigants were widows and single women, others were married women whose work supported families or supplemented other family income.[54]

Some urban housekeepers turned their homes into inns or shops; others took in sewing or laundry. In the eighteenth and nineteenth centuries, laundry was probably some of the hardest physical work that women did. Hauling water, lifting water-soaked fabrics, heating irons, stirring, rinsing, and wringing were only some of the steps that might have been involved. A study of the process at its most elaborate, as it would have been done in a wealthy household in the first half of the nineteenth century, outlines some ten steps altogether, including scrubbing especially dirty clothes on a washboard; the addition of blueing to prevent linens from turning yellow; starching; and putting large items through long wooden rollers known as "mangles" to wring out the water and flatten them.[55]

Another remunerative occupation, and one that women shared with men, was schoolteaching. In the eighteenth century and the first half of the nineteenth, it was relatively easy for women to teach, because most schools were domestic affairs. Indeed, the word "school" referred more to the teacher and her pupils than to whatever housing a school might have. The schoolmistress advertised her skills in the instruction of reading and writing, or of sewing, French, or fine arts, and waited at home for her pupils — as indeed did the vast majority of schoolmasters. When the teacher moved, so did her school; her pupils came on an irregular basis, attending only when they could be spared from their tasks at home. As the numbers of towns and newspapers expanded in British North America, so did the ads and the schools — which, like farming, fishing, or fur trading, were often family enterprises. A widow and her daughters, a husband and wife, or two sisters might set up a school together; the combinations varied, as did the subjects offered and the clientele. What is certain is that these domestic or private schools often taught quite large numbers of children and were important educational resources in their communities, as well as vital sources of income for the schoolmistresses and their families.[56]

Angélique and Marguerite Nolin are just one of many examples of sisters who taught. After their father died (sometime in the 1820s), these young mixed-blood women were persuaded to set up a school in Red River in 1829 by the Roman Catholic bishop of the region, Joseph-Norbert Provencher. The record does not supply details about the content of their lessons, but their pupils were undoubtedly the Métis children of French-Canadian fur traders and their Native wives, whose families had started to settle in the Red River area.[57]

It was also in the 1820s that Kate Andrews opened a "private school" in the "ample basement flat of her . . . commodious residence" in Liverpool, Nova Scotia, shortly after her second marriage. Her chronicler notes that the schoolmistress was self-educated.

> By conversation with broadly educated persons with whom she came in contact, by perusal of books and periodicals, as well as by practical definite study, she had informed herself on many subjects. Her reading manner was delightful, her calligraphy elegant in style. With this acquired knowledge, and her art in needlework, she at length felt well equipped for imparting instruction to the children of the town.

The school, which was mainly for day pupils but always had a few boarders as well, moved with its teacher when she moved house, but continued for some 50 years, touching nearly every family in the community for three or four generations. Kate taught with the assistance of a servant and later that of a niece. "Gentility" as well as the three Rs and needlework constituted the curriculum.[58]

There were many such schools in British North America by the early decades of the nineteenth century. Some catered to the well-to-do; others had a fairly representative clientele of pupils. Anne Langton, an Upper Canadian spinster who taught school two days a week in the rural household that she managed for her brother and elderly parents, saw her work as charity toward the local poor.[59] But more often than not, domestic schools provided women with a livelihood or with a way to supplement the family income. A schoolteacher from a later era, reminiscing about her own education in Quebec and Montreal in the 1830s, was able to recall at least seven private teachers with whom she had studied during that decade, both before and after a six-year period in the Ursuline convent school in Quebec City.[60]

Women of African origin were deeply involved in teaching in British North America. In Brindley Town, Nova Scotia, the black Loyalist teacher Joseph Leonard was assisted by his daughter, who taught sewing to the girls in the school; in Preston, the black school was entirely under the direction of Mrs. Catherine Abernathy.[61] When the fugitive slave migration brought a new black population to Canada West, women teachers were among these migrants as well. One was Mary Miles Bibb,[62] who had graduated from the Massachusetts State Normal School and taught in elementary schools in Boston and Albany, as well as in the Hiram S. Gilbert High School for black children in Cincinnati, before her marriage to fellow abolitionist Henry Bibb. In 1850, the Bibbs came to Sandwich, Canada West, where Mary Bibb helped found the Windsor Anti-Slavery Society, assisted other migrants through the Refugee Home Society, and also found time to work on her husband's newspaper, the *Voice of the Fugitive*. But her primary work was probably teaching, which she carried on in Canada West at various times and in a variety of settings, first when married to Henry Bibb, later as a widow, and again when she remarried and became Mrs. Isaac Cary. An abolitionist traveller writing about Canada West in 1861 felt that his readers would already know about Mary Bibb's work and so did not feel called upon to describe it in detail, but his admiration was obvious.

> Her labours during the lifetime of Mr. Bibb, in connection with him, for the fugitives, and her exertions since, are too well known for me to make mention here. Mrs. Cary has a private school with about 40 pupils, mostly of the better class of Windsor.[63]

Mary Bibb had married the brother-in-law of another famous black abolitionist and teacher, Mary Ann Shadd — later Mary Shadd Cary. Like Bibb, Shadd Cary taught in a number of places in Canada West before she returned to the United States during the Civil War.[64]

Perhaps the most difficult to document of women's vocations in the pre-industrial era was also one of the most important: the vocation of healer or midwife. Part of the problem of documentation is no doubt the fact that healing and midwifery were arts practised to some degree by all women in caring for their families and helping their neighbours. But as there had been in New France, so in British North America there were also women who were renowned and sought-after for their knowledge of herbs and for their midwifery skills. The importance of the woman healer to her community is illustrated by the story of Elizabeth Doane, an eighteenth-century immigrant to Nova Scotia. A thrice-married mother of eleven, Doane migrated from New England to Nova Scotia before the American Revolution, settling in the town of Barrington. Her knowledge of herbs, surgery, and midwifery was so highly prized by her neighbours that when her husband considered returning to New England in 1770 because his business was not prospering, 35 petitioners supported Elizabeth Doane's request for a land grant from the town proprietors so that she could build a house and stay. There must have been hundreds of such women in British North America, although so far the detailed stories of only a few have been discovered.[65]

Elizabeth Innes, a New Brunswick midwife, kept a diary but began it only on her sixtieth birthday. The diary recorded cures for rheumatism and a recipe for plastering a weak joint, as well as the various deaths, accidents, and other calamities that occurred in her family and neighbourhood. Under the heading "Nursing," she noted that in her time she had nursed "168 women in their Confinement and 150 Labour."[66] Probably most women who were literate kept records of medicinal remedies for use when their families became ill; the non-literate learned from watching and helping older relatives, and passed the treatments on orally to younger generations. Catharine Parr Traill combined her interest in the medicinal uses of plants with a passion for Canadian flora in general. As prolific a writer as her sister Susanna Moodie about life in the backwoods, Traill also made a name for herself as a botanist by sending specimens of Canadian plants to scientists in England.[67]

Catharine Parr Traill, Elizabeth Doane, Mary Bradley, and Elizabeth Innes, or Mrs. Willard, Mrs. Caffrey, and Mrs. Claris, or even possibly the Misses Nolin, Kate Andrews, Mary Bibb, and Mary Shadd Cary, may have made little distinction between their housework and their other activities. While most of their domestic employments were unpaid, such activities as weaving, millinery, dressmaking, laundry, schoolteaching, and midwifery could and did bring in income — income that was often essential. Nearly all of this work nevertheless took place in "domestic space."

Countless were the women, also, who ran small inns or taverns in their homes, or who accepted boarders. The latter was an especially vital occupation for townswomen. For example, the census for Hamilton, Canada West, records that 29 percent of all households in that community contained boarders in 1851.[68] Since a woman who took in boarders often provided a laundry service as well as meals for her boarders, the work involved was far from minimal. Like domestic service, weaving, laundry, and sewing — and even teaching and healing — keeping boarders was an expansion of women's traditional role, a way in which women could respectably earn their livings or assist in the maintenance of their families without straying very far from either their homes or their communities' expectations.

Prostitution was another, if less respectable, way of earning money. British North America was a military garrison, and there is no doubt that prostitution was a temporary or supplementary employment for many women, especially in the ports and garrison towns. But "Prostitute" and "Keeper of house of ill-fame" were also among the occupations that appeared on the 1851 census returns for Hamilton, Canada West, suggesting that one census taker at least was thinking in terms of more-permanent labels or identities.[69]

Interestingly enough, "Widow" and "Spinster" were also designated occupations on the census. In both cases, this presumably reflected the understanding that a woman's marital status had an effect on what she did. Certainly a woman who had lost her husband would have been anxious to have remunerative employment of some kind, unless she had been provided for by her family prior to her widowhood. Women who did not marry also increasingly needed paid work. We know that many widows and single women either sought or created employment for themselves. Rose Fortune, a black Nova Scotian, was among the more enterprising. Fortune set herself up as a carter to move baggage from ship to shore in Annapolis Royal in the 1820s, eventually creating a transport business that was to remain in her family for 125 years.[70] More typically, women sought work in domestic service, or worked as daughters and wives within their own households.

Yet if the word "Wife" was occasionally to be found in the column for occupations on the census, this column was generally left blank opposite the names of married women. Did most census takers believe, therefore, that wives did not work? Or was their work so taken for granted that it did not need to be itemized on the census? Perhaps the answer lies in the fact that wives' roles were too diverse and variable to be easily pinned down. An additional answer is to be found in the perception, increasingly powerful as we move into the nineteenth century, of a growing gulf between two newly defined worlds: the personal, domestic world of women and the family, where it was assumed that traditional female work would and should continue to go on; and a newly developing public world, from which wives and children were most appropriately excluded. "Work" or employment that could be dignified by the title of an "occupation" would increasingly be seen as belonging to the latter sphere, the sphere governed and occupied chiefly by men. The mid-nineteenth century was still a period when extraordinary numbers of people in British North America — perhaps the majority — had more than one occupation. To identify men or women by a *single* profession or kind of work, as the census did, was itself a move toward altering people's perceptions of what they did with their lives and who they were.

Men's occupations expanded in number and began to move out of the household; in some cases, they became specialized, full-time vocations. Women's domestic employments began to seem, in contrast, rather limited, unspecialized, and poorly remunerated.[71] Yet in British North America, this was largely an urban phenomenon and one that was not noticeable until the middle decades of the nineteenth century. Probably relatively few British North American women were greatly affected by the new attitudes toward women's work that were developing in England and New England, where things were patently changing far more rapidly.

Nevertheless, upper- and middle-class emigrants from New England and England could not and did not leave their belief in the ideology of "domestic" or "true" womanhood behind when they came to British North America. They adhered to it as best they could, aligning themselves with those in the colonies who seemed sympathetic. Such would be the men and women who understood women's work to be largely "ornamental," like Harriet Cartwright's painting perhaps, and wanted to believe that every woman was supported by a father, a brother, or a husband. Two of Anne Powell's three daughters did not marry, but there was no question of either woman's being allowed to "work" for her living — despite Anne's own history of employment in a millinery shop in Boston, where she had been set up in business by her eminently successful businesswoman aunt in the 1780s. Of the two unmarried daughters, Anne and Elizabeth, only Elizabeth successfully adapted to the pursuit of good works and ornamental dependency that was considered appropriate for a

A sketch of Rose Fortune, whose family trucking business, begun in Annapolis Royal about 1825, supported her descendants for several generations.

....

Source: Black Cultural Centre for Nova Scotia.

respectable single woman in the Powell circle by the early 1800s. Daughter Anne clearly craved something different, but was not permitted to found the school that she coveted and thus seek a life of her own. The tragic result was mental illness. In an ill-fated attempt to escape from what eventually became an unbearable situation at home, Anne finally lost her life in a shipwreck off the coast of Ireland in 1822.[72]

In the upper-middle-class and affluent circles of families like the Powells, traditional class prejudice began to share mental space with a new ideology of domesticity that — in theory, at least — emphasized the differences between women and men more than the differences between the classes. But in the world of British North America, this ideology denied what the vast majority of women, even those in the urban middle classes, actually experienced: the absolute necessity of work and sometimes of "hard labour" in the household, on the farm, or wherever they lived, to keep body and soul together and the family going. It also denied the vital contribution British North American women made to family and community economies by their reproductive and productive labour. In the former category, they had babies and raised children; they also fed, clothed, cared for, and otherwise "reproduced" the paid labour force. In the second, they did work that not only was essential to the survival of their families, but often made all the difference to the family's ability to accumulate capital as well.

With a few exceptions, the vast majority of British North American women were probably beyond the reach of the disabling beliefs that so negatively affected the life of Anne Powell's daughter Anne. If women were not supposed to engage in productive or remunerative work, most British North American women did not know it. Or, if they thought that this was the case, they were soon disabused of the notion. Even Susanna Moodie disciplined herself "to learn and practice all the menial employments which are necessary to a good settler's wife." She admired Canadian women, who possessed the "excellent practical abilities" that were so essential on the frontier, and eventually prided herself not only on her neat rows of potatoes, but also on her ability to bring in some much-needed cash through her literary and artistic productions. Finally, Susanna Moodie learned that chaos and difficulty did not last forever and could even be productive of good. Indeed, she found that it was when their situation appeared most desperate that they "were on the threshold of a new state of things, which was born out of that very distress."[73]

NOTES

1. Marilyn Porter, " 'She Was Skipper of the Shore-Crew': Notes on the History of the Sexual Division of Labour in Newfoundland," *Labour/Le travail* 15 (Spring 1985), 109.
2. Diane Bélanger et Lucie Rozon, *Les religieuses au Québec* (Montréal: Libre Expression, 1982), 294; Sister Maura, *The Sisters of Charity, Halifax* (Toronto: Ryerson Press, 1956).
3. W.A. Spray, "The Settlement of the Black Refugees in New Brunswick, 1815–1836," in P.A. Buckner and David Frank, eds., *Atlantic Canada Before Confederation: The Acadiensis Reader* (Fredericton: Acadiensis Press, 1985); Sylvia Hamilton, "Naming Names, Naming Ourselves: A Survey of Early Black Women in Nova Scotia," in Peggy Bristow, co-ord., et al., *"We're Rooted Here and They Can't Pull Us Up": Essays in African Canadian Women's History* (Toronto: University of Toronto Press, 1994), 13–40.
4. Adrienne Shadd, " 'The Lord Seemed to Say "Go" ': Women and the Underground Railroad Movement," and Peggy Bristow, " 'Whatever You Raise in the Ground You Can Sell It in Chatham': Black Women in Buxton and Chatham, 1850–65," in Bristow et al., *"We're Rooted Here,"* espec. 53–54, 81–82, 96.
5. Elva E. Jackson, "The True Story of the Legendary Granny Ross," *Nova Scotia Historical Quarterly* 8, 1 (1988), 42–61.
6. James W. St. G. Walker, *The Black Loyalists: The Search for a Promised Land in Nova Scotia and Sierra Leone, 1783–1870* (Toronto: University of Toronto Press, 1992).
7. Beth Light and Alison Prentice, eds., *Pioneer and Gentlewomen of British North America, 1713–1867* (Toronto: New Hogtown Press, 1980), 1–12; Elisabeth de Moissac, "L'éducation à la Rivière Rouge (1844–1870): Les Soeurs Grises," Canadian Catholic Historical Association, *Report* (1948–49), 39–45; Jan Gould, *Women of British Columbia* (Saanichton, B.C.: Hancock House, 1975), chap. 2.
8. Janice Potter-Mackinnon, *While the Women Only Wept: Loyalist Refugee Women in Eastern Ontario* (Montreal and Kingston: McGill-Queen's University Press, 1993).

9. L. Lee, "The Myth of Female Equality in Pioneer Society: The Red River Colony as a Test Case," University of Manitoba, M.A. Thesis, 1978, 14.

10. H.C. Burleigh, "A Tale of Loyalist Heroism," *Ontario History* 42, 2 (1950), 91–99; Potter-Mackinnon, *While the Women*, espec. 50–51, 108, 1150–52.

11. *The Canadian Encyclopedia* (Edmonton: Hurtig, 1985), vol. 1, 431.

12. Wallace Brown, *The Good Americans: The Loyalists in the American Revolution* (New York: Morrow, 1969), 140–41, 206.

13. Mary Beacock Fryer, "Sarah Sherwood: Wife and Mother and Invisible Loyalist," in Phyllis R. Blakeley and John N. Grant, eds., *Eleven Exiles: Accounts of Loyalists of the American Revolution* (Toronto: Dundurn Press, 1982), 245–64.

14. Potter-Mackinnon, *While the Women*, espec. chaps. 2–4.

15. Beatrice Ross Buszek, " 'By Fortune Wounded': Loyalist Women in Nova Scotia," *Nova Scotia Historical Review* 7, 2 (1987), 54.

16. Sylvia Hamilton, "Our Mothers Grand and Great: Black Women of Nova Scotia," *Canadian Woman's Studies/Les cahiers de la femme* 11, 3 (Spring 1991), 46; Walker, *Black Loyalists*, 48–49 and chap. 5.

17. Susanna Moodie, *Roughing It in the Bush or Life in Canada* (London, 1852; Virago Press edit., 1986), espec. 342; Elizabeth Hopkins, "A Prison-House for Prosperity: The Immigrant Experience of the Nineteenth Century Upper Class British Woman," in Jean Burnet, ed., *Looking into My Sister's Eyes: An Exploration in Women's History* (Toronto: Multicultural History Society of Ontario, 1986); Marian Fowler, *The Embroidered Tent: Five Gentlewomen in Early Canada* (Toronto: Anansi, 1982); Carl Ballstadt, Elizabeth Hopkins, and Michael Peterman, eds., *Susanna Moodie: Letters of a Lifetime* (Toronto: University of Toronto Press, 1985); Carole Gerson, "Canada's Early Women Writers: Texts in English to 1859," *CRIAW Papers* No. 33 (Ottawa: Canadian Research Institute for the Advancement of Women, May 1994).

18. Diary of Anne Powell, Diaries Collection, Public Archives of Ontario.

19. Marianne McLean, *The People of Glengarry: Highlanders in Transition, 1745–1820* (Montreal and Kingston: McGill-Queen's University Press, 1991), espec. 139–41.

20. See, for example, D. Suzanne Cross, "The Neglected Majority: The Changing Role of Women in 19th Century Montreal," in Susan Mann Trofimenkoff and Alison Prentice, eds., *The Neglected Majority: Essays in Canadian Women's History* (Toronto: McClelland and Stewart, 1977), vol. 1, 66–86; Michael B. Katz, *The People of Hamilton, Canada West: Family and Class in a Mid-Nineteenth-Century Canadian City* (Cambridge, Mass.: Harvard University Press, 1976), 265; Jane Errington, "Single Pioneering Women in Upper Canada," *Families* 31, 1 (February 1992), 5–19.

21. Gretchen Green, "Molly Brant, Catharine Brant, and Their Daughters: A Study in Colonial Acculturation," *Ontario History* 81, 3 (September 1989), 235–50.

22. Sylvia Van Kirk, " 'Women in Between': Indian Women in Fur Trade Society in Western Canada," *Historical Papers/Communications historique* (1977), 30–47; Van Kirk, " 'What If Mama Is an Indian?': The Cultural Ambivalence of the Alexander Ross Family," in John Foster, ed., *The Developing West* (Edmonton: University of Alberta Press, 1983), 125–36; Van Kirk, *"Many Tender Ties": Women in Fur Trade Society, 1670–1870* (Winnipeg: Watson and Dwyer, 1980), espec. chap. 8.

23. Sylvia Van Kirk, "The Impact of White Women on Fur Trade Society," in Trofimenkoff and Prentice, eds., *Neglected Majority*, vol. 1, 27–48; Van Kirk, *"Many Tender Ties,"* chap. 8.

24. See Jennifer S.H. Brown, "Ultimate Respectability: Fur Trade Children in the 'Civilized World,' " *The Beaver* (Winter 1977), 4–10 and (Spring 1978), 48–55.

25. Van Kirk, *"Many Tender Ties,"* 111–13, 156, 208–9, and 237; Van Kirk, " 'Women in Between' "; Gould, *Women of British Columbia,* chap. 2.

26. Ingeborg Marshall, "Disease as a Factor in the Demise of the Beothuck Indians," *Culture* 1, 1 (1981), 71–77; Virginia P. Miller, "The Decline of Nova Scotia Micmac Population, A.D. 1600–1850," *Culture* 2, 3 (1982), 107–20; Ruth Holmes White-head, "Christina Morris: Micmac Artist and Artist's Model," *Material History Bulletin* 3 (Spring 1977), 1–14; Keith Winter, *Shawanditti: The Last of the Beothucks* (North Vancouver: J.J. Douglas, 1975). On peoples of the northwest who managed to remain relatively isolated and escape the worst aspects of cultural conflict, see Julie Cruikshank, "Becoming a Woman in Athapaskan Society: Changing Traditions on the Upper Yukon River," *Western Canadian Journal of Anthropology* 5, 2 (1975), 1–14; Robin Ridington, "Stories of the Vision Quest among Dunne-Za Women," *Atlantis* 9, 1 (Fall 1983), 68–88.

27. Ellen M. Thomas Gee, "Marriage in Nineteenth-Century Canada," *Canadian Review of Sociology and Anthropology* 19, 3 (August 1982), 315–20; Katz, *People of Hamilton,* 271–72.

28. Jacques Henripin, *La population canadienne au début du XVIII siècle,* Institut nation-ale d'études démographiques: Travaux et documents, Cahier No. 22 (Paris: Presses universitaires de France, 1954); David Gagan, *Hopeful Travellers: Families, Land, and Social Change in Mid-Victorian Peel County, Canada West* (Toronto: University of Toronto Press, 1981), 70–73; Chad Gaffield, "Canadian Families in Cultural Context: Hypotheses from the Mid-Nineteenth Century," *Historical Papers/Communi-cations historiques* (1979), espec. graph 4; Katz, *People of Hamilton,* 34, 233; Roderic P. Beaujot and Kevin McQuillan, "Social Effects of Demographic Change: Canada 1851–1981," *Journal of Canadian Studies* 21, 1 (Spring 1986), 57–59.

29. Katherine M.J. McKenna, *A Life of Propriety: Anne Murray Powell and Her Family, 1755–1849* (Montreal and Kingston: McGill-Queen's University Press, 1994), espec. 197.

30. Margaret Angus, "A Gentlewoman in Early Kingston," *Historic Kingston* 24 (March 1976), 73–95.

31. Katz, *People of Hamilton,* 255.

32. Katz, *People of Hamilton,* 223; Gagan, *Hopeful Travellers,* 64–65; Sheva Medjuck, "Family and Household Composition in the Nineteenth Century: The Case of Moncton, New Brunswick, 1851–1871," *Canadian Journal of Sociology* 4, 3 (Summer 1979), 275–86.

33. Katz, *People of Hamilton,* 249, 255.

34. F.K. Donnelly, "Occupational and Household Structures of a New Brunswick Fish-ing Settlement: Campobello Island, 1851," in R. Chanteloup, ed., *Labour in Atlantic Canada* (Saint John: Social Service Monographs, 1981), vol. 4, 55–63; Katz, *People of Hamilton,* 250. See also Gagan, *Hopeful Travellers,* 65–67.

35. J.M. Bumsted, "The Household and Family of Edward Jarvis, 1828–1852," *The Island* 14 (Fall–Winter 1983), 22–28.

36. Claudette Lacelle, "Les domestiques dans les villes canadiennes au XIXe siècle: Effectifs et conditions de vie," *Histoire sociale/Social History* 15, 29 (May 1982), 181–207; Katz, *People of Hamilton,* 27.

37. Frances Stewart, *Our Forest Home, Being Extracts from the Correspondence of the Late Frances Stewart,* compiled and edited by her daughter, E.S. Dunlop (Toronto, 1889), 78–79; Audrey Saunders Miller, ed., *The Journals of Mary O'Brien* (Toronto: Macmillan, 1968).

38. Moodie, "The Walk to Dummer," *Roughing It in the Bush,* 446–82.

39. Elsie Gregory MacGill, *My Mother the Judge: A Biography of Helen Gregory MacGill* (Toronto: Peter Martin Associates, 1981), 6, 9, 32.

40. Stewart, *Our Forest Home*, 80–81.

41. Lacelle, "Les domestiques"; Katz, *People of Hamilton*, 260, 270.

42. Leone Banks Cousins, "Woman of the Year — 1842: The Life of Eliza Ruggles," *Nova Scotia Historical Quarterly* 6, 4 (December 1976), 349–76.

43. Elizabeth Gillan Muir, "Delayed but Not Forgotten: Methodist Women Called to Preach," unpublished paper, Faculty of Religious Studies, McGill University, 1980, 35; and Muir, *Petticoats in the Pulpit: The Story of Early Nineteenth-Century Methodist Women Preachers in Upper Canada* (Toronto: United Church Publishing House, 1991), 75.

44. John E. McDowell, "Madame La Framboise," *Michigan History* 56, 3 (Winter 1972), 271–86; McDowell, "Thérèse Schindler of Mackinac: Upward Mobility in the Great Lakes Fur Trade," *Wisconsin Magazine of History* 61 (Winter 1977–78), 125–43.

45. W. Kaye Lamb, "The Mystery of Mrs. Barkley's Diary," *British Columbia Historical Quarterly* 6, 1 (1942), 31–59; Margaret Conrad, "Recording Angels: Private Chronicles of Maritime Women, 1800–1950," *in* Alison Prentice and Susan Mann Trofimenkoff, eds., *The Neglected Majority: Essays in Canadian Women's History* (Toronto: McClelland and Stewart, 1985), vol. 2, 41–60.

46. Heather Fawcett, "The Same and Different: Women in the Unitarian and Universalist Church in Canada, 1830–1945," unpublished paper, University of Waterloo, 30; Porter, "She Was Skipper," 105–23. See also Phillip McCann, "Class, Gender and Religion in Newfoundland Education, 1836–1901," *Historical Studies in Education/Revue d'histoire de l'éducation* 1, 2 (Autumn 1989), 180–81.

47. Ephraim W. Tucker, *Five Months in Labrador and Newfoundland during the Summer of 1838* (Concord: 1838), 119–20.

48. Françoise Noel, " 'My Dear Eliza': The Letters of Robert Hoyle (1831–1844)," *Histoire sociale/Social History* 26, 51 (May 1993), 115–30.

49. David-Thiery Ruddel, "Consumer Trends, Clothing, Textiles and Equipment in the Montreal Area, 1792–1835," *Material History Bulletin* 32 (Fall 1990), 45–64. See also Judith Buxton-Keenleyside, *Selected Canadian Spinning Wheels in Perspective: An Analytical Approach* (Ottawa: National Museums of Canada, 1980), 285; and Jan Noel, " 'Femmes Fortes' and the Montreal Poor in the Early Nineteenth Century," *in* Wendy Mitchinson et al., eds., *Canadian Women: A Reader* (Toronto: Harcourt Brace, 1996), 68–85.

50. Marjorie Griffin Cohen, "The Decline of Women in Canadian Dairying," *in* Prentice and Trofimenkoff, eds., *Neglected Majority*, vol. 2, 61–83.

51. Conrad, "Recording Angels," 44–45.

52. Conrad, "Recording Angels," 44.

53. *Census Reports of the Canadas*, 1851: Upper Canada, vol. 1, 520; Lower Canada, vol. 1, 546.

54. Jane Errington, "She Merchants, Milliners and Mantua Makers: Surrogate Husbands and Independent Business Women in the Upper Canadian Market Place," paper presented to the Canadian Historical Association, Calgary, 1994; and Errington, "Single Pioneering Women"; Julian Gwyn, "Female Litigants in the Civil Courts of Nova Scotia, 1749–1783," paper presented to the Atlantic Canada Studies Conference, Fredericton, May 1994.

55. Christina Bates, "Blue Monday: A Day in the Life of a Washerwoman, 1840 . . . ," *Canadian Collector* (July/August 1985), 44–48.

56. For a discussion of domestic schools and their teachers in Upper Canada, see Susan E. Houston and Alison Prentice, *Schooling and Scholars in Nineteenth Century*

Ontario (Toronto: University of Toronto Press, 1988), chap. 3; and Jane Errington, "Ladies and Schoolmistresses: Educating Women in Early Nineteenth-Century Upper Canada," *Historical Studies in Education/Revue d'histoire de l'éducation* 6, 1 (Spring 1994), 71–96.

57. Donald Chaput, "The 'Misses Nolin' of Red River," *The Beaver* (Winter 1975), 14–17.

58. Grace McLeod Rogers, "Kate Andrews, Schoolmistress," *Maritime Advocate and Busy East* 32 (1942), 5–10.

59. H.H. Langton, ed., *A Gentlewoman in Upper Canada: The Journals of Anne Langton* (Toronto: Clarke, Irwin, 1950).

60. Light and Prentice, eds., *Pioneer and Gentlewomen*, 73–74.

61. Walker, *Black Loyalists*, 80–84; Hamilton, "Our Mothers," 46.

62. Afua Cooper, "Black Women and Work in Nineteenth-Century Canada West: Black Woman Teacher Mary Bibb," in Bristow et al., *"We're Rooted Here,"* 143–170; and Cooper, "The Search for Mary Bibb: Black Woman Teacher in Nineteenth-Century Canada West," *Ontario History* 83, 1 (March 1991), 39–54.

63. Cooper, "Black Women" 157–58.

64. Adrienne Shadd, "300 Years of Black Women in Canadian History: Circa 1700–1980," *Tiger Lily* 1, 2 (1987), 7; Bristow, " 'Whatever You Raise,' " 98 and 105–107. See our Chapter Five for more on Shadd Cary's work in Canada.

65. Phyllis R. Blakely, "And Having a Love for People," *Nova Scotia Historical Quarterly* 5, 2 (June 1975), 165–75.

66. Elizabeth W. McGann, ed., *Whispers from the Past: Selections from the Writings of New Brunswick Women* (Fredericton: Fiddlehead/Goose Lane Editions Ltd., 1986), 145–50.

67. Elizabeth McCallum, "Catharine Parr Traill: A Nineteenth Century Ontario Naturalist," *The Beaver* (Autumn 1975), 39–45; Marianne G. Ainley, "Last in the Field?: Canadian Women Natural Scientists, 1815–1965," in Ainley, ed., *Despite the Odds: Essays on Canadian Women and Science* (Montreal: Vehicule 1990), 28.

68. Katz, *People of Hamilton*, 222.

69. Katz, *People of Hamilton*, 348.

70. Hamilton, "Our Mothers," 46; Shadd, "300 Years," 6.

71. In the list of occupations for Hamilton, 21 appear to be clearly women's; men's occupations numbered several hundred (Katz, *People of Hamilton*, appendix two).

72. McKenna, *Life of Propriety*, chap. 9.

73. Moodie, *Roughing It in the Bush*, espec. 296 and 342.

CHAPTER FOUR

Women and the Public Order

British North Americans lived in a society regulated by popular custom and belief, by social hierarchy, by the rules of churches (where these existed), and, of course, by government and law. In French Canada, the Roman Catholic priest, the notary, and the *seigneur* exercised authority; there and in the rest of what was to become Canada there were also priests and other clergymen, magistrates, military or trading company officers, and large landowners who exercised power. These authority figures were all men, and their range of activity was wide.

Sometimes they enforced unwritten codes. Such was the case at Fort Detroit in the 1780s, when Pierre Frechette, the local priest, simply expelled two "disreputable" women from his parish. He reported to his bishop that he had forced the badly behaved Mme Moisseau to leave Simon's Mill; Mme Tourangu he had likewise "chased away."[1] These were not isolated or atypical events. In the absence of prisons, asylums, or police forces, vagrants and criminals were frequently driven from communities that did not want them.

Two other women who got into trouble with British North American authorities, in part because they had disguised themselves as men, illustrate the gradual encroachment of more formal regulation. One, known to history as the "Orkney lad," had come by sea to the northwest in 1806 disguised as a Hudson's Bay Company servant (possibly in order to be with the father of her expected child); her identity was discovered only when she gave birth. Isabel Gunn was no longer allowed to do the work of a company servant and was instead given employment as a washerwoman. Although she managed to stay in Rupert's Land for three years, Gunn was finally shipped back to Scotland by company authorities, who were enforcing a code that discouraged white women from entering or living in fur trade country. Some fifteen years later, Mary Palmer seems to have aggravated her disobedience of the law by cross-dressing: she was arrested in Halifax for causing a disturbance on the streets one night while wearing an officer's uniform. But although Mary had to spend the night in the watchhouse and appear before the magistrate in the morning, she got away with a reprimand, a small fine, and a warning. Equally resistant to incarceration was Sall Ross, who was arrested for breaking into a Halifax store in 1825; this was her fourth arrest in as many years. Borrowing two babies from a friend, she somehow persuaded the judge that she was a nursing mother who should not be sent to jail whatever her supposed misdeeds.[2]

As these stories suggest, female crime in British North America was generally minor in character. The offenders were chiefly young women who got into trouble with the law for drunkenness, theft, or prostitution. Yet the law could sometimes be severe, as the punishment of an eighteenth-century Halifax servant proved. She had misplaced some household silver, probably when cleaning it. After her trial and execution for theft, the missing goods were found outside, where they had been covered with snow.[3]

In the British colonies and in Hudson's Bay Company territory, women of all conditions, ranks, and stations found their lives increasingly affected by church regulation, British law, or new legislation passed by colonial legislatures. Some of these regulations and laws perpetuated traditional sexual inequalities or divisions of labour, or extended them to the new public world that men were in the process of creating. Women were not without recourse in this world, however. Canada's first comic novel, Frances Brookes's account of manners and morals as she experienced them in Quebec in the early days of British rule,[4] reveals a community in which upper-class women (English or French) exercised considerable social power, if no official authority. The extent of this power — and the various forms of self-empowerment or resistance practised by non-elite women — are not easy to assess. But historians are finding increasing evidence on which to base discussions of women's place in the emerging public worlds of British North America.

— emergence of public sphere

REGULATING WOMEN

Jane Beaver and her husband, Herbert — the Hudson's Bay Company chaplain — complained bitterly of many things they found wrong with Fort Vancouver on the Columbia River in the 1840s. But their greatest grief was the "country" marriages between traders and Native women. Because of their protests, several long-married couples, including James and Amelia Douglas, were married for a second time in the Church of England by Herbert Beaver; the church thus successfully "regulated" the custom of two centuries.[5]

Church authorities no doubt found reason to complain in other parts of British North America about casual attitudes to marriage. Owing to the shortage of persons authorized to marry them officially, many couples cheerfully lived together without benefit of religious rites. As the clergy became more numerous, efforts were made to alter this state of affairs, and accounts abound of couples, from Newfoundland to the west coast, whose several children were present at their weddings. One traveller to Canada West in 1842 met an informant who was proud of the fact that when she had married, her daughter had already been 2 years old. He claimed that Canadian girls preferred this practice and that Canadians considered ridiculous the "correcter feelings on this subject, of females from the old country." What this traveller either did not know or did not remember is that the high value placed on fertility and child labour in rural Europe had long been the source of similar attitudes. In Canada too, as he himself was quick to point out, children were "so valuable a possession" that bringing "two or three into the world in this irregular fashion, instead of being a bar to marriage, proves . . . an additional attraction, making the young lady a species of heiress." It followed that the producer of Canadian children was highly valued. "After marriage," the traveller went on, the Canadian "makes an active industrious wife, but expects from her husband much deference, and even that he should wink at occasional frailties."[6]

Courtship and parental arrangement of upper- and middle-class marriages also followed age-old patterns. Although the evidence is scattered and incomplete, we know that upper-class parents were especially concerned about controlling their children's choice of marriage partners. As in Europe, in urban centres young women met men in formalized situations, at balls and parties in wintertime, and at various meetings connected with their churches. Young men requested permission to call, or were invited to young women's homes. Taking a young woman for a drive, if one was wealthy enough to command a sleigh or a carriage, was a customary way to pay her court; if not, taking her for a walk, or walking her home from an event, was another. Tradition has it that in the County of Beauce on the south shore of the St. Lawrence, when a girl was ready for courting, her brother took her to church and escorted her to a similarly minded group of young women who stood apart from their families.[7]

In the countryside the process of daily life brought the sexes together, despite the divisions of labour that generally prevailed. Although work was hard and time for courting and lovemaking may have seemed limited, people appear to have had a relatively open approach to sexuality, albeit one in which men had greater power and freedom than women. Respectable courting went on more or less under the watchful eyes of the young woman's elders. In the Ottawa Valley as late as the 1860s, a young man named Thomas Dick and his female friends still seemed to be operating along the old lines. Thomas Dick went to "tea meetings," to church, and to what he invariably referred to as "sinning school," although we can presume he meant "singing." He called on neighbourhood girls in their homes, sitting and chatting with them, sometimes after the parents had gone to bed. He walked them home and he

A humorous view of courtship in Quebec City. The officer and his lady are being driven toward the Lower Town.

....

Source: James Hope-Wallace (June 7, 1807–Jan. 7, 1854)/National Archives of Canada/C-040288.

A country walk might provide an opportunity for courtship or private discussion. By James Pattison Cockburn, circa 1810.

Source: National Archives of Canada/C-043906.

discussed them with his male friends. Family sanctions sometimes operated to discourage rather than support courtship and marriage; in Dick's case, marriage may have been delayed because his mother was a widow. Despite his evident interest in courting in 1867, he waited until after his sisters had married and his mother had died before embarking on matrimony, some twenty years after the beginning of his diary.[8]

There was a clear sense of family involvement when a decision to marry was made. Rebecca Byles of Halifax discussed her engagement with relatives before she accepted her future husband's proposal in 1785. More than four decades later, Mary Gapper O'Brien hesitated for some time over her proposed marriage in Upper Canada, consulting parents and siblings on both sides of the Atlantic to make sure that her services, as the one remaining unmarried daughter in the family, could be spared. In many parts of British North America, community surveillance of marriage was to be expected. This sometimes erupted into the traditional wedding-night rioting known as the "charivari." Young male revellers, often in disguise, besieged the newlyweds in their home, demanding gifts. A charivari might happen when one spouse was much older than the other, or there was some other large social gulf between them.[9]

In Quebec, the French Civil Code — and thus French marriage law — prevailed after the British takeover, and remained in effect in the lower St. Lawrence colony of Lower Canada after new boundaries came into effect in 1791. As revised on a number of occasions between the Conquest and 1795, the law of Quebec and then Lower Canada required the agreement of both parties, the publication of banns, and a ceremony performed by an Anglican or Catholic priest for the marriage to be legal. The wedding also had to be witnessed and registered with the civil authorities. Eventually it became a little easier to get legally married: between 1827 and 1845, clergy from other religious denominations were given the power to officiate. While the French provision for the "community of property" continued to be operative, it would appear that new practices were beginning to favour the separation of property. But whereas before 1820, between 60 and 90 percent of couples in Quebec or Lower Canada signed marriage contracts, in the city of Montreal after that date, the proportion dropped sharply among both Protestants and Catholics. By the 1840s in Montreal, 12 percent or less signed such contracts before they married. Those who did so were mainly members of the wealthy classes, who had real property to be concerned about.[10]

Elsewhere in British North America, British common law governed marriage. To paraphrase Blackstone's famously terse dictum, in common law the husband and wife were considered one person — and that person was the husband. The wife's property and person, therefore, came entirely under the control of her husband. In the eyes of the law, a husband could not rape his wife; a wife could not sue her husband or testify against him in court. The families of well-to-do women sometimes attempted to protect them by marriage contracts similar to those used in Lower Canada, in order to keep brides' funds and inheritances safe from unscrupulous or incompetent husbands. But contracts do not seem to have been drawn up in great numbers by English-speaking British North Americans, suggesting that few women had such protection.[11]

Under British common law a married woman had the right to dower — a lifetime interest in one-third of her husband's property. In Lower Canada, the Registry Act of 1841 eliminated the automatic right to dower, which was seen as an obstacle to commercial transactions. But even when and where it was operative, dower became effective only upon the death of the husband; thus, although a woman was guaranteed some support during widowhood, no law protected her economic interest in the case of marriage breakdown. Most women who separated from their husbands lost their right not only to the use of whatever property the family had accumulated, but also to the custody of their children. At a time and in a place where children's labour was extremely valuable, the loss of their children constituted more than an emotional loss to those women who endured such separations.[12]

Divorce was possible, but difficult, and the law varied from colony to colony. There were several attempts to establish divorce courts in Upper and Lower Canada between 1833 and 1859, but these failed; in the Canadas, divorce had to be obtained through a special act of the legislature that was difficult and costly to achieve. Only in the Maritimes were there provisions for divorce courts. In Nova Scotia, the legislature granted the governor and council the authority to hear divorce cases in 1758; it took a subsequent law to settle the grounds, but these were fairly extensive and included impotence, adultery, and cruelty, as well as kinship within the prohibited degree, and bigamy. This relatively liberal legislation may have had some relation to initial shortages of women; it is also true that the Nova Scotia law was probably influenced by the New England "planters," the settlers who were moving into the colony in the mid-eighteenth century and diluting the power of the Anglican establishment in government. New Brunswick passed a law similar to Nova Scotia's in 1791, but the grounds for divorce were slightly different, as cruelty was not included.

In the 1830s, Prince Edward Island introduced a law identical to New Brunswick's; with some amendments, it received royal assent in 1836. Yet, despite the more liberal laws and divorce courts, divorce remained unusual even in the Maritime colonies.[13]

Women's lack of economic protection in marriage and the difficulty of divorce were hard enough. But even more damaging to some women was the common law's assumption of the husband's right to control his wife's person, which included control over her earnings as well as a veto over the possibility of her working for wages outside the home, control over the location of the household, the right to "confine" her to it under certain conditions, and even the right to mete out what was considered a "reasonable" amount of physical punishment. Of course, not everyone accepted the subordination that the law and legal marriage rites prescribed. An Upper Canadian traveller told the story of an American bride who simply walked out of the church when she discovered that the wedding ceremony required that she promise to obey, choosing to join the many couples who at that time lived as husband and wife without benefit of clerical or legal intervention in their affairs.[14]

Public protest against the injustice of British laws regarding marriage began to be heard early in the nineteenth century. In 1826, the *Nova Scotian* reprinted a letter (originally sent to an English newspaper) that was deeply critical of the laws governing marriage. Its author demanded legal changes in three areas: to prevent husbands squandering their wives' property; to give widows better access to the estates of their deceased husbands; and to prevent or stop domestic violence. Yet despite attempts to bring about reform of the married women's property law in Nova Scotia and evidence of concern elsewhere, change in this and other areas was slow to come.[15]

In the meantime, women coped as best they could. Ann Melvin, a mid-nineteenth-century Upper Canadian woman, was married to a man who would not permit her to go out of the house without his leave. She wrote to her sister in 1851 that she would rather live "in some Desert on bread and water" than remain married, but her offer to take the children away and "work out" to support them was scorned by the man who had become her jailor. Some wives in such untenable situations, especially women with economic resources, managed to arrange for legal separations, and to survive by moving back to parents or finding homes with friends. Others acted more precipitously. Ads in which husbands announced their refusal to pay debts incurred by runaway wives were by no means unusual in British North American newspapers. They testify to the fact that some women dealt with their unhappy marriages by simply walking out the door and down the road.[16]

The ad that Charles Wright placed in the *Nova Scotia Gazette and Weekly Chronicle* on September 13, 1775, described his wife's behaviour and also illustrated his concern for his patriarchal rights. Hannah Wright, the ad claimed, had "been very remiss in her duty" toward her husband and children, "living in idleness and such like vicious acts and practices, as tend wholly to subvert all kind of family order and Government." Hannah had evidently not only kept bad company, but had carried off and sold a large part of the household furniture before she finally "eloped" from his "bed and board." Wright intended to prosecute anyone who harboured his wife, and declared that he would pay no debts that she contracted. On the other hand, he was willing to repay to "all good people" any money advanced on the furniture, should they return it in the same condition that it was in when taken away.[17]

Probably the most common response to a problematic marriage was endurance, or even transformation of personal unhappiness into just another hardship to be conquered. Mary Bradley, whose weaving made such an important contribution to the economic success of her first marriage, sought solace in religion when she found her husband overbearing and unkind. Fortunately, after her first husband died, her second choice made her happier.[18]

Although the movement to reform the marital property provisions under English law did not result in change in the first half of the nineteenth century, in other areas affecting women, legal change—although not necessarily "reform"—did occur in British North America. Altered laws relating to infanticide, abortion, seduction, and rape reveal much about the changing politics of male/female relations.

Early British North American law on infanticide exactly duplicated an English statute from the seventeenth century. Christian law forbade infanticide, and under English common law child murder was a felony punishable by death. But if a newborn was dead, it was difficult to establish why it had died or even whether it had been born alive. The law on infanticide therefore made it a crime, also punishable by death, to conceal the birth of a "bastard," illegitimate children being the most likely to be simply done away with. The intriguing thing about these brutal laws on infanticide is their ineffectiveness. At first the laws applied only to illegitimate births, and the cases that were heard applied only to unmarried women; very few were convicted. When Angélique Pilotte, a 20-year-old Native servant, was given the death sentence for "concealment," there was a public outcry, and later a royal pardon. Pilotte's defenders pointed out that the defendant knew nothing of Christianity and was guilty only of the "invariable custom of Indian women to retire and bring forth their children alone and in secret."[19]

In 1803, with a view to obtaining convictions where they had failed in the past, the English lawmakers decided that the ordinary rules of murder trials were to apply to infanticide; if there was an acquittal, a verdict of concealment could be substituted, now punishable by imprisonment for a maximum of two years. The British North American colonies followed suit, all passing similar laws between 1810 and 1840. Further legislation increased the scope of the law to include married women in the 1830s and 1840s; in New Brunswick and Nova Scotia, persons other than mothers were included in the workings of the law in 1849 and 1851, respectively. There were still very few convictions, however, suggesting that the courts had some compassion for the women—who, it must have been clear, were victims themselves.[20]

Before 1803, under British law, abortion had been legal before "quickening" —that is, at any stage before the fetus's movements were felt. British legislation in 1803 criminalized all abortion, but still maintained the distinction between abortion before and after quickening. The latter was punishable by death, the former by lesser sentences such as imprisonment or transportation; the criminal in both cases was the abortionist. Most British North American colonies gradually enacted similar legislation in the first decades of the nineteenth century, with New Brunswick the first. By 1837, British legislators had abolished the distinction between the periods before and after quickening but reduced the maximum sentence to three years. This time British North American legislators, with the exception of Newfoundland, did not follow the British model in its entirety, tending to be more severe. New laws were passed in both Upper Canada and New Brunswick in the 1840s that also eliminated the distinction, but maximum sentences remained harsh: imprisonment for life in Upper Canada, and for fourteen years in New Brunswick. In 1849 and 1851, respectively, New Brunswick and Nova Scotia shifted ground substantially: in a move that was unprecedented, except in the State of New York, they made it a criminal offence for the woman herself to obtain an abortion at any stage of her pregnancy.[21]

One reason for the increasing criminalization of abortion was the growth of doctors' opposition to the procedure. In 1832, the human ovum was discovered. Until then, the association between menstruation and reproduction was only speculative. Since doctors no longer thought of quickening as the start of life, they were increasingly reluctant to interfere with what they now thought of as a continuous process that began with conception. At the same time, abortions continued to be performed, for it remained difficult to diagnose pregnancy before quickening made it unmistakable. Earlier in a pregnancy, remedies aimed at regulating or re-establishing menstruation were not easily distinguishable from remedies aimed at producing abortion, either by medical assistants or by the women concerned.[22]

Rape, like abortion and infanticide, came under the criminal code, and was punishable by death; the related crime of seduction was a civil offence. In both cases, it was not the woman who was held to be the victim, but her father. We know little about the enforcement of the law with regard to rape in British North America, although some Upper Canadian cases reported between 1824 and 1850 suggest that violent resistance had to be proved—and even then the all-male juries were reluctant to convict. Two convicted rapists were sentenced to death during this period; a number of others were given prison sentences of varying lengths.[23]

Infinitely more numerous than rape trials were the lawsuits generated by the unique Upper Canadian law of 1837 dealing with seduction. Under common law, seduction had been a crime against "masters" as well as parents, the offence being that it deprived a young woman's master or father of her services during the pregnancy and childbirth that resulted from an illicit relationship. The 1837 law may have recognized a new situation: young unmarried women who had emigrated before their parents, worked as servants, and were particularly vulnerable to the attentions of the men who were in fact their masters. It was thus fathers, not masters, who needed to be defended against the "ruin" of their "chaste" daughters, and they needed this protection even if their daughters were no longer living at home. The law also recognized that it was not loss of services *per se* that was at issue but, as the attorney-general of Upper Canada put it, "the wound given to parental feelings, the disgrace and injury inflicted upon the family of the person seduced." Except in Prince Edward Island, where an 1852 statute allowed the woman herself to sue, the injury to the women themselves seems to have been ignored in seduction legislation. In contrast to the punitive rape law, the law on seduction was frequently called upon in the colonies.[24]

The existence of the tort of seduction entrenched in civil law a father's right to his daughter's services. In addition, the new statute stated that his property interests took precedence over her sexuality and reputation. Certainly it denied in a fundamental way the autonomy of the woman concerned. Indeed, all of the laws affecting sexuality, marriage, and motherhood might be regarded as evidence of new kinds of intrusions into women's lives, as male lawgivers attempted to reinforce or reinterpret traditional male controls over, as well as their protection of, women in a changing world. In the 1840s, when criminal law came under the jurisdiction of the two Canadas, another British statute — this time the law with respect to abduction —was altered. The ancient British law had criminalized the abduction of a propertied daughter against her father's wishes; the Canadian version applied to all daughters, but distinguished between the majority of women (to whom the law applied only until they were 16) and heiresses (who were covered until the age of 21).[25]

How did women react to these laws? Anna Jameson, the British writer who visited Upper Canada in the 1830s, expressed what might be described as a feminist reaction to the 1837 seduction legislation. It was only a passing comment, but she seemed to imply that women needed less to be protected by their fathers and the law than to be equal and held responsible for their own persons and acts.[26] To achieve such equality and responsibility, however, women needed to be able to earn an independent living. This would gradually come to mean the right to enter the public sphere and seek employment outside the home.

BEYOND THE HOUSEHOLD

The early stirrings of industrial and urban development gradually affected life in British North America. By the mid-nineteenth century, a traveller in New Brunswick would notice the decline of household spinning, as even farm women began to purchase the textiles that originated in the manufactories of Britain or New England.[27] Family patterns were being changed by these trends, and daughters as well as sons increasingly sought remunerative work outside the home. For most of British North America's history, at the same time, the household economy continued to prevail, and a daughter's wages were a vital part of the family subsistence — hence the view that a workingman was indeed injured if he was deprived of his daughter's earnings. The single woman's right to an independent living was an idea whose time had not yet come. But the single woman's obligation to work for her family did nevertheless enable her to move toward employment in the new "public" sphere that was coming into being.

The transition from domestic to public employment was a subtle one and varied according to the type of work in question. One version of the process can be seen in the development of women's involvement in public education. A first step came when a few British North American married women, who had been teaching in their own homes, applied for and received certification as teachers eligible to receive the newly available provincial school grants; their household schools thus became public schools by virtue of this new source of income, although they continued to conduct them at home. The more typical process in the nineteenth century, however, was in the reverse direction, as the school itself moved out of domestic space and into public space — the tax-supported schoolhouse — and the teacher moved with it. Initially the distance was not great. Most publicly employed schoolmistresses were young unmarried women or widows who taught in a schoolhouse not far from home. Often they taught only in the summer, when male teachers were less available and the pupils tended to be younger. But by mid-century, women were teaching winter schools too.[28]

Ann Stewart had been in charge of her parish school in Newcastle, New Brunswick, for nearly three years when it was examined by a government inspector in 1844. A 32-year-old widow, Mrs. Stewart lived in the schoolhouse and had an average attendance of about twenty girls, to whom she taught reading (but not writing) along with plain and ornamental needlework and knitting. Her discipline consisted of "admonition" and "slight corporal punishment"; she did not employ rewards. The inspector believed that the schoolbooks currently supplied by the friends of the scholars were insufficient, although under the heading of "Books and Apparatus used in the School" he commented only that "being a female School there are few apparates [sic] needed." But this did not mean that the visitor found Mrs. Stewart's school up to standard; his final assessment was that Ann Stewart was not really competent to teach either reading or writing, and was employed by the local community only "with a view to the wants of the female children of the neighbourhood." It was because of these "peculiar circumstances" alone that the Board of Education had "passed" Mrs. Stewart and permitted her to collect the government allowance for elementary schoolteachers.[29]

By 1851, almost one-fifth of Nova Scotian parish or "common" schoolteachers were women; in Upper Canada, the proportion was about the same. But in New Brunswick, almost half the teachers were women by mid-century; in Lower Canada, the proportion who were women was higher still. Both the Lower Canadian and the New Brunswick examples alert us to the fact that the trend toward women teaching in the public schools did not necessarily originate in cities. Urban schools were beginning to be interested in employing female teachers as assistants, but even at mid-century their numbers were still tiny. Indeed, a study of teachers in central Canada during the middle of the nineteenth century suggests that rural poverty and the lure of resource industries for young men explain in part the preferential hiring of young women in the common schools. In addition, as rural school trustees and commissioners candidly admitted, female teachers could be got for "half the price"; when local funds to match the government grant for salaries were pitifully small, male teachers were simply beyond the community's reach.[30]

Some schoolmasters, bent on improving the status of the profession for men, railed against the advent of the woman teacher, claiming that the entry of women into public-school teaching prevented the payment of good wages to men. And in some regions, even poverty did not lead to the hiring of many women. In Newfoundland, school inspectors in the mid-1840s turned up a total of only four Roman Catholic and nine Protestant women teachers in the whole colony, and it was clear that both inspectors shared a preference for schoolmasters.[31] But such critics did not stop the hiring of women in state-funded schools. Increasingly, public-school teaching vied with domestic service as an occupation for girls who sought employment after their own schooling was over.

Less numerous than the female teachers employed in publicly supported elementary schools, but highly influential all the same, were the women teachers who worked in the larger Protestant and Roman Catholic academies. Many elite Protestant families sent their daughters to the Lower Canadian convent schools that the sisters of the *Congrégation de Notre-Dame* and the Ursulines continued to operate in the late eighteenth and early nineteenth centuries. Some of the new Protestant institutions may well have been created in response to the obvious attraction of these influential Catholic schools. But the new non-Catholic institutions that began to appear in British North America also had their roots in the American and British academy movements. And despite their apparent competition, Protestant and Catholic schools for young ladies differed very little in their educational offerings. Both emphasized the genteel arts, strict timetables, and social supervision. In both Catholic and Protestant girls' schools, and even in the co-educational academies, girls were offered basic instruction in English or French; arithmetic, geography, and perhaps history;

and a wide variety of the practical as well as the "ornamental" arts. Generally un-available to girls were such subjects as higher mathematics or classical languages, subjects that educators tended to define as "masculine." In the same way, in the public schools that girls attended and that were often co-educational, girls could be denied access to advanced arithmetic. In elementary schools, wherever female teachers were employed, girls were nearly always taught sewing in addition to the three Rs.[32]

Whether they were in public schools or domestic schools, Protestant academies or Catholic convent schools, women participated in varying degrees in a female culture that increasingly valued learning. Women were taught what was considered suitable to their sphere, and by the middle of the nineteenth century it was much expanded from what had been made available to most women of previous genera-tions. Those women who were aware of the growing international agitation for female "improvement" believed that a more advanced education was essential to fit women for their vital and enhanced educational role as mothers and teachers.

Mary Electa Adams was affected by this movement. The daughter of Loyalists who had settled first in Lower Canada, then in Upper Canada, Mary Electa was educated by her parents until, at the age of 17, she was sent to Vermont's Montpelier Academy, the school that had been attended by her mother. There she was admitted to the study of the classics and advanced mathematics. After a year at Montpelier, the young scholar returned to Upper Canada to study at the Cobourg Ladies' Sem-inary, founded when girls were excluded from the Upper Canada Academy when it became Victoria College and a school for boys only. The Seminary offered a diploma thought suitable for young ladies: the M.L.A. or "Mistress of Liberal Arts." Adams obtained the diploma and then remained at the Seminary to teach until its director and her husband moved their school to Toronto, where it reopened as the Adelaide Academy in 1847. It is not clear whether Adams made this move as well, but by 1849 she had embarked on a career of her own in the administration of girls' acad-emies. She went from the Picton Lady's Academy in Prince Edward County, Upper Canada, to Michigan, and then to New Brunswick, where she was "Lady Preceptress" of the women's department of Mount Allison University in the 1850s before returning to Canada West to head first the Wesleyan Female College in Hamilton, then an academy of her own known as Brookhurst, and finally the Ontario Ladies College in Whitby.[33]

The educational impulse took women in two somewhat contradictory direc-tions. On the one hand, it led to an expansion of all-female institutions, like those with which Ann Stewart and Mary Electa Adams were associated. This was partic-ularly true in Roman Catholic Lower Canada, where seven new female religious communities were established between 1842 and 1851, four of them devoted to the provision of schooling for girls or for poor children. English-speaking convents devoted to education were also established in centres like Halifax and Toronto at mid-century. Like the larger female academies and the small girls' parish schools, these institutions took girls and women out of the private household, but remained all-female enclaves. They provided forums where women could exercise power, but only by separating both teachers and students from the public world.[34]

The alternative route, which affected more British North American women in the long run, was the move into co-educational public schooling, where women worked and learned in closer proximity with men. This avenue was made more attractive to women by their admission to most of the "normal" schools, which were opened by the governments of nearly every British North American colony in the 1840s and 1850s for training teachers. In French Canada, the normal schools remained strictly male institutions, and the training of women teachers was undertaken by female religious orders, most notably the *Congrégation de Notre-Dame* and the Ursulines. Indeed, convent women had been engaged in the formal training of teachers in Lower Canada since the 1830s. But elsewhere in British North America, women moved into the same institutions and buildings as the men. Their position was by no means the same as that of their male counterparts, however. In Toronto, when women were admitted to the newly founded normal school in 1848, they were much younger on the average than the male teachers being trained there; they were also less advanced in their preparation, for many of the men had already taught school. Finally, the women were treated differently, streamed into lower levels of teacher certification, and more strictly supervised. Interaction between male and female students was largely forbidden. Martha Hamm Lewis, who petitioned the governor for permission to attend New Brunswick's normal school in Fredericton in 1849, was required to wear a veil when attending the school. She also had to arrive in class before the arrival of her fellow students, and leave well after the men had left.[35]

Interpreting what educational innovation meant for British North American women in the first half of the nineteenth century is a subtle exercise. There is no doubt that the more rapid advancement of education for boys and young men put girls and young women at a disadvantage. The first colleges and universities were exclusively male institutions. Yet, as mid-nineteenth-century observers recognized and the early normal schools demonstrated, simply admitting girls to boys' schools or colleges could also be problematic. Should young men and women study the same things together? Or should they be in separate departments studying different things? The latter was the solution chosen by most of the early co-educational academies. Government-funded grammar schools in Canada West, on the other hand, often admitted girls and offered them a curriculum almost the same as that offered to the boys.[36]

In the end, no solution really worked in the context of a society in which educational norms were established with young men's needs in mind, and in which the worlds of men and women seemed to be drifting apart. Advanced formal education was increasingly replacing apprenticeship for men who were preparing for professional roles. If this was so, what was the purpose of such education for women — who, those in authority believed, were properly excluded from the learned professions? The new medical schools that began to be founded for men in the 1830s and 1840s did not admit women; nor did the law schools. Nor could women train for the ministry. The established denominations placed great emphasis on learning and on a proper training in theology at a college or university for their priests and ministers, an ideal in which women had no place.[37]

Yet, as we have seen, prophesying and preaching women were not unknown in British North America, at least among the more radical sects. In the great religious revival known as the Second Awakening, which swept across North America in the late eighteenth and early nineteenth centuries, women and children were active participants. "Protracted" revival meetings engulfed communities for weeks, and prayer meetings went on day and night; both appeared to provide release and even leading roles for the young and female members of communities, whose lives were normally more constrained. As well, religious revivalism encouraged more permanent ministries among women. Bible Christian and Primitive Methodists, Universalists, and some Wesleyan Episcopals briefly supported women missionaries, and some of these made their way to the British colonies in North America. Elizabeth Dart Eynon came to the Cobourg area in the 1830s with her recently converted husband, John Hicks Eynon; both were itinerants in that region for several decades, often travelling and preaching separately. Eliza Barnes was a Wesleyan Episcopal who preached in the Canadas in the 1820s, but settled down to run a school for Native children when she married her fellow Methodist missionary William Case in 1833. Perhaps the most vibrant-sounding of the Methodist women preachers was the American Ellen Bangs, who "exhorted like a streak of red-hot lightning" on the Niagara circuit at the turn of the century. Another American, Barbara Heck, is credited with having founded the first Methodist congregation in Upper Canada. No less important were the women who led "class meetings" among the Methodists. Ann Jane Robinson led such a meeting, comprising both men and women, in St. Stephen, New Brunswick, from 1841 until she died in 1853 and was succeeded by her son.[38]

The less public role of class leader was one that women were able to carry on, in some communities, into the latter part of the nineteenth century. But the woman preacher was increasingly regarded as an anomaly. By the middle of the century, even evangelical sects had begun to adopt more-conservative notions about the need for a professionally trained ministry — and women called to preach rarely had access to the kind of education church leaders had in mind. Preaching women, moreover, were probably associated with "religious enthusiasm," itself identified by many British North Americans as a Yankee import and a danger to the dignity and safety of the imperial state. In the end, women remained largely excluded from the evangelical ministry, as they did from the other learned professions.

Perhaps Quaker women were most successful in creating an equal space for themselves in the public conduct of religion. Members of the Society of Friends who came to British North America brought with them the tradition of the separate women's meeting, in which women's concerns were discussed and validated. The minutes that survive of the Quaker women's meeting in Norwich, Upper Canada, show no deference whatsoever toward the men's meetings. They reveal, rather, that women used their meeting to discuss issues, such as marriage and children's education, that the whole community regarded as vitally important.[39]

If women found quasi-public roles in education and religion, they also challenged and subverted the separate-spheres ideology and the meaning of domestic space through the act of writing. Anne Powell, thwarted in her desire to open a school, threw herself into the private instruction of her nieces and the intense practice of her religion. But she probably also engaged, at least once, in the semi-public act of writing, anonymously, to her church newspaper.[40] Nor was this an isolated act: literate women of British North America were far more involved in writing for publication than has previously been acknowledged. Through these writings, educated women sought influence in the worlds outside their families and familiar communities. To the extent that they were successful in getting their words into print, they introduced the idea of women's voice — and women's authority — into the realm of public discourse.[41]

Women authors were often seeking to augment their incomes through their writing, but only a few (chiefly those who had already had established writing careers before they came to the colonies) were successful for any length of time. Many began writing with private circulation only in mind, but — like poet and schoolmistress Deborah How Cottnam of Nova Scotia and New Brunswick or, later on, romantic novelist Julia Beckwith Hart of New Brunswick and Upper Canada — found their financial circumstances altered or were encouraged by friends to publish their works for the enjoyment and edification of larger audiences. Both Julia Hart and Mary Eliza Herbert, who founded a literary periodical called *The Mayflower* in mid-century Halifax, had to face patronizing criticism and, in Herbert's case, total condemnation of her efforts as unsuitable for the "parlour or boudoir." By the 1850s, whether or not respectable women should seek remuneration for their writing — or even a public voice in the first place — was proving controversial, as ideology about women's proper sphere hardened in British North America. Nevertheless, women wrote. Mary Eliza Herbert was unable to sustain her journal, which eventually foundered, lacking sufficient contributors and subscribers; for reasons unknown, she also failed to publish a novel that began to probe quite deeply the subject of women's dissatisfactions. But she and others like her were nevertheless beginning to make the point that women had something to say and needed to be heard.[42]

And, sometimes tentatively, sometimes unabashedly, their ideas were political. In Pictou, Nova Scotia, Jane McPhail attempted to rouse her community to support her campaign against slavery and capital punishment, circulating her copy of *Uncle Tom's Cabin*, and sending Mi'kmaq crafts to bazaars to support the abolitionist cause in Boston. In Lower Canada, "Adelaide" tried to influence opinion in a letter to the Patriot journal *La Minerve*, arguing for a recognition of the French-Canadian nation as one that promoted equality between the sexes. Her concern was that married women, who had previously used their own parental family names, were beginning to sign contracts using their husbands' names, a practice that she felt might undermine women's equality.[43]

WOMEN, GOVERNMENT, AND POLITICS

If barring women from the learned professions and from the training that led to them, along with attempts to bar women from public discourse, were among the great exclusions of British North American history, another was the exclusion of women from direct participation in government. Men were active in politics in growing numbers as the imperial authorities established elected assemblies in the British North American colonies and introduced franchises based on increasingly generous property qualifications. The franchise was exercised, in this period before the secret ballot, in public election meetings — rowdy and highly contentious events that could last several days. At first it was not entirely clear what women's position might be under the rapidly changing political conditions of British North America. New Brunswick regulations specifically excluded women from voting in 1785; a law passed ten years later had no provision regarding women. In the other colonies, the laws with respect to voting were similarly non-specific. People simply assumed that most women would not exercise the franchise. According to one constitutional historian, women had not voted in British elections "for centuries," although there was no formal legal restraint.[44]

Yet, intriguingly, it appears that propertied women were not fully aware of their supposed exclusion. There is clear evidence that women voted occasionally in

New Brunswick and exercised the franchise somewhat more frequently in Lower Canada. A study of the Lower Canadian pollbooks that remain to us discovered more than 900 women voters in various elections between 1791 and 1849. A nineteenth-century history of the Papineau family described Montreal women voting in the election of 1809, noting particularly one "elderly lady, long a widow, but notwithstanding her age, still fresh and vigorous." When she was asked for whom she wished to vote, "she answered with a voice strong and filled with emotion 'For my son, M. Joseph Papineau, for I believe that he is a good and faithful subject.' " Evidently there was no protest, and the voter's son, Louis-Joseph Papineau, was elected for the East Ward of Montreal.[45]

Women in Bedford County and the borough of Three Rivers exercised the franchise in the election of 1820. The Bedford County case was disputed, however, because the votes of 22 married women had duplicated the votes of their husbands on the same properties. The Assembly declared that the election was void, and that voting by wives was illegal whether or not the husbands voted. Clearly the notion of an individual franchise was meaningless to these early nineteenth-century legislators. It was property that voted, as represented by male heads of families. By the late 1820s, the question of women at elections had begun to arouse more extensive controversy. In 1828, the election of the previous year in Quebec Upper Town was called into question because a widow had been refused permission to vote. Petitioners called this a lapse of justice, declaring that "it would be impolitic and tyrannical to circumscribe [woman's] efforts in society, — to say that she shall not have the strongest interest in the fate of her country, and the security of her common rights." Pointing out that women were responsible for rearing and educating men, they added that "widows exercise, generally, all the rights of men, are liable to most of the same duties towards the State, and can execute them as well."[46]

Public opinion and the views of British North American legislators and their imperial governors were moving inexorably in the other direction, however. In that same 1828 election in the "Borough of William Henry," a counter-petition claimed that there had been a miscarriage of justice because "many women" had been permitted to exercise the franchise. In the debate, one of the two members for Quebec Upper Town based his objection to women's participation in politics on historical tradition: "It was incontrovertibly the practice of all representative governments, both ancient and modern, to exclude women from any share therein," he explained; therefore, he could not "decide in favour of the ladies." In 1832, as part of an act concerning controverted elections, the Assembly included a measure specifically prohibiting the exercise of the franchise by women; the Reform Act in Britain made the same provision in the same year. The Canadian law was disallowed by the British authorities for reasons unrelated to its content, but there seems to be no further record of women going to the polls in Lower Canada. In 1844, shortly after the union of Upper and Lower Canada, seven women evidently managed to vote in Canada West, and the election was upheld. But in 1849 a Reform government finally passed a law excluding women from the franchise in both of the Canadas. Prince Edward Island and New Brunswick had passed similar laws in 1836, and Nova Scotia would do so in 1851.[47]

Something of the flavour of male attitudes to the idea of women voting comes through in an account of an election that took place in Nova Scotia before women's official exclusion. The incident was a hot contest in Annapolis County, reported in the *Novascotian* of December 3, 1840, by a supporter of the Reform party. He had gone into Annapolis in the middle of the election to see what the Tories there were doing and found that they were up to mischief:

> Getting all the old women and old maids, and everything in the shape of pet-ticoats to be carried up to the hustings the next and last day to vote for [the Tory candidate] Whitman. As it was 9 o'clock in the evening no time was to be lost. I . . . rode all Tuesday night, and roused up every farmer; and what was the result, they harnessed up their horses, went off, and each one by 10 o'clock, was back with a widow or a fair young fatherless maid, to vote against the Tory women from Annapolis Royal.[48]

It is not clear, in the end, if any of these Nova Scotia women actually managed to exercise the franchise. What is clear is that the attempt of women to vote was finally to be dismissed as no more than a partisan "manoeuvre" or perhaps, at the most, an occasion for a clever story. Reformers in the colonies did not take up votes for women for any length of time as a serious political cause. Louis-Joseph Papineau and other Lower Canadian Reformers evidently espoused the idea in the 1820s, but a violent by-election in Montreal West in 1832 changed Papineau's mind. Men and women alike were intimidated, he claimed; three people were killed, and women were being "drawn to the hustings by their husbands or their guardians, often against their wills." Papineau finally concluded that such scenes were against the "public interest, decency, and the natural modesty of the sex." It has been suggested that he was also responding to the fact that, unlike his mother, the majority of qualified female property-holders in Lower Canada were anglophones who could not be expected to support his party.[49]

Women in British North America were gradually disenfranchised, but it would be wrong to imply that they played no political roles whatever. On the contrary, the women of the colonial political elites — and even women who were not in the official governing classes — sometimes had considerable influence, particularly in times of stress. In New Brunswick, Lois Paine prevailed upon her husband, who was a member of the legislature, to get up a petition for the founding of a "Provincial Academy of the Arts and Sciences." He did what she asked in 1785; the result was a land reserve that would eventually support the creation of the University of New Brunswick. Probably Molly Brant was the most effective female political actor during the American revolutionary war. The third wife of the British Indian agent Sir William Johnston, and the sister of the Mohawk chief Joseph Brant, Molly Brant was a leading matron of her extensive and important tribe. She exerted a steady influence on her people and helped persuade them to continue their support for the Six Nations' alliance with the British. When the war forced the Mohawk to abandon their ancestral territories in New York State for a new home in Upper Canada, she continued to work for the best possible conditions for their settlement.[50]

Laura Secord also won fame for warning British officers of an impending American attack during the War of 1812. The record is unclear, but it appears that Secord walked the entire day of June 22, 1813, and a distance of some 30 kilometres, to carry this message. The entire American detachment of about 400 men was captured. The British officer in charge later described the event and his indebtedness to Secord: "The weather on the 22d was very hot and Mrs. Secord whose person was slight and delicate . . . no doubt was much exhausted by the exertion she made coming to me." He added that, since Secord and her family were "entire Strangers" to him before June 22, her "exertions . . . could have been made for public motive only." He therefore recommended her to the "favourable consideration" of the provincial government. But no reward was forthcoming, and Secord was left to live in poverty with the husband she had earlier saved from death in battle. In 1828, finally, he — not she — was rewarded with a series of local offices. Left with nothing after her husband's death in 1841, Laura Secord taught school in her home in Chippewa until, at age 85, she received a small reward of her own from the Prince of Wales.[51]

There was another kind of politics in which the wives of military and government officials in British North America's capital cities were active. Heavily involved in the production of social relations that defined rank and could cement (or destroy) political alliances, elite women could play powerful roles, making or breaking the political careers of their male relatives or enemies, or promoting the political goals of their choice. Women were intensely involved in the social round of Upper Canada's capital in the 1790s and early 1800s, choosing to call on certain "ladies" but not on others. Their choices were not without political impact. Wives were also not wholly silent or inactive in the reform movements that began to affect the colonies in the 1820s and 1830s. In Toronto, Isabel Mackenzie, the wife of Upper Canada's most famous rebel, was later characterized by her son-in-law as a more ardent opponent of the ruling Family Compact than William Lyon Mackenzie himself, during the period when he was becoming enmeshed in the movement that would lead to the 1837–38 Rebellions in the Canadas.[52]

A portrait of Anne Murray Powell, arbiter of social life in early Upper Canada's capital. The picture was made in 1834.

Source: From a painting by Stuart Gilbert (1834). Reprinted by permission of the Bureau of Michigan History, Lansing, Michigan.

The Rebellion in Lower Canada offers the historian a fascinating case study in attitudes toward women's roles in politics, as well as changing historical interpretations of those roles. Some appraisals of this event have produced evidence of women's participation in the Patriot cause. Women, for example, formed the *Association des dames patriotiques du comté des Deux-Montagnes* in the summer of 1837 and became involved in a campaign to boycott the goods of British merchants. Soon women in Montreal joined the movement, pledging to wear only French-Canadian homespun clothing and to avoid all but the most necessary purchases of imported materials. Individuals and groups of women also made flags, manufactured armaments, lent their homes for meetings, and even carried arms. Cordelia Lovell, a Lower Canadian who wrote to her sister about her alarm at the deteriorating political situation in November 1837, wondered if her sister would think she had become a *"politicienne."* She assured her that she had not, but that on the other hand it was not possible to avoid politics altogether. The political question preoccupied everyone and was "the subject of all conversation."[53]

Lovell's unease about politics may have stemmed from alarm about the violence that was about to unfold, an alarm that may have been as typical of women's response as more active involvement. A recent analysis of the Rebellion suggests that Patriot rhetoric was, moreover, far from supportive of the idea of women's intrusion into the world of politics, espousing rather the increasingly dominant myth of separate spheres. Misogynous verbal attacks on Queen Victoria were accompanied, in this rhetoric, by the notion that assertive women produced effeminate men; the latter, Patriots argued, were susceptible to tyranny. This assessment argues that the evidence of active female participation in the Rebellion itself is slight, and that the most assertive individual women were, in fact, pro-government.[54]

After the fighting was over, women did what they could to assist imprisoned rebels and win better treatment or reprieves for them, or to influence the climate of opinion in favour of the defeated rebels. Eugénie Saint-Germain petitioned the wife of the governor in 1838, begging that her husband be spared from death for his part in the Rebellions. Her pleas had no effect; under the law, neither Mme Saint-Germain nor Lady Colborne was in a position to exercise genuine political power, despite their membership in the elite circles of their respective societies. For such women power was, at the most, influence on those who were in a position to make decisions. During his exile in the United States in 1839, Louis-Joseph Papineau wrote to his friend Louis Perrault about the passionate defence of the rebel cause by Perrault's mother. She had exerted such an influence that an important American official had written to England, attempting to explain the extent of nationalist feeling in Lower Canada and urging a more moderate policy toward the Patriots.[55] But it is not clear what such efforts gained, and the aftermath of rebellion meant grief for many women. When Isabel Mackenzie followed her husband, William Lyon Mackenzie, into exile in December 1837, she had to leave five daughters under the age of 11; she did not see them again until navigation reopened the following spring. William's depressions, the death of one child, the birth of three more, and the necessity of moving house almost yearly did not make it easy for Isabel to endure their 12-year exile.[56]

Women's political involvement could take forms other than indirect influence, or actions for or against men's rebellions. Women were sometimes more directly involved on their own or others' behalf. Fighting for one's own liberty was a political act: at least two black women went to court in Nova Scotia in the late eighteenth century in an attempt to claim their freedom from abusive masters who had unlawfully treated them as if they were slaves. They were just two among the substantial number of eighteenth-century Nova Scotia women, the court records reveal, who were willing to sue in order to obtain justice. Taking flight from oppression was also a political act, as was supporting others who were refugees. Loyalist women were involved in such acts, as were the women of the underground railroad that brought runaway slaves to Canada after an imperial statute abolished slavery in all British territories in 1834. Usually these women worked in clandestine ways, but when necessary their actions could be overt.[57] Anna Jameson reported the excitement that developed among both white and black inhabitants of the Districts of Gore and Niagara when Upper Canadian authorities were preparing to deliver an escaped slave to his former owner. Because the man had stolen a horse to effect his escape, he was considered a felon; and by an agreement between the British and American governments, all felons had to be extradited. Drawing upon older traditions of popular political action, a black mob assembled and began to riot when the man was led out of jail; in the ensuing melee, he escaped. What fascinated Jameson was "the conduct of the women":

> They prevailed upon their husbands, brothers, and lovers, to use no arms, to do no illegal violence, but to lose their lives rather than see their comrade taken by force across the lines. They had been most active in the fray, throwing themselves fearlessly between the black men and the whites. . . . One woman had seized the sheriff, and held him pinioned in her arms; another . . . held [one of the artillerymen] in such a manner as to prevent his firing.[58]

A woman had been the mob's leader: a former slave from Virginia who had been treated well by her owners, she had nevertheless run away when her master died and it appeared that she would be sold. Anna Jameson asked to meet this black leader and was impressed by her passion as well as her courage. She expressed a fiery determination to live where she could be safe. If her people could not be safe on British ground, the woman told Jameson, she would go "to the end of the world" to find a country where they could be.

Still another form of politics was the use of petitions. Loyalist women used petitions in their attempts to win compensation for their losses or assistance in times of particular distress. One such petitioner was Sally or Sarah Ainse, an Oneida Loyalist who signed "eight petitions and half as many letters" between 1789 and 1808, regarding her legal entitlement to lands on the Thames River. In the end, the government refused to recognize that the land had been deeded to her by the Chippewa, but did give her title to some 1600 acres. And petitioning did not stop with the Loyalists. A study of New Brunswick women petitioners of the mid-nineteenth century found widows continuing the tradition of asking for compensation for family services rendered to the state; schoolmistresses who petitioned to receive the school grant for their teaching; and widows petitioning to promote their business interests after the death of husbands.[59]

Nor were the petitioners of government the only women to use this form. In 1846, Barbe Desroches, a New Brunswick midwife, organized a petition in support of a priest she preferred to his rival in the village of Saint-Antoine; she threatened to withdraw her services as midwife from those who failed to sign. Desroches presented her petition to the bishop in person and appears to have won the day. The defeated priest was outraged but powerless. Barbe Desroches, he wrote, intended to "hold the keys" of the church when it was built. Indeed, so powerful was this "wicked woman" that it was she, he maintained, who governed "the whole village" of Saint-Antoine.[60]

FORMALIZING COLLECTIVE ACTION

Such petitioning demonstrates that, although women were cut off from the ballot and from much political action by the mid-nineteenth century, they were not powerless. Nor were they cut off from each other. Pioneer women were lonely in British North America, because farms were often isolated and travel was difficult. But as quickly as they could, women attempted to re-establish their traditional patterns of female sociability and co-operation. Thus quilting and sewing bees, co-operative cooking for festivals, all-female gatherings to attend a birth, and long-term visiting by aunts, sisters, mothers, daughters, and friends continued to reinforce women's sense of community and common interest in a world in which, as a sex, some may have perceived themselves as increasingly isolated.

New outlets in religious work offered opportunities for individual expression as well as for collective action. Very few Protestant women could become itinerant preachers, class leaders, or settled ministers. But many more were able to immerse themselves in the Sunday-school movement that had begun in the Maritime colonies and had spread to the Canadas by the early nineteenth century. Young middle-class women wanting useful religious work found it in teaching poor children the three Rs and giving Bible lessons at Sunday schools, which often lasted for the whole day. Other women led prayer groups, such as the Maternal Association of Milltown/St. Stephen, founded in 1836 as a support group for mothers. Occasionally, religious belief provided the possibility of escaping from a patriarchal religious atmosphere at home or made possible a marriage in the face of parental disapproval. Such was the case for Nancy Lawrence, the daughter of a Nova Scotian Congregationalist minister; she became a "New Light" in the 1780s and, to her parents' distress, married a widower with three children because he shared her newfound religious enthusiasm. For Roman Catholic women, the revival of religious and particularly of convent life provided important opportunities for individual choice and socially useful work. Francophone sisters continued to run the hospitals that had served Montreal and Quebec for generations and to care for foundlings. But their work in all fields expanded; by 1825, there were four times as many nuns as priests in the city of Montreal, as increasing numbers of women chose the religious path.[61]

Women turned to social activism when they saw around them what seemed to be increasing levels of social distress and crime, as migration and economic dislocation wrought major changes in town and country. It is unclear whether the growing numbers of people arrested and jailed in the nineteenth century represent real increases in criminal activity or a growing unwillingness in urban centres to tolerate public drunkenness, prostitution, and vagrancy. But there is no doubt that in some localities more women were being jailed. In many jails, young and old, petty criminals and the mentally disturbed, mixed with members of both sexes who had

The Hôpital Général de Montréal, *founded by the Grey Sisters, as it appeared in an 1844 sketch by J. Duncan.*

Source: Hôpital Général de Montréal (Soeurs-Grises), 1844, by James Duncan. Musée de l'Amérique Française, Archives et Bibliothèque du Séminaire de Québec.

committed serious crimes.[62] Protestant and Roman Catholic women alike responded to such problems by banding together to create new charitable and religious associations to address the problems of unwed mothers, starving families, or orphaned children, or to try to reform their communities in ways that would make them better places for women and children. In this way they continued and extended the well-established tradition of mutual assistance and care for the needy. In small communities, informal home visiting continued to seem adequate to meet the needs of the poor and destitute; in larger centres, women began to move toward more-formal solutions and organized efforts.

By the middle decades of the nineteenth century, Protestant women's benevolent or missionary societies had sprung up in nearly every major town or city. The Prince Town Female Society for Propagating the Gospel and Other Religious Purposes was founded by Presbyterian women in Prince Town, or Malpeque, Prince Edward Island, in 1825, and included among its missions the distribution of Bibles to the families of isolated fishermen in the colony. In Montreal, three Church of Scotland women banded together with their friends in 1815 and founded the Female Benevolent Society to give aid to the distressed immigrants of the city. In Upper Canada, Hamilton's Ladies' Benevolent Society was, like its Montreal counterpart, interdenominational and devoted to visiting and distributing assistance to the poor. Toronto's Queen Victoria Benevolent Society was probably a largely Methodist organization. Serving the needs of indigent black women in the city, this association was founded by Ellen Abbott, herself a former domestic servant who had married a free black in the United States and immigrated to Upper Canada in 1835. Another society founded by Upper Canadian black women was known as the Daughters of Prince Albert. Both were burial societies that also cared for the poor and the sick. Many of the new associations involved women ministering to women, but some had children as their special care. The Montreal Protestant Orphan Asylum, a foundation of the Female Benevolent Society, came into existence in 1822.[63]

The need for such charities demonstrates that British North American society, for all its increasing idealization of motherhood and family, was a less than ideal world for many women and children. Unmarried mothers and poor widows did not fit the idealized view of the family that was emerging in the third and fourth decades of the nineteenth century, nor did the few women who chose not to marry and attempted to live independently. Even the Protestant and Catholic women's associations that tried to alleviate the poverty and distress they saw around them sometimes ran into male opposition. In French Canada, the church discouraged laywomen's organizations and channelled women's efforts into the development of religious orders. One group of laywomen under the direction of Emélie Gamelin had sick and destitute women as its special concern in a charity that dated from 1828; it was transformed into the Sisters of Providence in 1843. The French-Canadian women who gathered around Montreal widow Rosalie Cadron-Jetté in the early 1840s ministered to unwed mothers. Persuaded by the city's Bishop Ignace Bourget that their work could best be accomplished if she and her assistants were bound by religious vows, this 50-year-old midwife became the founder and first superior of the *Soeurs de la Miséricorde*, a community devoted at first to assisting unmarried mothers, and eventually to caring for their "orphaned" children as well.[64]

Eventually, some women began to recognize that their charitable and educational efforts, for all their worthwhile character, were to some extent "Band-Aids" in a social system that required more radical attention to the causes of social distress. This certainly was the view of the Saint John Ladies' Total Abstinence Society. In 1847 the society petitioned the New Brunswick legislature, asking for a ban on "strong drink," the evil that this group identified as the source of much of the city's social dislocation. Their petition met with no response.[65]

NOTES

1. Beth Light and Alison Prentice, eds., *Pioneer and Gentlewomen of British North America, 1713–1867* (Toronto: New Hogtown Press, 1980), 213–14.
2. Sylvia Van Kirk, *"Many Tender Ties": Women in Fur-Trade Society, 1670–1870* (Winnipeg: Watson and Dwyer, 1980), 175–77; Malvina Bolus, "The Son of I. Gunn," *The Beaver* (Winter 1971), 23–26; Light and Prentice, eds., *Pioneer and Gentlewomen*, 215–16; D. Owen Carrigan, *Crime and Punishment in Canada: A History* (Toronto: McClelland and Stewart, 1991), 250 and 253.
3. Carrigan, *Crime and Punishment in Canada*, 444.
4. Frances Brookes, *The History of Emily Montague* (London, 1769; Toronto: McClelland and Stewart, 1961).
5. Van Kirk, *"Many Tender Ties,"* 154–57.

6. Light and Prentice, eds., *Pioneer and Gentlewomen*, 120.

7. Peter Ward, "Courtship and Social Space in Nineteenth Century English Canada," *Canadian Historical Review* 68, 1 (March 1987), 35–62; Madeleine Ferron et Robert Cliché, *Les Beaucerons, ces insoumis: Suivi de Quand le peuple fait la loi* (La Salle, Qué.: Hurtubise, 1982), 279–80. See also Peter Ward, *Courtship, Love, and Marriage in Nineteenth-Century English Canada* (Montreal and Kingston: McGill-Queen's University Press, 1990).

8. Light and Prentice, eds., *Pioneer and Gentlewomen*, 99–101.

9. Audrey Saunders Miller, ed., *The Journals of Mary O'Brien* (Toronto: Macmillan, 1968), 84, 88–89; Ward, *Courtship*, 137; Bryan D. Palmer, "Discordant Music: Charivaris and Whitecapping in Nineteenth-Century North America," *Labour/Le travail* 3 (1978), 5–62.

10. Bettina Bradbury et al., "Property and Marriage: The Law and the Practice in Early Nineteenth-Century Montreal," *Histoire sociale/Social History* 26, 51 (May 1993), 9–39.

11. Constance B. Backhouse, "Married Women's Property Law in Nineteenth-Century Canada," in Bettina Bradbury, ed., *Canadian Family History: Selected Readings* (Toronto: Copp Clark Pitman, 1992), 320–359; and Backhouse, *Petticoats and Prejudice: Women and Law in Nineteenth-Century Canada* (Toronto: Osgoode Society, 1991), passim.

12. Bradbury et al., "Property and Marriage," 13–14; Rosemary Ball, " 'A Perfect Farmer's Wife': Women in 19th Century Rural Ontario," *Canada: An Historical Magazine* 3, 2 (December 1975), 2–21.

13. Constance B. Backhouse, " 'Pure Patriarchy': Nineteenth Century Canadian Marriage," *McGill Law Journal* 31, 2 (March 1986), 264–312; Backhouse, *Petticoats*, chap. 6; B. Hovius, *Family Law* (Toronto: Carswell, 1987), 110; Kimberley Smith Maynard, "Divorce in Nova Scotia, 1750–1890," in Philip Girard and Jim Phillips, eds., *Essays in the History of Canadian Law, Vol. 3: The Nova Scotia Experience* (Toronto: University of Toronto Press, 1990), 232–72; Wendy Owen and J.M. Bumsted, "Divorce in a Small Province: A History of Divorce on Prince Edward Island from 1833," *Acadiensis* 20, 2 (Spring 1991), 86–104.

14. Light and Prentice, eds., *Pioneer and Gentlewomen*, 119.

15. Philip Girard, "Married Women's Property, Chancery Abolition, and Insolvency Law: Law Reform in Nova Scotia, 1820–1867," in Girard and Phillips, eds., *Essays in the History of Canadian Law, Vol. 3*, espec. 80–92.

16. Light and Prentice, eds., *Pioneer and Gentlewomen*, 125–26 and 163–64; Margaret Conrad, "Recording Angels: Private Chronicles of Maritime Women, 1800–1950," in Alison Prentice and Susan Mann Trofimenkoff, eds., *The Neglected Majority: Essays in Canadian Women's History* (Toronto: McClelland and Stewart, 1985), vol. 2, 41–60.

17. Light and Prentice, eds., *Pioneer and Gentlewomen*, 163.

18. Conrad, "Recording Angels," 44–45.

19. Constance B. Backhouse, "Desperate Women and Compassionate Courts: Infanticide in Nineteenth-Century Canada," *University of Toronto Law Journal* 34, 4 (Fall 1984), 450–52; also Backhouse, *Petticoats*, chap. 4.

20. Backhouse, "Desperate Women"; Backhouse, *Petticoats*.

21. Constance B. Backhouse, "Involuntary Motherhood: Abortion, Birth Control and the Law in Nineteenth Century Canada," *Windsor Yearbook, Access to Justice* 3 (1983), 61–130; and Backhouse, *Petticoats*, chap. 5.

22. Richard A. Leonardo, *History of Gynecology* (New York: Froben, 1944), 255.

23. Ruth A. Olson, "Rape — An 'Un-Victorian' Aspect of Life in Upper Canada," *Ontario History* 68, 2 (June 1976), 75–79; Backhouse, *Petticoats*, chap. 3.

24. Constance B. Backhouse, "The Tort of Seduction: Fathers and Daughters in Nineteenth Century Canada," *Dalhousie Law Journal* 10, 1 (June 1986), 50; also Backhouse, *Petticoats*, chap. 2; Martha J. Bailey, "Servant Girls and Upper Canada's *Seduction Act:* 1837–1946," in Russell Smandych, Gordon Dodds, and Alvin Esau, eds., *Dimensions of Childhood: Essays on the History of Children and Youth in Canada* (Winnipeg: Legal Research Institute of the University of Manitoba, 1991), 159–82. Bailey's interpretation takes issue with the view of Backhouse (and the apparent assumption of Anna Jameson, noted below) that young women servants were in any position to defend themselves and act autonomously.

25. Backhouse, "Tort of Seduction"; Backhouse, *Petticoats*; Bailey, "Servant Girls"; and Karen Dubinsky, *Improper Advances: Rape and Heterosexual Conflict in Ontario, 1880–1929* (Chicago: University of Chicago Press, 1993), 81.

26. Light and Prentice, eds., *Pioneer and Gentlewomen*, 208–10.

27. Abraham Gesner, *New Brunswick: With Notes for Emigrants* (London: Simmonds and Ward, 1847), 241.

28. For Ontario, see Susan E. Houston and Alison Prentice, *Schooling and Scholars in Nineteenth Century Ontario* (Toronto: University of Toronto Press, 1988), espec. chaps. 2 and 3.

29. Light and Prentice, eds., *Pioneer and Gentlewomen*, 75–78.

30. Alison Prentice, "The Feminization of Teaching," in Susan Mann Trofimenkoff and Alison Prentice, eds., *The Neglected Majority: Essays in Canadian Women's History* (Toronto: McClelland and Stewart, 1977), vol. 1, 49–65; Marta Danylewycz, Beth Light, and Alison Prentice, "The Evolution of the Sexual Division of Labour in Teaching: A Nineteenth Century Ontario and Quebec Case Study," *Histoire sociale/ Social History* 16, 31 (May 1983), 81–109; and Marta Danylewycz and Alison Prentice, "Teachers, Gender, and Bureaucratizing School Systems in Nineteenth Century Montreal and Toronto," *History of Education Quarterly* 24, 1 (Spring 1984), 75–100.

31. Phillip McCann, "Class, Gender and Religion in Newfoundland Education, 1836–1901," *Historical Studies in Education/Revue d'histoire de l'éducation* 1, 2 (Fall 1989), 186.

32. Houston and Prentice, *Schooling and Scholars*, chap. 3; Johanna Selles-Roney, " 'A Realm of Pure Delight': Methodists and Women's Education in Ontario, 1836–1925," University of Toronto, Ed.D. Thesis, 1993, chap. 1; Elizabeth Smyth, " 'A Noble Proof of Excellence': The Culture and Curriculum of a Nineteenth Century Ontario Convent Academy," in Ruby Heap and Alison Prentice, eds., *Gender and Education in Ontario: An Historical Reader* (Toronto: Canadian Scholars' Press, 1991), 273–294.

33. Elsie Pomeroy, "Mary Electa Adams," *Ontario History* 41, 3 (1949), 106–17; Alison Prentice, "Scholarly Passion: Two Women Who Caught It," in Alison Prentice and Marjorie R. Theobald, eds., *Women Who Taught: Perspectives on the History of Women and Teaching* (Toronto: University of Toronto Press, 1991), 258–83.

34. Diane Bélanger et Lucie Rozon, *Les religieuses au Québec* (Montréal: Libre Expression, 1982), annexe 2, 294–315; Sister Marthe Baudoin, "The Religious of the Sacred Heart in Canada, 1842–1980," Canadian Catholic Historical Association *Study Sessions* 48 (1981), 43–60; Sister Maura, *The Sisters of Charity, Halifax* (Toronto: Ryerson Press, 1956); Smyth, " 'Noble Proof.' "

35. Jeanette Létourneau, *Les écoles normales de filles au Québec* (Montréal: Fides, 1981), espec. chaps. 1 and 2; Alison Prentice, " 'Friendly Atoms in Chemistry': Women

and Men at Normal School in Mid-Nineteenth Century Toronto," in David Keane and Colin Read, eds., *Old Ontario: Essays in Honour of J.M.S. Careless* (Toronto: Dundurn Press, 1990), 285–317; Light and Prentice, eds., *Pioneer and Gentlewomen*, 216–18.

36. For Ontario, see R.D. Gidney and W.P.J. Millar, *Inventing Secondary Education: The Rise of the High School in Nineteenth-Century Ontario* (Montreal and Kingston: McGill-Queen's University Press, 1990), passim.

37. For Ontario, see R.D. Gidney and W.P.J. Millar, *Professional Gentlemen: The Professions in Nineteenth-Century Ontario* (Toronto: University of Toronto Press, 1994).

38. G.A. Rawlyk, *Ravished by the Spirit: Religious Revivals, Baptists and Henry Alline* (Montreal and Kingston: McGill-Queen's University Press, 1984), espec. 76–79, 120–28; Jean Bannerman, *Leading Ladies: Canada 1639–1867* (Galt, Ont.: Highland Press, 1967), 25; Elizabeth Gillan Muir, "Delayed but Not Forgotten: Methodist Women Called to Preach," unpublished paper, Faculty of Religious Studies, McGill University, 1980; *Dictionary of Canadian Biography* (Toronto: University of Toronto Press, 1985), vol. 8, 200–1. Also see Muir, *Petticoats in the Pulpit: The Story of Early Nineteenth-Century Methodist Women Preachers in Upper Canada* (Toronto: United Church Publishing House, 1991), passim; Hannah M. Lane, " 'Wife, Mother, Sister, Friend,': Methodist Women in St. Stephen, New Brunswick, 1861–1881," in Janet Guildford and Suzanne Morton, eds., *Separate Spheres: Women's Worlds in the 19th-Century Maritimes* (Fredericton: Acadiensis Press, 1994), 111–12.

39. Cecilia Morgan, "Gender, Religion, and Rural Society: Quaker Women in Norwich, Ontario, 1820–1880," *Ontario History* 82, 4 (December 1990), 273–88.

40. Katherine M.J. McKenna, *A Life of Propriety: Anne Murray Powell and Her Family, 1755–1849* (Montreal and Kingston: McGill-Queen's University Press, 1994), 218.

41. Anne Innis Dagg, "Canadian Voices of Authority: Non-Fiction and Early Women Writers," *Journal of Canadian Studies* 27, 2 (Summer 1992), 107–23.

42. Carole Gerson, "Canada's Early Women Writers: Texts in English to 1859," *CRIAW Papers* No. 33 (Ottawa: Canadian Association for the Advancement of Women, 1994); Douglas Lockhead, "Introduction" to Julia Catherine Beckwith Hart, *St. Ursula's Convent or the Nun in Canada* (Ottawa: Carleton University Press, 1991); and Gwendolyn Davies, *Studies in Maritime Literary History, 1760–1930* (Fredericton: Acadiensis Press, 1991), 71–87.

43. Davies, *Maritime Literary History*, 78–79; Alan Greer, *The Patriots and the People: The Rebellion of 1837 in Lower Canada* (Toronto: University of Toronto Press, 1993), 207.

44. Elspeth Tulloch, *We, the Undersigned: A Historical Overview of New Brunswick Women's Political and Legal Status, 1784–1984* (Moncton: New Brunswick Advisory Council on the Status of Women, 1985), 3; John Garner, *The Franchise and Politics in British North America 1755–1867* (Toronto: University of Toronto Press, 1969), 156.

45. Tulloch, *We, the Undersigned*, 3–4; Bradbury et al., "Property and Marriage," 13; William Renwick Riddell, "Woman Franchise in Quebec a Century Ago," Royal Society of Canada, *Proceedings and Transactions* Series 3, 22 (1928), 87–88.

46. Garner, *Franchise*, 157, 88–89; Light and Prentice, eds., *Pioneer and Gentlewomen*, 211–13.

47. Garner, *Franchise*, 155.

48. Garner, *Franchise*, 156.

49. Garner, *Franchise*, 156–58; Le Collectif Clio, *L'histoire des femmes au Québec depuis quatre siècles* (Montréal: Quinze, 1982), 126.

50. Tulloch, *We, the Undersigned*, 5; Pearson Gundy, "Molly Brant — Loyalist," *Ontario History* 45, 3 (1953); Helen Caister Robinson, "Molly Brant: Mohawk Heroine," in Phyllis R. Blakeley and John N. Grant, eds., *Eleven Exiles: Accounts of Loyalists of the American Revolution* (Toronto: Dundurn Press, 1982); Jean Johnston, *Wilderness Women: Canada's Forgotten History* (Toronto: Peter Martin Associates, 1973).

51. Ruth Mackenzie, "Laura Ingersoll (Secord)," *Dictionary of Canadian Biography* (Toronto: University of Toronto Press, 1976), vol. 9, 405–7; John S. Moir, "An Early Record of Laura Secord's Walk," *Ontario History* 51, 2 (Spring 1959), 105–8. See also Cecilia Morgan, " 'Of Slender Frame and Delicate Appearance': The Placing of Laura Secord in the Narratives of Canadian Loyalist History," *Journal of the Canadian Historical Association*, n.s., 5 (1994), 195–212.

52. Katherine M.J. McKenna, "The Role of Women in the Establishment of Social Status in Early Upper Canada," *Ontario History* 83, 3 (September 1990), 179–206; McKenna, *Life of Propriety*, espec. chap. 3; Nancy Luno, "Domestic History: Following the Paper Trail of the W.L. Mackenzie Family," paper presented to the Ontario Women's History Network, Toronto, February 1994.

53. Le Collectif Clio, *L'histoire des femmes*, 144–49; Marcelle Reeves-Morache, "La canadienne pendant les troubles de 1837–1838," *Revue d'histoire de l'Amérique française* 5, 1 (juin 1951–52), 99–117.

54. Greer, *Patriots,* 190–218.

55. See Light and Prentice, eds., *Pioneer and Gentlewomen,* 165–66.

56. Greer, *Patriots*, 353; Nancy Luno, *A Genteel Exterior: The Domestic Life of William Lyon Mackenzie* (Toronto: Toronto Historical Board, 1990).

57. Julian Gwyn, "Female Litigants in the Civil Courts of Nova Scotia, 1749–1783," paper presented to the Atlantic Canada Studies Conference, Fredericton, May 1994; Janice Potter-Mackinnon, *While the Women Only Wept: Loyalist Refugee Women in Eastern Ontario* (Montreal and Kingston: McGill-Queen's University Press, 1993); and Adrienne Shadd, " 'The Lord Seemed to Say "Go" ': Women and the Underground Railroad Movement," in Peggy Bristow, co-ord., et al., *"We're Rooted Here and They Can't Pull Us Up": Essays in African Canadian Women's History* (Toronto: University of Toronto Press, 1994), 41–68.

58. Light and Prentice, eds., *Pioneer and Gentlewomen,* 191–96.

59. Patricia Kennedy, "Voices in the Shadows," *The Archivist* 20, 1 (January/February 1993), 2–4; Gail G. Campbell, "Disfranchised but Not Quiescent: Women Petitioners in New Brunswick in the Mid-19th Century," in Guildford and Morton, eds., *Separate Spheres*, 39–66.

60. Tulloch, *We, the Undersigned*, 5.

61. Alan Greer, "The Sunday Schools of Upper Canada," *Ontario History* 67, 3 (September 1975), 169–84; Marguerite Van Die, " 'A Woman's Awakening': Evangelical Belief and Female Spirituality in Mid-Nineteenth Century Canada," in Wendy Mitchinson et al., eds., *Canadian Women: A Reader* (Toronto: Harcourt Brace, 1996), 49–68; Elizabeth W. McGann, ed., *Whispers from the Past: Selections from the Writings of New Brunswick Women* (Fredericton: Fiddlehead/Goose Lane, 1986), 106–09; Rawlyk, *Ravished by the Spirit*, 124–27; Marta Danylewycz, *Taking the Veil: An Alternative to Marriage, Motherhood and Spinsterhood in Quebec, 1840–1920* (Toronto: McClelland and Stewart, 1987); Jan Noel, " 'Femme fortes' and the Montreal Poor," in Mitchinson et al., eds., *Canadian Women: A Reader*, 68–85.

62. On crime and the perception of crime in this period, see Roger Lane, *Policing the City: Boston 1822–1885* (Cambridge, Mass.: Harvard University Press, 1967); John

Weaver, "Crime, Public Order and Repression," *Ontario History* 78, 3 (September 1984), 191–92.

63. J.T. McNeil, *The Presbyterian Church in Canada 1875–1925* (Toronto: General Board of the Presbyterian Church in Canada, 1925), 140, 142; *Halifax Woman's Christian Temperance Union* (1890), 40; Haley P. Bamman, "The Ladies' Benevolent Society of Hamilton, Ontario: Form and Function in Mid-Nineteenth Century Urban Philanthropy," in Michael B. Katz and Paul H. Mattingly, eds., *Education and Social Change: Themes from Ontario's Past* (New York: New York University Press, 1975); Noel, " '*Femmes fortes*' "; Robin Winks, *The Blacks in Canada: A History* (Montreal and Kingston: McGill-Queen's University Press, 1971), 328–29; Shirley J. Yee, *Black Women Abolitionists: A Study in Activism, 1828–1860* (Knoxville: University of Tennessee Press, 1992), 80.

64. Le Collectif Clio, *L'histoire des femmes*, 124; Danylewycz, *Taking the Veil*, 20, 47; D. Suzanne Cross, "The Neglected Majority: The Changing Role of Women in 19th Century Montreal," in Trofimenkoff and Prentice, eds., *Neglected Majority*, vol. 1, 79.

65. Maritime Woman's Christian Temperance Union, *Annual Report* (1890), 40.

PART TWO

The New Pioneers: The Mid-Nineteenth Century to the End of the Great War

Historians have been fascinated by the period that stretches from the middle of the nineteenth century to the end of the Great War. The tremendous changes that occurred in those years laid the groundwork for Canadian society as we know it. In 1867, the colonies of Canada East and Canada West, New Brunswick, and Nova Scotia joined in Confederation; in the decades that followed, the goal of a Dominion from sea to sea was completed. During the same era, the burgeoning women's groups that existed across the country began to unite in more formalized associations; in the National Council of Women of Canada, they formed a single umbrella organization that joined in the unifying and expansionist impulses of the nascent national community.

The background to these political events was the continuing economic development of the nation. The staple economy expanded into the new pioneer areas of the north and west. In the settled regions, household production gave way to the beginnings of a factory system that co-existed with sweatshops, the "putting out" of industrial work into workers' homes, and artisan workshops. The vast forest, mineral, and hydro-electric resources of central British Columbia, Ontario, and Quebec helped fuel this development, as did foreign capital from Great Britain and increasingly from the United States. By the end of World War I, a full-blown industrial society had emerged, albeit with strong remnants of the earlier economic systems still in place in various regions and locales.[1] The resulting regional disparities are still with us.

The two decades following Confederation saw a boom in the Maritime economy, and it appeared that the provinces of New Brunswick and Nova Scotia in particular would benefit from industrialization. But the boom was not to continue, and by the early decades of the twentieth century the eastern regions had lost ground to the more industrially developed southern regions of Quebec and Ontario. Westerners too had their complaints about the distribution of economic benefits — specifically, the effects of the 1879 Conservative National Policy. High protective tariffs had the result of filling the coffers of eastern banks and enriching central Canadian industrialists at the expense of agricultural producers.

Class differences also created inequities. Industrial development was predicated on cheap labour; thousands of immigrants, especially those from non-English countries, paid a high price for their entry into Canada. They and other working-class

Photo on previous page: An Alberta woman after a successful hunt, 1917. Source: Mrs. Mary Denning (1892–1994) holding grouse and gun (NA 2674–17), Glenbow Archives, Calgary, Alberta.

Canadians endured harsh and unsafe working conditions and low pay with little public acknowledgement of their plight or appreciation of their efforts. Yet they continued to come, underlining the even harsher realities of the societies they were leaving behind.

Gender cut across regional, class, race, religious, and ethnic divisions, for women participated fully in the economic transformation of Canada in all regions and in all groups. Indeed, without them it is unlikely that the transformation would have occurred. Besides bearing children, who were the workforce of the future, women themselves provided a cheap and efficient workforce. Most of their work was unpaid, absorbed into the family economy; but even when irregular or unpaid, it was vital.

A massive growth in Canada's population accompanied and contributed to these economic changes. From approximately 2.5 million people in 1851, the population grew to nearly 9 million by 1921.[2] But population growth was not even. During the economic recession of the 1880s and early 1890s, hundreds of thousands of Canadians left the country to seek their fortunes elsewhere. Nevertheless, as a result of a high birth rate, the population did increase, and by 1900 the exodus had been stemmed. At the turn of the century, new immigrants flooded into Canada, not only from Great Britain and the United States—the two nations from which Canada had always attracted settlers—but now also from all parts of the European continent and from some parts of Asia and the West Indies. As a result, Canadians of British origin decreased from 60 percent of the population in 1871 to 55 percent in 1921, and those of French origin from 31 percent to 28 percent.[3] The host community sometimes displayed overt hostility to these latter immigrants, but many Canadians could see the benefits of a growing population, and immigrants, including young women (whom the federal government viewed as potential childbearers), continued to be encouraged to settle here.

Many of the immigrants who came in the early years of the twentieth century were attracted by the offer of free homestead land in the region west of Ontario. Not only did they help open up and develop this area, but their presence was strongly felt, since the host community was so small. In 1901, the foreign-born share of the population of British Columbia, the Northwest Territories, and Manitoba was 26, 30, and 15 percent, respectively. For the country as a whole, it was only 3 percent.[4]

The gender composition of the population also changed. Between 1851 and 1891, young men flocked to the Prairies, the Northwest Territories, and the United States in search of greater economic opportunities; as a result, women of marriageable age outnumbered men in the same age range in the original British North American provinces. In Manitoba and British Columbia, on the other hand, the 1881 and 1891 censuses revealed that men significantly outnumbered women.

At the same time as new regions were being settled, many Canadians and immigrants moved into urban areas. In 1851, more than four-fifths of the British North American population lived in rural regions; by 1901, the proportion of rural dwellers had declined to two-thirds. By 1921, the number of rural and urban Canadians was about equal.[5] Women continued to lead this shift in the population, because they moved to the cities for employment opportunities that the rural areas could not offer them. Consequently, women outnumbered men in most cities, just as men tended to form the majority in rural and frontier areas.[6]

The tremendous changes in the demographic and economic makeup of Canada — from an economy that stressed the ownership of land to one that emphasized wage labour, and from a society in which prestige devolved from who one's parents were to a society that placed value on what one did — gave many Canadians a sense that they were part of a modern and developing nation, and that this called for some adjustments in their institutions. One example was the franchise, which was changed to almost universal manhood suffrage. The general enfranchisement of women, however, continued to be denied until after the outbreak of World War I; indeed, the Dominion Franchise Act that governed the federal franchise between 1885 and 1898 specified that for the purposes of voting, a person was defined as a "male person, including an Indian and excluding a person of Mongolian or Chinese race.[7] It took nearly half a century of determined struggle on the part of women activists and their allies to secure votes for women.

Canada's expansion, industrialization, and rapid urbanization resulted in densely populated areas that accentuated the problems of poor sanitation and contagious disease. The concentration of factories in certain sections of the larger industrial centres created pollution and filth in the areas surrounding them. Intemperance, crime, delinquency, and prostitution were seen as social problems and appeared to be worsening. Nor was life in the rural areas idyllic. Many farmers' sons and daughters were lured to cities by the prospect of paid employment, a trend that resulted in rural depopulation in some regions and a sense of an agrarian lifestyle under siege.

Canadians responded to these problems in various ways. By the turn of the century, a vigorous — generally white and middle-class — reform movement was in place in which thousands of Canadian women were active. The existing women's organizations expanded the range of their activities. Improved transportation and communication networks began to overcome the vast distances of Canada's geography, and some women developed an enlarged sense of common identity. The growth of a female paid workforce in education, health, business, and industry also strengthened this spirit of sisterhood and increased the potential for organization. The isolation of rural women often made getting together difficult; nonetheless, their efforts to counter this isolation led to an enhanced awareness of shared experiences and problems, and ultimately to the creation of their own organizations.

At the same time, the women's movement responded to the nationalism and imperialism of the era, sharing in a patriotic concern both to protect the country's stability and future vitality, and to maintain and reinforce strong links with the British empire. Most English Canadians hoped that the territorial expansion of Canada would lead to a glorious future for the nation at the centre of the British empire, and the more imperialistic among them pressured the Canadian government into supporting the British in the 1899 Boer War. Women who shared these aims formed the Imperial Order Daughters of the Empire to look after the graves of those Canadian soldiers who had fallen on the foreign battlefield. Women were also enthusiastic supporters of Empire Day celebrations in the various schools throughout English-speaking Canada. Such patriotic activities reached their zenith during World War I.[8] The more-extreme imperialist and nationalist attitudes could shade into nativism, which at times rested on theories based on eugenics. Canadian-born, English-speaking

Canadians worried about the growing numbers of non-English-speaking immigrants, and the high birth rate of French Canadians. Women activists frequently shared these anxieties.

At the opposite end of the political spectrum, women supported socialist solutions to Canada's problems. Pacifism was attractive to some, who saw it as a natural expression of women's nurturing role. French-Canadian women in particular had reason to be opposed to war, for, unlike their anglophone sisters, they did not identify with British imperialist dreams of grandeur. French Canadians proudly asserted that their loyalty was undivided, and that their identity was rooted solidly in Canadian soil. Any affinity they had once had with Great Britain was largely destroyed as English-Canadian imperialists invoked their belief in the superiority of the Anglo-Saxon race, and of all things British, to justify their attacks on French-Canadian rights outside Quebec. School crises in New Brunswick, Manitoba, the Northwest Territories, and Ontario; the violent reactions of English Canadians to the two Riel uprisings (1869–70 and 1885); and the ongoing debate over the status of the French language underscored anglophone intentions to limit the French presence to Quebec. The result was a turning inward, a concentration on *la survivance*. A key element in the French-Canadian strategy for survival has been dubbed "the revenge of the cradle"—an emphasis on having large families to offset the tide of immigration that was swelling the ranks of non-French Canadians. This strategy was, of course, dependent on the labour of women, and reinforced an ideology that exalted women's role in the home. The Anglo-Protestant reform movement that was intended to accord most women increased economic and eventually political rights was generally unacceptable in Quebec. Nonetheless, as elsewhere in Canada, French-Canadian Catholic women did organize, and challenged the constraints on their activities. They also concentrated on initiating social reforms in response to the problems generated by industrialization and urbanization.

The grand themes for the nation as a whole during this period have been identified as "urbanization" and "industrialization." Only local studies can reveal how people integrated change into their lives. Canadians experienced urban or industrial development differently: the pace varied depending on region, class, race, ethnicity, and gender. They were active participants in the process, not the passive victims of inevitable economic, political, or demographic forces utterly beyond their control. Many nevertheless perceived change through the eyes of a bygone age. Attitudes had a tendency to shift more slowly than social reality, especially when the social reality was altering at a pace hitherto unknown.

Contemporary historians, including historians of women, have studied this period of our history more than any other period. As a result, we have been able to draw on a wealth of secondary literature that reflects rich primary sources. The number of newspapers and magazines expanded dramatically during these years. So did interest in women: the proper sphere of women was an obsession for Victorian and Edwardian Canadians, and they delighted in writing about it. Women were told what it meant to be a woman and the proper way to behave. At mid-century, religious authorities were the most significant voice in this discussion. However, with the increased commercialization of society, with the challenge to accepted faiths presented by Darwin's evolutionary theory, and with the questions that critical analysis of the bible posed regarding the literal truth of the scriptures, new experts appeared. Science in particular gained an aura of authority in the late nineteenth century, and those who invoked it, such as physicians, could bask in its reflected glory.

More reliable than the stereotypes in the written materials produced by male pundits are the records generated by women themselves: their actions, their words, and their artifacts. Diaries and letters were generally written by educated women, however, and by no means reflected the lives of all. This is true as well of the abundant records belonging to women's groups of this period. The evidence of material culture that has come down to us — the kitchen utensils, the new household appliances, the dresses—is also from relatively affluent homes. Not all women could afford to save things or not wear them out before new purchases were made. Yet these items are important, for they allow us to get closer to individual women and to flesh out impressions based on less-personal data.

The evidence from such sources can be supplemented by that contained in census returns and other quantifiable data. Comprehensive censuses of the British North American colonies, first taken in 1851, were repeated at ten-year intervals thereafter. In Catholic parishes, manuscript census returns augment the continuing parish records. In non-Catholic communities, these returns are often the only source of demographic data; they enable us to estimate the number of children women had, the age at which they married, and their life expectancies. From birth intervals, we can even infer whether or not they used birth control.

It is from many kinds of evidence, then, that we are now beginning to piece together a picture of women's experience in the second half of the nineteenth century and in the early decades of the twentieth. It is not always easy, however, to interpret that experience, for it is difficult to know how much women internalized the ideal concept of themselves. This is particularly true when it is remembered that the ideology of domesticity applied to a private or intimate culture. We know about women's public activities, their involvement in the paid labour force, and their participation in a myriad of women's organizations; we also know that such experiences were not as divorced from the private sphere as the domestic ideology suggested. But what did such experiences mean for women? Did they perceive any contradictions between the popular perceptions of women and the reality of their own lives?

NOTES

1. Bryan D. Palmer, *Working-Class Experience: The Rise and Reconstitution of Canadian Labour, 1800–1980* (Toronto: Butterworths, 1983), 67.
2. F.H. Leacy, ed., *Historical Statistics of Canada*, 2nd ed. (Ottawa: Statistics Canada, 1983), A1 14.
3. Leacy, ed., *Historical Statistics*, A125–63.
4. *Canadian Annual Review* (1905), 589.
5. L.O. Stone, *Urban Development in Canada*, 1961 Census Monograph, Dominion Bureau of Statistics (Ottawa: Queen's Printer, 1967), 29.
6. Ellen M. Thomas Gee, "Marriage in Nineteenth-Century Canada," *Canadian Review of Sociology and Anthropology* 19, 3 (August 1982), 318, 320.

7. Catherine L. Cleverdon, *The Woman Suffrage Movement in Canada*, 2nd ed. (Toronto: University of Toronto Press, 1974), 108.

8. Nancy M. Sheehan, "Women's Organizations and Educational Issues, 1900–1930," *Canadian Woman Studies/Les cahiers de la femme* 7, 3 (Fall 1986), 91.

CHAPTER FIVE

Continuity and Change in Women's Work

When two young sisters of Irish descent, Hannah and Alice Bailey, were wed in a

double ceremony in Ingersoll, Ontario, on February 26, 1908, neither could possibly

have imagined how utterly different their lives as married women would be.

Hannah's marriage was an unhappy one, but fortunately she was a plucky and hard-

working woman who outlived not only her first husband, but two others as well.

She raised seven children, and lived past the age of 90. Fate, however, was not so

kind to her younger sister Alice. Buoyed by the dream of owning their own farm,

she and her husband, Thomas, set out for Saskatchewan shortly after their marriage.

In the little loghouse they constructed on their homestead, Alice subsequently bore
two daughters; but, worn out by the hard work of pioneer life, she died of consumption when she was only 29.

In the period between 1851 and 1921, women's lives were marked by an
intriguing interplay of continuity and change. Increasingly, young women in rural
areas sought work off the farm. For most of the period, the major employment for
women was the traditional one: domestic service. The primary or resource sector of
the economy had not in the past afforded women significant opportunities for earning wages, but women were moving into new areas of wage labour after 1850. With
industrialization and the growth of secondary industry, thousands of women found
paid work within labour-intensive manufacturing enterprises. Moreover, by the end
of the nineteenth century, the tertiary or service sector of the economy was expanding
rapidly, and it afforded many women additional employment opportunities in fields
such as teaching, nursing, and clerical work. Indeed, by World War I, there were
more women holding down white-collar jobs than there were women engaged in
manufacturing. The work women did was remarkably varied, not only at any one

time but over an individual woman's life cycle. Their enterprise (paid or unpaid) contributed to the development of the economy and of society.

For all women, there was the tension between the ideal of the woman at home and the reality of women's work — whether inside or outside the home. Canadian women from the mid-nineteenth century on protested some of the conditions that working women faced, married or single, young or old. They rarely spoke with a united voice; for example, women in one class were not always sympathetic to the protests of women in another class. But isolated as their voices sometimes were, the emerging picture is one of a growing, if tentative, strength. Women workers began to recognize common problems and a common cause. Their collective efforts and the increased visibility of women's employment outside the home prompted public awareness of the new shape of women's lives.

MIGRATION

The pioneer experience did not disappear with the beginning of industrialization; thousands of Canadians continued to move into the less-populated areas of the new nation. For many women, the opportunities afforded by migration outweighed its disadvantages; but for others, giving up a home in a settled part of the country was not easy. Some refused to move, like Rebecca Ells of Port Williams, Nova Scotia, who with her son ran a mixed commercial farm while her husband went off to the Klondike for twelve years.[1] Some did not want to move, but had no choice. This was the situation of Mrs. Carmichael of Sunnyside, New Brunswick. Her husband insisted on selling the family farm and moving farther north. Her daughter recalled her mother's tears and her initial refusal to sign away her share of the farm. But in the end, seeing no alternative, she signed and the family made its move.[2]

By the late nineteenth and early twentieth centuries, more and more single women were also moving west. Some came on their own or with migration agencies; some were motivated by the high wages offered to domestic servants in a labour-scarce region; others were attracted by matrimonial offers. One such woman, the bride-to-be of a Mountie, made the trip out west; but when she arrived in town, her prospective groom, unbeknown to her, was looking her over from a distance. Deciding that she did not suit his needs, he sent a message to her and paid her way home.[3]

Immigrants also continued to move to Canadian farms from other countries. Between 1901 and 1921 alone, 644 089 men and women came from the British Isles and 246 125 from the United States.[4] Although Canadian customs and environments must have seemed very different, at least there was a shared language. Women who spoke languages other than English or French had more to contend with. Between 1901 and 1921, some 500 000 immigrants entered Canada from southern, central, and northern Europe or from Asia. The women among them, like many women migrants, often felt they had little choice in moving. Ida Bronowoski left Poland to join her 20-year-old husband in Canada because "I hear lots in Poland come from Canada, they talk. Man stay in rooms there, he forget wife and kids. I not trust."[5] In addition to the language barrier Ida faced when she arrived, she and women like her often had to cope with cultural, racial, or religious hostility. Racism kept some groups of women — blacks and Asians — from entering Canada in any significant numbers.

One of the largest groups of non-Anglo-Saxon immigrants to arrive during this period were the Ukrainians. From fewer than 6000 in 1901, their numbers swelled to more than 75 000 just ten years later. The influx of Ukrainian women to the prairie provinces, particularly Alberta, was a source of great concern to local women's organizations there, appalled as they were by the low status of women immigrants and the "abomination of child marriages among the Galicians [Ukrainians]."⁶ A similar concern was expressed about the Japanese "picture brides" — young women who arrived in Canada to marry, sight unseen, Japanese men who had decided to settle permanently in this country. Community reaction to Asian settlement was extremely hostile, for most Canadians considered "Orientals" to be unassimilable. From 1886 until 1923, when they were barred as permanent settlers, nearly all Chinese wishing to come to Canada had to pay a head tax. Beginning in 1904, the fee was set at the very high level of $500. This measure effectively kept female immigration to a minimum, since most Chinese men could not afford to bring their wives, and most single women did not have the resources to pay for themselves. Only Chinese women who had non-Chinese husbands, or were the wives of Chinese clergymen or merchants, were exempt from the tax. As a result, many of the women who did immigrate were "slave girls" brought in by Chinese businessmen, who claimed them as either wives or daughters. These young women were bought from their impoverished parents in China to work as domestic servants, waitresses, or prostitutes in British Columbia.⁷

Women from all cultures often experienced dire poverty in the course of their immigration. In the spring of 1905, Ottilia Tetzlaff Doering, pregnant with her eighth child, left Russia for Canada with her husband and seven children. En route, the wagon in which all their possessions were packed caught fire; only a samovar survived. During the voyage over (on what was essentially a cattle boat), Ottilia became

Haw Chow Shee was one of the few Chinese women who managed to immigrate to Canada in the late nineteenth century. She is depicted here with her son George and infant daughter Avis Haw in 1897.

Source: Photo by William Notman & Sons, 1897. Reprinted by permission of Professor Douglas H. Lee.

ill and would have died but for the captain's taking the entire family into his quarters. With only 50 cents to their name on arrival, the family accepted the help of an immigrant aid committee, which provided the fare to Manitoba. There Ottilia's husband ran church services and taught, her sons worked as farm labourers, and her daughters worked as kitchen helpers, until the family saved enough to build a log-house on a homestead in Chevlin. Ottilia died of tuberculosis a few years later and did not see the fruits of these efforts.[8]

At least Ottilia had a family with whom to share her trials. Single women of all groups lacked even that comfort, although their willingness to move suggests an independence and strength that would serve them well. Not all single women, however, moved freely. The Chinese "slave girls" and the Japanese "picture brides" of the early twentieth century clearly did not. Nor did the thousands of young "home girls" sent to Canada from various agencies in Great Britain, who were apprenticed out to local families as domestic servants.[9]

Migration to agricultural or northern frontiers was not the only migration of the era. Women also left the rural areas to seek their fortunes in the cities, pushed by the difficulties or loneliness of country life and pulled by new economic opportunities. By the turn of the century and increasingly afterward, columnists writing in farm newspapers acknowledged this rural exodus. They blamed it on the harshness of farm life for young people, and especially for young women, who felt they had no prospects on the farms, particularly in the less prosperous regions. Few wanted to end up as one 40-year-old farm woman did — left on her father's death with only a cow and 100 dollars to show for her lifelong work on the farm, when each of her three brothers had inherited a 320-acre farm. At least the cities offered women a chance to work for pay. Soon women were moving to urban centres in massive numbers. By 1871, women in Montreal outnumbered men in every age category. Nor was Montreal an anomaly. By 1921, women between the ages of 15 and 29 outnumbered men of the same age range in most urban centres in Canada.[10]

Migration to and between cities was equally the experience of immigrant women and Canadian-born women. Despite the fact that government policy encouraged immigrants to settle in agricultural regions, many chose cities or towns instead. The average rate of increase in the urban population after mid-century was 34 percent per decade. As well, many urban Canadians were transients in the decades after the middle of the century: in the centres that have been studied, 50 to 75 percent of city residents in a given year cannot be traced ten years later. The cities of Canada did offer opportunities to women. Between 1891 and 1901, women in the paid labour force increased by 41 959 or 21.4 percent, and most of these were in the urban centres.[11]

WORK OUTSIDE URBAN CENTRES

Women in rural regions and on the frontier continued to perform labour-intensive work for little or no pay. Russian Mennonite women newly arrived in Manitoba found that their work had increased: they laboured in the fields for the first year or so, something they had not done in the old country.[12] Although women engaged in farm work far more than men engaged in domestic work, labour on the farm continued to be gender-specific. Women scrubbed clothes on scrub boards (if they were lucky enough to have one), hauled water from the creek or the well, cooked on wood stoves, and made most of the family's clothes. In addition, they grew vegetables, gathered fruit, preserved and baked, and looked after their children. The domestic work of women was seldom easy. Susan Dunlap's diary of 1866–68, written when she was a young girl in Stewiacke, New Brunswick, details the household chores performed by her sister, her mother, and her. These included churning butter; washing, picking, and carding fleeces; spinning; weaving; and "pulling, setting, breaking, hackling, and scutching . . . of the flax." Even Christmas Day was not free from labour. In 1866 she wrote, "Christmas day and a rainy one. Mother and Mary scoured fifty skanes [skeins] of filling. Mother spun 2 skanes. Mary made Howard's cap. Aunt Ellen was over. Mother stitched a sack [dress] for Mary." These chores not only saved money but also, in some families, generated income. The butter Susan churned every day was sold and the money used to help support the family. The Ungava Inuit women of the Belcher Islands used eider skins for clothing by first pulling the skin away from the muscles, then sucking the fat out of the skins, and finally cutting the skin into pieces for sewing.[13]

Mi'kmaq women in the 1890s in Nova Scotia continued to bring in money with their basket work, and this money tended to be the most dependable source of family income. In addition, many of these women were doing most of the work on their farms. As the Indian agent in 1893 noted, "those Indians living on the reserve have done much more planting this spring than at any time previous, the women doing a large part of the work while the men are employed on the streets [in Yarmouth] at good pay."[14] Halfway across the continent, Dominko Roshko and her mother, pioneering in early twentieth-century southern Manitoba, dug seneca roots and sold them at 35 cents a pound for medicinal purposes, or traded them for supplies. The money these women earned helped their families to survive and also stimulated the economy. But selling their produce could be difficult for Native women. Those on prairie reserves were encouraged by the Indian agents to be agricultural producers and to sell their surplus eggs and butter, as white women did. However, each woman on the reserve needed the permission of the agent to do so — permission that was not always forthcoming. Newfoundland women, too, had difficulty participating directly in the market economy. Caught up with subsistence production tied to the fishery, they had little time to produce other goods for purchase or trade.[15] Market-oriented or not, women needed ingenuity in order to survive. In 1884, when her hens and a rooster were killed by a mink and her one remaining hen froze its foot, Harriet Neville fashioned an artificial leg and foot for it out of whalebone, wire, and a kid glove. The hen went on to raise several clutches of chicks.[16]

Although farm women, particularly pioneer women, continued many of the work patterns of their mothers and grandmothers, change did occur during the second half of the nineteenth century. When farms became prosperous, the money women generated was no longer as necessary for survival, although it still often represented a regular source of income for their families. Those women who continued to bring in money welcomed it for the independence it gave them, and the chance to buy things for their families and homes without feeling they were "robbing" the farm.

At the same time that the farm's financial needs were shifting, large-scale and centralized production often took over some of the work that traditionally had been women's, such as spinning and weaving, and the making of cheese and butter. In 1851, 32.4 million pounds of butter and 4.8 million pounds of cheese were home-produced in Canada. By 1891, it was 111.6 million and 6.3 million, respectively. That increase, however, occurred simultaneously with the even greater increase of cheese and butter production in factories. In 1864, the first cheese factory in Ontario opened. By 1900, there were 200 cheese factories in Oxford County alone; the share of cheese produced on Ontario farms declined steadily. Milk production increased to meet factory demand, and care of the growing dairy herds passed from the hands of the farm women into the hands of their husbands and farm labourers. In general, there was a decline in skilled work for farm women and a resulting decline in the money a farm woman was able to earn, leaving her with very little visible or recognized economic input. Yet when specifically asked whether the development of cheese factories had altered their financial position, Ontario farm women in 1903 said it had not: their focus was on how their lives related to others, how the family worked together, the family's well-being, and that of the farm economy.[17]

Many farmers acknowledged the work women did; in rural areas it was well known that bachelors were less successful at farming than were married men because the work done by wives and children remained so essential. In the early 1860s, the Agricultural Association of Upper Canada stated explicitly that "a good wife" was "indispensable" to a farmer.[18] Seeing firsthand the work that women performed in early twentieth-century Saskatchewan, settler Georgina Binnie-Clark could only concur with this judgement. She believed she owed one important debt to her life on the prairie: "a fair appreciation" of her own sex.[19] Yet few farm wives received *tangible* recognition. Farmers were notorious for purchasing new equipment for the barn or fields but refusing to buy anything for the house. Nor did the government of Canada recognize the work farm women did: in the census, farm wives — like other wives who worked in their homes — were listed as having "no occupation."[20]

According to both law and custom, a farm wife had little or no legal claim on family property that had been acquired partly as a result of her labours. The land was owned by her husband, and he had the right to sell it at any time unless she was protected by dower right. Increasingly, Canadian men viewed the buying and selling of land, including the family farm, as a way to get ahead, and saw dower

Women doing farm work in early twentieth-century Manitoba.

Source: Provincial Archives of Manitoba: East Kildonan — Farms. (N-12950). Women harvesting onions.

right as an anachronistic holdover from an earlier time when agricultural property seldom changed hands. The hostility to dower was particularly strong in the territories, where the right was abolished in 1886.[21]

Even if the land was not sold, a woman who outlived her husband often found her position tenuous. Frequently, widows found that the farm had been left to a son, and that they had little beyond their dower portion and some form of limited maintenance. Sometimes even this much was conditional on the wife's "good behaviour" — in particular, her willingness to remain a widow. In Richibucto, New Brunswick, in 1856, a widow discovered that her husband's will specified she would lose her right to the use of the family property if she remarried.[22] Control "from the grave" continued in many farming regions well into the twentieth century, as Lucy Maud Montgomery observed in connection with her grandmother in 1905.

> Uncle John and Prescott have been using grandmother shamefully all summer. In short, they have been trying to turn her out. . . . Grandfather's absurd will put her completely in their power — the power of selfish, domineering men eaten up with greed. Grandmother told them she would *not* leave the home where she had lived and worked for sixty years and since then Uncle John has never spoken to her or visited her.[23]

In the west the situation was worse, for widows there had no legal rights of inheritance. Widows in the Native community, too, were affected. The 1884 revisions of the Indian Act insisted that widows had to be "of moral character" in order to inherit. Indian agents also were reluctant to allow widows property unless there was a son to inherit from the mother. Those married to white men without benefit of clergy were particularly vulnerable. In 1878 a young South Peigan woman, Awatoyakew — also known as Mary Brown — was living with Nicholas Sheran. When he died, neither she nor the two sons she had had with Sheran received anything from his estate. His sister — who became the administrator of Sheran's estate and knew of Mary and her sons — claimed that her brother had been a bachelor. Mary returned to her own people, and Sheran's sister placed the two boys in a Catholic orphanage. In some cultures, inheritance practices encouraged extreme self-denial on the part of women.[24] In 1888, an elderly Inuit woman whose health had been declining for several years decided to follow the custom of her people, and asked her son to abandon her on an island to die. What prompted her to this decision was not only her failing health, but the knowledge that if she died in her son's home he, by custom, would have to throw away his clothes. His wife had already died that year; the mother decided that her son could not afford to lose a second set of clothes.

The relative lack of financial control over their future added to the decline in status that widows frequently experienced. Often the widow was no longer the mistress of her own house but, like Lucy Maud Montgomery's grandmother, a guest of her son and daughter-in-law, or of other younger family members. Nor were her daughters any better off. Except among such groups as the Russian Mennonites, they too rarely inherited family farms — and their portions of estates were usually smaller than those given to their brothers. The idea of women farming on their own did not appeal to Victorian public opinion — or to Victorian legislators, for that matter, as the 1872 Dominion statute governing public lands made clear. Only women with dependent children were permitted to homestead on their own. At least one woman is known to have disguised herself as a man when, after her husband died, she decided to carry on with the couple's scheme to raise horses on the Canadian Prairies, possibly in order to get access to public land. For the most part, women who wanted to be farmers had to accumulate enough capital to purchase land that had already been developed.[25]

Few farm women actually sought public recognition for their work. Their reward was the well-being of their families, even if they personally did not always have an equal share of the material benefits. Many delighted in living close to nature and building something for the future. One woman captured this faith in the following terms:

> I no longer utter a mental protest against the prairie as a final resting place. Our western life is too real, too vital to waste time in gloomy speculation. It is enough that you are alive and can take your chances in the great future that lies just at hand.[26]

Knowing that they were working for the good of their families helped offset the loneliness felt by many women in farming and rural communities. In the older, more prosperous farming districts, roads and railways gradually made access to and from rural areas easier, and speeded the delivery of mail. Yet even in such communities, women could be isolated: they generally had too little leisure time to enjoy contact with neighbouring friends and kin. In the outport villages of Newfoundland and in other remote regions, women could be cut off from their friends and relatives; in the case of frontier towns dependent on single resources such as mining and lumbering, the problem for women was the sense that they were living in a largely male environment. Those on prairie homesteads were among the most isolated. Neighbours were not close, and women were often hundreds, if not thousands, of kilometres from extended-family members and childhood friends. Johanne Fredericken, who came from Denmark in 1911 to join her husband homesteading in Saskatchewan, described the implications of this isolation: "Everything depends on the mother, one cannot share the responsibility with the shoemaker, tailor and baker, school or priest, and therefore, one stands by oneself poor and powerless."[27] As a sympathetic male commentator noted in 1913, the isolation of the frontier was difficult for all, but "especially for the women to whom the little amenities of social intercourse mean so much."[28]

It was an isolation not all could tolerate. While many women coped reasonably well, helped by husbands and children, newly made friends, and a belief in their contribution to the future, heartbreaking stories abound of women whose physical and mental health broke down. Letitia Youmans noted in her 1893 autobiography that farm women seemed to be particularly numerous in one Ontario asylum — because, according to the superintendent's laconic observation, of "hard toil and monotonous mode of living."[29]

Many women worked vigorously to decrease their isolation and to improve their situations, by maintaining ties with friends and family from whom they were separated, and by creating new ones with other women in their adopted communities, especially with those of the same religious, racial, or ethnic origin. Together they ensured that there were schools for their children, libraries for their neighbourhoods, and social occasions at which people could meet, talk with, and court one another. Women were often the chief supporters of institutional religion and were among the first to encourage the establishment of churches in isolated areas. Their interests encompassed the quality of life and thus the support and preservation of cultural traditions. Unfortunately, their efforts in this direction were not without victims, for they often closed out those who could not or would not conform. Indian and mixed-blood women were among those who suffered particular discrimination at the hands of English-speaking settlers in the west, convinced as the latter were of the superiority of their culture over all others.[30]

WOMEN'S WORK IN THE URBAN HOME

Farm women's lives, while changing, maintained a strong continuity with the past. The work performed in the home by urban women changed more. Industrialization had the effect of accentuating the division between paid and unpaid work, with most paid work now being performed outside the home. There was an increasing acceptance of the idea that it was the husband's responsibility to bring home a "family wage" — one that would support both the worker and his family — and a wife's to see to it that the wage covered the needs of the family. Women became involved in the network of home manufacture created by the "putting out" system. Employers avoided the necessity of renting or buying factories and passed on overhead costs to workers, employing subcontractors or middlemen who distributed work to women in their homes. In the garment trade, for instance, the employer or his agent might sell or rent sewing machines to home workers; he often deducted the cost of the needles, thread, or material from the women's wages. Domestic manufacture was paid by the piece, so that it was the worker, not the employer, who absorbed the cost of low production because of faulty equipment, crowded or difficult working conditions, or irregular demand. But many women who had families to care for at home were willing to put up with this situation: this way they could make some money without leaving home, and even their small children could be conscripted to accomplish simple parts of the work.

In towns and cities, there were other ways women at home continued to receive an income, such as taking in laundry or boarders. The income earned by such work came in irregularly in some cases, but it was often crucial for the continued well-being of the family.[31] Yet, because the income generated by women in the home was not as visible as wages earned outside it, few Canadians recognized the important role women's earnings played in a family's survival. Certainly the government did not. Its statistics on women's employment never acknowledged this kind of income, with the result that the percentage of women in paid employment was greatly underestimated.

Even more significantly, official statistics did not acknowledge the unpaid work that women did and its contribution to the country's wealth and prosperity. And women continued, of course, to work extremely long hours at the traditional tasks associated with housekeeping, childrearing, and general family management. As the life of the family increasingly ran on a cash basis, the stretching or reorganization of funds became an important part of women's work. Many working-class women stretched the family budget by keeping gardens, raising animals, making their own soap, and (once glass bottles became reasonably priced), canning their own fruits and vegetables. Some even stinted on their own food intake to ensure that the principal breadwinner was sufficiently fed. Women also assisted their husbands by their savings. They saved on medical costs by "doctoring" those around them, using Balm of Gilead for blisters, mustard plasters for colds, milk and bread poultices for boils, soda for bites, cold tea leaves for burns, salt water for sore throats, and senna tea for constipation.[32]

For urban women, however, the character of housekeeping and childcare was gradually changing. As children spent more time at school and as families became smaller, fewer children were at home to help with household chores or mind younger siblings; as well, fewer young girls were looking for jobs as domestic helpers. Partly in response to the fact that there were fewer hands to do the housework, and partly because of a whole new range of technological developments, housework was becoming more mechanized. The development of technology applied to domestic work had the potential to change household routines radically. The ideal woman portrayed in advertisements had at her disposal a factory: her servants were the workers, and they used such devices as carpet sweepers and washing machines. The only problem was that few of these ideal women — those having both the servants and the money necessary to purchase the new appliances — existed.

All women had to contend with apparently ever-rising expectations as new standards of cleanliness and efficiency developed. The recently discovered germ theory of disease propagation made dirty clothes or a dirty house seem tantamount to family neglect, as public health nurses and doctors tied childhood illness and high infant mortality rates to mothers' ignorance of the need to keep their households and children clean. The introduction of the hand-powered washing machine in the 1890s made washing easier, so laundry could be done more often. There seemed little or no excuse for soiled clothing or linens: "labour-saving" technology combined with new standards could actually mean an increase in the housekeeper's workload. For the urban poor, it was becoming more difficult to keep their households clean. Even if they could have afforded the new technology, dirt was endemic in the slums and working-class sections of Canada's growing industrial and commercial cities and towns. If women opened the windows to let in fresh air, as recommended by the health authorities, dirt would come in as well. Even in rural areas, opening windows to fresh air could, depending on the season, let in all sorts of infestations.

Technology was a double-edged sword, and not always the progressive change that manufacturers claimed.[33] Women's traditional lore and experience declined in value with developments in household technology, and also as new consumer goods replaced the products that women had once made themselves. In the cities, for public health reasons, municipal bylaws ended the keeping of the pigs, cows, and hens that had been so important to the traditional household economy. As stores distributing mass-produced goods proliferated, and as "store-bought" became the standard by which to measure "home-made" products such as bread and dresses, the items women used to make for their families in the home were increasingly replaced by factory-produced goods. As a result, women's work in the home declined in variety, although not in intensity. The noted feminist Nellie McClung recalled seeing her first ready-made dress, which a "daring" Manitoban woman had ordered from Montreal. She and other women waited with bated breath to see this "new" phenomenon, and were pleasantly surprised when it turned out to be attractive.[34] More women of all classes entered a new world — a world in which it was possible to be consumers of goods they had not produced themselves and in which "it was wonderful to imagine everything coming from a store."[35] But shopping carefully and effectively was itself work, as was accumulating the cash necessary to buy the new goods that seemed increasingly necessary.

OLD AND NEW KINDS OF EMPLOYMENT

Domestic service continued to be the single most important paid employment for women in Canada; in 1891, 41 percent of all working women were employed in this type of work. But it was work that increasing numbers of Canadian-born women spurned. As early as 1868, the *Globe* reported that "our working women dread household service, and hundreds would perhaps rather famish than apply at a servants' agency."[36] By 1921, only 11 percent of working women were in domestic service.[37] Domestics tended to be young girls—immigrants, more often than not—with little or no training. However, for immigrant women, particularly the Irish of the nineteenth century and the eastern Europeans of the early twentieth century, domestic service was at least a paid job and could represent upward mobility. The demand for servants was so great that the federal government and many women's organizations in fact encouraged British and European domestic servants to come to Canada. Domestic service provided an entry into the Canadian paid workforce not only for European women, but also for many farm girls. It was a job for which they were considered ideally suited, since they were familiar with household work and with conditions in Canada. From their parents' point of view, the occupation sometimes seemed preferable to others, since it at least took place in a family environment. Above all, domestic service was considered suitable for women because it prepared them for their eventual role as housewives. Government officials encouraged Native women to become domestics, viewing this as evidence of successful acculturation. To ensure that this would happen, Mi'kmaq women in Nova Scotia at the turn of the century were excluded from industrial employment in towns and considered suited only for domestic work. Most whites also deemed domestic service especially suitable for black women, although this attitude did not translate into any support for the immigration of black domestics. When an immigration scheme to bring West Indian domestics to Montreal from Guadeloupe began in 1911, it was quickly stopped due to the vocal opposition of white Canadians.[38]

Domestic work was only as good as the mistress for whom one worked. Since there were no employment standards to govern either work or living conditions, both could be very bad. "Living in" meant that one did not have to pay for room and board, but employers of live-in servants were known to hold back wages to ensure that their employees would remain. Some domestics had to spend entire days bent over the washtub; others were given next to no time off, and few servants had any privacy. Life could also be lonely, since few families could afford more than one servant, and class, race, and ethnic differences frequently prevented warm servant/mistress relationships.[39] Not all domestics were willing to play a subservient role, however. Nellie McClung recounted the story of a servant girl who was told that she must take a bath on her day off at the YWCA—not in the family tub. Her response was, "No bath, no work."[40]

A black nanny with her charges in Guysborough, Nova Scotia, at the turn of the century.

....

Source: W.H. Buckley Collection, 34.4.6 (N-6066), Public Archives of Nova Scotia.

Perhaps the most serious problem of the domestic servant, if she was far from the protection of friends or family, was her vulnerability to sexual exploitation. Olive Savariat, a 17-year-old domestic in the Clarenceville, Quebec, home of James Collins in the early 1860s, was one of the countless servants who were made pregnant by their employers. Olive's story ended tragically in her employer's barn, where she died as a result of an abortion he had arranged. In 1863, Reverend Corbett, an Anglican priest near the Red River settlement, was arrested for attempting to perform an abortion on his servant, Maria Thomas—a young half-Cree woman whom Corbett had drugged and raped. Corbet received a six-month jail term.[41] Yet not all young women were as easily victimized as Olive or Maria. In 1915, Carrie Davies, an 18-year-old servant of Charles Albert Massey, a scion of the wealthy Toronto family, shot and killed her employer because of his sexual advances. Davies did not escape trial, but about 1000 sympathetic supporters contributed to her defence fund, and the jury acquitted her. Davies's reaction was extreme, but the law certainly did not provide much protection for women like her. Between 1880 and 1930, not one Toronto employer charged by a domestic with rape or indecent assault was convicted.[42]

The more typical response of the exploited servant, whatever the form of exploitation, was simply to leave. The turnover rate in domestic service was very high, as domestics searched for better positions or left to get married. For this reason, up to one-third of Canadian employment agencies specialized in women workers.[43] For a domestic, it was better to leave than to be fired, since all servants depended to some extent on personal references. Most domestics lived in the homes of their employers; if they lost their jobs, they also lost their homes. For this reason, servants who were dismissed by their employers were extremely insecure. Those who had lost their virginity and might therefore have difficulty making a "respectable" marriage, and lonely immigrant women who were far from family and friends, were particularly vulnerable to the entreaties of madams and pimps who offered them lodgings and companionship. The low status accorded domestics may also have facilitated the entry of former servants into prostitution. For many, prostitution was one of the few options available for earning a living, especially in areas where there were few employment opportunities for women. Especially at risk were Chinese women, some of whom had been brought to Victoria's Chinatown to be prostitutes or servants without pay. At risk also were Native women; a national scandal broke out in 1886 when some employees of the federal Indian Affairs Department were charged with trafficking in Indian women.[44]

One of the positive features of domestic service that governments and women's organizations liked to stress was the level of remuneration. At the turn of the century, in western Canada, "general" servants made from $10 to $20 monthly. In the east, they could earn $8 to $14 per month (except for black domestics there, who made much less).[45] Wages paid to white servants were comparable to, and in some cases higher than, those earned by women in other occupations, because domestics did not have to pay for room and board.

With the development of Canadian industry after mid-century, young women were increasingly employed in factories or at piecework in the home. By 1871, women and children constituted 42 percent of the industrial workforce in Montreal and 34 percent in Toronto. Many young women remained close to home or actually lived at home while they were working at paid employment. At times their pattern of work was interrupted, because they frequently left paid work to help out at home.[46] Women played a particularly important role in the Canadian textile industry. Girls entered the mills as young as 11 and 12 in the 1880s, and at 13 and 14 at the turn of the century. In the Quebec cotton industry in 1908, almost half the operatives were women. Indeed, so tied to the industry were Quebec women that when jobs were scarce, a veritable exodus occurred to the mill towns of New England. Single women and men were often the first to go; as they became established, other family members followed. In 1909 alone, more than 10 000 people left Quebec for the United States in search of jobs.[47] This exodus was of particular concern to the church and government in Quebec, sensitive as they were to the issue of *la survivance* of the French culture within the larger English milieu of Canada. Priests and politicians alike did not want to see future childbearers leaving the province. However, Quebec was not the only province to see many of its energetic young people leave. Between 1881 and 1921, more than 165 000 Maritime women also left Canada to try their luck in the more industrialized and more lucrative job markets on the eastern seaboard of the United States. And jobs did seem easy to get. When Ada Williams left her fishing village in Nova Scotia for Boston in 1907, she quickly gained employment in a box factory, and when laid off had no difficulty finding another job, this time in an ice-cream parlour.[48]

By 1901, women represented 25 percent of the Canadian workforce engaged in manufacturing and mechanical work; in 1921, they still constituted 24 percent of a much-expanded industrial labour force.[49] Factory work was hard and involved long hours, despite the introduction of legislation to protect women and adolescents who were employed in industrial establishments. In 1884, Ontario became the first province to pass such a law; for young women it set the age at which they could begin factory work at 14 (for young men, the age was set at 12). The hours that women, girls, and youths could work were limited to 10 per day or 60 per week,

Women doing traditional spinning and weaving in New Brunswick. Note the young age of the girl on the right.

Source: Provincial Archives of New Brunswick, George Taylor Photograph, P5/651.

with an hour provided each day for a noon meal. Employers could apply for, and often received, special permits that enabled them to work their employees up to 72 hours per week for a maximum of 6 weeks each year. Concern for women's safety and especially for their reproductive potential was reflected in the portion of the law that prohibited their being employed in situations in which their health might be permanently damaged; however, the principal onus was placed on the worker to protect herself. Rather than require employers to install guards on dangerous machines, the law stipulated that women workers should wear hairnets to prevent themselves from being scalped.

Similar protective legislation applicable to factory work was passed by the Quebec Assembly in 1885. It took the government of Ontario two years to set up a system of factory inspectors to enforce its 1884 legislation, and the government of Quebec three years before it appointed its first factory inspector. By the 1890s, both governments had appointed female factory inspectors to visit those manufacturing establishments that employed large numbers of women and children; but as late as 1913 there were only two badly overworked female factory inspectors in each province. Although in 1900 the federal government passed the Fair Wage Resolution Act to prevent abuses resulting from subcontracting, the legislation was inadequate for women, since it focussed on industries where women were not workers. In 1913, women in Ontario and Quebec factories still routinely worked 55–60 hours a week and up to 70 hours in rush seasons.[50] But at least the hours were defined and at the end of the working day the time remaining was a worker's own. Factory work also seemed more "modern" and therefore more exciting than domestic employment. It usually provided the opportunity to talk and make friends with other women. In the factory, and during free time after work, a young woman was able to meet young men, and perhaps develop a relationship that would lead to marriage and the establishment of her own home.

The hierarchical work relations of factories proved as potentially abusive as those in domestic service. When the Royal Commission on the Relations of Capital and Labor reported in 1889, it described the case of Georgina Loiselle, a worker in a Montreal cigar factory. When this young woman refused to make another hundred cigars, her employer attempted to spank her; she fell to the ground, where he pinned her and struck her with a cigar mold. However, it was not the beating that concerned the Commission, but the propriety of "a man placing a girl of eighteen in that position."[51] The entry of women into the industrial workforce engendered concern about immorality, the future of the family, and even the future of the race. Ironically, this concern in turn created new employment opportunities for at least a few women. After 1910, many cities in Canada appointed women police officers to work on morality squads to help protect the thousands of young women coming to the cities in search of work.[52]

Whatever concerns women might have had about the relations of men and women in the workplace, they continued to seek industrial jobs. Many working-class families depended on the wages of their children. In 1891, more than 7000 females under the age of 16 were employed in industrial establishments. Unfortunately, women's ability to contribute to the family income was limited by the comparatively poor wages they received. According to early twentieth-century census returns, average earnings for women in central and eastern Canada, where most female industrial workers were situated, remained at 55 to 60 percent of male earnings. Moreover, neither male nor female earnings kept pace with inflation. In 1901, a Toronto woman was working for the equivalent of 2 cents per hour; and as late as 1921, factory women in Montreal received only half the wages men did.[53] One of the reasons for this large discrepancy was that women were employed on piecework more often than men. Since employers based piecework rates on the output of the fastest workers, the less speedy — that is, the majority — earned less than a living wage.

Women working in a modern garment factory in Quebec City early in the twentieth century.

Source: Fonds Fernand Pouliot, Archives nationales du Québec à Québec. Cote: P535, PN79-12-43.

In fact, most female workers barely made a living wage. In 1889, the Ontario Bureau of Industries provided a cost-of-living analysis for women workers without dependents. Average annual earnings were calculated to be $216.71, and average annual costs to be $214.28, leaving a grand surplus of $2.43! Female workers with dependents faced a yearly deficit of $14.23.[54] Not only did women receive less pay than men, but their wage-earning patterns were also different. A study of working women in three Nova Scotia communities—Sydney Mines, Yarmouth, and Amherst —in 1921 revealed that women's earnings gradually increased over their work lives, peaking at age 30, after which they declined. Men's wages increased significantly after age 20, peaking between 31 and 40 and only gradually declining after age 50. Women's pay did not improve greatly with time or with the introduction of new technology. Although machines did away with brute strength as a prerequisite for many jobs, sexual stereotypes remained. Women who worked machines were not identified as skilled operatives, as their brothers were, but only as "alert" and "nimble" workers (who were paid accordingly).[55]

At the same time that industrial work was opening up for women, there was a movement of domestic skills from the home into society. For example, women found employment as laundresses in commercial laundries, as waitresses in restaurants, and as cooks. But the work tended to be hard and poorly paid. Women who worked the Labrador fishery as cooks, for instance, received one-third the wages paid to men doing the same work. Some women, however, were able to take advantage of opportunities. Julia Hernandez and her sister, African-Americans attracted by the Fraser River gold fever, came to British Columbia, where Julia found a job as a cook that paid her $100 a week.[56]

Other new areas of work, chiefly for white women, emerged in the clerical and retail sectors. For all of the nineteenth century and even in the early decades of the twentieth century, clerical work was still considered men's work. When the Bank of Nova Scotia in St. John's, Newfoundland, hired a woman stenographer in 1898, it was described as an " 'experiment' . . . courageously and gallantly undertaken."[57] But women gradually found openings. In 1901, only one in twenty female workers were clerical workers, and they accounted for only one-fifth of all clerical workers; ten years later, approximately one in every ten gainfully employed women was a clerical worker, and one-third of all such workers were female.[58]

Clerical work at first seemed to offer considerable opportunity for upward mobility, and was valued as clean, "white-collar" work. And some women were indeed able to launch innovative careers by taking advantage of the need for clerical workers. For instance, Mary Frances Forbes, a student at Dalhousie University in 1896–97, eventually made a career for herself as principal of the Forbes Shorthand School in Halifax.[59] When the typewriter was introduced, women quickly made it their own, opening up a new area of employment for themselves. When Cora Hind first moved to Winnipeg, she created a job for herself as a "lady typewriter" by renting a typewriter and teaching herself how to work it. She eventually moved on to journalism and a career as a wheat crop forecaster. Gwen Cash was hired in 1917 by the Vancouver *Daily Province* "upon promising to learn typing."[60] However, for most women, having access to office work would prove less fulfilling. Clerical work, once an avenue to learning the business, gradually became routine and mechanical, characterized as women's work, and without prospects for advancement. Women did not replace male clerical workers so much as they filled a need for a new type of office worker. Secretarial work, while requiring special skills, was not always recognized as skilled labour, although in the years 1901 to 1921 those women in higher-status clerical jobs (such as stenographers and bookkeepers) were paid on a par with women teachers and nurses.[61]

Retail work grew quickly in the late 1890s with the re-emergence of economic prosperity. Women were preferred to men as sales personnel because they were considered to be more polite to the customers, particularly now that women were increasingly the purchasers of household goods. Even more to the point, perhaps, women sales clerks accepted low wages compared to men. By 1921, one in every four clerical and sales workers was a woman.[62] These jobs were seen as a step up for many young working-class women: as sales clerks, they could at least work in a clean environment compared to women in factories. Their work was less isolating than domestic service, less menial, and more respectable. But in reality, the pay was low, the hours were long (often longer than in a factory), and the physical strain was high, as sales clerks were required to stand for hours on end. Such jobs, too, required a certain outlay of money for clothing. Owing in large measure to pressure from women's organizations concerned about the long hours "shop girls" had to stand — and the possible negative effects on their capacity to bear children — some provincial governments introduced legislation setting minimum standards for women working in the retail trade. By 1897 Ontario had amended its original Shops' Regulation Act (1888) to limit women's employment to the hours between 7:00 A.M. and 6:00 P.M., and to require employers to provide seats for sales clerks to use when they were not working.[63]

WOMEN IN THE "PROFESSIONS" AND BUSINESS

By the last few decades of the nineteenth century, the occupation that engaged the most women, after domestic service, was teaching. Indeed, the number of women teachers became so great that they were largely responsible for the high percentage of individuals designated "professionals" in turn-of-the-century census returns. For example, almost half of those individuals were women, and well over 80 percent of these women were teachers in 1901. After that date, the percentage of professionals who were teachers decreased, because the census began to incorporate nurses and religious workers in the professional category. Yet the status of a teacher was ambiguous; the occupation might represent upward mobility for a farm girl, but not for a middle-class girl. Who was classified as a teacher was equally unclear. In the 1891 aggregate census, religious women who taught were classified as "Non-productive" (along with Indian Chiefs, paupers, asylum inmates, retired people, pensioners, and students).[64]

As public schooling expanded and became more complex after mid-century, educational systems provided women with increasing opportunities for both work and training. There were more normal schools, and some provinces also provided model schools authorized to give temporary teaching certificates. The development of secondary schooling and the continuation of private schooling provided additional opportunities. Overall, the need for teachers vastly increased, and employing women continued to be the solution for school boards that were hard-pressed for funds. In addition, educators and trustees alike were convinced that women made ideal assistants in schools where the senior grades and the schools as a whole were governed by men. Not all school boards agreed with this approach. Catholic boards in Quebec obtained higher provincial grants if they hired male teachers; and in 1903, the board in Victoria, British Columbia, determined "that in the interests of tactful discipline and the cultivation of strength and character in the boys," they should hire more male teachers. Partly for this reason, the feminization of teaching occurred later in British Columbia than in other provinces.[65] Nevertheless, at the turn of the century, women dominated the profession numerically: in 1901, three-quarters of all those engaged in the educational profession in Canada were women. In 1920, women constituted 83 percent of public-school teachers, but subsequently the rate for hiring men teachers exceeded that for women.[66]

But was teaching really a profession? Teachers, whether women or men, did not control entry into their field, nor did they make the regulations that controlled their workplace; they had little choice regarding the curriculum or the books used in their classrooms, and they were increasingly subject to an extraordinary degree of regulation by their local school boards, as well as by provincial school authorities.[67] The conditions of work may gradually have improved in some urban centres over time, but many teachers in rural areas continued to teach all ages in one classroom. Given the deeply rooted belief that women teachers were best supervised by men, it is somewhat ironic that they were entrusted with complete responsibility in rural schools, although the trustees were never very far away. Rural teachers boarded with students' families and so, like domestics, had little or no privacy. Indeed, the parallel with domestic service can be taken further: many teachers had to do the cleaning in their schools and, in the early years, even perform light duties for the families with whom they boarded.

Still, teaching was a respectable job that provided some upward mobility and a modicum of financial security for women who needed to work in order to support themselves or their dependents. A western Canadian remembered that when he started school, the women teachers of his community exuded authority. They had been to normal school in Brandon, Manitoba, and the fact that they had done so and were teaching meant "that they had been out in the great world, had met its demands and had proved themselves. They were, even after only a year, professionals and knew their job. It was an unusual thing for students, encountered only, and that rarely, in the local doctor and the local lawyer."[68] But there were limits to women teachers' prestige. Women continued to be paid less than men, even when equally qualified. In Toronto in 1870, the average salary for a woman teacher was $220–$400 per year; a man earned $600–$700. In rural areas of Ontario, the average pay for women and men teachers was $187.00 and $260.00, respectively.[69] Astonishingly, many women were able to save enough money from teaching to further their education and their careers. Dr. Elizabeth Margaret MacKenzie from Prince Edward Island taught for three years before attending the Dalhousie Medical School, from which she graduated in 1900.[70] Certainly there was little room for advancement within the teaching profession itself. A few women became principals and even inspectors; in the Catholic school systems, where the sexes were segregated and many of the teachers were nuns, there were far more opportunities for such administrative positions. But overall, promotions were rare. They were certainly the preserve of the unmarried career teacher. Indeed, as the occupational structure of teaching changed in the second half of the nineteenth century, so did the employment opportunities for married women in schools. Gradually, schools taught by married couples or married women working with sisters or daughters disappeared; more and more often, women teachers lost their jobs if they married.

The higher up the educational ladder one went, the scarcer women teachers became. Grammar-school teachers — and, later, high-school teachers — usually possessed a university degree, a requirement that posed a barrier for women, as did the assumption that older pupils needed a male teacher to guide them. In 1900, only 17.3 percent of secondary-school teachers in Ontario were women, although by 1920 this proportion had increased to 50.9 percent. Concern about this situation led one educator to point out what he saw as the reason for the decline in male interest in high-school teaching: "if women receive the same pay as men, men will not go into the profession."[71] Barriers to women's employment as university teachers were greater than at any other level of the educational system. In 1901, of the 857 professors listed in the census, only 47 were women. One of the most successful was scientist Carrie Derick, who received her B.A. from McGill in 1890 and her M.A. in 1896. She also studied at leading institutions in the United States, Great Britain, and Germany. In 1891 she was the first woman appointed to McGill's academic staff when she became a demonstrator in botany; in 1912, she became the first woman in Canada to be named a full professor. Her own struggle for recognition within the academic world led Derick to an active involvement in the women's movement, and to her assertion that "the professions should be open to men and women alike. It is just a question of the survival of the fittest."[72]

Like teaching, nursing had an ambiguous and changing status. For generations, religious nursing orders had enjoyed a high reputation, along with individual nursing sisters, who became legends in their communities. When Sr. Ste. Thérèse, who acted as a pharmacist in the Red River settlement, was recalled by her order to Bytown (Ottawa) in 1859, the father of Louis Riel voiced the objections of the people who had depended on her, and had her kidnapped and returned to the settlement. The Sisters of Saint Ann not only worked in St. Mary's Hospital in Dawson but provided financial assistance as well. At the turn of the century, two of their members covered 475 miles in 28 days, collecting money from miners for support of the hospital: they raised $10 000.[73] Unlike nursing sisters, lay nurses at mid-century were not held in such high esteem. Hospitals were designed for the poor and destitute; the nurses who worked in them were essentially servants who were unable to find employment elsewhere. Florence Nightingale's campaign to make nursing respectable began to have an impact in Canada by the latter part of the century, and with the opening of the first training school in St. Catharines in 1874, nursing began a new era. But change was slow. The young nurses in training were used as a source of cheap labour in the hospitals, taking their classes in between their regular duties, which could last from 7:00 A.M. to 7:00 P.M. As long as hospitals continued to depend on nursing students for their labour force, the only work for graduates was private-duty nursing, which also shared many features with domestic service.

Nurses made various attempts to change their situation. Some tried to expand their area of expertise: the Victorian Order of Nurses (VON) was formed in 1897 with the intention of allowing some of its members to act as midwives. The medical profession opposed this proposal so vigorously, however, that it never became a reality. Nonetheless, the VON created a model national public health nursing service, dedicated to sending trained nurses to people's homes, particularly in sparsely populated communities. Trained nurses in Alberta were legally permitted to attend births in 1919, but only in remote areas where a physician was not available.[74] Doctors were also hostile when nursing education seemed to take a professional turn. As one physician put it in 1906, nurses ought to forgo scientific study and return to the "gentle touch."[75] Municipal public health nurses, who emerged as a separate group in the early twentieth century, were more successful in exerting their power, perhaps because they tended to work in teams and were able to control their work with little interference from doctors. As a result, they were also able to develop an *esprit de corps* that gave them a sense of worth and identification with their calling. School nurses, too, had more control over what they did than did hospital or private-duty nurses.[76]

While teaching and nursing remained the largest professions to attract women, others gradually opened up, although not without a struggle. Jennie Trout and Emily Howard Stowe, the two women most responsible for advancing medical training for women in Canada, were both trained as physicians in the United States, since no medical school in Canada in the 1860s and mid-1870s would accept women. Women had traditionally been healers, and caring for the sick was not a departure from woman's traditional sphere; but being highly educated to do so and being paid for it were. When they had finished their training and returned to Canada, Trout and Stowe pushed for the admission of women to medicine. The major obstacle to medical training for women was the problem of co-education, particularly when the subject was the human body. So antagonistic were Canadians to the idea of allowing women into existing medical schools that two separate women's training facilities were established in 1883. The Kingston Women's Medical College was affiliated with Queen's University, and Woman's Medical College, Toronto, was affiliated with the University of Toronto and with the University of Trinity College. Beginning in 1890, women in Montreal were also able to study at the Faculty of Medicine established by Bishop's University. In 1895, that institution graduated Regina Lewis-Landau, the first Jewish woman to gain a medical degree in Canada. But the required education was only the first barrier women had to face in their quest to practise medicine. Few hospitals would provide them with the opportunity to gain clinical experience. To be admitted to the Quebec College of Physicians and Surgeons in 1903, Dr. Irma Levasseur, who had trained in the United States, had to win authorization through a private member's bill in the legislature. Once licenced, women doctors were unlikely to attract enough patients to make private practice economically viable.[77]

Despite the obstacles, many of these early women physicians went on to distinguished careers. In the early years, many women doctors chose to leave Canada and become medical missionaries. Maud Menten, who graduated with a medical degree in 1911 from the University of Toronto, travelled to Germany, where, with Dr. Lenore Michaelis, she studied the properties of enzymes; together they devised the Michaelis–Menten Equation, which provided a theoretical framework for further studies and research on enzymes. Women were also attracted to alternative medicine. Between 1915 and 1926, they constituted a significant portion of both the student body and the faculty at chiropractic schools, as well as practising chiropractors.[78]

Law degrees came later than medical degrees, perhaps because there was no equivalent in the legal profession to the image of woman as healer. In *The Canada Monthly* in 1872, the distinguished journalist and former academic Goldwin Smith argued that the physical attraction between the two sexes made it highly improper for women to be admitted to the bar, for "it would be present when a female advocate rose to address male jury men and judges; and perhaps the class of women who would become advocates would not be those least likely to make an unscrupulous use of their power of appealing to emotions subversive of the supremacy of justice."[79] As a result of this kind of attitude, Clara Brett Martin, the first woman trained in law in Canada and in the British empire, had to face much opposition.

An exceptionally bright student, Martin graduated at 16 in 1890 from Trinity College with an honours degree in mathematics. The following year she applied for admission as a student to the Law Society of Upper Canada, but was rejected on the grounds that the Society's regulations restricted admission to "persons" — and, since women were not legally "persons," they were thus ineligible to study law. This decision failed to dampen Martin's determination. Championed by Dr. Emily Stowe and the Dominion Women's Enfranchisement Association, she used all the means in her power to pursue her goal. She succeeded in having a bill passed by the Ontario legislature making it possible for women to study law. Martin's victory was partly owing to the personal support she received from Sir Oliver Mowat, the premier and attorney-general, who had been under pressure from the suffragists for some time to enfranchise women. His support appears to have been a compromise measure designed to appease the suffrage forces without succumbing to their more controversial demand. The new legislation allowed women to be considered by the Law Society for admission, and to be permitted to practise as solicitors but not as barristers. This meant they could not appear in court to present and argue cases. Even so, the Law Society responded by declaring that it was "inexpedient" to frame rules for the admission of women. As persistent as ever, Martin persuaded Mowat to intervene with the Society on her behalf. This he did, and by 1892 Martin was able to pursue her studies. But her troubles were not yet over. Throughout her student years she endured the taunts and ridicule of male classmates, teachers, and the press. Before graduating in 1895, she decided to petition the Law Society for admission as a barrister. She received extensive public support, including that of Lady Aberdeen, the wife of the governor-general, and that of the recently formed National Council of Women of Canada. Premier Mowat again brought pressure to bear on the Law Society. Finally the Society grudgingly amended its regulations, thereby allowing Clara Brett Martin to become, in 1897, a fully fledged member of the legal profession, and the first woman to practise law in the British empire.[80] Women aspiring to careers in the law were not as successful in Quebec. Although the first woman in that province to graduate with a law degree did so in 1914, women there were not allowed to practise law until 1941.[81]

Other occupations that opened up to women did not need the intensive training that law and medicine required. The rapid growth of the Salvation Army in the 1880s in English Canada required the recruitment of preachers; 56 percent were women, who challenged Victorian stereotypes of womanhood by marching in the streets and calling attention to themselves. Their largely working-class origin and following may have made it easier to flout convention, as did the fact that the work they did was for others, not themselves. Between 1881 and 1921, the Woman's Missionary Society of the Methodist Church hired more than 300 women to be missionaries both at home and abroad. Isabel Grant, an honours mathematics graduate from Dalhousie University, became, in 1911, the federal government's first woman actuary and insurance expert. Family lore has it that she applied for the job using her initials, and when her application was accepted and she reported for work, her employers were shocked when a woman appeared.[82] Many women made their living or supplemented the family income with their novels and poetry; Félicité Angers (Laure Conan) was the first French-Canadian woman novelist; Margaret Marshall Saunders was the first person in Canada to sell one million copies of a book (her 1894 novel *Beautiful Joe*).[83] With the publication of *Anne of Green Gables*, L.M. Montgomery became not only one of Canada's most beloved writers but an international figure. Fame also came to Pauline Johnson, a Mohawk from Ontario. She was celebrated for her poetry; her white audiences viewed her as a representative of her people, whom many in her audiences believed to be a "Vanishing Race."[84] Angers, Saunders, Montgomery, and Johnson were all single women who needed to write to support themselves.

Women also entered journalism. When Cora Hind applied for a job on the *Free Press* in Winnipeg in 1881, she met with shocked disbelief on the part of the editor. "It would never do to have a woman in the newspaper business," he argued; it was a business "marked by hard, rough work, late hours, and sometimes involved meeting not quite nice people."[85] Nevertheless, women before and after Cora Hind flocked to work that was respectable, clean, a bit daring, and different, and that offered them a public vehicle for their thoughts. Many exploited the fact that women were major consumers of reading material by writing columns for and about their sex. Some of these were shortlived, but others, like Francis Beynon's column in the *Grain Growers' Guide*, became an essential part of their paper's popularity. One of the most famous journalists was "Kit" Coleman, whose "Women's Kingdom" page in the Toronto *Mail* helped boost the circulation of that paper. Her work, however, went beyond the women's page. In 1898, she made her way to Cuba to cover the Spanish–American War; in 1906, she described the aftermath of the San Francisco earthquake.[86] Women journalists became so successful and numerous that they set up the Women's Press Club in 1904. Some women even helped establish and edit newspapers. One of the earliest was Mary Ann Shadd, who established and edited the *Provincial Freeman* in the mid-1850s to publicize the plight of the black people of Canada and to give them a voice. When she moved to Chatham in 1856, she resigned the editorship and bade farewell to her readers, writing that "we have worked . . . through difficulties such as few females have had to contend against."[87] Two other influential women were editors of widely read women's magazines: Mme Josephine Marchand of *Le coin du feu*, 1893–99, and Robertine Barry of *Le journal de françoise*, 1902–1909.[88] Sara McLagan published the Vancouver *World* after her husband's death, thereby becoming the first woman newspaper publisher in Canada.

Other creative fields attracted women, particularly the visual and performing arts, at both the amateur and the professional level. Those working as professionals usually did so as teachers. Emma Lajeunesse from Chambly, Quebec, took the late-nineteenth-century opera world by storm as Mme Albani. When she retired in 1896, she had performed 43 starring roles. Pauline (Lightstone) Donalda, daughter of a Jewish immigrant family in Montreal, made her debut in France; while she never sang in Canada, she helped establish the Montreal Opera Company in 1937. Elizabeth Ann Thomas Johnson was a well-known singer of spirituals and Jubilees in the late nineteenth century. Women musicians seldom played professionally except when there were not enough men to fill orchestra positions. Emma Scott Raff helped found the little-theatre movement in Canada through the Margaret Eaton School of Literature and Expression in Toronto.[89] Canadian-born actresses such as Marie Dressler and Mary Pickford became moving-picture stars, and Margaret Anglin had a noted career on the stage. All three found success in the United States and became household names. Despite the few who won acclaim, however, most went unsung. Canadians tended to view the stage as not quite respectable, and associated actresses with dancehall girls.[90]

Women visual artists also had difficulty achieving public recognition and supporting themselves with their art. Emily Carr ran a boardinghouse for a number of years because she needed the money to continue her painting. And Mary Riter Hamilton, whose realistic scenes of World War I won her acclaim from the French government, was ignored by her own.[91] Less well-known were women photographers. At least twenty women were working in professional photography in Ontario alone by the 1860s. In 1894, women were admitted to the newly formed Toronto Camera Club, although until 1943 they were prohibited from using the darkroom, and then only during the day.[92]

Like many of the women photographers, other women were self-employed and ran their own businesses. We know that some women were hotel and tavern keepers; others owned brothels, ran their own millinery and dressmaking businesses, operated their own private schools, or ran their own ranches. Much of this work could be done from their own homes and thus remained an ongoing challenge to the ideology of separation of spheres. However, census returns often did not distinguish between those who worked for someone else and those who worked for themselves; thus the extent of entrepreneurial endeavour is difficult to trace. It was often difficult for women on their own to gain access to capital or credit, although by the end of the century this situation had improved. And there were startling success stories. For example, Belinda Mulrooney came to the Klondike during the Gold Rush from Pennsylvania on a steamship, working as a stewardess. In the exceptional circumstances of boomtown Dawson, she ran a lunch counter, started a contracting business, and later opened a roadhouse. She then built the elegant Fairview Hotel in Dawson and subsequently became part owner of a mining company and a telephone syndicate.[93]

WOMEN WORKERS ORGANIZE FOR CHANGE

Women workers had little power to improve their working conditions. Yet some did become involved with unions or form their own associations; they were also involved in protests and strikes. In the textile and garment trades, unions had to come to terms with the presence of large numbers of women workers. The Knights of Labor, a unique trade union organization in the late nineteenth century, believed that most workers — whether skilled or unskilled, male or female — should be organized. As a way of attracting women workers to the union, the Knights held "socials" that brought together female and male workers. They also asked Leonora Barry, who was the General Investigator of Women's Work and Wages for the Knights in the United States, to come to Toronto to help organize female workers. These efforts met with some success. In 1884, Local Assembly 3040 of the Knights was formed among the woollen-mill operatives in Hamilton, and included women within its ranks. The women later broke away and formed the exclusively female Excelsior Local Assembly

3179, led by Katie McVicar. McVicar was a young, single worker who was devoted to improving the lot of women workers. She stressed the need for organized labour to change its usual recruiting techniques to meet the needs of women, who were unlikely to participate in mass rallies or to be swayed by vague promises of improved conditions. Unfortunately, her untimely death at age 30 robbed the women's union movement of one of its most forceful leaders. In 1885, another women's local, the Hope Local Assembly, was established in Toronto, primarily by garment workers.[94] The Knights were a shortlived phenomenon whose impact in provinces other than Quebec greatly diminished after 1890. By 1902 they had been reduced to a mere remnant in Quebec also.

The majority of women workers were not members of male trade unions; nonetheless, on many occasions they demonstrated a high degree of militancy, devotion to working-class solidarity, and commitment to advancing their own economic interests. In 1880 in Hochelaga, Quebec, female weavers initiated a strike to protest an increase in the work week. Although the strike included some men, the Montreal *Gazette* reported that the men "were not so nearly demonstrative as the women."[95] White-collar workers were in a different situation. The public perceived their "respectable" work as less onerous, and so it was with surprise that Toronto citizens faced a strike by 400 Bell telephone operators in 1907. In fact, the job of a telephone operator was fatiguing and stressful; it could even be dangerous, for severe electric shocks on the long-distance lines gave some workers convulsions. The strike began when the company decided to increase the hours of work and eliminate overtime. The workers protested and eventually went out on strike on January 31. The women's solidarity during the strike was impressive — as was public support for them, since the telephone monopoly had earned little sympathy. William Lyon Mackenzie King, the deputy minister of labour, intervened in the strike and persuaded the women to go back to work in return for a public inquiry. Most of the testimony at that inquiry supported the workers, and Bell agreed to a settlement that reduced their hours of work. Take-home pay, however, remained inferior to what it had been under the overtime system.[96]

In 1912 almost 1000 workers from the T. Eaton Co. factory in Toronto, many of them women, went out on strike to protest the firing of some co-workers. The strike spread to Montreal, and sympathetic garment workers in Kingston threatened to strike firms that did business with Eaton's. In addition, Toronto's immigrant Jewish community ran an effective boycott of Eaton's goods, thanks to the support of the women. However, gender was not always a predictor of support: during the 1911 strike of Jewish cloakmakers and shirtmakers at the Toronto Puritan factory, women were on both sides of the picket line. Even among the most isolated of female workers, there were attempts at organization. In British Columbia, a group of domestic workers established the Home and Domestic Employees Union in 1913 to work toward obtaining a nine-hour day and minimum wages. Given the enormous obstacles the Union had to confront in its attempt to organize domestics, most of whom worked alone in individual households, it is not surprising that the Union dissolved within two years.[97]

Despite their militancy, women did not play a significant role within the union movement. This was partly because of the practical problems involved in organizing them. Even women who worked in manufacturing were frequently employed in such small shops dispersed around the city that they were difficult to bring together. For example, in 1891 more than 2000 Toronto women worked in either dressmaking or tailoring, but they were divided among 614 different workplaces.[98] In addition, unions were generally restricted to workers who were considered "skilled," of whom few were women. The work performed by women, whatever its characteristics, was usually labelled "unskilled." Unions during this period were very fragile and vulnerable, and were convinced that they had more than enough to do trying to organize male workers. Women workers presented union organizers with additional problems: compared to men, women had high turnover rates, since many left their jobs when they married. In addition, female wage earners often had family or domestic obligations that prevented them from attending union meetings in the evenings.

Of equal significance, however, was the ambivalence or outright hostility many union members and leaders felt toward the idea of women working in the public labour force. In 1898 the Trades and Labour Congress, the largest grouping of organized labour, declared its support for the "abolition . . . of female labor in all branches of industrial life such as mines, factories, workshops, etc."[99] By the turn of the century, many male workers saw women as competitors for their jobs, even though statistics indicated that women and men workers seldom performed the same kind of work. Even when both sexes worked in the same industry, a closer examination indicates that the separation of the sexes into specific job categories was maintained. In the cotton industry, while female and male operatives worked alongside each other in the weave rooms, other departments were overwhelmingly composed of either female or male workers. Ring spinners looked after a stationary frame on which the cotton yarn was drawn onto spindles by means of a ring travelling around a small circular track; such spinners were almost exclusively female, since manual dexterity was the principal requirement for the successful ring spinner. Mule spinners, by contrast, were always male, since the mule-spinning frame was a large, complex machine with a moving carriage, a machine that was considered too difficult for women to operate. Not surprisingly, this job and that of loom fixer, another exclusively male occupation, constituted the highest-paying manual work in the mills.

Male workers also believed that women workers caused wages to be low. If the only way to counteract this influence was to bring women into a union, it would sometimes be done — but often more for the benefit of the male members than for the female ones. As the *Palladium of Labor* pointed out in 1894, "place the sexes upon equal pay for the same kind of service and man has the advantage."[100] Indeed, insistence on economic equality with men in the workforce often cost women their jobs. This seemed to be the case in the cigar industry of late-nineteenth-century Toronto. As one commentator explained, "in Toronto there are very few women employed in cigar-making. The reason being that all the employés [sic] belong to a union which insists on all workers being paid alike, and the employers prefer to employ men, because they are likely to remain longer in the business."[101]

The intersection of class and gender was complex and highly charged. Underlying much of the uneasiness toward women workers was the growing belief, in the latter half of the nineteenth century, in the idea of the "family wage." Workers believed that if a family wage were paid to men, women would not need to seek paid employment. They could then remain in their proper sphere — the home. This belief, of course, assumed that most women had a male protector, and overlooked the fact that many women did not: indeed, many had dependents of their own for whom they were responsible, while others simply wanted to work outside the home.

Working men also saw the workplace as morally dangerous for women.[102] Even labour radicals did not question the accepted norms of gender relations. For them class was central, not gender.

Women continued to enter the paid workforce — especially the service sector and the new or growing women's "professions" — in massive numbers. In these areas, poor working conditions and low pay often brought women together in an effort to improve their situations. The first associations of women teachers were formed in towns and cities, where it was easier both to organize and to see the extent to which women were discriminated against compared to the men who taught in the public schools. Eight women created the original Women Teachers' Association of Toronto in 1885; teachers in Montreal and in several smaller Ontario cities soon followed suit. Teachers were ambivalent about their organizing efforts, caught as they were between an image of "professionalism" and the realities of their working conditions and their pay. In Toronto, for example, the more-radical members of the Women Teachers' Association considered affiliating with the Trades and Labour Council in the early 1900s, but caution won out and the affiliation never happened. Energies went, rather, into campaigns for better wages and working conditions, and into making connections with other groups. In 1918 the various Ontario groups formed the Federation of Women Teachers' Associations of Ontario and began the long process of building a province-wide organization. In the same year, the Saskatoon Women Teachers' Association was formed by fifteen teachers. Campaigning for better contracts, equal pay for equal work, and the retention of married women teachers, they too demonstrated an awareness of women's disadvantages in the labour force and of the need to organize in order to seek improvement.[103]

Catholic teachers were also struggling to improve their lot. In Montreal the Catholic association for laywomen teachers and the Protestant women teachers' association combined forces to fight for improvements in Quebec teachers' pension pay, which was manifestly unfair to women. They made some headway, but eventually Joséphine Samson became so frustrated with the grievances of the Catholic teachers in particular that she initiated a campaign of her own, which she finally carried to the office of the prime minister. It would be a gross miscarriage of justice, Samson pointed out, if Catholic women teachers should end their days "having only black bread to eat" because they had taught practically for free. It was galling to think that two other categories of retired teachers would do better: not only all male teachers, but even Protestant women teachers, because their salaries had been greater than those paid to the Catholic women, would eat "white bread" as pensioners. In Quebec urban centres the majority of women teachers were members of religious orders, and they perhaps had a greater sense of control over their conditions of work. On the other hand, teaching sisters were not immune from the interference of school officials and bishops. In Halifax the Sisters of Charity came into conflict with their new archbishop in 1876, when he attempted to prevent the attendance of the laity at the graduation exercises of Mount Saint Vincent Academy, and to institute other reforms not to the liking of the teaching sisters. A deputation to Rome eventually succeeded in having the order placed under the authority of their friend the bishop of Antigonish. In Montreal, the sisters of the *Congrégation de Notre-Dame* fought a battle with a Catholic school commission that was perennially short of money and seemed to believe that nuns did not need to be paid a living wage for their work.[104]

Nurses also organized to improve their working conditions. In 1905 the Alumnae Association of the Toronto General Hospital School of Nursing inaugurated a journal called *The Canadian Nurse*, which concerned itself with such issues as the need for registration. Nurses believed that registration would attest to their training and skill, thus raising their status in the eyes of other professionals and the public.[105] From 1912 on, the Canadian National Association of Trained Nurses, formed originally to affiliate with the International Council of Nurses in 1897, struggled to obtain registration laws in the various provinces.

WORK AND WAR

Canada's involvement in World War I had important repercussions for women's work, not all of them positive. Among those women whose ethnic background was the same as that of the "enemy," some found that holding onto a job was not always easy. Others found themselves placed in internment camps along with their husbands.[106] For most women workers, however, the war created opportunities—especially after 1915, when the recruitment of thousands of young men into the armed forces resulted in serious labour shortages. Daisy Phillips of Athalmer, British Columbia, expressed the consequences to her sister: "Fancy all the men having to go at a moment[']s notice without time to make arrangements but I suppose the women will just carry on as best they can. . . . [T]hat is the other part of our Duty if we cannot fight."[107] As Canada increased its agricultural exports to hard-pressed Britain, women were called upon to assume an even larger part of farm work. During the summer months, farm wives and daughters were aided in their efforts by hundreds of female students housed in camps and hostels run by the Young Women's Christian Association. In 1917 and 1918, there were more than 2000 young women in these camps in Ontario alone. They worked at every job: "besides picking and packing fruit, [they] handled horses, pitched hay, drove motor trucks to market and sold the fruit[,] . . . took charge of chicken houses, worked in canning factories, put handles on baskets, [and] hoed for ten hours a day."[108] Not all farmers were convinced that young women should do such heavy work. One even worried about whether a woman could carry a ladder. Government officials also expressed concern about work in the canning factories, since the women who took those jobs had to "mix so much with foreigners."[109]

Urban working women saw their employment opportunities change. Although many continued to enter domestic service, still the largest employer of women, new jobs opened up as the wartime economy moved into full gear after 1916. The most widely publicized were in the munitions industry, since before the entry of the United States into the war in 1917, Canada was a major supplier of munitions to Great Britain. To meet its commitment to supply arms, the Canadian government actively recruited female workers for the munitions factories, and by 1917 more than 35 000 women in Ontario and Quebec were producing shells for the Allies. Although the munitions manufacturers paid wages well above those earned by women in traditional occupations, female munitions workers in 1917 earned only 50 to 83 percent of what their male co-workers earned.[110] In addition, the wartime emergency was used to justify extremely long hours (13 to 14 hours a day) and deplorable working conditions.

The brief but impressive economic boom and the manpower shortage engendered by the war enabled women to move into areas of employment normally reserved for men. In Montreal alone, more than 2300 women were employed by the railways and by the steel and cement industries in jobs formerly held by men only. That women were becoming telegraph messengers was headline news.[111] In October 1917, Maude Chart made history in Kingston by becoming the first street-railway "conductorette" in Canada; soon all male conductors in Kingston had been replaced by women. The insatiable demand for men to serve overseas — a demand that resulted in conscription late in 1917 — also facilitated the entry of women into white-collar work previously performed by men. Between 1911 and 1921, the number of female clerical workers nearly tripled (rising from 33 723 to 90 577); by 1921, they accounted for nearly 42 percent of all clerical workers and for more than 18 percent of all paid women workers in Canada. In English-speaking Canada, even the most renowned bastions of male clerical work, the banks, were motivated by a combination of male-labour shortages and increased task specialization to hire women as tellers and clerks. In 1916, more than 40 percent of the clerks employed by the Bank of Nova Scotia in Ontario were women, compared to fewer than 10 percent five years earlier.[112] Racial and ethnic barriers still persisted, however.

The proportion of married women working in industry also increased in these years. In 1921, for example, 22 percent of the female munitions workers in the

Women boat builders at the end of the war in Baddeck, Nova Scotia, 1918.

Source: Canadian Heritage — Parks Canada, Alexander Graham Bell National Historic Site.

Montreal area were married, although married women made up only 2 percent of all gainfully employed women.[113] Of course, young single women continued to constitute the vast majority of female workers. But the war established, once and for all, the propriety of women working for wages before marriage, even when the young woman belonged to the middle class. In "respectable" work like teaching, women continued to replace men teachers at the elementary- and secondary-school levels. In Alberta, for example, there were 630 more women teachers in 1916 than there had been in 1914.[114]

The armed services also recognized the potential of women's work, but only as nurses. In 1885 during the Riel Rebellion, at the invitation of the minister of militia and defence, seven Church of England nursing sisters had travelled to the Northwest Territories to tend the wounded. The Boer War presented Canadian nurses with another opportunity to serve in battlefield hospitals, and in 1901 the Canadian Nursing Service was created as a part of the Army Medical Corps. During World War I, 2504 members were actively involved in overseas duties; all told, 46 nurses died while in the service of their country.[115] The dedication and heroism of the wartime nurses contributed much to enhancing the status of the nursing profession. On the home front, women worked through the Red Cross and St. John Ambulance Corps. Women's new work during the war had been part of the war effort — as men had assumed military responsibilities, so too had women, but as supporters of the soldiers. As a result, the ideology of femininity was not radically altered.[116] Many of the trends in women's employment were reversed after the war's end. Women were treated essentially as a "reserve army of labour." When there were labour shortages, women were pulled into the workforce, including into jobs from which they had been traditionally excluded. But when the special need was over, the traditional gender division of work roles was re-established.[117] Nonetheless, owing to the terrible casualties among the young men of Canada, many women could not expect to marry. With these women in mind, the Women's War Conference of February 1918, which had been convened by the federal government to ensure women's continued support for the war effort, passed resolutions in favour of equal pay for equal work, technical training, and a minimum wage for women.[118]

Although the war focussed increased attention on women in paid employment, it was difficult for many Canadians to accept with equanimity the idea of the working woman. As more women entered the workforce from the mid-century to the end of the Great War, the reality of their doing so could not be ignored. It seemed increasingly acceptable for young women to work before marriage, and a small but important group of women were already making lifelong careers for themselves. They represented the "new woman" of the late Victorian and Edwardian period.

More representative of women of this era were those who married, bore children, and devoted themselves to ensuring a better life for the next generation. In untold cases this seemingly simple task involved enormous courage and sacrifice, as it did for Lillie Davis. It was during World War I that she and her husband, DeCourcy, decided to emigrate with their two young children from England to Canada. Just before they set sail, however, DeCourcy died. Undaunted by her loss, Lillie decided to emigrate anyway. After surviving a German attack on her ship during the crossing, she began a new and ultimately successful life for herself and her children in Canada.[119]

NOTES

1. Margaret Conrad, " 'Sunday Always Makes Me Think of Home': Time and Place in Canadian Women's History," in Veronica Strong-Boag and Anita Clair Fellman, eds., *Rethinking Canada: The Promise of Women's History* (Toronto: Copp Clark Pitman, 1986), 72.

2. Beth Light and Joy Parr, eds., *Canadian Women on the Move, 1867–1920* (Toronto: New Hogtown Press and OISE Press, 1983), 169–70.

3. Linda Rasmussen et al., eds., *A Harvest Yet to Reap: A History of Prairie Women* (Toronto: Women's Press, 1976), 26.

4. Canada, Dominion Bureau of Statistics, *Origin, Birthplace, Nationality and Language of the Canadian People* (Ottawa: King's Printer, 1929), 42.

5. Dominion Bureau of Statistics, *Origin*, 42; Carolyn Moore, *Our Land, Too: Women of Canada and the Northwest 1860–1914* (Whitehorse: Government of the Yukon, 1992), 18.

6. F.H. Leacy, ed., *Historical Statistics of Canada*, 2nd ed. (Ottawa: Statistics Canada, 1983), A110–53; Howard Palmer, *Patterns of Prejudice: A History of Nativism in Alberta* (Toronto: McClelland and Stewart, 1982), 39.

7. Tamara Adilman, "A Preliminary Sketch of Chinese Women and Work in British Columbia, 1858–1950," in Barbara K. Latham and Roberta J. Pazdro, eds., *Not Just Pin Money: Selected Essays on the History of Women's Work in British Columbia* (Victoria: Camosun College, 1984), 54–57.

8. Information provided by Ottilia Doering's great-granddaughter, Bonnie Shettler.

9. Joy Parr, *Labouring Children: British Immigrant Apprentices to Canada, 1869–1924* (Montreal: McGill-Queen's University Press, 1980), 88.

10. Rasmussen et al., eds., *Harvest*, 22; Paul Phillips and Erin Phillips, *Women and Work: Inequality in the Labour Market* (Toronto: James Lorimer, 1983), 6; Leacy, ed., *Historical Statistics*, A94–109.

11. Warren E. Kalbach and Wayne W. McVey, *The Demographic Bases of Canadian Society*, 2nd ed. (Toronto: McGraw-Hill Ryerson, 1971), 136; Emily Nett, "Canadian Families in Social–Historical Perspective," *Canadian Journal of Sociology* 6, 3 (Summer 1981), 245; *Census of Canada* (1921), vol. 4, xiv.

12. Royden K. Loewen, *Family, Church, and Market: A Mennonite Community in the Old and the New Worlds, 1850–1930* (Toronto: University of Toronto Press, 1993), 101.

13. G.G. Campbell, "Susan Dunlap: Her Diary," *Dalhousie Review* 46, 2 (Summer 1966), 218–19; Jill Oakes, "Eider Skin Garments Used by the Ungava Inuit from the Belcher Islands, Northwest Territories: Construction and Context," *Clothing and Textiles Research Journal* 10, 2 (Winter 1992), 4.

14. Ellice B. Gonzalez, *Changing Economic Roles for Micmac Men and Women: An Ethnohistorical Analysis* (Ottawa: National Museums of Canada, 1981), 86, 91.

15. Anne B. Woywitka, "Homesteader's Woman," *Alberta History* 24, 2 (Spring 1976), 21; Pamela Margaret White, "Restructuring the Domestic Sphere — Prairie Indian Women on Reserves: Image, Ideology and State Policy 1880–1930," McGill University, Ph.D. Thesis, 1987, 132; Linda Kealey, "Introduction," in Kealey, ed., *Pursuing Equality: Historical Perspectives on Women in Newfoundland and Labrador* (St. John's: Institute of Social and Economic Research, Memorial University, 1993), 9.

16. Harriet Neville, "Pioneering in the North-West Territories, 1882–1905," *Canada: An Historical Magazine* 2, 4 (June 1975), 29.

17. Sarah Kolasiewicz, "Outstanding Women of Oxford County," *Canadian Women's Studies/Les cahiers de la femme* 3, 1 (1981), 50–1; Marjorie Griffin Cohen, "The Decline of Women in Canadian Dairying," in Alison Prentice and Susan Mann Trofimenkoff, eds., *The Neglected Majority: Essays in Canadian Women's History* (Toronto: McClelland and Stewart, 1985), vol. 2, 71–83; Terry Crowley, "Mechanization, Proletarianization, and the Gendered Division of Labour: The Rural Crisis in Late Nineteenth-Century Ontario Reconsidered," paper presented to the Canadian Historical Association, Charlottetown, 1992, 13–14.

18. Beth Light and Alison Prentice, eds., *Pioneer and Gentlewomen of British North America, 1713–1867* (Toronto: New Hogtown Press, 1980), 160.

19. Susan Jackel, "Introduction" to Georgina Binnie-Clark, *Wheat and Woman* (Toronto: University of Toronto Press, 1979), xvii.

20. Light and Parr, eds., *Canadian Women on the Move*, 189–90.

21. Anita Penner, "Emily Murphy and the Attempt to Alter the Status of Canadian Women, 1910–31," Carleton University, M.A. Thesis, 1979, 46.

22. Nanciellen Davis, " 'Patriarchy from the Grave': Family Relations in 19th Century New Brunswick Wills," *Acadiensis* 13, 2 (Spring 1984), 95.

23. Mary Rubio and Elizabeth Waterson, eds., *Selected Journals of L.M. Montgomery, Vol. 1 (1889–1910)* (Toronto: Oxford University Press, 1986), 310.

24. Jo-Anne Fiske, "Child of the State Mother of the Nation: Aboriginal Women and the Ideology of Motherhood," *Culture* 13, 1 (1993), 18; Alex Johnston, "Nicholas and Marcella Sheran: Lethbridge's First Citizens," *Alberta History* 31, 4 (Autumn 1983), 1–10.

25. "How the Chamberlains Found Canada," *Women's Work in Western Canada* (Canadian Pacific Railway, 1906), 63–66; Georgina Binnie-Clark, *Wheat and Woman* (Toronto: William Heinemann, 1914).

26. Rasmussen et al., eds., *Harvest*, 60.

27. Jorgen Dahlie, "Learning on the Frontier: Scandinavian Immigrants and Education in Western Canada," *Canadian and International Education* 1, 2 (December 1972), 64.

28. Light and Parr, eds., *Canadian Women on the Move*, 168.

29. Letitia Youmans, *Campaign Echoes: The Autobiography of Letitia Youmans* (Toronto: William Briggs, 1893), 81.

30. Sylvia Van Kirk, "The Impact of White Women on Fur Trade Society," in Susan Mann Trofimenkoff and Alison Prentice, eds., *The Neglected Majority: Essays in Canadian Women's History* (Toronto: McClelland and Stewart, 1977), vol. 1, 27–48.

31. Bettina Bradbury, "The Fragmented Family: Family Strategies in the Face of Death, Illness and Poverty, Montreal, 1860–1885," in Joy Parr, ed., *Childhood and Family in Canadian History* (Toronto: McClelland and Stewart, 1982), 109–28; Bradbury, "Pigs, Cows and Boarders: Non-Wage Forms of Survival among Montreal Families 1861–1891," *Labour/Le travail* 14 (Fall 1984), 9–48; see also Bradbury, *Working Families: Age, Gender, and Daily Survival in Industrializing Montreal* (Toronto: McClelland and Stewart, 1993).

32. Light and Parr, eds., *Canadian Women on the Move*, 27; Rasmussen et al., eds., *Harvest*, 70.

33. See Ruth Schwartz Cowan, *More Work for Mother: The Ironies of Household Technology from the Open Hearth to the Microwave* (New York: Basic, 1983).

34. Nellie McClung, *The Stream Runs Fast* (Toronto: Thomas Allen, 1945), 47.

35. Light and Parr, eds., *Canadian Women on the Move*, 61.

36. Ian Davey, "Educational Reform and the Working Class: School Attendance in Hamilton, Ontario, 1851–1891," University of Toronto, Ph.D. Thesis, 1975, 175.

37. Phillips and Phillips, *Women and Work*, 12.

38. White, "Restructuring the Domestic Sphere," 149; Gonzalez, "Changing Economic Roles," 94; Marlene Epp, "West Indian Domestics to Canada in 1911: A Study of Discrimination in Immigration," paper presented to the Canadian Historical Association, Victoria, 1990, 1.

39. Phillips and Phillips, *Women and Work*, 12; Cassie Palamar, "The Treatment of Issues Affecting Women by the Knights of Labor in the *Palladium of Labor*, 1883–86," unpublished paper, Ontario Institute for Studies in Education, 12.

40. McClung, *The Stream Runs Fast*, 259.

41. Peter Gossage, "Absorbing Junior: The Use of Patent Medicines as Abortifacients in Nineteenth Century Montreal," *The Register* 3, 1 (March 1982), 2–3; Erica Smith, "Sexual Discourse and Ambiguity in the Trial of Rev. G.O. Corbett: Notes Towards Research," paper presented to the Canadian Historical Association, Ottawa, 1993, 7–8.

42. Genevieve Leslie, "Domestic Service in Canada, 1880–1920," in Janice Acton, Penny Goldsmith, and Bonnie Shepard, eds., *Women at Work: Ontario 1850–1930* (Toronto: Canadian Women's Educational Press, 1974), 94; Carolyn Strange, "Wounded Womanhood and Dead Men: Chivalry and the Trials of Clara Ford and Carrie Davies," in Franca Iacovetta and Mariana Valverde, eds., *Gender Conflicts: New Essays in Women's History* (Toronto: University of Toronto Press, 1992), 177.

43. Robin John Anderson, "Domestic Service: The YWCA and Women's Employment Agencies in Vancouver, 1898–1915," *Histoire sociale/Social History* 25, 50 (November 1992), 308.

44. Tamara Adilman, "A Preliminary Sketch of Chinese Women and Work in British Columbia, 1858–1950," in Gillian Creese and Veronica Strong-Boag, eds., *British Columbia Reconsidered: Essays on Women* (Vancouver: Press Gang, 1992), 314; Lori Rotenberg, "The Wayward Worker: Toronto's Prostitute at the Turn of the Century," in Acton et al., eds., *Women at Work*, 33–69; Constance B. Backhouse, "Nineteenth-Century Canadian Prostitution Law: Reflection of a Discriminatory Society," *Histoire sociale/Social History* 18, 36 (November 1985), 387–423.

45. Agnes Calliste, "Race, Gender and Canadian Immigration Policy: Blacks from the Caribbean, 1900–1932," *Journal of Canadian Studies* 28, 4 (Winter 1993–94), 132.

46. Phillips and Phillips, *Women and Work*, 8; Bradbury, *Working Families*, 142.

47. Albert Faucher, "Explication socio-économique des migrations dans l'histoire du Québec," in Normand Séguin, *Agriculture et colonisation au Québec* (Montréal: Boréal Express, 1980), 114.

48. Light and Parr, eds., *Canadian Women on the Move*, 100–1; Betsy Beattie, " 'Going Up to Lynn': Single, Maritime-Born Women in Lynn, Massachusetts, 1879–1930," *Acadiensis* 22, 1 (Autumn 1992), 65–86.

49. Ceta Ramkhalawansingh, "Women during the Great War," in Acton, Goldsmith, and Shepard, eds., *Women at Work*, 281.

50. Bob Russell, "A Fair or a Minimum Wage? Women Workers, the State, and the Origins of Wage Regulation in Western Canada," *Labour/Le travail* 28 (Autumn 1991), 70–71; Wayne Roberts, "Honest Womanhood: Feminism, Femininity and Class Consciousness among Toronto Working Women 1893–1914," in R. Douglas Francis and Donald B. Smith, eds., *Readings in Canadian History: Post Confederation*, 2nd ed. (Toronto: Holt, Rinehart and Winston, 1986), 240; Terry Copp, *The*

Anatomy of Poverty: The Condition of the Working Class in Montreal 1897–1929 (Toronto: McClelland and Stewart, 1974), 45.

51. Susan Trofimenkoff, "One Hundred and Two Muffled Voices: Canada's Industrial Women in the 1880's," *Atlantis* 3, 1 (Fall 1977), 67–68.

52. Carolyn Strange, "The Perils and Pleasures of the City: Single, Wage-Earning Women in Toronto, 1880–1930," Rutgers University, Ph.D. Thesis, 1991, 20; Tamara Myers, "Women Policing Women: A Patrol Woman in Montreal, 1918," paper presented to the Canadian Historical Association, Ottawa, 1993, 7.

53. *Census of Canada* (1891), 186; Phillips and Phillips, *Women and Work,* 22; Wayne Roberts, *Honest Womanhood: Feminism, Femininity and Class Consciousness among Toronto Working Women, 1893–1914* (Toronto: New Hogtown Press, 1976), 37; J.T. Copp, "The Conditions of the Working Class in Montreal, 1897–1920," in Francis and Smith, eds., *Readings in Canadian History*, 2nd ed., 227.

54. Rotenberg, "The Wayward Workers," 48–49.

55. D.A. Muise, "The Industrial Context of Inequality: Female Participation in Nova Scotia's Paid Labour Force, 1871–1921," *Acadiensis* 20, 2 (Spring 1991), 19; Roberts, "Honest Womanhood," 242.

56. Roberts, *Honest Womanhood*; Linda Cullum and Maeve Baird with the assistance of Cynthia Penney, "A Woman's Lot: Women and Law in Newfoundland from Early Settlement to the Twentieth Century" in Kealey, ed., *Pursuing Equality*, 116; Sherry Edmunds-Flett, "The Family and Community Life of British Columbia's 19th Century African-Canadian Women," paper presented to the Canadian Historical Association, Charlottetown, 1992, 10.

57. Barbara Hansen, "A Historical Study of Women in Canadian Banking, 1900–1975," *Canadian Women's Studies/Les cahiers de la femme* 1, 2 (Winter 1978/79), 17.

58. Ramkhalawansingh, "Women during the Great War," 280–81.

59. Judith Fingard, "The New Woman Goes to College: Dalhousie Coeds, 1881–1921," unpublished paper, Dalhousie University, 1986, 9.

60. Kennethe Haig, "E. Cora Hind," in Mary Quayle Innis, ed., *The Clear Spirit: Twenty Canadian Women and Their Times* (Toronto: University of Toronto Press, 1966), 120–41; Gwen Cash, *Off the Record: The Personal Reminiscences of Canada's First Woman Reporter* (Langley, B.C.: Stagecoach, 1977), 12.

61. Graham Lowe, "Class, Job, and Gender in the Canadian Office," *Labour/Le travail* 10 (Autumn 1982), 20, 28; see also Lowe, *Women in the Administrative Revolution* (Toronto: University of Toronto Press, 1987).

62. Phillips and Phillips, *Women and Work*, 25.

63. Linda Bohnen, "Women Workers in Ontario: A Socio-Legal History," *University of Toronto Faculty of Law Review* 31 (1973), 47.

64. *Census of Canada* (1921), vol. 4, 6–7; Elizabeth Smyth, "Teacher Education within a Community of Religious Women in Nineteenth Century Ontario: The Teaching Sisters of the Congregation of the Sisters of St. Joseph, Toronto 1851–1911," paper presented to the Canadian Historical Association and the Canadian Society of Church History, Kingston, 1991, 29.

65. J. Donald Wilson, Robert M. Stamp, and Louis-Philippe Audet, eds., *Canadian Education: A History* (Scarborough: Prentice-Hall, 1970), 317; Jean Barman, "Birds of Passage or Early Professionals? Teachers in Late Nineteenth-Century British Columbia," *Historical Studies in Education/Revue d'histoire de l'éducation* 2, 1 (Spring 1990), 18.

66. Patrick Harrigan, "The Development of a Corps of Public School Teachers in Canada, 1870–1980," *History of Education Quarterly* 32, 4 (Winter 1992), 489.

67. Alison Prentice and Marta Danylewycz, "Teacher's Work: Changing Patterns and Perceptions in the Emerging School Systems of Nineteenth- and Early Twentieth-Century Central Canada," *Labour/Le travail* 17 (Spring 1986), 65.

68. W.L. Morton, "Furrow's End," *Journal of Canadian Studies* 21, 3 (Fall 1986), 29.

69. Elizabeth Graham, "Schoolmarms and Early Teaching in Ontario," in Acton, Goldsmith, and Shepard, eds., *Women at Work*, 194.

70. Saskatoon Women's Calendar Collective, "Medical Women of Prince Edward Island," in *Herstory* (Sidney, B.C.: Gray's Publishing, 1981), 12.

71. Susan Gelman, "The 'Feminization' of the High Schools? Women Secondary School Teachers in Toronto: 1871–1930," *Historical Studies in Education/Revue d'histoire de l'éducation* 2, 1 (Spring 1990), 123–25, 129.

72. Margaret Gillett, *We Walked Very Warily: A History of Women at McGill* (Montreal: Eden Press, 1981), 227, 306; see also Alison Prentice, "Bluestockings, Feminists, or Women Workers? A Preliminary Look at Women's Early Employment at the University of Toronto," *Journal of the Canadian Historical Association*, New Series 2 (1991), 231–61.

73. Sr. Marie Bonin, "The Grey Nuns and the Red River Settlement," *Manitoba History* 11 (Spring 1986), 13; Sister Margaret Cantwell, *North to Share: The Sisters of Saint Ann in Alaska and the Yukon Territory* (Victoria: Sisters of Saint Ann, 1992), 87–88.

74. Judi Coburn, " 'I See and Am Silent': A Short History of Nursing in Ontario," in Acton, Goldsmith, and Shepard, eds., *Women at Work*, 150.

75. Colin Howell, "Reform and the Monopolistic Impulse: The Professionalization of Medicine in the Maritimes," *Acadiensis* 11, 1 (Autumn 1981), 20.

76. Heather MacDougall, " 'Guides, Philosophers and Friends': The Development of Public Health Nursing in Toronto, 1907–1932," paper presented to the Canadian Historical Association, Winnipeg, 1986, 1–2; Kari Dehli, " 'Health Scouts' for the State? School and Public Health Nurses in Early Twentieth-Century Toronto," *Historical Studies in Education/Revue d'histoire de l'éducation* 2, 2 (Fall 1990), 247–64.

77. A.A. Travill, "Early Medical Co-Education and Women's Medical College, Kingston, Ontario, 1880–1894," *Historic Kingston* 30 (January 1982), 86; Micheline Dumont-Johnson, "History of the Status of Women in the Province of Quebec," in Royal Commission on the Status of Women in Canada, *Cultural Tradition and Political History of Women in Canada*, Study 8 of the RCSW (Ottawa: Information Canada, 1971), 29; Elizabeth Hearn Milner, "Bishop's Medical Faculty 1871–1905: Its Jewish Dean, Aaron Hart David, and Its Jewish Students," *Canadian Jewish Historical Society Journal* 6, 2 (Fall 1982), 74; see also Veronica Strong-Boag, "Canada's Women Doctors: Feminism Constrained," in Linda Kealey, ed., *A Not Unreasonable Claim: Women and Reform in Canada, 1880s–1920s* (Toronto: Canadian Women's Educational Press, 1979), 109–29.

78. Strong-Boag, "Canada's Women Doctors," 109–29; Heather Fawcett, "Not Just Stackers of Bones: The History of Chiropractic in Canada," unpublished paper, University of Waterloo, 1992.

79. A Bystander, "The Woman's Rights Movement," *The Canada Monthly* (March 1872), 255.

80. Constance B. Backhouse, " 'To Open the Way for Others of My Sex': Clara Brett Martin's Career as Canada's First Woman Lawyer," *Canadian Journal of Women and the Law* 1, 1 (1985), 1–41. For a discussion of Martin's anti-Semitism, see Backhouse, "Clara Brett Martin: Canadian Heroine or Not?" *Canadian Journal of Women and the Law* 5, 2 (1992), 263–79; Lita-Rose Betcherman, "Clara Brett

Martin's Anti-Semitism," *Canadian Journal of Women and the Law* 5, 2 (1992), 280–97; Brenda Cossman and Marlee Kline, " 'And If Not Now, When?': Feminism and Anti-Semitism beyond Clara Brett Martin," *Canadian Journal of Women and the Law* 5, 2 (1992), 298–316; Lynne Pearlman, "Through Jewish Lesbian Eyes: Rethinking Clara Brett Martin," *Canadian Journal of Women and the Law* 5, 2 (1992), 317–350; Backhouse, "Response to Cossman, Kline, and Pearlman," *Canadian Journal of Women and the Law* 5, 2 (1992), 351–54; Betcherman, "Response to Cossman, Kline and Pearlman," *Canadian Journal of Women and the Law* 5, 2 (1992), 355–56.

81. Dumont-Johnson, "History," 28–29.

82. Lynne Marks, "Working-Class Femininity and the Salvation Army: Halellujah Lasses in English Canada, 1882–1892," in Strong-Boag and Fellman, eds., *Rethinking Canada*, 189–90; Rosemary R. Gagan, "More than 'A Lure to the Gilded Bower of Matrimony': The Education of Methodist Women Missionaries, 1881–1925," *Historical Studies in Education/Revue d'histoire de l'éducation* 1, 2 (Fall 1989), 239–59; Fingard, "New Woman," 46.

83. Our thanks to Margaret Conrad for this information.

84. Daniel Francis, *The Imaginary Indian: The Images of the Indian in Canadian Culture* (Vancouver: Arsenal Pulp Press, 1992), 118–19; Elizabeth Loosley, "Pauline Johnson" in Innis, ed., *Clear Spirit*, 74–90.

85. Isabel Bassett, *The Parlour Rebellion: Profiles in the Struggle for Women's Rights* (Toronto: McClelland and Stewart, 1975), 154.

86. Barbara Freeman, " 'Every Stroke Upward': Women Journalists in Canada, 1880–1906," *Canadian Woman Studies/Les cahiers de la femme* 7, 3 (Fall 1986), 44–45.

87. Peggy Bristow, " 'Whatever You Raise in the Ground You Can Sell It in Chatham': Black Women in Buxton and Chatham, 1850–65," in Peggy Bristow, co-ord., et al., *"We're Rooted Here and They Can't Pull Us Up": Essays in African Canadian Women's History* (Toronto: University of Toronto Press, 1994), 105; Paula Giddings, *When and Where I Enter: The Impact of Black Women on Race and Sex in America* (New York: Bantam, 1984), 69.

88. Mary Jean Green, "The Literary Feminists in the Fight for Women's Writing in Quebec," *Journal of Canadian Studies* 21, 1 (Spring 1986), 129.

89. K. Linda Kivi, *Canadian Women Making Music* (Toronto: Green Dragon, 1992), 19–24. The information on Johnson comes from the Black Cultural Centre for Nova Scotia; *The Canadian Encyclopedia* (Edmonton: Hurtig, 1985), vol. 1, 35; and Heather Murray, "Making the Modern: Twenty Five Years of the Margaret Eaton School of Literature and Expression," *Essays in Theatre/Études théâtrales* 10, 1 (November 1991), 39.

90. Carol Budnick, "The Performing Arts as a Field of Endeavour for Winnipeg Women, 1870–1930," *Manitoba History* 11 (Spring 1986), 51.

91. Maria Tippett, *Emily Carr: A Biography* (Toronto: Oxford University Press, 1979), 118–19; Angela F. Davis, "Mary Riter Hamilton: Manitoba Artist 1873–1954," *Manitoba History* 11 (Spring 1986), 23–25.

92. Laura Jones, "Rediscovery," *Canadian Woman Studies/Les cahiers de la femme* 2, 3 (1980), 5–6; Diana Pedersen and Martha Phemister, "Women and Photography in Ontario, 1839–1929: A Case Study of the Interaction of Gender and Technology," *Scientia Canadensis* 9, 1 (June 1985), 34.

93. Peter A. Baskerville, "She Has Already Hinted at 'Board': Enterprising Urban Women in British Columbia, 1863–1896" *Histoire sociale/Social History* 26, 52

(November 1993), 224; Laurie Alberts, "Petticoats and Pickaxes," *Alaska Journal* 7, 3 (Summer 1972), 146–59.

94. Gregory S. Kealey and Bryan D. Palmer, *Dreaming of What Might Be: The Knights of Labor in Ontario, 1880–1900* (New York: Cambridge University Press, 1982), 106.

95. Jacques Ferland, "When the Cotton Mills 'Girls' Struck for the First Time: A Study of Female Militancy in the Cotton and Shoe Factories of Quebec (1880–1910)," paper presented to the Canadian Historical Association, Winnipeg, 1986, 18–19.

96. Joan Sangster, "The 1907 Bell Telephone Strike: Organizing Women Workers," *Labour/Le travail* 3 (1978), 109–30.

97. Ruth Frager, "Sewing Solidarity: The Eaton's Strike of 1912," *Canadian Woman Studies/Les cahiers de la femme* 7, 3 (Fall 1986), 96–97; Frager, *Sweatshop Strife: Class, Ethnicity, and Gender in the Jewish Labour Movement of Toronto, 1900–1939* (Toronto: University of Toronto Press, 1992), 92–93; Star Rosenthal, "Union Maids: Organized Women Workers in Vancouver, 1900–1915," *BC Studies* 41 (Spring 1979), 50.

98. Roberts, "Honest Womanhood," 243.

99. Margaret E. McCallum, "Keeping Women in Their Place: The Minimum Wage in Canada 1910–25," *Labour/Le travail* 17 (Spring 1986), 37; Christina Burr, " 'Defending Art Preservative': Class and Gender Relations in the Printing Trades Union, 1850–1914," *Labour/Le travail* 31 (Spring 1993), 47–74.

100. Palamar, "Treatment," 9.

101. Ruth Frager, "No Proper Deal: Women Workers and the Canadian Labour Movement, 1870–1940," in Linda Briskin and Lynda Yanz, eds., *Union Sisters: Women in the Labour Movement* (Toronto: Women's Press, 1983), 52.

102. A.M. Givertz, "Considering Race and Class in the Regulation of Sexuality and the Prosecution of Sexual Assault in Hamilton, Ontario, 1880–1929," paper presented to the Canadian Historical Association, Ottawa, 1993, 13.

103. Prentice and Danylewycz, "Teacher's Work," 76; Alison Prentice, "Themes in the Early History of the Women Teachers' Association of Toronto," in Paula Bourne, ed., *Women's Paid and Unpaid Work: Historical and Contemporary Perspectives* (Toronto: New Hogtown Press, 1985), 97–121; Pat Staton and Beth Light, *Speak with Their Own Voices: A Documentary History of the Federation of Women Teachers' Associations of Ontario and the Elementary Public School Teachers of Ontario* (Toronto: FWTAO, 1987), chap. 3; Apolonja Maria Kojder, "In Union There Is Strength: The Saskatoon Women Teachers' Association," *Canadian Woman Studies/ Les cahiers de la femme* 7, 3 (Fall 1986), 82–84.

104. Ruby Heap and Alison Prentice, " 'The Outlook for Old Age Is Not Hopeful': The Struggle of Female Teachers over Pensions in Quebec, 1880–1914," *Histoire sociale/Social History* 26, 51 (May 1993), 91; P.B. Waite, *The Man from Halifax: Sir John Thompson Prime Minister* (Toronto: University of Toronto Press, 1985), 61–65; Marta Danylewycz, *Taking the Veil: An Alternative to Marriage, Motherhood and Spinsterhood in Quebec, 1840–1920* (Toronto: McClelland and Stewart, 1987), 95.

105. Margaret Street, *Watch-Fires on the Mountains: The Life and Writings of Ethel Johns* (Toronto: University of Toronto Press, 1973), 43.

106. Cash, *Off the Record*, 19.

107. Charles W. Humphries, "Keeping the Home Fires Burning: British Columbia Women and the First World War," paper presented to the Canadian Historical Association, Charlottetown, 1992, 4.

108. Mary Quayle Innis, *Unfold the Years: A History of the Young Women's Christian Association in Canada* (Toronto: McClelland and Stewart, 1949), 80.

109. Margaret Kechnie, " '. . . This Is Not a Paying Job . . .': The Farmerette Movement in Ontario during the Great War," paper presented to the Canadian Historical Association, Ottawa, 1993, 17.

110. Ramkhalawansingh, "Women during the Great War," 279.

111. Ramkhalawansingh, "Women during the Great War," 275; Shirley Tillotson, " 'We May All Soon Be "First-Class Men" ': Gender and Skill in Canada's Early Twentieth-Century Urban Telegraph Industry," *Labour/Le travail* 27 (Spring 1991), 110.

112. Graham S. Lowe, "Women, Work and the Office: The Feminization of Clerical Occupations in Canada, 1901–1931," in Strong-Boag and Fellman, eds., *Rethinking Canada*, 109–14.

113. Ramkhalawansingh, "Women during the Great War," 276.

114. John Herd Thompson, *The Harvests of War: The Prairie West, 1914–1918* (Toronto: McClelland and Stewart, 1978), 110.

115. G.W.L. Nicholson, *Canada's Nursing Sisters* (Toronto: Hakkert, 1975), 4, 98.

116. Kori Street, "More Than Bombs and Bandages: Women Who Served on the Homefront during the Great War," paper presented to the Canadian Historical Association, Charlottetown, 1992, 2, 7, 8.

117. See Patricia Connelly, *Last Hired, First Fired: Women and the Canadian Work Force* (Toronto: Women's Press, 1978), 10–22.

118. Margaret McCallum, "Keeping," 34.

119. Frances Mitchinson, pers. com.

CHAPTER SIX

Women's Sphere

Distressed by the Canadian government's failure to recognize the contribution of Laura Secord to her nation's sovereignty in the debate over pensions for veterans of the War of 1812, Sarah A. Curzon took up her pen in 1876 and wrote a play focussing on Secord's heroic deeds. In her preface to "Laura Secord, the Heroine of 1812," Curzon pointed to the injustice of showering so much attention on the male heroes of the war. "To save *from* the sword is surely as great a deed as to save *with* the sword; and this Laura Secord did, at an expense of nerve and muscle fully equal to any that are recorded of the warrior." In the play itself, Curzon had Colonel Fitzgibbon, the officer who made his military reputation as a result of Secord's warning, deliver the moral that Canadians ought to draw.

> Men, never forget this woman's noble deed.
> Armed, and in company, inspirited
> By crash of martial music, soldiers march
> To duty; but she alone, defenseless,
> With no support but kind humanity
> And burning patriotism, ran all our risks,
> Of hurt, and bloody death, to serve us men,
> Strangers to her save by quick war-time ties.
> Therefore, in grateful memory and kind return,
> Ever treat women well.[1]

With these words and by her play, Curzon acknowledged the link between her generation and Secord's, a link that many Canadian women of her time felt profoundly. For all their sense that they were living in a new era, they recognized how close they still were to the women before them.

It was true that women were increasingly entering the labour market. But they tended to do so when they were single and young, working between the ages of 15 and 24. In 1891, in fact, only 11 percent of women over 15 were "employed," according to the official record of the census; in 1911 the figure had risen to a mere 14 percent.[2] What such statistics ignored, of course, were the thousands of women who toiled in their own homes as their mothers and grandmothers had done before them.

That women were crucial to the household had long been recognized, even — perhaps especially — in the days when the household and the workforce were less clearly separated. Women's identity had always been centred on the family. But in the nineteenth century, as some women moved into an identifiable, non-domestic world of work, the family and women's role in it seemed threatened. In response, nineteenth-century ideologues promoted the concept of separate spheres for women and men and, most significantly, prescribed a domestic and maternal role for women that was highly idealized. Clergymen, doctors, and other male "experts" in fact had much to say about the nature of womanhood and about what the ideal woman should or should not do. Notions of appropriate behaviour were culturally specific. Until the end of the nineteenth century, a few Kaska women in the Yukon could cross the gender divide and for all social and economic purposes become male. Among the Naskapis, gender roles remained relatively fluid and uninfluenced by the intrusion of commercial interests in the area around Fort McKenzie. For some Inuit women, conforming to their cultural norm might result in ceremonial partner exchange. In Haida culture, some traditions survived — girl children were preferred, since they ensured the continued expansion of their family in the future. Ukrainian elites had their own concept of how Ukrainian women should behave so as to maintain their culture and advance the group's status in Canada. Ukrainian women were to ensure the survival of the language, marry within the Ukrainian community, and see that their homes remained culturally separate from mainstream society.[3]

Women were not silent on the subject of the ideology of woman's proper sphere. In the second half of the nineteenth century, a growing number of women, mostly drawn from the middle class, began to propose solutions to what was increasingly identified as the "woman question" or the "woman problem." Many argued that education was the way to improve women's condition, but two different directions were proposed: one sought a more practical training geared to the reality of woman's work in the home, and led to the domestic science movement; the other demanded access to higher education and to the professions, and led to the movement of small numbers of women into the universities. Another burning issue was women's reproductive behaviour. Since motherhood was so inextricably linked to the image of the ideal woman and the continuation of "the race," it was with great consternation that many realized that women were apparently abandoning this role and having fewer children.

THE IDEALIZATION OF DOMESTICITY

Victorian Canadians of all persuasions were assaulted by an ideology that saw women as the embodiment of purity, and as both physically and financially dependent. Home was a woman's "proper sphere." In 1851 the *Voice of the Fugitive*, a newspaper predominantly directing its words to the black population of southwestern Ontario, instructed women about their importance. "The most powerful and beneficial of the influences ordinarily at work in the formulation of human character is that of woman. . . . Man in life is what he is, to a great extent by the power of woman. His infancy being committed to her charge and his childhood spent in her society."[4] Woman, the ideal proclaimed, was man's equal, but equal did not mean identical. Women were different, and from this difference complementary roles and responsibilities naturally evolved. As the Reverend Robert Sedgwick explained to a group of young men in 1856,

> Woman is the equal of man, alike in the matter of intellect, emotion, and activity, and . . . she has shown her capabilities in these respects. . . . It would never do, however, from these premises, to draw the conclusion that woman . . . is bound to exert her powers in the same direction and for the same ends as man. This were to usurp the place of man — this were to forget her position as the complement of man, and assume a place she is incompetent to fill, or rather was not designed to fill.[5]

Two decades later, another commentator could only concur. "Woman's first and only place is in her home," this writer explained. "She is destined by Providence to make her home . . . a cloister wherein one may seek calm and joyful repose from the busy, heartless world. . . . The land she governs is a bright oasis in the desert of the world's selfishness."[6] Since most women married and indeed expected to make home and children their main concerns, the ideal was not completely divorced from reality. If it had been, it would not have been so powerful. What was new and confining about the ideal of domesticity was the increasingly sharp distinction it made between the domestic world of women and the public world of men, the growing emphasis on the mothering role, and the negative reactions that greeted most deviations from the norm.

Several groups of men were heavily involved in public discussion of the question of woman's proper sphere. Among the first to take up the issue were clergymen like Robert Sedgwick. Clerics continued to preach and write on women's place and possibilities throughout the latter part of the nineteenth century and on into the twentieth century. Within the Roman Catholic church, there were two possible roles for women: wife and mother, or member of a religious order. For members of religious communities, a variety of paths was possible, since the church fostered and supported contemplative orders like the Carmelites as well as more active ones involved in teaching or social work. What the church frowned on were sisterhoods of laywomen. Women who tried to organize communal life for charitable purposes were urged to take permanent vows and bring their associations under church control. Catholic religious orders expanded phenomenally between the middle of the nineteenth century and the first two decades of the twentieth century; existing orders established many new foundations and saw their numbers mushroom, while across the country, at least two dozen new orders of women religious came into being during this period.[7] These orders were responding to the needs not just of the church but of the women who entered them. But male clerics continued to see themselves as the proper interpreters of women's roles, both inside and outside the convent. Women were "naturally" separate and different from men, as a French-Canadian priest explained in 1918.

Hazel Purdy of Bear River, Nova Scotia, having tea with her dolls, circa 1896.

Source: Armstrong-Archibald Collection #20 33.4.6 (N-1346). Public Archives of Nova Scotia.

> Equality, whatever it is before God, in no way implies the parity of roles in society. One forgets that woman, by her very sex, by her physical structure and her moral qualities, by her tastes, talents, and tendencies, absolutely differs from man, and that this radical difference between the sexes results in no less a difference in their duties.[8]

Protestant clergymen of all denominations also felt called upon to pronounce on women's proper roles and duties. Whereas earlier in the century some sects had encouraged women to speak out at meetings or even to preach, by the third quarter of the nineteenth century the practice was condemned. Woman's Christian vocation was to be silent; the woman's place was in the home. "Bad" mothers, moreover, were increasingly held responsible for "delinquent" children, whether drunken sons or fallen daughters. By the early twentieth century, the leading Methodist reformer J.S. Woodsworth had no doubt that mothers who went out to work were to blame for a good deal of "truancy and juvenile crime."[9]

Physicians were a second group of men who had much to say on the subject of women and their roles. And in an era when religious faith was being challenged and when physicians were working very hard to upgrade their profession and gain control of health care, the voice of doctors was an increasingly powerful one. Like clergymen, they wrote in the popular press. But they also wrote a great deal for each other in the medical press. Physicians tended to emphasize women's physical frailty, reflected in every aspect of the biological life cycle. The weakness began with puberty. This difficult and mysterious stage appeared to heighten the physical, mental, and emotional differences between the two sexes. A pubescent woman's energies evidently became so concentrated on the development of her reproductive system that there was little energy left for anything else — certainly not for higher education or for sports. Some doctors warned that the woman who did continue her studies during this crucial stage might well damage her reproductive system forever, as her vital energies would go to her brain instead of her uterus. Medical experts encouraged girls to engage in appropriate physical activity, but the sports recommended were very different from those recommended for their brothers. Walking was good for girls; running was not. As we have seen, where Native women were able to maintain their traditions, the practice of having pubescent girls withdraw to menstrual huts continued well into the twentieth century. Among the Wet'suwet'en, the period of retreat could last from a few months to several years. The young women observed dietary restrictions and were not to gaze into the faces of others. They were visited and taught by the older women of their communities. At the end of their seclusion, a ceremony celebrated their reintegration into society. Unlike Euro-Canadian society, Native culture continued to acknowledge the power of menstruating women and treated puberty as a time for young women to learn their culture and traditions.[10]

Even when a woman passed the precarious age of puberty, her reproductive system continued to control every aspect of her being. "Woman exists for the sake of the womb," declared a popular health manual of the 1890s.[11] Doctors also believed that the complexity of a woman's reproductive system made her especially subject to disease. This placed women at risk throughout their lives, and the risk permitted the medical profession to speak out on a number of topics. Women were urged, for example, to cast off their corsets and wear clothing that was both more comfortable and healthy, and less likely to damage their childbearing capacity.

Physicians acknowledged woman's sexuality, but interpreted it in their own way. They comforted themselves by arguing that it existed to encourage conception, and they developed fascinating theories about the relationship between sexual excitement and its results. The *Canadian Practitioner* of 1886, for example, republished a review from an American journal, which solemnly informed its readers that "at the generation of male offspring the mother must be in a higher state of excitement than the father. And, conversely, at the generation of female offspring the father must be in a higher state of such excitement than the mother."[12] In general, doctors believed that a woman's sex drive was not nearly as strong as a man's, and that it was a woman's responsibility to keep both under control (since men could not). Nor should women attempt to avoid the repercussions of their sexuality. If they remained virgins or practised birth control, they risked physical breakdown.

Even after the childbearing years were over, medical experts thought that woman's reproductive system continued to exert its unremitting control — menopausal women were irrational and liable to "every form of neurasthenia, neuralgia, hysteria, convulsive disease, melancholia," and even insanity.[13] Doctors believed women to be highly susceptible to emotional disorders, particularly hysteria. Their belief in "reflex action" — that is, the tendency of healthy parts of the body to be weakened by diseased parts — persuaded some doctors that certain cases of insanity in women could be reversed by curing them of their gynecological disorders. As a result, hundreds of insane women were given gynecological operations, from simple curettage or cleansing of the diseased surface to complete hysterectomies. A middle-aged woman who was subjected to "curettage and amputation of the cervix" in the London, Ontario, insane asylum in 1898 had been diagnosed as suffering from a "subinvoluted uterus and cystic and hypertrophied cervix" as well as a perineum that was "slightly torn." She reported that her husband neglected and abused her and consorted with other women. According to her file, her insanity was a form of pyromania: she "gathers anything she can and burns it." Whatever the relationships between the various aspects of her case, the operation was declared to have been a success and the patient discharged.[14]

Performing operations on women judged insane was an extreme approach. More typically, physicians avoided discussing the causes of women's emotional disabilities. It was simply accepted that women were weaker and less emotionally stable than men. This led easily to the view that they needed to be both protected and controlled. Yet at the same time, it was believed that because women were more moral and less sexually excitable, they should be able to control themselves. Such contradictory views permeated the thinking of lawmakers and judges, another group of men who routinely differentiated between the sexes and made pronouncements, both overt and implicit, about women's capabilities and roles. Their views had practical as well as ideological force. Adolescent girls who were convicted of offences, for example, received longer sentences than boys did in the new reformatories that were being set up for young offenders. Magistrates and legislators were also more willing to incarcerate adult women for "moral" offences than men. An 1871 statute stipulated five years' imprisonment for Quebec women convicted of vagrancy for a second time; no such law applied to men.[15]

Canadian divorce law also continued to embody the double standard. In 1857 the British Matrimonial Causes Act was adopted in the province of Canada; as we saw in Chapter Four, similar laws were in effect in most of the other provinces. Typically, a husband might win a divorce if his wife was proven to have committed adultery. It was still the case that a wife could obtain a divorce only if her husband was proven guilty of adultery coupled with desertion without reason, extreme cruelty, incest, or bigamy, or if he was convicted of raping another woman or of sodomy.[16] In general, the law and its enforcement seemed to be saying that men needed some freedom; women should be content with their lot in the home, no matter what their circumstances. For them, no transgressions were permitted. However, in Quebec it was declared in 1866 that marriage for Roman Catholics was dissoluble only by death.

Laws governing Native women also reflected the view that a woman's place was with her husband. The Indian Act of 1869 excluded Native women from Indian status if they married non-status men. White husbands of Native women were seen as a threat to the resources of various bands; white wives of Native men did not, it was believed, constitute such a threat, and consequently on marriage they were granted Indian status. The government did acknowledge the validity of Native marriages according to their own customs, but it refused to sanction their traditional practices with respect to divorce.[17]

The double standard in many provinces regarding divorce extended to the status of married women. After the 1870s, a woman could sue her husband, but only for damages to her property, not to her body. Ontario judges continued to cite an 1844 court decision that had stated that it was a wife's duty "to conform to the tastes and habits of her husband, to sacrifice much of her own comfort and conven-ience to his whims and caprices, [and] to submit to his commands." If the husband was violent, it was the wife's role "to endeavour . . . to induce a change and alteration" in his behaviour.[18] Wives who attempted to sue for divorce after repeated beatings were chastised for failing to leave after the first beating — they were held to have condoned their husbands' actions. On the other hand, wives who did leave after only one or two beatings were chastised for being insufficiently patient with their husbands. Nonetheless, in what can be seen as an act of resistance, many women resorted to the courts in an effort to curb their husbands' violence.[19] In both murder and assault cases where wives were the victims, judgements often suggested that the women involved were somehow themselves to blame for inciting their husbands to these acts. And, for all the increasing emphasis on motherhood and the importance of this role for women, women did not have equal guardianship rights over their children. Only unwed mothers had rights over their children, and even then an 1859 Upper Canadian statute prevented the prosecution of any man who abducted a child, and who "claim[ed] to be the father."[20] Finally, the wife's disability and the double standard extended beyond her husband's death. In any province that provided relief for widows, the woman was deprived of her right to it if she had committed adultery.[21]

The courts had little sympathy for women who deviated from the domestic ideal. In the case of prostitutes, the women who solicited, not their clients, were viewed as the criminals. They, after all, were the ones who made the money. Nor were the courts particularly sympathetic to women who were the subjects of men's violence outside marriage. It was still rare for rapists to be prosecuted, and even more rare for them to be convicted. Non–English-speaking immigrant women were especially vulnerable, since the courts and the press often treated sexual assault against them as simply "the outcome of a row among foreigners."[22] As in an earlier period, the courts were reluctant to find women guilty of infanticide, but the reason for this leniency was the demeaning view that women were uninformed and therefore morally incapable. Newfoundland courts, on the other hand, were much harsher in sentencing women. The view of women as being morally incapable also emerged when women turned their violence against themselves. Coroners and jurors inves-tigating female suicide in British Columbia were convinced that respectable European women would resort to suicide only if they were insane. Those not deemed respect-able — prostitutes, Native women, or immigrant women — were considered sane, and their culture was blamed for the suicides.[23]

In looking at this kind of evidence, we have come a long way from woman as the embodiment of purity and gentleness, a creature in need of man's protection. In fact, a good deal of what late-Victorian Canadians said about women suggested that they were to be feared rather than protected. At the very least, a woman outside her "place" was a woman in danger — or a woman who did not deserve protection and invited ridicule. One group of lower-class white-collar male workers in Saint John who called themselves the Polymorphians mocked "hen-pecked" husbands and parodied women who had the temerity not to stay at home. In 1882 they rigged a float entitled "Colored Voters" that ridiculed the women of Loch Lomond, a nearby black settlement, for making and selling brooms in order to help support their families.[24] One feminist argued that "so persistently [are women workers] ignored by the advocates of 'women's proper sphere,' we are forced to the conclusion that female wage earners are not to be ranked as women." But staying in the home provided little protection: even there, women could find themselves at risk of attack by relatives and friends.[25]

WOMEN'S LIVES

Women themselves had a much richer, more complex, and more positive concept of their own roles and lives. The centre of their world was indeed the home — but for many the home was a base of power and influence, not a refuge. They were ritualists, remembering family events and family history, and celebrating occasions as a reminder of family connections. The physical surroundings of home, garden, dairy, and poultry house was their landscape, not the quarter-section or more that was the basis of the farm. They devoted much time to decorating the interior space so as to transform a house into a home.[26] They recognized the importance of their ties to other women, particularly the relationships between sisters and between mothers and daughters. As a young girl in boarding school in the late 1870s, Margaret Marshall Saunders wrote to her mother in Halifax quite explicitly about her feelings: "I do not believe a child ever loved her mother as much as I love you. I would be willing to die to ensure your happiness, my darling. I hope the dear Lord Jesus will keep you safely till I come back."[27] There was also a sense that family obligation fell more on women than on men, and that this was appropriate. It seemed right that they should help to care for younger siblings or for their parents as they aged. When Elizabeth Smith wanted to enter medical school in 1877, her best friend, Maud Rankin, tried to dissuade her because of the duty she owed her parents. "Lay aside those silly thoughts and you will be a better woman," Rankin urged. "I know that you are wishing to do something grand [,] something that will carry your name on to further ages . . . but are you neglecting no home duties . . . ? Lizzie [,] your first duty lies there, you never can repay your father and mother for all they have done for you."[28] At times, caring for parents delayed or prevented any chance a woman had to lead a full life of her own. In her personal recollections, Alice Chown had much to say about the constraints on women. Only after the death of her widowed mother, when Alice was 40, did she finally have some control over her own fate.

> During the next few months I shall have all the struggle for life and breath that an infant has, for I shall be breaking away from all the old walls that have surrounded me, from all the old environments that have enfolded me, that have kept me hidden from life and have forced me to live only through others.[29]

Chown celebrated her liberation by throwing herself into labour politics. Other women, forced almost against their will into domesticity, reacted more dramatically. Flora McPhee was a single woman who had made her life in Montreal, but was called home to Campbellville, Ontario, to nurse her mother, who treated her like a servant. When her mother died in 1920, free at last, McPhee expressed her rebellion by going out to the barn and chopping "into little pieces the old spinning wheel and loom. . . . She said she needed kindling." What she really needed, the niece who tells her story believes, "was to destroy the symbols of her bondage."[30]

The role of the helping daughter, sister, or aunt was one that not all enjoyed. Many single women admitted that they coveted domesticity, and they usually meant married domesticity. Love was becoming the measure of a successful marriage, and many women's diaries and letters testify to its reality in their lives. Marriage represented a sense of place, of creating a family of one's own, and of shaping and controlling the next generation. In the words of a woman banker quoted in the 1915–16 *Journal of the Canadian Bankers' Association*, "When the opportunity offers the most successful banking women amongst us will cheerfully retire to her own hearthstone, preferring the love of a husband and little children to thousands a year and a seat in the council of the mighty!"[31] Indeed, professional single women were sometimes the most vociferous promoters of the domestic ideal. Many were sure that the employment of the married woman outside the home meant that her family would suffer. In her 1910 "Report on Infant Mortality in Toronto," Dr. Helen MacMurchy took these sentiments to their ultimate conclusion: "Where the mother works," she stated, "the baby dies."[32] Certainly most women agreed about the importance of the family and of their own role in keeping it together. They argued that, as the family went, so went the nation. So focussed were women on their role as mothers that Nellie McClung felt she could safely declare that "every normal woman desires children."[33]

Unfortunately, to the extent that they accepted their role as the exclusive moral guardians of children and the family, women left themselves open not only to the barbs of male moralists and clergymen when their children transgressed, but also to feelings of guilt and self-blame. Even "good" mothers puzzled over how best to train their children. One Victorian mother, who kept a running diary of her child's development, recorded a constant state of worry over her daughter's moral health. How was she to train her daughter and ensure that she would "grow up a good woman?"[34] Women were also not above blaming each other. In 1911, the Presbyterian Woman's Home Missionary Society criticized Ruthenian immigrant women for lacking the ideals and morals needed to raise their children as proper Christian Canadians.[35]

Despite the primacy of family for most, women did not define themselves solely by their familial roles and obligations. Victorian and Edwardian women also saw themselves increasingly as individuals in their own right, with obligations and friendships outside the family. The opportunity to make female friends was one reason unmarried working-class women gave for preferring factory work to domestic service. Friendships were also formed through the numerous organizations and clubs that were developed by women and for women during this era. Some women's friendships became passionate attachments, but such relationships between women were becoming suspect and the object of repression. In a small village in Quebec in the 1880s, a teacher named Elizabeth Hébert was persecuted because of her intimate friendship with an older woman in the community; she lost her position as a result, but was "exonerated" in the hearing that the Quebec Department of Public Instruction held at her request. Female sociability was adaptive. When the telephone was introduced in the late nineteenth century, it was envisioned to be an aid to business. However, women quickly added a social dimension to the new instrument, using it to keep track of friends and relatives. In rural areas, the party line became a way for many women to participate in community life.[36]

Family and close friendships do not constitute the total picture. For many women—perhaps most of the women who put their thoughts on paper during this

Three young women enjoying a good laugh together.

....

Source: J.A. Irvine Album, 37 #145,
36.5.4 (N-6766). Public Archives of
Nova Scotia.

period — religion was a major focus. For them and other women, faith gave meaning to their existence and was the foundation for their work in the larger world. In 1878, medical student Elizabeth Smith thanked God in her diary for her religion: "It is my rock of strength — it has never failed me yet — it never will."[37] Others — particularly those newly emigrated to the country — found special comfort in their religion in a strange and often uninviting land. Still others found in religion the route to collective action, for women frequently outnumbered men in their congregations, and saw themselves as the special carriers of the Christian message. Laura Haviland was a Quaker for whom religious faith led to a mission to former American slaves. In addition to helping fugitive slaves escape the United States, she set up a Christian Union church for blacks in the Puce River area of Canada West in the early 1850s. Black women were the backbone of their respective churches — filling the membership rolls, raising money, teaching, and even physically helping to build them. Women were also the majority of those attending Salvation Army meetings, although they were more reluctant than men to give public testimony about their faith, thus conforming to expected gender roles. Women were particularly active in the Protestant Social Gospel movement at the turn of the century, a movement with links to earlier evangelicalism and devoted to the establishment of God's Kingdom on earth and thus to the reform of the temporal world. To work for social reform seemed to the women in the movement a logical extension of their maternalism; in this context, they developed many new roles. Toronto's first settlement, Evangelia House, opened in 1902: women students from the university supported it and found some employment opportunities there. Beatrice Brigden was hired in 1913 by the Methodist church to work with girls, and became a travelling lecturer on sex, hygiene, and young women's social problems.[38]

Catholic women similarly found their roles expanding through their work in the church. Between 1851 and 1911, the number of nuns in the province of Quebec increased from 650 (representing just over 1 percent of single women over the age of 20) to 13 579 (or 9 percent). In English Canada, several religious orders were introduced—at mid-century, the Sisters of Charity in Halifax and the Sisters of Saint Joseph in Toronto and Hamilton; and in the early 1860s, the Ursulines in Chatham and the Sisters of Providence in Kingston. Through the church, nuns could find and maintain a status in society outside of marriage. Outlets for Catholic laywomen also increased. In the 1860s devotional organizations developed, dominated by women. Two of the largest in Toronto were the Sodality of the Blessed Virgin Mary and the Association of the Children of Mary. These groups, which appealed to all classes of women, provided an emotional intensity that focussed on Mary and on the saying of the rosary; they gave new meaning and authority to these women's role in the home. After the 1890s laywomen as well found in the church more than a spiritual source of strength, as they joined with nuns to further Christian education or supported the sisters' social activism.[39] Jewish women from eastern Europe played a subordinate role in their religion, but in their case this circumstance was offset by an acceptance of their active participation in the marketplace. They were seen as more practical and more worldly than men; in their case, the domestic ideology was not played out in the same way it was for many other Canadian women.[40]

Although women were very active participants in organized religion, they were not necessarily unquestioning believers. Through the diaries and letters of some Canadian women, we can glimpse a refusal to be told what to believe. Henriette Dessaulles, who grew up in the village of St. Hyacinthe in the 1870s, went to confession, but she learned to tell the priest only what she wanted him to know. And when he criticized her friendship with a young man, Henriette rejected his opinion out of hand. Henriette was also critical of the conformity to rules and formalized ritual that she found among the nuns at her convent school and in the church generally. Similarly, in 1910, Lucy Maud Montgomery made it clear that church attendance for her was part of a social ritual and a way of focussing on her own spiritual development. It did not signify acceptance of the formalized doctrine that her church espoused, even though she was engaged to a minister.[41]

Women saw themselves as more than spiritual beings; they were physical beings as well. Victorian Canadians seldom discussed their bodies openly, but there are suggestions of what they thought. Privileged young women who had leisure to do so engaged in a variety of physical activities, and revelled in the opportunities they had for play. In their diaries they wrote about the pleasure they derived from walking, riding, playing hockey, curling, skating, dancing, and, at the end of the century, from the new craze of bicycling. In 1893 the Brampton *Conservator* felt that the idea of a woman riding a bicycle was novel and important enough to report. Miss Lillie Roberts had "the proud distinction of being Brampton's first lady bicyclist," the newspaper noted. "The graceful appearance she presents while passing through the town on her wheel will no doubt lead others to take up the healthy pastime." For many women, the bicycle represented increased mobility and independence. Predictably, some men disapproved, among them the trustees of the Toronto Public School Board when one of the city's teachers was seen riding in public.[42] Women were enthusiastic travellers, composing up to 20 percent of those who toured the Klondike at the turn of the century.[43] While the automobile might seem likely to have made travelling easier for women, in the early years of the twentieth century it sometimes curtailed their activities, especially in rural areas. Susie Campbell from Brampton, Ontario, complained that automobiles on the road made it difficult to control a horse and buggy; as a result, many women she knew were unable to go out. As with the bicycle, the auto had its critics: some felt that its use "[made] men effeminate and women neurotic."[44] Opportunities for team sports were also increasing. By the 1890s there were lawn tennis and curling championships for women, and in 1903 a women's rink from Quebec City defeated a men's curling team from the Royal Caledonian in Scotland. Sport reformers, who had encouraged women to participate in moderate physical activity to promote health, became concerned about the competitive nature of team sports and the physical strength they required. By the early twentieth century, they had altered their emphasis to focus on proper behaviour and appearance for women engaged in sports.[45]

Women's fashions also called attention to their bodies. At mid-century, the bustle accentuated the hips; then and later, corsets emphasized not only the hips but the breasts as well. In looking back on the buttoned gloves they wore, one woman recalled that "[b]oy friends, then known as sweethearts, would tenderly stroke the small area of flesh exposed between those buttons, sending delicious thrills through maidenly breasts."[46] Yet the dictates of fashion could interfere with healthy activity. Increasingly, when dress interfered with what women wanted to do, it was altered. As women started to bicycle, play tennis, and swim, new and more comfortable fashions made their appearance. Bloomers or a divided skirt were worn for bicycling. The shirtwaist, a garment that was slightly more comfortable and plainer than the fitted bodice, reflected the impact of the "working girl" on the fashion industry. The shirtwaist had the additional advantage of being inexpensive, because it required less measuring and sewing and could be mass-produced.

Victorian and Edwardian women rarely discussed their sexuality; when they did, it was usually to emphasize their own self-control. Control seemed necessary to most women who wrote on the subject, since it was women who paid the price of sexual pleasure in the fact of childbirth. Women gained moral stature and a certain amount of domestic power through affirming their sexual purity, and some were

Young women playing field hockey, Manitoba, 1912.

Source: National Archives of Canada/C-030935.

willing to carry that image into public life. They were particularly concerned about the fate of innocent young girls attracted to urban centres and susceptible to the sexual entreaties of immoral men. Young immigrant girls were thought to be especially at risk. Working men, too, believed that young women were vulnerable to attacks from wealthy men. The *Palladium of Labor* in 1885 asked, "Would you not 10,000 times rather your beautiful daughter had a dagger put through her heart or a bullet through her brain, than she should be doomed to die in agony of suffering brought on by being forced to submit to inhuman, diabolical outrages, to the nature it is impossible even to allude."[47] The Woman's Christian Temperance Union (WCTU) was more pragmatic; in 1894, the Ontario WCTU threatened to publish the names of prostitutes' clients so that mothers could protect their daughters from such men. At times women resorted to violence when men transgressed sexual norms. In a tragic case of domestic violence, Annie Robinson had to face the fact that her husband had committed incest with their two daughters. Her response was infanticide — she killed the two infants born from this incest.[48]

Many women felt they had the right to protect themselves and their daughters against sexual exploitation by unscrupulous men. Venereal disease was recognized as a threat to prostitutes and, indirectly, to all women. Indeed, the danger from venereal disease was very real, and it gradually became another topic that women were willing to discuss. Some physicians in the late nineteenth century estimated that 15 percent of gynecological disorders, including sterility, were the result of women having contracted venereal disease from their husbands, who had acquired it before or outside of marriage. The Haven, a Toronto charity, provided shelter for young women who had contracted venereal disease; its members refused to give in to public pressure to stop doing so.[49] In 1917, the National Council of Women urged "a Dominion campaign for the study and control of venereal diseases."[50]

The concern about the dangers of sexuality and the belief in the need for control over sexual feelings were part of a larger "moral panic" created by social change, but should not be equated with the non-existence of sexual feelings among Victorian women.[51] Elsa Gidlow recalled how, as a young woman living in Montreal, she had fallen in love with her "best friend," Frances, and had written "about her eyes like bits of smiling skys on a sunny day, her red-gold hair and graceful body." So limited was her own knowledge about sexuality that it was some time later before she realized she was a lesbian.[52] Lucy Maud Montgomery poured out her feelings about an early love in her diary on April 8, 1898. Looking back on her passion for Herman Leard, a man with little education and few prospects, she recalled that she had loved him "with a wild, passionate, unreasoning love that dominated my entire being and possessed me like a flame — a love I could neither quell nor control — a love that in its intensity seemed little short of absolute madness. Madness! Yes!" But she controlled the madness, for, as she concluded, Herman had been "impossible, viewed as a husband."[53] Montgomery eventually chose to marry someone she deemed more suitable — someone who, she believed, could provide her with the kind of home and family life she wanted.

With Montgomery, we come full circle to the centrality of marriage and family to Victorian Canadians. Montgomery tempered her own emotions and chose a marriage partner on the basis of practical considerations. The vast majority of women — pioneer and working-class women especially — must have had similarly practical notions, and probably took the idealization of their situation with a grain of salt.

A Klondike dancer.

....

Source: E.A. Hegg/National
Archives of Canada/
PA-013284.

Certainly Alberta farm women seldom romanticized their positions as wives. When reflecting on their marriages later in life, they tended to focus on the economic nature of these partnerships. Bella Harris, a Cree whose parents arranged her marriage in 1913 (when she was 15), recalled the event with a certain wry humour.

> Your parents choose the guy you going to marry. You don't even know the man. Here comes your husband. I was fifteen. After the dance some people came to visit and they were having dinner. I was in the kitchen washing dishes and all at once I heard my mother say, "Oh yes, she'll marry him." And that's it. And I'm wondering who was going to marry who. And it was me they were talking about.[54]

But for most young women, courtship was now occurring outside the boundaries of the home and family; they made their own decisions about whom to marry, although they still sought parental blessing.[55]

The idealization of home and family made a mockery of some women's lives. The domestic ideal depicted a woman with a man to protect her. But in Winnipeg in 1916, more than 20 percent of women between the ages of 35 and 64 were single, widowed, or divorced.[56] Looking at the realities that many of their sex faced, women found new ways to protest society's unwillingness to support women's domestic role with something more concrete than rhetoric. Most large newspapers introduced women's columns. That of the *Grain Growers' Guide* in the early twentieth century chastised farmers who took advantage of their wives' good will and self-sacrifice. Women's testimony before various government commissions spelled out the harsh conditions under which many married and single women in paid employment worked and lived.

The ideal had little to offer a woman like Mary Gorman, who never really had a chance to achieve it. Born in 1858 in Ontario to a mother who was a prostitute, Mary had few advantages and certainly little if any chance to learn the codes of Victorian respectability. Arrested at age 9 for being drunk and disorderly, she served 30 days at hard labour. By age 10 she had been convicted at least three times and served more time at hard labour. From age 10 to age 14, she worked as a servant but was also convicted four more times. At age 14, she was listed as a prostitute in the gaol records, which also noted that she was illiterate.[57] For this young girl, the cult of domesticity was irrelevant; life in Victorian Canada was ugly and hard.

THE QUEST FOR EDUCATION

That Mary Gorman's illiteracy was noted was symptomatic of the nineteenth-century concern for education. Everywhere the socially concerned were promoting more-regular and improved schooling for both sexes as a solution to many of the social ills of their time. Educators were another group that spoke at length about the differences between men and women, focussing on the kind of training appropriate to each.

Educational reformers believed that more-systematic school attendance, in state-supported institutions designed to uplift as well as to inform, had the potential to prevent the social, economic, and moral ruin of girls like Mary. The hope was that they would grow up to follow the ideals that men were putting forward for the women of their time. Governments worked to achieve the aims of educational reform by legislating free schooling and compulsory school attendance, along with programs designed to improve what went on in schools. By 1905, all provinces except Quebec and the colony of Newfoundland had laws requiring young children (initially those between the ages of 7 and 12) to attend school for certain minimum periods. Although some families resisted, many parents saw the economic and social value of schooling, and were motivated to send their children to school more regularly and for longer periods. Attendance continued to be sporadic and geared to the requirements of the family rather than the school, but gradually more young people attended classes for more months of the year and stayed in school for more years altogether. By 1911, Canadian girls and boys typically spent almost eight years in classrooms. Nevertheless, in the same year, only slightly over 44 percent of all 15-year-old girls were attending school.[58]

Old patterns of girls' school attendance persisted, especially in rural or isolated areas. Many working-class and immigrant families who needed their girls at home also retained traditional practices, such as rotating school attendance among their daughters. Where young women had access to jobs, as they did in towns with textile mills or food-processing plants, working-class girls tended to leave school early. Attendance also varied according to race, ethnicity, and class.[59] In parts of the country, black children had to attend separate black schools, which often lacked money, equipment, and well-trained instructors. British immigrant children who came to Canada through such organizations as the Barnardo Homes were less likely to attend school than Canadian-born children. In 1896 a woman who had migrated to southern Ontario through another child immigration agency, Annie Macpherson's House of Industry, was made an apprentice and evidently obtained no schooling whatever. She wrote back to the House, saying that she was ashamed of her poor writing.

> The people you let take me and raise as their child they would not sent me to school and mistreat me. . . . I run away when I was 15 year old I wish I could see you.[60]

Beyond the common- or elementary-school level, access to education was uneven and varied. After mid-century, there were still many small private schools for girls, along with a number of grammar schools, academies, and colleges that either admitted girls or were designed for them alone. But in the co-educational institutions, girls were often treated as second-class citizens. In the 1860s a debate developed in Ontario over the conditions under which girls could attend state-subsidized grammar schools: the government decided that female students who were not studying the classics were worth only half the subsidy paid for male students.[61] Supporters of grammar schools, however, were aware that girl students were needed to make the schools an economic reality, and advocates of woman's intellectual equality with man furnished them with a theory that would allow the schooling of girls without changing the grammar-school curriculum. By 1871 Ontario had a new system of secondary education that was more accessible to girls; but few secondary schools in any province were free, and few parents could afford to subsidize the costs of their daughters' attendance even when they were. In all provinces the number of teacher-training institutions increased, as did the number of young women who attended them. These schools opened up to women the prospect of superior or better-paid teaching jobs and the chance to save money to further their education in other fields. Still, the normal schools contributed to the doctrine of separate spheres in their unequal treatment of the sexes. In Toronto, a separate training institute was founded in the 1880s, chiefly for men who would go on to teach in the secondary schools; in the early twentieth century, the creation of a Faculty of Education associated with the University of Toronto (later the Ontario College of Education) was also motivated by the concern to foster an elite corps of male secondary-school teachers. In Quebec, all Roman Catholic teacher education continued to be segregated by gender.

Girls' academies, while often providing an excellent grounding in academic and cultural areas, varied in quality. Many considered their primary task to be the training of young ladies. Such goals did not necessarily negate good scholarly training, and the calendars of some of these colleges reveal a rigorous academic program. Many such schools seemed designed, however, to keep particular groups of girls apart from the less "respectable" parts of society. And the All Hallows School for Girls in Yale, British Columbia, which had once mixed its Native and white students, was by 1891 advertising its strict separation of the two groups.[62]

In English Canada, public elementary schools initially appeared to make no distinction between the sexes as far as curriculum was concerned, but separate playgrounds, school entrances, and seating in classrooms proclaimed the message that boys and girls needed to be separated. In urban schools, which were largely taught by female instructors labelled "assistants," the male principals and superintendents provided a message of masculine authority that was not lost on the children who attended. At the high-school level, a further message was embedded in differing curricula for young men and young women. Only the former were encouraged to take the classics or the more advanced mathematics required for university entrance and the professions. When physical education was introduced, it was segregated, with the girls engaged in calisthenics and excluded from the rougher games of boys, while the latter were also given military drill. Finally, the latter years of the nineteenth century witnessed the beginning of a new educational campaign to provide practical training in the schools for young men and women. Gradually, public secondary schools took over from private colleges the commercial courses that were so popular with middle-class youth. In response to the rapidly changing commercial workplace at the turn of the century, the business curriculum also became increasingly gendered, as boys enrolled in subjects like accounting, while girls were steered into stenography and typing. In both elementary and secondary schools, boys were offered manual training and girls domestic science.[63]

There were at least two fundamental motives behind the domestic science movement. On the one hand, there was the problem of girls like Mary Gorman, who so clearly and tragically lacked any kind of schooling and who required some practical training. On the other hand, there was the housewife and mother, who increasingly laboured alone and could use trained help. To make a point, some middle-class women exaggerated the repercussions of not having adequate help. When faced by the lack of domestic help, one newspaper columnist named "Gwen" questioned "Why should we women be forced to give up our homes, why should we be forced to neglect our children, our sewing and our requisite rest and recreation."[64] Young girls were reluctant to choose domestic service if they could find paid work elsewhere; too often, those who did go into service seemed poorly educated or socially unsuited to the work. Commentators offered two solutions to the servant shortage. One was to encourage the government of Canada to bring over immigrant women to replace the dwindling pool of Canadian-born domestics. The second and more innovative project was to improve the status of domestic work through domestic science education. Young women would then be attracted to domestic service, it was argued, because the work would be considered educated, professional work. At the same time, those trained in domestic science would be properly prepared for their future roles and more capable of running their own households and families.

Needlework had always been taught in girls' schools. Quebec's convent schools had been renowned since the seventeenth century for their teaching of fine embroidery and other kinds of needlework.[65] But the way sewing was taught began to change toward the end of the nineteenth century, as the domestic science movement took hold. Teachers were now given detailed and often rigid instructions about the needlework lessons they were to teach. By the early twentieth century, classes in the new subject of domestic science were formally established in most school systems, and cooking and nutrition were added to the subjects girls studied. By 1903, advanced training in domestic science was being provided at the Macdonald Institute in Guelph, Ontario; later it was made available at the University of Toronto, and at McGill (Macdonald College in Ste. Anne de Bellevue), Acadia, and Mount Allison universities. Although the expansion of domestic science classes was impressive, it was largely an urban phenomenon. In 1905–1906, fewer than 6 percent of the girls in elementary school took formal domestic science classes in Ontario cities; by 1920–1921, the figure had risen to 70 percent. In rural schools, however, it remained below 7 percent.[66]

Obviously the courses were not popular with everyone. The supporters of domestic science education argued that with more young women entering the workforce, daughters would no longer learn household skills from their mothers, and had to be trained in scientific and hygienic ways. But these courses emphasized woman's domestic role to the exclusion of all others, and critics complained about their lack of intellectual content, as well as about their remoteness from some girls' realities. Domestic science courses promoted the latest technology — technology that girls rarely found in their homes — and also subtly undermined the work women had traditionally done and the way students or their mothers still did it. The emphasis was on what women were doing wrong, not on what they were doing right. And as governments sponsored lectures and organized leaflet campaigns designed for adult learners, mature farm women and housewives joined schoolgirls as recipients of the messages of the domestic science movement. Many women were grateful that someone was taking enough interest in what they were doing to proffer advice, and they certainly enjoyed the excuse to meet and chat with other women. But their own wisdom and experience were often ignored. As one woman complained to the *Grain Growers' Guide* in 1916, such educational programs seemed designed "for very young schoolgirls." She had more than one question to ask: "Does this program speak to your head and intellect? Does this program give us a larger field than the usual 'women's yard'? Always suggestions about housework, knitting, and the main woman's destination 'preparing of dainty side-dishes and salads'. Kitchen, kitchen, and again kitchen!"[67] In Industrial Schools on the Prairies, Native girls found their education dominated by "hands-on" domestic training — they were expected to do the housework, sew, knit, mend, and wash, with the "washing for the school only taking a little over two one half days per week." On reserves, Native women were encouraged to learn "domestic" skills, meaning the skills of white homemakers; their teachers were often the unpaid wives of the Indian agents.[68]

The most vociferous and lengthy debate in education was over the question of women at university. When New Brunswick's Mount Allison University granted a B.Sc. degree to Grace Annie Lockhart in 1875, it was the first university in the British empire to graduate a woman.[69] Nova Scotia's Acadia University soon followed. Other universities in the country were not as open to change, but eventually yielded to pressure as more women acquired the necessary entrance qualifications. Young women desperately wanted the chance to learn. Quebec's Maude Abbott, who eventually became a renowned doctor and medical researcher, wrote in her diary in 1884 about her "selfish" desire to go to school.

> I do so *long* to go. And here I go again, once begun dreaming of the possibilities and I become half daft over what I know will never come to pass. Oh, *to think* of studying with other girls! Think of learning German, Latin, and other languages in general. Think of the loveliness of thinking that it entirely depended on myself, whether I got on and that I had the advantages I have always longed for.[70]

Such women would not be denied, and their campaigns for advanced schooling initiated a wide-ranging discussion on woman's role in society and the kind of education she needed.

Some ridiculed the idea of the educated woman. In 1872 a writer in the *Christian Guardian* snidely remarked that "very intellectual women are seldom beautiful; their features, and particularly their foreheads, are more or less masculine."[71] Others were concerned about the more serious effects of educating women. Dominion statistician George Johnson announced that the decline in the birth rate was "due to the spread of education which enables females to become better wage earners and therefore less interested in marriage."[72] Johnson's perception was not inaccurate — about half of the 392 women who studied at Dalhousie University between 1885 and 1900 remained single, a high figure compared to the 10 percent of the whole population that did not marry.[73]

Most Canadians who wrote on the subject supported higher education for women, as long as women were educated separately and differently from men. But the question of separate facilities remained an issue of critical importance. Many feared that it was dangerous to educate young women and men in the same classrooms during the years when they were reaching sexual maturity. Although there were some attempts to found ladies' colleges, few succeeded in establishing themselves as university-level institutions. One of the institutions that came closest to success in English Canada was Mount Saint Vincent Academy in Halifax. Established by the Sisters of Charity in 1873, it was recognized by the government in 1895 as a teacher-training school for the members of that order. By 1915 many of the teaching sisters had obtained advanced degrees, and the Academy, in association with Dalhousie University, was permitted to offer university-level courses for a degree that the latter would confer. In Quebec, the Sisters of the *Congrégation de Notre-Dame* also moved into higher education for women when they founded the *École d'enseignement supérieur* (later the *Collège Marguerite Bourgeoys*) in 1908.[74]

Heavy costs prevented the development of other colleges for women; but heavy operating costs at the universities, along with a shortage of qualified male students, were also partly responsible for the fact that women were finally admitted to those

This admonition to women students was being written in one of the classrooms of McGill University, circa 1912.

Source: Nevil Norton Evans Collection/ National Archives of Canada/PA-122876.

once exclusively male halls of learning. The process of women's acceptance was slow, however. In the case of McGill, women's higher education began in 1857, when the new McGill Normal School admitted both men and women. In 1870, a meeting of Montreal citizens convened by the McGill Board of Governors unanimously adopted a resolution to extend university benefits to women as soon as possible; the following year, the Ladies' Educational Association was formed to provide lectures for women and to look into the establishment of a women's college connected with the university. The founding of a high school for girls by the Protestant Board of School Commissioners in Montreal was a necessary first step. Girls at that school took exams that McGill considered matriculation or successful completion of high school, but they were still not permitted to enter the university. Only in 1884, when Donald Smith gave McGill a substantial sum earmarked for the higher education of women, did the university finally open its doors to them. Even then, the step was taken reluctantly, and for many years the university did all it could to educate its women students, nicknamed "Donaldas," separately and differently from the men.[75]

The three Rs, domestic science, art, music, and literature were generally accepted as appropriate subjects for women. Few objected to their training to be teachers or to be better wives and mothers. But opposition was acute to the idea of women entering the medical or law schools, for this suggested that women intended to be doctors and lawyers rather than wives and mothers.

Emily Howard Stowe, along with Jennie Trout, did the most to break down the barriers to the entry of women into medicine in Canada. Born in 1831 in Norwich, Upper Canada, the eldest daughter of a Quaker family, Emily Howard was raised to believe in religious freedom and the equality of women. Like so many young women of her era, she began teaching school when she was 15. But like no others in her period that we know of, she also had the audacity to apply for admission to the University of Toronto. Her application rejected, Howard continued to teach and save money so she could attend the Normal School in Toronto, from which she graduated in 1854 with a first-class certificate. Armed with her certificate, Emily Howard captured a job as the principal of a Brantford elementary school, and thus became the first Canadian woman to hold such a position in the public-school system. Two years later she married, and by 1863 she was the mother of a daughter and two sons. When her husband contracted tuberculosis, she determined to become a physician. After returning to teaching to support her family and to earn the money she would require for further study, she was again denied admission to the University of Toronto. Undeterred, this tenacious woman finally earned her degree from the New York Medical College for Women in 1867.[76]

But this was not the end of Emily Stowe's battle. When she tried to establish a practice, she found herself at odds with the provincial requirement that all doctors obtain a licence from the College of Physicians and Surgeons of Ontario, which refused certification to doctors who had trained outside the province until they had first attended a series of lectures given by a provincial school of medicine, and then been examined by the College. The problem was that no medical school in Ontario yet admitted women. Finally, in the 1870s, Stowe was allowed to attend the necessary courses, but she refused to submit to the required examination, practising without a licence until 1880, when she finally received provincial accreditation. Jennie Trout, who attended the courses with Stowe, did take the exams and so became the first licenced woman physician in Canada.

The first women actually admitted to Canadian medical schools did not necessarily have better experiences. When Elizabeth Smith and a handful of women colleagues attended medical lectures at Queen's in the 1882–83 session, some of the male medical students staged a revolt and threatened to transfer to another school. This and other hostile behaviour — on the part of the professors as well as that of the male students — took its toll. The women felt excluded. As Smith put it, her early medical school experience was like going through a "furnace fiery & severe."[77]

Similar resistance was encountered across the country: some universities refused to admit women altogether, while others denied their entry to particular faculties. Nevertheless, by 1900, 11 percent of college and university students in Canada were women, and by 1919–20 the percentage had risen to 13.9. The majority of women students were concentrated in the undergraduate faculties of arts and education, but some found their way into other faculties; a few even braved graduate study. In 1903, Emma Baker became the first woman to gain a Ph.D. in philosophy from a Canadian university when she graduated from the University of Toronto.[78]

Women (and men) who attended university were a tiny fraction of the total population. But despite their limited numbers and despite the fact that, for many, higher education for women was accepted only reluctantly and with a view to reinforcing women's traditional roles, the new graduates began to alter women's public image. Certainly there was now evidence that women were capable of advanced learning and of taking on the professional work that such learning could lead to. Bigoted views could still be openly expressed, however. In Quebec, a vice-rector at Laval University warned of the dangers of failing to measure out knowledge according to "the nature and scope" of young girls' minds, and of what would happen if women students were not immunized against "stupid pride or ambition." This cleric believed that higher education might easily be the means of launching such young women "on a disastrous course . . . no longer preparing them to be generous and devoted companions of man, but rather his inhibiting and, in all instances, misunderstood rivals." The news that the first graduate of the new *Congrégation de Notre-Dame* college for women had come first in the Quebec provincial examinations was deliberately kept quiet, as were similar "compromising incidents."[79]

Women proved in their university work that they were the intellectual equals of men. They also proved that educated women could marry and have children, even if they did so less frequently than other women. After all, half of Dalhousie's women graduates had in fact married. A university education also opened up new careers and employment possibilities to women. While a woman lawyer or doctor was still atypical in 1920, she was no longer an anomaly. The first generation of women graduates also had a sense that they were special. They formed long-lasting friendships with each other, and codified them through the formation of the Canadian Federation of University Women in 1919.

CHILDBEARING AND CHILDREARING

Women graduates provided a new dimension to the concept of womanhood but did not change its underlying premises. Women continued to be seen in terms of their destinies as wives and mothers. Indeed, on one level, the world of women was remarkably stable: the majority of women married and had children. But on another level, women's family lives were dramatically altered. The timing of family events changed. The age at which women experienced puberty was dropping in the western world — Canadian evidence is not available, but according to British studies, if fell from about 16 at mid-century to around 15 by the 1890s.[80] Yet, despite the lengthening of the potential childbearing years, the fertility rate for legitimate births underwent a marked decline. In addition, fewer women in fact married; in Canada, the percentage of single women between the ages of 45 and 49, which was 8.2 in 1851, rose to 11.1 by 1921.[81]

The number of children women bore varied according to region, religion, ethnicity, and class. The newly settled prairie provinces had a higher birth rate than the older provinces, and Quebec also maintained a high rate (although in the 1850s and 1860s, Nova Scotia's was higher still). The 1871 census showed that women of Scottish origin and women of French-Canadian origin had higher marital fertility rates than women of Irish or German backgrounds — who, in turn, had higher rates than women of English origin. Between 1900 and 1910, the birth rate of Native people increased, but after that it began a slow decline. In terms of class, a study of Hamilton, Ontario, between 1851 and 1871 reveals that fertility rates among the middle class decreased, whereas those of skilled and unskilled workers increased as both groups took advantage of labour opportunities for their adolescent children. When these opportunities lessened, fertility rates declined. The general decline in fertility rates was also a result of older women limiting the number of children they had, for women under 25 continued to have high rates. The net result of declining fertility may be seen in the changing average size of completed families. Whereas in 1851 a woman who had come to the end of her childbearing years would have borne on average 7.02 children, by 1921 the average had dropped to 3.54.[82]

Another important factor contributing to the declining birth rate was the rising average age at first marriage; later marriage shortened the total number of years that a woman might bear legitimate children, and also resulted in the bypassing of several years of potentially high fertility. In 1851 the average age at first marriage for women was 23; by 1871 it was 25.4; and by 1891 it had risen to 26. The economic recession of the 1880s was a possible related cause.[83] Although the average age at first marriage for women declined again to 24.9 in 1911 and to 24.3 in 1921, it still remained higher than it had been in the middle of the nineteenth century, reflecting both a cautious approach to the future and the increasing material aspirations that accompanied the expanding economy.[84]

Among some groups, delayed marriage was a deliberate strategy for limiting family size. Some Canadians were also intentionally limiting the sizes of their families by using birth control. *Coitus interruptus* or withdrawal was probably the most widespread birth control method used during this period. But many others were also known. Advertisements in late-nineteenth-century newspapers attest to the use of condoms, which, when rubber was vulcanized at mid-century, became less expensive than they had been previously. Condoms were not deemed respectable, however, as they were associated with prostitution and the prevention of venereal disease. Abstinence from sexual intercourse was another method of birth control that couples practised. Women also shared information about how to prevent pregnancy through the use of herbs or the insertion of vaginal sponges or pessaries, often home-made. One recipe that a young woman actually passed on to her mother called for cocoa butter, tannic acid, and boric acid.[85] It has been suggested that the declining birth

TABLE 6.1 *Average Age at First Marriage and Sex Ratios, 1851–1891*

	Average Age at Marriage		Number of Men Aged 20–49
	Men	Women	per 100 Women Aged 17½–47½
1851			
Quebec	25.4	23.7	89.1
Ontario	26.7	22.4	103.7
1861			
Nova Scotia	28.8	26.8	85.2
Quebec	26.5	24.7	91.9
Ontario	27.2	23.9	97.5
1871			
Nova Scotia	29.4	26.6	87.0
New Brunswick	28.8	26.0	90.8
Quebec	26.9	25.3	86.0
Ontario	28.4	25.0	92.5
1881			
Prince Edward Island	30.1	26.9	88.1
Nova Scotia	29.8	25.9	89.0
New Brunswick	29.4	25.4	91.4
Quebec	26.7	24.9	87.5
Ontario	28.0	25.3	91.4
Manitoba	28.3	20.1	147.7
British Columbia	29.3	20.0	173.7
1891			
Prince Edward Island	31.1	27.9	89.6
Nova Scotia	30.1	26.4	92.0
New Brunswick	29.4	26.3	90.8
Quebec	27.5	25.3	89.1
Ontario	29.3	26.6	91.9
Manitoba	29.8	23.8	134.7
British Columbia	32.7	22.3	231.2

Source: Ellen M. Thomas Gee, "Marriage in Nineteenth-Century Canada," *Canadian Review of Sociology and Anthropology* 19, 3 (August 1982), p. 321.

rate in other countries in this period could be construed as evidence of a kind of "domestic feminism," as married women achieved a greater measure of control over their bodies and over an important area of their lives through insisting on the use of birth control.[86] This may well have been true for some Canadian women.

Not all birth control methods were reliable, however, nor were all men co-operative. Women frequently faced unwanted pregnancies, and many continued to seek abortions. As with birth control, women's traditional knowledge included ways of inducing miscarriage using herbs. Among the Nuu'chah'nulth of the west coast in the 1870s, women mashed the roots of "a three-leaved plant" in water and drank

An elaborate wedding party in Nova Scotia at the turn of the century.

Source: Notman Photographic Archives, McCord Museum of Canadian History.

the infusion once or twice a day to induce abortion.[87] Elsewhere a variety of home remedies were known, although they were not necessarily effective or safe. These ranged from jumping off a hay wagon, taking excruciatingly hot baths, or drinking carbolic acid or a mixture of turpentine and sugar, to even more dangerous methods involving the insertion of instruments like scissors or knitting needles to bring on miscarriage. Scores of patent medicines were thinly disguised abortifacients, among them Dr. Holloway's Pills, which were advertised as being designed to cure "female irregularities."[88] Throughout the period, women who could afford to do so also sought the services of abortionists. In Toronto "Mamma [Lyyli] Anderson" ran an abortion service as well as a hostel and job exchange for Finnish domestic servants.[89]

While abortion before quickening had once been legal and had not been regarded by the society at large as a moral problem, the practice was increasingly condemned in the course of the nineteenth century. Everywhere in the western world, moral and legal barriers were gradually raised against it. Nativists of British origin worried about what they and other middle-class moralists referred to as the "race suicide" of the Anglo-Saxon population. The logical outcome of such thinking was to condemn not just abortion but all methods of birth control. In 1892, Section 179 of the Criminal Code of Canada read as follows:

Everyone is guilty of an indictable offense and liable to two years' imprisonment who knowingly, without lawful excuse or justification, offers to sell, advertises, publishes an advertisement of or has for sale or disposal any medicine, drug or article intended or represented as a means of preventing conception or causing abortion.[90]

This law remained unchanged until 1969.

The birth rate continued to decline, however, particularly among the middle classes and in urban centres, but also among the working class and in rural areas.[91] By 1921, the fertility of urban couples was approximately 20 percent lower than that of rural couples. Children were not as useful in the urban economy, where family costs were higher, as they were in the countryside. Child labour laws, compulsory education laws, and parents' changing attitudes to children all conspired to make large families seem impractical, if not irresponsible. And even farm families experienced pressures to limit their fertility as the future on the land, especially in older settled regions, began to seem less promising than it had in the past.[92] The decline of the family as a unit of economic production accounts for the variation in fertility patterns by region. It was in Ontario that the rate plummeted most sharply; in Nova Scotia, the rate dropped between 1871 and 1891, when industrialization first became a major factor there. Elsewhere the decline came later; for cultural reasons, the decline was especially delayed in Quebec.

A further reason for declining family size was the more positive factor of declining mortality rates. Many couples still experienced the tragedy of children dying young. But by 1920, infant mortality had decreased significantly (to approximately 102 deaths per 1000 population, compared to 184 per 1000 in 1851).[93] However, the decline in the birth rate pre-dates, by at least a generation, the decline in infant mortality. Thus we know that the expectation that more children would live can only be part of the cause of family limitation. However, declining infant mortality did mean that fewer women would undergo the heartbreak of losing a child and living with the loss, as did one woman who, eight years after the death of her son, wrote in her diary: "Oh how I miss him yet — that dear sweet face — but God knows best and I am sure he is better off—But O I miss him all the time."[94]

A positive result for women of the decline in fertility was the reduced physical toll of childbearing, which in turn increased women's average life expectancy. However, childbirth remained a major cause of death among women of childbearing age, and puerperal infection continued to be common, despite the medical knowledge that it was preventable with the use of antiseptic techniques. In 1921 the Canadian maternal mortality rate was 4.7 per 1000 live births, a rate higher than that experienced in most other western countries.[95]

Physicians argued that their scientific expertise and access to medical technology justified their increasing control of childbirth, and made the process safer. In 1874, the medical journal *The Canadian Lancet* explicitly called for women's gratitude to the male medical profession.

But if woman could only be made intimately acquainted with the truth, that the cultivation of obstetrics by men has been to their advantage by immense odds over what could have been expected of its continued practice by women, what a debt of gratitude would the sex be sensible of owing to man.[96]

Many women accepted such arguments, believing that doctors' scientific knowledge was more valuable than the experiential wisdom of midwives and grandmothers. Childbirth came to be regarded more as a medical than as a natural phenomenon, and as a matter for a woman and her physician rather than for midwives, women friends, and families. Midwives continued to practise in remote regions, among many immigrant groups, and within Native communities, but doctors were taking control of childbirth in urban centres. Almost all births, however, still took place in the home. Only the unmarried or the very poor gave birth in hospitals, or lying-in homes, where infant mortality rates were shockingly high, although by the second decade of the twentieth century, medical authorities were beginning to persuade other women that hospitals were the safest places to give birth.

Childrearing began to change as well. For much of the nineteenth century, there was typically a 40-year span between the birth of a woman's first child and the departure of the last one from home.[97] Smaller families did not alter this situation; the tendency for children to stay in the home longer and marry later initially meant little change in the number of years that women devoted to children at home. Now mothers had to cope with the newly defined period of "adolescence" in their children, as earlier puberty and later marriage resulted in young people who were sexually mature but still dependent. For most Canadians, the onset of puberty began to be seen as a "problem," as there was less work for the young to do on the farm, in the home, and in the public labour force, and schooling extended longer into the teenage years. Mothers also found that the state was increasingly intervening in how they raised their children. Public health officers could enter their homes and examine their children; truant officers enforced compulsory education. Yet motherhood was more than birthing, coping with adolescence, and putting up with others telling a woman how to care for her family. Carrie Best, a black Nova Scotian, tells a story about her mother: at the end of World War I there was a race riot in New Glasgow, Nova Scotia; fearing for her son, who had not returned home from work, Best's mother went out at night, walked through an angry crowd, and brought her son home to safety.[98]

Many women had to raise their families alone. Some were deserted by husbands, but many others were widowed at a young age. These latter women tended to support themselves with the help of older children. In Haida culture, a young widow was expected to remarry within her husband's lineage, whereas a widower was under no obligation to his wife's family once he had given a mortuary potlatch for his wife.[99] About older women we know very little. Perhaps this is because so much emphasis was placed on woman as mother; when a woman stopped being able to bear children, she became less visible. We do know that there was a great difference in life expectancy among people over 60. At mid-century, men outlived women at this age level, but by the end of the century this trend had reversed. Some old-age homes were built to cater to (predominantly female) paying customers. Evidence suggests that in the late nineteenth century, however, more elderly women than elderly men were able to avoid institutions through some form of family co-residency. These women could still make contributions to the household and so were welcomed. Those poorer women who were not were dependent on charity or the poorhouse to look after them in their old age. When Newfoundland (which was still a British colony) in 1911 introduced the first state-run old age pension program, only men could receive it. In Native cultures, older women were particularly esteemed; in some cases their status increased, since they now had access to areas of endeavour previously prohibited during their menstrual years.[100]

What women experienced during this period, then, was on the one hand, greater opportunity to educate themselves for wider roles, but on the other hand, increasing pressures to espouse domestic life, and particularly an intensification of the role of motherhood. Books devoted to advising women on childcare proliferated, along with books for children. The number of children might be fewer, but the task of raising them became more complex. Where women had once seen raising children as part of the many things they did, it now seemed their most important responsibility, and one that, according to the prescriptive literature, belonged chiefly to them. The tensions produced by this new vision were multiple, but three were particularly important. Women were told that they bore the responsibility for their children's lives, but the reality was that more and more of their children's time was in fact controlled by schools. Women were to take responsibility for the young; but at the same time, their real sphere was the supposedly separate one of the home. The public world, the world that affected all their children and in which their grown sons would have to spend their working lives, was controlled by men. Finally, increasing numbers of women were educated and/or had a period of employment outside the home; but much of what they learned at school or at work had little bearing on their future lives as wives and mothers.

It was these realities and conditions that late-nineteenth-century and early twentieth-century women faced and turned to account as they increased their demand for a voice in the public realm. Many of them were already "voting with their wombs" by having fewer children as they recognized the complexities of childrearing in the new industrial age. Drawing on the powerful ideology of separate spheres and on a culture of womanhood that celebrated not only the home but also the bonds between women, they now proclaimed that as mothers and the managers of families or as single professional women they had both the need and the right to influence what went on in the world outside the home.

NOTES

1. Anton Wagner, ed., *Women Pioneers: Canada's Lost Plays* (Toronto: Canadian Theatre Review Publications, 1979), vol. 2, 94–5, [our emphasis], 95, 136–37.
2. Paul Phillips and Erin Phillips, *Women and Work: Inequality in the Labour Market* (Toronto: James Lorimer, 1983), 8.
3. Evelyn Blackwood, "Sexuality and Gender in Certain Native American Tribes: The Case of Cross-Gender Females," *Signs* 10, 1 (Autumn 1984), 27–42; Danielle Desmarais, Carole Levesque, et Dominique Raby, "La contribution des femmes naskapies aux travaux de la vie quotidienne à l'époque de Fort McKenzie," *Recherches féministes* 7, 1 (1994), 39; G. Oosten Jaarich, "Male and Female in Inuit Shamanism," *Études/Inuit/Studies* 10, 1–2 (1986), 119; Margaret B. Blackman, *A Haida Woman* (Vancouver: Douglas and McIntyre, 1982), 26; Frances Swyripa, *Wedded to the Cause: Ukrainian-Canadian Women and Ethnic Identity 1891–1991* (Toronto: University of Toronto Press, 1993), 60–61.
4. Peggy Bristow, " 'Whatever You Raise in the Ground You Can Sell It in Chatham': Black Women in Buxton and Chatham, 1850–65," in Peggy Bristow, co-ord., et

al., *"We're Rooted Here and They Can't Pull Us Up"*: Essays in African Canadian Women's History (Toronto: University of Toronto Press, 1994), 84.

5. Ramsay Cook and Wendy Mitchinson, eds., *The Proper Sphere: Woman's Place in Canadian Society* (Toronto: Oxford University Press, 1976), 9.

6. "Woman's Sphere," *The Harp* (December 1874), 25.

7. Diane Bélanger et Lucie Rozon, *Les religieuses au Québec* (Montréal: Libre Expression, 1982), 294–319, annexe 2; Michel Thériault, *The Institutes of Consecrated Life in Canada* (Ottawa: National Library of Canada, 1980).

8. Cook and Mitchinson, eds., *Proper Sphere*, 86–87 [our translation].

9. Michael Owen, "Keeping Canada God's Country: Presbyterian Perspectives on Selected Social Issues 1900–1915," University of Toronto, Ph.D. Thesis, 1984, 114.

10. Jo-Anne Fiske, "Gender and Politics in a Carrier Indian Community," University of British Columbia, Ph.D. Thesis, 1989, 109–11; Margaret B. Blackman, "The Changing Status of Haida Women: An Ethnohistorical and Life History Approach," in Donald A. Abbott, ed., *The World as Sharp as a Knife: An Anthology in Honour of Wilson Duff* (Victoria: British Columbia Provincial Museum, 1981), 67; see also Edward Sapis, "A Girl's Puberty Ceremony among the Nootka Indians," Royal Society of Canada, *Proceedings and Transactions* Series 3, 7 Part 2 (1930), 67.

11. M.L. Holbrook, "Parturition without Pain," in George Napheys, *The Physical Life of Woman* (Toronto: 1890), 312.

12. *Canadian Practitioner*, reprinted from N.Y. Med. Recorder (January 1886), 43.

13. J. Thorburn, *A Practical Treatise of the Diseases of Women* (London: 1885), 192–93. See also Wendy Mitchinson, "Causes of Disease in Women: The Case of Late 19th Century English Canada," in Charles G. Roland, ed., *Health, Disease, and Medicine: Essays in Canadian History* (Toronto: Clarke, Irwin, 1984), 381–95.

14. Wendy Mitchinson, "Gynecological Operations on Insane Women, London, Ontario, 1895–1901," *Journal of Social History* 15, 3 (Spring 1982), 467–84; Public Archives of Ontario, Case Files of London Ontario Asylum for the Insane, Case No. 4269, E.F.; see also Wendy Mitchinson, *The Nature of Their Bodies: Women and Their Doctors in Victorian Canada* (Toronto: University of Toronto Press, 1991).

15. Constance B. Backhouse, "Nineteenth-Century Canadian Prostitution Law: Reflection of a Discriminatory Society," *Histoire sociale/Social History* 18, 36 (November 1985), 416–17.

16. Linda Silver Dranoff, *Women in Canadian Life: Law* (Toronto: Fitzhenry and Whiteside, 1977), 62, 64.

17. Sally Weaver, "The Status of Indian Women," in Jean Leonard Elliott, ed., *Two Nations, Many Cultures: Ethnic Groups in Canada* (Scarborough: Prentice-Hall, 1983), 58–59; Douglas Sanders, "Indian Women: A Brief History of Their Roles and Rights," *McGill Law Journal* 21, 4 (Winter 1975), 663.

18. Erin Breault, "Educating Women about the Law: Violence against Wives in Ontario, 1850–1920," University of Toronto, M.A. Thesis, 1986, espec. 39.

19. Bernadine Dodge, "Gendered Discourses: Women and the Law in Ontario, 1850–1900," University of Toronto, Ph.D. Dissertation, 1993, chap. 6.

20. Dranoff, *Women in Canadian Life: Law*, 20–23.

21. Dranoff, *Women in Canadian Life: Law*, 58.

22. Constance B. Backhouse, "Nineteenth Century Canadian Rape Law 1800–92," in David Flaherty, ed., *Essays in the History of Canadian Law* (Toronto: Osgoode

Society, 1983), vol. 2, 200–47; A.M. Givertz, "Considering Race and Class in the Regulation of Sexuality and the Prosecution of Sexual Assault in Hamilton, Ontario 1880–1929," paper presented to the Canadian Historical Association, Ottawa, 1993, 38.

23. Linda Cullum and Maeve Baird with the assistance of Cynthia Penney, "A Woman's Lot: Women and Law in Newfoundland from Early Settlement to the Twentieth Century," in Linda Kealey, ed., *Pursuing Equality: Historical Perspectives on Women in Newfoundland and Labrador* (St. John's: Institute of Social and Economic Research, Memorial University, 1993), 111; Susan Johnston, " 'Mother Was Never Very Happy': Women and Suicide in Late Nineteenth-Century British Columbia," unpublished paper, University of Victoria, 1988, 52–54.

24. Bonnie Huskins, "The Ceremonial Space of Women: Public Processions in Victorian Saint John and Halifax," in Janet Guildford and Suzanne Morton, eds., *Separate Spheres: Women's Worlds in the 19th-Century Maritimes* (Fredericton: Acadiensis Press, 1994), 151.

25. Sharon Myers, " 'Not to Be Ranked as Women': Female Industrial Workers in Turn-of-the-Century Halifax," in Guildford and Morton, eds., *Separate Spheres* 176; Karen Dubinsky, *Improper Advances: Rape and Heterosexual Conflict in Ontario, 1880–1929* (Chicago: University of Chicago Press, 1993).

26. Jeanne Kay, "Landscapes of Women and Men: Rethinking the Regional Historical Geography of the United States and Canada," *Journal of Historical Geography* 17, 4 (October 1991), 446; Jenny Cook, "Bringing the Outside In: Women and the Transformation of the Middle-Class Maritime Canadian Interior, 1830–1860," *Material History Review* 38 (Fall 1993), 36–46.

27. Karen Sanders, "Margaret Marshall Saunders: Children's Literature as an Expression of Early Twentieth-Century Social Reform," Dalhousie University, M.A. Thesis, 1978, 20.

28. Maud Rankin to Elizabeth Smith, September 1877. Elizabeth Smith Shortt Papers, Doris Lewis Rare Book Room, University of Waterloo.

29. Alice Chown, *The Stairway* (Boston: Cornhill, 1921), 11.

30. Janet McPhee, "The Campbellville Chronicles," unpublished paper, 1987.

31. Barbara Hansen, "A Historical Study of Women in Canadian Banking, 1900–1975," *Canadian Women's Studies/Les cahiers de la femme* 1, 2 (Winter 1978/79), 18.

32. Michael Piva, *Conditions of the Working Class in Toronto — 1900–1921* (Ottawa: University of Ottawa Press, 1979), 125.

33. Veronica Strong-Boag, "Introduction," to Nellie McClung, *In Times Like These* (Toronto: University of Toronto Press, 1972), 22.

34. Alison L. Prentice and Susan E. Houston, eds., *Family, School and Society in Nineteenth-Century Canada* (Toronto: Oxford University Press, 1975), 267.

35. Owen, "Keeping Canada God's Country," 85.

36. John Abbott and Alison Prentice, "Policy, Gender and Conflict: Teachers and Inspectors in Ontario and Quebec in the 1870s and 1880s," paper presented to the Canadian History of Education Association, Halifax, October 1986; Michèle Martin, *"Hello, Central?": Gender, Technology, and Culture in the Formation of Telephone Systems* (Montreal and Kingston: McGill-Queen's University Press, 1991), chap. 6.

37. Elizabeth Smith, *"A Woman with a Purpose": The Diaries of Elizabeth Smith 1872–1884*, edited and with an introduction by Veronica Strong-Boag (Toronto: University of Toronto Press, 1980), 22.

38. Robin Winks, *The Blacks in Canada: A History* (Montreal and Kingston: McGill-Queen's University Press, 1971), 243; Shirley J. Yee, "Gender Ideology and Black Women as Community Builders in Ontario, 1850–70," *Canadian Historical Review* 75, 1 (March 1994), 63–65; Lynne Marks, "The 'Hallelujah Lasses': Working-Class Women in the Salvation Army in English Canada, 1882–92," in Franca Iacovetta and Mariana Valverde, eds., *Gender Conflicts: New Essays in Women's History* (Toronto: University of Toronto Press, 1992), 79; Sara Z. Burke, "Science and Sentiment: Social Service and Gender at the University of Toronto, 1888–1910," *Journal of the Canadian Historical Association*, New Series 4 (1993), 80–82; Beatrice Brigden, "One Woman's Campaign for Social Purity and Social Reform," in Richard Allen, ed., *The Social Gospel in Canada* (Ottawa: National Museums of Canada, 1975), 36–62.

39. Marta Danylewycz, *Taking the Veil: An Alternative to Marriage, Motherhood and Spinsterhood in Quebec, 1840–1920* (Toronto: McClelland and Stewart, 1987), 134–37; *The Canadian Encyclopedia* (Edmonton: Hurtig, 1985), vol. 1, 341; Brian P. Clarke, *Piety and Nationalism: Lay Voluntary Associations and the Creation of an Irish-Catholic Community in Toronto, 1850–1895* (Montreal and Kingston: McGill-Queen's University Press, 1993), chap. 6.

40. Ruth A. Frager, *Sweatshop Strife: Class, Ethnicity and Gender in the Jewish Labour Movement of Toronto, 1900–1939* (Toronto: University of Toronto Press, 1992), 150–53.

41. Henriette Dessaulles, *Hopes and Dreams: The Diary of Henriette Dessaulles, 1874–1881*, translated by Liedewy Hawke (Willowdale, Ont.: Hounslow, 1986), espec. 64; Mary Rubio and Elizabeth Waterson, eds., *Selected Journals of L.M. Montgomery, Vol. 1 (1889–1910)* (Toronto: Oxford University Press, 1986), 263.

42. Jean Cochrane, Abby Hoffman, and Pat Kincaid, *Women in Canadian Life: Sports* (Toronto: Fitzhenry and Whiteside, 1977), 25–27; Honora M. Cochrane, ed., *Centennial Story: Board of Education for the City of Toronto, 1850–1950* (Toronto: Thomas Nelson, 1950), 173.

43. Charlene Porsild, " 'Accidental Tourists': Men and Women Travellers to the Klondike, 1896–1900," paper presented to the Canadian Historical Association, Charlottetown, 1992, 13–14.

44. Kristopher Churchill, "Harnessing the Auto: Motorization and the Countryside in Ontario," paper presented to the Canadian Historical Association, Charlottetown, 1992, 12–13; Stephen J. Davies, "Men Effeminate and Women Neurotic: Rural Ontario and the Automobile, 1900–1925," paper presented to the Canadian Historical Association, Charlottetown, 1992, 3–4.

45. Cochrane, Hoffman, and Kincaid, *Women in Canadian Life: Sports*, 25–27; Michael J. Smith, "Graceful Athleticism or Robust Womanhood: The Sporting Culture of Women in Victorian Nova Scotia, 1870–1914," *Journal of Canadian Studies* 23, 1–2 (Spring/Summer 1988), 133.

46. Gwen Cash, *Off the Record: The Personal Reminiscences of Canada's First Woman Reporter* (Langley, B.C.: Stagecoach, 1977), 13.

47. Givertz, "Considering," 10–11, 20.

48. Dubinsky, *Improper Advances*, 104.

49. *Dominion Medical Monthly and Ontario Medical Journal* (February 1897), 146–47; John R. Graham, "The Haven, 1870–1930: A Toronto Charity's Transition from a Religious to a Professional Ethos," *Histoire sociale/Social History* 25, 50 (November 1992), 296.

50. Jay Cassel, *Venereal Disease in Canada, 1838–1939* (Toronto: University of Toronto Press, 1987), 156. See also Suzann Buckley and Janice Dickin McGinnis, "Venereal Disease and Public Health Reform in Canada," *Canadian Historical Review* 63, 3 (September 1982), 337–54.

51. Mariana Valverde, *The Age of Light, Soap and Water: Moral Reform in English Canada, 1885–1925* (Toronto: McClelland and Stewart, 1991).

52. Elsa Gidlow, "Casting a Net: Excerpts from an Autobiography," *The Body Politic* (May 1982), 27–30; "Elsa Gidlow: Memoirs," *Feminist Studies* 6, 1 (Spring 1980), 107–127.

53. Rubio and Waterson, eds., *Selected Journals*, 209–10.

54. Eliane Leslau Silverman, "Women's Perceptions of Marriage on the Alberta Frontier," in David C. Jones and Ian MacPherson, eds., *Building beyond the Homestead* (Calgary: University of Calgary Press, 1985), 55.

55. See Peter Ward, *Courtship, Love, and Marriage in Nineteenth-Century English Canada* (Montreal and Kingston: McGill-Queen's University Press, 1990).

56. Mary Horodyski, "Women and the Winnipeg General Strike of 1919," *Manitoba History* 11 (Spring 1986), 29.

57. Backhouse, "Nineteenth-Century Canadian Prostitution Law," 404–5.

58. Frederick Elkin, *The Family in Canada* (Ottawa: Vanier Institute of the Family, 1964), 113; Jean Barman, "Youth, Class and Opportunity in Vancouver," paper presented to the Canadian Historical Association, Vancouver, 1983, 5.

59. Ian Davey, "Educational Reform and the Working Class: School Attendance in Hamilton, Ontario, 1851–1891," University of Toronto, Ph.D. Thesis, 1975, 134–35.

60. Joy Parr, *Labouring Children: British Immigrant Apprentices to Canada, 1869–1924* (Montreal and Kingston: McGill-Queen's University Press, 1980), 109.

61. Marion V. Royce, "Arguments over the Education of Girls — Their Admission to Grammar Schools in This Province," *Ontario History* 67, 1 (March 1975), 1–13.

62. Donna Varga Heise, "Gender Differentiated Teacher Training. The Toronto Normal School, 1877–1902," University of Toronto, M.A. Thesis, 1987; R.D. Gidney and W.P.J. Millar, *Inventing Secondary Education: The Rise of the High School in Nineteenth-Century Ontario* (Montreal and Kingston: McGill-Queen's University Press, 1990); Susan Gelman, "Women Secondary Teachers: Ontario, 1871–1930," University of Toronto, Ph.D. Thesis, 1994, chap. 3; Dunham Ladies' College Calendar (1883–84), 7; Jean Barman, "Separate and Unequal: Indian and White Girls at All Hallows School, 1884–1920," in Jean Barman Yvonne Hébert, and Don McCaskill, eds., *Indian Education in Canada, Vol. 1: The Legacy* (Vancouver: University of British Columbia Press, 1986), 114.

63. Nancy S. Jackson and Jane S. Gaskell, "White Collar Vocationalism: The Rise of Commercial Education in Ontario and British Columbia, 1870–1920," in Ruby Heap and Alison Prentice, eds., *Gender and Education in Ontario: An Historical Reader* (Toronto: Canadian Scholars' Press, 1991), espec. 174–85.

64. Patricia E. Roy, *A White Man's Province: British Columbia Politicians and Chinese and Japanese Immigrants, 1858–1914* (Vancouver: University of British Columbia Press, 1989), 180.

65. Joyce Taylor Dawson, "A Note on Research in Progress: The Needlework of the Ursulines of Early Quebec," *Material History Bulletin* 5 (Spring 1978), 73–80.

66. Barbara Riley, "Six Saucepans to One: Domestic Science vs. the Home in British Columbia 1900–1930," in Barbara K. Latham and Roberta J. Pazdro, eds., *Not*

Just Pin Money: Selected Essays on the History of Women's Work in British Columbia (Victoria: Camosun College, 1984), 168, 100; Marta Danylewycz, Nadia Fahmy-Eid, et Nicole Thivierge, "L'enseignement ménager et les 'home economics' au Québec et en Ontario au début du 20e siècle: Une analyse comparées," *in* J. Donald Wilson, ed., *An Imperfect Past: Education and Society in Canadian History* (Vancouver: Centre for the Study of Curriculum and Instruction, University of British Columbia, 1984), 109.

67. Linda Rasmussen et al., eds., *A Harvest Yet to Reap: A History of Prairie Women* (Toronto: Women's Press, 1976), 132.

68. Pamela Margaret White, "Restructuring the Domestic Sphere — Prairie Indian Women on Reserves: Image, Ideology and State Policy 1880–1930," McGill University, Ph.D. Dissertation, 1987, 114–19, 131–41, 171–72.

69. Beth Light and Alison Prentice, eds., *Pioneer and Gentlewomen of British North America, 1713–1867* (Toronto: New Hogtown Press, 1980), 82.

70. Hugh Ernest MacDermot, *Maude Abbott: A Memoir* (Toronto: Macmillan, 1941), 10.

71. *Christian Guardian* (October 30, 1872), 346.

72. Alan A. Brookes, "The Golden Age and the Exodus," *Acadiensis* 11, 1 (Fall 1981), 67.

73. Judith Fingard, "College, Career, and Community: Dalhousie Coeds 1881–1921," *in* Paul Axelrod and John G. Reid, eds., *Youth, University and Canadian Society: Essays in the Social History of Higher Education* (Montreal and Kingston: McGill-Queen's University Press, 1989), 26–50.

74. Sister Maura, *The Sisters of Charity, Halifax* (Toronto: Ryerson Press, 1956), 24, 34, 77–78; Danylewycz, *Taking the Veil*, 146.

75. Donna Ronish, "The Development of Higher Education for Women at McGill University from 1857 to 1907," McGill University, M.Ed. Thesis, 1972; Paula J.S. LaPierre, "Separate or Mixed: The Debate over Co-Education at McGill University," McGill University, M.A. Thesis, 1983; Margaret Gillett, *We Walked Very Warily: A History of Women at McGill* (Montreal: Eden Press, 1981).

76. Catherine L. Cleverdon, *The Woman Suffrage Movement in Canada*, 2nd ed. (Toronto: University of Toronto Press, 1974), chap. 2; Deborah Gorham, "Singing Up the Hill," *Canadian Dimension* 10, 8 (June 1975), 29; Carlotta Hacker, *The Indomitable Lady Doctors* (Toronto: Clarke, Irwin, 1974), chap. 2; Veronica Strong-Boag, "Canada's Women Doctors: Feminism Constrained," *in* Linda Kealey, ed., *A Not Unreasonable Claim: Women and Reform in Canada, 1880s–1920s* (Toronto: Canadian Women's Educational Press, 1979), 109–30; J.E. Thompson, "The Influence of Dr. Emily Howard Stowe on the Woman Suffrage Movement in Canada," *Ontario History* 54, 4 (December 1962), 253–66.

77. A.A. Travill, "Early Medical Co-Education and Women's Medical College, Kingston, Ontario, 1880–1894," *Historic Kingston* 30 (January 1982), 72.

78. *Canada Year Book* (1918–19); *Report of the Royal Commission on the Status of Women in Canada* (Ottawa: Information Canada, 1970), 68; see also John A. Reid, "The Education of Women at Mount Allison, 1854–1914," *Acadiensis* 12, 2 (Spring 1983), 38.

79. Danylewycz, *Taking the Veil*, 146–47.

80. Peter Laslett, "Age at Menarche in Europe since the Eighteenth Century," *in* Theodore K. Rabb and Robert I. Rotberg, eds., *The Family in History: Interdisciplinary Essays* (New York: Harper and Row, 1971), 29.

81. Ellen M. Thomas Gee, "Marriage in Nineteenth-Century Canada," *Canadian Review of Sociology and Anthropology* 19, 3 (August 1982), 315; Gee, "Female Marriage Patterns in Canada: Changes and Differentials," *Journal of Comparative Family Studies* 11, 4 (Autumn 1980), 460.

82. Lorne Tepperman, "Ethnic Variations in Marriage and Fertility: Canada, 1871," *Canadian Review of Sociology and Anthropology* 11, 4 (November 1974), 331; A. Romaniuc, *Fertility in Canada: From Baby-Boom to Baby-Bust* (Ottawa: Statistics Canada, 1984), 19; Bryan Palmer, *Working Class Experience: Rethinking the History of Canadian Labour, 1800–1991* (Toronto: McClelland and Stewart, 1992), 100; Jacques Henripin, *Trends and Factors of Fertility in Canada* (Ottawa: Federal Census Bureau, 1972), 39; Roderic P. Beaujot and Kevin McQuillan, "Social Effects of Demographic Change: Canada 1851–1981," *Journal of Canadian Studies* 21, 1 (Spring 1986), 57–59.

83. Gee, "Marriage in Nineteenth-Century Canada," 315.

84. Gee, "Female Marriage Patterns," 460.

85. Terry Chapman, "Women, Sex, and Marriage in Western Canada, 1890–1920," *Alberta History* 33, 4 (Fall 1985), 8; Rasmussen et al., eds., *Harvest*, 72.

86. Daniel Scott Smith, "Family Limitation, Sexual Control, and Domestic Feminism in Victorian America," *Feminist Studies* 1 (Winter/Spring 1973), 40–57.

87. Gilbert Malcolm Sproat, *The Nootka: Scenes and Studies of Savage Life* (1868), West Coast Heritage Series (Victoria: Sono Nis Press, 1987), 169.

88. Peter Gossage, "Absorbing Junior: The Use of Patent Medicines as Abortifacients in Nineteenth Century Montreal," *The Register* 3, 1 (March 1982), 6.

89. Varpu Lindström-Best, *Defiant Sisters: A Social History of Finnish Immigrant Women in Canada* (Toronto: Multicultural History Society of Ontario, 1988), 81.

90. Angus McLaren and Arlene Tigar McLaren, *The Bedroom and the State: The Changing Practices and Politics of Contraception and Abortion in Canada 1880–1980* (Toronto: McClelland and Stewart, 1986), 19.

91. Henripin, *Trends*, 81.

92. Joy Parr, "Hired Men: Ontario Agricultural Wage Labour in Historical Perspective," *Labour/Le travail* 15 (Spring 1985), 91–103.

93. Beaujot and McQuillan, "Social Effects," 59.

94. Margaret Conrad, " 'Sunday Always Makes Me Think of Home': Time and Place in Canadian Women's History," in Veronica Strong-Boag and Anita Clair Fellman, eds., *Rethinking Canada: The Promise of Women's History* (Toronto: Copp Clark Pitman, 1986), 74.

95. Beth Light and Joy Parr, eds., *Canadian Women on the Move, 1867–1920* (Toronto: New Hogtown Press and OISE Press, 1983), 112.

96. *The Canadian Lancet* 7 (October 1874), 57.

97. Light and Parr, eds., *Canadian Women on the Move*, 153.

98. Carrie Best, *That Lonesome Road* (New Glasgow, N.S.: Clarion Publishing, 1977), 43–44.

99. Lorna R. McLean, "Single Again: Widow's Work in the Urban Family Economy, Ottawa, 1871," *Ontario History* 83, 2 (June 1991), 127–150; Blackman, "Changing Status," 68.

100. F.H. Leacy, ed., *Historical Statistics of Canada*, 2nd ed. (Ottawa: Statistics Canada, 1983), A78–93; Tom Belton, "Homes for the Aged in Ontario, 1870–1920," unpublished paper, University of Waterloo, 1986; Teresa A. Bishop, "Peel Industrial Farm and House of Refuge: A Case Study in Institutional

Development," University of Toronto, M.A. Thesis, 1982, 35–75; Stormie Elizabeth Stewart, "The Elderly Poor in Rural Ontario: Inmates of the Wellington County House of Industry, 1877–1907," paper presented to the Canadian Historical Association, Charlottetown, 1992, 9, 14; James G. Snell, "The Newfoundland Old Age Pension Programme, 1911–1949," *Acadiensis* 23, 1 (Autumn 1993), 86–109.

CHAPTER SEVEN

The "Woman Movement"

For Canada's women reformers, the impulse for social change often began with a personal experience. Letitia Youmans recalled how, as a child, she saw the rotting body of a local drunkard, "swarming with worms" after he had lain dead and unmissed for several days. "This was my first impressive temperance lesson," she wrote, "and I still look back to it with horror."[1] While not all women activists could recall such an early and telling awakening, all could, like Youmans, document a growing awareness of needs and problems in the society surrounding them. They coupled these concerns with a growing dissatisfaction with the constraints of their prescribed roles. And co-operation with and for other women also became an identification with shared problems.

For most women, religious faith was the underpinning for their activism, just as it was the underpinning for their work in charitable associations. As Canadian women organized to change society, they found it necessary to defend explicitly the goals they had always taken for granted; as their efforts expanded in scope and scale, becoming visible and effective, activists became the objects of public criticism and even abuse. The arguments they used in response were the basis of the "woman movement," incorporating the two perspectives that continue to be influential today. The first of these, and the most characteristic of Canadian feminism, was "maternal" or "social" feminism, based on woman's role as guardian of the home. Arguing that women had special experience and values that would be crucial to society, if society would only allow them free rein, women activists insisted on their responsibility to establish order and well-being, not just for their families, but for the country. Indeed, how could they care for their families unless conditions were improved in the country? And they came to believe that, unless women had the same political rights as men, and particularly the right to vote, society would never be reformed as they wanted.

At the same time, a version of feminist beliefs often called "equal rights" or "equity" feminism focussed more directly on arguments of simple justice. This viewpoint stressed how much women resembled men, and how unjust it was that they should have fewer rights. As human beings, women were endowed with souls and abilities, but they were barred by custom and law from participating in public life. In such a context, the vote became the symbol of citizenship. A number of women had the property qualifications that would have let them vote if they had been men. Yet assemblies of men, elected by other men, continued to decide what women might or might not do. It was infuriating, quite apart from noble ideals for reforming society. Amazingly, the vote was at that time a "radical" issue that respectable women hesitated to endorse, mainly because many respectable, otherwise reasonable men found the idea outrageous.[2]

While the arguments used by the women can be labelled, the women themselves cannot. Most accepted both types of feminist arguments, emphasizing one or the other as seemed most useful or appropriate, apparently without feeling any contradiction. Most of them would have been reluctant to adopt the term "feminist," which at that time meant a quite extreme degree of commitment to women's issues. They preferred instead to speak of what was then called the "woman movement"; in this, all kinds and groups of women could co-operate.

The "woman movement" was not unique to Canada. Similar ideas and reform movements were present in other western societies. Leading feminists toured each other's countries and read each other's publications, and there is evidence of considerable cross-fertilization.[3] However, the development of the women's movement in Canada was distinctive in a number of ways. Tactics involving deliberate flouting of the law were never used in Canada, and only a few of the Canadian leaders approved of the attacks on property and politicians organized by the British militants. The traditional methods of the disenfranchised — petitions, lobbying, publicity, and private efforts at influence — remained their preferred weapons. In addition, although a national umbrella organization, the National Council of Women of Canada, played a significant role, the Canadian women's movement derived its success from the diversity and strength of many organizations rather than from a single unified or national force. Finally, in Canada, winning the franchise did not become the obsessive goal it did in some other countries.

THE POLITICS OF WOMANHOOD

Women's politics, like all Canadian politics in the latter half of the nineteenth century, was heavily influenced by religion. After 1850, evangelicalism — the belief that the world could be perfected by individual moral behaviour and efforts and that a rejuvenated evangelical social order could be achieved — became a key component of Protestant conviction. A central tenet held individuals responsible to Christ, to themselves, to their families and friends, and to the extended society. Evangelicals attributed moral superiority and redemptive power to Christian women, and especially mothers. This understanding both motivated and justified women's involvement and expanding role first in church-based organizations and later in wider-ranging activities on behalf of the family and society.[4]

The church-affiliated women's organizations were originally directed by the male governing bodies of the various denominations, but eventually some became truly independent. In the Maritimes, for example, Protestantism stimulated the growth of church societies with local women's auxiliaries. As the local Protestant churches joined together into larger national organizations, their proselytizing efforts expanded to include overseas missions in such areas as the West Indies, India, China, and Japan. The male-controlled missionary societies refused, however, to sponsor women missionaries. In Canso, Nova Scotia, Baptist women inspired by Hannah Norris formed the first separate female missionary society in 1870; similar local groups then grew rapidly. Norris was a teacher active among the poor; she learned the Mi'kmaqs' language in order to work with them. Converted as an adult and baptized in the cold waters of Canso harbour in March 1869, she applied to go to "Burmah" as a missionary. When the Baptist Foreign Mission Board rejected her application, she turned to the women of the church, who established the first female fundraising society. Soon there were thirty-two Baptist Woman's Missionary Aid societies, and with their guarantee of financial support, Hannah Norris sailed for Burma, where she served for forty-two years, as well as marrying and raising three children.[5]

The women's missionary societies grew rapidly and were successful in all the Protestant denominations. Although Baptists constituted a smaller percentage of the population in Quebec and Ontario than they did in the Maritimes, a Baptist board was formed for these provinces in 1876. And by 1885 there were 123 Baptist Woman's Missionary Aid societies in small towns and villages across the Maritimes, operating under a central regional board after 1884. Presbyterian women in Quebec established a Ladies' Auxiliary (1864), which became the Ladies' French Evangelization Society (1875), and then in 1882 became part of the Montreal Woman's Missionary Society for Home, French and Foreign Work. The Presbyterian Woman's Foreign Missionary Society, with a Western Division for Ontario, Quebec, and the western provinces and an Eastern Division for the Maritimes, was established in 1876. As for Methodist women, they created a similar association in 1881. The Anglican women's efforts were the last to get under way, starting in 1885, when seven women approached the Domestic and Foreign Missionary Society to offer the services of women as an auxiliary. The Anglican women did not get independence from their general missionary society until 1911.[6]

Women's roles in the new societies differed significantly from their earlier ones in church auxiliaries. They now raised funds for their own organizations, funds that they controlled. The amount of money raised was truly remarkable, considering that most of it came from women themselves through weekly pledges, special collections, donations, and the sale of literature and reports. In 1899, Presbyterian women from the Western Division collected no less than $45 513 from 21 000 members; in 1900, Baptist women collected $10 000 in the Maritimes alone; in 1901, Methodist women raised more than $50 000.[7] With this money the societies supported female missionaries throughout the world, and by 1899 the Western Division of the Presbyterian Woman's Foreign Missionary Society was supporting seventeen women in India and four in China. Many of the early women missionaries trained as teachers or doctors specifically for this work; one of the first three women who graduated from the Kingston Women's Medical College, Dr. Elizabeth Beatty, went to India under the sponsorship of the Presbyterian Woman's Foreign Missionary Society.[8]

Female missionaries increased the overseas effort at little cost to the churches. They were valuable to the missions because they had access to women. Canadian missionary women's educational and medical work benefitted many individual women. For example, in central India they established local dispensaries and clinics that provided valuable health-care services, while mission medical schools trained Indian women doctors. On the other hand, the imposition of western and Christian values often caused social and cultural isolation. Similar problems occurred as a result of the activities of the home-based women missionaries among Native and immigrant women.[9] Religious ideology and deep personal spirituality inspired missionary society women; at the same time, their activities also had significant institutional consequences. They challenged men's control of important work both at home and abroad. Most did not see themselves as part of a larger women's movement. Nevertheless, co-ordinating female missionary societies' activities provided many women with their first chance to develop leadership and administrative skills. Their societies were the first large-scale women's organizations in which women were able to act independently and to develop confidence in their own abilities.

Unlike the female missionary societies, the Woman's Christian Temperance Union (WCTU) was from the very start strongly identified with Canadian women's causes and concerns at home. It began as a women's group and closely guarded its independence from male intrusion, allowing men to be honorary members but not to vote. Yet there were similarities between the women's missionary movement and the temperance movement. Both were deeply Christian and drew heavily on rural communities for their members; both provided a valuable training in public speaking and in parliamentary procedure. And both were crucial to the development of the women's movement in Canada.

Letitia Youmans founded the first Canadian local of the WCTU in Picton, Ontario, in 1874. Although a women's temperance society called the Ladies' Prohibition League was established early the same year in Owen Sound, Ontario, by Mrs. R.J. Doyle, Youmans is rightly regarded as the pioneer organizer of Canadian women's temperance activities. A former ladies' academy teacher who, at age 23, married a widower with eight children, Youmans was inspired to form the Picton local after attending the founding meeting of the American WCTU. As a Methodist Sunday-school teacher, she had been horrified by the harm caused by alcohol among her students' families; in response, she had started a non-denominational temperance group for children. Youmans then progressed from local community involvement to leadership at the provincial and national levels, eventually becoming first president of both the Ontario and the Dominion Unions (in 1877 and 1883, respectively).[10]

Letitia Youmans was one of a number of Canadian women activists who earned a considerable international reputation. She was prominent in the World WCTU, whose founder, Frances Willard, wrote of how Youmans had been "loved and honored" in the United States as well as Canada, and how her powerful voice "electrified . . . her American sisters."[11] It obviously electrified Canadians also, for by 1891 there were more than 9000 members of WCTU locals in Canada. While Ontario claimed the largest number of dues-paying members — more than 4000 — British Columbia women participated to the greatest extent in proportion to the female population in that province.[12]

At its beginning stages, the WCTU focussed on the evils associated with alcohol consumption; temperance was a pressing moral and religious issue. Members were convinced that government intervention was necessary and that only complete prohibition could save society from crime, male violence, family breakdown, political corruption, and immorality. For WCTU women, the beliefs and the cause they espoused grew out of their evangelical roles and perspectives as middle-class wives and mothers, and their acknowledged responsibility to convert sinners and to protect the family from the results of male intemperance and moral weakness.[13] Most members had seen the tragic results of drunkenness, even if less horrific than Letitia Youmans's tale of a maggot-infested corpse; Youmans herself recounted many more-commonplace episodes of family disruption and domestic violence. Practical concern for the victimized wives and children led the organization to a truly radical departure from women's traditional charity to the needy. WCTU members believed they had identified a primary cause of want and disorder, and they hoped to eradicate misery at its source. But by the 1880s the organization had enlarged its analysis to advocate a wide variety of reforms, all designed to achieve a new evangelical social order.

Until the 1890s the WCTU directed its energies toward membership recruitment, individual temperance pledges, and petitions asking various levels of government to adopt prohibition. These were formidable tasks. Thousands of signatures testify to the endless hours of trudging from door to door. Attending and addressing public meetings was also a triumph for many women, who faced audiences unaccustomed and frequently hostile to the idea of women speaking in public. The members of the Picton WCTU were typical as they presented their first prohibition petition to the all-male town council. Fearing that their appearance would be regarded as "bold . . . and unwomanly," they met and prayed before entering the

A typical family temperance pledge signed by adults and children.

....

Source: Women's and Labour Studies Resource Room, Monarch Park Collegiate.

council chamber "with palpitating hearts." When the mayor insisted that the ladies should defend their own petition instead of having a council member do so, they "looked at each other in blank despair." But Letitia Youmans rose to the challenge and aroused the room with an account of "the suffering families, the freezing in the snow-drift under the influence of drink, and the amputations resulting therefrom."[14]

Through their Evangelical Departments, local WCTU members ministered to "needy" groups, especially women and children, and established a variety of social services, including reading rooms, homes for prostitutes, and visitations to the elderly, ill, and imprisoned.[15] Members also sought to have temperance teaching and materials used in both Sunday and public schools, and tried to influence doctors to cease prescribing liquor as medicine. Gradually, as all these activities proved unfruitful, the Union became convinced that the major obstacle to the achievement of its goal was the political powerlessness of women.[16] From religion-based ideas that men were morally weak and women were morally strong, they forged a demand for women to have more practical power within both family and society. This conviction was increasingly shared by other women activists, some of whom focussed more directly on women's rights.

THE QUEST FOR POLITICAL POWER

The last half of the nineteenth century saw a number of changes in married women's property law. The first known shift occurred in 1851, when New Brunswick passed "An Act to Secure to Married Women Real and Personal Property Held in Their Own Right." This legislation stated that a married woman's property, whether acquired before or after marriage, was her own separate property and, as such, was exempt from responsibility for her husband's debts and liabilities. Married women were not, however, given the right to sell or otherwise dispose of their assets. The motivation behind this early legislation appears to have been primarily economic in nature. From the late 1840s to 1851, New Brunswick experienced a financial crisis that resulted in many business failures and bankruptcies. Under the existing British common law, which gave total control over a wife's property to her husband, creditors could and did seize it to repay debts accumulated by the husband. The 1851 statute was therefore intended to protect this separate property and to preserve at least some family assets in times of economic emergency.[17]

Between 1852 and 1857, three groups of women petitioned the legislature of Canada West, requesting the passage of a married women's property act giving them some degree of freedom from control of their property by their husbands. These are the first records we know of women going to the legislature on behalf of their own property rights. Anne Macdonald "and other ladies" made the appeal in 1852, Elizabeth L. Hawley "and others" petitioned in 1856, and Elizabeth Dunlop "and others" did the same the next year. We know little about the petitioners, though Elizabeth Dunlop, at least, was apparently active in women's issues; her name appears on the list of prominent women attempting to incorporate the Toronto Magdalen Asylum and Industrial House of Refuge in 1858, to provide assistance to prostitutes and unmarried mothers.[18] These sources show that, by the 1850s, some Canadian women were increasingly concerned about their economic dependence and had organized to seek remedies. And they seem to have produced results. The 1856 petition had asked for legislation like that in New York State. In 1859 an Upper Canadian law without any British precedent recognized a married woman's right to own property. Although she could not sell it, her consent was now required if her husband wished to make the sale. Like the earlier New Brunswick measure, the Ontario legislation was, in part, designed to insulate a married woman's property from seizure by her husband's creditors. In Ontario, there was also concern for cases where drunken or improvident husbands would dispose of women's earnings, savings, or other assets, and the Women's Rights petition supporting the measure noted specifically "the injury sustained by women of the lower classes," whom common law deprived "of all pecuniary resources."[19] The drafts of the law even included permission for married women to retain their earnings. But a more moderate version was passed, and judicial interpretations tended, in practice, to restrict women's right to manage or get benefits from their property. In 1872 an Ontario statute — this time following a previous British one — gave married women control over their own earnings.[20]

At approximately the same time as the earliest-known groups of women were presenting petitions relating to married women's property, there is the first evidence of public interest in women's rights. The Toronto *Provincial Freeman* reported in 1855 that Lucy Stone, the well-known American feminist, "held forth to crowded audiences on the subject of 'WOMAN'S RIGHTS.'" Editor and abolitionist Mary Ann Shadd was encouraged that "in Toronto, with the strong attachment to antiquated notions respecting woman and her sphere, so prevalent, she was listened to patiently, applauded abundantly, and patronized extensively."[21] There was an early association between the anti-slavery movement and the budding women's rights movement. For example, in 1858, the ninety-one black members of Halifax's Cornwallis Street Baptist Church sponsored and attended two lectures: one by an escaped slave who was raising money for refugee slaves in Dresden, Ontario; the other by a former member of the British regiment on the subject of the "Rights of Women."[22] In 1871 Susan B. Anthony, the American suffragist, gave a series of lectures to enthusiastic Victoria, British Columbia, audiences. She "thundered out, night after night" that the local women were "meek, milk and water and had no rights of their own."[23] Although there is no record of a British Columbia woman's suffrage organization during the 1870s, a bill supporting the provincial vote for women was introduced into the provincial legislature in 1872. It received the support of only two members. British Columbia women property-holders did receive the municipal franchise in 1873, however, becoming the first women in Canada to be granted the right to vote after their mid-century exclusion from the franchise. Moreover, the right was given to both married and unmarried women. In January 1875, three eligible women, organized by the doughty widow Silvestria Theodora Smith, actually voted in the municipal election in spite of "jibes and catcalls."[24]

Only in 1876, it seems, was an organization formed explicitly to address women's lack of access to the political process. A small group of women founded the Toronto Women's Literary Club, whose name and subsequent history suggest that its founders felt the need to disguise its major political objectives. Discussions of educational, social, political, and economic issues, however, supported the conviction that little could be done to advance women's status — literary or otherwise — until they acquired the vote. The dynamic leader of the Toronto Women's Literary Club, Dr. Emily Howard Stowe, had confronted women's exclusion from the public realm in her own struggles to enter the medical profession. Along with other Literary Club members, she was concerned about women's educational and professional rights, the inadequate protection of women in the workplace, married women's property rights, and the need to acquire the vote. The Club facilitated the discussion of these topics; although small, it became an important catalyst for reform. Its educational program was enhanced in 1881 when one of its members, the witty and urbane Sarah Curzon, became associate editor of *Canada Citizen*, a weekly temperance newspaper, and started a regular column outlining the Club's activities and urging the adoption of woman suffrage.[25]

The Club's members must have been pleased when, in 1882, an Ontario law gave the right to vote on municipal bylaws to spinsters and widows with the requisite property qualifications, even though the full municipal franchise and the eligibility to hold office were still denied to women. In spite of, or perhaps because of, the partial character of this victory, the Literary Club discarded its disguise and publicly proclaimed the suffrage cause, adopting the following motion on February 1, 1883:

> That in view of the end for which the Toronto Women's Literary Club was formed, having been attained, viz., to foster a general and living public sentiment in favor of women suffrage, this Club hereby disband, to form a Canadian Woman Suffrage Association.[26]

To implement this motion, a quite remarkable turnout of 130 men and women attended a meeting in the Toronto City Council Chamber and agreed to organize the Canadian Women's Suffrage Association, as well as a Toronto local named the Toronto Women's Suffrage Association; both endorsed equal suffrage as their major aim.

The next two years, which saw no progress in respect to the vote, nevertheless saw additional gains in Ontario in the quest for equality with men. Women were admitted to the University of Toronto (1884), and medical colleges for women were established in both Toronto (1883) and Kingston (1883). In 1884 the full municipal franchise was extended to unmarried women with the appropriate property qualifi- cations, although without the right to hold public office. Married women were once again excluded, although in that same year Ontario passed a Married Women's Prop- erty Act giving married women the right not only to own separate property but also to deal with it — rent or sell it — without their husbands' consent. In addition, married women were for the first time allowed to enter into contracts with respect to their separate property.[27] Although this Act was limited in its effect (because few married women actually owned property), its provisions did substantially improve on existing rights. It was not until 1897 that the Ontario law was changed to permit a married woman to sign a contract whether or not she owned property, a provision that was a crucial condition of carrying on business independently.

On the Prairies, isolation, the sparseness of population, and the strenuous work of frontier homesteading and community-building limited the establishment of reform or feminist networks until the twentieth century. While there were a few non- religious women's organizations in Quebec before 1893, the major growth of women's activism took place within the Catholic church and the women's religious orders, which were growing vigorously by the second half of the nineteenth century. Old orders expanded and new ones were founded as French-Canadian women confronted the social problems that Protestant women were tackling in their benevolent and missionary societies or through the WCTU. There is intriguing evidence that some

URGENT!

Thousands of nice girls are wanted in THE CANADIAN WEST.

Over 20,000 Men are sighing for what they cannot get-WIVES! Shame!

Don't hesitate-COME AT ONCE. If you cannot come, send your sisters.

So great is the demand that anything in skirts stands a chance.

**No reasonable offer refused
They are all shy but willing.
All Prizes! No Blanks.**

Hustle up now Girls and don't miss this chance. Some of you will never get another.

Special Application Card from

An advertisement directed to single women urging them to move to the Canadian west.

Source: Courtesy of Betty Tomlinson Anderson. Donated to Centre for Women's Studies. Ontario Institute for Studies in Education.

nuns and laywomen fashioned feminist alliances to address the problems and inequities confronting women in Quebec society. But the primary responsibility for the care of the needy resided with the nuns, and their efforts in social and political reform always remained under the control of male-dominated church hierarchies.[28] Not surprisingly, convent women for the most part immersed themselves in the necessary social work rather than pressuring government to pass social reform legislation. The *religieuses* nevertheless did important innovative work; in Montreal, for example, the Grey Nuns organized and operated urban *salles d'asile* or daycare centres for the children of working women.[29]

Public service often led women to a deeper involvement in the political questions of the day. In 1885 the national WCTU formalized an effective nation-wide structure. The evangelical reform impulse had generated other socially concerned groups; by the 1890s, they too had been transformed into national organizations. An especially important example is the Young Women's Christian Association (YWCA), while the Girls' Friendly Society, an Anglican organization very much like the YWCA, was also prominent at this time. Both provided reception centres, shelters, and educational programs for single working-class women.[30] The varied objectives of these organizations

Inside the Ottawa Home for Friendless Women, 1895. Notice the babies in the basket and the elderly woman sitting at the front.

Source: William James Topley/National Archives of Canada/PA-027434.

capture the dynamism of the women's movement; together, they provided a range of opportunities for women who wished to expand their concerns beyond the home. Membership in such groups appealed to women at different stages of their life cycles. Those with young families and little free time tended to join local organizations focussed on issues affecting children. As their family responsibilities diminished, women involved themselves with broader issues at the provincial and national levels. Letitia Youmans, for instance, waited until all of her stepfamily was grown before becoming heavily involved in the public domain. But she was unusual in having not just the approval but the active support of her husband, who eventually accompanied her on temperance lecture tours.

The YWCA, the Girls' Friendly Society, the missionary societies, and the WCTU all adopted a maternal or social-feminist stance, imbued with a strong sense of Christian morality. The WCTU was initially the only group that espoused this philosophy and also articulated the need for equal political rights in order to achieve its main objective. Even then, only certain locals shared these political aims. In Victoria, British Columbia, the local WCTU unsuccessfully petitioned for the provincial vote in 1883 and repeated the process with the same result in 1885. On the east coast, the Nova Scotian WCTU locals succeeded in pressuring their legislators to introduce a municipal suffrage bill in 1884. The bill failed, but three years later unmarried women were at last granted the municipal franchise; New Brunswick women had obtained this right the previous year. These suffragist initiatives of WCTU locals were always tied to evangelical goals. For some the evangelical vision was more compelling than the reform goals. Indeed, as Ontario WCTU President, Mrs. Chisholm, told annual-meeting listeners in 1887,

> I have sometimes feared . . . when all our efforts were turned to the legal side of the question, we were in danger of forgetting to be as earnest as before with the gospel part of our work. Therefore, I would urge again upon our Unions that more attention be paid to evangelistic work and more time given to gospel temperance meetings . . . the stated object of which shall be not only to induce men and women to sign the pledge but to take the first step in a new and better life.[31]

Pragmatism more than unquestioning adherence to any particular feminist philosophy guided most women activists. Between 1884 and 1893, the Woman's Christian Temperance Union continued its educational and social service programs and intensified political activities through its national, provincial, and local organizations. In 1891 it formally endorsed woman suffrage at all levels of government. Repeated petitions, delegations to provincial and federal governments, and demands for plebiscites kept the question of votes for women before the public. This tireless work played a crucial role in bringing Canadians to accept the notion of political rights for women.

The Toronto-based Canadian Women's Suffrage Association, in the meantime, seems to have been relatively inactive in the second half of the 1880s, after a very energetic and effective first year. There are a number of possible explanations for this hiatus. Activists may have been temporarily satisfied with the real, though limited, gains that women had made. The leaders may well have felt the need to rest, to recharge their energies, and to plan future directions for the movement; Emily Stowe and her daughter Augusta Stowe-Gullen were both heavily involved in their professional lives at this time. In addition, according to Stowe, the presence of men sapped the organization of its vitality:

> We admitted the opposite sex as members and the effect was demoralizing. The old idea of female dependence crept in and the ladies began to rely on the gentlemen rather than upon their own efforts.[32]

Whatever the reason for the lull, the Canadian Women's Suffrage Association entered into a renewed phase of activity in 1889. Meeting in Emily Stowe's home, members agreed to engage Dr. Anna Howard Shaw, the eloquent American suffragist and preacher, to address a Toronto public meeting. The enthusiasm generated by this event led to the creation of a renewed and more effective suffrage organization, the Dominion Women's Enfranchisement Association. Stowe was elected the group's first president.

Immediately after its founding, the Association took action, along with the Toronto WCTU, to support passage of a suffrage bill for Ontario sponsored by John Waters, a Liberal member of the provincial legislature. Waters had introduced

suffrage proposals every year beginning in 1885, some aimed at extending the municipal franchise to married women, others at giving the provincial vote to unmarried
women; it was clear that his efforts needed organized support. But although Emily
Stowe was described as addressing legislators "in a style that would have done justice
to an Oxford lecturer," the bill was defeated; Stowe commented tartly that she wished
Attorney-General Mowat, who had voted against woman suffrage, had been "less the
politician and more the Christian."[33] During its first year, the Dominion Women's
Enfranchisement Association also mounted a lecture series to increase public knowledge about and sympathy for its causes, bringing Dr. Shaw back and ending with a
stirring presentation by Susan B. Anthony. The success of this series convinced the
Association that it could command broader support; it hired an American organizer
to establish branch associations, and in 1890 it held its first national convention. A
number of Canadian delegates from outside Ontario attended, as did several representatives of the American movement, but only a few branches were organized. The
Dominion Women's Enfranchisement Association's national aspirations remained
elusive. Like the earlier Canadian Women's Suffrage Association, it was Toronto-
based, was directed and dominated by Toronto members, and never fully succeeded
in the difficult task of organizing a nation-wide suffrage group.[34]

THE 1890s: CONSOLIDATION

In the 1890s the women's movement continued to pursue other political goals.
Toronto feminists celebrated a notable success in 1892, when three women won
election to the Toronto School Board as trustees. Arguing that education was of
particular interest to women because of their maternal role, movement activists had
evidently persuaded a larger public that women should participate in school management. The right was of particular interest to women teachers, who felt that female
trustees would understand their problems and work harder to improve their conditions of work. One of the first women trustees was Augusta Stowe-Gullen. As a
young woman she had participated in the discussions of the Toronto Women's Literary Club; she later became the first woman doctor to graduate from a Canadian
medical college and the first woman staff member of the recently established Toronto
Woman's Medical College. A founding member of the Dominion Women's Enfranchisement Association, she followed her mother as its president in 1903.[35]

The 1890s witnessed a general broadening of middle-class women's reform
aspirations and activities. The Dominion Women's Enfranchisement Association was
one of the women's groups that supported Clara Brett Martin's struggle to become
a lawyer. The passage of the 1892 Ontario statute permitting women to study and
practice law in the province was greatly assisted by the co-operative efforts of mainstream women's groups; such co-operation was now more than ever characteristic
of the women's movement.

It was increasingly apparent that women's roles and status in society were
undergoing a transformation, a transformation that, although uneven across the
Dominion, was in evidence everywhere as Canada changed from a rural to an urban
society. For middle-class city women, the problems associated with urban industrial
development gave rise to a variety of new causes. Women reformers responded by
founding hostels for immigrant women; housekeeping and health standards became

an issue; conditions in jails and prisons developed into another.[36] Nor did temperance and suffrage cease to be important issues. Rather, they became the central foci for a variety of concerns emphasizing woman's role as protector of the home. As Canadian women approached the end of the nineteenth century, they asserted their right and responsibility to be "housekeepers" of the public realm.

The flowering of reform interest led, in 1893, to the establishment of the National Council of Women of Canada (NCWC), an umbrella group that comprised representatives from national women's organizations. Affiliated Local Councils of Women (LCWs) served likewise as umbrella groups for organizations operating within their communities, usually including branches of national women's groups like the YWCA, and local societies such as women teachers' associations. The Council's major objective was to encourage and support the extension of women's domestic roles into the larger society, as its constitution made clear:

> We, Women of Canada, sincerely believing that the best good of our homes and nation will be advanced by our own greater unity of thought, sympathy, and purpose, and that an organized movement of women will best conserve the greatest good of the Family and State, do hereby band ourselves together to further the application of the Golden Rule to society, custom and law.[37]

The founder of Canada's National Council of Women was the indefatigable Lady Ishbel Marjoribanks Gordon, Countess of Aberdeen. Lady Aberdeen was elected president of the International Council of Women during its Congress at the Chicago World Fair in 1893. An enthusiastic and energetic supporter of reform causes, Lady Aberdeen was well known to many Canadian women reformers for her work on behalf of British women and children. She first visited Canada with her husband in 1890 and helped found the Aberdeen Association to provide reading materials for isolated settlers. Lady Aberdeen came to Canada for a longer stay when her husband was appointed governor-general in 1893. The Victorian Order of Nurses, first proposed by the Vancouver Local Council of Women, also benefitted by the sponsorship of Lady Aberdeen. This organization, established in 1897, provided visiting nurses for areas not served by trained medical help. Lady Aberdeen held the dual presidency of the Canadian and International Councils of Women until her husband's tour of duty in Canada ended in 1898. Devoting both time and money to the National Council's development, she remained a staunch supporter of its activities until the 1920s.[38]

Aware of the potential divisiveness of political and religious differences, Lady Aberdeen, with difficulty, got agreement at the outset that Canada's National Council would avoid activities or positions that allied it with any particular creed or political organization. Although personally sympathetic to woman suffrage, she refrained from publicly endorsing it so as not to alienate more-conservative women. Largely through her influence, the National Council also adopted silent instead of spoken prayer in the hope of attracting Catholic, Jewish, and other non-Protestant women's groups while still remaining acceptable in an overwhelmingly Protestant society. Seven urban Jewish women's groups affiliated with the NCWC through locals in Hamilton, Montreal, and Toronto before the turn of the century, but they made up only 3 percent of the locals' membership. Although they constituted some 5 to 10 percent of the membership, Catholic women also did not join the NCWC in large numbers. Despite

Lady Aberdeen and a farm woman, Manitoba, 1890.

....

Source: Provincial Archives of Manitoba (N7573). Photo by Lord Aberdeen.

its official constitution as a non-sectarian organization, the NCWC and the majority of its members promoted and followed the strongly held religious beliefs of the Protestant middle-class majority. In the 1890s, especially at the Local Council level, religious or broadly defined moral or spiritual societies dominated the membership and policy development.[39] As with other women's groups, the impulse to convert people and to improve society underscored the work of NCWC members and contributed substantially to the rapid spread of Local Councils.

But the decision against audible prayer so alienated the Methodist, Presbyterian, and Congregational women's missionary societies that they did not affiliate — nor did they accept the invitation to attend the NCWC's second annual meeting in 1895 as "fraternal" observers.[40] The NCWC's public non-denominational stance also lost it the immediate support of the Dominion WCTU, the largest (and the only effective) nationally organized women's reform association at the time. Although the Woman's Christian Temperance Union was officially non-denominational, its members believed that their Union and its causes were essentially and rigorously Christian, as their name stated. For them, silent prayer was an unacceptable denial of the need for an explicit religious commitment. The Dominion WCTU consequently refused to affiliate with the newly formed National Council, as did other Christian women's associations (including the National YWCA). As it turned out, the National YWCA eventually affiliated in 1914, and the Dominion WCTU did so in 1921; some local branches of the YWCA and the WCTU joined Local Councils of Women even earlier.[41] The early hostility between the Dominion WCTU and the National Council reflected in part the different origins of the two groups' leaders: the WCTU tended to draw on small communities and the middle or lower middle class; the National

Council was led by upper-middle-class women from small towns and cities. Lady Aberdeen herself disapproved of some aspects of the WCTU, noting acidly in her journal, "They train their younger women to be so painfully aggressive and self-asserting on all matters & on all occasions. They are essentially *American*."[42]

Although the National Council had difficulty encompassing all women's groups, its organizational structure did create a nation-wide network for organized women's activities and communication. Within six years of its founding, seven Dominion-wide societies affiliated: the Victorian Order of Nurses, the Girls' Friendly Society, the Dominion Women's Enfranchisement Association, the Dominion Order of King's Daughters, the Lady Aberdeen Association for Distribution of Literature to Settlers in the West, the Women's Art Association of Canada, and the National Home Reading Union. Also, within six years, twenty-three Local Councils were set up in towns and cities from Charlottetown to Victoria. For example, the Winnipeg LCW, founded in 1894, affiliated members of the Children's Home, the Women's Hospital Aid Society, the Central Woman's Christian Temperance Union, the Free Kindergarten, the Woman's Christian Union, the Young Women's Temperance Union, and the Lady Aberdeen Association.[43] Once the basic structure was in place, local and national resolutions determined Council programs. Members discussed, studied, and recommended reforms relating to such diverse areas as dental and medical health, "pernicious" literature, truancy, prostitution and the "white slave trade," the provision of recreational facilities, and immigration policy. In some instances, they set up standing committees to examine a cluster of related concerns, as with the important committees on laws for the protection of women and children, and issues related to public health. The Council's approach reflected its basically Christian, upper-middle-class, and urban membership, but its programs, while cautious, nevertheless contained the seeds of significant reform.[44]

For rural women, physical isolation created sets of problems and responses that were different from those of city women. At the same time, they too were affected by the changing commercial and industrial scene. Concern for their children, for themselves, and for other rural women, and a sense that rural problems also demanded political solutions, drew rural women into new organizations focussing on their own particular needs. As with many urban activists, it was often a personal experience or observation that prompted a reform response. Such was reportedly the case for Adelaide Hoodless, whose youngest child died as a result of drinking impure milk. Galvanized to action, she determined to eradicate this common cause of infant mortality. Working initially through the Hamilton, Ontario, Young Women's Christian Association, Hoodless concentrated on the need for educational programs dealing with nutrition and sanitation. She soon became an influential advocate of public-school domestic science courses, "pure milk" legislation, and the public health movement. Already familiar with the activities of the Farmers' Institutes, a men's organization designed to improve agricultural practices, she told an audience of Wentworth County women that they too needed an organization to promote their interests; she proposed an affiliated institute to foster homecraft and educated motherhood. Spurred on by this suggestion, the women established in February 1897 a separate, rather than an affiliated, organization: the Women's Institute of Saltfleet (Stoney Creek). Its stated objectives were ambitious and optimistic, emphasizing the role of science in the home:

to promote that knowledge of household science which shall lead to the improvement in household architecture with special attention to home sanitation, to a better understanding of economics and hygienic value of foods and fuels, and to a more scientific care of children.

Their goal was "raising the general standards of health of our people."[45]

Although Hoodless was made honorary president of this first Women's Institute, she did not become involved in its work, concentrating instead on promoting school-based domestic science. The Women's Institutes spread slowly at first, hampered by the problems of organization within isolated rural communities, and by the lack of money to hire qualified resource people. By 1900 there were only three branches. Convinced of the advantages to rural society, the Ontario provincial government offered assistance in organizing Women's Institutes, including cash subsidies for hiring lecturers and demonstrators to teach courses in hygiene, nutrition, cooking, home nursing, and sewing. The response was overwhelming, and by 1903 there were fifty-two branches throughout the province, with a dues-paying membership of 4151. As their popularity suggests, the Women's Institutes met important needs for rural women. They also played a significant role in the early development of continuing education for adults, as branches extended their initial concerns beyond the farm home itself, seeking to improve rural schools, introduce preventive health measures for children, and set up cultural programs for both men and women in their communities.[46]

Other women reformers shared the Women's Institutes' interest in improving household management and childrearing practices in accordance with anglo-Canadian and middle-class standards. The National Council of Women had already resolved in 1894 to lobby for domestic science courses in the schools, an initiative designed not only to further women's education as "proper" wives and mothers, but also to provide better-trained domestics for those who could afford them.[47] Similarly, during the 1890s the Woman's Christian Temperance Union expanded its plan for a "moral society" to include domestic science education and manual training.

All women's organizations of this period had an expanding and diverse range of reform interests. The WCTU, for instance, initiated "social purity" campaigns in the hope of ridding society of such perceived evils as prostitution and gambling, both of which all too often accompanied excessive drinking. Some carried such programs further, worrying about the effects of nude art or even of allowing young women and men to dance together in modern dances such as the waltz. Members urged mothers to protect their daughters from temptation for their own sake and in society's interest. By 1900 the WCTU boasted 26 different departments organized around separate issues but united in the belief that social reform could be achieved through female activism. Yet prohibition remained a primary goal. The federal government's refusal to enact temperance legislation prompted the WCTU to pursue its suffrage campaign with increased vigour.

THE TACTICS OF REFORM

Endorsement of suffrage as the means of achieving prohibition quickly became part of the platform of the Manitoba WCTU, organized in the early 1890s by a committed group of Winnipeg women. This innovative group — which included Dr. Amelia Yeomans, journalist Cora Hind, and Mrs. J.A. McClung, a temperance advocate who was the future mother-in-law of Nellie McClung — staged a "Mock Parliament" in 1893, with the women taking roles for and against suffrage. The event forcefully demonstrated the absurdity of much of the opposition to female suffrage and received favourable publicity in the local press, as did a similar 1896 Mock Parliament staged by the Dominion Women's Enfranchisement Association in co-operation with the Ontario WCTU. While these tactics did not result in legislation, they did serve to draw attention to the suffrage cause. In Manitoba the renewal of publicity, fired by WCTU disillusionment with the negative legislative response to a prohibition petition, led to the founding of the Manitoba Equal Franchise Club in 1894. The crucial factor in the founding of this, the first English-speaking suffrage organization west of Ontario, was the appointment of Yeomans as the provincial president of the Dominion Women's Enfranchisement Association. The Winnipeg-based Club provided information and public education about women's political rights, although it cannot be described as having exerted a lasting influence.[48]

The Icelandic community in Manitoba generated one of the earliest expressions of pro-suffrage opinion. An Icelandic population was firmly established in the province by the 1890s, but it remained isolated from the Anglo-Saxon majority by its different language and culture. A major distinction between the two communities was the role and status of women. The cultural, economic, and political participation of Icelandic women drew not only on a solid community base, but also on a long tradition of equal rights for women. An active Icelandic Women's Society existed in Winnipeg as early as 1881. In that year, the Society staged a full-length play and held a tombola and other fundraising activities. The results were impressive. Records detail donations of $65 to the newspaper Franfar, $122 to school work by the Progressive Society, $87 to pay the tuition of two women attending a convent school, and $50 toward the erecting of a monument to Passion Hymn author Rev. Hullgrimur Petursson. At the end of the year, $150 remained in reserve. One generous teacher, Gudrun Jonsdottir, contributed half her monthly wages of $15 to support the school work. Also under the Society's auspices a regular column, written by various Icelandic women, began publication on January 16, 1890, in the newspaper Heimskringla. Not all Icelandic men supported the women's initiative: one critic called the articles "nonsense" and condemned the paper for their publication.[49]

Determined to regain in Canada the status that they had enjoyed before emigrating, Icelandic women mounted a sustained campaign, forming suffrage associations and petitioning the legislature. In 1890 a platform debate on suffrage engaged those attending at the Argyle settlement. Margret J. Benedictsson became a major force in the Icelandic suffrage movement. Born in Iceland in 1866, and orphaned at age 13, she learned to care for herself. She emigrated in 1887 to North Dakota but subsequently moved to Winnipeg, where she studied shorthand and typing at business college. Between 1898 and 1910, Benedictsson and her husband, Sigfus, published a magazine called Freyja (Woman); its articles advocated political, social, legal, and economic equality for women. In 1908 Benedictsson founded an Icelandic suffrage association, Tilraum (Endeavour), in Winnipeg. A second society, Sigurvon (Hope of Victory), worked in Gimli from 1910. Despite a concern for temperance shared with anglophone women, and contacts with the Manitoba Equal Franchise Club, Icelandic feminists remained relatively separate from the wider women's movement. Certainly Benedictsson's outspoken views on women's rights tended to set her apart from many suffrage supporters.[50]

The difficulties of building a strong common front among women of different economic and cultural backgrounds are further illustrated in Quebec. However, while the mainstream Manitoba suffrage activists appear to have made little effort to communicate or co-operate with Icelandic women, the very active Montreal Local Council of Women initially consisted of both French and English women's groups. It strongly supported suffrage from the outset. Local Council women struggled valiantly, if largely unsuccessfully, to open the professions and higher education to women, to effect urban reforms, and to abolish legal discrimination against women. Eventually, however, the French women involved in the Montreal Local Council came to realize that the Council's ideas and activities reflected British Protestant values unacceptable to the vast majority of French-Canadian Catholic women. Influenced also by the Catholic feminism then developing in France, in 1907 Marie Gérin-Lajoie, Caroline Béique, and Joséphine Marchand-Dandurand, all prominent leaders in French-Canadian society, founded an explicitly francophone, Catholic, and separate organization. Organized along lines similar to the Montreal Local Council of Women and often collaborating with it, the *Fédération nationale Saint-Jean-Baptiste* linked the few existing French-speaking laywomen's groups and established three areas of concern —charity, education, and economics. Under the latter heading, the *Fédération* sought to improve the plight of working women, and fostered the establishment of associations for store employees, factory workers, office employees, servants, teachers, and businesswomen. These associations acted as mutual aid societies and provided

An 1888 newspaper drawing of a charitable lady distributing coupons to a poor family in Montreal. The coupons could be exchanged for food or other family necessities.

Source: *Une Visite chez les Pauvres, Le Monde* illustré, no. 254 (16 mars 1889), p. 364. Courtesy of Bibliothèque nationale du Québec.

members with religious support as well as technical and homemaking courses. While the need for political rights was recognized by *Fédération* members, who encouraged women to exercise those municipal rights that they had obtained, escalating opposition by the Catholic church inhibited full support for suffrage.[51]

The role of religion in relation to women's public activities was also evident in the Maritime provinces. There Protestantism provided the major outlet for female energies; women perhaps felt less need for involvement in reform causes, such as a major campaign for the vote, that would take them beyond the church. The relatively small size of the urban middle class also likely limited the range of causes adopted by activist wives and daughters. Nevertheless, temperance, prostitute "rescue and prevention," and child welfare caught the attention of urban reformers in Nova Scotia, where WCTU locals actively supported suffrage from their formation in the early 1880s through the mid-1890s.[52] Leaders of the Halifax WCTU organized a Local Council of Women in 1893, which continued support for the cause. Their zeal and work for the franchise is shown by the annual doubling of pro-suffrage petition signatures from 3000 in 1893 to between 6000 and 7000 the next year, and more than 12 000 names in 1895.[53] After 1895, interest in suffrage apparently waned in the midst of a wave of anti-feminist propaganda, much of it emanating from the Roman Catholic archbishop of Halifax. The evidence suggests that Halifax feminists did not abandon the suffrage question, but instead avoided confrontation by pragmatically shifting their emphasis toward achievable social reform goals (such as the organization of a branch of the Victorian Order of Nurses). These tactics enabled the Halifax Local Council to attract support, and eventually — in 1910, when progress appeared more likely — once again to endorse suffrage.[54]

Suffrage was also a topic on the mind of a New Brunswick-born Acadian woman teaching in Nova Scotia. Between 1895 and 1898 Emilie Carrier LeBlanc, under the pseudonym of "Marichette," wrote a series of thirteen letters about the lives and aspirations of Acadian women to *L'Evangeline*, the major French Maritime newspaper. An avowed supporter of temperance and of women's education, in a February 1895 letter Marichette addressed the question of the female franchise, punning on the word "suffrager" to describe the "suffering" of Acadian women impatiently awaiting suffrage. And in March 1895 she supported women's claim to the vote with a witty and impertinent version of God's creation of Eve:

> When He was making woman, He found Adam, "le boss" of all men, dozing with the sun shining on his belly, too lazy to work in his garden. He ripped out Adam's brain and took the best stuff out of it and made woman, who has saved man from disaster.

For Marichette, women were superior to men, and should have "worn the pants and governed the country."[55] Evidently her stance provoked *L'Evangeline*'s readers, editors, or owners, for within two months the paper editorially opposed woman's suffrage and announced its intention not to publish favourable views from other writers on the question. However, owing to Marichette's popularity, the newspaper did continue to publish her letters, in spite of their controversial content.[56]

The only recorded separate women's suffrage association to exist in the Maritimes and Newfoundland before World War I, the Women's Enfranchisement Association of New Brunswick, was organized in 1894 and articulated equal rights arguments to advance its cause. The provincial WCTU remained the major pro-suffrage supporter, doing so from a social-feminist perspective that focussed on women's special nurturing and domestic roles. These ideological differences prevented a close relationship between the two groups, while the Saint John Local Council of Women refused to support suffrage for any reason. The Women's Enfranchisement Association attempted to co-operate with both the Local Council, of which it was an affiliate, and the WCTU. Increasingly frustrated by the Council's unwillingness to endorse woman suffrage, the Association developed its own political agenda. Between 1899 and 1902, it expressed support for equal pay for equal work and argued that there was a need for more-collectivist approaches to social life, as well as for equality between men and women. The alienated Local Council responded by being outspokenly critical of such ideas at its 1902 annual meeting, precipitating the withdrawal of the Enfranchisement Association. That withdrawal, though it proved only temporary, was nevertheless evidence of the way in which feminist forces could polarize. During the early 1890s, WCTU members campaigned for suffrage in Newfoundland. The issue was debated twice in the legislature and defeated on both occasions. The narrow base of evangelical support limited WCTU activities in this province, where suffrage did not re-appear as an issue until after World War I. In Prince Edward Island, even women active in the WCTU showed little interest in the question of suffrage. By 1900, the province had already adopted prohibition; evidently less-radical tactics had succeeded in achieving WCTU members' most cherished goal.[57] The situation in British Columbia was very different. There suffrage and temperance reform remained closely linked. Until the formation of the Political Equality League in 1910, the only formal voice petitioning and supporting bills in the cause of suffrage was that of the anti-liquor lobby. In this respect British Columbia resembled Manitoba and Ontario, where temperance women continued to be the primary suffrage agitators between 1896 and 1905.

As time went on, organized middle-class women demonstrated their distinct and separate ability to perceive and respond to social problems. Although disagreements existed between individual women and women's groups, a measure of unity was fashioned at the community, provincial, national, and even international levels. The WCTU, missionary societies of various denominations, and suffrage organizations affiliated formally or linked themselves informally with other organizations such as the YWCA, Women's Institutes, and NCWC, to take advantage of the power that comes with organization and to break down the isolation of women in their homes. Together they moulded a lobby committed to reform.

The work of enrolling members and of developing organizations that dominated these years taught women the techniques of public speaking and of pressure politics. Although the provincial and federal franchises had yet to be won, a number of other political efforts bore fruit. Women became eligible to be elected to school boards, and could vote in municipal elections in many jurisdictions. Between 1872 and 1907, Married Women's Property Acts were passed in all the common-law provinces except Alberta.[58] A married woman's personal property, including her earnings, were at last her own.

Laws were also passed to help deserted wives. In Newfoundland, legislation dated from 1872, and in 1888 Ontario followed suit, pegging assistance at $5 per week. Wives who left husbands because they were cruel or refused to support them were not eligible for the assistance, because they rather than the husbands had technically deserted. Still, such laws were a beginning, and between 1900 and 1911, Manitoba, British Columbia, and Saskatchewan also passed laws designed to help women who had been abandoned by their husbands.

The legislation that women reformers lobbied for and won was designed to uphold the family and to protect women. This protection did not, however, extend to married Native women. Under the 1876 Indian Act and its 1884 revisions, the federal government took away their property rights on reserves and severely restricted the inheritance right of widows.[59] Yet for other women, whether working, married, or deserted, the new laws constituted progress. They also showed that organized women could have a positive influence. In some instances, however, such as activities directed at "Canadianizing" immigrants and imposing middle-class values and standards of "proper" behaviour upon them and working-class women, the influence was less positive.

Although the activist groups never represented all Canadian women, for those involved, they nevertheless provided a resource for action and sisterhood. Few organizations attempted to forge alliances across race, ethnic, or class lines, but most were not completely unresponsive to the concerns of women different from their own members. For their part, members of these excluded groups developed or joined organizations that served their own communities and encouraged their participation. Within the Salvation Army, for example, working-class women in the 1890s found a more congenial outlet than that offered by the mainstream Protestant churches for combining religious fervour with work directed at reducing male drunkenness and protecting the family. In like manner, adhering to traditional female roles and responsibilities, black women in Chatham, Ontario, organized the Victoria Benevolent Society to provide money and social relief to members of their community. On the west coast, the Vancouver Island Committee of Coloured Ladies raised funds to assist ex-slaves. The religious impulses that underpinned these charitable activities were explicitly articulated in the 1882 formation of the Black Women's Home Missionary Society of Amherstburg, Ontario. Although considerably smaller than its white Protestant counterparts, the Society also marked the emergence of women into leadership positions in their church for the first time and provided opportunities for some to undertake overseas conversion work in Africa.[60]

Despite differences in focus and size, and in the race, class, and ethnicity of members, all of these organizations shared traditional interests in the new, wider view that they brought to problems concerning other women, children, the family, the church, and the community. And in that continuity, reform-minded women found a respectable, acceptable rationale for their activities and for the expansion of their field of endeavour.

NOTES

1. Letitia Youmans, *Campaign Echoes: The Autobiography of Letitia Youmans* (Toronto: William Briggs, 1893), 42.
2. Naomi Black, *Social Feminism* (Ithaca, N.Y.: Cornell University Press, 1989).
3. Deborah Gorham, "English Militancy and the Canadian Suffrage Movement," *Atlantis* 1, 1 (Fall 1975), 83–112; Gorham, "WSPU Deputation to Prime Minister

Borden, 1912," *Atlantis* 5, 2 (Spring 1980), 188–95; Ian Tyrrel, *Women's World, Women's Empire: The Women's Christian Temperance Union in International Perspective* (Chapel Hill: University of North Carolina Press, 1991); Margot I. Duley, *Where Once Our Mothers Stood We Stand: Women's Suffrage in Newfoundland 1890–1925* (Charlottetown: gynergy books, 1993), 55–57, 77–78.

4. Sharon Anne Cooke, " 'Continued and Preserving Combat': The Ontario Woman's Christian Temperance Union—A Study in Evangelical Feminism," paper presented to the Canadian Historical Association, Kingston, 1991.

5. E.C. Merrick, *These Impossible Women: The Story of the United Baptist Woman's Missionary Union of the Maritime Provinces* (Fredericton: Brunswick Press, 1970), 13–16.

6. Wendy Mitchinson, "Aspects of Reform: Four Women's Organizations in Nineteenth Century Canada," York University, Ph.D. Thesis, 1977, 69, 76.

7. Wendy Mitchinson, "Canadian Women and Church Missionary Societies," *Atlantis* 2, 2 (Spring 1977), 60–62.

8. Carlotta Hacker, *The Indomitable Lady Doctors* (Toronto: Clarke, Irwin, 1974), 68–69; Loraine Gordon, "Doctor Margaret Norris Patterson: First Woman Police Magistrate in Eastern Canada—Toronto—January 1922 to November 1934," *Atlantis* 10, 2 (Autumn 1984), 97.

9. Ruth Compton Brouwer, *New Women for God: Canadian Presbyterian Women and India Missions, 1876–1914* (Toronto: University of Toronto Press, 1990); Rosemary R. Gagan, *A Sensitive Independence: Canadian Methodist Women Missionaries in Canada and the Orient, 1881–1925* (Montreal and Kingston: McGill-Queen's University Press, 1992); Margaret Whitehead, " 'A Useful Christian Woman': First Nations' Women and Protestant Missionary Work in British Columbia," *Atlantis* 18, 1–2 (Fall/Winter 1992; Spring/Summer 1993), 142–166; Michael Owen, " 'Lighting the Pathways for New Canadians': Methodist and United Church WMS in Eastern Alberta, 1904–1940," in Catherine A. Cavanaugh and Randi R. Warne, eds., *Standing on New Ground: Women in Alberta* (Edmonton: University of Alberta Press, 1993), 1–18; Mariana Valverde, " 'When the Mother of the Race Is Free': Race, Reproduction and Sexuality in First-Wave Feminism," in Franca Iacovetta and Mariana Valverde, eds., *Gender Conflicts: New Essays in Women's History* (Toronto: University of Toronto Press, 1992), 10–11.

10. Wendy Mitchinson, "The Woman's Christian Temperance Union: A Study in Organization," *International Journal of Women's Studies* 4, 2 (March/April 1981), 143–56.

11. Frances Willard, "Introduction," in Youmans, *Campaign Echoes*, 18; Suzanne M. Marilley, "Frances Willard and the Feminism of Fear," *Feminist Studies* 19, 1 (Spring 1993), 130–131.

12. Mitchinson, "Woman's Christian Temperance Union," 148–49.

13. Cooke, " 'Continued and Preserving Combat,' " 5.

14. Youmans, *Campaign Echoes*, 106–7.

15. Cooke, " 'Continued and Preserving Combat,' " 13.

16. Wendy Mitchinson, "The WCTU: For God, Home and Native Land: A Study in Nineteenth-Century Feminism," in Linda Kealey, ed., *A Not Unreasonable Claim: Women and Reform in Canada, 1880s–1920s* (Toronto: Canadian Women's Educational Press, 1979), 155.

17. Constance B. Backhouse, "Married Women's Property Law in Nineteenth-Century Canada," in Bettina Bradbury, ed., *Canadian Family History: Selected Readings* (Toronto: Copp Clark Pitman, 1992), 329–30.

18. Communication from Mary Jane Mossman.
19. *The Globe* (January 9, 1857), 1.
20. Backhouse, "Married Women's Property Law," 330–42.
21. Jim Bearden and Linda Jean Butler, *Shadd: The Life and Times of Mary Shadd Cary* (Toronto: NC Press, 1977), 160–61.
22. Allen P. Stouffer, "Towards a Redrawing of Nova Scotia Black History: A First Look at Mid Nineteenth Century Halifax," paper presented to the Canadian Historical Association, Ottawa, 1993, 5.
23. Elizabeth Forbes, *Wild Roses at Their Feet: Pioneer Women of Vancouver Island* (Vancouver: Evergreen, 1971), 27–28.
24. Forbes, *Wild Roses*, 7; Michael H. Cramer, "Public and Political — Documents of the Woman's Suffrage Campaign in British Columbia, 1871–1917: The View from Victoria," in Barbara Latham and Cathy Kess, eds., *In Her Own Right: Selected Essays on Women's History in B.C.* (Victoria: Camosun College, 1980), 79–100.
25. Edith M. Luke, "Woman Suffrage in Canada," *Canadian Magazine* 5 (1895), 330.
26. Luke, "Woman Suffrage in Canada," 330.
27. Linda Silver Dranoff, *Women in Canadian Life: Law* (Toronto: Fitzhenry and Whiteside, 1977), 45–59; Backhouse, "Married Women's Property Law," 341.
28. Jan Noel, " 'Femmes Fortes' and the Montreal Poor," in Wendy Mitchinson et al., eds., *Canadian Women: A Reader* (Toronto: Harcourt Brace, 1996), 68–85; Marta Danylewycz, *Taking the Veil: An Alternative to Marriage, Motherhood, and Spinsterhood in Quebec, 1840–1920* (Toronto: McClelland and Stewart, 1987), espec. chap. 5.
29. See D. Suzanne Cross, "The Neglected Majority: The Changing Role of Women in 19th Century Montreal," in Susan Mann Trofimenkoff and Alison Prentice, eds., *The Neglected Majority: Essays in Canadian Women's History* (Toronto: McClelland and Stewart, 1977), vol. 1, 75–77; Micheline Dumont-Johnson, "Des garderies au XXIXe siècle: Les salles d'asile des Soeurs Grises à Montréal," *Revue d'histoire de l'Amérique française* 34, 1 (juin 1980), 27–55.
30. Diana Pedersen, " 'Keeping Our Good Girls Good': The YWCA and the 'Girl Problem' 1870–1930," *Canadian Woman Studies/Les cahiers de la femme* 7, 4 (Winter 1986), 20–24; Josephine P. Harshaw, *When Women Work Together: A History of the Young Women's Christian Association in Canada, 1870–1966* (Toronto: Ryerson Press, 1966); Mary Quayle Innis, *Unfold the Years: A History of the Young Women's Christian Association in Canada* (Toronto: McClelland and Stewart, 1949); Pedersen, "Providing a Woman's Conscience: The YWCA, Female Evangelicalism, and the Girl in the City, 1870–1930," in Mitchinson et al., eds., *Canadian Women: A Reader*, 194–210.
31. Annual Report of the Woman's Christian Temperance Union, Ontario (1887), 40.
32. Joanne Emily Thompson, "The Influence of Dr. Emily Howard Stowe on the Woman Suffrage Movement in Canada," *Ontario History* 54, 4 (December 1962), 259.
33. Thompson, "Influence," 260–61.
34. Catherine L. Cleverdon, *The Woman Suffrage Movement in Canada*, 2nd ed. (Toronto: University of Toronto Press, 1974), 22–26.
35. Hacker, *Indomitable Lady Doctors*, 26–35.
36. John R. Graham, "The Haven, 1878–1930: A Toronto Charity's Transition from a Religious to a Professional Ethos," *Histoire sociale/Social History* 25, 50 (November 1992), 283–306.
37. Veronica Strong-Boag, *The Parliament of Women: The National Council of Women of Canada 1893–1929* (Ottawa: National Museums of Canada, 1976), 81.

38. Strong-Boag, *Parliament of Women*, 131–46; N.E.S. Griffiths, *The Splendid Vision: Centennial History of the National Council of Women of Canada, 1893–1993* (Ottawa: Carleton University Press, 1993), 13–47, 65.

39. Beverly Boutillier, "Gender, Faith and the Ideal of Female Unity in Late Victorian Canada: The National Council of Women and the Silent Prayer Debate of 1895," unpublished paper, 1994, 7, 26 n. 14, 8.

40. Boutillier, "Gender," 28 n. 26.

41. Mitchinson, "Woman's Christian Temperance Union," 152–53; Strong-Boag, *Parliament of Women*, 78–79; Griffiths, *Splendid Vision*, 13–15.

42. Lady Aberdeen, *The Canadian Journal of Lady Aberdeen*, edited by J.T. Saywell (Toronto: University of Toronto Press, 1960), 258, August 2, 1895.

43. Griffiths, *Splendid Vision*, 14.

44. Griffiths, *Splendid Vision*, 13–47.

45. Ruth Howes, "Adelaide Hoodless," in Mary Quayle Innis, ed., *The Clear Spirit: Twenty Canadian Women and Their Times* (Toronto: University of Toronto Press, 1966), 114.

46. Terry Crowley, "Madonnas before Magdalenes: Adelaide Hoodless and the Making of the Canadian Gibson Girl," *Canadian Historical Review* 67, 4 (December 1986), 520–47; "The Origins of Continuing Education for Women: The Ontario Women's Institutes," *Canadian Woman Studies/Les cahiers de la femme* 7, 3 (Fall 1986), 78–81.

47. Robert Stamp, "Teaching Girls Their 'God Given Place in Life': The Introduction of Home Economics in the Schools," *Atlantis* 2, 2, part 1 (Spring 1977), 18–34.

48. Cleverdon, *Woman Suffrage Movement*, chap. 3.

49. W.J. Lindal, *The Icelanders in Canada* (Ottawa/Winnipeg: National Publishers/Viking Printers, 1967), 160–61; Hrund Skulason, "The Battle of the Sexes," *Icelandic Canadian* (Winter 1975), 47.

50. Mary Kinnear, "The Icelandic Connection: *Freyja* and the Manitoba Woman Suffrage Movement," *Canadian Woman Studies/Les cahiers de la femme* 7, 4 (Winter 1986), 25–28.

51. Yolande Pinard, "Les débuts du mouvement des femmes à Montréal, 1893–1902," in Marie Lavigne et Yolande Pinard, eds., *Travailleuses et féministes: Les femmes dans la société québécoise* (Montréal: Boréal Express, 1983), 194–96; Le Collectif Clio, *L'histoire des femmes au Québec depuis quatre siècles* (Montréal: Quinze, 1982), 329; Marie Lavigne, Yolande Pinard, and Jennifer Stoddart, "The *Fédération nationale Saint-Jean-Baptiste* and the Women's Movement in Quebec," in Kealey, ed., *A Not Unreasonable Claim*, 71–88.

52. Margaret Conrad, "Recording Angels: Private Chronicles of Maritime Women, 1800–1950," in Alison Prentice and Susan Mann Trofimenkoff, eds., *The Neglected Majority: Essays in Canadian Women's History* (Toronto: McClelland and Stewart, 1985), vol. 2, 41–60; Judith Fingard, "The Prevention of Cruelty, Marriage Breakdown, and the Rights of Wives in Nova Scotia, 1880–1900," *Acadiensis* 22, 2 (Spring 1993), 87.

53. Luke, "Woman Suffrage in Canada," 335–36.

54. Ernest Forbes, "The Ideas of Carol Bacchi and the Suffragists of Halifax," *Atlantis* 10, 2 (Spring 1985), 119–26.

55. Pierre M. Gérin et Pierre Gérin, "Une femme à la recherche et la défense de l'identité acadienne à la fin du XIXe siècle, Marichette," *La revue de l'Université de Moncton* 11 (mai 1978), 22 [our translation].

56. Elspeth Tulloch, *We, the Undersigned: A Historical Overview of New Brunswick Women's Political and Legal Status, 1784–1984* (Moncton: New Brunswick Advisory

Council on the Status of Women, 1985), 43; Pierre M. Gérin et Pierre Gérin, "Qui êtes-vous Marichette?" *Cahiers de la société historique acadienne* 8, 4 (décembre 1977), 165–72; Gérin et Gérin, "Une femme," 17–26.

57. Tulloch, *We, the Undersigned*; Duley, *Where Once*, 14–38; Cleverdon, *Woman Suffrage Movement*, chap. 6.

58. Susan Altschul and Christine Carron, "Chronology of Some Legal Landmarks in the History of Canadian Women," *McGill Law Journal* 21, 4 (Winter 1975), 476–94; Backhouse, "Married Women's Property Law," 337–345.

59. Jo-Anne Fiske, "Child of the State Mother of the Nation: Aboriginal Women and the Ideology of Motherhood," *Culture* 13, 1 (1993), 18.

60. Lynne Marks, " 'The Hallelujah Lasses': Working-Class Women in the Salvation Army in English Canada, 1882–92," in Iacovetta and Valverde, eds., *Gender Conflicts*, 67–117; Adrienne Shadd, "300 Years of Black Women in Canadian History: Circa 1700–1980," *Tiger Lily* 1, 2 (1987), 9–10; Shirley J. Yee, "Black Women as Community Leaders in Ontario, 1850–70," *Canadian Historical Review* 85, 1 (March 1994), 53–73; Sherry Edmunds-Flett, "African-Canadian Family and Community Life in Nineteenth-Century British Columbia," paper presented to the Canadian Historical Association, Ottawa, 1993, 16.

CHAPTER EIGHT

Marching into the Twentieth Century

The dawning of the new century stimulated many Canadians to assess — formally and informally — the country's past, present, and future. After half a century of collective endeavours, the time was propitious for Canadian women to reflect on their progress. Judging by sheer numbers and diversity of activities, women's organizations were a great success. Female reform groups representing a wide range of causes were thriving in urban and rural communities throughout the country. Alongside them existed a rich mosaic of women's cultural and artistic organizations dedicated to personal and communal improvement.

The progressive optimism voiced by many Canadians at the start of the new century was not shared by everyone. While some suffragists believed that the tide of public support and legislative debate on the vote had turned in their favour, and that female enfranchisement was imminent, others expressed concern about the rising anti-suffrage voice and the conservatism of provincial and federal legislators. Nevertheless, members of religious, social, and reform organizations could and did take great pride in the scope of their activities and achievements, and in the expansion of organizational activity among concerned women. Nowhere was this self-confidence more evident than in the National Council of Women of Canada and its written assessment of the roles and status of Canadian women, produced for the Paris International Exposition in 1900.

This report, *Women of Canada: Their Life and Work*, was funded by the federal government, and was the first published national portrait of Canadian women.[1] As well as documenting women's status, roles, and condition, it also set an agenda for mainstream women's reform activities in the years to come. *Women of Canada*'s program for change was not stated in so many words; it was, rather, implied by the careful chronicling of achievements and remaining challenges. Introducing this survey of the organizations in which the Canadian woman "realizes the power of a corporate life," the compilers signalled their confidence in organized, activist women.[2] The book reviewed women's group activities and problems in the legal and political realms, the professions, trades and industries, education, literature, the arts, the churches, charitable and reform work, and social life. As a comprehensive reflection of women's associational life in Canada, *Women of Canada* was less than perfect. Short sections were devoted to non–Anglo-Saxon immigrants and Native women, but apart from a note by Native poet Pauline Johnson, the volume did not provide them any opportunity to present their own personal or group perspectives. Nor was there any reference to labour unions, although the volume did refer to protective legislation for working women. What *Women of Canada* did provide were insights into the leadership and the themes that would dominate the mainstream Canadian women's movement in the next two decades.

THE FLOWERING OF THE WOMEN'S MOVEMENT

The vast majority of organized women belonged to local groups, frequently developed by local women themselves and devoted to improving the quality of community life. This was particularly so in the frontier areas of the nation. Mrs. McNeil of Leslieville, Alberta, is a case in point. When the McNeils arrived in Leslieville in 1907, most of the residents were preoccupied with homesteading. The determined Mrs. McNeil, convinced that her community needed an interdenominational church, set about organizing local women. The women held a series of community "bees" at which the menfolk constructed the building while the women did finishing work such as plastering and painting; the women also supplied the meals. When interest lagged at various stages of the construction, Mrs. McNeil rose to the occasion, one time mailing cards around and another posting a placard that read "WANTED — 1,000 men for a worthy cause! Payment — Virtue is its own reward." Mrs. McNeil got her church built, and the women's group continued as a spiritual, educational, and fundraising force in the community.[3]

Women's auxiliaries, like the one in Leslieville, proliferated across the country and became the mainstays of many churches, schools, and other community activities. Depending on their denominational affiliation, the women called themselves sewing circles, ladies' aids, mothers' meetings, or guilds. While designed to tend to the social and spiritual needs of their members, these groups also engaged in charitable work and did much to advance the material circumstances of their communities. Native women in Split Lake, Manitoba, for example, formed an Anglican auxiliary in 1913 to supply equipment necessary for their church and to co-operate with other women's auxiliaries in local and international mission work. Lara Bjarnason brought the pressing need for a home for the aged to the Ladies Aid of the First Icelandic Lutheran Church in Winnipeg early in 1901. The members began fundraising; by 1916, they had purchased a building and opened the Betel home in Gimli. Similarly inspired to serve their community's need, the Saint John, New Brunswick, Daughters of Israel created and maintained the Mikvah (ritual bath). Nova Scotian black women in the Halifax Baptist church constituted themselves informally in 1917 as the "Women at the Well," with the purpose of supporting education for their community. In 1918 the African Baptist Association passed a resolution calling on every local church to organize a Ladies Auxiliary. The Ladies Auxiliaries worked tirelessly to raise money for the Nova Scotia Home for Coloured Children.[4]

Already by 1900, clubs promoting social interests — the arts, handicrafts, drama, music, history — had been established in such great numbers as to occupy one-tenth of the 442 pages in *Women of Canada*. The founders in most cases had a particular interest or expertise in the arts and sought to extend their enjoyment and knowledge to other women in the community. A variety of cultural interests occupied Anna Leonowens during the decade she spent in Halifax. A former teacher in the court of Siam (her story became the basis for Margaret Landon's book *Anna and the King of Siam*, and later for the musical *The King and I*), Leonowens organized a women's book club and a Shakespearean Society, as well as playing a leadership role in the Local Council of Women.[5] By 1920 all the major centres — and many of the smaller communities, as well — could boast a host of women's clubs devoted to the various arts and crafts.

In the first two decades of the new century, some Canadian women became more active in their professional organizations. As they advanced in such fields as teaching, journalism, social work, and public health, and began to make advances in medicine and law, their involvement in the political reform movement also increased. Toronto's female teachers, for example, formed a separate teachers' franchise club in 1909. Activity aimed at gaining the franchise also grew within the National and Local Councils of Women, culminating with the National Council's endorsement of suffrage at its 1910 annual meeting. The Council's philosophy evolved after 1900, and the organization less frequently justified its public involvement by citing the benefits of women's influence. By 1914, the NCWC asserted that women's right to power in public policy derived from their indispensable role in society.[6] New and expanded suffrage undertakings, including visits by American and British suffrage leaders, also brought energy to the movement. The Dominion Women's Enfranchisement Association changed its name in 1907 to the Canadian Suffrage Association. One of the earliest groups to affiliate with it was the Icelandic Suffrage Association. In 1909, the Canadian Suffrage Association collaborated with the WCTU in a monster demonstration at the Ontario legislature. A vigorous new group of progressive and professional members were attracted to the cause, along with members of the Toronto Local Council of Women, most of whom were wives of the city's leading businessmen.[7]

An unorthodox new participant in the Toronto movement, Flora MacDonald Denison, quickly made her voice heard. Born in 1867, she spent her childhood and youth in impoverished circumstances brought on by her father's business losses, drunkenness, and unemployment. Although she taught for a short time, she eventually trained in a private commercial school and worked for a Toronto insurance company, later moving on to journalism in Detroit. There she met and married Howard Denison in 1892. After the birth of a son, the family returned to Toronto, where Flora Denison worked first as a dressmaker, then as a "modiste" for Simpson's, and eventually opened her own dressmaking business. By 1898 Denison was also writing for *Saturday Night*, frequently drawing on her experiences and observations of the sweated needle-trades for her articles. In 1903 Denison met Emily Stowe, who introduced her to the Toronto women's movement and encouraged her to become actively involved in it. Within three years, Flora Denison held the post of secretary of the Dominion Women's Enfranchisement Association and was appointed the official Canadian delegate to attend the third World Conference of the International Woman Suffrage Alliance in Copenhagen. Denison increasingly expounded her view of a widely democratic, egalitarian feminism. She adopted a position that was intensely critical of capitalist society and orthodox Christianity, a position that most women found unacceptable.[8] Denison's "democracy" did not, however, extend to Canada's recent male immigrants. She labelled them "illiterate and often the scum of the earth" and complained that "in a few years they will be empowered to vote and make laws for the women of our land." In the use of such nativist stereotypes, Denison voiced opinions current among reformers that were openly used to press for women's rights.[9]

The majority within the small Canadian suffrage movement wanted to continue the cautious route of petitioning, issuing pamphlets, public speaking, and letter-writing campaigns. They argued for restraint and for the pursuit of other reforms in times of anti-suffrage hostility, moving toward more active pressure when public sentiment seemed less hostile to female enfranchisement. Some of the new members, particularly Denison, increased tension by advocating more militant strategies for getting the vote. They were impressed by and sympathetic to the arguments, slogans, and strategies adopted by the Women's Social and Political Union founded in Manchester, England, in 1903. Led by Emmeline Pankhurst and her daughters, Christabel and Sylvia, the "suffragettes," as they were eventually labelled, conducted a militant campaign for votes for women: their tactics included heckling politicians, chaining themselves to fences, breaking shop windows, and resorting to arson. Like the majority of Canadian suffrage supporters, Flora MacDonald Denison initially rejected the tactics of the British suffragettes, labelling them "unwomanly" in a 1906 interview. However, the International Woman Suffrage Alliance conference that same year, which she attended, changed her mind. Speaking on her return, she explained:

> I am inclined to think that the press has woefully exaggerated the behaviour of the women who are not lunatics or fanatics, but earnest women anxious and willing to sacrifice themselves that the race may be benefitted and moved nearer to an ideal civilization of cooperative brotherhood and sisterhood.[10]

Denison helped arrange for Emmeline Pankhurst to speak in Toronto in 1909, and Denison's column in the *World* regularly and sympathetically reported the activities of the British suffragettes. In 1913, at the height of the Women's Social and Political Union campaign of violence, Denison changed the name of her column to "Stray Leaves from a Suffragette's Notebook," becoming one of the few Canadian women to identify herself publicly as a suffragette. The hostility engendered by Denison's open espousal of British militant suffragette tactics led to a split in the Toronto movement. In 1912 members of the Toronto Local Council of Women founded a separate franchise organization, the Equal Franchise League. Unlike Denison, this group of women argued for the vote not as a natural right but as a means of achieving other necessary reforms. A letter in Denison's papers suggests that some may also have been uneasy with her working-class background and connections.[11]

Hostilities and tensions among reformers were not new. A rift over ideological differences had occurred in 1902 in New Brunswick between the Women's Enfranchisement Association and the Saint John Local Council of Women. Class, religious, rural/urban, philosophic, racial, and ethnic differences also worked against female unity. The influx of large numbers of non–Anglo-Saxon immigrants, especially after 1896, heightened nativist concerns. The larger families, non-Protestant backgrounds, and higher birth rates of the newcomers encouraged xenophobia, as did immigrants' supposedly lenient attitudes toward alcohol and prostitution. Some women activists were strongly attracted to eugenics, which, at its most extreme, advocated selective breeding of the fittest and compulsory sterilization for those considered inferior.[12] Their aim was the "regeneration" of the "Anglo-Saxon" race, a cause that could only alienate those belonging to other groups.[13] Only a minority of reformers thoroughly supported eugenics; its premise that heredity determined all was contrary to the belief in social change and Christian perfection. Most hoped that, through education, conversion to Protestantism, and improvement of their social environment, immigrants' problems — or the "problem" of the immigrant — could be overcome.

Aggressive Protestant evangelical missions directed at converting the youth of Toronto's Jewish community in the first decade of the century sparked an immediate response. Ida Siegel organized a Hebrew Ladies Sewing Circle in 1906, the same year that the Presbyterian Jewish mission opened. Initially conceived to provide girls in the Ward (a working-class district of Toronto) with sewing skills and to distribute the clothing they made to the poor, the Circle soon expanded its efforts to counter the successful recreational programs of the missions. For example, the ladies organized a picnic for children on Centre Island and drew 200 participants. The next year, the largely East European group again enlarged its interests to include education, medical care, domestic assistance, and food for new mothers and infants — activities reflected in their new name: Hebrew Ladies' Maternity and Child Welfare Society. Expansion of the sewing school and girls' club continued, and in 1912 the institution added a library for those who wished to read in English. By then called the Jewish Endeavour Sewing School, it held classes after regular school hours and taught girls not only sewing but also Jewish religion, history, and Zionism. In 1913, 200 elementary-school girls attended.

The energetic Ida Siegel also arranged additional efforts through the local public school. She won permission for a Jewish girls' club to meet Saturday afternoons at the school. Using community concerns about idle children shoplifting in nearby department stores as her rationale, Siegel initiated the club's program to teach young Jewish girls values at an age earlier than the formal religious education available within the East European community. Members of a mothers' club also began to learn about child welfare issues. While all these efforts fostered Jewish cultural and religious identity, they also facilitated adaption to Canadian life. Group leaders and teachers served as role models, and the groups provided a safe environment in which the participants could develop familiarity with English.[14]

Resistance to the evangelizing activity of the Methodist Woman's Missionary Society took a different form at the Chinese Rescue Home, founded in 1887 in Victoria, British Columbia, to rescue, convert, and "civilise" Victoria's Chinese prostitutes or "slave girls." Over time, the Chinese clients developed strategies that enabled them to use the home only for services they valued — namely childcare and education. This shift led the mission to redefine its role and redirect its energies to concentrate on providing such services. The change in the institution's primary role was acknowledged when, in 1908, the WMS constructed a new building and named it the Oriental Home and School.[15]

In general, women most frequently identified with and organized within their own cultural or racial settings, either separately or as auxiliaries to male associations. In Montreal, for example, black women began to meet informally in 1900 for mutual support and friendship, the first known example of organized black women's solidarity in that community. Although the census recorded only 191 Montreal blacks in 1901, by 1902 the women had formalized their organization as the Coloured Women's Club of Montreal.[16] The members recognized that social agencies in the city were not paying attention to the hardships and problems suffered by black families, especially by new arrivals from the West Indies. The Coloured Women's Club initiated a number of relief and benevolent services, providing warm clothing for newly arrived families, introducing them to the existing black community, and suggesting strategies for dealing with discrimination.[17]

In Saskatchewan, participants in the women's congress held at the annual Saskatchewan Grain Growers' Association (SGGA) convention in 1913 debated appropriate organizational forms and identities. Among the speakers

> there was a great discussion as to whether they should become Homemakers' Clubs or evolve an organization of their own. The preponderance of opinion was that they should become a part of the farm people's organization and so strengthen the hands of all concerned.[18]

As farm women, they felt more comfortable and effective creating a Women's Section of the 10 000-member-strong SGGA than in a not exclusively farm-based group like the Homemakers' Clubs. Violet McNaughton, who began organizing Women's Grain Growers Clubs after the convention, summed up the farm women's feelings about the Homemakers' Clubs:

> They are doing splendid work, but are distinctly a women's organization; also, being under the government or university control, [they] are much restricted in their topics.[19]

Despite the decision to organize separately within the SGGA, the two clubs developed co-operation and exchanged ideas.

A similar organizational perspective developed in Alberta. In a 1916 letter to McNaughton, Irene Parlby, president of the United Farm Women of Alberta (UFWA) commented on the differences from the Women's Institutes:

> Their [Women's Institutes] line of work to tell you the truth does not interest me very much — there is too much of the housekeeping business about it, and . . . I think the farm women want to be taken out of their housekeeping troubles and made to realize there are other things of interest in the world, and that they do their housework all the better for thinking of outside affairs.[20]

As the UFWA's membership drive expanded, conflict with the Women's Institutes increased, and partisan political battles developed.

Parlby's comments notwithstanding, the Alberta Women's Institutes (AWIs) attracted many women by offering them a reprieve from the isolation of farm life. Activities that extended beyond the domestic included educational programs designed to improve farm management and to expand their knowledge of political issues and legislation affecting women and children. Although some Alberta women joined both organizations, more opted for the AWI which by 1920 comprised 265 Institutes with a total membership of 13 150. At its peak in 1921, the UFWA counted 309 locals representing 4536 women. Differences not noted by Parlby accounted for the AWI's larger numbers. It was open to all rural and urban women while the UFWA restricted membership to wives and daughters of farmers. And the AWI was officially non-partisan, whereas the UFWA was the women's branch of the United Farmers (who formed the government in Alberta from 1920 to 1935).[21]

While the AWIs accommodated city and farm women, rural/urban differences in other locales divided female social reformers. The Winnipeg Political Equality League was founded in 1912 and subsequently renamed the Manitoba Political Equality League in 1913. Like its predecessor, the Manitoba Equal Franchise Club, it did not attract many members among ethnic or rural women. Rather, it appealed to urban Social Gospellers, who believed that the church should play a major role in eradicating the problems of cities, and saw women as an essential force for social and political reform. Progressive women's campaigns for temperance, social purity, improved public welfare, the franchise, and urban renewal meshed with the evangelical impetus to rid society of its imperfections.[22] Reformers were also joined by businessmen, who supported a moral reform movement that would increase the respectability of their cities and so promote expansion and investment in them.[23]

The Manitoba Political Equality League's success in attracting male support and involvement is aptly illustrated in the Mock Parliament staged at the Regina Walker Theatre in Winnipeg in 1914. Men were not only well represented in the audience but also participated in the entertainment itself. Presented the day after Manitoba Premier R.P. Roblin had rejected the suffrage petition of a women's delegation to the Legislative Assembly, the play was entitled *How the Vote Was Not Won*. To the tremendous amusement of all, this Mock Parliament, like its two predecessors, forcefully exposed the sanctimonious and contradictory arguments used by male politicians to deny female suffrage. The curtain parted to reveal the women sitting at desks, posing as legislators receiving a deputation of vote-seeking men who were pushing a wheelbarrow full of petitions. The "Premier," the witty and well-known Nellie McClung, congratulated the men on their "splendid appearance" but told them that "man is made for something higher and better than voting":

> Men were made to support families. What is a home without a bank account? . . . In this agricultural province, the man's place is the farm. Shall I call man away from the useful plow and harrow to talk loud on street corners about things which do not concern him! Politics unsettle men, and unsettled men mean unsettled bills — broken furniture, and broken vows — and divorce. . . . When you ask for the vote you are asking me to break up peaceful, happy homes — to wreck innocent lives. . . .

"It may be that I am old-fashioned," she concluded. "I may be wrong. After all, men may be human. Perhaps the time will come when men may vote with women." And she assured them solemnly that "the man who pays the grocer rules the world."[24] She was faithfully echoing the words and tone used by Premier Roblin when speaking to the suffragists the day before, and the crowd roared in recognition.

THE VOTE GIRL

I WANT THE VOTE, AND I MEAN TO HAVE THE VOTE; THAT'S THE SORT OF GIRL I AM

This pro-suffrage postcard was reproduced in the Grain Growers' Guide *on July 8, 1914.*

Source: From *Grain Growers' Guide* (July 1914).

THE PUBLIC DEBATE

The Mock Parliament was but one vehicle used by supporters of the suffrage cause to get their message across to the public. They—along with their opponents—also expounded their views in lectures, sermons, books, magazines, and newspapers. One of the earliest and least-known contributors to the debate was Ontario schoolmaster Donald McCaig, who published in the United States a yawn-inducing 241-page attempt to rebut John Stuart Mill's *The Subjection of Women*.[25] Better known was the Toronto journalist and former academic Goldwin Smith. In an essay entitled "Woman Suffrage," Smith acknowledged that some women's reform work was a logical extension of their mothering role, but argued that the exercise of political rights was men's business and quite inappropriate for women. Woman's enfranchisement would, he suggested, lead to "national emasculation" and the disruption of home lives, as spouses supported different candidates and fought over politics. Smith, who prior to coming to Canada had resigned his Cornell University post in protest against that institution's decision to admit women, claimed that women did not need the vote. They already had, he maintained, equal access to education and equal opportunities in the professions.[26]

Some twenty years later, Canadian economist and humourist Stephen Leacock expressed his own opposition to women's suffrage. He argued that woman's true and only role was motherhood, and that society should recognize and uphold women in this role. The problem was that society did not truly value or support women's work in the home or deal adequately with the visible fact of women's necessary dependency in a harsh and frequently uncaring world.

Women need not more freedom but less. Social policy should proceed from the fundamental truth that women are and must be dependent. If they cannot be looked after by an individual (a thing on which they took their chance in earlier days) they must be looked after by the State. To expect a woman, for example, if left by the death of her husband with young children without support, to maintain herself by her own efforts, is the most absurd mockery of freedom ever devised.[27]

Quebec anti-suffragists voiced their opposition to suffrage even more strongly. Alarmed by the threats to family life posed by industrialization and urbanization, Henri Bourassa, an outspoken French-Canadian nationalist and founder of the influential Quebec newspaper *Le Devoir*, condemned anything that drew women's attention from the home, including the vote.[28]

Male anti-suffrage writers were not alone in their views. Their theories and arguments were echoed across the country and struck a chord not only in the minds of anxious men, but also in those of concerned women. Adelaide Hoodless was one of the women who were never persuaded that the vote was the answer to women's problems. She believed that women exerted their most effective influence on government through the education of their sons. Although she admitted a possible role for unmarried women in municipal affairs, she maintained that the role of the married woman was essentially domestic and that proper training would reveal this to be true; "any girl or woman who has been brought face to face with the great truths presented through a properly graded course in domestic science or Home Economics in its wider interpretation," Hoodless felt sure, would never be found "in the ranks of the suffragettes."[29] French-Canadian women who were against the franchise may have been influenced by nationalist writings to see women's suffrage as an Anglo-Saxon, foreign idea that was inimical to the interests of their people.

On the other hand, supporters of the vote for women could be found in all provinces. In general, the progressive press was supportive, and in some cases ran separate women's columns addressing the need for improving women's status. The *Manitoba Free Press*, for example, devoted articles to these concerns from at least 1890 on. The existence of separate women's columns facilitated both the debate on women's issues and the emergence of women journalists, such as Francis Beynon and Isabel Graham and others, who tended to be strong advocates of reform. Labour, farm, and socialist newspapers also provided a forum for discussing the unequal treatment of women. The *Grain Growers' Guide* actively promoted suffrage, along with a host of other feminist reforms, including reformed dower law and improved homesteading, property, and guardianship rights for women.

Men in western Canada appear to have been especially sympathetic to the suffrage cause. Dissatisfaction with government policies toward farmers was strong, and female suffrage would have strengthened the farm vote: this motivation probably affected both men and women in the prairie provinces. It is possible also that western men were aware of the pioneering efforts of their spouses, regarding them as equal partners entitled to the vote. However, some of these men adamantly opposed the granting of equal property rights to women, and it was in these regions that women lost their already meagre dower rights. It seems more likely that some men, at least, were responding to women's perceived role as moral and spiritual guardians of the home, who would use the vote for reforms essential for the maintenance of a stable social order. Certainly this was the motivation of the supporters of temperance and, more widely, of the Social Gospellers.

The possible influence of the massive and relatively recent immigration into the prairie provinces should also be noted. The experience of resettlement may itself have played some liberating role, and so may the fact that a significant number of western settlers came from those American states where women had already won the vote. Finally, there is the less positive influence of nativism. There was growing prejudice against the non–Anglo-Saxon immigrants, accompanied by concern about purchase and manipulation of votes. Some were offended that illiterate "foreign" men could vote, while relatively well-educated Anglo-Saxon women could not. They were convinced that foreign women, educated or not, would counterbalance their more easily corrupted spouses. But whatever their motivation, rural western men, individually and collectively—through such organizations as the United Farmers of Alberta and the Saskatchewan Grain Growers' Association, and through newspapers like the *Grain Growers' Guide*—vigorously supported the suffragist efforts.[30]

For its part, organized labour was ambivalent in its support for suffrage. When it was supportive, it generally equated the franchise with workers' rights. Labour newspapers emphasized the need to increase the power of labour generally, and also hoped that working-class women might help elect a labour government and bring about reforms that organized labour endorsed. Socialist writers discussed a variety of women's issues in the press. *Cotton's Weekly*, a socialist newspaper published in the eastern townships of Quebec, included columns in its first year (1908–1909) on the problems of working women, as well as on women's "emancipation" and the problems of women in the home. Its columns addressed prostitution, sexuality, and even "free love." The paper strongly supported suffrage, and advocated both socialist and feminist activism to bring it about. On the other hand, the Socialist Party of Canada and its newspaper, the *Western Clarion*, displayed considerable uncertainty regarding both suffrage and the "woman question," arguing that the task of replacing capitalism should take precedence over addressing women's issues.[31]

Socialist Party women did, however, press their issues and interests. At the first convention of the Ontario section in 1908, delegates brought the question of women's suffrage to the floor. One of the women present was Sanna Kannasto, whom the party approved as its first paid organizer for the Finnish Socialists. Although still in her twenties at the time, Kannasto already had an established reputation as a speaker, writer, and organizer in the United States. Touring northern Ontario, she tirelessly recruited members in the distant mining towns, rural villages, and lumber camps. Where possible she arranged additional, separate meetings for women, at which she encouraged and facilitated the formation of women's groups, explored questions on women's role in socialism, and provided information and opinion on marital concerns and birth control. Sanna Kannasto's efforts met with success. By the summer of 1913, 562 women had become members of the party, while many others had been influenced by Kannasto's tours and the resultant women's groups. One measure of the influence exercised by Kannasto is the attention she attracted from the RCMP. Officers closely monitored her activities, labelled her a "dangerous radical," and recommended her deportation. In 1920, Sanna Kannasto, arrested while on a speaking tour in western Canada, wrote from jail:

Finnish women in northern Ontario march for voting rights.

....

Source: The Thunder Bay Finnish Canadian Historical Society Collection, The Chancellor Paterson Library Archives, Lakehead University.

I am not nervous, I am made of iron, I have not shed a single tear, although I have been in cruel cross-examinations. Despite everything, I am happy and I try to joke and keep up the humour with my prison guards.[32]

The gruelling pace of organizational work, agitation and travel took its toll on the woman made of iron, however, contributing to the end of her common-law relationship. Increasing police harassment, added to the time and attention demands of motherhood, led Kannasto to less activity and eventually retirement.[33]

The existence of separate radical women's groups kept women's concerns on the socialist agenda in this period. Similarly, the development of a separate women's press heightened publicity for the women's reform cause. Periodicals like Quebec's *Le coin du feu* and *Le journal de françoise*, the Icelandic women's paper *Freyja*, and British Columbia's *The Champion*, produced by and for women, devoted all of their pages to an examination of the major issues facing women. In addition, most of the women's organizations had papers, bulletins, or reports that were widely distributed.

Female supporters of suffrage continued to move easily between causes, all of which were connected to their concern for reforming society. Nellie Letitia Mooney McClung worked for prohibition, factory laws for women, compulsory education, prison reform, and changes to the existing laws affecting women and children; it was to effect reforms in these areas that she and other feminists fought so hard to get the vote. A particularly vibrant personality, McClung has come to epitomize the first-wave Canadian feminist movement. Certainly she has become its best-known advocate from the west. Born in Ontario's Grey County in 1873, McClung participated in the Ontario migration to the west, moving with her family to Manitoba in 1880, and later as an adult to Alberta and British Columbia. By the time she reached her forties, McClung, the mother of five children, had become a best-selling author of socially conscious novels, and a rip-roaring public speaker.[34] Basing her approach on social feminism, McClung explained women's public role in terms of their special capacity as women. Addressing the argument that politics were too corrupt for women, she retorted:

> What would you think of a man who would say to his wife: "This house to which I am bringing you to live is very dirty and unsanitary, but I will not allow you — the dear wife whom I have sworn to protect — to touch it. It is too dirty for your precious little white hands! You must stay upstairs, dear. Of course the odor from below may come up to you, but use your smelling salts and think no evil. I do not hope to ever be able to clean it up, but certainly you must never think of trying." . . . Women have cleaned up things since time began; and if women ever get into politics there will be a cleaning-out of pigeon-holes and forgotten corners, on which the dust of years has fallen, and the sound of the political carpet-beater will be heard in the land.[35]

McClung was similarly comfortable advocating women's right to participate equally with men in the political realm, and frequently voiced the equal rights appeal to plain justice:

> We went there to the Manitoba Legislature asking for plain, common justice, an old fashioned square deal, and in reply to that we got hat-lifting. I feel that when a man offers hat-lifting when we ask for justice we should tell him to keep his hat right on. I will go further and say that we should tell him not only to keep his hat on but to pull it right down over his face.[36]

Nellie McClung saw no contradiction between arguments from women's special gifts and arguments from justice. Women and men, she believed, were different but equal.

WORKING FOR LEGAL CHANGE

The campaign for legal reform gained momentum in the second decade of the twentieth century. The laws relating to property continued to be a concern everywhere, but were particularly in need of reform in the prairie provinces, where women were still largely excluded from homesteading rights and, unprotected by dower laws, had no control over the disposal or use of family property. In addition, widows had no legal guarantee of inheritance. The *Grain Growers' Guide's* women's section crystallized and actively developed the public demand and campaign for dower laws. The first success came in 1910, partly through the efforts of writer and reformer Emily Murphy: Alberta legislators passed the Married Women's Relief Act, which entitled a widow to receive through the courts something of her husband's estate if he had not adequately provided for her. However, dower law supporters intensified their campaign, insisting that women's claims be legally recognized as rights not subject to

Left to right: Suffragists Nellie McClung, Alice Jamieson, and Emily Murphy. Jamieson was one of the earliest women judges.

Source: British Columbia Archives and Records Service, HP39854.

the discretionary decision of a husband or judge. Farm women's concern for this question brought many of those who sought property and homesteading reform to support the right to vote; farm women's and suffrage organizations worked in common. When travelling on the Prairies in 1913–14, Scottish suffragist Elizabeth B. Mitchell described the link between the two issues, observing that the

> special trouble which has turned the prairie women's minds to politics is connected with the land. The woman so obviously shares with her husband in making the "improved farm" . . . that it is felt to be an injustice that this product of their joint labour becomes the sole property of the man.[37]

Between 1910 and 1919, all three prairie provinces passed legislation guaranteeing wives' inheritance rights and restricting a husband's ability to sell or mortgage property without his wife's consent.[38] The impetus behind this legislation was to regularize credit relationships, rather than to recognize wives as equal partners with their husbands. Consent was not required for the husband to sell or dispose of farm equipment, livestock, seed, furniture, or any item other than the family home. Nor did the law acknowledge the contributions of separated or divorced wives who were forced to leave the farm.[39]

The law governing homesteading was an even harder nut to crack. The homestead act provided that all men, but only some women — widows and deserted, separated, and divorced women with dependents under the age of 21 — had the right to homestead, entitling them to free legal title to frontier lands when they met specified conditions. The movement for reform to allow wives and unmarried women homestead rights began as sporadic, unco-ordinated protests in a number of communities. The issue was eventually taken up by two influential activists, Georgina Binnie-Clark and Isabel Beaton Graham. Isabel Graham, who emigrated west from Ontario with her husband in 1885, was a founding member of the Winnipeg Women's Press Club, honorary secretary of that city's Women's Canadian Club, and women's editor of the *Grain Growers' Guide* from 1909 to 1911. Her November 1909 column featured a theoretical and practical discussion with Georgina Binnie-Clark on women's right to homestead. Binnie-Clark, a British journalist turned prairie wheat farmer, was the most prominent advocate of equality in homestead laws, and through her two books, *A Summer on the Canadian Prairie* and *Wheat and Woman*, the major publicist of this cause.[40] Although some western men supported the extension of homesteading rights to wives and unmarried women, the campaign for this reform encountered strong, highly organized, and politically influential opposition. In 1912, for example, delegates to the annual meeting of the Saskatchewan Grain Growers' Association rejected a motion to extend homesteading privileges to women. The battle continued unresolved until the 1930s, when control of public lands passed from the federal to the provincial governments. Manitoba and Saskatchewan eliminated homestead rights for everyone; Alberta drew up its own legislation allowing "every person" who met specific conditions the right to obtain a homestead.

Important legal battles were also fought in the early twentieth century in British Columbia. Such leaders as Helen Gregory MacGill studied, discussed, and lobbied for improvements in family law affecting the lives of women. Born to an elite family in 1864 in Hamilton, Ontario, Helen Gregory graduated from Toronto's Trinity College with Bachelor of Music, Bachelor of Arts, and Master of Arts degrees. She became a journalist, and while travelling across the Prairies met and married her first husband. Pregnant and with a broken leg, she continued to Japan on her own to complete a newspaper assignment. After her return, she lived with her husband in San Francisco and subsequently Minnesota. When her husband died, she was left to support two young sons and her mother. Two years later, Helen married lawyer James MacGill, and by 1901 they had settled in Vancouver. There, as she had in San Francisco and Minnesota, she involved herself in women's organizations, including the Women's Musical Club, the Vancouver Women's Press Club, and the University Women's Club. In working with and for other women, Helen Gregory MacGill followed a family tradition established by her mother and grandmother. Her daughter and biographer, Elsie MacGill, recalled:

> In each new society [i.e., community] a compulsion forced her to work toward a particular goal of her own, the radix of the force being that disturbing thrust of intellect that had pushed her into Trinity, over to Japan, into writing, publishing, crusading.[41]

In British Columbia, that goal came to be the protection and improved status of women and children. In 1912, with the backing of the Vancouver University Women's Club, MacGill produced a booklet outlining the inequities women faced before the law. British Columbia became the first province to enact an equal guardianship and custody law in 1917, giving mothers the same rights as fathers with respect to their children. Later the same year, the province established a juvenile court and appointed MacGill as one of its first two judges.

The plight of paid women workers was another focus of attention in British Columbia. Low wages, long hours, and miserable working conditions motivated suffrage and labour activist Helena Rose Gutteridge to work to unionize women and to demand improved conditions. This militant British suffragette, socialist, and Labour Party member arrived in Vancouver in 1911 and quickly immersed herself in reform activities. Gutteridge helped organize city laundry and garment workers, took a prominent role in the Vancouver Trades and Labour Council, and campaigned for the minimum wage for women as well as pensions for mothers left without other means of support. The passing of a 1918 law restricting hours of work for women was, in part, the result of her efforts. Similar campaigns to ameliorate women's working conditions were continuing in other provinces, and by 1920 a variety of further protective measures for female employees had been legislated in the Maritimes, Ontario, Quebec, and the Prairies.[42]

Hand in hand with British Columbia women's interest in legal and labour law reform went a renewed commitment to suffrage. From its founding in 1911, the provincial Political Equality League organized delegations, circulated petitions, and ran public meetings.[43] It garnered support from various men's and women's organizations, including the British Columbia Federation of Labour, the Local Option League, the WCTU, and the provincial opposition Liberal Party, but could not unite all political rights reformers. After 1911, a variety of more radical but shortlived suffrage associations appeared in the province. One in particular, Gutteridge's British Columbia Woman's Suffrage League, objected to the Political Equality League's conservatism, its failure to involve working-class women, and its use of exclusively maternalist arguments. The aims of Gutteridge's group extended beyond obtaining the vote to dealing "with all matters connected with the interests of women, particularly those things that affect women out in the labour market."[44]

While support for women's suffrage in British Columbia appeared to grow, women activists in the Maritime provinces continued to struggle against a current of strong anti-feminist sentiment. Although sporadic attempts to raise the franchise question continued to come from WCTU or Local Council women in all three provinces, the separate suffrage associations floundered. Internal division apparently crippled the cause in New Brunswick, where there is no evidence of activity by the Women's Enfranchisement Association between 1903 and 1907.[45] Revitalized in 1907, the Association began to work for the passage of a suffrage bill drawn up by one of its own members, Mabel French, New Brunswick's first female lawyer. In this effort and subsequent ones, the women met with increasingly overt mockery, insult, and even sexual harassment from some provincial legislators. The presence in 1909 of seven suffrage supporters at a hearing by the legislative Committee of the Whole on a bill to enfranchise unmarried women brought catcalls of "Help" and "Police," the ringing of the division bells, and open laughter at a coarse "verse" directed at the women. Despite this public abuse, the Local Council of Women and the Sons of Temperance endorsed suffrage in 1910, and a well-publicized visit to Saint John was made in 1912 by British suffragette Sylvia Pankhurst.

The same year saw the establishment of an Equal Franchise League in Moncton, and the publication by the Saint John *Globe* of a cogent letter to the editor, simultaneously rebuffing the abusive legislators and aggressively supporting equal political rights for women. The writer of the letter, Ella Hatheway, secretary-treasurer of the Women's Enfranchisement Association and wife of a sympathetic member of the legislature, recalled the appalling treatment of the 1909 delegation, of which she had been part, and outlined the similarly uncouth reaction she had encountered when an attempt was made to introduce a bill in 1912. Maintaining that women refused to be intimidated and would never abandon their just cause, she went on to outline her reasoning:

> The woman suffrage movement, the world over, has broadened and intensified during the past year. In no way is this shown more than in the growing demand from women that they shall no longer be regarded by men as sex beings, but as human beings; that they shall be recognized, politically and economically, as persons, not as females merely.[46]

In Nova Scotia, the local newspapers' prominent coverage and condemnation of the growing violence of the suffragettes in England inhibited overt suffrage support. Following the defeat of the suffrage bills in the 1890s, the movement's leaders had made a pragmatic decision to pursue other reform work through the Local Council of Women until some later date when, as leader Eliza Ritchie put it, "the time was ripe" for a return to explicit suffrage activities.[47] Certainly there was plenty to be done, and Council members had used their time and energy to advocate and advance a number of reform programs. Beginning in 1908, they lobbied local and provincial authorities, and later the federal Royal Commission on Technical Education, for the establishment of a vocational school to train women for a variety of industrial occupations. Halifax Local Council women also engaged in a major public health campaign. They raised funds for the Victorian Order of Nurses through tag days, formed an anti-tuberculosis league, and educated the public about the causes and prevention of infant mortality. Through such activities they hoped to dispel public criticism of the women's movement, and particularly that coming from the city's Catholic clergy.[48]

The lack of separate suffrage organization and activity in Prince Edward Island during the first two decades of the twentieth century may have similarly stemmed from women's concentration on alternative reform work; or the winning of prohibition may have taken the wind out of the reformers' sails. The only documented motion in favour of the franchise was passed in 1913 at the regional WCTU convention in Summerside. Otherwise, women activists in Prince Edward Island appear to have maintained a discreet silence on the subject. In Newfoundland, no separate suffrage activity existed until the founding of the Newfoundland Women's Franchise League in 1920.[49]

Like their east coast sisters, Quebec's women activists experienced a severe anti-feminist backlash prior to World War I. At the turn of the century, French-Canadian lay and clerical elites increasingly responded to urban industrial growth, social dislocation, growing Anglo–American influences, and new public initiatives by women with an aggressive, conservative nationalism. In their blueprint for a better society there was no place for the "new woman." Yet in fact, concerned nationalists, the leaders of the Catholic church, and the emerging lay feminist organizations were all addressing, albeit in different ways, perceived threats to the social order and its basic unit, the French-Canadian Catholic family. In some cases, they co-operated in social, charitable, and educational action, but with increasing frequency both lay nationalists and church leaders allied themselves against feminism in any form. French-Canadian women's organizations nevertheless persevered.[50]

The founding of the *Fédération nationale Saint-Jean-Baptiste* in 1907 provided francophone women's associations with a united voice and a public alliance with their sisters in the convents. Although the *Fédération's* feminism was not overt, it successfully co-ordinated Catholic women in their work to benefit society. Members' and affiliated groups' activities before World War I were diverse. Some, for example, set up commercial, technical, and household science classes; others addressed the problems of factory women, establishing sickness and mutual aid funds, employment bureaus, and boardinghouses for working women. Partly as a result of *Fédération* work, by 1914 Quebec women teachers' pensions had improved, factory lighting had improved, pure milk depots or "*gouttes de lait*" had been established to reduce rampant infant mortality, and legislation had been passed making it mandatory to provide female store clerks with chairs. Perhaps the *Fédération's* greatest contribution, however, was in uniting with the sisters of the *Congrégation de Notre-Dame* to achieve in 1908 the establishment of the *École d'enseignement supérieur*, the first institution to offer higher education to francophone women.[51]

There was little explicit franchise activity in Quebec's francophone community at this time. It was the members of the anglophone Montreal Local Council of Women who founded the Montreal Suffrage Association in 1913. Their major efforts were educational, involving the distribution and sale of literature about suffrage and about the legal inequities affecting women.

WAR

By the outbreak of World War I, Canadian women had organized around a remarkable number of social, political, cultural, and economic issues. Overlapping memberships in women's associations were common, and female voluntary organizations frequently adopted and supported each others' causes. Involvement in specific social reform often seemed to lead individual women into a broad reform program.

Emily Murphy was an excellent example of this progression. The daughter of a well-to-do Ontario family, Murphy married a popular preacher. By 1910 she had settled with her husband in Edmonton and was beginning to find her niche as a journalist and popular novelist, known to her large public as "Janey Canuck." In addition to an active participation in the Canadian Women's Press Club, the effervescent Murphy lent her name, acumen, and energy to the cause of reform. She worked to establish a local Victorian Order of Nurses, police courts for female offenders, public playgrounds, and municipal hospitals, as well as the right for women to be elected as school trustees in Edmonton. Campaigns for a provincial dower law and tuberculosis prevention also occupied her attention, as did provincial and national drives for suffrage. During the war years she added to her list of activities the registration of female wartime volunteers, and participation in the War Council of Women. Like other maternal feminists, Murphy based her claim for equality on arguments about women's moral superiority. As an Edmonton magistrate, her treatment of young female offenders was sometimes unsympathetic. Her drive to control moral depravity also led Murphy to echo the racist sentiments of many social reformers in questioning the advisability of admitting non-British immigrants, whom she saw as particularly prone to sexual precociousness and promiscuity.[52]

National commitment to the war effort provided many opportunities for individual and group endeavours. Spurred on by personal economic need as well as patriotic fervour, thousands of women entered the paid workforce, filling jobs vacated by enlisted men.[53] Others undertook a host of volunteer labours designed to aid the overseas campaign. They knitted socks, preserved foods, and salvaged clothing. Prominent Canadian women such as Lady Drummond, the first president of the Montreal Local Council of Women and widow of the president of the Bank of Montreal, offered their English homes as hospitals and created an Information Department of the Canadian Red Cross Society, which became the main channel of communication between the soldier and his family. They also established Maple Leaf Clubs for soldiers on leave. Two Toronto women, Mary Plummer and Joan Arnoldi, formed the Canadian Field Comforts Commission to oversee the distribution of clothing and other supplies assembled by women throughout Canada to soldiers in England and on the Continent. Although many women worked separately, most joined existing, pro-British women's groups or reform organizations that adapted or enhanced their programs by emphasizing war service. Some suffragists persisted in their campaign, but established Suffragists' War Auxiliaries, which became involved in local recruitment drives and organized women to fill available jobs vacated by male service volunteers.[54] In some communities, suffrage activists planned future suffrage campaigns during sessions for making soldier comforts and bandages for the Red Cross.

The visible, publicly acknowledged wartime work of women encouraged many reformers to press their more comprehensive demands. Despite the opposition of local employers, the Halifax Local Council of Women created a women's employment bureau in order to promote better industrial career training, occupational access, and advancement.[55] A Canadian Patriotic Fund was set up through which women's groups could work together to provide financial help and advice for families of enlisted men; as the war went on, the Fund became what can only be described as a national welfare service for them.[56] Reformers pointed to the example of the improved living conditions for soldiers' dependent wives and children achieved by the Fund, and lobbied for mothers' pensions, day nurseries, improved urban housing, and health inspection. Wartime inflation and deprivation revived interest in the economy and domestic consumption, and Household Leagues, formed just prior to the turn of the century and affiliated with the National Council of Women of Canada, became particularly visible in Victoria, Halifax, and northern Ontario. Members demanded government regulation of prices and quantities, the standardization of sizes in manufactured and canned goods, and the control of local food production and distribution. The Ottawa League investigated co-operative buying, while a similar association, the Calgary Consumers' League, put that idea into practice. Particularly concerned by high prices for the necessities of life in the fall and winter of 1914–15, the Calgary women brought carloads of flour and frozen fish into the city market, which they sold to members at substantial reductions. They also counteracted soaring fuel costs by arranging for discounted coal purchases.[57] Strategies such as these expanded in the later war years as the government launched thrift, food conservation, and "self-denial" campaigns. By 1917 the Quebec Housewives' League had 10 000 members, and other Leagues had expanded on a similar scale.[58]

More-spontaneous and more-radical responses to specific price increases also occurred. In May 1917, for example, when Jewish bakers in Toronto announced a 12-cents a-loaf increase in the price of bread, the angry women of the Ward and Spadina Avenue community organized a committee and began a boycott of the bakeries. They canvassed neighbourhood homes and businesses for support, petitioned the federal government for the appointment of a food commissioner, and picketed all fifteen bakeries, forcing their temporary shutdown. As the boycott grew, protesters broke bakery windows and damaged flour and bread. They disrupted and virtually halted bread delivery. *The Telegram* reported:

> The bakers say the safety of their drivers was in danger and some were attacked by infuriated women, who pulled their hair and upset their bread baskets on the street.

The women did not give up until the price of bread eased.[59]

Wartime patriotism directly benefitted many of the established women's organizations by attracting new members. The National Council of Women, the YWCA, the Women's Institutes, and the Imperial Order Daughters of the Empire (IODE) all experienced spectacular increases in membership. By 1915, the Women's Institutes had attracted 29 045 women to a total of 892 branches. During World War I, the Institutes spread beyond Canada's borders to England and eventually to other European countries.[60] The IODE's first chapters had been founded in 1900 in Fredericton and Montreal in response to the Boer War, and by the end of World War I it had become one of the nation's largest women's voluntary associations. In just three years, 1915–1917, IODE membership increased by 10 000, and nearly 100 new chapters were formed. The IODE's primary purpose was to mobilize women and children to support the British empire, and to appreciate its history. During World War I, the IODE founded Red Cross branches, organized the Canadian Women's Hospital Ship Fund, sent gifts to soldiers overseas, assisted in recruitment, badgered those who did not enlist, and organized material and emotional support for soldiers' families. By 1917 the Daughters had collected more than $1.5 million to finance their efforts.[61] In reviewing these large numbers and broad activities, it is easy to overlook the innumerable local fundraising and unpaid women's hours required. Johanna Gudrun Skaptason formed the Jon Sigurdsson Chapter, IODE, in Winnipeg in 1916. Her daughter recalled:

> Twice annually during those first war days our home became parcel packing-headquarters, with cartons, and cases of food, socks, etc., piled ceilingward and women working day after day, pausing only for coffee.[62]

Although its members were concerned about women's problems, the IODE's pronounced patriotism and enthusiasm for things British occasionally put its members at odds with other women's organizations. They protested, for example, the National Council of Women of Canada's affiliation with the International Council of Women, which, they argued, also included "enemy" affiliates.[63]

Through their organized reform activities in the late nineteenth and early twentieth centuries, women had developed and refined the skills of organizing and fundraising. In the war years the government needed civilian assistance in drives to recruit men and to raise war funds, and found ready-made support in existing women's organizations. Prime Minister Robert Borden estimated in 1916 that Canadian women had raised the immense sum of between $40 and $50 million since the war began. In Newfoundland, as well, women had raised $205 614 in cash and supplies for the war effort by 1916.[64] Women also responded when wartime disaster struck. The Halifax explosion of December 6, 1917, which destroyed more than 2000 homes, killed 1600 people, and injured an additional 9000, activated the city's women and their organizations. Women from all walks of life participated in the rescue work under the leadership and initiative of prominent feminists and Local Council leaders. Leading women's movement activists such as May Sexton, Eliza Ritchie, and Agnes Dennis organized nursing care and co-ordinated the distribution of food and clothing.[65]

In a symbolic recognition of the huge range and intensity of women's voluntary and emergency efforts, a Women's War Conference, also known as the War Council of Women, was convened in 1918 at the request of the Cabinet War Committee. Conference resolutions ranged widely, covering the major unachieved reform platforms, including suffrage, that the National Council of Women of Canada, along with its affiliates and supporters, had been espousing for over two decades.[66]

While World War I had a positive effect on the image and prestige of organized women, it also accentuated old divisions and raised some new ones. In Winnipeg in 1918, the Local Council of Women, concerned about maintaining communications necessary to the war effort, acted as scab workers, replacing—and undermining the cause of — women telephone operators who were on strike.[67] Organized women also divided sharply on the issues of conscription and the Union government, which federal Liberals and Conservatives formed in 1917 to pursue the national war effort. In Saint John, the refusal of Women's Enfranchisement Association members to endorse Prime Minister Borden's Union government sparked the resignations of its president and vice-president.[68]

It was perhaps Canada's involvement in the war in the first place that presented the greatest challenge to female reformers. Central to the ideology of feminism lay a strong condemnation of violence, associated with men and male power. The Maritimes WCTU had been involved in the 1890s, for example, in a campaign for peace through international arbitration.[69] Flora MacDonald Denison was among the prominent women reformers who had written on the subject in the years before the war. Her *War and Women*, published by the Canadian Suffrage Association in 1914, blamed militarism on the domination of public life by men.[70] Nellie McClung's *In Times Like These* (1915) included one of the most eloquent condemnations of all forms of war.

> But although men like to fight, war is not inevitable. War is not of God's making. War is a crime committed by men and, therefore, when enough people say it shall not be, it cannot be. This will not happen until women are allowed to say what they think of war. Up to the present time women have had nothing to say about war, except pay the price of war—this privilege has been theirs always.[71]

McClung and Denison were two feminists for whom the reality, as opposed to the abstraction, of war presented painful problems of personal conscience. Both had been against war; both had dearly loved sons who enlisted; both eventually came to support the Allied cause. Only a few Canadian women sustained their pacifist opposition to violence. These included Winnipeg writer Francis Marion Beynon, British Columbia's Helena Gutteridge, and Toronto peace activist Laura Hughes, all of whom consistently and publicly condemned Canada's participation in the war. Beynon's refusal to alter her pacifist stance resulted in her forced resignation from her job as a respected journalist on the *Grain Growers' Guide*, and led to her self-imposed exile in the United States.[72] Early in the war, pacifism also inspired the president of the Toronto Business Women's Club, Mrs. C.R. Barker, to resign her presidency rather than share in the Club's war work. But these women and others who spoke or wrote publicly against the war found themselves increasingly isolated. Looking back in 1945, Nellie McClung recalled:

> The fall of 1914 blurs in my memory like a troubled dream. The war dominated everything. Some of my friends were pacifists and resented Canada's participation in a war of which we knew so little. . . . Chief among the Empire's defenders among the women was Miss Cora Hind. Her views were clear cut and definite. We were British and must follow the tradition of our fathers. She would have gone herself if women were accepted. Miss Hind saw only one side of the question and there were times when I envied her, though I resented her denunciations of those who thought otherwise.
>
> The old crowd began to break up, and our good times were over.[73]

VICTORY

In spite of obstacles and disagreements, women continued to campaign for suffrage. The turning point in the long battle finally came in 1916, when the vigorous suffrage campaign waged by western women culminated in their enfranchisement in Manitoba, Alberta, and Saskatchewan. A year later, British Columbia and Ontario followed suit; women in Nova Scotia, New Brunswick, Prince Edward Island, and Newfoundland won the vote in 1918, 1919, 1922, and 1925, respectively. In all cases except New Brunswick and Ontario, the right to vote was accompanied by the right to hold office; New Brunswick women became eligible to hold office in 1934 and Ontario women in 1919. Only Quebec held back and refused to grant the vote to women.

At the federal level, women's franchise was achieved in three phases. The Military Voters Act in 1917 gave the vote to women nurses serving in the war. Later that year, the Wartime Elections Act extended the franchise to the wives, widows, mothers, sisters, and daughters of those, alive or deceased, who had served or were serving in the Canadian or British military or naval forces. This Act, designed to help re-elect Borden's Union government and endorse its mandate for conscription, drew both praise and outrage from suffrage advocates.[74] Support came primarily from people who, in the wartime context, believed in the superiority of the Anglo-Saxon race and saw the vote as a way of reshaping society according to their values. Opponents, like the Victoria and Regina Local Councils of Women, both of which passed resolutions protesting the law, also saw the vote as an instrument for achieving social change, but objected to the Act's discriminatory provisions, maintaining that valid change could be achieved only when all women acquired equal political rights with men.[75] Their political objective was finally met in 1918 with the passage of the federal Women's Franchise Act, which gave the vote to women who were over the age of 21 and British subjects, and who possessed the same qualifications as men required for the provincial franchise. Women of Asian descent, like their menfolk, could not vote, because they were not eligible to become British subjects. The unrestricted right to the federal vote was also denied to Native women — who, along with Native men, remained disenfranchised under the terms of the Indian Act until 1960. Full political participation in band politics had also been denied to Native women by the federal government in 1869.[76] Eligible Canadian women had, however, achieved the franchise before women in Great Britain and, as far as the federal government was concerned, in the United States as well. The following year, the federal government enacted legislation enabling women to be elected to the House of Commons.[77]

The timing of these victories has generated considerable discussion among historians. Why did most of Canada's governments acquiesce to the campaign for the suffrage between 1916 and 1925? Why, in contrast, did Quebec not participate in the general trend? The first question is perhaps the easiest to answer. Certainly "political motives" are obvious major factors in the 1917 federal decision. Borden's Union government clearly had much to gain from the prospect of a loyal voting block of newly enfranchised women, at the height of bitterness over the conscription issue. In British Columbia and Manitoba, suffrage had become a partisan issue; newly elected Liberal governments were simply fulfilling their campaign promises. In Ontario, the incumbent Conservative government under Premier William Hearst gradually recognized the expediency of accepting female suffrage; in addition, Hearst was evidently pressured by Prime Minister Borden to adopt the cause. Concern about capturing women's votes undoubtedly motivated the Alberta and New Brunswick Liberal governments as well.

This 1917 newspaper cartoon equates conscription with defending the honour of womanhood and the sentimentality of patriotism.

Source: Racey, 1917,
The Montreal Daily Star.

The suffrage movement in Newfoundland developed strong links to the international movement through its membership in the International Woman Suffrage Alliance.[78] International influences may also have played a part in other victories. After 1910 a revitalized feminist movement was sweeping Europe and North America, making it more difficult for Canadian legislators to justify women's continued exclusion. A negative stance became even harder to defend in the light of women's acknowledged and valued contributions to the war effort. Speeches introducing franchise measures certainly often cited these contributions as a major rationale. It has also been suggested that the growth of a female labour market increased women's visibility as an independent force and gradually paved the way for the acceptance of equal political rights. Ultimately, the extraordinarily persistent efforts of the suffragist campaigners paid off. The campaign, after all, had taken some 60 years to win. From the time it began, thousands of women and hundreds of organizations had been involved in the fight for political rights. Even during periods of apparent inactivity and division, the movement never completely lost its focus or momentum.

The reform movement that had claimed more than half a century of women's attention could boast other important victories by 1920. Through their work aimed at counteracting the problems associated with urbanization, improving the status and well-being of women in the workplace, and eradicating the inequities faced by women in family law, Canadian feminists never lost sight of the importance of family and children. They idealized the family and believed that a stable family life could both prevent and counteract social degeneration and promote moral regeneration. This led to a call for state support for the family. Rather than providing for children in state institutions, feminist reformers and their allies sought and won channels for legal adoptions, and in some provinces the establishment of Children's Aid Societies. By 1920, allowances for mothers to tide them over economically difficult times were available in Manitoba (1916), Saskatchewan (1917), Alberta (1919), and British Columbia and Ontario (1920). Reform-minded women had also been involved over the years in the kindergarten movement and the founding of Home and School Associations. They had advocated and achieved separate courts, trials, and institutions for the group of children and adolescents increasingly identified as "juvenile delinquents." Gradually, various provinces accepted the need to provide separate facilities for female offenders.[79]

Reformers could take pride in all these accomplishments, but by far the greatest victory they achieved was the implementation of prohibition throughout Canada during the war years. The spirit of sacrifice, the strong commitment to the reformation of society, and the growing acceptance of government intervention in the lives of Canada's citizens, all evoked by the war, created a climate of opinion extremely favourable to the prohibitionists' cause. Supporters equated the corrupting liquor trade with the evil enemy, Kaiser Wilhelm, arguing that both were scourges of western civilization. Why sacrifice innocent young men to the Allied cause, only to have them frequent "wet" canteens and fall victims first to drink and then, in their vulnerable state, to prostitution and venereal disease? Moreover, prohibition advocates argued that it was inefficient to use valuable grain for the manufacture of alcohol when it might better be sent to the starving Allied nations.

On the basis of these and similar arguments, the prohibitionists' long-standing cry for the banishment of bottle and bar caught the attention and support of unprecedented numbers of Canadians, many of whom had previously been indifferent or overtly opposed to the temperance movement. Prohibitionist sentiment was strongest in the prairie provinces, whose politicians were unable to ignore it. Newfound allies for the prohibitionists included the Imperial Order Daughters of the Empire, the Orange Lodge, and the Anglican church. Significant numbers of immigrants, who had previously been resistant to temperance overtures, converted to the cause. Following the holding of provincial referenda, by the end of 1916 all three prairie governments had enacted prohibitory legislation. Within a year, all other provinces, with the exception of Quebec, also endorsed prohibition. In 1918 the Dominion government used its powers under the War Measures Act to apply prohibition to that province also, and to stop interprovincial trade in liquor.

Victory was now complete, but was prohibition the panacea that the WCTU and other supporters claimed it would be? Initially at least, they could take great satisfaction in the results: in Manitoba during the seven months following the introduction of prohibition, arrests for drunkenness fell by 87 percent, and all other crimes by nearly one-third; in Alberta, arrests for drunkenness declined by 90 percent in 1917 and 1918. People also praised the effectiveness of the new legislation in creating a safer and more wholesome environment. One enthusiastic Saskatchewan farm wife proudly informed the provincial premier that her small community, "formerly a drunkard's paradise, since the banishment of the bars and dispensaries has assumed an air of thrift and sobriety."[80]

The women's associations of the late nineteenth and early twentieth centuries met important needs. Accessible both to women who were able to make a full commitment and to those who could be involved only part time, the women's movement reached out to a remarkable number of women in Canadian society in one way or another. By 1916, journalist Marjory MacMurchy could proclaim that one out of every eight women in the Dominion belonged to the network of women's societies.[81] Organized activity not only provided a sense of purpose for many women, but also prevented their personal isolation and — through exposure to and participation in the community of like-minded women — intensified their common identity. Through their clubs, members learned the organizational and public skills essential to their greater participation in the urbanized and industrialized world of the twentieth century. The lobbying skills and national and international networks developed by women enabled them to mobilize as the need arose. For example, in 1911, when Angelina Napolitano of Sault Ste. Marie, Ontario, faced the death penalty for killing her abusive husband, organizations including the WCTU, the NCWC, and various suffrage societies from outside Canada mounted a clemency campaign that resulted in the commutation of the death sentence to life imprisonment.[82]

Although Canadian women reformers personally claimed victory for many of the social, economic, and political reforms of this period, the extent to which these can be described as uniquely women's victories is debatable. In certain areas, such as the temperance and suffrage movements, a direct relationship between women's efforts and the reform in question can be traced — although the efforts of male supporters of these causes clearly cannot be dismissed. In others, perhaps, men's and women's efforts were about equal. Male collaboration in feminist reform reflected the acceptance of women's movement goals by increasing numbers of Canadians. The thrust of the movement, with its emphasis on protecting the home and family life, perhaps posed no major threat to male supremacy. But it did challenge the exclusive nature of men's public power. Feminist thought radically challenged the supposed division of the world into men's and women's spheres by continuing to erode the boundaries between public and private activities. In the context of turn-of-the-century Canadian middle-class Christianity, the work of female reformers was genuinely radical. If their efforts fell short of social revolution, they nevertheless paved the way for more-revolutionary activity to come.

In the final analysis, although most historians identify "maternal" or "social" feminism as the dominant philosophy of this first-wave Canadian women's reform movement, the radical character of some aspects of the movement cannot be overlooked. From an early expression by the Toronto Women's Literary Club, the argument for equal rights evolved with, and often merged with, the idea of women's special maternal and nurturing role. Canadian middle-class women believed that, as mothers and as homemakers, they had knowledge and skills that were as valuable as and equal to men's knowledge and skills. In a just society, their value ought to be acknowledged and rewarded. These views challenged the unequal power balance within the family unit, and the issues of the times appeared to call forth women's talents; between 1850 and 1920, a growing body of educated women were sensitized to the need for public action. Ultimately, realistic appraisals of what was practical and generally acceptable guided women reformers.

NOTES

1. National Council of Women of Canada [NCWC], *Women of Canada: Their Life and Work* (Ottawa: NCWC, 1900, reprinted 1975).
2. NCWC, *Women of Canada*, 3.
3. Beth Light and Joy Parr, eds., *Canadian Women on the Move 1867–1920* (Toronto: New Hogtown Press and OISE Press, 1983), 187–88.
4. Mary Kinnear and Vera Fast, *Planting the Garden: An Annotated Archival Bibliography of the History of Women in Manitoba* (Winnipeg: University of Manitoba Press, 1987), 209; W.J. Lindal, *The Icelanders in Canada* (Ottawa/Winnipeg: National Publishers/Viking Printers, 1967), 304; Marcia Koven, *Weaving the Past into the Present: A Glimpse into the 130 Year History of the Saint John Jewish Community* (Saint John, N.B.: Saint John Jewish Historical Museum, 1989), 26–7; Robin Winks, *The Blacks in Canada: A History* (Montreal and Kingston: McGill-Queen's University Press, 1971), 348; Sylvia Hamilton, "The Women at the Well," in Linda Carty, ed., *And Still We Rise: Feminist Political Mobilizing in Contemporary Canada* (Toronto: Women's Press, 1993), 189–203.
5. Jean Bannerman, *Leading Ladies Canada* (Belleville, Ont.: Mika Publishing, 1977 Rev. ed.), 67; P.R. Blakeley, "Anna of Siam in Canada," *Atlantic Advocate* (January 1967), 41–45; Ernest Forbes, "Battles in Another War: Edith Archibald and the Halifax Feminist Movement," in his *Challenging the Regional Stereotypes* (Fredericton: Acadiensis Press, 1989), 71.
6. N.E.S. Griffiths, *The Splendid Vision: Centennial History of the National Council of Women of Canada, 1893–1993* (Ottawa: Carleton University Press, 1993), 91.
7. Catherine L. Cleverdon, *The Woman Suffrage Movement in Canada*, 2nd ed. (Toronto: University of Toronto Press, 1974), 29–33.

8. Deborah Gorham, "Flora MacDonald Denison: Canadian Feminist," in Linda Kealey, ed., *A Not Unreasonable Claim: Women and Reform in Canada, 1880s–1920s* (Toronto: Canadian Women's Educational Press, 1979), 47–70.

9. Karen Dubinsky, *Improper Advances: Rape and Heterosexual Conflict in Ontario, 1880–1929* (Chicago: University of Chicago Press, 1993), 140.

10. Gorham, "Flora MacDonald Denison," 56–57.

11. Gorham, "Flora MacDonald Denison," 58–60; Cleverdon, *Woman Suffrage Movement*, 36; Deborah Gorham, "English Militancy and the Canadian Suffrage Movement," *Atlantis* 1, 1 (Fall 1975), 83–112; Carol Bacchi, *Liberation Deferred?: The Ideas of the English-Canadian Suffragists 1877–1918* (Toronto: University of Toronto Press, 1983), 37–38.

12. Veronica Strong-Boag, "Canada's Women Doctors: Feminism Constrained," in Kealey, ed., *A Not Unreasonable Claim*, 124–26; Kathleen McConnachie, "Methodology in the Study of Women in History: A Case Study of Helen MacMurchy, M.D.," *Ontario History* 75 (March 1983), 61–70; Angus McLaren, "The Creation of a Haven for 'Human Thoroughbreds': The Sterilization of the Feeble-Minded and the Mentally Ill in British Columbia," *Canadian Historical Review* 67, 2 (June 1986), 127–50; Terry L. Chapman, "The Early Eugenics Movement in Western Canada," *Alberta History* 25 (1977), 9–17.

13. Carol Bacchi, "Race Regeneration and Social Purity: A Study of the Social Attitudes of Canada's English-Speaking Suffragists," *Histoire sociale/Social History* 11, 22 (November 1978), 460–74; Mariana Valverde, " 'When the Mother of the Race Is Free': Race, Reproduction and Sexuality in First-Wave Feminism," in Franca Iacovetta and Mariana Valverde, eds., *Gender Conflicts: New Essays in Women's History* (Toronto: University of Toronto Press, 1992), 15–21.

14. Stephen A. Speisman, *The Jews of Toronto: A History to 1937* (Toronto: McClelland and Stewart, 1987), 149–53; Luigi G. Pennacchio, "The Defence of Identity: Ida Siegel and the Jews of Toronto versus the Assimilation Attempts of the Public School and Its Allies, 1900–1920," *Canadian Jewish Historical Society Journal* 9, 1 (Spring 1985), 41–60; Irving Abella, *A Coat of Many Colours: Two Centuries of Jewish Life in Canada* (Toronto: Lester and Orpen Dennys, 1990), 153.

15. Marilyn Färdig Whitely, " 'Allee Sammee Melican Lady': Imperialism and Negotiation at the Chinese Rescue Home," *Resources for Feminist Research/Documentation sur la recherche féministe* 22, 3/4 (Fall/Winter 1993), 45–50.

16. *Census of Canada* (1901), Table 11, "Origins of the People." It is likely that census takers underestimated the size of the community.

17. Carrie Best, *That Lonesome Road* (New Glasgow, N.S.: Clarion Publishing, 1977), 189.

18. Georgina M. Taylor, " 'A Splendid Field before Us': Violet McNaughton and the Development of Agrarian Feminism in Canada, 1909 to 1926," paper presented to the Canadian Historical Association, Ottawa, 1993, 5.

19. Taylor, " 'Splendid Field,' " 5.

20. Taylor, " 'Splendid Field,' " 25.

21. Catherine C. Cole and Ann Milovic, "Education, Community Service, and Social Life: The Alberta Women's Institutes and Rural Families, 1909–1945," in Catherine A. Cavanaugh and Randi R. Warne, eds., *Standing on New Ground: Women in Alberta* (Edmonton: University of Alberta Press, 1993), 20–25.

22. Richard Allen, ed., *The Social Gospel in Canada* (Ottawa: National Museums of Canada, 1975), espec. Beatrice Brigden, "One Woman's Campaign for Social Purity and Social Reform," 36–62.

23. Paul Voisey, "The 'Votes for Women' Movement," *Alberta History* 23, 2 (Summer 1975), 17.

24. Candace Savage, *Our Nell: A Scrapbook Biography of Nellie L. McClung* (Saskatoon: Western Producer Prairie Books, 1979), 89.

25. Donald McCaig, *A Reply to John Stuart Mill on the Subjection of Women* (Philadelphia: J.B. Lippincott, 1870).

26. Goldwin Smith, "Woman Suffrage," in his *Essays on the Questions of the Day, Political and Social* (New York, 1893).

27. Stephen Leacock, "The Woman Question" in his *Essays and Literary Studies* (New York: John Lane, 1916).

28. Susan Mann Trofimenkoff, "Henri Bourassa and 'the Woman Question,'" *Journal of Canadian Studies* 10, 4 (November 1975), 3–11.

29. Terry Crowley, "Madonnas before Magdalenes: Adelaide Hoodless and the Making of the Canadian Gibson Girl," *Canadian Historical Review* 67, 4 (December 1986), 532.

30. Carol Bacchi, "Divided Allegiances: The Response of Farm and Labour Women to Suffrage," in Kealey, ed., *A Not Unreasonable Claim*, 89–108; Christine MacDonald, "How Saskatchewan Women Got the Vote," *Saskatchewan History* 1, 3 (October 1948), 1–9; Voisey, "'Votes for Women,'" 10–23; Cleverdon, *Woman Suffrage Movement*, chap. 3; Nellie McClung, *In Times Like These*, introduction by Veronica Strong-Boag (Toronto: University of Toronto Press, 1972), 54–55.

31. Janice Newton, "Women and *Cotton's Weekly*: A Study of Women and Socialism in Canada, 1909," paper presented at the fifth conference on Workers and their Communities, Toronto, 1984; Linda Kealey, "Prairie Socialist Women and WW I: The Urban West," paper presented to the Canadian Historical Association, Winnipeg, 1986.

32. Varpu Lindström-Best, *Defiant Sisters: A Social History of Finnish Immigrant Women in Canada* (Toronto: Multicultural History Society of Ontario, 1988), 151.

33. Lindström-Best, *Defiant Sisters*, 147–52.

34. Veronica Strong-Boag, "'Ever a Crusader': Nellie McClung, First-Wave Feminist," in Veronica Strong-Boag and Anita Clair Fellman, eds., *Rethinking Canada: The Promise of Women's History* (Toronto: Copp Clark Pitman, 1986), 178–90; Mary Hallett and Marilyn Davis, *Firing the Heather: The Life and Times of Nellie McClung* (Saskatoon: Fifth House, 1993).

35. McClung, *In Times Like These*, 48.

36. McClung, *In Times Like These*, 87.

37. Margaret E. McCallum, "Prairie Women and the Struggle for a Dower Law, 1905–1920," *Prairie Forum* 18, 1 (Spring 1993), 28.

38. Linda Silver Dranoff, *Women in Canadian Life: Law* (Toronto: Fitzhenry and Whiteside, 1977), 49.

39. Alvin Finkel, "Populism and Gender: The UFA and Social Credit Experience," *Journal of Canadian Studies* 27, 4 (Winter 1992–93), 80–81.

40. Georgina Binnie-Clark, *Wheat and Woman*, introduction by Susan Jackel (Toronto: University of Toronto Press, 1979); and Binnie-Clark, *A Summer on the Canadian Prairie* (London: Edward Arnold, 1910).

41. Elsie Gregory MacGill, *My Mother the Judge: A Biography of Helen Gregory MacGill*, introduction by Naomi Black (Toronto: Peter Martin Associates, 1981), 115.

42. Susan Wade, "Helena Gutteridge: Votes for Women and Trade Unions," in Barbara Latham and Cathy Kess, eds., *In Her Own Right: Selected Essays on Women's History in B.C.* (Victoria: Camosun College, 1980), 187–204; Dranoff, *Women in Canadian*

Life: Law, 70–73; Margaret E. McCallum, "Keeping Women in Their Place: The Minimum Wage in Canada, 1910–25," *Labour/Le travail* 17 (Spring 1986), 29–56.

43. Michael H. Cramer, "Public and Political— Documents of the Women's Suffrage Campaign in British Columbia, 1871–1917: The View from Victoria," in Gillian Creese and Veronica Strong-Boag, eds., *British Columbia Reconsidered: Essays on Women* (Vancouver: Press Gang, 1992), 60–64.

44. Wade, "Helena Gutteridge"; Cleverdon, *Woman Suffrage Movement*, chap. 4.

45. Elspeth Tulloch, *We, the Undersigned: A Historical Overview of New Brunswick Women's Political and Legal Status, 1784–1984* (Moncton: New Brunswick Advisory Council on the Status of Women, 1985), 44–45.

46. Tulloch, *We, the Undersigned*, 47–48.

47. Ernest Forbes, "The Ideas of Carol Bacchi and the Suffragists of Halifax," *Atlantis* 10, 2 (Spring 1985), 121.

48. Forbes, "Battles in Another War."

49. Cleverdon, *Woman Suffrage Movement*, 201–2; Margot I. Duley, *Where Once Our Mothers Stood We Stand: Women's Suffrage in Newfoundland 1890–1925* (Charlottetown: gynergy books, 1993), 78–95.

50. For an overview, see Susan Mann Trofimenkoff, *The Dream of Nation: A Social and Intellectual History of Quebec* (Toronto: Macmillan, 1982), chap. 6. On lay and religious women, see Marta Danylewycz, *Taking the Veil: An Alternative to Marriage, Motherhood, and Spinsterhood in Quebec, 1840–1920* (Toronto: McClelland and Stewart, 1987), espec. chap. 5.

51. Marie Lavigne, Yolande Pinard, and Jennifer Stoddart, "The *Fédération nationale Saint-Jean-Baptiste* and the Women's Movement in Quebec," in Kealey, ed., *A Not Unreasonable Claim*, 71–88; Yolande Pinard, "Les débuts du mouvement des femmes à Montréal, 1893–1902," in Marie Lavigne et Yolande Pinard, eds., *Travailleuses et féministes: Les femmes dans la société québécoise* (Montréal: Boréal Express, 1983), 177–98; Ruby Heap and Alison Prentice, "'The Outlook for Old Age Is Not Hopeful': The Struggle of Female Teachers over Pensions in Quebec, 1880–1914," *Histoire sociale/Social History* 26, 51 (May 1993), 67–94.

52. Christine Mander, *Emily Murphy: Rebel* (Toronto: Simon and Pierre, 1985); Byrne Hope Sanders, *Emily Murphy Crusader* (Toronto: Macmillan, 1945); Rebecca Priegert Coulter, "Between School and Marriage: A Case Study Approach to Young Women's Work in Early Twentieth Century Canada," *History of Education Review* 18, 2 (1989), 26–27.

53. Barbara M. Wilson, *Ontario and the First World War* (Toronto: Champlain Society, 1977), lxxxv–xcv and 101–47.

54. Wilson, *Ontario and the First World War*, lxxxvi.

55. Forbes, "Ideas of Carol Bacchi," 121–22.

56. Veronica Strong-Boag, *The Parliament of Women: The National Council of Women of Canada 1893–1929* (Ottawa: National Museums of Canada, 1976), 323–24.

57. Strong-Boag, *Parliament of Women*, chap. 7.

58. *Canadian Annual Review* (1917), 432.

59. Speisman, *The Jews of Toronto*, 195–97.

60. Crowley, "Madonnas before Magdalenes," 520–47.

61. *Canadian Annual Review* (1915, 1916, 1917).

62. W. Kristjanson, "Johanna Gudrun Skaptason," *Icelandic Canadian* (Winter 1960), 39.

63. Strong-Boag, *Parliament of Women*, 329; Griffiths, *Splendid Vision*, 166–67.

64. *Canadian Annual Review* (1916), 419; Duley, *Where Once*, 67–68.

65. Judith Fingard, "The New Woman Goes to College: Dalhousie Coeds, 1881–1921," unpublished paper (1986), 41–42; and Forbes, "Battles in Another War," 82–84.

66. Strong-Boag, *Parliament of Women*, 324–25.

67. Strong-Boag, *Parliament of Women*, 305, 329–32.

68. Tulloch, *We, the Undersigned*, 61.

69. Forbes, "Ideas of Carol Bacchi," 122.

70. Flora Denison, "War and Women," in Ramsay Cook and Wendy Mitchinson, eds., *The Proper Sphere: Woman's Place in Canadian Society* (Toronto: Oxford University Press, 1976), 249–52; Deborah Gorham, "Vera Brittain, Flora MacDonald Denison and the Great War: The Failure of Non-Violence," in Ruth Roach Pierson, ed., *Women and Peace: Theoretical, Historical and Practical Perspectives* (London: Croom Helm, 1987), 137.

71. McClung, *In Times Like These*, 15.

72. R.R. Warne, "Nellie McClung and Peace," in Janice Williamson and Deborah Gorham, eds., *Up and Doing: Canadian Women and Peace* (Toronto: Women's Press, 1989), 35–47; Barbara Roberts, "Women against War, 1914–1918: Francis Beynon and Laura Hughes," in Williamson and Gorham, eds., *Up and Doing*, 48–65.

73. Savage, *Our Nell*, 109–10.

74. Gloria Geller, "The Wartimes Elections Act of 1917 and the Canadian Women's Movement," *Atlantis* 2, 1 (Autumn 1976), 88–106.

75. *Canadian Annual Review* (1917), 428.

76. T. Bettel Dawson, *Relating to Law: A Chronology of Women and Law in Canada* (North York, Ont.: Captus, 1990), 36–37; Jo-Anne Fiske, "Child of the State Mother of the Nation: Aboriginal Women and the Ideology of Motherhood," *Culture* 13, 1 (1993), 18.

77. Cleverdon, *Woman Suffrage Movement*, chap. 5.

78. Duley, *Where Once*, 55, 77–78.

79. Neil Sutherland, *Children in English-Canadian Society: Framing the Twentieth-Century Consensus* (Toronto: University of Toronto Press, 1976).

80. John Herd Thompson, *The Harvests of War: The Prairie West, 1914–1918* (Toronto: McClelland and Stewart, 1978), 98–106.

81. Marjory MacMurchy, *The Woman Bless Her* (Toronto: S.B. Gundy, 1916).

82. Karen Dubinsky and Franca Iacovetta, "Murder, Womanly Virtue and Motherhood: The Case of Angelina Napolitano," *Canadian Historical Review* 72, 4 (December 1991), 505–31.

PART THREE

The Promised Land?
The End of the
Great War to the
Beginning of
World War Two

On a moonlit evening in May 1918, Allied encampments near Étable in France suffered a prolonged bombardment. By the time the seemingly endless attack was over, two Canadian field hospitals had been seriously damaged and four Canadian nursing sisters were dead or lay dying. Other nurses made heroic efforts to save the wounded: among them were the first nurses to receive the Military Medal for bravery.[1] The activities of the Canadian nursing sisters overseas dramatically illustrated the new responsibilities Canadian women had assumed, and the sacrifice they had made for the war effort. Women's wartime contribution was one of the principal arguments used to justify the granting of the federal franchise to the majority of women in Canada, which occurred in May 1918.

The contribution of both women and men to the Allied cause was used by the Canadian government to claim a more prominent position for the Dominion within the British empire. Prime Minister Robert Borden was one of the signatories to the Versailles Treaty at the end of World War I, the first Canadian representative to sign an international treaty in his own right. The subsequent gradual recognition of Canada as an entity with its own identity and interests laid the foundation for the evolution of the British empire into the Commonwealth. In 1931, the Statute of Westminster officially confirmed Canada's transformation from a dependent colony into a sovereign state.

World War I, then, was a turning point for Canada as a nation. The Canada of 1919 was profoundly different from the Canada of 1914 in several fundamental aspects — demographic, economic, political, and social. Wracked internally by divisions between French and English, east and west, labour and capital, and plunged into a serious recession, the emerging nation stood poised on the brink of an uncertain future. Most Canadians could scarcely imagine that only twenty years later they would be at war again, or that many would welcome war's arrival as a way to escape the grinding poverty and unemployment produced by the Depression of the 1930s.

The Canadian inter-war experience can best be described as turbulent. The transition from a wartime to a peacetime economy was a painful one, particularly for women workers; jobs generated by wartime production ceased, and both unemployment and inflation rose during the post-war depression. In this difficult economic climate, labour militancy intensified, as working men and women sought to protect or improve their standard of living. Radical new organizations, such as the One Big Union, brought together industrial workers regardless of their trade or skill, and led

Photo on previous page: Elsie Hall, first woman graduate of The College of Law, University of Saskatchewan, 1920. Source: College of Law, University of Saskatchewan.

many Canadians to fear that Bolshevism, recently triumphant in Russia, was about to wreak havoc in their own backyard. Thus, when workers initiated massive walkouts across the nation in the spring of 1919, the full weight of the Canadian state was ranged against them. The ensuing defeat of labour precipitated a rapid decline in union membership throughout the 1920s, and left the labour movement dispirited.

The expanding economy of the middle and late 1920s, particularly buoyant in central and western Canada, did result in new job opportunities and unprecedented prosperity for some segments of the Canadian population. The most significant economic growth occurred in the resource-related industries, especially in pulp and paper and in mining, but these industries provided few employment opportunities for women. Women had been urged by public officials to give up their paid employment at war's end; pressured by economic need, poor women and women from ethnic and racial minorities paid no heed. With the return of prosperity, young single white women were once again actively recruited into the workforce, mainly in the growing clerical and service sectors. In the manufacturing sector, owners and managers used new technologies and "scientific management" techniques to rationalize their operations and to reduce labour costs. Many skilled jobs were eliminated and replaced by repetitive assembly work; skilled workers were often pitted against unskilled workers, female workers against male workers.

The improved economic conditions of the mid-1920s did make it possible for some male workers to support their families on their own wages—the "family wage" was becoming a reality. Conversely, the traditional family economy, to which all able-bodied members of the family were expected to contribute, was under attack. Smaller families, and legislation in most provinces extending compulsory school attendance, reduced the number of children in the paid labour force and reinforced married women's roles as mothers and consumers; their participation in the economy as paid workers was increasingly criticized as unnecessary and ill-advised.

Yet with the onset of the Great Depression in 1929, few families could rely on one male wage earner. Among the western industrialized countries, Canada was one of the most adversely affected by the economic downturn, since its economy was so dependent on the export of commodities. Between 1926 and 1933, the price of wheat fell from $1.09 to 35 cents per bushel, and that of newsprint from $70 to $41 per ton.[2] Entire single-industry towns were abandoned as families moved, usually to the larger urban centres, in a frenzied attempt to find jobs. In many families, only wives and daughters were able to find employment; but as the Depression deepened, women found it extremely difficult to keep their paid work, and as unemployment soared, married and single women were blamed for contributing to the nation's problems by taking jobs away from men. Thousands of men, and some women, jumped on freight trains and travelled across the nation searching for jobs. Although there were several indicators that the worst of the Depression was over by 1937, for hundreds of thousands of Canadians conditions improved only after Canada entered World War II in September 1939.

The wildly alternating cycles of bust—boom—bust from 1919 to 1939 created enormous fluctuations in population growth. Although the population increased from nearly 9 million in 1921 to 11.5 million by 1941, the pace of growth slowed and was at its lowest during the Depression years. For the first time since official records were begun in 1851, the number of births dropped during an intercensal period: between 1931 and 1941, there were only 2.29 million births, compared to 2.42 million during the previous decade. The most startling demographic change was the sharp decline in immigration after 1931, as economic conditions worsened and the Canadian government restricted immigration: a mere 149 000 immigrants arrived between 1931 and 1941, the lowest number recorded for any decade since 1851. Just as immigration plummeted during the Depression, so too did emigration, most notably to the United States. During the 1920s, 970 000 residents left Canada; but in the following decade, the United States tightened its immigration policies, and fewer than a quarter of a million Canadians left their native or adopted land to re-establish themselves elsewhere.

The impact of the Depression on population was most noticeable in Saskatchewan. The collapse of wheat prices, prolonged drought, and the plagues of grasshoppers that devoured the few existing crops proved too much for many of the province's residents. Over 150 000 more people left the province than entered it, and in spite of natural increase, there were 25 000 fewer inhabitants in 1941 than there had been ten years earlier. The pace of urbanization also slowed during the Depression: the proportion of all Canadians who resided in urban settings grew only 3 percent, reaching a level of 55.7 percent in 1941. As in the past, there were more women than men in the urban centres, especially in the 15–29 age group. For the first time since the census began in 1851, there were also more women than men urban residents in the 30–34 age group, reflecting both the increased employment opportunities for women in this age group in the cities, and the departure of some of the men to perform military service.

Fluctuations in the nation's economy and population in the inter-war period created an atmosphere conducive to political change. Discontent with the Borden administration's wartime policies combined with the economic and social turmoil that enveloped the nation immediately after the war to produce new political movements and parties. Across the nation, farmers deserted the traditional parties to support emerging organizations such as the Progressive movement in western Canada and the United Farmers of Ontario. Workers, returned veterans, and other disaffected groups variously sought to register their protest during federal and provincial elections by supporting socialist and labour parties, or independent candidates. The formation of the Communist Party of Canada, at a secret meeting held in a barn near Guelph, Ontario, in 1921, provided those on the left with yet another vehicle for political protest. These alternative political parties gave newly enfranchised women new avenues of political involvement. It soon became apparent, however, that women and men voters preferred the two traditional parties, particularly the Liberal Party. For most of the 1920s, federal politics were dominated by the back-and-forth struggle for power between the bland but adroit Liberal leader, William Lyon Mackenzie King, and the brilliant but hapless Arthur Meighen, who had replaced Borden at the helm of the Conservative Party in 1920. With the exception of a few brief days, King managed to hold onto power for the Liberals by his skilful courting of the west and of Quebec.

Even King's political finesse, however, was no match for the cataclysmic impact of the Great Depression, and in 1930 he was defeated by the Conservatives, now led by millionaire R.B. Bennett. Before King left office, however, Canadian women had the small satisfaction of seeing him name the first woman senator. The Liberal defeat was only a preliminary indication of a substantial political upheaval engendered by the Depression. At the federal level, the Co-operative Commonwealth Federation (CCF), formed in Calgary in 1932, and the Reconstruction Party led by maverick Tory H.H. Stevens offered new alternatives for voters in the election of 1935. Like most other leftist political organizations, the CCF officially endorsed the full participation of women and provided many women with a forum for involvement in the political process. Agnes Macphail, Canada's first woman MP, was among its founding members. Canadians, however, were in a cautious mood and preferred reinstating King and the Liberals to engaging in political experimentation. The advent of new parties and colourful leaders was more momentous at the provincial level. Duff Patullo and the Liberals in British Columbia, "Bible Bill" Aberhart and the Social Credit in Alberta, Mitchell Hepburn and the Liberals in Ontario, and Maurice Duplessis and the *Union Nationale* in Quebec all rode to power on a wave of protest against incumbents long ensconced in their respective legislatures.

One of the new tools that this generation of politicians had at their disposal was the radio. Radio broke down much of the isolation that had been a hallmark of living in Canada, putting Canadians in contact not only with one another but also with the rest of the world. It often provided women at home with their only form of entertainment, and it served as a powerful instrument for the dissemination of information and mass culture. The other major technological innovation of the inter-war period that brought Canadians into closer contact was the automobile; by 1930 there were more than 1.2 million motor vehicles registered in Canada. The car made it possible for workers to commute longer distances and so stimulated the growth of suburban areas. This one development alone had important ramifications for thousands of married women, whose own workplace, the home, was consequently changed. Households tended to become smaller and more private; increased emphasis was put on the nuclear family as a unit of consumption rather than of production, and on married women's role in making the home a haven in an increasingly complex society. As scientific management principles were applied to the household, women were expected to save time and energy through more efficient home management, and spend more time with their children and husbands.

Capturing the essence of women's experience during this exciting phase of Canadian history is both easier and more difficult than for earlier periods. For this period, oral sources are available to feminist scholars; these can be used to supplement traditional written sources. New magazines directed chiefly at middle-class women made their appearance during the 1920s, and provide a fascinating window on women's domestic and public life. This period also saw the first tentative steps toward the welfare state, with the implementation of programs such as mothers' allowances and old age pensions. Government bureaucracies generated masses of documents on many aspects of women's lives. On the other hand, it is more difficult to locate personal letters and diaries for the inter-war years. Women probably wrote fewer letters because the telephone was becoming more available, and new forms of entertainment took up their limited spare time. Moreover, personal documents such as diaries and letters may not yet be deposited in archives. This period has also received somewhat less attention from historians than that between 1850 and 1918. The study of women's organizations after World War I, for example, is less extensive than it is for the earlier period.

This may explain the belief— only recently challenged— that the women's movement in Canada disappeared after the achievement of suffrage. Careful reconstruction of the activities and issues that mainstream women's organizations pursued during the inter-war years is beginning to reveal that, on the contrary, many groups continued to work actively for the transformation of Canadian society in accordance with their interpretation of feminist principles. This finding raises the important question of why women's issues failed to generate the public attention they had attracted during the suffrage campaign.

Other questions focus on technology. What was the impact, as far as women were concerned, of the changes that were introduced into the home and factory in the name of improved efficiency? New and improved appliances and products became available in the majority of middle-class urban households as the distribution of electricity widened. Did their use significantly lighten women's load, or did these changes create new demands on women's time and energy? Finally, recent studies of women during the Depression have raised questions about how major economic change affects the role and status of women over time.

NOTES

1. G.W.L. Nicholson, *Canada's Nursing Sisters* (Toronto: Hakkert, 1975), 92–93.
2. A.E. Safarian, *The Canadian Economy in The Great Depression* (Toronto: McClelland and Stewart, 1970), 196, 202.

CHAPTER NINE

New Opportunities, Old Obstacles: Women in the Corporate Economy, 1918–1939

It is a natural conviction that enfranchised Canadian women will apply them-

selves intelligently and with energy to the basic economic problems of national

existence. It is only through the help of women that the future can be made

secure. The co-operation of Canadian women in industrial life and reconstruction

is indispensable.[1]

So wrote Marjory MacMurchy, a well-known journalist, at the end of World War I. The gains women had made in the labour force during the war inspired considerable optimism; reformers like MacMurchy and Nellie McClung believed that, since women had proven invaluable to the war effort and had won the vote, a new era of social reform and advancement for women was certain to follow. For them, "reconstruction" meant not the restoration of Canadian society as it existed prior to 1914, but rather its reorganization and renovation into a more perfect society.

At the same time, most Canadians remained convinced that women's primary place was in the home. It was taken for granted that when the hostilities ceased and the men returned, women would cheerfully surrender their newly acquired positions in the workforce. To make certain that women understood this, the federal government bombarded them with a poster campaign. "Do you feel justified in holding a job which could be filled by a man who has not only himself to support, but a wife and family as well?" one such poster demanded: "Think it over."[2] Women were urged to seek "feminine" areas of employment where they would not threaten the position of male workers.

Much attention was now focussed on new opportunities for single, educated women to engage in work that was light, clean, and non-threatening to their womanhood. Education was stressed for all young women; if women were transient, low-wage workers, it was because they had failed to equip themselves adequately for the workplace.[3] Occupations such as nutritionist, social worker, journalist, sales clerk, stenographer, and librarian were highly recommended for the educated woman. One brochure extolled the advantages of secretarial work for university-trained women and, lest any old-fashioned prejudice remain against higher education for women, an American study was cited showing that the infant mortality rate for mothers with university training was less than half that for mothers of similar social standing but with less schooling.[4]

Indeed, most commentators continued to stress motherhood as the principal and most rewarding career for Canadian women. While there was a new emphasis on vocational training and higher education for women, and a wider acceptance of single women in paid employment, women were expected to work at jobs for only a few years before marriage. Women were reminded that "no other work that a woman can do is as important to Canada as making a home and taking care of children."[5] Given the loss of 60 000 Canadian lives during the war, full-time mother-hood acquired an enhanced practical and symbolic importance, however much an unreality it was for many women. Those from minority races or ethnicities, as well as aboriginal women, remained likely to seek work all of their adult lives. So too did those who, from necessity or choice, did not live with a wage-earning man: war widows, those whose fiancés were killed in the war, lesbians. All continued to receive lower wages than men for the same or comparable work; legislation and public attitudes remained unresponsive to such problems as sexual harassment and job segregation.

THE MODERN "WORKING GIRL"

The tremendous social and economic dislocation the nation experienced at war's end reinforced the pre-war belief that women should not compete for men's jobs. Massive unemployment, labour unrest, and political ferment characterized the last years of the war and the immediate post-war era. By 1918, female unemployment had risen significantly; it was one of the issues discussed at the Women's War Conference in February of that year. Thousands of female workers suffered enormous hardships as jobs became scarce, wages were cut, and inflation soared. Although the Women's Department of the Reconstruction Association proclaimed that this was the age of the woman at work, it too counselled women to avoid direct competition with men for jobs: experienced female munitions workers were not to take employment in machine shops where there was already an excess of male workers. Only highly skilled, extraordinarily strong women with exceptional financial needs, it was argued, were justified in continuing to work in the metal trades, and even they were cau-tioned to avoid undercutting male wages. When women could secure employment, they often had to be content with traditional female jobs and inadequate wages. According to a sympathetic observer in Hamilton, Ontario, some were forced into prostitution to support themselves and their dependents.

> And they are all working girls! Here was the dressmaker's apprentice who could not live on nothing a week, there the worker in the jam factory who was out of work for three months and had to find her bread on the street. . . . Clerks, barmaids, factory hands, servants, laundry workers, every trade was represented in which women are over-worked and exploited.[6]

Given women workers' low wages and acute vulnerability to the ravages of post-war inflation, it is not surprising that they played an active part in the labour unrest that swept through many communities after the war. Women were the first to walk out in the Winnipeg General Strike on May 15, 1919, when some 500 telephone operators left their jobs shortly after dawn; hundreds of confectionery workers and sales clerks subsequently joined them. One of the most visible strike organizers was Helen Armstrong, president of the city's Women's Labour League. She was arrested several times and, on one occasion, jailed for several days for urging workers to strike and for inciting strikers to violence. Under Armstrong's direction, the Women's Labour League, a progressive, non-partisan, working-class group, provided up to 1500 meals daily to women strikers and others in need. In addition, the League gave cash grants to women who were on strike to cover the cost of their rent. Merchants or their agents who sought to carry on business as usual incurred the wrath of women who supported the strike; one company had three delivery wagons destroyed, and its drivers assaulted. A detective sent out to investigate warned men not to go to that district for "his life is in danger if these women find out that he is at work, or had been working during the strike." Not all women, however, supported the strike; some worked to undermine it by crossing picket lines to provide what they considered essential services.[7]

The telephone operators in Vancouver played a visible but costly role in the general strike called there to support the Winnipeg workers. They did not join the initial walkout, since they were classified as essential workers by the strike committee; but 300 operators left their jobs at the peak of the strike in the middle of June. Although the Vancouver General Strike came to an end on July 3, the operators remained on strike until the middle of the month to protest the telephone company's policy of replacing striking supervisors and senior employees with strikebreakers. In the end the operators had to return to work on the company's terms, and within a year the telephone operators' union disappeared.[8]

In Toronto, some women workers actively supported the union movement — especially the attempt of less-skilled workers to organize on an industrial rather than on a craft basis. By the end of 1919, hundreds of women telephone operators had secured substantial improvements in their working conditions through unionization, and a newly established union of bank employees claimed that over half of all bank clerks, many of whom were women, had joined its ranks. Other groups of women who had traditionally been considered unorganizable, such as domestic servants and waitresses, also joined unions. During the sympathy strike called in mid-May to support Toronto metal workers, approximately 2000 garment workers joined in a show of solidarity.[9]

By 1921, more than 17 percent of all Canadian women over the age of 15 were counted as members of the paid labour force, and they constituted 15 percent of all paid workers. There was considerable regional variation: female labour-force participation rates were higher in Ontario and Quebec (19 percent), and considerably lower in Prince Edward Island (13.5 percent) and in Saskatchewan and Alberta (13 percent). In the latter two provinces, there were so few jobs for women that they constituted fewer than one in ten paid workers. Even after the severe recession of the early 1920s gave way to the relative national prosperity of the latter part of the decade, female workers everywhere continued to experience the injustices arising from the ghettoization of women's work. Domestic service; the textile, clothing, and food industries; clerical work; teaching; and nursing — all were characterized by low wages, poor working conditions, and limited job opportunities.

Staff of the Newfoundland Hotel dining room in the 1930s: waitresses and their (male) supervisor.

Source: Provincial Archives of Newfoundland and Labrador, Hayward 1546.

As in previous decades, the majority of women who worked outside the home were young and single. According to one Vancouver survey, eight out of ten working women in that city were under 25 years of age. The 1920s has been portrayed as a period during which young people asserted their independence and challenged the moral and social dictates of their parents; but in reality, the lives of working-class daughters throughout Canada largely replicated those of their mothers.[10] Economic necessity still compelled thousands of girls under the age of 15 to go out to work. Most unmarried employed women continued to live at home or under the watchful eye of relatives or other surrogate parents, and to hand over a significant portion of their meagre earnings to their families. Quebec textile workers in the 1920s, for example, reported that they kept only a small portion of their bi-monthly pay for themselves; in some cases this amounted to just a few cents. Single Jewish women working in Toronto's garment industry did the same, as did Chinese store clerks in British Columbia and Ukrainian daughters on the Prairies.[11] Because family was considered so important, young working women did not generally object to this custom. Even had they wanted to live away from home, their low wages would have prevented most of them from doing so.

For women living in small or remote communities, domestic service frequently continued to be the only form of paid employment available. "I had to go out and earn my own bread," Elizabeth Goudie of Labrador recalled.

> I never was home much after the age of fourteen. The wages were very low. I went to work for two dollars a month. If the family was very poor you only got your food or maybe the makings of a new dress. This work wasn't easy. You had to do everything by hand: scrub, wash, bring wood and water, help to cook and mend clothing.[12]

As most Canadian-born white women continued to reject the long hours, low wages, demeaning status, and lack of privacy of household service, the federal government increased its efforts to encourage the immigration of foreign-born domestics. The majority still came from Great Britain; in the decade after the war, some 80 000 British women, including large numbers of working-class women sponsored by the Salvation Army, entered Canada as domestic servants. Domestic service was also still being advocated as a suitable occupation for British "gentlewomen," who were provided accommodation in hostels such as the Queen Mary's Coronation Hostel in Vancouver, where they were also given six- to eight-week training courses to enable them to secure employment as "home helps." The promoters of this type of work, usually pursued in rural areas for $20 to $25 per month, claimed that it was appropriate for British "ladies" since they were to be placed with families of similar social standing to their own, and to be treated as one of the family.[13]

There was a substantial increase in non-British domestic servants during the 1920s, however. One-quarter of all immigrant domestics in Ontario in 1931 were from continental Europe; those from Germany and the Scandinavian countries were preferred. For all its constraints, domestic service could have several positive features: steady employment, room and board, an opportunity to learn English or French and to become familiar with middle-class Canadian customs. Angelina, a Mi'kmaq of Prince Edward Island, escaped from a "terrible childhood" and left home at age 15 in 1919.

> I did not want to live there. I could only get three cents a quart for blueberries
> and I resented the fact that I could barely speak English, that I had no education,
> that all I could do was wash dishes and scrub floors.

She left the reserve to take a domestic job in Springhill, Nova Scotia, that paid the greater amount of $5 a month. Later, she moved to the United States; there she married and remained until widowed. In 1969, hoping to use her savings to retire to her homeland on Lennox Island, she discovered that by marrying a non-Indian she had lost her Indian status and her right to live on the reserve.[14]

Domestic service frequently provided a means of economic improvement for women. Finnish servants, who constituted 8 percent of all immigrant domestics in the 1920s, took great pride in their work; for them, to be a servant was to be far from servile. When conditions proved unsatisfactory, they reacted energetically and in a variety of ways, ranging from frequent changes of employer to collective organization. Indeed, during the 1920s Finnish maids' organizations were established in a number of urban centres.[15]

The newly created Woman's Branch of the Department of Immigration also recruited women from central and eastern Europe for household service. All unaccompanied immigrant women were put under the supervision of federally appointed train conductresses, who were to prevent their charges from being enticed away with offers of employment before they reached their intended destinations. Yet escapes occurred. From one party of twenty-five women, three ran away in Montreal, and another two were caught trying to climb through the window minutes before the train's departure.[16]

Domestic service was also the lot of many of the Chinese and Japanese women who managed to circumvent the severe restrictions placed on immigration from Asia. In 1923 even this trickle of female immigrants from China was stemmed when the federal government, in response to the deep-rooted racism of most Canadians and to continuing hysteria about the "yellow peril," passed the Chinese Exclusion Act, which excluded all Chinese people from permanent settlement in Canada. This legislation remained in force until 1947. Although Japanese and South Asian women were not explicitly barred from entry into Canada, a number of policies adopted by the Department of Immigration effectively kept their numbers low during the interwar period. Willingness to work as a domestic could ease entry to Canada. Almost twice as many black women as men entered Canada via ocean ports between 1916 and 1928. Of the 411 black women admitted to the country, the vast majority (329) came as domestic servants.[17]

The trend away from live-in domestics to household helpers hired on a daily basis became firmly established during the decade following World War I.[18] After the war, many married immigrant women were engaged as daily household workers when their husbands were unable to find employment; the men stayed home to look after the children. Such arrangements made it possible for the family to survive, but could result in strained relationships.

In western Canada, immigrant husbands and wives were frequently employed together as agricultural labourers. When Helen Potrebenko's parents first arrived in Alberta in 1928, her mother "fed the pigs in the morning, milked five cows, separated the milk, washed the separator, then repeated the whole thing in the evening. In between, she picked roots on newly-broken land," all for $1 per day. Even when women stooked grain all day long in the fields as efficiently as their husbands, they were paid less than the men.[19] Women also constituted half the seasonal workers in the fruit-growing areas of Ontario's Erie and Niagara regions in 1930. Similarly, British Columbia farmers relied heavily on women workers. Chinese women have since recalled their experience of this work. Ruth remembered: "The women used to take me to the farms when I was four or five in the summers. My mom weeded for 10 cents an hour in the 1920s." As a teenager in the late 1930s, by picking at least 100 pounds of beans a day, Ying could earn between $3 and $5.[20]

Women workers in urban areas could usually count on better wages and shorter hours than they could obtain as domestic or agricultural workers. However, they remained clustered in certain industries and confined to low-paying jobs. Even in industries where they formed a significant proportion of the workforce, women rarely posed a direct threat to male employment, since jobs were generally assigned on the basis of gender and race. A complex interplay of factors determined the sexual division of labour in this period. In general, women were excluded from skilled positions or from exercising control over the work process or over other workers. "Foreladies" were rare, and exercised authority only over other female operatives. In work resembling that done in the home, women were still relegated to positions with less control and fewer rewards than those held by men. In the clothing industry, men had more-prestigious and better-paying positions as cutters and pressers, while women lined, hemmed, and finished the garments. When women and men did the same work, they often worked on different shifts—the women during the day, the men at night. Most factory departments were therefore predominantly of one sex, thus enhancing solidarity among workers of the same sex but impeding a sense of common interest between the sexes. When women and men performed the same tasks and were paid on an hourly basis, the men were nearly always paid at a higher rate. In the Toronto garment industry, the average female wage was one-half to two-thirds of the average male wage.[21]

During the 1920s, industrial workers of both sexes had to contend with the consequences of an increased emphasis on efficiency and scientific management techniques. As a result of time studies and technological innovation, operatives faced speed-ups and ever-mounting production quotas. Women workers, on the whole, were more vulnerable to the negative effects of technological change, since they were virtually excluded from the decision-making process and were more often paid piece rates. When workers consistently achieved their quotas, unscrupulous employers cut their piecework rates. Prostitutes were always paid "piece rates," but at least their rates were higher. In some Montreal brothels, the prostitutes were said to entertain up to 40 clients a night, and they were able to keep half of the $1 each client was charged.[22]

The nervous strain created by the hectic pace of production in manufacturing took its toll on the workers' health. In one Winnipeg clothing factory, a labour newspaper reported that the "girls" were seated side by side on long benches, and all sewing machines were operated by a single motor. As a result, the individual operators could not leave their machines without causing all to fall behind. The only respite from this incredibly arduous regimen was the half-hour the workers were allowed for lunch, which they were compelled to eat in the workroom.[23]

Despite the introduction in most provinces during the 1920s of legislation setting minimum standards for wages, hours, and conditions for female workers in industrial establishments, abuses were rife. There were too few factory inspectors to provide effective enforcement, and the worst injustices occurred in individual households under the system of sweated labour. Entire families, often recent immigrants, basted, hemmed, cut out appliqués, or sewed on buttons at wages well below those paid in factories. Such workers were generally at the mercy of the clothing subcontractors, and were not protected by legislation of any sort. Home work, for all its problems, was nevertheless the preferred form of employment for Italian women, since it allowed them to work with other family members and to combine paid employment with domestic responsibilities. Nor was such work confined to the garment trade; in Toronto one food company sent out bushels of onions to Italian women for peeling and washing, and then collected them for further processing at its plant.[24]

Working in a lobster cannery, New Brunswick, 1920.

Source: E.M. Finn/National Archives of Canada/C-053850.

Given the difficult conditions, limited opportunities, and low status of women workers in manufacturing, clerical work became an increasingly attractive option. In 1929 the Toronto Local Council of Women surveyed 300 stenographers and secretaries. They found that 79 percent lived with their employed husbands and 57 percent had children. The largest number (35 percent) said that they worked to support themselves. Other reasons for working, in descending order, included the following: to assist with their children's education, to live more comfortably, to support their mothers, and to meet liabilities. Slightly more than half saw their work as long-term, giving responses such as "always" to a question about how long they intended to work.[25]

By the early 1920s there was already a glut of stenographers and typists; ironically, these women shared a common fate with their supposed social inferiors, the "factory girls." Some stenographers and secretaries continued to perform skilled work, but with the increased specialization that took place after 1920, many female office workers were relegated to subordinate positions that were routine, low-paying, and dead-end. Like the factory operatives, clerical workers experienced the negative effects of mechanization: work became fragmented, the pace of work increased, and supervision intensified.[26] For visible-minority women, there was the added problem of racial discrimination. Businesses routinely refused to hire Chinese or black women with secretarial training and, as one observer noted in 1930 with respect to black women in Montreal, "unless they have no negroid features coloured girls cannot obtain work in offices and stores."[27]

The influx of women into the federal civil service during the first decades of the twentieth century had been a source of great concern for male bureaucrats, who feared the large numbers of women would deter bright young men from pursuing careers in government. After 1910 the most important positions were reserved for men. In 1918 additional restrictions were placed on female employment, and by 1921 women were virtually excluded from all permanent positions in the federal bureaucracy. Female employees who married were required to hand in their resignations. These stringent measures achieved their goal: between 1921 and 1931 there was a 13 percent decline in the number of female civil servants working in Ottawa, while the number of male civil servants increased by more than 6 percent.[28] Other white-collar occupations generally regarded as appropriate for women were those of sales clerk and telephone operator. In these positions too, women were subject to a rigid sexual division of labour, intense competition from other women workers, low wages, and long hours.

Women's opportunities for advancement in the business world were extremely limited. Deeply rooted misogynist views surfaced in articles such as "Woman in Business Is Still at Heart a Woman," in which the author pontificated, "A man can do business very successfully with someone he dislikes but I have never met a woman who could."[29] Since it was assumed that women were destined for marriage, it seemed a waste of time and money to train them for more-responsible positions. Nevertheless, wives were often indispensable to the successful operation of small family businesses such as restaurants, laundries, grocery stores, and shoeshine parlours. As one Canadian-born Chinese woman recalled,

> My mother helped out for many long hours in the laundry. She did not even go out to shop. She worked the longest. My mother worked six days and also Sunday. . . . Sometimes she had to cook for thirteen.[30]

Rosetta Amon Richardson, the Toronto-born daughter of an underground railroad refugee, owned and operated the city's first Soul Food Restaurant with her husband before setting up and running a lunch counter at the Canadian National Exhibition.[31]

Traditional skills continued to be valuable sources of family income. Black women sold baskets at Halifax's city market, as they had since at least the mid-nineteenth century. In 1928, at age 8, Edith Clayton of East Preston, Nova Scotia, made her first maple basket for sale, thereby maintaining a six-generation family tradition. Across the continent in British Columbia, grandmother Mollyann of the Sechelt band also wove baskets, using the cedar roots she collected. She traded these to clothe her fifteen children and later her grandchildren. Mi'kmaq women of Prince Edward Island applied their traditional skills to resist government initiatives to keep them and their families as stationary farmers at the Lennox Island Reserve. Cash earned through selling baskets and other crafts supported the Mi'kmaq in maintaining, albeit at near starvation-level wages, the migratory way of life they had historically preferred. Flower-selling, fishing, and blueberry- and potato-picking supplemented Mi'kmaq women's craft income. In the outports of Newfoundland, wives earned much-needed cash through their berry-picking, and continued their management of the complex, all-important processing of the cod catch on shore. Resourceful women everywhere capitalized on or created opportunities to develop lucrative businesses. For example, Finnish women bootleggers or *Koiratorpparit* (doghouse/blind pig keepers) in the male-dominated resource towns (as well as in the urban centres) of the 1920s, controlled the illegal liquor business within their communities.[32]

The majority of "professional" women during this period were teachers and nurses still struggling to obtain self-regulation, status, and appropriate monetary rewards. In the field of education, the proportion of women hired as full-time university faculty increased during the 1920s; but, as studies of women employed at Dalhousie University and at the Universities of Toronto and Manitoba show, most women with advanced degrees occupied the lower-paid and less prestigious jobs of instructor or demonstrator.[33] The extraordinary heroism of the Canadian nursing sisters who served overseas during the war, and the important role nurses played in combatting the horrendous Spanish influenza epidemic of 1918–19 that resulted in 50 000 Canadian deaths, greatly enhanced the public image of nursing, especially in English Canada. Attempting to capitalize on their new respectability, determined nurses engaged in an intensified campaign to control their profession. In 1919, the first university degree program in nursing in the British empire was established at the University of British Columbia. Similar study programs designed to meet the urgent need for nursing teachers, nursing administrators, and public health nurses were initiated at the University of Toronto and at McGill University during the 1920s. These initiatives did not win unanimous approval either inside or outside the profession. Most nurses could not afford to take the five-year degree course and opted instead, if they could gain acceptance, for the three-year courses offered by the hospitals. Chinese women seeking training and employment as nurses in British Columbia hospitals like the Vancouver General faced explicit exclusion under racist policies. Similar bans blocked women of other races. In 1937, a Nova Scotia woman named Marie gave up her dream of being a nurse and decided to train as a teacher because Nova Scotia barred black nurses' training until 1945.[34]

White hospital trainees often resented what they perceived as the preferential treatment of the select number of students who were enrolled in the university programs. Of greater concern to the proponents of higher education for nurses was the opposition they encountered from doctors. In 1920, for example, the College of Physicians and Surgeons in British Columbia stated that two years of training was quite sufficient for nurses and proclaimed that "the overtraining of nurses is not desirable and results largely in the losing of their usefulness."[35]

Nurses throughout the country did achieve some success in gaining control over who could be a member of the profession. By 1922 all provinces had enacted legislation setting out the education and training required for registered nurses, and investing the power of registration in the hands of the provincial nursing associations. Religious and linguistic differences complicated the process in Quebec. There, the 1920 legislation that had given the anglophone registered nurses' association exclusive control over registration was amended two years later at the insistence of francophone nurses and doctors, diluting the criteria for registration and breaking the association's control over registration.[36]

A national survey of nursing education reported in 1929 that the *raison d'être* of the nursing schools continued to be the provision of cheap labour for the hospitals. Most student nurses put in a twelve-hour work day (nine hours on the wards, and three hours of lectures and study). During their first year of training, in particular, they were required to perform many heavy housekeeping duties. Once trained, most were replaced in hospitals by a new group of unpaid student nurses; in 1929, 60 percent of graduate nurses continued to be employed as private-duty nurses in patients' homes, where domestic work was often expected of them. During times of economic crisis, private-duty nurses found it difficult to secure full-time employment and had to compete with untrained women who were willing to provide similar services for lower wages. Among the private-duty nurses who participated in the 1929 survey, 60 percent stated that they were not able to save for their retirement. Since nine out of every ten nurses were unmarried, their futures were bleak.[37]

During the 1920s, a general shortage of nurses was keenly felt in the area of public health nursing, as provincial and some municipal health services grew. Still, by 1922 there were more than 1000 public health nurses in Canada.[38] In addition to receiving higher wages than nurses who worked in hospitals or private homes, these specialized nurses also enjoyed a greater degree of autonomy from physicians, especially when they were posted to remote areas. Nonetheless, public health nurses frequently met with hostility or indifference from doctors and other male community leaders when they sought to establish much-needed services that were aimed primarily at women and children. After three years of a provincially supported program undertaken in 1920 to place nurse educators in Ontario communities, only eight communities had engaged public health nurses. When two provincially sponsored nurses arrived in Kenora in northern Ontario, they were advised not to ask the prosperous town for money, and so used their bedrooms at the local hotel as their offices.[39]

ATTEMPTS AT IMPROVEMENT: MINIMUM WAGES AND UNIONS

During the 1920s, there was little improvement in female workers' hours and wages. Responding to pressure from women's groups to protect and improve the position of female workers, and from organized labour to limit female competition, provincial governments extended "protective" legislation. In 1917, Alberta became the first province to adopt a minimum wage law for women. Most provinces followed suit: British Columbia and Manitoba did so in 1918, Saskatchewan and Quebec in 1919, and Nova Scotia and Ontario in 1920. By the end of the decade, only New Brunswick and Prince Edward Island still had not passed such laws. But it took Alberta until 1924 to set up a permanent wage board, and minimum wage legislation was not actually put into force until 1927 in Quebec, and until 1930 in Nova Scotia.[40]

The stated purpose of minimum wage laws was not only to ensure "the right of the worker to live from her work," but also "to preserve the health, morals and efficiency of that large class of women dependent on their daily wage for a living."[41] As the number of young, Canadian-born women entering the labour force continued to mount, so did concern over the future of the Anglo-Saxon race: those very same women who toiled in industry, it was pointed out, would one day be the mothers of the nation. Concerns about inter-racial contact led the combined forces of organized labour, business, religion, and moral reform to support discriminatory legislation, colloquially known as "white women's labour laws," that prohibited the employment of white women by Asian-Canadians.[42] Few white women opposed this racist law, but, as in other industrialized nations, they remained divided on other aspects of the issue of protective legislation. Some prominent feminists, such as British Columbia's Helen Gregory MacGill, served on provincial wage commissions, but others were firmly opposed to minimum wage laws, and the pros and cons of protective legislation for women became the focus of vigorous debate. Maud Petitt Hill, a middle-class journalist and reformer, declared that protective legislation was highly desirable because women workers were even less unionized than men. In 1912 Hill had disguised her origins and had gone to work in a Toronto biscuit factory. Using the pseudonym "Videre," she had written a series of articles about female factory workers in which she expressed an overriding concern for their moral condition and their weakness for "finery."[43] In the 1920s she continued to argue that working "girls" had to be protected from themselves; otherwise, they might "overwork with the mere ambition of owning silken hose and patent pumps" and subsequently "produce an inferior race." Further, it was undesirable to have women working night shifts and "walking the streets alone at night."[44]

Other supporters of minimum wage laws for women, such as the British Columbia union activist Helena Gutteridge, were more clearly motivated by concern for the female worker's economic status. They firmly believed that such laws would result in improved wages and a better standard of living for women. Gutteridge also urged the organization of unions and championed equal pay for equal work.[45] Other concerned women criticized protection as unwarranted privilege and a poor substitute for equality. Because protective laws would render women less competitive, the principal beneficiaries of the maximum hours and minimum wages that applied only to women would be male workers. Moreover, the argument that such legislation would help preserve their morality was insulting to the women workers.

Minimum wage commissions began their work by establishing the basic weekly amount a single female worker required to keep herself in a respectable, if somewhat impoverished, state. There was no acknowledgement that many female wage earners had dependents to support. The budget the commissioners invented was based on a full year's employment, an unattainable goal for many women. A third highly questionable assumption was that only a few unscrupulous employers were paying unconscionably low wages. There was no provision for retirement savings or vacations. Minimum wage rates varied from province to province and from industry to industry, and a separate order had to be issued to cover women in each trade. Within a province, the rate for women in the same type of employment might differ according to the size of community in which the worker resided, her age, and her experience. By the end of the decade, the majority of provinces had set minimum wages for most large groups of female employees. The exceptions, however, were notable: all those engaged in agriculture, domestic service, banking, teaching, and nursing. Initially, the wage commissions had no authority to regulate hours, a situation that many employers exploited by simply offsetting mandatory higher wages with longer hours. Eventually, however, this power was conceded to all provincial commissions except the one in Quebec.

In Ontario and Quebec, the highest minimum wage (for experienced female workers in certain industries in the largest urban centres) was set at $12.50 per week; the lowest (for the youngest and least experienced) was $8.00. In Alberta, the minimum was set at $12.50. Unfortunately, the minimum rate rapidly became the maximum most women could earn — and even these low wages were not guaranteed to all workers. In Ontario, for example, inexperienced workers or minors under the age of 18, who did not have to be paid the minimum, could legally constitute up to half of an employer's workforce, depending on the type of industry. In the case of piece workers, only 80 percent had to attain the minimum rate. Exemptions were also granted for "handicapped" workers, the elderly, and some juvenile workers under 18 years of age.[46]

The problems created by the legal loopholes were exacerbated by those related to enforcement. There were few inspectors, and the fines for contravening the law were paltry: $50 in Quebec, for example, and $100 in Saskatchewan. Employers frequently claimed ignorance of the law, and many employees were unaware of its existence or were too intimidated to invoke it. In the needle trades, those piece workers who were furthest from earning the minimum wage at week's end, and therefore would be the most costly for employers to "bonus up" to the required level, were subject to layoffs or dismissal. When, in December 1924, the King Edward Hotel in Toronto posted an increase in chambermaids' weekly hours from 54 to 69, without any pay increase, 25 women struck and took their case to the Ontario Minimum Wage Board. Their employer, however, refused to attend with any organized labour representation; the Board closed the file without any improvement to the chambermaids' pay.[47] Several other methods employers used to contravene the legislation included having more than one employee punch in on the same time card, switching workers from job to job or firing and rehiring them so that they could continue to be classified as inexperienced, or using so many different piecework rates that it was virtually impossible for workers and inspectors to comprehend how the wages had been calculated. Although wage commissions continued to claim that employers who resorted to such practices were rare exceptions (and primarily of "foreign" origin), many respectable and well-known establishments such as the T.E. Eaton Company and the Robert Simpson Company were also among the offenders. The Minimum Wage Boards had initially reassured nervous employers that female wages would not rise drastically, and they were right; women workers continued to earn on average 54 to 60 percent of what men earned.

Was there a better alternative to government intervention to improve the lot of women workers? Many believed that there was: unionization. Outspoken female champions of working women, such as Communist activists Annie Buller, Becky Buhay, Bella Hall Gauld, and Florence Custance, argued that only by recognizing the class origins of their exploitation and by organizing themselves could working women effect significant changes in their lives. Buller, who had been sent at the age of 13 to work in a Montreal tobacco factory, worked her way up from sales clerk to department store buyer; in the end, however, she turned her back on what appears to have been a highly desirable position and devoted herself to Marxist politics and labour activism. She and her friends Buhay and Gauld were instrumental in setting up the Montreal Labour College in 1920 to promote the study of Marxism and to provide a meeting place for workers. Florence Custance was similarly involved in the Toronto Labour College. Through their writings, their speaking tours, and their participation in various important strikes — and in some cases through their arrests — these women worked on behalf of both female and male workers in industries as diverse as the needle trades and mining, and became well-known figures in the labour movement in several regions of Canada. Jeanne Corbin, a young francophone woman from northern Alberta, was another important activist. Recruited by Buhay and Buller in 1929 to contribute to Communist labour publications in both Ontario and Quebec, Corbin became an organizer among miners and bush workers in northern Ontario and Quebec, and was later imprisoned for her involvement in the 1934 miners' strike in Noranda, Quebec.[48]

During the 1920s, however, few Canadians of either sex embraced communism or unions; after 1923, only one out of every eight non-agricultural paid workers was a union member. According to one estimate, fewer than 1 percent of female wage earners were unionized.[49] Employers had a variety of tactics at their disposal for discouraging unionization, including threatening workers with dismissal, moving their factories, and establishing "shop" unions that were pro-management. The craft unions of skilled workers continued to dominate the Canadian labour scene, confining their activities to industrial settings in which there were few women. In any event, they had a tradition of excluding women. Many male unionists still considered female workers unlikely and undesirable union members; one concluded that because women did not have a long-term commitment to paid employment, and because they did not "possess that spirit of solidarity, characteristic of men in industry," female workers were "the most difficult workers to organize."[50]

Such negative assessments failed to recognize that it was often male unionists' indifference or overt hostility to female workers, and their failure to deal with issues of importance to women such as sexual harassment or unhygienic working conditions, that caused many women to spurn unions. In the 1920s unions made little effort to eliminate the pay differential between male and female workers, and by insisting on across-the-board raises they effectively increased the wage gap. Union halls were primarily male clubs. Although women were hired occasionally by the international unions to act as organizers in industries with large numbers of female workers, they too suffered the familiar inequities in pay. In the early 1920s, for example, Mary McNab was hired as an organizer by the Amalgamated Clothing Workers in Hamilton, and paid half the salary typically given to male organizers. In unions where women workers dominated the membership rolls, leadership roles sometimes became available. Women delegates, however, remained a minority on urban Trades and Labour Councils.[51]

Despite the obstacles to organization, women in manufacturing did score some notable successes during the 1920s, especially in the garment and textile industries, although inter-union rivalries as well as ethnic divisions complicated organizational efforts among the garment workers. Three major unions with American or international connections — the Amalgamated Clothing Workers of America, the International Ladies' Garment Workers of America, and the Communist-supported Industrial Union of Needle Trades Workers — sought to establish their pre-eminence. In Quebec these unions also faced a strong challenge from the newly organized *Confédération des travailleurs catholiques du Canada* (Canadian Catholic Confederation of Labour). Formed in 1921 under the aegis of the Catholic church, this organization sought to protect Catholic workers not only from the exploitation inherent in unfettered capitalism, but also from what many French Canadians perceived as essentially atheistic, foreign-controlled international unions. By 1921 there were eight women's locals of the Catholic Confederation in Hull and one in Montreal; in addition, other female workers were organized along with their male co-workers into "mixed" locals. All told, approximately 2200 women belonged to exclusively female Catholic unions, and another 600 to the mixed Catholic unions; but together they accounted for only 3 percent of all the women workers in Quebec industry and commerce.[52]

Despite women's membership in the union movement, male leaders continued to regard the presence of women in the labour force as symbolic of an unhealthy industrial order in which a man could not earn enough to support his family. Once the "family wage" was secured, they argued, there would be no reason for daughters and wives to desert hearth and home. Such arguments ignored the continuing economic contribution made by working women, their right to work for wages outside the home, and the fact that many women workers had no male "breadwinner" to rely on. The right of married women to work and even the right of women to work became much-debated topics throughout the 1920s and 1930s.[53]

Women workers, whether unionized or not, were far from passive. As individuals, they reacted to unsatisfactory work situations by changing jobs or getting married; collectively, they helped each other meet production quotas or engaged in militant activities such as slowdowns, walkouts, and strikes. In August 1921, hosiery workers in Stratford, Ontario, set up picket lines to try to win union recognition and improvements in wages. As in most labour–management disputes, the full force of the law was used against the strikers: fifteen were arrested, two of whom had to be tried in juvenile court. Despite widespread local support, after two months the strike failed. Another example of female workers' activism occurred in Hull, Quebec, in 1924. In this instance, without notifying their union, the women at the E.B. Eddy factory walked off the job to protest the firing of their female supervisors and management's attempts to force the workers to sign "yellow dog" contracts renouncing union membership. They were more successful in pummelling the plant manager into temporary submission, however, than in achieving their long-term goals. Although a settlement was reached and the workers were rehired, the company refused to reinstate the female supervisors or to permit ongoing union activities.[54]

For those women engaged in the clerical and retail trades, both unionization and strike activity were rarer, partly because of the safer working conditions, and because of their perception of themselves as a better-educated, higher-status occupational group for whom trade union activities were inappropriate. Moreover, managers often pre-empted attempts at organization by providing employee welfare schemes such as company cafeterias, recreational facilities, pensions for loyal long-term workers, and piecemeal benefits for the "deserving." In Montreal the associations for women in white-collar occupations that had been created by the *Fédération nation-ale Saint-Jean-Baptiste* before World War I continued to operate. But total member-ships never exceeded a few hundred women, and the major objective of these associations remained the educational and moral betterment of their members rather than fighting for better working conditions or pay. Secretaries, stenographers, bank and assorted clerks, and other white-collar women workers formed the backbone membership of the Canadian Federation of Business and Professional Women's Clubs (CFBPWC, or BPW for short). Their growth is evidence of the importance of mutual support and belonging among this group of workers.[55]

In some regions, on the other hand, female white-collar workers recorded considerable progress in union organizing during this decade. In 1918 local women teachers' organizations had formed the Federation of Women Teachers' Associations of Ontario. Given the chronic post-war inflation and inadequate salaries for its mem-bers, the Federation assigned top priority to equal pay for equal work and to contract protection. Within a year, more than one-third of the province's women teachers had joined the Federation. The militancy of some women teachers was demonstrated in 1922, when several in Owen Sound threatened strike action to support their demands for a decent wage. The local Board of Education conceded by raising the minimum salary for female teachers to $1200. In western Canada, female teachers also sought to improve their position by joining forces. Many Calgary teachers joined the Dominion Labour Party. Between 1918 and 1936, their support helped elect and maintain a Labour woman on the school board. Trustees like Amelia Turner pressed teachers' collective bargaining rights and equality for female teachers.[56] The Saskatoon Women Teachers' Association continued to campaign for better contracts, equal pay for equal work, and the retention of married women as teachers. This activism not-withstanding, women in the teaching profession were still treated as second-class citizens. Their salaries lagged significantly behind those of men teachers; those who married generally lost their permanent contracts or were dismissed, while their male counterparts received bonuses. Enrollment in the women teachers' associations remained strictly voluntary, and only a minority of rural teachers belonged, a fact that restricted both financial stability and bargaining power.[57]

Similarly, nurses continued to press for better working conditions and a greater degree of professional recognition and self-regulation. In 1928, student nurses at Guelph General Hospital reacted to the heavy workload and the regimentation by launching a strike that lasted for two days. Although it appears to have resulted only in the departure of some of the nurses involved, the strike demonstrated that even the most powerless of women were prepared on occasion to strike back at the "system."[58]

Women's militancy in the 1920s was not confined to those who worked for wages. In several instances workers' wives, mothers, and daughters lent both imme-diate and longer-term support to their male family members' labour struggles. In coalminers' strikes in Nova Scotia (1922) and Alberta (1923), the militancy of the miners' wives was a significant factor in the collective demonstration of solidarity the men were able to mount.[59] One Ukrainian woman in Edmonton recalled her first involvement in a labour dispute:

> In 1921 there was a strike. We walked the picket line. We left at four in the morning. The police prevented us from going and pushed us with rifle butts. I

was afraid. There I met other women, and we went to the Labour Temple for meetings.

In Cardiff, Alberta, women armed with sticks engaged in a pitched battle with police and strikebreakers or "scabs," and some were subsequently arrested and convicted of disturbing the peace.[60]

A MOST DEPRESSING DECADE

If the 1920s were difficult years for women workers, the 1930s were disastrous. Wages plummeted, working conditions deteriorated, union membership declined, and women's right to work was even more seriously challenged. For women who worked at home, there was enormous pressure to replace unemployed family members in the labour force, to supplement the reduced wages of those still working, and to intensify their domestic labour to make ends meet. As the Depression deepened, millions of Canadians experienced unprecedented deprivation and an immeasurable loss of dignity. Although governments clumsily attempted to attenuate the worst effects of the economic crisis, they directed most of their efforts toward aiding men. Once again it was assumed that the vast majority of women would be looked after by their families, and women who had no one able or willing to support them were initially left to fend for themselves. Yet, while it is difficult to assess the actual numbers, we know that a large percentage of women in the labour force were supporting themselves, and many were responsible for the support of dependents.[61]

At first the world-wide economic crisis that began in October 1929 appeared to stimulate the entry of women into the labour force. In many families the role of breadwinner was transferred from men, who were now unemployed, to daughters and wives able to find work in traditionally female areas of employment. By 1931 there was already a 2 percent increase in the labour-force participation rate of women aged 10 and over, compared to ten years earlier. However, much larger increases occurred among women in their twenties and thirties; there was a 7 percent increase for those aged 20 to 24 years, and a 4.5 percent increase for those between 25 and 34 years old. Evidence presented in 1934 before the Special Committee on Price Spreads and Mass Buying emphasized the vital role women were playing:

> Of 30 women from one non-union shop, practically all of whom were earning less than $12.50 per week, . . . 21 were married and were the sole providers for the family or were happy to support them; eight were single, but were helping to support their families, while only one girl had no dependents and no family obligations.[62]

As the crisis grew and the national unemployment rate mounted to almost one-third of all workers, resentment against wage-earning women increased. The deep-seated prejudice against married women working outside the home intensified, and the appropriateness even of single women working for wages, widely conceded during the 1920s, was now called into question. These convictions transcended regional, ethnic, class, and, to some extent, gender boundaries. Whether it was the westerner who counselled Prime Minister R.B. Bennett to end unemployment by firing all single young women, or the leaders of the Canadian Catholic Confederation of Labour, including those representing female textile workers, who petitioned the Quebec government to bar all women from working for wages except in cases of absolute necessity, the message was the same: get the women out of the paid labour force. Men contended that they were being replaced by unskilled female workers. Women in business and the professions were also accused of taking away men's jobs. Stories abound of women who had to be content with lengthy engagements, clandestine relationships, or secret marriages in order to retain their jobs. For Native, ethnic, and visible-minority women, the discrimination encountered in securing employment was exacerbated by pervasive prejudice. Anti-Semitism was also especially rife during the 1930s: one woman in Winnipeg was able to obtain and keep an office position only because, since she was tall and blonde, her employers did not realize that she was Jewish.[63]

Despite the widespread perception of the threat women posed to male employment, there is incontrovertible evidence that desperate male workers were undercutting women's wages and supplanting women in several industries. In the garment, textile, and leather industries, the practice of giving preferential treatment to male workers was common. Married female operatives, some with many years' experience, were dismissed so that their work could be re-allocated to male workers, often at rates of pay well below the minimum required for women workers. In the cotton industry, ring spinning, a job consisting of minding sets of spinning frames, had previously been considered women's work. During the Depression years it was assigned to men as well, and female spinners at the Magog mill in Quebec reported being replaced by male textile workers from Sherbrooke. Thus the minimum wage legislation that had been intended to protect women often proved their undoing. At one textile mill in Valleyfield, Quebec, a group of female apprentice weavers signed a petition imploring the provincial government not to apply minimum wage legislation to them so that they could keep their jobs. The substituting of lower-paid male for female workers became so widespread that, in order to maintain male wage levels, the provincial governments of Ontario and Quebec extended their minimum wage legislation to include men. British Columbia had already made a similar move in 1934. Legislation that had originally affected only women thus finally generated an important new category of wage support for industrial workers. In Paris, Ontario, skilled female operators constituted the majority of the knit goods workforce, and they continued to enjoy greater security of employment than their male relatives.[64]

But often, when women were successful in securing or maintaining positions, they experienced drastic wage cuts and deteriorating working conditions. In Ontario, the Factory Act was amended to allow the implementation of a double shift for women and youths between 6 A.M. and 11 P.M. The fact that so many of Canada's female wage earners were concentrated in industries characterized by low capital investment and intense competition rendered them all the more vulnerable to exploitation. This was particularly true of the garment trade, where many small, undercapitalized entrepreneurs fought to maintain their markets by slashing production costs. Even large, well-established companies such as the T.E. Eaton Company cut wages, reduced the number of employees, and increased production quotas. Mrs. Annie Wells, an examiner who began work at Eaton's in 1916, testified before the Royal Commission on Price Spreads that she was not allowed to sit down during her eight-hour shift, and that after 1931 she was not able to make the minimum wage because the piece rates had been so greatly reduced. The price for sewing a dozen dresses was cut from $5 per dozen before 1929 to $3 by 1934. The resulting physical and nervous exhaustion of the workers led another witness, Miss A. Tucker, to declare that

> the girls were just about insane. In fact it got to such a climax that they were threatening to commit suicide and even I myself was contemplating the same thing.

Another employee revealed that she had gone out only once in 1934 — to celebrate her birthday — the only time she attended a movie in three years.[65] But once again it was home workers who suffered the most. In one Quebec home, a woman and her daughter produced a dozen pair of boys' short pants for 30 cents minus 5 cents for the thread they used. Their average daily production was one dozen pairs of pants.[66]

Whatever limited occupational mobility had existed for women workers now vanished. In one large Quebec cotton mill, young girls — who would normally have progressed from learners to weavers within a few months — now spent several years toiling at unskilled jobs. For many women there was only downward mobility into domestic service; between 1921 and 1931, there was a 7 percent increase in female wage earners employed as domestics, and a 6 percent decline in those engaged in manufacturing. For Canadians with fixed or steady incomes, the standard of living improved as prices dropped, and many families found they could afford a domestic helper. In Vancouver, a domestic servant could be engaged for as little as $10 per month plus room and board. Local relief officers encouraged young women without jobs or families to support them to become servants, and the only major initiative to reduce female unemployment undertaken by governments was the development of domestic training programs. At the end of 1936, only an estimated 400 single women had met government relief requirements in Vancouver; two-thirds were over 50 years old. Young, healthy unemployed female workers could not receive relief as long as domestic service jobs at any wage continued to be available.[67]

Municipalities did not initially provide relief for single women; indeed, their first priority was to try to provide what limited assistance they could afford to married men. This usually took the form of make-work projects (such as street improvements, and highway and sewer construction) that required the use of many unskilled labourers. Similarly, the federal government gave subsidies to the provinces to undertake highway and railroad construction work, which provided jobs almost exclusively for men. Although municipal relief for single men was often poorly organized and inadequate, usually some attempt was made to provide food and hostel accommodation; responsibility for single women was generally relegated to their families or to private charitable organizations. Indeed, the existing limited welfare programs all derived from the assumption of a male breadwinner supporting dependent women and children.[68] Women were not perceived as posing a serious threat to the social order, as did the roaming bands of unemployed young men who "rode the rods," in spite of the fact that "girl hoboes were frequently encountered."[69] Even when women could qualify for financial assistance, relief officers could be sexist and insensitive. Some women were told that "with figures like theirs" they did not need relief. According to C.G. MacNeil, the Member of Parliament for Vancouver North, relief payments to women were so inadequate that they are compelled to live in only the most disreputable parts of the city, denied any chance to dress respectably . . . ready material for prostitution in its most sordid forms.[70]

For some women, prostitution was the only way they could eke out a livelihood during the Depression. Immigrants who could not get jobs faced double jeopardy. If they had been in Canada less than five years, they could be deported if they went "on relief."

Women's ability to adapt to changing economic circumstances can be seen in the experience of Wet'suwet'en women in British Columbia. Before World War I, settlement, railroad, and highway development replaced the fur trade, and Wet'suwet'en men moved in increasing numbers into the paid labour force. Women continued their responsibility for fishing, farming, trapping, and berry-picking, and families of wage earners relied on this supplemental work. When, in 1911, the federal government abolished the use of large salmon weirs, catching and preserving salmon became exclusively women's work. Wet'suwet'en women's enlarged economic role, however, was balanced by men's earning power — until the Depression virtually eliminated male wage opportunities. One woman recalled her experience of the 1930s with pride:

> We stayed put while the men went all over for work. We did the fishing, had our big gardens in them days too. You bet, them days we fed the men. They sure were glad for us women. It was our catches that kept their bellies full.

Not only did they feed their families but they also produced food for use by the community and for trade. Wet'suwet'en women peddled house to house or traded in town for clothing, fabric, flour, tea, and sugar. They shared fish and meat with neighbouring indigent white farm women. Within their communities, the Wet'suwet'en women enjoyed increased prestige as a result of these roles and control of wealth.[71]

The wives of those men who had lost their jobs strained to cope with the financial, social, and psychological repercussions of living with an unemployed breadwinner. Finnish immigrant wives frequently turned their household skills to domestic service and may have gained status and power by having money to spend.[72] Married women's right to work, however, remained a continuing target as the male breadwinner's role was threatened by the economic depression.[73] Husbands frequently left their families to search for work elsewhere, and sometimes deserted them altogether rather than face the humiliation of failing to provide. The number of female heads of households in Edmonton, for example, rose from 978 in 1921 to 2653 ten years later.[74] The social stigma associated with being "on the dole" was crushing: the relief authorities confiscated all possessions they considered luxuries, such as cars, radios, and jewellery. Persons receiving relief had to hand in their liquor permits, and if they owned a telephone it was removed. The limited financial assistance successful applicants received usually took the form of vouchers for food and rent; no provision was made for the replacement of clothing or for the sundry items most Canadians considered essential. When their silk stockings wore out, women powdered their legs and drew a black line down the back. Wives, mothers, and sisters made clothing from flour bags, and mended, patched, and darned until the cloth disintegrated; sometimes women and children became virtual prisoners in their homes because they lacked suitable clothing to go out. Women also often lacked the cooking facilities and fuel they needed to prepare what little food they had. They substituted chicory or roasted grain for coffee, used game instead of butcher's cuts, and invented an endless variety of "mock" dishes. To obtain additional milk and clothing for her children, one woman consented to have sexual relations with her relief officer.[75] When their myriad and continuous efforts to sustain the family failed, a few women appealed directly to the prime minister for help. Their letters reveal not only the pathetic state to which many had been reduced, but also their habit of putting husbands and children first, and their unshakeable faith in God and country. The moving entreaty from Mrs. C.L. Warden of Lambert, Saskatchewan, written in the winter of 1934, speaks for itself:

> Your Honor:
> I am writing you regarding Relief. Will you please tell me if we can get Steady Relief and how much we should be allowed per week we have three children, 2 of school age. . . . There are times we are living on potatoes for days at a time. . . . I am five months pregnant and I haven't even felt life yet to my baby and its I feel quite sure for lack of food . . . the two oldest children and I are suffering from abscess teeth can we get them out and have the town pay for the Dental Bill.[76]

For some women even the opportunity to appeal to public authorities was brutally denied. When Stepan Chiruk was imprisoned for three months for killing a moose and her calf in order to feed his family of six, his wife was told that she must agree to have him sterilized or the entire family would be deported. Zosya Chiruk refused, distributed her children among the neighbours, and went into hiding in the bush in northern Alberta. Eventually Zosya hired a lawyer, who advised her to return home with her children; this she did, only to find the police at her doorstep. Since there were many neighbours present, the police promised Zosya that the family would not be deported, and that her husband would be allowed to return. Later that same night, when the neighbours had all gone, the police returned and took away Zosya and the children. The entire family was sent back to Ukraine.[77]

Life during the Depression was also very harsh for many older women who were separated, divorced, or widowed. Their sex and age combined to reduce their chances of employment. One particularly poignant story involved a needy and resourceful 77-year-old English widow who advertised for a pensioner husband to supplement her small income. Although she did find a husband by this means, he was under 70 and therefore not yet a pensioner; consequently, when his son reneged on a promise to provide his father with $20 a month until he reached pensionable age, the woman's financial situation was ironically made more precarious.[78] Hard work and Christian faith sustained Christina Elizabeth Jenkins Howson of London, Ontario. In 1923, with her husband, she founded *The Dawn of Tomorrow*, a widely circulated newspaper that focussed on black concerns and causes, and she assumed full editorial responsibility in 1931 when her husband died. Circulation fell off under the economic pressure of the Depression, until only two issues appeared in 1939. The editor did not accept defeat, however, and redoubled her efforts to increase circulation. In 1950, *The Dawn of Tomorrow* finally achieved its previous circulation level of 5000 copies.[79]

Women of all ages and regions fought back against the indignities and deprivations with whatever limited means they possessed. In Vancouver, the *Unemployed Worker* reported groups of white and sometimes Asian women pressing a variety of demands at local relief offices. Among the reported results of political community action in 1933, the newspaper listed the provision of milk for women with babies; relief for ailing single women; clothing allowances for mothers and their children; medical care during pregnancy; and relief for destitute Japanese and Chinese families. Radical working-class women belonging to the Single Women's Protective Association in Vancouver launched a campaign in 1936 to achieve equal relief rates with men but were ultimately unsuccessful.[80] Rural women on the Prairies, who confronted drought, dust, grasshoppers, sheriffs' writs, and bank foreclosures, found support in women's organizations and new political parties such as the CCF (Co-operative Commonwealth Federation) and Social Credit. In 1932 Jewish women in Toronto, including labour militants, factory workers, and housewives, organized a boycott of kosher butchers, who were charging exorbitant prices for their products.

> Every butcher was picketed each morning by small groups of women, often starting at 6:00 A.M. They tried to prevent anyone from going in, and often ripped the meat out of the hands of those who did buy, and threw it into the street.[81]

As for unions, membership fell sharply during the worst years of the Depression as competition for jobs intensified. Workers were afraid to join unions for fear of losing their jobs; and in any case, they often could not afford to pay the union dues. Nonetheless, there were some significant organizational initiatives. In 1936, Laure Gaudreault, who had started teaching 30 years earlier at the age of 16, formed an association of female rural schoolteachers in the Chicoutimi area of Quebec. Created to protest the provincial government's failure to implement a promised salary increase, this group developed within a year into the *Fédération catholique des institutrices rurales*. Under Gaudreault's leadership, it undertook a vigorous campaign to improve the desperately low salaries and primitive working conditions that women teachers in rural schools had so long endured. Rural teachers in British Columbia had also reached the limit of their patience. Frustrated by the lack of action by government and the Department of Education and angry over low salaries, poor housing and working conditions, and lack of bargaining power, the women formed the Rural Elementary Teachers' Association in 1938. Vancouver waitresses engaged in ten separate strikes during the 1930s and emerged as one of the most militant groups of organized women. Significant gender-based pay differences fuelled their activism. The waitresses forced their agenda for equality, and equal pay for waiters and waitresses at $12 per week became a union and strike demand for the first time in 1933. Throughout the Depression, in aggressively pressing the right to work, to relief, and to equality in pay regardless of marital status, militant Vancouver women began to express an enlarged feminist consciousness and to challenge underlying social and economic assumptions.[82]

In Montreal and Toronto, leftist activists such as Lea Roback and Pearl Wedro worked to attract garment and fur workers into unions. The only unions to demonstrate any increase in membership during the early 1930s were those affiliated with the Workers' Unity League, which had been organized in 1929 by the Communist International and the Communist Party. In 1934 alone, the Workers' Unity

Miners' wives barricade the entrance to the Flin Flon community hall to stop a back-to-work meeting during the 1934 strike.

Source: Provincial Archives of Manitoba.

League organized 109 strikes involving some 50 000 Canadian workers. Prominent among its affiliates was the Industrial Union of Needle Trades Workers, which was involved in the Toronto dressmakers' strike in February 1931, and the Montreal garment workers' strike of August 1934. In the latter, thousands of young women, primarily of Jewish and French-Canadian origin, took to the streets; when attacked by mounted police, the women fought back by stabbing the horses with pins.[83] It was surely no coincidence that, during the course of this violent strike, which lasted more than six weeks, the Quebec Minimum Wage Commission announced a slight upward adjustment of wages for female operatives in the garment industry, and reduced the work week from 55 hours to 48 hours. When the workers returned to work, however, the battle for union recognition was lost, and within a year the Workers' Unity League had been disbanded.

Cross-class solidarity among women was vividly illustrated in 1934 during a strike in the Eaton's dressmaking department by workers who belonged to the International Ladies' Garment Workers' Union. Members of the Toronto Local Council of Women and other middle-class women's organizations raised funds for the strikers, lobbied government officials to force a settlement, and even joined the picket line. When the strike failed, the Local Council provided funds to help some of the strikers set up their own co-operative dressmaking shop. The organized women's movement's willingness to help the largely Anglo-Celtic workers in 1934 contrasted with the general lack of support from this sector for the mostly Jewish women garment workers during their 1912 strike against Eaton's.[84]

In April 1937 it was the International Ladies' Garment Workers' Union that led yet another strike of Montreal women garment workers, popularly called "midinettes." After four weeks on the picket line, the workers won a general wage increase of 10 percent, a 44-hour work week, and, more importantly, the "closed shop" — only workers belonging to the Union could be engaged by those companies that signed the collective agreement. Subsequently, further significant improvements in salary were established through arbitration, but the workers' victory was shortlived. Many employers simply reneged on the terms of the agreement. Among the first to join the Union was Yvette Charpentier. Sent to work at age 10, she became an active organizer among workers in the dress industry, and eventually became the Union's director of educational services. Four months later, in August 1937, even more women were on strike in Quebec as a result of a province-wide walkout in the textile industry. This strike, which was led by the Canadian Catholic Confederation of Labour and lasted more than a month, ended with an agreement, arbitrated by Cardinal Villeneuve, that won only minor improvements for the workers.

After long and bitter conflicts, the immediate gains of these strikes were either negligible or minimal, but such confrontations constituted important demonstrations of female workers' solidarity. The strike of the "midinettes" or female garment workers in Montreal was especially significant, for it demonstrated the militancy of women previously considered unorganizable, and their ability to transcend the ethnic and linguistic divisions that employers had previously exploited to keep the workers from uniting. Moreover, a new generation of female organizers, such as Lea Roback and Yvette Charpentier, emerged from the strike to carry on what would become a successful struggle for unionization over the next two decades.

NOTES

1. Marjory MacMurchy, *Women and Reconstruction* (Toronto: Canadian Reconstruction Association, n.d.), 9.
2. Ceta Ramkalawansingh, "Women during the Great War," in Janice Acton, Penny Goldsmith, and Bonnie Shepard, eds., *Women at Work: Ontario, 1850–1930* (Toronto: Canadian Women's Educational Press, 1974), 288.
3. Ontario, Department of Labour, *Vocational Opportunities in the Industries of Ontario*, 1 (1920), iii.
4. *What Shall I Do Now? How to Work for Canada in Peace* (Toronto: Canadian Reconstruction Association, Women's Department, 1919), 7.
5. *What Shall I Do Now?*, 3.
6. Juliet Stuart Poyntz, "Problems of the Working Woman," *The New Democracy* (May 29, 1919).
7. Mary Horodyski, "Women and the Winnipeg General Strike of 1919," *Manitoba History* 11 (Spring 1986), 28–37; J.M. Bumsted, "The Winnipeg General Strike Reconsidered," *The Beaver* 74, 3 (June/July 1994), 37–39.
8. Elaine Bernard, "Last Back: Folklore and the Telephone Operators in the 1919 Vancouver General Strike," in Barbara K. Latham and Roberta J. Pazdro, eds., *Not Just Pin Money: Selected Essays on the History of Women's Work in British Columbia* (Victoria: Camosun College, 1984), 279–86.
9. James Naylor, "Toronto 1919," *Historical Papers/Communications historiques* (1986), 44, 50.
10. Saskatoon Women's Calendar Collective, "Vancouver Working Women, 1920," in *Herstory* (Sidney, B.C.: Gray's Publishing, 1982), 96.

11. Gail Cuthbert Brandt, " 'Weaving It Together': Life Cycle and the Industrial Experience of Female Cotton Workers in Quebec, 1910–1950," *Labour/Le travail* 7 (Spring 1981), 164–66; Ruth A. Frager, *Sweatshop Strife: Class, Ethnicity, and Gender in the Jewish Labour Movement of Toronto, 1900–1939* (Toronto: University of Toronto Press, 1992), 166; Rebecca Coulter, "Teen-Agers in Edmonton, 1921–1931: Experiences of Gender and Class," University of Alberta, Ph.D. Thesis, 1987, 56; Tamara Adilman, "A Preliminary Sketch of Chinese Women and Work in British Columbia, 1858–1950," in Gillian Creese and Veronica Strong-Boag, eds., *British Columbia Reconsidered: Essays on Women* (Vancouver: Press Gang, 1992), 327; Frances Swyripa, "Nation Building into the 1920s: Conflicting Claims on Ukrainian Immigrant Women," in Manoly R. Lupul, ed., *Continuity and Change: The Cultural Life of Alberta's First Ukrainians* (Edmonton: University of Alberta Press, 1988), 140.

12. Elizabeth Goudie, *Woman of Labrador* (Toronto: Peter Martin Associates Limited, 1975), 7–8.

13. Nicholas Mew, "The Migration of Domestics from the United Kingdom to Canada through the Salvation Army, 1925–1931," (Wilfrid Laurier University: Cognate Essay, 1994); Marilyn Barber, "The Gentlewomen of Queen Mary's Coronation Hostel," in Latham and Pazdro, eds., *Not Just Pin Money*, 141–58.

14. Olga McKenna, *Micmac by Choice: Elsie Stark — An Island Legend* (Halifax: Formac, 1990), 164.

15. Varpu Lindström-Best, " 'I Won't Be a Slave!': Finnish Domestics in Canada, 1911–30," in Jean Burnet, ed., *Looking into My Sister's Eyes: An Exploration in Women's History* (Toronto: Multicultural History Society of Ontario, 1986), 33–53.

16. Helen Potrebenko, *No Streets of Gold: A Social History of Ukrainians in Alberta* (Vancouver: New Star, 1977), 180.

17. Adilman, "Preliminary Sketch," 309–39; Mahinder Kaur Doman, "A Note on Asian Indian Women in British Columbia 1900–1935," in Latham and Pazdro, eds., *Not Just Pin Money*, 99–104; Dorothy W. Williams, *Blacks in Montreal 1628–1986: An Urban Demography* (Cowansville, Que.: Éditions Yvon Blais, 1989), 117.

18. Robin John Armstrong, "The YWCA and Women's Employment Agencies in Vancouver, 1898–1915," *Histoire sociale/Social History* 25, 50 (November 1992), 309.

19. Potrebenko, *No Streets of Gold*, 186.

20. Joy Parr, "Hired Men: Ontario Agricultural Wage Labour in Historical Perspective," *Labour/Le travail* 15 (Spring 1985), 102; Adilman, "Preliminary Sketch," 329.

21. Margaret E. McCallum, "Separate Spheres: The Organization of Work in a Confectionery Factory — Ganong Bros., St. Stephen, New Brunswick, 1900–1945," *Labour/Le travail* 24 (Fall 1989), 69–90; Frager, *Sweatshop Strife*, 121; Gail Cuthbert Brandt, "The Transformation of Women's Work in the Quebec Cotton Industry 1920–1950," in Bryan D. Palmer, ed., *The Character of Class Struggle: Essays in Canadian Working-Class History, 1850–1985* (Toronto: McClelland and Stewart, 1986), 115–37; Joy Parr, "Disaggregating the Sexual Division of Labour: A Transatlantic Case Study," unpublished paper, Queen's University, November 1986.

22. Andrée Lévesque, "Putting It Out: Social Reformers' Efforts to Extinguish the Red Light in Montreal," paper presented to the Canadian Historical Association, Hamilton, 1987, 29; Lévesque, "Le bordel: Milieu de travail contrôlé," *Labour/Le travail* 20 (Fall 1987), 13–31.

23. Jack Gregg, "Girls Live Only to Create Profits for a Boss," *The Young Worker* (May 1926), 2.

24. Franc Sturino, "The Role of Women in Italian Immigration to the New World," in Burnet, ed., *Looking into My Sister's Eyes*, 27–28.

25. N.E.S. Griffiths, *The Splendid Vision: Centennial History of the National Council of Women of Canada, 1893–1993* (Ottawa: Carleton University Press, 1993), 186–87.

26. Graham S. Lowe, "Women, Work and the Office: The Feminization of Clerical Occupations in Canada, 1901–1931," in Veronica Strong-Boag and Anita Clair Fellman, eds., *Rethinking Canada: The Promise of Women's History* (Toronto: Copp Clark Pitman, 1986), 116.

27. Women's Book Committee, Chinese National Council, *Jin Guo: Voices of Chinese Canadian Women* (Toronto: Women's Press, 1992), 146; Dionne Brand, " 'We Weren't Allowed to Go into Factory Work until Hitler Started the War': The 1920s to the 1940s," in Peggy Bristow, co-ord., et al., *"We're Rooted Here and They Can't Pull Us Up": Essays in African Canadian Women's History* (Toronto: University of Toronto Press, 1994), 177; as quoted in Adrienne Shadd, "300 Years of Black Women in Canadian History: Circa 1700–1980," *Tiger Lily* 1, 2 (1987), 10.

28. Veronica Strong-Boag, "The Girl of the New Day: Canadian Working Women in the 1920s," *Labour/Le travail* 4 (1979), 146.

29. M.E. Clark, "Woman in Business Is Still at Heart a Woman," *Canadian Magazine* 69 (January 1928), 27.

30. Dora Nipp, " 'But Women Did Come': Working Chinese Women in The Interwar Years," in Burnet, ed., *Looking into My Sister's Eyes*, 189.

31. Rella Braithwaite and Tessa Benn-Ireland, *Some Black Women: Profiles of Black Women in Canada* (Toronto: Sister Vision, 1993), 35.

32. Sylvia Hamilton, "Our Mothers Grand and Great: Black Women of Nova Scotia," *Canadian Woman Studies/Les cahiers de la femme* 11, 3 (Spring 1991), 46; Theresa M. Jeffries, "Sechelt Women and Self-Government," in Creese and Strong-Boag, eds., *British Columbia Reconsidered*, 91; McKenna, *Micmac by Choice*, 4, 50–51, 53; Marilyn Porter, " 'She Was Skipper of the Shore-Crew': Notes on the History of the Sexual Division of Labour in Newfoundland," *Labour/Le travail* 15 (Spring 1985), 112–16; Varpu Lindström-Best, *Defiant Sisters: A Social History of Finnish Immigrant Women in Canada* (Toronto: Multicultural History Society of Ontario, 1988), 102–3.

33. Judith Fingard, "Gender Inequality at Dalhousie: Faculty Women before 1950," *Dalhousie Review* 64 (1984–5), 687–703; Alison Prentice, "Bluestockings, Feminists, or Women Workers? A Preliminary Look at Women's Early Employment at the University of Toronto," *Journal of the Canadian Historical Association*, New Series 2 (1991), 231–61; Mary Kinnear, "Disappointment in Discourse: Women University Professors at the University of Manitoba before 1970," *Historical Studies in Education* 4, 9 (1992), 269–87.

34. Adilman, "Preliminary Sketch," 323; Hamilton, "Our Mothers," 47.

35. Margaret M. Street, *Watch-Fires on the Mountains: The Life and Writings of Ethel Johns* (Toronto: University of Toronto Press, 1973), 128–29.

36. Yolande Cohen et Michèle Dagenais, "Infirmière: Un métier ou une carrière? Savoirs féminins et reconnaissance professionnelle," paper presented to the Canadian Historical Association, Hamilton, 1987, 41–45; Johanna Daigle, "Devenir infirmière: Les modalités d'expression d'une culture soignante au XXe siècle," *Recherches féministes* 4, 1 (1991), 67–86; Yolande Cohen et Louise Bienvenue, "Émergence de l'identité professionelle chez les infirmières québécoises (1890–1927)," *Bulletin canadien d'histoire de la médécin* (août 1994); André Petitat, *Les infirmières: De la vocation à la profession* (Montréal: Boréal Express, 1989).

37. Judi Coburn, " 'I See and Am Silent': A Short History of Nursing in Ontario," *in* Acton, Goldsmith, and Shepard, eds., *Women at Work*, 142–47; Barbara A. Keddy, "Private Duty Nursing Days of the 1920s and 1930s in Canada," *Canadian Woman Studies/Les cahiers de la femme* 7, 3 (Fall 1986), 99–102; Natalie Nitia Riegler, "The Work and Network of Jean L. Gunn, Superintendent of Nurses, Toronto General Hospital 1913–1941: A Presentation of Some Issues in Nursing during her Lifetime 1882–1941," University of Toronto, Ph.D. Thesis, 1992.

38. Coburn, " 'I See and Am Silent,' " 148.

39. Meryn Stuart, " 'Let Not the People Perish for Lack of Knowledge': Public Health Nursing in Ontario, 1920–1925," paper presented to the Canadian Society for the History of Medicine, Hamilton, 1987, 8–9, 12.

40. Margaret E. McCallum, "Keeping Women in Their Place: The Minimum Wage in Canada, 1910–1925," *Labour/Le travail* 17 (Spring 1986), 29–56.

41. Ontario, *Sessional Papers*, Annual Report of the Minimum Wage Commission (1920), 5.

42. Constance Backhouse, "White Female Help and Chinese-Canadian Employers: Race, Class, Gender, and Law in the Case of Yee Clun 1924," *in* Wendy Mitchinson et al., eds., *Canadian Women: A Reader* (Toronto: Harcourt Brace, 1996), 280–99.

43. Alice Klein and Wayne Roberts, "Besieged Innocence: The 'Problem' and Problems of Working Women — Toronto, 1896–1914," *in* Acton, Goldsmith, and Shepard, eds., *Women at Work*, 211–12.

44. E.M. Murray and Maude Pettit Hill, "Do Women Want Protection? Yes and No," *Chatelaine* 1, 6 (August 1928), 7.

45. Susan Wade, "Helena Gutteridge: Votes for Women and Trade Unions," *in* Barbara Latham and Cathy Kess, eds., *In Her Own Right: Selected Essays on Women's History in B.C.* (Victoria: Camosun College, 1984), 196–97; McCallum, "Keeping," 37.

46. Ontario, *Sessional Papers*, Annual Report of the Minimum Wage Commission (1921), 14.

47. McCallum, "Keeping," 54.

48. Louise Watson, *She Never Was Afraid: The Biography of Annie Buller* (Toronto: Progress Books, 1976), 1–11, 82.

49. Joan Sangster, "The Communist Party and the Woman Question, 1922–1929," *Labour/Le travail* 15 (Spring 1985), 34.

50. H.A. Spencer, "Minimum Wage Laws for Women," *Canadian Congress Journal* 4 (March 1925), 37.

51. Frager, *Sweatshop Strife*, 135; Gillian Creese, "The Politics of Dependence: Women, Work, and Unemployment in the Vancouver Labour Movement before World War II," *in* Creese and Strong-Boag, eds., *British Columbia Reconsidered*, 372.

52. Soeur Marie Gérin-Lajoie, "Le syndicalisme féminin," *in* Michèle Jean, ed., *Québécoises au XXe siècle* (Montréal: Éditions Le jour, 1974), 104–6.

53. Creese, "The Politics of Dependence," 365; Margaret Hillyard Little, "The Regulation of Ontario Single Mothers during the 'Dirty Thirties,' " paper presented to the Canadian Historical Association, Charlottetown, 1992, 8; Margaret Hobbs, "Equality and Difference: Feminism and the Defence of Women Workers during the Great Depression," *Labour/Le travail* 32 (Fall 1993), 20–23.

54. Strong-Boag, "The Girl of the New Day," 155–56; Michelle Lapointe, "Le syndicat catholique des allumetières de Hull, 1919–1924," *Revue d'histoire de l'Amérique française* 32, 4 (mars 1979), 603–28.

55. Gérin-Lajoie, "Le syndicalisme féminin," 107; Joan Sangster, "The Softball Solution: Female Workers, Male Managers and the Operation of Male Paternalism at

Westclox, 1923–1960," *Labour/Le travail* 32 (Fall 1993), 167–200; Hobbs, "Equality and Difference," 210–13.

56. Patricia Roome, "Amelia Turner and the Calgary Labour Women, 1919–1935," in Linda Kealey and Joan Sangster, eds., *Beyond the Vote: Canadian Women and Politics* (Toronto: University of Toronto Press, 1989), 89–117.

57. Pat Staton and Beth Light, *Speak with Their Own Voices: A Documentary History of the Federation of Women Teachers' Associations of Ontario and the Women Elementary Public School Teachers of Ontario* (Toronto: FWTAO, 1987), chap. 3; Apolonja Kojder, "In Union There is Strength: The Saskatoon Women Teachers' Association," *Canadian Woman Studies/Les cahiers de la femme* 7, 3 (Fall 1986), 82–84; Doris French, *High Button Bootstraps* (Toronto: Ryerson Press, 1968), 43.

58. Registered Nurses' Association of Ontario Foundation, *1987 Appointment Book* (Toronto: RNAOF, 1986).

59. Stephen Penfold, " 'Have You No Manhood in You?': Gender and Class in the Cape Breton Coalmines, 1920–1926," *Acadiensis* 2 (Spring 1994), 21–44.

60. Potrebenko, *No Streets of Gold*, 169; Anne B. Woywitka, "A Pioneer Woman in the Labour Movement," in Strong-Boag and Fellman, eds., *Rethinking Canada*, 196–97.

61. Creese, "The Politics of Dependence," 369.

62. Canada, House of Commons, Special Committee on Price Spreads and Mass Buying, *Proceedings and Evidence* (1934), vol. 1, 113.

63. Sybil Shack, *Saturday's Children: Canadian Women in Business* (Toronto: Faculty of Education, University of Toronto, 1977), 29.

64. Brandt, "The Transformation of Women's Work," 128; Joy Parr, *The Gender of Breadwinners: Women, Men, and Change in Two Industrial Towns 1880–1950* (Toronto: University of Toronto Press, 1990).

65. Canada, Royal Commission on Price Spreads, *Minutes of Proceedings and Evidence* (1935), 4410, 4433, 4569, 4554.

66. Canada, *Report of the Royal Commission on Price Spreads* (Ottawa: King's Printer, 1935), 110.

67. Creese, "The Politics of Dependence," 308.

68. Hillyard Little, "Regulation," 8.

69. L. Richter, ed., *Canada's Unemployment Problem* (Toronto: Macmillan, 1939), 118.

70. "Single Women on Relief," *Canadian Forum* 16, 15 (March 1937).

71. Jo-Anne Fiske, "Gender and Politics in a Carrier Indian Community," University of British Columbia, Ph.D. Thesis, 1989, 89, 87–90; Fiske, "Carrier Women and the Politics of Mothering," in Creese and Strong-Boag, eds., *British Columbia Reconsidered*, 203.

72. Lindström-Best, *Defiant Sisters*, 91.

73. Margaret Hobbs, "Rethinking Antifeminism in the 1930s: Gender Crisis or Workplace Justice? A Response to Alice Kessler-Harris," *Gender and History* 5, 1 (Spring 1993), 4–15.

74. Rebecca Coulter, "Teen-Agers in Edmonton," 36.

75. Barry Broadfoot, *Ten Lost Years, 1929–1939: Memories of Canadians Who Survived the Depression* (Toronto: Doubleday, 1973), 280, 74–75.

76. L.M. Grayson and Michael Bliss, eds., *The Wretched of Canada: Letters to R.B. Bennett 1930–1935* (Toronto: University of Toronto Press, 1971), 75–77.

77. Potrebenko, *No Streets of Gold*, 250–52.

78. James Gray, *The Winter Years: The Depression on the Prairies* (Toronto: Macmillan, 1966), 63–66.

79. Braithwaite and Ireland, *Some Black Women*, 65.

80. Creese, "The Politics of Dependence," 380–81.

81. Dorothy Kidd, "Women's Organization: Learning from Yesterday," in Acton, Goldsmith, and Shepard, eds., *Women at Work*, 340.

82. Le Collectif Clio, *L'histoire des femmes au Québec depuis quatre siècles* (Montréal: Quinze, 1982), 299–300; Donald Wilson, "Lottie Bowron and Rural Women Teachers in British Columbia, 1928–34," in Creese and Strong-Boag, eds., *British Columbia Reconsidered*, 357–58; Creese, "The Politics of Dependence," 372, 383.

83. Evelyn Dumas, *The Bitter Thirties in Quebec* (Montreal: Black Rose Books, 1975), 49.

84. Ruth A. Frager, "Class, Ethnicity, and Gender in the Eaton Strikes of 1912 and 1934," in Franca Iacovetta and Mariana Valverde, eds., *Gender Conflicts: New Essays in Women's History* (Toronto: University of Toronto Press, 1992), 189–228.

CHAPTER TEN

Training Women to Keep Their Place

The disruption to family life brought about by World War I strengthened the desire

for a return to peacetime lifestyles. For women, this meant a reaffirmation of estab-

lished roles as wives and mothers at a time when increased educational and job

opportunities appeared to offer more choice than ever before. These seemingly par-

adoxical attitudes and assumptions about women's place did not result in major

changes in women's lives. Rather, they coalesced, as the image of the "new woman"

was incorporated into a value system that reasserted and redefined the female traits

of femininity, domesticity, and dependence.

Whether women wanted or expected a return to pre-war "normalcy" or not, social, economic, and demographic changes were shifting what was normal. By 1921 nearly half the Canadian population was living in urban centres. Urbanization continued to increase throughout the inter-war years, while family size declined, particularly among the working class. Even in the rural areas, families were smaller. Analysts of 1931 census data suggested that working-class couples were making a conscious decision to limit the size of their families in order to escape poverty and to improve their social position.[1] The average number of children born per Canadian woman fell from 3.2 in 1930 to 2.7 during the Depression decade, in large part because of delayed marriages.[2]

Better public health practices altered the life expectancy of both men and women, primarily by reducing infant mortality—although mortality rates remained unconscionably high among Native children, with 21 percent dying before their first birthday.[3] A Canadian woman born in 1931 who survived infancy could expect to live to 62.1 years of age, and a man to 60 years; a woman born a decade later had a life expectancy of 66.3, while that of a man was 63.[4] Since most Canadians got married, their longer life expectancy increased the average length of marriages. This,

Jennie Kanajuq was 12 or 13 when this photograph was taken in 1916. In 1931 Jennie died of tuberculosis.

Source: Canadian Museum of Civilization, MCC/CMC No. 51231.

combined with smaller family size, extended the time between children leaving home and the death of the husband or wife. Couples who married in 1920 could expect this postparental period to be almost seven years longer than it had been for those who had married in 1900.[5] Women immigrants to Canada during this period may not have experienced the same patterns as those emerging among the Canadian-born. Among West Indians, it was women who tended to immigrate rather than men. Indeed, they entered Canada at a rate 15 times that of West Indian men, with the result that, for many West Indian women, marriage partners were hard to find. The Chinese Exclusion Act of 1923 prohibited the entry of wives and children of Chinese men already resident in Canada, although some senators proposed allowing entry to those wives who were aged 50 or older — that is, women past their child-bearing years.[6]

Neither the larger demographic changes nor immigration drastically altered women's major role within the family, but the nature and performance of that role was subjected to increasing scrutiny and pressure during the inter-war years. Through educational systems, newspapers, books, and magazines, new ideals and standards for women were created, all aimed at preserving the "best" of the old attitudes and assumptions about proper female roles while accommodating the "best" of the new.

CREATING THE EDUCATED HOUSEWIFE
....

Training for adult roles was increasingly the concern of formal educational institutions and systems, as young people generally spent more of their formative years in school. School-leaving age varied from province to province, and even within provinces, ranging from 14 in New Brunswick and Manitoba to 16 in cities in Ontario, Alberta, British Columbia, Saskatchewan, and Nova Scotia. There was still no compulsory attendance law in Quebec or Newfoundland. Attendance requirements reflected rural or urban realities and economic conditions — legislation allowed exemptions if children were required during the fishing and fruit-picking seasons, or for other seasonal labour on farms, for necessary household duties such as the care of siblings, or for "personal maintenance" to support themselves or their families.

A young person's ability to take advantage of education, along with the quality of her or his schooling, continued to vary according to class, gender, race, ethnicity, religion, and rural or urban residence. Nevertheless, by their early teens, nearly all children had received some formal schooling.[7] On average, Canadian boys and girls spent almost ten years in the classroom by 1931.[8] However, formal education for Native youth was limited to residential schooling. Some of those living in remote areas could participate through correspondence courses, which were introduced across the country during the 1920s, and through the school radio broadcasts that began in the 1930s.[9] For most girls in remote areas, instruction continued to be interrupted by seasonal farm or domestic labour. The letters of 12-year-old Edna Snyder of Ashcroft, British Columbia, to her correspondence teacher provide a typical example. In the first month of 1927 she wrote to her teacher explaining, "I have only been to school for three years. I have gone since I was nine years old and only had one whole year, [as] the others were only parts. I am also teaching my brother." Two months later Edna had to abandon her lessons to help her father haul hay. The 1934–39 correspondence between Alma Paubst and her teacher reflects the similar frustration this teenager experienced. Alma routinely had to put up with interruptions in her formal learning during the farming season or when family members were ill. Non-routine farm tasks also claimed her time, as she noted in a letter dated May 14, 1937: "I haven't much time to do lessons now. We have to build a new barn before haying time and now that we have a cow we have to put up all new fences and plant the garden."[10]

Urban girls too, and not exclusively those in working-class families, were expected to sacrifice lessons when other chores, paid or unpaid, demanded their time. Nevertheless, increasing numbers of girls completed elementary school, and more young women enrolled in secondary schools and in the universities than in the pre-war period. Enrollment of women undergraduates reached its peak in 1930, when 23.5 percent of all undergraduate students were women. The ratio of female to male undergraduates declined slightly throughout the 1930s, although in absolute numbers, undergraduate female enrollment increased (from 7428 in 1930 to 8107 in 1940). The proportion of women in the total graduate enrollment also dropped during this decade, going from 26 percent in 1930 to 20 percent in 1940. By contrast to undergraduates, the actual number of women graduate students declined slightly, from 352 in 1930 to 326 a decade later.[11] Within the universities and colleges, moreover, women were channelled into "female" departments: home economics, nursing, and such courses as secretarial science (first offered at the University of

A classroom in St. Mary's School on the Blood Reserve, Cardston, Alberta, 1933.

....

Source: Provincial Archives of Alberta, O.M.I. Collection, Ob 10558.

Western Ontario in 1925). In the prestigious faculties of medicine, law, and engineering, women remained a tiny minority. In 1920–21, 18 percent of National Research Council grant holders were women; in 1930–31, women constituted only 10 percent.[12]

In addition to basic literacy skills, elementary- and secondary-school curricula emphasized the development of vocational skills designed to prepare women for marriage and motherhood, and for careers that complemented these roles. Throughout the 1920s and 1930s, provincial departments of education, pressured by the established women's organizations and by new ones like the United Farm Women of Alberta, expanded domestic science programs in the public elementary and secondary schools. These programs now reached greater numbers of girls than previously and could be followed to a higher degree of specialization. For girls in Quebec, domestic science classes frequently replaced academic subjects like science in the province's secondary and normal schools.[13] British Columbia appointed its first director of home economics in 1926. At that time, 55 home economics teachers were employed in elementary and secondary schools, teaching some 11 955 students, or close to 25 percent of the girls enrolled in public schools. In keeping with the application of scientific principles to household management, British Columbia's courses stressed order, cleanliness, and the use of "good" equipment. Classroom visitors and reporters remarked on the regimentation and attention to detail. After visiting a class, one commentator noted that the teacher gave her students

> a thorough training in systematic methods, the work of her classes being performed with almost military promptness and precision, each dish in each girl's cupboard being in its exact place, and even the knives, forks and spoons being ranged like a row of little soldiers.[14]

Many parents and taxpayers criticized the programs as a waste of time and money. Some complained of the lack of attention to practical activities and the overemphasis on order and theory embodied in prescribed lectures on hygiene and nutrition. Others worried about students' possible frustration and dissatisfaction when they were unable to apply the prescribed theories and practices in their own homes. In class, girls cooked on modern electric stoves and ironed with electric irons, but rural and working-class girls went home to the reality of wood or coal stoves and flat-irons.

Teachers stressed standardization of recipes, a practice impossible in a home without measuring utensils, and at odds with family recipes handed down from generation to generation and calling for a "handful" of this and a "pinch" of that. Interviews with students exposed to domestic science training in British Columbia's schools during the 1920s suggest that most school-taught practices and recipes were rejected in favour of the training received at home. One former student recalled the dreadful indigestion she suffered after eating a Waldorf salad prepared at school. Her digestive system could not tolerate the celery and nuts, ingredients beyond the financial means of her family and thus new to her.[15] The tension between home and school created by the content of the domestic science curriculum was exacerbated by the perception of many working-class mothers that such classes undermined their authority and denigrated their personal role in educating their daughters. For Native girls, too, domestic training was a key component of their schooling. The principal of the Lejac Residential School in central British Columbia did not question the limitations of an education that predominantly stressed domestic skills — what more could Native girls expect or want? But at least they received more classroom learning than did boys, who spent most of their time farming. Native girls living at home also found traditional ways of learning being undermined. Among the Haida, the puberty potlatch was no longer performed because "they became ashamed of it."[16]

Proponents continued to stress the role of domestic science in training working-class girls, particularly those from ethnic and racial minorities, both to ensure "better-run" working-class households and to provide a supply of trained servants for middle- and upper-class households. This latter rationale became particularly important in the 1920s, when the women who once might have gone into service increasingly opted for factory or other jobs. Many girls, including those from middle-class homes, now spent their formative years in classrooms and moved on directly from school into the working world. As a result, it was believed that all girls lacked sufficient opportunity to learn household skills from their mothers. Increasingly, middle-class "professional" women, such as teachers, nurses, and secretaries, married after living away from home in boardinghouses or other non-domestic settings. Without school-based instruction, domestic science advocates maintained, these women would lack the necessary skills in scientific homemaking when they needed them. Paradoxically, they were implicitly accepting women's increased participation in the workforce while simultaneously developing various rationales for domestic science training that reinforced traditional attitudes about women's domestic role.[17]

Young girls doing early morning calisthenics at the Girl Guide Camp, French Village, Nova Scotia, circa 1933.

Source: St. Margaret's Bay Historical Society, Collection #215, 34.4.5 (N-2639). Public Archives of Nova Scotia.

Outside the school, youth clubs developed their own educational programs. Organizations such as the Girl Guides of Canada, the Canadian Girls in Training, and the Girls' and Boys' Clubs of Canada (later the 4-H Club), added new objectives to their earlier goals of developing moral, upstanding citizens. They encouraged female independence while at the same time emphasizing domestic activities related to girls' future roles as wives and mothers. In 1935, some 1200 4-H Club girls in Manitoba independently organized and ran their own clothing and food projects. Although there was no prize money, the girls set up competitions and sold home-made goods, using the profits to assist themselves and their families.[18] Paralleling the pattern of groups for older women, organizations like the 4-H Club and the Girl Guides provided opportunities for camaraderie, leadership, and the development of decision-making skills.

The stress on the development of both domestic skills and independence was in keeping with the expectations held for adolescent girls once they left school. Canadians increasingly assumed that nearly all girls, whether working-class or middle-class, would seek employment. Organizations like the YWCA, business girls' clubs, and settlement houses continued their educational and support services for single working women living away from home, attempting to re-create a family atmosphere by fostering individual and group morality as well as homemaking skills.

Services provided by such groups were regarded as essential in the 1920s in a society alarmed by the media image of the "flapper" — the girl who indulged in "immoral" pursuits such as drinking, smoking, wild dancing, and party-going. The author of the 1922 *Maclean's* magazine article "Is the Flapper a Menace?" confirmed society's worst fears, even though she admitted that the majority of young Canadian women followed more "chaste" lifestyles. Three flappers, aged 17, 18, and 20, all from middle-class homes, had described to the author a motoring outing where such large quantities of bootlegged liquor were consumed that one of the flappers declared, "It was a wonder we got back without an accident." Another told of "fussing" parties, "where each girl sits on a boy's knee and lets him kiss her all he wants to do. Sometimes the kissing goes on for hours." According to the flappers, unchaperoned parties were commonplace, and mothers were too innocent to know what was going on at them.[19] In her book *The Black Candle*, Judge Emily Murphy combined anecdotes from her courtroom experience with national and international statistics to link contemporary evidence of youthful women's moral laxity to drug trafficking, prostitution, and the white slave trade. Inter-racial intimacy was also deemed cause for alarm. In 1930 in Oakville, Ontario, when it appeared that a white girl had married a black man, the Ku Klux Klan protested.[20]

Ultimately, the "independence" Canadian women gained from paid employment was considered by most to be temporary; marriage and leaving the labour force remained the goal for most women, however much an unreality it was for many. The media bombarded women with anxious pronouncements on the virtual impossibility and, above all, the undesirability of combining marriage with a career. Short stories telling of independent young women happily trading their jobs for marital bliss appeared frequently in widely read magazines like the *Canadian Home Journal* and *Maclean's*. Sometimes the stories related the unhappy lives of married women who attempted to be both housewives and paid workers, but eventually found true happiness by staying at home. Given that the circulation figures for these magazines were relatively high, the impact of such stories was potentially significant.[21] Canadian women's interest in having their own magazine was illustrated by the fact that

70 000 entries were submitted in the contest to name a new magazine. The winner, Mrs. Hilda Paine of British Columbia, received a cheque for $1000. Her suggestion, *The Chatelaine*, was chosen because it "seemed to have about it a feminine grace. . . . In one word, it expressed women and Canada."[22]

For those working women who traded their jobs or careers for marriage, a real or potential conflict did exist. Given women's typically low pay, their social and economic status usually improved with marriage. But it now reflected their husband's position, not their own. A number of factors helped ease the transition from a limited form of independence, where women had some money of their own to spend, to marital dependence. First of all, most young single women from the working class continued to reside at home and contribute most of their wages to their families. In addition, women continued to be socialized and trained from their earliest years for their wifely role, and many preferred this role to the alternative of poorly paid work and the frequently denigrated role of spinster. Relatively new forces were also at work. The burgeoning household technology industry and the mass media increasingly defined homemakers as new "professionals"; household management itself was touted as a "career." The customary, supposedly haphazard, approach to housework and childcare were to be replaced by the principles of science and business.

The promises of the new technology were especially appealing to those middle-class women who could not find or afford to employ domestic servants. The growth in the number of families with disposable income coincided with the application of new technologies developed during World War I to domestic uses. Such products as instant coffee, tinned goods, and rayon were aggressively advertised in the mass media; increasingly, these ads were directed toward women, reflecting a recognition of the family's growing role as a unit of consumption, and that a woman's job was buying.[23] The key to the new domestic technology was electricity, which became available in the majority of built-up areas by the end of the 1920s. According to the 1941 census, nearly all urban homes had electricity. Some 60 percent of rural non-farm homes used electricity, but only one in five farm households had it.

TABLE 10.1 *Amenities Present in Canadian Households, 1941*

	% Electric Lighting	% Inside Running Water	% Telephone	% Refrigeration	% Flush Toilet (Private)
Rural					
Farm areas	20.2	12.2	29.3	22.2	8.1
Rural non-farm	59.5	41.0	27.8	35.9	32.8
Urban					
<1000	75.0	35.0	24.7	35.0	27.7
1000–5000	94.1	81.6	34.0	56.3	66.5
5000–15 000	97.2	94.4	45.0	66.1	82.8
15 000–30 000	98.7	96.4	53.8	67.4	85.2
>30 000	99.4	98.5	57.3	79.2	88.9
Canada Total	69.1	60.5	40.3	50.9	52.1

Source: Drawn from *Census of Canada* (1941). Reproduced by authority of the Minister of Industry, 1995.

Electricity meant a clean, safe, and efficient method of lighting and cooking. The electric stove not only cooked food but also helped ensure a constant supply of hot water; the electric refrigerator preserved food more efficiently than iceboxes, and made less mess; the electric washing machine, in conjunction with the new easy-care fabrics, abolished many heavy and time-consuming laundry chores. Women greeted these appliances with enthusiasm. At the same time, however, standards of family nutrition and cleanliness continued to rise. Appliances like the washing machine also brought back to the urban household tasks that had been removed during the earlier industrial period. Urban women who had sent laundry out to commercial laundries or self-employed home laundresses now found themselves washing clothes. The actual benefits of appliances such as vacuum cleaners and floor polishers are questionable. There is no doubt that the new appliances greatly decreased the physical effort involved in household labour, a fact much appreciated by housewives, most of whom now worked alone. But rising standards of house-keeping meant that they won little free time as a result.

Acquiring all these appliances made it necessary to reorganize the kitchen, and a new art of kitchen planning developed. Based in industrial organization, it stressed convenience and efficiency. For the minority of families able to afford such renovations, built-in cupboards replaced movable cabinets and open shelves, providing increased storage space. Cupboards, countertops, and appliances were positioned to minimize unnecessary walking, bending, and climbing. Articles and intensified advertising in women's magazines and local newspapers praised the advantages of the changing technology and the streamlined kitchen. Encouraged by media and advertising campaigns, and by the exposure in domestic science classes, many women became convinced of the benefits of change.

Women's actual financial control over household purchases was, of course, limited by their economic dependence and their ability to persuade husbands to spend the money. This was clearly demonstrated in the advertising campaign by the Dominion government in connection with its 1936 Home Improvement Plan. Designed as a means of promoting employment within the depressed construction industry, and clearly directed at middle-class men, the plan provided low-interest loans to property owners for repairing and modernizing homes. The government also recognized women's vital importance to the plan's success, however. Promotional literature focussed on their role as financial managers and consumers; the advertising assumed that women needed little convincing of the advantages of modernization.

Two women with a new electric washing machine and iron, Ontario, 1921.

Source: Ontario Hydro Corporate Archives.

Joined by the media, and by manufacturers of household equipment, the government urged women to convince their husbands to take out loans to create new kitchens, bathrooms, dens for men, "rumpus" rooms for children, or "recreation" rooms. Only after meeting the needs of husbands and children was it suggested that women plan rooms entirely for their own use, perhaps a sewing room in the attic.[24] Certainly, women who could afford to do so welcomed opportunities to modernize their homes and equip them with the latest technology. Consumer credit companies such as Household Finance Corporation also promoted the idea of borrowing money for these purposes. Part of this consumerism was fired by the expansion of department stores, three of which controlled 80 percent of all department store sales by 1929. Many women found the advertisements of these stores and others appealing, and believed that they would be happier, freer wives and mothers as a result of spending less time on household chores. Farm women must, in any case, have welcomed any possibility of reducing their double load of domestic chores and farm work.[25]

THE EDUCATED MOTHER

The time women supposedly saved from domestic toil was to be spent on the now magnified responsibilities of caring for husband and children. During the 1920s and 1930s, medical and other experts bombarded women with popularized versions of new theories about childbirth and childcare. Scientific approaches were to replace instinct, intuition, and informal advice. The new methods, like those for household management, required more time, but smaller families meant that the mother could pay more attention to each child. High maternal and infant mortality rates had worried late nineteenth- and early twentieth-century social reformers, but their efforts at reversing these trends at first met with limited success. The loss of life in World War I motivated a renewed and systematic campaign to ensure "the production of future generations of healthy Canadians."[26] The campaign was fuelled by the findings of a number of studies on maternal and infant mortality by Dr. Helen MacMurchy, perhaps the best-known publicist of the infant welfare movement in Canada. Appointed by the Ontario government in 1910 to study and make recommendations on the problem of infant mortality, Dr. MacMurchy produced reports that brought her to national prominence as a doctor, writer, lecturer, and government official. When the federal government created the Child Welfare Division of the Department of Health in 1919, MacMurchy became its chief.

Her 1926 report confirmed the extent of maternal mortality, but did not address itself to solutions. A number of women's organizations, medical associations, and government agencies then studied and recommended ways to combat the problem of infant and maternal mortality. Three major needs emerged: formalized pre-natal education and care, increased medical competency, and improved socio-economic conditions. Government and other appropriate agencies directed their efforts toward the first two areas; for the most part, they ignored the low standard of living that jeopardized the health of many pregnant women and their babies.

Reformers adopted the strategy of educating women and providing them with what was perceived as the correct information. Health-care authorities advised that women should improve their physical health long before they became pregnant. Pregnant women should be monitored by a doctor or through medically supervised pre-natal clinics. Government and public health agencies published and distributed brochures written by doctors. The most famous of these, *The Canadian Mother's Book*, available in English or French from the Child Welfare Division of the federal Department of Health, had more than 200 000 copies in print by 1922. Childbirth itself was to be supervised by a doctor; it more frequently took place in a hospital. It was not long before half of all births took place in hospitals in the more populous provinces: in British Columbia by 1929, in Ontario by 1938, and in Quebec by 1945.[27] For many women the hospital experience was a positive one, providing them with a chance to rest and be looked after before returning home to normal household activities, care of the new baby, and, in most cases, other children. Leila Middleton's March 29, 1930, diary entry expressed this fact. After one miscarriage, one stillbirth, and two home deliveries, she gave birth to her third and fourth children in the hospital in Clinton, Ontario. Since she also had three stepchildren at home, it is not surprising that she wrote, "I enjoyed my hospital stay."[28] The drawback was that doctors increasingly treated the process of giving birth not as a natural event but as a medical one. Cesarean section rates increased to almost 5 percent of all hospital births — a rate that some physicians believed was too high. Intriguingly, such operations were performed more often on private than on public ward patients. The medicalization of childbirth undermined women's traditional support networks and practices. In Newfoundland, those networks and practices survived, with neighbourhood women acting as midwives. But even these women were influenced by medical techniques: they began to insist that during labour, women should no longer take whatever position they found comfortable but rather remain in bed, preferably on their backs.[29]

Once the child had been born, experts from the fields of psychology, education, and social welfare prescribed correct methods for mothering. Women who failed to heed this advice were viewed as irresponsibly endangering the survival, health, and character of their children. Popular articles, well-baby clinics, radio talks to mothers, pamphlets produced by governments and businesses, visits by public health nurses, and lectures to women's organizations — all ensured that more and more Canadian women received instruction in "approved" childrearing practices.

No aspect of infancy, childhood, or adolescence remained untouched by the new scientific authorities. Beginning at birth, prescribed feeding times, especially for bottle-fed babies, allowed for no deviation. Breast-feeding was preferred, but for those who could not or would not, the correct methods of formula preparation were widely publicized. Unless there was a good reason to the contrary, weaning was to take place at nine months of age. Age (rather than the baby's state of readiness) also determined the timing for toilet training. Regimented sleeping and exercise patterns rounded out the infant's schedule. Strict adherence to all these methods, mothers were told, would promote not only physical but also emotional health. Behavioural and other problems in later life were attributed to the mother's failure to establish the discipline required by industrial society. Anything that detracted from the formation of appropriate regular habits was frowned upon.

While the literature urged parents to love their babies, it advised against outward signs of affection, such as hugging and kissing, on the grounds that this behaviour would be likely to produce spoiled, nervous, and irritable children. Furthermore, medical experts suggested that excessive handling of infants could lead to a variety of physical problems, including bone deformities and spinal curvatures.[30]

Of course, not all women followed the advice of the experts. In rearing her first-born infant, Phyllis Knight, a working-class woman who had immigrated to Canada in the late 1920s, rejected "silly psychological books," preferring instead instinct, tradition, and observation.[31] But not all mothers may have been so strong-minded.

The mothers of school-age and older children also received instruction about how to oversee their physical, emotional, and intellectual development. Children's prompt and regular school attendance, their cleanliness and health, and their attitudes toward school and learning all demanded the mother's co-operation with, and support of, the educational and public health professionals' efforts. The authorities insisted on their right to intervene in the parent–child relationship by virtue of their scientific approach.

Mothers were also active in disseminating these values. In Baddeck, Nova Scotia, they formed the first Canadian Home and School (or Parent–Teachers' Association) group in the 1890s; during the first two decades of the twentieth century, the movement slowly spread. The major expansion of these associations occurred during the 1920s and 1930s, when both local groups and provincial federations flourished. A national federation, devoted to the training and guidance of children and youth both during and after their school years, was established in 1929. The federation's growth during the inter-war period indicates an acceptance of the partnership between parents — usually mothers — and experts, while the fact that recommendations for changes in the school curriculum frequently originated with parents shows that their involvement was not purely passive. Music and home economics, for instance, were two subjects vigorously promoted and actively organized by parent members of Home and School groups. Rural mothers also became involved in the education of their children through women's organizations. The United Farm Women of Alberta's Education Committee, for example, sought to improve rural education both inside and outside the classroom by emphasizing educational experiences that were both social and practical.[32]

The duty of monitoring the time children spent outside school was no longer the parents' alone. Social reformers and professionals railed against the effects of child employment; against unchaperoned co-educational activities; and against idleness. As alternatives, they suggested protected, supervised home or group cultural pastimes.[33] A particularly strong media campaign in the 1920s linked the social immorality of modern life and the problems of youth to parental failure in rearing and supervising their sons and, particularly, their daughters. One 1926 study of delinquent girls identified a form of parental failure ignored by most experts: sexual abuse in the home.[34]

One proposal for combatting problems caused by idle time was to convince school and municipal authorities to allow the use of school equipment and playground facilities after hours and during vacations for activities organized by trained instructors.[35] Another, perhaps more successful, one suggested the organization of athletic clubs and youth sport groups. Interest and participation in sporting activities promoted healthy alternatives to evil temptations, it was argued, not only during the school years but also into adulthood. Although the question of women's biological fitness for physical activity continued to be debated, physical-education teachers and medical authorities generally agreed that suitable types of exercise programs were beneficial. Sports for girls were encouraged so long as they were neither too aggressive nor too competitive. Organizers were cautioned about the possible adverse effects of strenuous activities during puberty. Care was to be taken to ensure that normal menstruation patterns were established and maintained, and that no damage occurred to the female reproductive system. Menstruation continued to be viewed as a disabling time during which girls were excused from gym classes and other sporting events. At the same time, gentle calisthenic exercises were promoted as a relief from menstrual pain and as a contribution to the development of good posture in young women.[36] For those young women able to afford them, the introduction of sanitary napkins eased their entrance into puberty; those unable to buy them were dependent on rags, which they either threw away when finished or washed to be used again. Some Native women used moss, which proved both hygenic and convenient.

Parental acceptance of the experts' views concerning the limitations that should be placed on girls' physical activities cost at least one young Maritimer the opportunity to compete in the 1928 Amsterdam Olympic Games. Gertrude Phinney, Canadian champion in the 220-yard dash, qualified for the Games but did not participate, because her father believed "that strenuous exercise such as that demanded of a track athlete would most certainly have adverse effects on child bearing and cause perhaps 'irreparable harm' to the mysterious workings" of her female body.[37] Some parents and their daughters were not so concerned: Corinne Cooper revelled in the joy of physical exertion to become, in the late 1930s, the best female sprinter in the country.[38]

It was generally the mother's responsibility to administer the experts' prescriptions for the proper physical, mental, and social adjustment of children, and the ultimate responsibility for a child's success or failure remained with her. Motherhood was promoted as a woman's patriotic and moral duty, as well as her lifelong profession. As Dr. Helen MacMurchy put it in 1922,

> being a mother is the highest of all professions and the most extensive of all undertakings. Nothing that she can know is useless to a mother. She can use it all. The mother reports for special duty about 250 days before the baby is born and she is never demobilised until she meets the Bearer of the Great Invitation. Mother, at ninety years, is still Mother.[39]

Fearing the harmful effects of feminist politics on Quebec families, Monseigneur Georges Gauthier, archbishop and coadjutor of the Montreal Diocese, used his 1930 New Year's Eve sermon to stress the moral aspect of women's proper role "as queen of the home, creator of the race." Monseigneur Gauthier concluded that, "through their noble maternal functions," women held in their hands "the education and moral formation of the future generation."[40]

The experts who extolled the virtues of the scientific, informed approach to motherhood promised that, if their advice was followed, it not only would produce well-adjusted and healthy offspring, but also would reduce the time involved in raising children. Little cognizance was taken of the contradiction in these arguments. In reality, acquiring, updating, and applying this information took more time than mothering had in the past. Mothers were now expected to read books, pamphlets, and relevant articles in the popular press, to attend baby and child health clinics, and to participate in mothers' clubs, parent–teacher associations, and the running of youth activities. Mothering, if one followed the experts, was becoming a full-time job. At the same time, experts ignored the economic reality of many women's lives. The literature advocated lengthy rest periods before, and recuperations after, pregnancy that were impossible for most working-class and farm women, or for those with other offspring and no domestic help. Similarly, both doctor care and hospitalization cost money, as did the long list of baby articles considered necessary for a baby's layette. But what choice did a mother have? If she believed in the literature, she might see her failure to provide the idealized home for her baby and growing child as seriously endangering its physical and emotional survival.

While the role of fathers was neither as circumscribed nor as scrutinized as that of mothers, it too was subjected to considerable attention. Preparation for "perfect" fatherhood, as with motherhood, was to begin long before birth. The ideal father was physically and morally fit, and a good provider. While mothers were assigned primary responsibility for childcare and for character and personality development, the father's role was to be supportive in every way possible. The literature accepted that men lacked their wives' patience, understanding, and time to study the new training methods, but suggested that they use their own business skills of efficiency and understanding to develop friendly relations with their children. The age of the tyrant father was over; instead, a father should provide an inspiring influence for his children. This meant taking time from his busy schedule to initiate and participate in such activities as ball games, fishing expeditions, and visits to the zoo or the circus. However, although experts did not assign father's role the importance of mother's with regard to the daily childcare responsibilities, they clearly recognized the father as the final authority and head of the family. "Bringing up children is a two parent job," commented one writer, "and almost always father sets the pace."[41]

THE IDEAL MARRIAGE

The experts intended that mothers' time, allegedly freed up through scientific childcare and household management, should be used primarily for the pursuit of an ideal home life. Family planning and birth control advocates suggested that reduced family size would lead to improved marital happiness; removing the fear of unwanted pregnancy, moreover, could lead to more satisfying sexual relations. Indeed, books and birth control advice frequently included counselling aimed at enhancing the sexual aspect of marriage. *Sex, Marriage and Birth Control*, a 1936 Canadian guidebook written by an Anglican clergyman, stated as a fact that "in the life of love that marriage implies, satisfactory sexual intercourse is the prime factor."[42] Intuition and instinct were no longer sufficient to ensure that couples would achieve the desired sexual relationship. They now were expected to study marriage manuals in order to learn about the workings of their bodies and the correct sexual responses. Expression of sexuality outside of marriage, however, was still considered unacceptable. Homosexuality was mentioned only to be condemned. For most women, cultural taboos continued to shroud the subject of sexual activity during menopause, and the attitudes of medical authorities toward menopausal problems remained ambivalent. By the end of the inter-war period, synthetic estrogen began to be manufactured and given to women during menopause — despite the fact that early studies were reporting its possible carcinogenic effects.[43]

The expanding cosmetics industry emphasized the role of physical attractiveness in promoting a satisfactory marital state. It advocated the use of face creams, cosmetics, mouthwashes, and deodorants as a means of promoting and maintaining an acceptable body image. Beauty parlours proliferated as new, shorter hairstyles required the attention of trained hairdressers. In fact, employment opportunities for women in this industry increased even during the severe unemployment of the Depression. Advertising downplayed the relationship between beauty and sexuality in favour of more acceptable campaigns stressing the retention of a youthful appearance and enhanced femininity. This theme was echoed in women's magazines, in articles in the popular press, and in books. In *Margaret Currie — Her Book*, the author, a columnist for the *Montreal Star*, devoted a chapter to "Beauty," outlining methods for skin care, weight loss, and hairstyling. Other chapters dealt with household financial management, laundry, cooking, and the "Middle Aged Wife."[44]

The focus on weight loss reflected another aspect of the contemporary preferred body image — slimness. World War I had had a liberating effect on women's clothes: short, loose dresses that de-emphasized breasts and hips became fashionable, encouraging the pursuit of a slim, boyish look. Corsets had earlier been discarded by young women in favour of bras and girdles. Now women were advised to maintain a "trim" figure through careful diet and exercise programs as well. For the plump or

A typical advertisement for patent medicines for women.

....

Source: Women's and Labour Studies Resource Room, Monarch Park Collegiate.

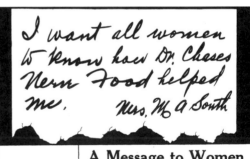

I want all women to know how Dr. Chase's Nerve Food helped me. Mrs. M. A. South

A Message to Women

From one who has learned to appreciate Dr. Chase's Nerve Food.

Modern life whether in the office, factory or home means an enormous strain on the more delicate nervous system of women. Whether it is the girl behind the counter or the lady going the round of society functions, the nerves are at high tension and require an abundance of rich, red blood if health is to be maintained.

Because Dr. Chase's Nerve Food forms new, rich blood, it is eminently successful in curing the ailments which cause the greater part of woman's suffering and has become duly popular among those who have learned of its merits.

Mrs. M. A. South, Grand Prairie, Alta., writes:—"I cannot begin to tell you how much good Dr. Chase's Nerve Food has done me. I was all run down, had no appetite, and suffered each month in a way only women will understand. After having followed this treatment for some weeks I feel like a different woman, sleep well, have a good appetite and am able to do my own work, even during the time that I formerly had so much suffering. I have no pains whatever now, which is an entirely new experience for me You may publish this letter as I want all women to know how Dr. Chase's Nerve Food has helped me, and I feel sure it will do as much for any woman."

Dr. Chase's Nerve Food, the greatest of restoratives, 50c. a box, 6 for $2.50, all dealers or Edmanson, Bates & Co., Ltd., Toronto

Dr.Chase's Nerve Food

As Your Druggist for Three Months Treatment, 12 Boxes for $5.00

big-breasted woman, these fashion prescriptions translated into painfully binding her breasts and starving herself into the fashionable silhouette. Aging or even mature women were out of style in the heyday of the cinema vamp.

Physical and sexual attractiveness were not all that was required of a wife. While it was acceptable for married women who could afford it to engage in hobbies like bridge, golf, and tennis, and cultural pursuits like piano playing, amateur acting, and painting, most "free" time was to be devoted to being a loving, supportive companion for their husbands. Of special concern were women who gambled or who played bingo to the detriment of their families. Women's magazines frequently exhorted their female readers to take up their husbands' interests and to educate themselves in order to augment their wifely roles.[45] The idea of the wife as a husband's "best friend" became increasingly popular; young people were counselled to seek marriage partners whose interests, education, and values reflected their own. In Quebec, where the Catholic church adamantly opposed any form of birth control, the clergy stressed the importance of friendship and companionship within marriage. Newly implemented marriage preparation courses used these ideas to reinforce the old prohibition against marriage outside the faith. Other churches were perhaps less explicit, but also encouraged marriage within the fold by sponsoring chaperoned activities for young adults. In some communities, such as the Inuit and Armenian, arranged marriages were still the norm.[46]

A Jewish ladies' "stag" party, Winnipeg, Manitoba, 1920.

Source: Provincial Archives of Manitoba (N-2448). Photo by Lewis B. Foote.

The idea of companionate marriage may in part have been a response to demographic factors. As family size fell and longevity for both sexes increased, it became more likely that couples would spend a longer time together after their children had grown up. The view of marriage as an equal partnership was also supported somewhat by changes that improved the legal status of wives within marriage. These included provincial equal guardianship laws and the 1925 federal divorce law, which finally allowed a woman to obtain a divorce on the same grounds as a man—namely, simple adultery. Some women came close to attaining the ideal marriage. Newfoundland suffragist Fanny McNeil found in her husband a supportive friend and companion. When pressured by the government to curb his wife's political activities, his response was "Go to the devil."[47] Yet for other women, marriage often meant support of, and submission to, husbands—who continued to be the heads of families both in theory and in fact. One Japanese woman in Vancouver recalled envying the single Anglican missionary women who worked in her community.

> One thing I noticed about the missionaries is that women usually lived alone and they were independent and they were so wrapped up in what they were doing. In most Japanese families the women had to obey and serve the man. I remember thinking, it must be nice to be able to do what you want to do.[48]

Husbands were rarely encouraged to take up their wives' interests; women continued to be responsible for the home. According to editorials in *Chatelaine*, it remained a wife's duty to create a smoothly run haven for her hard-working husband. When problems arose, it was her responsibility to solve them.[49] Fearing possible rising divorce rates after the enactment of the divorce laws in 1925, the popular press constantly reminded women that it was their duty, honour, and privilege to preserve family stability for the benefit not only of the family but also of the nation. Throughout the Depression, this same press exhorted women to budget wisely, and to provide emotional support for unemployed husbands. Self-sacrifice and restraint of selfish desire were the hallmarks of the "good" wife in the ideal family setting.

Difficult as it was for middle-class women to attain the high standards expected of them in all areas, for most working-class, rural, or immigrant women the ideal was impossible. Almost all rural families still used outhouses and depended on outside water supplies.[50] Gwen Lefort, a 16-year-old World War I war bride, discovered as much on her arrival in Canada in 1918. Her French-Canadian husband had told her "glowing stories" about Canada, none of which prepared her for life in Cheticamp, Cape Breton, where she spent fifteen years before moving to the nearby town of New Waterford. In Cheticamp she raised nine children and, as she later recalled,

> I cooked meals and scrubbed floors and washed my kids clothes on the scrubbing board you know. And drew water from the well — there was no indoor plumbing or anything.[51]

Many of the basic amenities lacking in her Canadian home were ones she had taken for granted while growing up in an English city. Her experience was not unique: many Canadian women coped with similar conditions. Even those who enjoyed comfortable material surroundings had little time for reading, let alone practising the experts' advice on being an ideal wife or perfect mother. In addition, of course, the advice literature could not be understood by women who were unable to read either English or French.

For most Canadians, moreover, the husband's wages, supplemented by a wife's or children's pay or by other household economic strategies, were barely enough to provide housing, food, and basic necessities. By 1928 it was for the first time theoretically possible for the average male manufacturing worker to earn sufficient wages to provide for a family on his own. But in 1929, 60 percent of Canadian working men and 82 percent of working women earned less than the minimum necessary for the support of a family of four.[52] The concept of the family wage was unrealistic at the best of times, and when strikes or unemployment hit, many women faced debilitating hardships. Following her 1925 visit to inspect conditions during the Glace Bay coalminers' strike, Canada's first woman MP, Agnes Macphail, criticized the federal government for its "neglect of humanity," particularly its failure to address the problems of the emotional and physical effects of this strike on women.

> I could not help but be struck by the tragedy of womankind in the place. Their youth is brief. Some young women are hotly resentful . . . but for the most part, especially if they have many children, their attitude is subdued and apathetic.[53]

For the wife who worked outside the home, or who raised livestock or took in boarders to make family ends meet, the time required to achieve the ideal household, children, or marriage was simply not available. One Winnipeg immigrant woman's inability to cope had a particularly tragic ending in December 1934. Despondent over her husband's continual lack of work and the prospect of a poverty-stricken Christmas, according to the newspaper account,

> she had just completed the hanging of Christmas decorations in her little home. Then with the home bravely adorned and spotlessly clean, she strangled one child, drowned the other in the bath, and killed herself by drinking a powerful germicide. There had not even been enough money in the house to buy the poison that killed her. She left a farewell note on the kitchen table bearing this out. "I owe the drug store 44 cents; farewell," it said.[54]

HELP FOR WIVES AND MOTHERS

Meeting the new standards was difficult for women who were poor, and impossible for poor women with large families. Yet the distribution of family planning information and the sale of birth control devices were both illegal. Moreover, for the women themselves the subject was often embarrassingly taboo. Throughout the 1920s, desperate Canadian women wrote seeking contraceptive advice from *The Birth Control Review*, a journal published in New York by Margaret Sanger, founder of North America's first birth control clinic. The following letter from a Saskatchewan woman was typical:

> I am a young married woman nineteen years old and I have a dear little baby boy five and a half months old, and I am expecting another baby in four months. Now, we are not in a position to support more than two children as my husband

and I both work hard for a living. I love my baby and I want to give him a fair chance in life. I have a good husband and he don't want to see a big family in want any more than I do. I have good health at present, but oh! Mrs. Sanger, how long would it be good if babies came to me that fast, and once health and happiness are gone, what is the use of asking help then? Now is the time, and if you could only tell me how to prevent conception you would make me the happiest woman in Canada.[55]

The pleas came from across Canada, from working-class and middle-class women and also from men. A college-educated woman related how, after three pregnancies, she had followed a neighbour's totally inadequate advice about birth control and given birth to two more children. Her health gone, she had decided "not to go back to my husband unless I can know of an absolutely certain contraceptive." Physical separation was the best advice that some doctors were willing to give, and a few still warned that mechanical methods of birth control were dangerous as well as disreputable. Most doctors, however, maintained a public silence on the issue.[56]

Women used a variety of contraceptive measures. But as the two letters to *The Birth Control Review* illustrate, their knowledge was limited and often incorrect, and such information was made available only by being passed privately from one woman to another. During the inter-war years, when the question of limiting family size moved from the private to the public arena, it was surrounded by controversy. Believers in the superiority of British stock continued to argue that the practice of family limitation among the Anglo-Saxon middle class would gradually but ultimately lead to "race suicide," because they would eventually be outnumbered by the larger immigrant and working-class families. A similar argument was put forward by French-Canadian nationalists, who feared for the survival of their culture should the francophone population decline. The United Church of Canada emphasized the use of contraception by married couples as essential for the promotion of companionate Christian marriages; but members of fundamentalist religions condemned the use of birth control as immoral and likely to contribute to sexual promiscuity, while the Catholic church proclaimed that marriage existed for procreation and that any attempt to thwart this purpose constituted a sin.

Despite these arguments, birth control advocates worked to educate women. Particularly influential were American birth control leaders like Margaret Sanger, or the anarchist Emma Goldman — who, during her exile in Canada, expounded her view that birth control was an individual woman's right, part of the right to control her own body, and also a necessary weapon in the workers' struggle against capitalism. This latter argument found favour among some Canadian socialist groups, who were convinced that the capitalist system encouraged large working-class families in order to have a cheap source of labour for its factories and cannon fodder for its armies. In 1924, British Columbia socialists founded the Canadian Birth Control League to educate the working class about these matters. Equally concerned about the physical and mental toll of unwanted pregnancies on farm and working-class wives, the women's branch of the United Farmers of Canada's Saskatchewan section passed the first public resolution on the matter at a 1929 convention. Calling on the government to rescind the ban on the distribution of birth control information, delegates requested the establishment of birth control clinics staffed by trained doctors.[57]

A birth control clinic founded in British Columbia in 1932 also counted among its objectives the need for "good breeding" and recommended the sterilization of the "unfit."[58] The use of such eugenic arguments became increasingly popular in the 1930s, when the ranks of the unemployed caused rising relief costs while deteriorating economic conditions raised fears of social unrest. Birth control clinics were established in at least three provinces: Ontario, Manitoba, and British Columbia. Rising relief costs also concerned Dr. Elizabeth Bagshaw, the pioneering medical director of a clinic in Hamilton, Ontario, from 1932 to 1966. But her main motivation—like Sanger's in the United States—was her genuine concern for the plight of working-class women facing repeated unwanted pregnancies. Founded and largely financed by Mary Hawkins, a wealthy Hamilton widow, the clinic was a godsend to many women, some of whom were given the contraceptive devices they were unable to pay for. This clinic also supported sterilization as a means of family limitation, and its dependence on doctors contributed to the medicalization of birth control.[59]

The debate about family limitation received national attention in 1936, when Dorothea Palmer was charged under the Criminal Code for distributing birth control information and devices to women in Eastview, a working-class, French-Canadian suburb of Ottawa. Palmer was employed by Alvin R. Kaufman, the wealthy owner of the Kaufman Rubber Company. Inspired by a growing personal conviction that limiting family size was essential for maintaining social order in a depressed economy, Kaufman had established the Parents' Information Bureau in Kitchener, Ontario, in 1929. The Bureau hired married women as field workers in many parts of Canada; at the time of Palmer's arrest, it employed 53 field workers to visit the homes of poor women and counsel them about birth control. During the Palmer trial, experts testified that it was "in the public good" to provide contraceptive information in areas like Eastview, with its large French-Canadian families and population of unemployed who were receiving public relief. More telling still were the 20 French-Catholic women who testified that Palmer's work was appreciated and that they saw nothing wrong with the contraception methods the Parents' Information Bureau promoted. The defence was successful: Palmer was acquitted on March 17, 1937, and an appeal of the verdict was dismissed. Yet, although the trial provided a platform for opponents and proponents of birth control, and had an undoubted effect, the law regarding the distribution of birth control information and devices was not rewritten.[60]

The economic hardships suffered by some families had been recognized in a limited way by governments through the introduction of mothers' allowances in Manitoba, Saskatchewan, Alberta, Ontario, and British Columbia between 1916 and 1920. Nova Scotia introduced them in 1930 and Quebec in 1937, leaving only Prince Edward Island, New Brunswick, and Newfoundland without this assistance during the inter-war years. Mothers who, through no fault of their own, were left alone with the responsibility of raising children, were eligible for the allowances, which were to be short-term supplements, not regular income. Both the eligibility requirements and the amounts provided varied from province to province. Widows were eligible recipients in all provinces; some provinces also paid allowances to deserted wives, wives whose husbands were physically and mentally handicapped, or wives of prisoners. Mothers with one dependent child qualified in certain provinces but not in others, and the maximum age of dependency varied from 15 to 16. In all provinces except Alberta and Saskatchewan, to qualify for assistance the mother had to be a married British subject, or the widow or wife of a British subject. This restriction resulted in

the disqualification of unwed mothers, women who lost their status as British subjects upon marriage, as well as many immigrant women. Many mothers fell through
the minimal safety net provided by the allowances. Heartrending ads show that some
felt they had no alternative but to put their children up for adoption. All recipient
mothers were encouraged to earn additional income when they could do so without
neglecting their family responsibilities. Applicants were scrupulously scrutinized,
especially if they were aboriginal or from a racial or ethnic minority, and recipients
were supervised to ensure that they were truly deserving.[61]

Mothers' allowances, like compulsory school attendance laws and child labour
legislation, represented an example of direct state intervention in family life in support
of a particular middle-class model of the family. The replacement of voluntary philanthropy with state assistance reflected the growing eagerness of the English-speaking
middle class to enlist the state in the campaign to support Canadian family life. Institutions like orphanages, refuges, and training and reform schools, and even foster
families, were increasingly under attack for their failure to produce good results. It
was best, it was now argued, to use means that encouraged mothers to remain at home
and keep their families together. During the Depression, relief was granted to women
on the basis of their respectability as women, not their willingness to work (as was
true in the case of men).[62] There was no recognition or financial support for women
who were responsible for elderly or handicapped adult dependents.

An astonishing case of state intervention in an individual family occurred in
Corbeil, Ontario, in 1934 with the birth of the famous Dionne quintuplets. The
poor, rural French-Canadian parents of these children were completely "relieved" of
the responsibility for raising their five girls, implying quite clearly that provincial
authorities disapproved of the parents' values and lifestyle. Within two months of
the birth, the provincial government placed Yvonne, Annette, Cécile, Emilie, and
Marie Dionne under the control of a board of guardians, which did not include their
parents.[63] In September of that year, the 5-month-old babies were moved from the
family farmhouse to a separate, specially equipped "hospital" building, and placed
under the care of Dr. Allan Roy Dafoe, the doctor who had delivered them. Dafoe
instituted what he called, in the foreword to his mothers' guidebook, "medical control," typified by rigorous monitoring of every aspect of the quints' lives and environment.[64] Although their parents might visit the girls, Elzire and Oliva Dionne
could not interfere in their care, despite Elzire's protests in favour of her own cultural
practices and her desire for an active role. In 1936 Dr. William Blatz, Canada's leading
child psychologist, took control, introducing his own system of disciplined, scientific
routine and child study. Only in 1938 did the Dionne parents' arguments, combined
with those of Catholic and Franco-Ontarian nationalists, succeed in restoring the
parents' authority. But the damage had been done. It was too late to heal the rift
that had developed between the quints and their family. The saga of the Dionnes
represented more than intervention on the part of the government. The experts
involved made their reputations and fortunes, and all Canadian women were treated
to yet another campaign designed to convert them to perfect, germ-free childrearing.

UNCONVENTIONAL WOMEN

Some women did not or could not conform to the idealized maternal role, with its
emphasis on self-effacing femininity or on scientific child-management, and righteous

moral indignation continued to haunt the lives of many of these women. Unwed mothers were seen as "weak and ignorant, strong-minded and wicked, or simple-minded."[65] The only exceptions tended to be those who were the victims of sexual abuse. The nuns who ran Montreal's *Hôpital de la Miséricorde* shielded their inmates from the outside world, but expected them to perform domestic duties both for their keep and as atonement for their transgressions. Wherever possible the unwed mother was encouraged to marry, even if the prospective husband was unsuitable, because marriage was seen as the only means of achieving a respectable living other than entering the convent. A more direct response to illegitimacy, in this case among women deemed mentally ill or feeble-minded, was sterilization. Between 1935 and 1945, 57 of the 64 patients sterilized at a British Columbia hospital were women. Of these, 46 were single women — mothers to a combined total of 33 illegitimate children.[66]

Little or no attention was paid to the situation of those women who, for reasons of choice or circumstance, did not marry. Yet some women challenged society's right to control their sexuality and restrict it to marriage. As knowledge of birth control spread, some women separated their sexuality from procreation. As early as 1928, a female Canadian university student questioned the assumption that she would marry, arguing that women should have the option to remain independent but not necessarily celibate. Introducing her discussion as a "protest and an explanation," this anonymous critic noted that she was not against marriage as a social institution, but rather was against having it thrown in her teeth as an "inevitable goal" or as "the simple panacea for all one's difficulties and ambitions."[67] A few women chose to fulfil a desire for motherhood and children despite their single status. Most single immigrant women came to Canada with cultural beliefs that emphasized the overriding importance of marriage, family, and motherhood. Some Finnish women who had come to Montreal as domestic servants seem to have consciously chosen to have children despite their unmarried state.[68]

Most people, however, believed that the only respectable lifestyle for an unmarried woman was celibacy. Many such women chose life in a Roman Catholic (or Anglican) religious order, and the number of sisters and the number of female orders, inside and outside Quebec, continued to expand. More than 15 000 women entered full-time religious life between 1921 and 1941. As well as offering a spiritual role, the convent still represented an important form of economic security, especially during the Depression years, including the possibility of self-development and a career. For some, it even provided a certain degree of independence.[69] But not all Catholic women wanted to join a religious order, and for most Protestant women, this option did not exist. In both French and English Canada, independent unmarried laywomen constituted an important group. There were few women whose occupations could adequately support separate households. In this period when marriage was so ardently promoted, close or lasting relationships among unrelated adult women were increasingly likely to attract social disapproval, and joint establishments with other women were suspect. Some women who recognized themselves as lesbians felt obliged to conceal their identity behind a façade of celibate friendship (the "old maid" companions); others continued an old tradition of mutual but non-sexual support among women. In Paris, Ontario, during the years when jobs for women were so easily available in the booming textile industry that a woman-centred culture evolved, some single women maintained shared households. Since most professions still barred married women, the few women professionals were likely to be unmarried, and some combined economic and emotional resources, often for substantial periods of their lives. Charlotte Whitton, a social worker and later executive secretary of the Canadian Council on Child Welfare (who gained further renown and some notoriety as mayor of Ottawa during the 1950s) lived with Margaret Grier, another federal civil servant, for almost 30 years, until Grier's death in 1947.[70]

Even married women could resist the conventional ideal of the housewife and mother depicted by the glossy magazines. The New Glasgow, Nova Scotia, temperance inspector Clifford Rose ran into a number of women who made ends meet for themselves and their families in ways that hardly accorded with the ideal. He recalled the notorious women, known as "mothers," who ran the "worst dives" in town. One, whose name was Delores, "was a mite of a woman [but] . . . her obscene and profane tongue was feared by friend and foe." Delores escaped prosecution for running an illegal tavern by smashing her rum bottles in the sink when the inspector was hammering on the door. The most famous of the women rumrunners, known as "the Queen," was the object of veiled admiration. A former nurse, horsewoman, and part-time movie actress in the United States, the Queen had returned to her native Nova Scotia with her husband in order to care for her aging parents. Attracted by the money to be made in smuggling rum, she used her commercial acumen — and her ability to bribe highly placed government officials — to create a business that even the inspectors had to admit was successful. Delores and the Queen were not atypical in their involvement with the illegal trade in alcohol during prohibition — the prohibition that other women had fought hard to obtain. In Peterborough, Ontario, arrests of women for making and selling alcohol increased markedly in the 1920s.[71]

Clearly, women like Delores and the Queen had not been able to depend on their husbands to make ends meet. Many other women did not have husbands, but nonetheless had children or other dependents to support. A family in which the mother stayed at home to look after the house and her children while her husband, as the sole breadwinner, supported the entire household was an ideal to which many — perhaps most — families could not conform.

The inadequacy of the family wage was finally recognized with the introduction by the federal government in 1944 of the family allowance, a monthly sum to be paid for each child. This controversial measure, as the debate surrounding its passage showed, was justified on the need to supplement the wages of the male breadwinner. Underlying the initiative was the assumption that, except in emergency situations, married women were responsible for childcare and ought not to be wage earners. Family allowance cheques were to be made out directly to mothers, a rule that initially was to be applied in all provinces but Quebec (there the cheques were to be made out to the fathers). It was Quebec feminist and politician Thérèse Casgrain who discovered this extraordinary plan and managed to stop it in its tracks before the first cheques were issued. After a delay of three weeks, Quebec women also received the family allowance cheque. Although the sums involved were small, family allowance legislation did benefit families in all provinces — and it was important that the money was controlled by women. At the same time, the scheme reinforced the traditional view that the man was the wage earner and that woman's proper role was a domestic one.[72]

NOTES

1. A.J. Pelletier, F.D. Thompson, and A. Rochon, *The Canadian Family*, Census Monograph no. 7 (Ottawa: J.O. Patenaude for the Dominion Bureau of Statistics, 1938), 19.
2. Roy H. Rogers and Gail Whitney, "The Family Cycle in Twentieth Century Canada," *Journal of Marriage and the Family* 43, 3 (August 1981), 734.
3. Canada, Dominion Bureau of Statistics, *Origin, Birthplace, Nationality and Language of the Canadian People* (Ottawa: King's Printer, 1929), 219.
4. Canada, Dominion Bureau of Statistics, *Vital Statistics 1964* (Ottawa: Queen's Printer, 1966), L2, 212.
5. Rogers and Whitney, "The Family Cycle," 729.
6. Dorothy W. Williams, *Blacks in Montreal 1628–1986: An Urban Demography* (Cowansville, Que.: Éditions Yvon Blais, 1989), 46; Tamara Adilman, "A Preliminary Sketch of Chinese Women and Work in British Columbia, 1858–1950," in Gillian Creese and Veronica Strong-Boag, eds., *British Columbia Reconsidered: Essays on Women* (Vancouver: Press Gang, 1992), 324.
7. Rebecca Coulter, "Rhetoric and Reality: The Experience of Teenagers in Edmonton," paper presented to the Canadian Historical Association, Vancouver, 1983, 14; Coulter, "The Working Young of Edmonton, 1921–1931," in Joy Parr, ed., *Childhood and Family in Canadian History* (Toronto: McClelland and Stewart, 1982), 146; Joy Parr, "Introduction," in Parr, ed., *Childhood and Family*, 14; Neil Sutherland, *Children in English-Canadian Society: Framing the Twentieth-Century Consensus* (Toronto: University of Toronto Press, 1976), 165.
8. Frederick Elkin, *The Family in Canada* (Ottawa: Vanier Institute of the Family, 1964), 113.
9. Beth Light and Ruth Roach Pierson, eds., *No Easy Road. Women in Canada, 1920s–1960s* (Toronto: New Hogtown Press, 1990), chap. 1; J. Donald Wilson, Robert J. Stamp, and Louis-Philippe Audet, eds., *Canadian Education: A History* (Scarborough: Prentice-Hall, 1970), 364–65.
10. Light and Pierson, eds., *No Easy Road*, chap. 1.
11. F.H. Leacy, ed., *Historical Statistics of Canada*, 2nd ed. (Ottawa: Statistics Canada, 1983), W340–438; Paul Axelrod, *Making a Middle Class: Student Life in English Canada during the Thirties* (Montreal and Kingston: McGill-Queen's University Press, 1990).
12. Marianne Gosztonyi Ainley and Catherine Miller, "A Select Few: Women and the National Research Council of Canada, 1916–1991," *Scientia Canadensis* 15, 2 (1991), 109.
13. Marta Danylewycz, Nadia Fahmy-Eid, et Nicole Thivierge, "L'enseignement ménager et les 'home economics' au Québec et en Ontario au début du 20e siècle: Une analyse comparée," in J. Donald Wilson, ed., *An Imperfect Past: Education and Society in Canadian History* (Vancouver: Centre for the Study of Curriculum and Instruction, University of British Columbia, 1984), 72.
14. Barbara Riley, "Six Saucepans to One: Domestic Science vs. the Home in British Columbia 1900–1930," in Barbara K. Latham and Roberta J. Pazdro, eds., *Not Just Pin Money: Selected Essays on the History of Women's Work in British Columbia* (Victoria: Camosun College, 1984), 168.
15. Riley, "Six Saucepans to One," 172.
16. Jo-Anne Fiske, "Gender and the Paradox of Residential Education in Carrier Society," in Jane Gaskell and Arlene McLaren, eds., *Women and Education:*

A Canadian Perspective, 2nd ed. (Calgary: Detselig, 1991), 137; Margaret Blackman, "The Changing Status of Haida Women: An Ethnohistorical and Life History Approach," in Donald A. Abbott, ed., *The World as Sharp as a Knife: An Anthology in Honour of Wilson Duff* (Victoria: British Columbia Provincial Museum, 1981), 75.

17. Riley, "Six Saucepans to One," 159–94; Danylewycz, Fahmy-Eid, et Thivierge, "L'enseignement ménager," 65–119.

18. *4-H Clubs in Manitoba* (Winnipeg: Historic Resources Branch, Manitoba Department of Cultural Affairs and Historic Resources, 1983), 8.

19. Gertrude E.S. Pringle, "Is the Flapper a Menace?" *Maclean's* (June 15, 1922).

20. Emily F. Murphy, *The Black Candle* (Toronto: Thomas Allen, 1922; reprinted Toronto: Coles Canadiana Collection, 1973); Joan Sangster, " 'Pardon Tales' from Magistrate's Court: Women, Crime, and the Court in Peterborough County, 1920–50," *Canadian Historical Review* 74, 2 (1993), 182; James W. St. G. Walker, *A History of Blacks in Canada* (Ottawa: Supply and Services Canada, 1980), 89.

21. Mary Vipond, "The Image of Women in Mass Circulation Magazines in the 1920s," in Susan Mann Trofimenkoff and Alison Prentice, eds., *The Neglected Majority: Essays in Canadian Women's History* (Toronto: McClelland and Stewart, 1977), vol. 1, 118–24.

22. Marjorie Harris, "Fifty Golden Years of *Chatelaine*," *Chatelaine* 51, 3 (March 1978), 43.

23. Christine Foley, "Consumerism, Consumption and Canadian Feminism 1900–1930," University of Toronto, M.A. Thesis, 1979, 23, 58–59.

24. Margaret Hobbs and Ruth Roach Pierson, "When Is a Kitchen Not a Kitchen?" *Canadian Woman Studies/Les cahiers de la femme* 7, 4 (Winter 1986), 71–76.

25. Cynthia Wright, " 'Feminine Trifles of Vast Importance': Writing Gender into the History of Consumption," in Franca Iacovetta and Mariana Valverde, eds., *Gender Conflicts: New Essays in Women's History* (Toronto: University of Toronto Press, 1992), 242; Linda Ambrose, "Teaching Gender to Junior Farmers: Agricultural Cartoons in the 1950s," unpublished paper, Guelph University, 1994, 18.

26. Suzann Buckley, "Efforts to Reduce Infant Matern[al] Mortality in Canada between the Two World Wars," *Atlantis* 2, 2, part 2 (Spring 1977), 76.

27. Norah L. Lewis, "Reducing Maternal Mortality in British Columbia: An Educational Process," in Latham and Pazdro, eds., *Not Just Pin Money*, 344; Jo Oppenheimer, "Childbirth in Ontario: The Transition from Home to Hospital in the Early Twentieth Century," *Ontario History* 75, 1 (March 1983), 36; France Laurendeau, "La médicalisation de l'accouchement," *Recherches sociographiques* 24, 2 (mai/août 1983), 204; Veronica Strong-Boag and Kathryn McPherson, "The Confinement of Women: Childbirth and Hospitalization in Vancouver, 1919–1939," *BC Studies* 69–70 (Spring/Summer 1986), 142–74.

28. Diary of Leila Middleton, March 29, 1930, courtesy of her granddaughter Sharon Trewartha; Katherine Arnup, *Education for Motherhood: Advice for Mothers in Twentieth-Century Canada* (Toronto: University of Toronto Press, 1994).

29. Janet McNaughton, "Midwifery, Traditional Obstetric Care and Change in Newfoundland," paper presented to the Ethnobotany/Ethnomedicine Group, Memorial University, December 1989, 8–9.

30. Veronica Strong-Boag, "Intruders in the Nursery: Childcare Professionals Reshape the Years One to Five, 1920–1940," in Parr, ed., *Childhood and Family*, 160–78; Norah L. Lewis, "Creating the Little Machine: Child Rearing in British Columbia, 1919–1939," *BC Studies* 56 (Winter 1982–1983), 44–60.

31. Phyllis Knight and Rolf Knight, *A Very Ordinary Life* (Vancouver: New Star, 1974), 165.

32. Charles Vincent Madder, *History of the Canadian Home and School and Parent–Teacher Federation 1895–1963* (Toronto: Canadian Home and School and Parent–Teacher Federation, 1964), n.p.; Kari Dehli, "For Intelligent Motherhood and National Efficiency: The Toronto Home and School Council, 1916–1930," in Ruby Heap and Alison Prentice, eds., *Gender and Education in Ontario: An Historical Reader* (Toronto: Canadian Scholars' Press, 1991), 147–64; L.J. Wilson, "Educational Role of the United Farm Women of Alberta," in David C. Jones, Nancy M. Sheehan, and Robert M. Stamp, eds., *Shaping the Schools of the Canadian West* (Calgary: Detselig, 1979), 124–35.

33. Coulter, "Rhetoric and Reality."

34. Murphy, *The Black Candle*; Pringle, "Is the Flapper a Menace?"; Tamara Myers, "Women Policing Women: A Patrol Woman in Montreal, 1918," paper presented to the Canadian Historical Association, Ottawa, 1993, 19.

35. Lola Martin Burgoyne, *A History of the Home and School Movement in Ontario* (Toronto: Charters, 1934), 27.

36. Coulter, "Rhetoric and Reality," 12; Helen Lenskyj, *Out of Bounds: Women, Sport and Sexuality* (Toronto: Women's Press, 1986), 33–53.

37. *Women at Acadia University: The First Fifty Years, 1884–1934* (Wolfville, N.S.: Acadia University, 1984), 12.

38. Leo W. Bertley, *Canada and Its People of African Descent* (Pierrefonds, Que.: Bilongo, 1977), 330.

39. Katherine Arnup, "Education for Motherhood: Government Health Publications, Mothers and the State," paper presented to the Canadian Sociology and Anthropology Association, Winnipeg, 1986, 21.

40. *La Presse* (2 janvier 1930), 1 [our translation].

41. Mabel Crews Ringland, "What about Father?" *Maclean's* (August 1, 1928), 59 61. See also Stella E. Pines, "We Want Perfect Parents!" *Chatelaine* 1, 7 (September 1928), 12–13.

42. A.H. Tyrer, *Sex, Marriage and Birth Control* (Toronto: Marriage Welfare Bureau, 1936), xiii.

43. Margaret Lock, *Encounters with Aging: Mythologies of Menopause in Japan and North America* (Berkeley: University of California Press, 1993), 341–42.

44. Margaret Currie, *Margaret Currie — Her Book* (Toronto: Hunter-Rose, 1924).

45. See, for example, "How to Be a Good Wife," *Chatelaine* 13, 2 (February 1940); Suzanne Morton, "Winning under Capitalism: Luck, Bingo and Lotteries in Canada, 1919–1939," paper presented to the Canadian Historical Association, Charlottetown, 1992, 14–24.

46. Light and Pierson, eds., *No Easy Road*, chap. 1; Janet Mancini Billson, "New Choices for a New Era," in Mary Crnkovich, *"Gossip": A Spoken History of Women in the North* (Ottawa: Canadian Arctic Resources Committee, 1990), 47; Isabel Kaprielian-Churchill, "Armenian Refugee Women: The Picture Brides, 1920–1930," *Journal of American Ethnic History* 12, 3 (Spring 1993), 3–29.

47. Margot Iris Duley, " 'The Radius of Her Influence for Good': The Rise and Triumph of the Women's Suffrage Movement in Newfoundland, 1909–1925," in Linda Kealey, ed., *Pursuing Equality: Historical Perspectives on Women in Newfoundland and Labrador* (St. John's: Institute of Social and Economic Research, Memorial University, 1993), 38.

48. Norman Knowles, "A Selective Dependence: Vancouver's Japanese Community and Anglican Missions, 1903–42," paper presented to the Canadian Historical Association, Calgary, 1994, 20.

49. Inez Houlihan, "The Image of Women in *Chatelaine* Editorials March 1928 to September 1977," University of Toronto, M.A. Thesis, 1984, 31–32.

50. A full 89.2 percent of farm families used outhouses, compared to only 11.9 percent of urban dwellers; 57.1 percent of farm households depended on outside water pumps, versus 7 percent of households in urban areas. *Census of Canada* (1941), vol. 9, Table 16, 73, and Table 14, 66.

51. "Gwen Lefort, War Bride in WW I," *Cape Breton's Magazine* 35 (1984), 49.

52. Bryan D. Palmer, *Working-Class Experience: The Rise and Reconstitution of Canadian Labour, 1800–1980* (Toronto: Butterworths, 1983), 192–93.

53. Margaret Stewart and Doris French, *Ask No Quarter: A Biography of Agnes Macphail* (Toronto: Longmans, Green, 1959), 92.

54. *Winnipeg Free Press* (December 18, 1934), as quoted in Canada, House of Commons *Debates* (January 22, 1935), 84–85.

55. Light and Pierson, eds., *No Easy Road*, chap. 2.

56. Angus McLaren and Arlene Tigar McLaren, *The Bedroom and the State: The Changing Practices and Politics of Contraception and Abortion in Canada, 1880–1980* (Toronto: McClelland and Stewart, 1986), 67.

57. Angus McLaren, " 'What Has This to Do with Working Class Women?': Birth Control and the Canadian Left, 1900–1939," *Histoire sociale/Social History* 14, 28 (November 1981), 435–54. See also McLaren and McLaren, *The Bedroom and the State*, chaps. 3 and 4; Angus McLaren, "The First Campaigns for Birth Control Clinics in British Columbia," *Journal of Canadian Studies* 19, 3 (Fall 1984), 50–64.

58. McLaren and McLaren, *The Bedroom and the State*, 64.

59. Marjorie Wild, *Elizabeth Bagshaw* (Toronto: Fitzhenry and Whiteside, 1984), 97; see Catherine Annau, "The Canadian Birth Control Movement in an International Perspective," McGill University, M.A. Thesis, 1992.

60. Le Collectif Clio, *L'histoire des femmes au Québec depuis quatre siècles* (Montréal: Quinze, 1982), 250–51; Diane Dodd, "The Canadian Birth Control Movement on Trial, 1936–1937," *Histoire sociale/Social History* 16, 32 (November 1983), 411–28.

61. National Archives of Canada, Canadian Council on Social Development, MG 28, I 10, vol. 13, file 497, *Aid to Dependent Mothers and Children in Canada: Social Policy behind Our Legislation*; Suzanne Morton, "Women on Their Own: Single Mothers in Working-Class Halifax in the 1920s," *Acadiensis* 21, 2 (Spring 1992), 95; Margaret Hillyard Little, "The Regulation of Ontario Single Mothers during the 'Dirty Thirties,'" paper presented to the Canadian Historical Association, Charlottetown, 1992, 29.

62. Theresa Healy, "Resisting State Sanctioned Violence — Women's Strategies versus State Policy: Vancouver Relief Programmes in the 1930s," paper presented to the Canadian Historical Association, Calgary, 1994, 7.

63. Pierre Berton, *The Dionne Years* (Toronto: McClelland and Stewart, 1977), 81; Mariana Valverde, "Representing Childhood: The Multiple Fathers of the Dionne Quintuplets," in Carol Smart, ed., *Regulating Womanhood: Historical Essays on Marriage, Motherhood and Sexuality* (London: Routledge, 1992), 119–46.

64. Allan Roy Dafoe, *Dr. Dafoe's Guidebook for Mothers* (New York: Julian Messner, 1936), xii

65. Andrée Lévesque, "Deviant Anonymous: Single Mothers at the *Hôpital de la Miséricorde* Montreal, 1929–39," *Historical Papers/Communications historiques* (1984), 175; see also Lévesque, *Making and Breaking the Rules: Women in Quebec, 1919–1939*, translated by Yvonne M. Klein (Toronto: McClelland and Stewart, 1994).

66. Angus McLaren, "The Creation of a Haven for 'Human Thoroughbreds': The Sterilization of the Feeble-Minded and the Mentally Ill in British Columbia," *Canadian Historical Review* 67, 2 (June 1986), 146.

67. Light and Pierson, eds., *No Easy Road*, chap. 3; see also Nicole Neatley, "Preparing for the Working World: Women at Queen's during the 1920s," in Heap and Prentice, eds., *Gender and Education*, 329–51; and Gwethalyn Graham, "Women, Are they Human?" *Canadian Forum* 16, 1 (December 1936), 21–23.

68. Varpu Lindström-Best, " 'I Won't Be A Slave!': Finnish Domestics in Canada, 1911–30," in Jean Burnet, ed., *Looking into My Sister's Eyes: An Exploration in Women's History* (Toronto: Multicultural History Society of Ontario, 1986), 35.

69. Micheline Dumont-Johnson, "Les communautés religieuses et la condition féminine," *Recherches sociographiques* 19, 1 (janvier/avril 1978), 90; Marta Danylewycz, *Taking the Veil: An Alternative to Marriage, Motherhood, and Spinsterhood in Quebec, 1840–1920* (Toronto: McClelland and Stewart, 1987), 17.

70. The Lesbians Making History Collective, "People Think This Didn't Happen in Canada — But It Did," *Fireweed* 28 (Spring 1989), 81–86; Joy Parr, *The Gender of Breadwinners: Women, Men, and Change in Two Industrial Towns 1880–1950* (Toronto: University of Toronto Press, 1990); Patricia T. Rooke, "Public Figure, Private Woman: Same-sex Support Structures in the Life of Charlotte Whitton," *International Journal of Women's Studies* 6, 5 (November/December 1983), 412–28.

71. E.R. Forbes and A.A. Mackenzie, eds., *Four Years with the Demon Rum 1925–1929: The Autobiography and Diary of Temperance Inspector Clifford Rose* (Fredericton: Acadiensis Press, 1980), 32–34, 42–43; Sangster, " 'Pardon Tales,' " 167.

72. Thérèse F. Casgrain, *A Woman in a Man's World*, translated by Joyce Marshall (Toronto: McClelland and Stewart, 1972), 112–14; Brigitte Kitchen, "The Introduction of Family Allowances in Canada," in Allan Moscovitch and Jim Albert, eds., *The Benevolent State: The Growth of Welfare in Canada* (Toronto: Garamond, 1987), 222–41.

CHAPTER ELEVEN

Proving Themselves in Public Life

Buoyed by their achievements and by the recognition they had received during

World War I, women's organizations entered the post-war period determined to

solidify their gains and extend their social, economic, cultural, and political influ-

ence. Even in the depths of the Depression this optimism was never completely

abandoned. Speaking to the Canadian Federation of Business and Professional

Women's Clubs in 1933, Josephine Dauphinee of Vancouver challenged the

members to

> study, read, discuss, . . . and learn to draw conclusions from your thinking. The
>
> men will welcome you to their councils and with equal rights, men and women
>
> will confer together over the problems of the day.[1]

Women's suffrage, of course, was no longer a shared goal once the federal franchise
had been achieved and women had won the provincial vote everywhere except in
Quebec. Temperance had also ceased to be a major issue with the introduction in
many provinces of government regulations controlling liquor distribution and sales.
New secular agencies took over many functions from evangelical-based organizations
such as the YWCA. The child welfare and public health programs long advocated
by women's groups gradually moved forward with the establishment of the Federal
Department of Health and its Child Welfare Division (1919), and the development
of similar provincial and municipal agencies. Staffed in some cases by former activists
from the women's reform movement, these agencies also opened up career opportunities for women as professional social work gradually replaced voluntary efforts.[2]

PROFESSIONAL ORGANIZATIONS

Career aspirations prompted many middle-class white women to join organizations focussing on an occupation and seeking to establish women's equality with men.[3] One example was the Federation of Medical Women of Canada, established in 1924 to provide women doctors with a forum in which to meet, exchange ideas, and discuss problems. A founding member was Dr. Elizabeth Bagshaw, who subsequently became the driving force of a birth control clinic in Hamilton. Within a year of its founding, the federation had 65 members on its rolls, drawn from all provinces. Another example of separate organizations for professional women was the Canadian Women's Press Club, which by the 1920s had branches in Winnipeg, Edmonton, Toronto, Vancouver, Ottawa, Halifax, and Saint John. These and other groups, such as the Federation of Women Teachers' Associations of Ontario and the Canadian Nurses' Association, were now able to launch vigorous campaigns aimed at enhancing the status of their members as professionals. During the 1930s, the Canadian Federation of University Women, for example, worked hard to find teaching positions for academic women who were on the job market. Women doctors, teachers, nurses, and journalists worked to improve their salaries and to develop special training and career opportunities. Their primary identification was with their chosen occupations; most members of these groups were single women, brought to activism through their professional connections.[4]

Local Business and Professional Women's Clubs had started before the war, beginning in Toronto in 1910; in 1930 they joined together in the Canadian Federation of Business and Professional Women's Clubs, chaired by Dorothy Heneker of Montreal, then the only Canadian woman to hold both Bachelor of Civil Law and Bachelor of Common Law degrees. Active in business, and working as a subordinate in her father's law firm because Quebec regulations would not allow women to practise law, Heneker was keenly aware of the disadvantages endured by women working in white-collar occupations. Others shared her concern, for by 1937 there were more than 2000 members in Business and Professional Women's Clubs in centres across Canada.[5] These clubs sought to improve the social and economic conditions of working women by promoting training and advancement for women in their careers. From their inception, the clubs were committed to equality between men and women. Armed with their own survey on unemployment, in 1933 the Federation's National Board endorsed the principle of unemployment insurance, but added the proviso that "any legislation which might be introduced in respect thereof shall apply equally to men and women."

The local clubs provided opportunities for women with similar jobs to meet socially and discuss issues of common interest. In the Montreal club, bi-weekly talks covered topics ranging from parliamentary procedure to industrial working conditions for women in China and Australia. The club worked to establish a national health insurance scheme; lobbied the Quebec government for provincial and municipal political rights for women; provided funding and volunteers for other groups such as the Big Sisters' Association and the Montreal Girls' Association; and during the Depression, co-operated with the YWCA in registering unemployed women and locating jobs for them. During the Depression, the Federation also protested the dismissal of female bank clerks.[6]

Professional organizations separate from men's did not, however, suit the aims and objectives of all career women. Rather than organize their own groups, women in the arts tended to join men in founding mixed societies dedicated to the promotion of their work. Possibly their limited numbers, along with the struggle for recognition and acceptance experienced by all artists, male and female alike, encouraged collective strength. A number of female writers participated in the founding convention of the Canadian Authors' Association, held in 1921, and women artists were among the founders and active members of the Canadian Group of Painters. In 1933 nearly one-third of the members belonging to the latter group were women; six years later, landscape artist Isabel McLaughlin was elected the organization's first female president. Women painters participated as founders in nearly all the major artistic organizing efforts of the inter-war years. In Montreal, the Beaver Hall Hill group (1920–21) brought together ten female and eight male artists who not only shared studio space but also contributed to the development of a co-operative modernist movement. Several women artists were invited by the all-male Group of Seven to include their works in its exhibitions and, in 1924, fifty-four works by thirty women artists were selected to represent modern Canadian art at the prestigious British Empire Exhibition held in England. Among Canada's internationally acclaimed visual artists were sculptors and long-time companions Frances Loring and Florence Wyle. Together with colleague Elizabeth Wyn Wood and two men, they established the Sculptors' Society of Canada in 1928, chartered in 1932. Women sculptors had benefitted from the post-war enthusiasm for municipal and other patriotic memorials, and for the first time they competed equally with men to produce major public pieces.[7]

The apparent breakdown of society during the Depression, and the emergence of new forms of political and social activism, challenged some women artists to address the question of the relationship of their work to social change. Such consciousness stirred poet Dorothy Livesay, who, with 34 others, began the Progressive Arts Club in 1932, linking writers and the left. Committed to social action in both

Internationally acclaimed sculptors and lifelong partners Frances Loring and Florence Wyle.

Source: Robert Flaherty (Canadian, 1884–1951): Portrait of Frances Loring and Florence Wyle, c. 1919. Art Gallery of Ontario, Toronto.

her poetry and her life, Livesay described the summer of 1932, after her return from Paris, as

> a crucial one for friendship and love. . . . My political convictions became the dominating obsession of my life. This lost me friends, split me away from parents, disrupted my relationship with my lover.[8]

Similarly arguing for political involvement, painter Paraskeva Clark wrote,

> those who give their lives, their knowledge and their time to social struggle have the right to expect help from the artist. I cannot imagine a more inspiring role than that which the artist is asked to play for the defense and advancement of civilization.[9]

COMMUNITY GROUPS

Other women worked within the community to advance culture and art through existing and new organizations. The Women's Art Association of Canada carried on the tradition of promoting public interest in art; among its varied activities, it encouraged the work of women artists. By the 1920s it had active branches in large and small urban centres throughout the nation, and in 1927 it arranged the first meeting between Emily Carr and the Group of Seven. Local groups like the Heliconian Club in Toronto sponsored a variety of cultural activities; others, like the Hawthorn Women's Club (established in Winnipeg in 1923), worked to foster the study of the arts. In Montreal, Lillian Rutherford organized the Phyllis Wheatley Art Club in 1922 for other black women and, in the mid-1930s, this club was reconstituted as the Negro Theatre Guild of Montreal. Women's auxiliaries provided funding and promotion for many theatrical companies, musical organizations, art galleries, and schools of art. In 1936, Mme Athanase David organized the first Montreal Music Festival. Many of the local literary clubs, Shakespearean societies, and musical societies that had been common in the later nineteenth century continued, or new ones were formed.[10]

During the 1920s, the dramatic economic and social changes occurring in the nation challenged the policies and structures of many of the older reform-oriented organizations. The religious home missions among the country's immigrant and Native female populations, established with the object of conversion and assimilation, continued to confront community resistance and began to alter their policies. For example, the Methodist and Presbyterian Woman's Missionary Societies that operated residential school homes for the daughters of Alberta's Ukrainian settlers gradually altered their narrow ethnocentric programs to emphasize integration and service to the community. As the school homes closed in the inter-war period, medical and community missions occupied increasing amounts of the Societies' time and resources; then, as government and Ukrainian-led community services grew, these activities also declined. Their efforts directed to conversion and acculturation failed. However, by providing essential medical, educational, and other services to neglected outlying communities, the religious societies met important needs.[11]

Sometimes the services provided unintentionally subverted the missionaries' aims. This was certainly the case for the young Wet'suwet'en girls who attended the

Lejac Residential School in British Columbia during the inter-war period. Run by the Oblates of Mary Immaculate, the school's curriculum was designed to provide basic domestic and literacy skills — that is, to train future farm wives. Not only did the school's students resist efforts to eradicate traditional practices, but in the 1940s they used the literacy skills developed at the school to spearhead community action and protests against harsh conditions at Lejac. In 1951, when the federal government ban against women's participation in band politics was removed, Wet'suwet'en women drew on these same skills, honed over the years, to run for and to win election to band councils.[12]

In the immediate post-war years, the National Council of Women of Canada (NCWC) continued to focus on motherhood and the protection of home life as necessary stabilizing factors after the upheavals of war. It largely ignored female career aspirations, or criticized them as a threat to the home, and promoted such occupations as domestic service, nursing, and teaching as suitable work for unmarried women. The NCWC's conservative orientation discouraged many young professional women from joining, and even antagonized former supporters. The Canadian Women's Press Club, for instance, disaffiliated from the NCWC in 1925, and twenty-three Local Councils made the same choice within the next five years. During the Depression years, when jobs were scarce, the National Council joined other Canadians in arguing that working women should not be competing with men for jobs. Both the National and Local Councils did debate the plight of unemployed women, and undertook relief work in many localities; the concern, however, that jobless women would turn to prostitution or the suspicion that they preferred relief to domestic service jobs, pervaded Council discussions. To counteract these perceived problems, the Council endorsed the upgrading of domestic work and the creation of self-help groups where unemployed women could come together to knit, sew, or quilt. Member associations were encouraged to establish domestic training courses, and the National Council adopted a Code for Household Workers, designed to improve working conditions and combat women's reluctance to accept domestic jobs.[13]

Within its family-oriented frame of reference, the National Council continued its reform work. NCWC membership grew from 150 000 in 1919 to half a million by 1940. Most of the increase came from new group affiliates at the local level in the growing towns and cities of Ontario, and these enlarged Local Councils increasingly came to dominate national policy formation.[14] The Council backed and monitored mothers' allowance legislation, and continued to address the issue of child welfare in the home, in institutions, and in schools. It urged equal treatment for male and female divorce petitioners, the establishment of divorce courts in all provinces, an increase in the age of consent for marriage, the treatment of adultery as a criminal offence, and enhanced legal remedies for deserted wives. To safeguard the financial position of wives and mothers, it proposed amendments to the provincial dower laws. On occasion, Local Councils also became involved in consumer issues, such as boycotts to eliminate large commercial and industrial profits on some products. The National Council's consumer policy, however, generally resembled that of the Canadian Manufacturers' Association, endorsing the latter organization's "Made-in-Canada" campaign and accepting, apparently uncritically, the growing role of advertising and the cult of household efficiency. The pro-manufacturing and central Canadian outlook of the national organization alienated many rural and western members; by the late 1920s, the major organized farm women's associations had ended their affiliations with the NCWC. Still, by the outbreak of World War II, National Council members had reason to feel that their work had helped to achieve considerable improvement in the quality of life enjoyed by Canadian women. The care of the old and the sick had improved, women had benefitted from mothers' allowances, infant mortality and tuberculosis rates had declined, new urban parks served children's recreational needs, and in some regions innovative education programs had been put into place.[15]

The Woman's Christian Temperance Union (WCTU) continued to make prohibition its primary focus and to work on a variety of fronts. Prison reform occupied some members; during the 1930s, a number of western locals were involved in the Canadian women's peace movement. After the defeat of absolute prohibition in various provinces in the 1920s and the introduction of government liquor control, the Union directed even more attention than previously toward educating the public about the dangers of alcohol. Members continued their campaigns for temperance textbooks and courses in schools, held essay contests, and encouraged teachers to inculcate the virtues of temperance in their classrooms. Their gains are hard to assess. Public drunkenness may have become less visible in Canada as a result of the organization's efforts, but a ban on alcohol consumption was impossible to achieve. Prohibition was increasingly out of step with a society that no longer regarded the use of alcohol as a major social evil.[16]

The difficulties faced by the WCTU, the home missionary societies, and, to a lesser extent, the NCWC were not shared by all volunteer women's organizations during this period. Some, notably the United Farm Women of Alberta and the Women's Institutes, expanded both their influence and their programs. Rural women, disillusioned with the essentially urban orientation of the National Council of Women, turned to associations whose aims and objectives reflected their own needs. Established in 1915 both to educate members for self-realization and to improve rural health services and education, the United Farm Women of Alberta (UFWA) was directed by a central board. It nevertheless encouraged its member groups to undertake local projects such as the construction of libraries, to which the central body donated books. Locals organized lectures and study groups on literature, music, immigration, rural health care, and schooling. Irene Parlby, elected under the United Farmers of Alberta banner as a member of the provincial legislature in 1921, recognized the constraints of rural life and saw the farm women's organization as a vehicle for a lifetime learning process, a practical outlet for her idealism and that of her peers. One of those very active and visionary peers was Susan Gunn, a former teacher, president of the United Farm Women of Alberta from 1924 to 1929, and a dynamic member throughout the 1920s of the Education Committee of both the women's organization and the men's association, the United Farmers of Alberta. Parlby and Gunn were dedicated to progressive educational reform, and through their countless speeches and writings did much to promote improvements in the province's rural schools. Speaking of her involvement in the agrarian movement during the inter-war period, Susan Gunn recalled:

> I was caught up in the work of the UFA and the UFWA. It was like a crusade, through co-operative effort we envisaged a new Heaven and a new earth, co-operative stores were started, municipal hospitals, the great wheat pools.

. . . Then along came the devastating thirties and we were flat on our backs. It took us a long and weary time to get on our feet.[17]

As Alberta's minister without portfolio from 1921 to 1935, Parlby continued to support and encourage farm women to think beyond domestic questions and to broaden their horizons. One of the many ways that the United Farm Women promoted this objective was to organize, in conjunction with the provincial Department of Agriculture, annual conferences known as "Farm Women's Week" at the University of Alberta. Efforts to make this event as accessible as possible included the provision for pre-school children to attend at no extra cost.[18]

The goal of providing continuing education for rural women, and close co-operation with provincial departments of agriculture, were also central characteristics of the Women's Institute movement that flourished after the war. The Institutes or Homemakers' Clubs engaged paid lecturers to speak about household science and agriculture, and these proved extremely popular. Although the development of domestic skills remained a primary concern, many local Institutes broadened their interests. The British Columbia Women's Institutes, for example, included business methods for young women as well as health care among the many other topics studied. When the province's Department of Health decided in the late 1920s to establish provincial health centres, it called on the Institutes for support to carry out its plan. The Alberta Women's Institutes undertook a wide range of community projects, including hot-lunch programs for schoolchildren, the establishment of public libraries, and relief work during the Depression.[19]

In Quebec, the convergence of government, clerical, and rural women's interests in strengthening rural life had fostered the development and growth of French-Canadian Women's Institutes, known as *Cercles de fermières*. In 1919 there were already 34 locals amalgamated under a provincial council, and the *Cercles* were among the founding members of the Federated Women's Institutes of Canada established in that year. Through their magazine, *La bonne fermière*, and through lectures, study groups, and exhibitions, the *Cercles* promoted the upgrading of homes and the development of farm skills.[20] Like the Women's Institutes, the *Cercles* were encouraged by the state; also like the Institutes, they reinforced the philosophy of separate spheres. They nevertheless provided opportunities for female organization and self-development. Perhaps more important, the Institutes and the *Cercles* opened new economic ventures for their members, and by publicizing rural women's traditional activities through exhibitions and sales, they validated farm women's work and attempted to professionalize it. Théodora Dupont, the vice-president of the Saint-Denis *Cercle*, established in 1921, recalled the economic advantages of her membership:

> The Minister of Agriculture gave us two hives of bees per circle. Selected by lot, I was the happy winner of one of the hives with all the necessary operating equipment. . . . The first beneficiaries of these gift-hives had to give their first swarm to another farm woman who did not have one, in my opinion an excellent idea. After that, an inspector came several times in the season, without charge, to give us the required instructions. The following spring, each farm woman received fourteen Plymouth Rock chicken eggs . . . for us to incubate, which gave us the chance to improve our flock.[21]

During the 1920s, Canadian rural women's organizations served as a model that women from other countries copied; in 1933, women from around the world met to create the Associated Country Women of the World.

The established women's organizations did not, for the most part, seriously court or attract minority women, who continued to organize and expand their own associations. Most of these had three related objectives: to preserve and enhance their group culture, to help members of their racial and ethnic communities adjust to Canadian life and overcome prejudice, and to maintain contacts with and assist members of their group outside Canada. Within black churches, women continued to play central financial and spiritual leadership roles:

> Missionary work was women's work . . . women . . . visited the sick, raised money for those in need here and in Africa and organized the social life of the Black community.[22]

Separate women's organizations, like the Eureka Club of Toronto, focussed on promoting black culture and welfare activities. By 1920, the existence of various religious, charitable, and educational groups organized by Nova Scotian black women prompted the holding of the first Convention of Coloured Women in Halifax. Another group, the Hour-A-Day Study Club, was established in Windsor, Ontario, in 1934 to bring black women together for self-improvement, to organize cultural programs and the study of black history, and to foster mutual understanding through involvement in the Windsor community. Mixed organizations such as the Universal Negro Improvement Association also benefitted from the significant contributions of black women, and many wives of black porters became active in auxiliaries of the Brotherhood of Sleeping Car Porters.[23]

Some Jewish women, mainly of western European origin, worked together in the 1920s and during the Depression in the National Council of Jewish Women and in other groups. Through fundraising and volunteer work they supported schools, scholarships, orphanages, care for the aged, and summer camps. In 1913, Mrs. Slova Greenberg founded the Ezras Noshim, a mutual benefit organization for Toronto immigrant women, to visit sick members and assist with housework during illness. As the organization matured, it enlarged its welfare mandate. Prompted by the case of a pious 90-year-old woman living in a home for incurables who, due to the language barrier, could not communicate her requirements for kosher food, the Ezras Noshim undertook the organization and completed the building of the Jewish Old Folks Home in 1920. The following year, with other women, they mobilized their members' considerable experience at door-to-door fundraising to the task of establishing a Jewish Hospital. Another group, the Zionist Hadassah, formed during World War I and dedicated to providing social services to Jews in Palestine, attracted more recently arrived eastern European Jewish women. This increased social action by Jewish women resulted not only from the growth of the community but also from increasing anti-Semitism during the period. Following a number of complaints in 1919, the Toronto Board of Education demanded that Ida Siegel's Mothers' Club at Hester How School discontinue the use of Yiddish at its meetings and ordered that only English be used.[24]

Ukrainian women, under the auspices of the Association of United Ukrainian Canadians, formed a Women's Section in 1922, and branches were organized in many localities. For their part, women in the Ladies' Section of the Macedonian Political Organization, founded in Toronto in 1927, dominated church and community social life. They raised funds and animated the community to support the achievement of a free and independent Macedonia while at the same time promoting and maintaining awareness of the Macedonian culture. Armenian women, although also few in number, joined the Armenian Relief Society, which had Canadian branches even before World War I. As survivors of the Turkish massacres arrived during the 1920s, membership and activities expanded to include assisting Armenians internationally and locally; supporting Armenian choirs, theatre, poetry, and lectures; and expanding knowledge of the language. Syrian women in Montreal founded a non-sectarian Ladies Aid Society in 1930 following the instigation of a visiting Lebanese educator, Mary Kassab. The object of the Society — to provide financial and other relief to needy Syrian families — met initially with opposition from the clergy, who claimed that no poor Syrian families existed. The women had amassed facts and figures, however, and eventually won support.[25]

Although group policy decisions were most often made by males among minority populations (as among majority ones), women made vital contributions to the maintenance of communal identity and adaptation. Moreover, not all women's groups were content to play merely supportive roles. The Pioneer Women's Organization, a Jewish socialist group composed mainly of working-class women born in eastern Europe, disaffiliated from the male-dominated Labour Zionist movement in 1925 because the women were disenchanted with their exclusion from the political process. This independent group pursued overtly feminist goals, supporting programs in Palestine and North America aimed at increasing women's and children's political and social awareness. Leaders of the various Zionist women's organizations that emerged after 1900, such as the Daughters of Zion or the Herzl Ladies Society, actively sought roles in Zionist politics.[26]

Women's clubs were the training ground for many of the women who were eventually to become active in public life. Florence Bird, later head of the Royal Commission on the Status of Women in Canada, gained organizational experience in Montreal and Winnipeg during the 1930s and early 1940s. An occasional columnist and magazine writer, Bird was "lonely and disoriented" when, in her twenties, she arrived with her husband from the United States.[27] They quickly developed friendships with the circle of Montreal progressive intellectuals who formed the League for Social Reconstruction. Bird also worked at a women's food depot several days a week, and joined with friends to form a women's Peace Study Group. At their semi-monthly meetings, members heard papers and discussed the causes of and cures for war. She later remembered preparing several talks for the group:

> Evidently some of the members thought well of them, because I was invited to give four lectures on current events by the Montreal Junior League. I worked hard preparing those lectures. I was excruciatingly nervous beforehand and was seized with violent diarrhoea before each.[28]

Her talks were the beginning of a "most interesting and rewarding career." Bird was paid to lecture to other organizations, although she continued to speak before groups of working women without charge. In 1937 Bird's husband accepted the job of assistant editor at the *Winnipeg Tribune*. The uprooted Florence once again found solace within women's organizations. She became active in the Social Science Study Club, an organization similar to the Peace Study Group she had left behind, and in the Winnipeg Junior League. Her early assessment of its members as "fat-cat women who amused themselves by playing the role of Lady Bountiful" changed as she underwent the requisite social work training course, and saw at first hand their community contributions. In her autobiography, she gives credit to these associations not only for their obvious contributions but also for their role in developing individual women's awareness of their potential.[29]

THE PURSUIT OF EQUALITY

Women's organizations, whether volunteer, cultural, or professional, shared a common theme: a desire for continuing self-education. Through formal and informal learning, women strove to improve their lives and those of other women. Many also recognized that self-realization for women required that young girls be trained to make decisions. With this goal in mind, the Canadian Girls in Training (CGIT) was founded in 1917 by the Young Women's Christian Association (YWCA) and the Protestant churches. Initially, the YWCA had sponsored Girl Guide companies, but its dissatisfaction with the Girl Guides' perceived secularism, imperialist and competitive spirit, and lack of opportunity for girls to participate in decision-making convinced the YWCA that a different organization was necessary. Canadian Girls in Training was the result. These groups met with their leaders at Sunday school and at mid-week sessions. Their activities reflected progressive educational theories, emphasizing research and discussion, co-operation, and independent thought. Adolescent girls from 12 to 17 were encouraged to participate in physical, religious, intellectual, and service activities, not for reward but for their intrinsic value. The enthusiastic response to the movement can be measured by its numbers; in 1925 there were 30 000 members in 3000 groups from Vancouver Island to Newfoundland. During the Depression (1933–34), numbers peaked at 40 000 in 1100 communities. Although the organizers assumed that marriage and motherhood were the ultimate goal for women, CGIT groups urged girls to pursue their education.[30]

Most youth-oriented groups, particularly the YWCA, stressed participation in physical education. Indeed, the 1920s and 1930s have been labelled the "Golden Age of Sports" for young women, in contrast to the previous generation. Organized physical activity and games for girls and women had the additional advantage that participants were supervised and kept out of mischief. School athletic programs expanded, and team activities such as basketball and baseball were popular, although after 1930 in eastern Canada, these games were usually played using "girls' rules" that restricted physical contact and limited physical exertion. The greatest development in women's sports was the expansion of women's amateur sports and athletic clubs. These separate organizations provided for women's participation not only as players but also as coaches, fundraisers, and administrators. Women's sports caught the imagination of spectators and the press; businesses sponsored them to an extent that has only recently been matched. Phyllis Dewar of Moose Jaw, Saskatchewan, became the first Canadian woman competitor to win four gold medals for swimming at the 1934 British Empire Games, a record that stood until 1966. Perhaps the most famous team accomplishment was that of the Edmonton Grads. Formed from students and graduates of an Edmonton high school, this basketball team amassed 502 wins and only 20 losses from 1915 to 1940. Recognized four times as world champions at international tournaments, the Grads were forced to disband at the beginning of World War II because the military took over their practice facilities.[31]

At universities, women's sports thrived as well, but there was a significant difference in levels of support for men's and women's activities. Although the number of women students had increased, campus facilities for women generally remained non-existent or pitifully inadequate. As early as 1911, female students at the University of Toronto had petitioned for a gymnasium. When Hart House was finally built in 1919 for sports and extracurricular activities, women were excluded. Although women at McGill had their own athletic facilities at Royal Victoria College, these were crowded and inadequate for the compulsory physical-education program. The new Currie Gym, built on the McGill campus in 1939, assigned last priority to women's space requirements and accepted women only "on sufferance."[32]

Not all student activities were organized for each sex separately. The Student Christian Movement (SCM), which was formed in 1920 from the student departments of the YWCA and YMCA, provided university and normal-school students of both sexes with an opportunity to examine and reflect upon the real and potential problems they faced. At some universities, the Student Christian Movement was co-educational; at others, men and women met separately. An offshoot of the Social Gospel movement, this Christian reform association organized study groups on most Canadian campuses throughout the 1920s and 1930s to re-examine traditional notions of Christianity and to address social problems. It became an outlet for spirituality and idealism and a training ground for students interested in social change and international co-operation.[33]

Through their Student Christian Movement activities, many women sharpened their interpersonal and organizational skills; both would prove useful for their future successful participation in public life.[34] One such woman, Marion Royce, was a driving force in the YWCA at both the national and the international levels during the 1930s and 1940s, and in 1954 became the first director of the federal Department

*A young woman learning to
ski in Ontario.*

Source: Reprinted by permission of
Katharine N. Hooke.

of Labour's Women's Bureau. The applied Christianity learned in the SCM also led some women into political activism. Both Marjorie Mann and Avis McCurdy, later active members of the Co-operative Commonwealth Federation (CCF), credited the student organization, at least in part, for their later political perspective. McCurdy, who came from a middle-class Maritimes family, recalled in a 1982 interview,

> I came straight to the CCF because I was convinced I had to be my brother's keeper. It was right out of my religious background — CGIT and SCM. I had also worked in business in my summers, and was overcome with the injustice and inequality.[35]

Women's desire for equal participation extended into the major Protestant churches. Both the Methodist and Presbyterian churches had admitted deaconesses from the 1890s, giving women an opportunity to participate in church life in a manner that mirrored their separate sphere: deaconesses visited the poor and the inmates of prisons, workhouses, and hospitals, and nursed the sick. Although some (like those who oversaw the daily activities of the Jost Mission for the poor in Halifax) undertook managerial work, their limited training and lack of financial compensation reflected the churches' continuing perception of women's volunteer role. Despite some improvements in training and salary by the 1920s, the failure of the female diaconate can be attributed partly to its inferior status within the church hierarchies. When a shortage of ordained ministers developed during and immediately after World War I, deaconesses had been called upon to take over many ministerial duties and responsibilities, but at the same time were prohibited from administering the sacraments or performing marriages. Dissatisfaction with these limitations in role and status caused many deaconesses to leave, taking jobs in the expanding fields of nursing and social work — areas where their skills were clearly welcomed. By 1925, the year of the Methodist, Presbyterian, and Congregational union as the United Church of Canada, there remained only 67 Presbyterian and 47 Methodist deaconesses in Canada.[36]

Separate auxiliaries and charitable associations within their churches remained the avenue for most Protestant women's achievements. Like the Women's Missionary Society of the United Church, Mennonite women's organizations provided an example of how women's strength could be perceived as a threat to the male establishment. Informal Mennonite sewing circles had long provided social contact while producing clothes for the needy. In 1908, however, Ontario Swiss women formalized their circle as a mission society, possibly the first Ontario Mennonite group to do so. By 1917 the various female Mennonite and Amish societies had expanded sufficiently to unite as a district, preceding the formal male conference unions by several years. Unification increased the strength of the women's missionary group and was perceived as a challenge to the power of the male Mennonite Board of Missions and Charities. In the late 1920s, the church reacted by placing the women's societies under the Board's control. At about the same time, strict new dress regulations, much more prescriptive and restrictive for women than men, came into effect.[37]

Frontier areas attracted women missionaries, some of whom, like Eva Hasell and Monica Storrs, came from Great Britain. Hasell began her work immediately after World War I. Trained in nursing, car maintenance, and driving, she conceived a plan to spread the Anglican Sunday-school movement to remote sections of the

Canadian Prairies and British Columbia, using vans as mobile churches. With financing partly from her own money and partly from the Western Canada Sunday School Caravan Fund, Hasell's commitment and personal work continued until 1972, when she was 84. In England in 1928, Eva Hasell met Monica Storrs, the then middle-aged daughter of an Anglican dean. Hasell convinced Storrs to undertake the mission of religious training in the Peace River area. Monica Storrs left for Canada in September 1929 to begin organizing Sunday schools, Boy Scouts, and Girl Guides for the children of Peace River.[38]

Other church women were involved directly in the fight for equality in their denominations. The slowly growing campaign for equal status within the Protestant churches realized one goal when the Methodist Assembly admitted women delegates for the first time in 1922. Nellie McClung, the seasoned women's rights activist, was instrumental in pushing forward this reform. She also urged that women be admitted as regular clergy. After the 1925 founding of the United Church of Canada, she devoted a major part of her energy to lecturing and writing on expanding the role of women in the church. The impetus for McClung, as for other women who advocated female ordination, was personal spiritual conviction as well as the quest for women's rights.[39]

The standard response of the church leaders—that they were willing to consider female ordination only if and when there was a candidate seeking it—was first put to the test when a request for ordination was received from Lydia Gruchy in 1926. Gruchy, a theology graduate and preacher, served three large Saskatchewan congregations. Her acceptance by the congregations, and her endurance of the physical exertions involved in tending to their spiritual needs, ought to have defused arguments that women ministers were unacceptable to church members and could not withstand the hardships of the extensive travel that was necessary in many rural areas. Still, Gruchy's application was refused by the 1926 meeting of the United Church's General Council, which instead recommended a new diaconate to which women could be ordained. This compromise was rejected by both Gruchy and her employer, the Saskatchewan Conference, which required a fully ordained minister capable of performing all the functions of that role. Continued requests for Gruchy's ordination were made by the Saskatchewan Conference, backed by Nellie McClung and a small but forceful group of supporters.[40]

The campaigners were disappointed by the lack of support received from the United Church's Women's Missionary Society, however. This Society—which was created, supported, and administered by women—raised and controlled a million-dollar budget in the 1920s, and maintained nearly 300 female missionaries in Canada and overseas. Perhaps the Society perceived that competition between itself and the ministry for female recruits would have an adverse effect on Women's Missionary Society membership and work. The Society may also have opposed female ordination because it believed that its own expanding organization provided sufficient career opportunities for capable, well-educated church women.[41] The fact that this strong organization was outside the control of the male church leaders certainly engendered feelings of anxiety if not outright hostility in the men. Indeed, the eventual reluctant acceptance of female ordination by the 1934 General Council has been attributed to the church leaders' determination to assimilate women's growing strength into the male-dominated church structure rather than tolerate it outside. Even after the ordination of Lydia Gruchy in 1936, the fight for equal rights in Protestantism was only beginning. Although in 1946 married women were also accepted as United Church ministers, most other Protestant churches remained closed to the idea of women assuming genuine leadership roles, whether married or single.

The lack of leadership and equal roles for women in the established Protestant churches may partly explain women's numerical dominance in the various religious sects that mushroomed, particularly in western Canada, before World War II.[42] One well-known example was the International Church of the Foursquare Gospel and its charismatic leader. Born on a dairy farm near Ingersoll, Ontario, in 1890, Aimee Semple McPherson was exposed to popular religion as a child through her mother's involvement in the Salvation Army and in evangelical camp meetings. By age 19 she had completed elocution lessons, won numerous medals in WCTU public-speaking contests, and married a Pentecostal preacher, Robert Semple. She travelled with him to China, where he died; she then returned, penniless and with an infant daughter to North America. Several years later, after an unsuccessful marriage to New York grocer Harold McPherson, Aimee left this second husband and returned with her children to Ingersoll to preach. Now known as Sister Aimee, she launched a continent-wide religious campaign that combined evangelism and drama. By the mid-1920s she had established a church, the Angelus Temple, in California. Her ability to attract followers was enhanced by her use of the media — which were infatuated with all aspects of her life, particularly her mysterious "disappearance" in 1926, and the numerous court cases related to her various marriages and her church's finances. In western Canada, McPherson founded and ran several churches and a Bible school. During the Depression she discovered a new vehicle in the radio, and became as well-known a radio preacher as the Social Credit premier of Alberta, William Aberhart.[43]

Within Roman Catholicism, it was difficult for women to move beyond the separate, subordinate roles that church authorities ascribed to them. In 1920, the Catholic Women's League was established to federate diverse groups of Catholic laywomen organized at the local diocesan level. League members responded to the needs of Catholic immigrants and working women, and supported the cause of Catholic education. By 1939 the League had 50 000 members in 554 divisions across Canada.[44] The church assigned service roles in public health and education to the female religious orders, as it assigned similar roles to women within the family. In Quebec this view of the appropriate activities of lay and religious women solidified in the 1920s and 1930s, as the perceived threat to French-Canadian nationalism posed by urbanization and industrialization intensified. Equal political, social, and economic rights for women continued to be viewed with horror by the male church hierarchy. To counter these ideas, the church assiduously promoted initiatives aimed at enhancing women's family role. In 1937 Cardinal Jean-Marie-Rodrigue Villeneuve directed Abbé Albert Tessier to spare no effort in mounting a campaign to persuade the public of the need to educate girls "to the vocation of wife and mother." For women to fail in their "great mission" would irreparably damage the Christian order. Under Tessier's leadership, the écoles ménagères (domestic science schools) were reorganized into instituts familiaux (family institutes), popularly called "schools for happiness"; the primary objective, however, remained unchanged — the education of women in a manner completely different from that of men.[45]

Clerical insistence on the maternal role left few respectable career alternatives for Catholic laywomen. Such attitudes may have contributed to the remarkable increase in the number of nuns and the expansion of the church's female orders, especially in Quebec, where ten new women's orders were added to the existing ones during the inter-war period.[46] The immense growth in the numbers of women entering convents provoked little comment — unlike the entry of women into politics.

WOMEN AND POLITICS

For the women who had fought for the vote, a key question of the 1920s was how women's suffrage would influence the political process. Initially, politicians were eager to court the new female electorate, for they accepted suffragists' arguments that women would vote as a bloc to reform society. It became apparent within the decade, however, that regional, class, cultural, and other differences divided women's political allegiances just as they did men's. In 1918, a group of Ontario women from the National Equal Franchise Union attempted to form a non-partisan Woman's Party working through the National Council of Women of Canada.[47] Their efforts were strongly opposed, especially by western Council members; the result was a shortlived and ineffective organization. More pragmatic was the practice that the National Council began of adopting a Canadian Women's Platform to identify women's issues to be pursued through the established political parties. The 1920 platform incorporated reform positions on the political equality of the sexes, equal pay for equal work, equal child guardianship, and a female minimum wage. The Council also continued to mount campaigns to educate women about their political responsibilities, and to encourage their participation in partisan politics. In Alberta, the UFWA adopted its own political education agenda — which included disseminating knowledge about public institutions and services, providing training in parliamentary procedure and the conduct of meetings, and helping women develop public-speaking skills.[48]

Such activities were more important than might be thought at first, for many women still found it very difficult even to cast their ballots. According to Elsie Inman, a founder of the Women's Liberal Club in Prince Edward Island, and later a senator, when Island women finally did get the provincial vote in 1922, many had to overcome their husbands' opposition in order to use it. In one case that she recalled, the woman "was scared to vote because her husband threatened her if he saw her at a poll." Working on the assumption that the man would not recognize his wife if she were attired differently, Inman took the woman home, dressed her in Inman's own clothes, coat, and veil, and successfully conducted her to the polling station. When Inman went to accompany another woman to vote, she was met by the irate husband, who accused her of trying to lead his wife astray. He sternly admonished her, "You're from a nice family, and have a good husband, you should be ashamed of yourself."[49]

Although a number of local women's auxiliaries to the two major political parties existed as early as 1906, they were not formally integrated into party structures. This changed in 1928, when the Liberal Party formed a national women's auxiliary, the Federation of Liberal Women of Canada, to attract women to the party. The Conservative Party followed suit shortly after. Both women's organizations were established to bring women to the parties as voters, with no intention of integrating them into strategic or leadership roles. Within the party organization, they were expected to carry out the essential day-to-day tasks of party maintenance, serving as the staffers who raised small-scale party funds, stuffed envelopes, distributed literature, answered telephones, and "minded" campaign offices. During elections, they became indispensable as canvassers, poll clerks, and scrutineers. In riding associations, they became secretaries and occasionally treasurers.[50] As valuable as these activities were, they were unlikely to provide opportunities for women to gain the skills, reputation, or political contacts necessary for party or public office. Legal equality did not bring inclusion as equals in political processes and organizations.

Many of the third parties that emerged or grew into prominence in Canada after World War I were relatively receptive to having women participate; these included the United Farmers' parties in Alberta, New Brunswick, Nova Scotia, and Ontario. The National Progressive Party and the Co-operative Commonwealth Federation (CCF), as well as the even smaller Socialist Party of Canada and Communist Party of Canada, were also less steeped in traditions that reflected a male dominance of politics. In addition, the philosophical orientation of many of the third parties embraced social and economic issues such as equal pay, protective labour legislation, and birth control — issues that had long been dear to reform-minded women.[51]

In their quest for members and for citizens willing to stand for office when there was little hope of winning, the newer parties actively recruited women. Agnes Macphail, Canada's first woman MP, was among the founders of the CCF, and the party relied heavily on the organizing work of women like Louise Lucas and Gladys Strum. Unlike their male colleagues, however, women organizers were not always paid. The UFWA president, for example, received only a reimbursement of expenses up to $500 per year and no salary, while the UFA president received an annual salary of $4000 and a $750 expense account.[52]

The parties' support of women's issues was limited in many ways. The example of the Communist Party of Canada illustrates the point. In the 1920s, this party took up the "woman question"; by the middle of the decade, the party had inaugurated a women's department with the object of advancing communism among women, established a women's column in its newspaper, and formed a national organization of working-class women. The Women's Labour Leagues, led by Florence Custance, numbered 37 by 1937. Finnish, Jewish, and Ukrainian Leagues predominated, reflecting the party's important ethnic connections. The Leagues emphasized the economic exploitation of women and attributed their subordination to the capitalist system. Despite this activity, women's issues never became a major priority for Canadian Communists; like other organizations, the party could not avoid reflecting structures of inequality in the larger society.[53]

The more influential Co-operative Commonwealth Federation was also committed to the emancipation of women but had similar difficulty living up to its promise. Concerned primarily with overcoming class inequality and getting candidates elected, the party relegated the cause of equal rights for women to the background. Nonetheless, many women worked at the local level for the CCF, as did Nellie Fraser. Fraser was widowed at the age of 32 in 1919. Her husband, who had been an agent with the Great West Life Company in Saskatchewan during the wheat boom, left her enough money to live on and to support their three children. In 1938, with her family grown up, she sold her home in Winnipeg, moved to Toronto, and became involved with the party, speaking on its behalf on local radio. A commitment to peace activism led her to work with the Women's International League for Peace and Freedom, eventually becoming president of its Toronto branch.[54]

Members of the Winnipeg Women's Labour League prepare relief bundles to support Nova Scotia coalminers in 1925.

....

Source: Provincial Archives of Manitoba (N-9343).

During the Depression years, when unemployment and economic problems dominated political life, socialist and communist women co-operated with each other and with women of other political persuasions on social and economic issues. In 1935, when relief camp internees in British Columbia went on strike and occupied the Vancouver post office, women from various local groups — including the Vancouver Communist Party, the CCF, the Local Council of Women, and the WCTU — joined together to form a Mothers' Council. It passed a resolution urging the federal government to provide genuine work and a living wage for the strikers. Led by women from the CCF and the Communist Party, the Mothers' Council participated in rallies and demonstrations supporting the unemployed, and organized the distribution of food, clothing, and shelter to the destitute. Similar groups in Saskatchewan and Alberta established women's committees to aid the "On To Ottawa" Trek of unemployed workers. After the 1935 crisis passed, interest in the Mothers' Council waned, although Communist Party of Canada involvement remained strong. In 1936 the Mothers' Council affiliated with the Local Council of Women and became the socialist voice on the latter's Unemployment Relief Committee.[55]

After 1921 women had another, more direct avenue to making their views known; they could be elected to legislative office federally and in most provinces. A small number of women entered the provincial legislatures and were able to further the social and welfare legislation that the newly enfranchised members of women's groups supported. There were many hurdles to be overcome, however.[56] The first woman seated in the federal House of Commons, Agnes Macphail, faced discrimination during all stages of the political process. Although Macphail won the United Farmers of Ontario federal nomination over ten men at the South-East Grey convention in September 1920, protests against her candidacy flooded the riding executive. Called before the executive and under pressure from some quarters to resign, she refused, arguing that she had been duly selected by the accredited delegates. During her election campaign, opponents attacked her religion — the Church of Jesus Christ of the Latter Day Saints — her sex, and her "mannish" behaviour, but on December 6, 1921, Macphail was duly elected. As a member of a third party and as the only woman member of the Commons, Macphail was an alien novelty, commented upon and scrutinized by other MPs, the public, and the press. Her first session, she herself admitted, was

Vancouver women demand the abolition of relief camps for the unemployed, 1935.

Source: National Archives of Canada.

miserable. . . . I was intensely unhappy. Some members resented my intrusion, others jeered at me, while a very few were genuinely glad to see a woman in the House. Most of the members made me painfully conscious of my sex.[57]

She did not shrink from the responsibility she had accepted, taking it so seriously that she rejected several marriage proposals in order to continue her work. Sensitive over being a "spinster" in an era when marriage was highly valued, Macphail took pains to announce the marriage offers publicly. She sat as the South-East Grey member, initially for the United Farmers of Ontario from 1921 until 1940. While she never lost sight of the interests of her agrarian constituency during her years in Parliament, Macphail also came to see herself as representing and acting for the women of Canada. In her day she was regarded, and criticized, as a feminist. She supported the struggle for women's suffrage in Quebec; fought successfully for the Archambault Royal Commission on prison reform and then for the implementation of its findings; and worked for peace and social welfare provisions, including unemployment insurance, family allowances, and pensions for the old, the blind, and the disabled. Defeated in 1940, partly because of her pacifism, Macphail later served as one of the first two women to sit in the Ontario legislature.[58]

Only five women were elected to the federal Parliament before 1950. Like Macphail, Dorise Nielsen and Gladys Strum, both from Saskatchewan, represented third parties; the other two, who sat for the major parties, were both cases of "widow's succession" — replacements for previously elected husbands. However, both of the latter two women — Cora Taylor Casselman, who was elected in an Alberta by-election following her Liberal husband's death; and Martha Black, who represented her Conservative husband's Yukon riding for five years when he was incapacitated by poor health — turned out to be excellent parliamentarians in their own right.[59] An American immigrant who was estranged from her first husband, Black had walked across the Chilkoot Pass in 1898 while pregnant with her third child. She settled near Dawson City and became a successful sawmill owner and operator. In 1904 she married George Black, who later became the territory's commissioner, and in 1921 its Member of Parliament. When 69-year-old Martha ran in his place in 1935, she faced a hard battle. Despite her husband's popularity, her victory was far from assured, and she won by only 134 votes. In her autobiography she recalled how she had to confront her hecklers:

> There were the younger women who said, "What can this damned old woman do for us at Ottawa?" That was hard to take, yet I hurled back, "You'll be lucky when you reach my age if you have my sturdy legs, my good stomach, my strong heart, and what I like to call my headpiece."[60]

Once in the Commons, she concerned herself with pensions and unemployment, and supported both cadet training and the imperial tie with Britain. When her husband was well enough to replace her in 1940, she retired.

It is clear that women came to the decision to seek elected office for a variety of reasons. Historians are only beginning to examine the growth of a feminist consciousness that occurred during the postsuffrage era as women recognized the continued presence of systemic barriers to their equal participation in public life. The inter-war political development of Margaret McWilliams is a case in point. The first woman to receive a degree in political economy from the University of Toronto, McWilliams actively participated in the Winnipeg Canadian Women's Club, the Local Council of Women, and the University Women's Club. Her belief that educated women had a responsibility to influence and lead in their local and national communities encouraged her to serve as first president of the Canadian Federation of University Women. In the early 1920s she believed that women could best influence and effect change through example, education, and reform organizations, but her actual experience of such work for and with other women altered her views. In 1933, with the considerable support of the Local Council of Women, she successfully ran in the municipal election in South Winnipeg and remained a city councillor for four terms.[61]

Margaret McWilliams was just one of eleven Winnipeg women who stood for aldermanic office between 1918 and 1939. Nineteen different women candidates ran for school trustee during the same period. The numbers of male candidates were 443 and 258, respectively. Like the men, the women politicians represented the range of class and ethnic politics in the city. The women candidates and elected officials focussed on gender issues and consciously identified with other women as a social group in their campaigns and political behaviour. In this feminism, we can see continuity with the pre-war movement and the seeds of the second wave to come. Although few in number, women entered municipal politics more frequently than at other political levels.[62]

At the provincial level, twenty-three women managed to win legislative seats between 1916 and 1949; nearly all were from Ontario and the west, for with the exception of one woman in the legislature of the newly created province of

Newfoundland, no women had been elected in Atlantic Canada or in Quebec. Most of these MLAs represented third parties. The CCF sponsored a number of female candidates, two of whom, Dorothy Steeves and Laura Jamieson, were elected during the 1930s to the British Columbia legislature.[63] Steeves's primary commitment was to socialism rather than women's issues, but Laura Jamieson, like many of the early women's activists, associated herself with a broad range of feminist causes and groups, including suffrage, the women's peace movement, the British Columbia Parent–Teacher Association, the Business and Professional Women's Club, and the Women's School for Citizenship. Before her election in 1939, Jamieson had served for eleven years as a Burnaby juvenile court judge.[64]

The United Farmers of Alberta was one of the few third parties to form a provincial government in this period, and therefore to gain the opportunity to legislate on women's issues. After its election in 1921, it appointed Irene Parlby as minister without portfolio. Aided and endorsed by the United Farm Women of Alberta, she became a spokesperson for women's issues, such as the provision of a minimum wage for women, married women's property rights, mothers' allowances, and children's welfare. The United Farmers of Alberta government passed 18 Acts that positively affected the welfare of women and children during its term. However, efforts by Parlby and some UFWA members to make wives co-equals with their husbands in the disposition of farm assets, and to recognize women's economic contributions in cases of separation and divorce, failed in face of opposition both by the UFA and by conservative UFWA women. Similar opposition combined to defeat the UFWA campaign aimed at legalizing contraceptive devices and at spending government money to disseminate information about contraception.[65]

A campaign of great symbolic significance that was visibly initiated and led to a successful conclusion by women was the action taken to gain Senate appointments for women. At issue was the exclusion of women from the upper house; some reform-minded women also believed that the Senate could be used as a platform from which to exert influence on public policy. In 1919 the first conference of the Federated Women's Institutes of Canada, presided over by Judge Emily Murphy, passed a resolution requesting that the prime minister appoint a woman senator. Surely women, now voters and eligible for election to the lower house of Parliament, ought to be among those "persons" who, if qualified, could be summoned to serve in the Senate. The National Council of Women and the Montreal Women's Club renewed the request, settling on Judge Murphy as their candidate. But the governments of both Arthur Meighen and Mackenzie King stalled, apologetically pointing out that women were precluded from eligibility under the terms of the British North America Act of 1867. After eight years of requests, refusals, and lack of progress, Murphy got together with four other prominent women, including Nellie McClung, Louise McKinney, and Irene Parlby, all of whom had served in the Alberta legislature, to mount a legal challenge. The fifth petitioner, Henrietta Muir Edwards, was very well known in women's organizations for her many years of service as convenor of laws for the National Council of Women. These women used an obscure section of the Supreme Court Act to petition the government for an Order-in-Council directing the Supreme Court to rule on the constitutional question of whether the term "qualified persons" in Section 24 of the BNA Act included women, and therefore whether women were eligible to be summoned to the Senate. The Supreme Court ruling in April 1928 held that the term "qualified persons" did not include women. The five petitioners then asked the government to allow an appeal of the judgement to the Judicial Committee of the Privy Council in England, at that time the highest court of appeal on questions related to Canadian law. The government agreed and the appeal was heard. On October 18, 1929, the Judicial Committee unanimously reversed the judgement of the Supreme Court of Canada and held that the word "persons" in Section 24 of the BNA Act did include women as well as men. Status Indian women, however, remained excluded under the terms of the Indian Act. Like their menfolk, Native women and women of Asian descent were also disqualified from voting in provincial or federal elections. However, only women status Indians shared with the *Québécoises* a sex-based bar from the franchise.

Emily Murphy was never invited to sit in the Senate; being a well-known Conservative, she was passed over by Mackenzie King in favour of Liberal Cairine Wilson, who was appointed the first woman senator in 1930. Even when the Conservatives returned to office later that year, and a Senate vacancy was created in 1931 by the death of a Catholic senator from Edmonton, Murphy was once again denied a seat, this time because she was a Protestant. Two years later, Emily Murphy died without achieving the appointment for which she had fought so long and hard. In 1935 a second woman, Iva Fallis, was named to the Senate.[66]

Montreal-born Cairine Wilson had not achieved the same recognition from the general public and the women's movement as Murphy, but she had devoted her married life to social and charitable reform causes, and (more importantly, from the point of view of the Senate appointment) to Liberal Party politics after 1921. An active volunteer with the Red Cross, the Victorian Order of Nurses, the Presbyterian Woman's Missionary Society, the Salvation Army, the YWCA, and the Ottawa Welfare Bureau, Wilson was a founder of the national Federation of Liberal Women. As a senator, she involved herself in divorce legislation, immigration, and the League of Nations. She was president of the Canadian League of Nations Society, and also one of the few Canadians to protest the restrictive immigration policies that prevented the entry into Canada of Jews fleeing Nazi persecution in the 1930s.[67]

Women were still unable to vote provincially and ineligible to hold public office in Quebec until 1940. Under pressure from the Roman Catholic church, the *Fédération nationale Saint-Jean-Baptiste* had abandoned its support for women's suffrage by 1920. For a short period there was no separate suffrage organization in Quebec, a situation remedied in 1922 by the formation of the Provincial Franchise Committee at the initiative of Marie Gérin-Lajoie, president of the *Fédération*. This organization consisted of two sections, one English and one French; the heads of each shared the new organization's leadership. Gérin-Lajoie became president of the French section, and Anna Lyman headed the English section. The Provincial Franchise Committee sent delegations to the provincial government, mounted education campaigns, and supported attempts to introduce the suffrage question in the province's Assembly.

Hopes for a continuing women's suffrage movement that would unite Local Council of Women and *Fédération* members were dashed in short order. When Archbishop Paul-Eugène Roy denounced suffrage in a 1922 pastoral letter, Gérin-Lajoie took her case and that of the women of Quebec to the International Union of Leagues of Catholic Women, hoping to win papal support. Although she was successful in getting the council to pass two favourable resolutions — one encouraging enfranchised women to exercise their rights, and another approving the civic, moral, and religious education of women — a third resolution tied any new suffrage activities to prior approval of the church in each country. When Gérin-Lajoie and the *Fédération* attempted to interpret the clause as relating to a local authority — the relatively progressive bishop of Montreal — the international body responded that approval was required from all the province's bishops.[68] The position of the Quebec church hierarchy was made clear by Cardinal L.N. Bégin in a letter supporting Archbishop Roy and sent to the newspaper *Le Canada* on March 19, 1922. "The entry of women into politics, even by merely voting," he emphasized, "would be a misfortune for our province. Nothing justifies it, neither the natural law nor the good of society."[69] This pressure forced the *Fédération* to withdraw its support for the Provincial Franchise Committee and Gérin-Lajoie to resign her presidency of the Committee.[70]

After this serious setback, the Provincial Franchise Committee marked time. In 1928 it was revitalized under the dynamic leadership of Thérèse Casgrain, and renamed the League for Women's Rights the following year. The daughter of an upper-class political family from Montreal (her husband served as Speaker of the House of Commons and as secretary of state in the Mackenzie King government), Casgrain used her influence and public prestige to campaign for political and professional rights for Quebec women throughout the 1930s. She was a tireless worker, championing the cause of Quebec women through her writings, lectures, and radio broadcasts.[71]

In 1927 a separate organization, the *alliance canadienne pour le vote des femmes du Québec*, had been formed under the leadership of Idola Saint-Jean, a McGill language professor. A member of the original Provincial Franchise Committee, Saint-Jean had resigned in January of that year to initiate her own campaign for the vote. The *alliance* attracted working-class francophone women; it operated alone and sometimes in unison with other suffrage forces to build what its founder called "a militant campaign."[72] Saint-Jean was at the heart of the struggle, writing for newspapers, magazines, and the group's own publication; lobbying the legislature; and presenting briefs to government commissions. By courageously running as an independent candidate in the 1930 federal election, Saint-Jean generated a great deal of publicity for the suffrage cause; although she lost, she did manage to win the support of nearly 3000 electors. The work of the various Quebec suffrage organizations and the support of other provincial women's associations, like the Montreal Local Council of Women, culminated in the endorsement of women's franchise by the Quebec Liberal Party at its 1938 convention, and the subsequent passage of the enabling legislation when that party assumed power in 1940. Thérèse Casgrain pressed for and secured the admission of delegates from the Association of Liberal Women to the provincial congress. It was from this political base that women's suffrage received a position on the official program.[73]

Quebec women were battling on a number of fronts during these years. Their inferior legal and economic status was also a major focus for organizational effort. Spurred on by improvements in the status of women in other provinces, both anglophone and francophone women sought similar reforms for themselves. In response to these demands and to divert attention from the suffrage issue, the Liberal government of Louis-Alexandre Taschereau set up the Commission on the Civil Rights of Women, headed by Judge Charles-Edouard Dorion, in 1929. The women who appeared before the Commission did not demand radical changes in their civil rights. Rather, they sought only to lessen restrictions on married women and to equalize

The Montreal Rosemount Community Centre's Adult Women's Club in the 1930s. The women are making clothes for unemployed families.

Source: McGill University Archives.

authority within the marital relationship, changes similar to those under discussion in France at the same time. A particular change they sought was the elimination of the double standard for legal separation. Under Quebec law a husband could seek a separation if his wife committed adultery, whereas, to be granted the same right, she had to prove that her husband kept his "concubine" in the family home. The primary demand, however, was that married women be legally entitled to control their own earnings. Even though no more than 10 percent of Quebec wives earned wages, witnesses testified about the hardships caused to women and children by husbands who refused to provide the necessities of life for their families and who squandered their wives' earnings.

Most briefs presented by delegations were extremely moderate, stressing the need to limit a husband's right to dispose of "community assets" for frivolous purposes without consulting his wife. No individual or group appearing before the Commission seriously challenged the patriarchal structure of Quebec families. No one threatened the sacrosanct role of the husband as *chef de famille* by suggesting that he no longer be accorded his wife's obedience, or that mothers and fathers share responsibility for family affairs. Nevertheless, faced with the hostility of the church, the legal profession, and the government, the Dorion Commission produced arguments for retaining the status quo, stating that "women themselves have not really evolved. Created to be the companions of men, women are always, and above all else, wives and mothers."[74] In the light of such sentiment, it is not surprising that the minor changes recommended by the Commission affected few women. They did include giving women the right to control their salaries and any goods or property brought with them into a marriage. But no other changes in the law respecting legal separations were recommended. The Commission, like the clerical and nationalist forces that opposed Quebec feminists in the first four decades of the twentieth century, echoed the powerful view that women had to remain in subordinate and familial roles if the French-Canadian nation was to survive. Assessing the Commission in her autobiography, Thérèse Casgrain wrote that "while the Dorion report brought a few amendments to our Civil Code, it did not go very far." She also believed that in the report's arguments against change, it was easy to observe the "scornful and haughty attitude of our masculine elite towards women."[75] The feminists were deeply disappointed, even though the Commission's deliberations and reports did provide a forum for the discussion of women's rights.

PEACE WORK

World War I had provoked for many an altered awareness of the nation's position in the world, and in the 1920s and 1930s some Canadian women developed and acted on a new international perspective. In 1929 Agnes Macphail was a member of the Canadian delegation to the League of Nations. Rejecting pressure that she sit on the committee dealing with welfare, women, and children, Macphail successfully insisted on becoming the first woman delegate to sit on the Disarmament Committee. Charlotte Whitton, while serving as the executive secretary for the Canadian Council on Child Welfare, represented Canada on the League of Nations' Commission on the Protection of Women and Children, and later on the League's Advisory Committee on Social Questions. She also served as a member of the Advisory Committee of Experts on the Protection of Women created by the International Labour Organization. Another prominent activist, Nellie McClung, was one of Canada's delegates to the 1938 session of the League of Nations.

These individual efforts were part of a larger movement of international co-operation among women and their organizations, which was by no means new. National organizations of farm, business and professional, and university women identified internationally with like women and linked their associations in international bodies. Connections between women's groups in Canada, the United States, and Great Britain were long-standing, as was the international outlook of the various Protestant missionary societies. The promotion of a world view and the eradication of racial prejudice and intolerance became goals for many groups. Within the various missionary societies, for instance, new theories of individual self-worth and cultural relativism replaced old ideas about Christian superiority.[76] The National Council of Women maintained its membership in the International Council of Women throughout the inter-war period. Consequently, some women were able to contribute at the international level, while local groups gained access to information and strategies concerning global issues that affected women. At the 1920 meeting, the delegates addressed women's rights as citizens, issues related to women's education, and concerns about health. International interests also frequently sparked national and local efforts on behalf of women. An international request for information about the experience of older, unemployed Canadian women prompted the National Council to activity regarding their situation in 1936.[77]

Canada's involvement in the war had not only highlighted the interdependence of nations but also produced a profound reaction to war itself. In the aftermath of the war, Canadian women and men had established in 1921 a national organization to support the efforts of the League of Nations in Geneva. Membership in the

Canadian League of Nations Society reached a peak in 1929 as a result of the work of women's organizations such as the WCTU and the National Council of Women of Canada, especially in the west. Although initially dominated by a male elite, the Society owed its survival to the efforts of its many women members. By the 1930s it had become in effect a women's peace organization, led by Cairine Wilson. In addition to taking up the League of Nations Society's cause, Local Councils of Women sponsored lectures, study groups, essay and speaking contests to promote the spirit of international understanding. Despite its tradition of avoiding controversial issues that could create tensions for some members, the National Council of Women of Canada lobbied Ottawa on peace issues, urging government support for the 1932 Disarmament Conference.

Even before the end of World War I, a group of women who were dissatisfied with the efforts of existing organizations had formed a separate peace party, the Canadian Women's Peace Party. It was one of the founding groups for the Women's International League for Peace and Freedom (WILPF). By the late 1920s, Canadian branches of the WILPF were active in Ontario and the west. More left-leaning than other peace organizations, the WILPF did not involve a large number of Canadian members, but it did attract women of high calibre. Violet McNaughton, editor of the women's page of the *Western Producer*, became a propagandist for the League, and she is credited with creating strong support for its activities among rural women in the west. Laura Jamieson, aided by various women's organizations, organized peace conferences in Vancouver, Winnipeg, and Saskatoon, and together with Violet McNaughton and Agnes Macphail represented Canada at the International Congress of the Women's International League for Peace and Freedom in Prague, Czechoslovakia, in 1929. Upon their return they determined to build a stronger movement in Canada, and in 1930 seventeen locals of the United Farm Women of Alberta and the Alberta WCTU joined the League.

A major goal for women's peace groups was the reorientation of Canadian education. They campaigned to replace cadet training in schools with physical education and to change textbooks and curricula that glorified the military and war. They also tried with some success to get their own members elected as school trustees in Winnipeg and Toronto in the 1930s. Although WILPF members co-operated with the League of Nations Society, the WCTU, and Local Council of Women branches, for the most part they found these groups unwilling to adopt many of the pacifist positions they promoted.

The increasing sympathy among the members of the Women's International League for Peace and Freedom toward radical social change accelerated during the Depression. McNaughton became active in the League for Social Reconstruction; Jamieson joined the Co-operative of Unemployed Workers and later the CCF. Pacifists faced a dilemma at the outbreak of the Spanish Civil War, when commitment to non-violence conflicted with commitment to social justice. Their dilemma intensified as dictators assumed power in Germany and Italy. Sharp divisions occurred within the membership of the Women's International League, with some persisting in their opposition to all war, while others concluded that war against the Nazis and Hitler was a regrettable necessity. Perhaps for this reason, by the late 1930s the organization had lost its base across the country and ceased to attract younger women.[78]

For Canadian women, as for all Canadians, peace and international understanding were elusive goals. The optimism that characterized the women's peace movement faltered in the face of deteriorating world conditions. Looking back over nearly two decades of women's active participation in domestic politics, some observers also felt discouraged. Even the normally irrepressible Nellie McClung was disillusioned:

> When women were given the vote in 1916–17 . . . we were obsessed with the belief that we could cleanse and purify the world by law. . . . But when all was over, and the smoke of battle cleared away, something happened to us. Our forces, so well organized for the campaign, began to dwindle.[79]

Not all suffragists concurred; Helen Gregory MacGill wrote an article in 1936 entitled "Canadian Women Have Not Failed in Politics." To prove her point, she cited a long list of important social and legal reforms — enacted at both the provincial and the federal levels — that were directly attributable to women's public involvement.[80] In the final analysis, however, the achievement of the vote was insufficient to bring about substantial political, economic, and social change for most women. Nevertheless, women's organizations had indeed continued to play a crucial role in extending the horizons of many Canadian women; and when Canada found itself at war in 1939, the women's organizations once again responded enthusiastically to the patriotic call for their selfless, unpaid efforts.

NOTES

1. Elizabeth Forbes, comp., *With Enthusiasm and Faith: History of the Canadian Federation of Business and Professional Women's Clubs . . . 1930–1972* (Ottawa: Canadian Federation of Business and Professional Women's Clubs, 1974), 7.
2. Diane Crossley, "The BC Liberal Party and Women's Reforms, 1916–1928," in Barbara Latham and Cathy Kess, eds., *In Her Own Right: Selected Essays on Women's History in B.C.* (Victoria: Camosun College, 1980), 229; Diana Pedersen, "Providing a Woman's Conscience: The YWCA, Female Evangelicalism, and the Girl in the City, 1870–1930," in Wendy Mitchinson et al., eds., *Canadian Women: A Reader*, (Toronto: Harcourt Brace, 1996), 194–210.
3. Gail Brandt, "Organizations in Canada: The English Protestant Tradition," in Paula Bourne, ed., *Women's Paid and Unpaid Work: Historical and Contemporary Perspectives* (Toronto: New Hogtown Press, 1985), 89.
4. Marjorie Wild, *Elizabeth Bagshaw* (Toronto: Fitzhenry and Whiteside, 1984), 57–58; Clara Thomas, "Women Writers of the Twenties: The Dynamics of Community," paper presented to the York–University of Toronto Women's Studies Colloquium, November 1978; Doris French, *High Button Bootstraps* (Toronto: Ryerson Press, 1968), 48; Pat Staton and Beth Light, *Speak with Their Own Voices: A Documentary History of the Federation of Women Teachers' Associations of Ontario and the Women Elementary Public School Teachers* (Toronto: FWTAO, 1987); Marion V. Royce, *Eunice Dyke, Health Care Professional* (Toronto: Dundurn Press, 1983), chap. 7.
5. Judi Cumming, "The Canadian Federation of Business and Professional Women's Clubs," *The Archivist* 14, 1 (January/February 1987), 4–5; Forbes, comp., *With Enthusiasm and Faith*, 15–32.
6. Forbes, comp., *With Enthusiasm and Faith*, 28–29, 15–17.

7. Thomas, "Women Writers of the Twenties"; Joan Murray, "Isabel McLaughlin," *Resources for Feminist Research/Documentation sur la recherche féministe* 13, 4 (December/January 1984/5), 17–20; Natalie Luckyj, *Visions and Victories: Ten Canadian Women Artists 1914–1945* (London, Ont.: London Regional Art Gallery, 1983), 3–14; Frances Rooney, "Frances Loring and Florence Wyle, Sculptors," *Resources for Feminist Research/Documentation sur la recherche féministe* 13, 4 (December/January 1984/85), 21–23; Rebecca Sisler, *The Girls: A Biography of Frances Loring and Florence Wyle* (Toronto: Clarke, Irwin, 1972).

8. Dorothy Livesay, *Right Hand, Left Hand* (Erin, Ont.: Press Porcepic, 1977), 48.

9. Luckyj, *Visions and Victories*, 16.

10. Luckyj, *Visions and Victories*, 109; Robin Winks, *The Blacks in Canada: A History* (Montreal and Kingston: McGill-Queen's University Press, 1971), 417; Adrienne Shadd, "300 Years of Black Women in Canadian History: Circa 1700–1980," *Tiger Lily* 1, 2 (1987), 11; Jean Bannerman, *Leading Ladies Canada* (Belleville, Ont.: Mika Publishing, 1977 Rev. ed.), 309.

11. Michael Owen, " 'Lighting the Pathways for New Canadians': Methodist and United Church WMS Missions in Eastern Alberta, 1904–1940," in Catherine A. Cavanaugh and Randi R. Warne, eds., *Standing on New Ground: Women in Alberta* (Edmonton: University of Alberta Press, 1993), 1–18; Frances Swyripa, "Nation Building into the 1920s: Conflicting Claims on Ukrainian Women," in Manoly R. Lupul, ed., *Continuity and Change: The Cultural Life of Alberta's First Ukrainians* (Edmonton: University of Alberta Press, 1988), 125–51.

12. Jo-Anne Fiske, "Gender and the Paradox of Residential Education in Carrier Society," in Jane Gaskell and Arlene McLaren, eds., *Women and Education: A Canadian Perspective*, 2nd ed. (Calgary: Detselig, 1991), 131–46.

13. Veronica Strong-Boag, *The Parliament of Women: The National Council of Women of Canada 1893–1929* (Ottawa: National Museums of Canada, 1976), 444; National Council of Women of Canada, *Yearbook* (1935, 1936).

14. N.E.S. Griffiths, *The Splendid Vision: Centennial History of the National Council of Women of Canada, 1893–1993* (Ottawa: Carleton University Press, 1993), 11, 162–3.

15. Strong-Boag, *Parliament of Women*, 357–58, 364–67; Christine Foley, "Consumerism, Consumption and Canadian Feminism 1900–1930, University of Toronto, M.A. Thesis, 1979; Anne Leger Anderson, "Regional Identity and Women's History," paper presented to the Canadian Historical Association, Calgary, 1994, 17; Rosa L. Shaw, *Proud Heritage: A History of the National Council of Women of Canada* (Toronto: Ryerson Press, 1957).

16. Nancy M. Sheehan, "Temperance, Education and the WCTU in Alberta, 1905–1930," *Journal of Educational Thought* 14, 2 (August 1980), 108–24; Sheehan, " 'Women Helping Women': The WCTU and the Foreign Population in the West, 1905–1930," *International Journal of Women's Studies* 6, 5 (November/December 1983), 395–411; Sheehan, "The WCTU and Educational Strategies on the Canadian Prairie," *History of Education Quarterly* 24, 1 (Spring 1984), 101–19; Sheehan, "The WCTU on the Prairies, 1886–1930: An Alberta–Saskatchewan Comparison," *Prairie Forum* 6, 1 (1981), 17–33.

17. L.J. Wilson, "Educational Role of the United Farm Women of Alberta," *Alberta History* 25, 2 (Spring 1977), 35.

18. Wilson, "Educational Role of the United Farm Women," 30.

19. Alexandra Zacharias, "British Columbian Women's Institutes in the Early Years: Time to Remember," in Latham and Kess, eds., *In Her Own Right*, 69; Catherine C.

Cole and Ann Milovic, "Education, Community Service, and Social Life: The Alberta Women's Institutes and Rural Families, 1909–1945," in Cavanaugh and Warne, eds., *Standing on New Ground*, 28–29.

20. Le Collectif Clio, *L'histoire des femmes au Québec depuis quatre siècles* (Montréal: Quinze, 1982), 307–9; Yolande Cohen, *Femmes de parole: L'histoire des Cercles de fermières du Quebéc 1915–1990* (Montréal: Éditions Le Jour, 1990).

21. Beth Light and Ruth Roach Pierson, eds., *No Easy Road: Women in Canada, 1920s–1960s* (Toronto: New Hogtown Press, 1990), chap. 5.

22. Dionne Brand, *No Burden to Carry: Narratives of Black Working Women in Ontario, 1920s–1950s* (Toronto: Women's Press, 1991), 18.

23. Sylvia Hamilton, "Our Mothers Grand and Great: Black Women of Nova Scotia," *Canadian Woman Studies/Les cahiers de la femme* 11, 3 (Spring 1991), 47; Brand, *No Burden to Carry*, 19, 16–17; "History of Hour-A-Day Study Club," *Impetus —The Black Woman: Proceedings of the 4th National Congress of Black Women in Canada* (1977), 8; Peggy Bristow, "The Hour-A-Day Study Club," in Linda Carty, ed., *And Still We Rise: Feminist Political Mobilizing in Contemporary Canada* (Toronto: Women's Press, 1993), 145–72.

24. Stephen A. Speisman, *The Jews of Toronto: A History to 1937* (Toronto: McClelland and Stewart, 1987), 305–7, 319–20.

25. Mary Prokop, "Looking Back on Fifty Years," *Ukrainian Canadian* (March 1972), 7–14; Lillian Petroff, "Macedonian Women in Toronto in 1940," *Polyphony* 8, 1–2 (1986), 24–28; Isabel Kaprielian, "Armenian Refugee Women and the Maintenance of Identity and Heritage," *Polyphony* 8, 1–2 (1986), 33; Baha Abu-Laban, *An Olive Branch on the Family Tree: The Arabs in Canada* (Toronto: McClelland and Stewart, 1980), 146. For a discussion of these and other ethnic organizations, see Jean Burnet, ed., *Looking into My Sister's Eyes: An Exploration in Women's History* (Toronto: Multicultural History Society of Ontario, 1986); Robert F. Harney, ed., *Gathering Place: Peoples and Neighbourhoods of Toronto, 1834–1934* (Toronto: Multicultural History Society of Ontario, 1985).

26. Paula J. Draper and Janice B. Karlinsky, "Abraham's Daughters: Women, Charity and Power in the Canadian Jewish Community," in Burnet, ed. *Looking into My Sister's Eyes*, 75–90; Irving Abella, *A Coat of Many Colours: Two Centuries of Jewish Life in Canada* (Toronto: Lester and Orpen Dennys, 1990), 153–4.

27. Florence Bird, *Anne Francis: An Autobiography* (Toronto: Clarke, Irwin, 1974), 114.

28. Bird, *Anne Francis*, 119.

29. Bird, *Anne Francis*, 141, 149.

30. Margaret Prang, " 'The Girl God Would Have Me Be': The Canadian Girls in Training, 1915–39," *Canadian Historical Review* 66, 2 (1985), 154–84.

31. Jean Cochrane, Abby Hoffman, and Pat Kincaid, *Women in Canadian Life: Sports* (Toronto: Fitzhenry and Whiteside, 1977); Helen Lenskyj, *Out of Bounds: Women, Sport and Sexuality* (Toronto: Women's Press, 1986); Lenskyj, "We Want to Play . . . We'll Play: Women and Sport in the Twenties and Thirties," *Canadian Woman Studies/Les cahiers de la femme* 4, 3 (Spring/May 1983), 11–18; Ron Hotchkiss, " 'The Matchless Six': Canadian Women at the Olympics, 1928," *The Beaver* (October/November 1993), 23–42.

32. Anne Rochon Ford, *A Path Not Strewn with Roses: One Hundred Years of Women at the University of Toronto 1884–1984* (Toronto: Governing Council, University of Toronto, 1985), 65–72; Margaret Gillett, *We Walked Very Warily: A History of Women at McGill* (Montreal: Eden Press, 1981), 245–46; Helen Gurney, *A Century*

to Remember 1893–1993: Women's Sport at the University of Toronto (Toronto: University of Toronto Women's T-Holders Association, 1993).

33. Paul Axelrod, "Moulding the Middle Class: Student Life at Dalhousie University in the 1930s," *Acadiensis* 15, 1 (Fall 1985), 117; Gillett, *We Walked Very Warily,* 231–32; Ruth Compton Brouwer, "Transcending the 'Unacknowledged Quarantine': Putting Religion into English-Canadian Women's History," *Journal of Canadian Studies* 27, 3 (Fall 1992), 53–4; Doris McCarthy, *A Fool in Paradise: An Artist's Early Life* (Toronto: Macfarlane, Walter and Ross, 1990), espec. chaps. 5 and 6.

34. Elizabeth Anderson, "Women in the Student Christian Movement of Canada 1921–1949," unpublished student paper, University of Toronto, n.d.

35. Joan Sangster, " 'Women and the New Era': The Role of Women in the Early CCF, 1933–1940," in J. William Brennan, ed., *"Building the Co-operative Commonwealth": Essays on the Democratic Socialist Tradition in Canada* (Regina: Canadian Plains Research Center, University of Regina, 1985), 72.

36. Christina Simons, " 'Helping the Poorer Sisters': The Women of the Jost Mission," in Veronica Strong-Boag and Anita Clair Fellman, eds., *Rethinking Canada: The Promise of Women's History,* 2nd ed. (Toronto: Copp Clark Pitman, 1991), 286–307; Diane Haglund, "Side Road on the Journey to Autonomy: The Diaconate prior to Church Union," in Shirley Davy, ed., *Women, Work and Worship in the United Church of Canada* (Toronto: United Church of Canada, 1983), 206–27; John D. Thomas, "Servants of the Church: Canadian Methodist Deaconess Work, 1890–1926," *Canadian Historical Review* 65, 3 (September 1984), 371–95.

37. Marlene Epp, "The Changing Role of Mennonite Women in Canada," paper presented at the Symposium on Mennonites in Canada, University of Winnipeg, May 1987, 10.

38. F. H. Eva Hasell, *Canyons, Cans and Caravans* (London: Society for the Propagation of Christian Knowledge, 1930); W.L. Morton, ed., *God's Galloping Girl: The Peace River Diaries of Monica Storrs, 1929–1931* (Vancouver: University of British Columbia Press, 1979); Lucille Marr, "Sunday School Teaching — A Women's Enterprise: A Case Study from the Canadian Methodist, Presbyterian and United Church Tradition, 1919–1939," *Histoire sociale/Social History* 26, 52 (November 1993), 329–44; Marr, "Hierarchy, Gender and the Goals of the Religious Educators in the Canadian Presbyterian, Methodist and United Churches, 1919–1939," *Studies in Religion/Sciences réligieuses* 20, 1 (1991), 65–74.

39. Randi R. Warne, *Literature as Pulpit: The Christian Social Activism of Nellie L. McClung* (Waterloo, Ont.: Wilfrid Laurier University Press, 1993).

40. Mary E. Hallett, "Nellie McClung and the Fight for the Ordination of Women in the United Church of Canada," *Atlantis* 4, 2 (Spring 1979), 2–16; Valerie J. Korinek, "No Women Need Apply: The Ordination of Women in the United Church, 1918–65," *Canadian Historical Review* 74, 4 (December 1993), 473–509.

41. Shelagh Parsons, "Women and Power in the United Church of Canada," in Davy, ed., *Women, Work, and Worship,* 172–88.

42. William E. Mann, *Sect, Cult and Church in Alberta* (Toronto: University of Toronto Press, 1955), 40.

43. Alvyn Austin, *Aimee Semple McPherson* (Toronto: Fitzhenry and Whiteside, 1980).

44. Valerie J. Fall, comp., *"Except the Lord Build the House . . .": A History of the Catholic Women's League of Canada 1920–1990* (Winnipeg: Catholic Women's League, 1990).

45. Evelyn M. Brown, *Educating Eve* (Montreal: Palm, 1957), xiv–xv; Sherene Razack, "School for Happiness: *Instituts familiaux* and the Education for Ideal Wives and Mothers," in Strong-Boag and Fellman, eds., *Rethinking Canada,* 2nd ed., 356–75.

46. Diane Bélanger et Lucie Rozon, *Les religieuses au Québec* (Montréal: Libre Expression, 1982), annexe 2, 294–319.

47. Carol Bacchi, *Liberation Deferred? The Ideas of the English-Canadian Suffragists 1877–1918* (Toronto: University of Toronto Press, 1983), 129–30; Georgina M. Taylor, " 'A Splendid Field before Us': Violet McNaughton and the Development of Agrarian Feminism in Canada, 1909 to 1926," paper presented to the Canadian Historical Association, Ottawa, 1993, 28.

48. Strong-Boag, *Parliament of Women*, 438–39; Ramsay Cook and Wendy Mitchinson, eds., *The Proper Sphere: Woman's Place in Canadian Society* (Toronto: Oxford University Press, 1976), 324–27; Nanci Langford, " 'All that Glitters': The Political Apprenticeship of Alberta Women, 1916–1930," in Cavanaugh and Warne, eds., *Standing on New Ground*, 73–6.

49. Douglas Baldwin, *Abegeweit: Land of the Red Soil* (Charlottetown: Ragweed, 1985), 328.

50. M. Janine Brodie and Jill McCalla Vickers, *Canadian Women in Politics: An Overview*, CRIAW Papers No. 2 (Ottawa: Canadian Research Institute for the Advancement of Women, 1982), 6; Patricia A. Myers, " 'A Noble Effort': The National Federation of Liberal Women of Canada, 1928–1973," in Linda Kealey and Joan Sangster, eds., *Beyond the Vote: Canadian Women and Politics* (Toronto: University of Toronto Press, 1989), 39–62.

51. Joan Sangster, "The Communist Party and the Woman Question, 1922–1929," *Labour/Le travail* 15 (Spring 1985), 25–56; John Manley, "Women and the Left in the 1930s: The Case of the Toronto CCF Women's Joint Committee," *Atlantis* 5, 2 (Spring 1980), 100–19; Sangster, "The Role of Women in the Early CCF, 1933–1940" in Kealey and Sangster, eds., *Beyond the Vote*, 118–38.

52. Georgina M. Taylor, "Gladys Strum: Farm Woman, Teacher and Politician," *Canadian Woman Studies/Les cahiers de la femme* 7, 4 (Winter 1986), 89–93; J.F.C. Wright, *The Louise Lucas Story* (Montreal: Harvest House, 1963); Alvin Finkel, "Populism and Gender: The UFA and Social Credit Experiences," *Journal of Canadian Studies* 27, 4 (Winter 1992–93), 79.

53. Sangster, "The Communist Party and the Woman Question," 27.

54. Her life story was told by her son, Craig Fraser, 1987.

55. Irene Howard, "The Mothers' Council of Vancouver: Holding the Fort for the Unemployed, 1935–1938," *BC Studies* 69–70 (Spring/Summer 1986), 249–87.

56. Langford, " 'All That Glitters,' " 71–85.

57. Margaret Stewart and Doris French, *Ask No Quarter: A Biography of Agnes Macphail* (Toronto: Longmans, Green, 1959), 74.

58. Terry Crowley, *Agnes Macphail and the Politics of Equality* (Toronto: James Lorimer, 1990); Doris Pennington, *Agnes Macphail Reformer: Canada's First Female MP* (Toronto: Simon and Pierre, 1989).

59. Sylvia B. Bashevkin, "Independence versus Partisanship: Dilemmas in the Political History of Women in English Canada," in Veronica Strong-Boag and Anita Clair Fellman, eds., *Rethinking Canada: The Promise of Women's History* (Toronto: Copp Clark Pitman, 1986), 258.

60. Martha Louise Black, *My Ninety Years* (Anchorage: Alaska Northwest Publishing, 1976), 137.

61. Mary Kinnear, *Margaret McWilliams: An Interwar Feminist* (Montreal and Kingston: McGill-Queen's University Press, 1991), 3–6.

62. Mary Kinnear, "Post-Suffrage Politics: Women Candidates in Winnipeg Municipal Elections, 1918–1939," *Prairie Forum* 16, 1 (Spring 1991), 41–57; Patricia Roome,

"Amelia Turner and the Calgary Labour Women, 1919–1935," in Kealey and Sangster, eds., *Beyond the Vote*, 89–117.

63. Susan Walsh, "The Peacock and the Guinea Hen: Political Profiles of Dorothy Gretchen Steeves and Grace MacInnis," in Alison Prentice and Susan Mann Trofimenkoff, eds., *The Neglected Majority: Essays in Canadian Women's History* (Toronto: McClelland and Stewart, 1985), vol. 2, 144–59.

64. Linda Louise Hale, "Votes for Women: Profiles of Prominent British Columbia Suffragists and Social Reformers," in Latham and Kess, eds., *In Her Own Right*, 294.

65. Finkel, "Populism and Gender," 81–4.

66. Olive M. Stone, "Canadian Women as Legal Persons," *Alberta Law Review* 17, 3 (1979), 370–71; Catherine L. Cleverdon, *The Woman Suffrage Movement in Canada*, 2nd ed. (Toronto: University of Toronto Press, 1974), 143–55.

67. Franca Iacovetta, "The Political Career of Senator Cairine Wilson, 1921–1961," *Atlantis* 11, 1 (Fall 1985), 108–23; Marion C. Wilson, ed., *Women in Federal Politics: A Bio-Bibliography* (Ottawa: National Library of Canada, 1975), 1.

68. Luigi Trifiro, "Une intervention à Rome dans la lutte pour le suffrage féminin au Québec (1922)," *Revue d'histoire de l'Amérique française* 32, 1 (juin 1978), 3–18.

69. Thérèse F. Casgrain, *A Woman in a Man's World*, translated by Joyce Marshall (Toronto: McClelland and Stewart, 1972), 54.

70. Marie Lavigne, Yolande Pinard, and Jennifer Stoddart, "The *Fédération nationale Saint-Jean-Baptiste* and the Women's Movement in Quebec," in Linda Kealey, ed., *A Not Unreasonable Claim: Women and Reform in Canada, 1880s–1920s* (Toronto: Canadian Women's Educational Press, 1979), 79; Marie-Aimée Cliche, "Droits égaux ou influence accrue? Nature et rôle de la femme d'après les féministes chrétiennes et les antiféministes au Québec 1896–1930," *Recherches féministes* 2, 2 (1989), 101–119.

71. Susan Mann Trofimenkoff, "Thérèse Casgrain and the CCF in Quebec," *Canadian Historical Review* 66, 2 (June 1985), 125–53; Casgrain, *A Woman in a Man's World*.

72. Cleverdon, *Woman Suffrage Movement*, 232.

73. Diane Lamoureux, "Féminisme de charme et féminisme du choc," in Anita Caron et Lorraine Archambault, eds., *Thérèse Casgrain: Une femme ténace et engagée* (Sainte-Foy: Presses de l'Université du Québec, 1993), 49.

74. Jennifer Stoddart, "Quebec's Legal Elite Looks at Women's Rights: The Dorion Commission 1929–1931," in D.H. Flaherty, ed., *Essays in the History of Canadian Law* (Toronto: Osgoode Society, 1981), vol. 1, 342.

75. Casgrain, *A Woman in a Man's World*, 62–63.

76. Owen, " 'Lighting the Pathways.' "

77. Griffiths, *Splendid Vision*, 167–9, 196–7, 212–3.

78. Donald M. Page, "The Development of a Western Canadian Peace Movement," in S.M. Trofimenkoff, ed., *The Twenties in Western Canada*, Mercury Series, Paper No. 1 (Ottawa: National Museum of Man, 1972), 81–89. Thomas Paul Socknat, *"Witness against War": Pacifism in Canada, 1900–1945* (Toronto: University of Toronto Press, 1987); Veronica Strong-Boag, "Peace-Making Women: Canada 1919–1939," in Ruth Roach Pierson, ed., *Women and Peace: Theoretical, Historical and Practical Perspectives* (London: Croom Helm, 1987), 169–90.

79. Candace Savage, *Our Nell: A Scrapbook Biography of Nellie L. McClung* (Saskatoon: Western Producer Prairie Books, 1979), 171.

80. Elsie Gregory MacGill, *My Mother the Judge: A Biography of Helen Gregory MacGill*, introduction by Naomi Black (Toronto: Peter Martin Associates, 1981), 218–19.

PART FOUR

The Unfinished Revolution: World War Two to the Present

"Our revolution is the most important revolution in the history of human beings."[1]

With this ringing proclamation, a small group of women calling themselves the "New Feminists" declared their intention to achieve a fundamental transformation of society — the destruction of gender roles for both Canadian women and Canadian men.

The New Feminists formed in 1969, at the end of a turbulent decade of dramatic change. Yet for them, as for many groups in Canadian society, the changes had not been as fast or as sweeping as they desired. Francophones, Native peoples, students, and women struggled, sometimes together but most often on parallel or even conflicting courses, to achieve a larger share in the "Just Society" promised by the newly elected prime minister, Pierre Elliott Trudeau. The social and political ferment represented by separatism, the Native rights movement, the student movement, and the women's liberation movement led many puzzled Canadians to look back longingly to the "good old days," when people seemed to know their place. Then, everyone appeared content to bask in unprecedented national prosperity, and to pursue single-mindedly the good life: a home of one's own, a car in the driveway, a fridge in the kitchen, and 2.5 kids in the "rec room" watching "Les Plouffes" or "Father Knows Best."

The prosperity Canadians were still enjoying in the late 1960s began when World War II brought the Great Depression to a close. Canadian participation in the war depended heavily on women's voluntary activities, as well as on their work in the paid labour force and, for the first time, in the armed services. After the continuous prosperity of the 1950s and 1960s, the economy experienced a series of slowdowns and mini-booms often characterized by inflation, rising unemployment, and skyrocketing interest rates. In the early 1980s, and again in the early 1990s, most regions of the country were fighting a full-fledged recession.

From a small, staid, white Anglo-Saxon country of just over 11 million inhabitants in 1939, Canada was transformed into a dynamic, officially bilingual, and multicultural society of over 28 million inhabitants by 1994. This population growth had three components: high rates of natural increase (the baby boom and declining death rates), the entry of Newfoundland into Confederation in 1949, and a massive influx of immigrants — some 8 million in 50 years. Population growth varied from region to region: Ontario, Quebec, and British Columbia attracted the bulk of the immigrants, but the highest percentage increases in population after the war were recorded in northern and western Canada, a result of the growth of resource-based industries there. In contrast, the proportion of the Canadian population located in the Atlantic region declined, despite the addition of Newfoundland. At the time of Confederation in 1867, more than one in five Canadians had lived in the Maritime provinces; by 1991, only one in twelve was located in the Atlantic region.

Photo on previous page: A Karate Black Belt, 1982. Source: Photo by E. Sim, 1982: Donna Sharkey (black belt).

Although the wave of immigration that began immediately after World War II was still overwhelmingly British and American in origin, by 1950 this was no longer the case. Immigrants made their way from the displaced-persons camps of war-torn Europe, and subsequently fled internal upheavals such as the Hungarian revolution; in 1951, seven out of every ten immigrants came from countries other than the United States and Great Britain. The ethnic composition of these "other" immigrants was increasingly diverse, as European immigrants were joined by large contingents from the West Indies, Asia, and Latin America. By 1990 more than 70 percent of immigrants were from non-traditional sources. Canada was not only a multicultural society, but also a multiracial society with significant visible minorities. Initially, after the war, the majority of those arriving at Canadian points of entry were men, but after 1958 female immigrants outnumbered male immigrants in most years.

The female immigrant experience was remarkably unchanged in the jet age. Successive groups of young single women — Italian, West Indian, then Filipina — were recruited for domestic service, and many suffered the same hardships of isolation and generally poor working conditions that British- and other European-born domestics had experienced in previous generations. The principal way for most women to enter Canada was as family members. Until the late 1980s, this meant that the majority of women immigrants were ineligible for the benefits and programs, such as government-sponsored language courses, that were available to adult male immigrants.

Immigrants of both sexes continued to prefer the cities to the country, and during this period the inexorable transformation of Canada from a rural and agricultural nation to an overwhelmingly urban and industrial society was completed. According to the 1991 census, nearly eight out of every ten Canadians lived in an urban setting. It is important to note, however, that the rate of urbanization varied considerably: Ontario remained the most highly urbanized province — 84 percent of its population was urban — while Prince Edward Island was the least urbanized at 45 percent. Increasingly, Canadians lived in very large centres. In 1991, 48 percent of the total Canadian population was to be found in metropolitan centres with populations of more than 500 000, double the proportion that lived in such large centres 40 years earlier; nearly 32 percent lived in Toronto, Montreal, or Vancouver. By 1981 Toronto had replaced Montreal as the nation's largest metropolitan centre, and movement west, especially to British Columbia and Alberta during the years of great prosperity for the resource industries, resulted in extremely rapid growth for Calgary, Edmonton, and Vancouver.

Within these internal migration patterns, there were some interesting cycles. During the 1950s, the greatest growth rates occurred in the suburban areas of the metropolitan centres: by 1961, 45 percent of all urban residents lived in the suburbs, and by 1991 a majority (57 percent) lived there. The back-to-the-land movement of the late 1960s and the early 1970s, however, sparked a small but not insignificant movement to rural areas beyond the cities and their suburbs, especially among the urban middle class. Then, within a decade, middle-class Canadians, sometimes even the same individuals, were turning to the inner city for housing. Many of these were affluent "yuppies" — young urban professionals — who played a role in the transformation of the inner cores of the larger metropolitan centres during the 1970s and 1980s.

Changes in the composition and distribution of the population were in large part responses to the ebb and flow of economic life. In general terms, Canadian economic development followed that of other western industrial nations, from the age of Sputnik to that of the information highway. The rapid pace of technological change was dramatically demonstrated by the development of computers: from bulky constructions taking up the space of a large room, they evolved into ever-smaller personal computers that transformed the ways in which many Canadians lived, thought, and communicated. The movement from an industrial to a post-industrial society was signalled in the 1950s by the declining importance to the national economy of primary (resource-based) industries and of secondary industry, such as manufacturing, and the continuous growth of the service and clerical sectors. By 1991 this latter area — known as the tertiary sector — comprised 73 percent of the labour force, compared to 48 percent in 1951.

This shift created massive employment opportunities for women, so that despite widespread opposition to their working for wages, increasing numbers of married women entered the labour force. Although public attitudes toward married women in gainful employment changed slowly, by the 1960s it had become widely accepted that childless married women, or those whose children were in school, could be in the labour force. However, it took another decade before it became common for women with pre-school children to work outside the home.

Married women's labour-force participation was greatly stimulated by the renewed emphasis on the production and purchase of consumer goods at war's end. Increased consumer spending and the creation of a national social welfare system were integral parts of the plan developed by C.D. Howe, the federal minister of reconstruction, for Canada's post-war recovery. Industries converted their tremendous capacity for wartime production to the manufacture of automobiles, appliances, and other household goods. The advent of television in the 1950s provided yet another medium — an even more powerful one — through which advertisers could convince Canadians that such products were essential to an improved standard of living. For most families, the purchase of expensive consumer items was possible only if there was more than one wage earner in the family. This role was increasingly filled by wives, since prolonged education for children, and legal restrictions on child labour, greatly reduced the number of young adolescents active in the full-time workforce.

The master plan of Mackenzie King's Liberal government for ensuring Canada's prosperity after the war also involved a massive development of the nation's natural resources, particularly in the west and north. To expedite this process, the government encouraged Americans to invest in such projects as the construction of a pipeline to carry gas and oil from Alberta to eastern Canada. As American investment in Canada grew by leaps and bounds, so too did concerns about the nation's sovereignty. Prominent Canadians like economist Harold Innis warned that the country was now in the process of becoming a colony once again, this time of an increasingly powerful American empire. In 1950 the Massey Commission, the royal commission appointed to report on the state of the arts and sciences in Canada, documented just how fragile Canadian culture was as a result of the pervasiveness of the American influence. The negative impact of Canada's reliance on the United States was a favourite theme of the Conservative opposition leader, populist John G. Diefenbaker, who made it a major issue of the 1957 general election campaign. After forming a minority government in 1957, and calling an election the following year, the Conservatives swept into power in 1958 with the largest parliamentary majority up to that time in Canadian history. Thus ended the federal Liberal rule that had been uninterrupted since 1935, and only briefly broken since 1896.

Diefenbaker's love affair with the Canadian electorate soon turned sour, however. Just four years after his apparently decisive victory, Diefenbaker was defeated at the polls by the Liberals, now led by the internationally renowned diplomat Lester B. Pearson, who formed a minority government in 1962, and then obtained a majority a year later. Scarcely had he taken office, Pearson found himself embroiled in controversy over the issue of Canadian sovereignty. Should the Canadian government permit the installation of nuclear warheads on missiles stationed in Canada? After much soul-searching, the prime minister permitted their installation, a decision that alienated Canadian women involved in the peace movement. Canadian women, in growing numbers, were participating in the protest against the war in Vietnam. More generally, a new dimension of women's lives during this period was their greater participation in both conventional and protest politics. Soon a resurgent women's movement would be launching public actions on behalf of women themselves.

Women would continue their increased political involvement during the decades that followed, decades that were dominated by the prime ministerial regimes of, first, the Liberal successor to Lester Pearson, Pierre Elliott Trudeau, and, later on, the Progressive Conservatives' Brian Mulroney. Among the issues crowding the political agenda were the quest for bilingualism in the aftermath of the 1967 report of the Royal Commission on Bilingualism and Biculturalism, the need to patriate the Canadian constitution, concern for Native self-government, and the debate over NAFTA (the North American Free Trade Agreement). As deficits loomed larger and larger, the federal government seemed determined to hand over its responsibilities for social welfare programs to the provinces; as their financial positions appeared to worsen, all levels of government seemed anxious to pass the buck to Canada's citizens. Whatever the issue, women were increasingly aware that they had interests to defend and that these interests needed to be represented.

The many changes in women's lives affect our study of them as we move into the present. Because of the importance our culture assigns to public and political activities, the historical sources dealing with such activities are relatively abundant. When we turn to other aspects of women's experience, the material is more difficult to find. Autobiographical and biographical accounts of prominent women continue to be a valuable source, although the limits of such material are obvious. The political activities of women on the margins of society — the poor and the powerless — are only now starting to gain attention. When the study of women's history began in earnest in the 1970s, the recent past was not much studied; researchers were preoccupied with exploring the historical roots of the Canadian women's movement. As a result, many dimensions of women's lives in the period from 1939 onward remain unexamined.

The task of locating sources for the most recent decades has been rendered more difficult by the fact that the telephone continues to replace the personal letter as a major means of communication. If diaries exist for this period, they are still relatively inaccessible, compounding the problem of understanding the private worlds of ordinary women. The newer women's organizations, committed to informal procedures and non-hierarchical structures, have so far generated fewer organizational records than traditional ones did, and often their newsletters and briefs are difficult to locate. Oral history is only beginning to provide exciting new documentation for the recent past. We have supplemented written and oral personal sources by using magazines and newspapers, but it remains difficult to capture the perspectives of all Canadian women in a period when, despite the diversity of women's experiences, the mass media continue to privilege mainstream views.

In addition to the problem of sources, there are new problems of interpretation. Historians venture into the realm of the present with considerable trepidation; the subjectivity involved in choosing personalities, events, and issues on which to focus is all too apparent. Here there is no accumulated body of historical scholarship to use as a reference point, and no consensus on what should or should not be included. The treatment of the contemporary women's movement embodies these problems, as does the whole question of possible improvement in the lives of women. Can we assert that women are better off today in Canada than they were 50 years ago? Sexism and heterosexism continue to be powerful constraints on even those women most privileged by class and race; the "superwoman syndrome" seems often to have produced an overload of roles and responsibilities. And what part, if any, did the women's movement play in the recent history of Canadian women, for good or for ill?

NOTES

1. "Dorothy," "Report of the Royal Commission on the Status of Women," *The New Feminist* 2, 2 (May 1971), 6.

CHAPTER TWELVE

Work: From the Bren Gun Girl to the Electronic Scanner

Looking back from the mid-1990s, it is possible to represent shifts in the work experience of Canadian women over the past half-century by a series of images. The war years evoke memories of thousands of women going off in their bandannas and coveralls to work in wartime industries such as aircraft factories and shipyards. By contrast, the typical adult woman of the 1950s is usually remembered as a contented homemaker, isolated from the world of paid work, and quietly living out her destiny with husband and children in the suburbs. And then there is the upwardly mobile, childless career woman of the 1980s, a glamorous "gladiatrix" in designer clothes off to do battle in the executive suite. Like most stereotypes, these images contain just enough truth to perpetuate themselves. The first reflects the vital participation of women in sectors of the economy where they had previously not been welcomed; the second, the reduced role of women in the labour force in the late 1940s. The third portrait attests to the greater likelihood of women attaining positions of power and prestige in traditional male preserves. However, these portrayals also mask some significant facts. The large-scale entry of married women into the paid workforce during World War II did not come to an abrupt end in the 1950s; rather, it was during this decade that their labour-force participation rate increased substantially. As for the woman worker of the 1980s, she was much more likely to be a secretary with dependent children than a corporate lawyer with none. Important regional, class, race, and ethnic variations in women's work experiences are also obscured by these distilled images.

WAR WORK

In 1939, Canadians were still preoccupied with the agonizingly slow recovery from the devastating impact of the Great Depression, but on September 17, they found themselves yet again propelled into an overseas conflict not of their own making. And once more Canadian women played a key role in the war effort through their multifaceted work in the nation's homes, fields, factories, and voluntary organizations. In addition, they were recruited for the first time into the ultimate bastion of male power, the armed forces.

As had been the case during World War I, the work that involved the greatest number of Canadian women was volunteer work. As individuals and as members of associations, they initiated an extensive and varied amount of work directly related to the Allied efforts to achieve victory. This time, however, their activities came to be closely co-ordinated and controlled by the federal government through the Women's Voluntary Services Division, created in the autumn of 1941. Some women's organizations resented this intervention, since they had already begun their own programs.[1] The Department of National War Services ran an extensive publicity campaign in both French and English aimed at involving Canadian housewives in the war effort. One advertisement, entitled "From the Frying Pan to the Firing Line," depicted three women pouring a panful of grease, which magically turned into bombs, over an enemy ship. "Work at munitions production in your own kitchen," the accompanying copy exhorted.[2] In response, thousands of women and children collected fats, paper, glass, metals, rubber, rags, and bones for recycling into munitions and other war matériel.

A World War II poster issued by the Department of National War Services encouraging women to salvage household materials for the war effort.

....

Source: National Archives of Canada/C-03344.

The government's management of the war economy depended heavily on women, since Canadian homemakers were responsible for more than 80 percent of the nation's retail purchases.[3] As wartime production expanded, employment levels soared, and the average Canadian's purchasing power grew rapidly. At the same time, there were fewer civilian goods available, and as a result there were shortages, a sharp increase in the cost of living, and the threat of an uncontrollable price–wage spiral. To control inflation, the federal government created the Wartime Prices and Trade Board to establish production quotas and maximum prices for many civilian goods. Various women's organizations, such as the National and Local Councils of Women, made it their responsibility to see that the Board's price guidelines were followed. Impressed by their price-monitoring activities, the board moved to create a Consumer Branch with the well-known editor of *Chatelaine*, Bryne Hope Saunders, as its head. Subsequently, 14 regional committees co-ordinated the efforts of more than 10 000 liaison officers supplied by women's voluntary organizations; these women informed consumers of the Board's regulations, policed prices, and laid the basis for the establishment of the Canadian Consumers' Association when the war ended. The federal government also relied on women to support its rationing system and wartime savings program, and to maintain the nation's nutritional standards. In addition, hundreds of thousands of women planted victory gardens, knitted and sewed articles of clothing for the troops, made up parcels for prisoners of war, ran hospitality centres and canteens for members of the armed forces, organized blood banks, practised civil defence procedures, or acted as spotters of enemy aircraft.

In rural areas the Women's Institutes were especially active in promoting women's war services, and in mobilizing women for agricultural production. In British Columbia and Ontario, dominion–provincial programs were established to mobilize farm labour; by 1943 nearly 13 000 farm women, urban working women, teachers, and students were enrolled in Ontario's program.[4] Across the nation wives and daughters supplemented the declining male agricultural workforce, as men signed up for military service or gravitated to more-attractive industrial work. For some farm wives, the war years brought not only an increased burden of work and responsibility, but also new opportunities for personal growth and accomplishment. "Dorothy," for example, tackled the heavy farm work during her husband's absence overseas, maintained the equipment, looked after the house and children, taught Sunday school, and still found time for curling and hunting. On her husband's return, she handed him the family bankbook and proudly declared, "There is more money in there than we ever had in our lives."[5]

The recruitment of women for agricultural production was part of a federal government campaign to manage the wartime labour force and to cope with labour shortages. Initially little government intervention was required, for there were some 900 000 unemployed Canadians when the war broke out. By 1942, however, this labour pool had been depleted as both industry and the armed forces expanded. In March of that year, Mackenzie King's government established the National Selective Service agency to oversee the recruitment and allocation of labour. Two months later, the Women's Division of the Selective Service agency was created under the direction of Fraudena Eaton of Vancouver; in September 1942, it undertook a national registration of women aged 20 to 24 in order to identify single women who could be recruited into war industry. Although married women in this age category were also required to register, the federal government hoped that if it created a pool of single workers, wives could stay at home. Once the registration exercise was complete, the National Selective Service initiated massive publicity campaigns and arranged for the relocation of single women from the Prairies and the Maritimes to central Canada to work in war industry.

As the war progressed and workers continued to be lured away by the higher wages offered by war industries, the demand for female employees rose, particularly in the garment, textile, and service industries. Now there was no choice but to turn to married women to take up the slack. Throughout the summer of 1943, with the help of Local Councils of Women, Selective Service mounted ambitious drives to recruit married women for part-time work in the service sector, in such establishments as laundries and hospitals. Housewives were also asked to work evening shifts, created especially for them, in essential war industries. Still the labour shortage remained acute, and the government in Ottawa introduced incentives to encourage the full-time employment of married women. In July 1942, the Income Tax Act was amended so that working wives were treated as full dependents no matter how much they earned. Previously, if a wife earned more than $750, her husband lost the "married status" exemption.[6] The other major initiative was the provision, for the first time, of government-funded daycare services. In July 1942, the federal government acknowledged the need for institutional childcare by introducing the dominion–provincial Wartime Day Nurseries Agreement. It provided for the two senior levels of government to share equally the costs of daycare services for children whose mothers were employed in war industries. However, only three provinces—Ontario, Quebec, and Alberta — signed the accord, and after further study Alberta decided not to implement the program. Eventually, twenty-eight day nurseries were established in Ontario and six in Quebec. These nurseries accommodated children between 2 and 6 years of age; in Ontario, homecare was arranged for children under the age of 2 and after-school daycare for those between the ages of 6 and 16. In keeping with the government's commitment to provide such services strictly to cope with the wartime emergency, only one-quarter of the available spaces could be given to the children of working mothers not employed in war industries. Eventually public pressure forced the government to amend the legislation to provide services for the children of all working mothers, but priority was still assigned to war industry employees.[7]

In Quebec, the few day nurseries established under the program primarily served the anglophone population. French-Canadian Catholic leaders in that province denounced the employment of mothers. Part of this negative reaction was the result of opposition to the war itself. Religious leaders and nationalists in Quebec roundly condemned those married women who "deserted" their families for lucrative work in munitions plants, and articles published in the influential Jesuit publication *Relations* branded government-sponsored daycare facilities communistic and destructive of the family. In an impassioned speech, one member of the Quebec Assembly condemned all women's work outside the home. Such work, he claimed, created a dangerous desire for emancipation, thereby destroying the family and "sabotaging what is most precious to us."[8]

Despite these vehement denunciations, thousands of French-Canadian mothers took on paid employment. Their primary reasons for doing so were economic. According to Florence Martel, Fraudena Eaton's Quebec assistant,

We were coming out of the Depression. There were no longer sheets on the beds, the children had no shoes and there were no more kitchen utensils. . . . Women lacked everything for a long time and they did not go to work to buy luxuries, as certain people accused them of doing.[9]

Indeed, across Canada, many women indicated that an improved standard of living, not the call to loyalty and service, had drawn them into paid employment.

As the labour shortage grew, women were admitted in increasing numbers into the dominion–provincial War Emergency Training Program and into non-traditional employment. By June 1943, about a quarter of a million women were working in war industries at such non-traditional jobs as welding, electronics, drafting, and industrial chemistry. But these apparent opportunities were of limited value. Government training programs for women were shorter than those for men, and most women received only two to six weeks' instruction. Commentators frequently drew analogies between women's war work and their usual domestic tasks: running a lathe was even easier than operating a vacuum cleaner, while filling a shell was no more difficult than making a cake.[10] Consequently, there was little opportunity for women to secure the specialized training that would ensure long-term employment or upward mobility.

Visible-minority women, who had previously found it particularly difficult to secure waged employment other than domestic work, now found job openings in industry and, to a limited extent, in clerical and retail settings. However, the positions

A woman working at shipbuilding in Pictou, Nova Scotia, 1943.

....

Source: National Film Board of Canada Collection/National Archives of Canada/PA 116153.

they were able to secure were often the least desirable. When the Cape Breton steel company employed women as production workers for the first time during the war, there were charges that it was slow to hire non-white women and that when they were hired, they were assigned the heaviest, dirtiest jobs — working at the coke ovens.[11] Other women did assume positions of authority, and immediately became the focus of media attention. They were held up as living examples of the emancipating effects of the war. Such was the case of Elsie Gregory MacGill, who was put in charge of all engineering work for Canadian production of the Hurricane and Helldiver fighter planes. The daughter of Helen Gregory MacGill, Elsie MacGill had been the first woman to graduate in electrical engineering in Canada. Far more typical of war workers, however, were young women like Veronica Foster, the 1941 "Bren Gun Girl," who was chosen to glamourize work on the assembly lines.[12]

WOMEN IN THE ARMED FORCES

The image of the emancipated woman was further enhanced during the war by the entry of women into the armed forces; yet here, as in war industry, equality was never gained. Before the war began, thousands of women across the nation had organized themselves into paramilitary groups. Modelled on the women's auxiliary of the British army, these organizations taught their members military drill, first aid, map reading, signalling, and transport driving; some even included rifle practice. Shortly after their formation, the women's corps lobbied vigorously for official recognition from the Department of National Defence, but this was withheld. Only when the manpower shortage grew serious, and pressure mounted from both home and abroad for Canada to use women in military support positions, did the government decide to form the Canadian Women's Army Corps (CWAC). Established in August 1941, it provided only partial recognition of the existing women's corps, which were used primarily as a source of recruits.[13]

Once again women's war initiatives were taken over and directed by a male-dominated bureaucracy. Since the CWAC was initially not integrated into the army, but constituted a separate organization, its officers did not enjoy the same ranks, authority, or insignia as men in the army did. Only in March 1942 was the CWAC integrated into the Canadian armed forces, and its members entitled to use the usual military titles and insignia. In 1941, the federal government also established the Canadian Women's Auxiliary Air Force, largely as a result of British inquiries about recruiting women to assist at Commonwealth Air Training Plan centres; in February 1942, the auxiliary was transformed into the Women's Division, Royal Canadian Air Force. In July 1942, the Women's Royal Canadian Naval Service was created. As the recruiting proceeded, issues arose concerning race, ethnicity, and language. One CWAC recruiting officer in Toronto considered it necessary to ask her superiors if a young woman of "Indian nationality," who was the top student in her drafting class, was admissible. In this case, the answer was an unequivocal yes. Initially, only bilingual French-Canadian women were recruited; however, after English-language training facilities were established in the latter half of 1942, unilingual francophones were accepted. Once inducted, they were dispersed among the various basic training camps so that they might be more readily absorbed into the predominantly anglophone military organization.[14]

Women who entered the armed forces encountered many of the same obstructive attitudes and practices that confronted women in civilian life. In all ranks, they received only two-thirds of the basic pay of men with equivalent rank. Confronted with vehement protests against these practices by servicewomen themselves and by the National Council of Women, and with the negative impact the poor pay was having on female recruitment, the Department of National Defence raised women's basic pay to 80 percent of that received by men of similar rank. Job segregation also remained a fact of life in the armed forces. It was understood that only the war emergency and the need to release able-bodied men for active duty justified the creation of the women's services. From the beginning, military authorities intended to use female recruits to replace support personnel such as clerks, cooks, telephone operators, and drivers. In all areas men remained firmly in charge. In the CWAC, the vast majority of recruits worked at typically female jobs: of nearly 6000 CWAC tradeswomen surveyed in March 1945, 62 percent were working as clerks. In comparison, the situation of recruits in the Women's Division of the RCAF (WDs, as they were called) was definitely better: by 1945, 65 percent of the trades in that service were open to women, while only 50 percent of army trades were open to CWACs. Pay scales were also higher in the air force, so although WDs also received only four-fifths of an airman's basic pay, they were better remunerated than their army counterparts.[15]

Most women who enlisted hoped to satisfy their spirit of adventure through an overseas posting; however, with the exception of the nursing sisters, only one in nine servicewomen served outside Canada. We can well imagine the anger and disappointment felt by one group of WDs in training at Ottawa's Rockcliffe base, who found themselves scrubbing the floors in the governor-general's residence. When they did manage to make it overseas, most CWACs found themselves assigned as clerks, laundry workers, and cooks; in fact, the first call for Canadian servicewomen to serve overseas came when Canadian Headquarters in London was unable to find sufficient laundry staff, and requested 150 CWACs to make up the shortfall.[16]

By the war's end, more than 43 000 women had enlisted in the armed forces: 21 000 in the Women's Army Corps, 16 000 in the Women's Division of the air force, and 6600 in the Women's Naval Service. In addition, some 2500 women joined the Nursing Service, and 38 women doctors signed up for medical duty. They came from all regions of the country, and from all walks of life. Some were underage, reportedly as young as 14; others were older women whose own sons were in the service. Some signed up out of a sense of adventure, while others did so for patriotic reasons. According to one study, more than 70 percent of female recruits were employed at the time they enlisted; many left their civilian jobs for the superior remuneration, benefits, and training offered by the women's branches of the armed forces.[17]

Despite the limitations and discrimination that women in the services frequently encountered, for many their wartime experience was exhilarating. "When you passed your exams and you received your flags," one member of the Women's Naval Service recalled,

> it was like getting your degree. It had a big effect on our lives. We were proud of ourselves as individuals as well as women, for we succeeded under the same conditions as the men, and for many this changed our outlook toward our place within society.[18]

Nonetheless, the official mottoes of the women's services — "We are the women behind the men behind the guns"; "We serve that men might fly"; and "We serve that men might fight" — cast them in a subsidiary role. Although the women's naval and military units played a crucial role in the war effort, and considerable pressure was exerted on the government to maintain them as part of Canada's reserve forces, once the hostilities ceased they were promptly disbanded.

Even before peace was achieved, most Canadians expected women, especially those who were married, to rededicate themselves to work in the home. Many feared a resumption of the severe recession and massive unemployment of the 1930s, or of the inflation and social unrest of the years immediately following World War I. Spurred on by these concerns, in March 1941 the Liberal government named an Advisory Committee on Reconstruction, consisting of six prominent men. Almost immediately, women began to petition for female representation, on the basis of women's important contribution to the war effort. Finally, in January 1943, the government established a new subcommittee to deal with the problems women in war industry were likely to encounter once the war ended. This subcommittee, whose terms of reference were soon expanded to allow it to report on post-war problems for all Canadian women, was headed by Margaret Stovel McWilliams, journalist, Winnipeg councillor, and prominent women's organization activist, and included nine other women from across the nation.[19]

At its initial meeting, the subcommittee adopted as its first principle the precept that women had a right to post-war employment, to equal remuneration, and to the same opportunity for advancement as men. The subcommittee's final report was a mixture of old and new. It recommended that women be able to access training and retraining programs on the same basis as men, but that most be trained for distinctive women's occupations, such as domestic service, nursing, teaching, and social work. Somewhat radically, the subcommittee proposed that "household workers" be included in any national labour code that might be forthcoming, so that they would be covered by minimum wage legislation, unemployment insurance, and workmen's compensation. The subcommittee members proposed that married women in the home be viewed as economic partners with their husbands, be included in social security schemes such as health insurance, receive family allowances, and have access to government-funded morning nursery schools. Hoping to arrest the wartime exodus of women from rural areas, it urged governments to extend electricity to more rural areas, supply household appliances at cost, improve communication networks, and expand rural educational, health, and recreational facilities. Some journalists described the report as a "charter of rights" or a "bill of rights" for Canadian women.[20] Yet despite its innovative character, the report received little public attention — apart from a few press accounts, which were usually consigned to the "women's pages." The federal government ignored most of the report's recommendations, as it did most of the recommendations of the Advisory Committee's other subcommittees.

A Gallup poll conducted in 1944 indicated that 75 percent of the Canadian men polled, as well as 68 percent of the women, believed men should be given preference in post-war employment.[21] Given the physical and emotional strain endured by those who combined paid employment with domestic labour, the aggravation of wartime shortages, and the anxiety caused by the absence of loved ones, many Canadian women themselves looked forward to a return to full-time home life at war's end. "When the Johnnys and Joes come marching home," a woman journalist noted, "just shopping for ham to cook ham and eggs — if she can get eggs — is apt to be important to a woman . . . even if she drops an odd pay envelope along the way."[22]

For many women, the war had been a devastating experience. There could be no return to normalcy for Japanese-Canadian women, whose families were forced by the Canadian government to leave their homes along the Pacific coast. They spent the war years in detention camps in the interior of British Columbia, or working on sugar beet farms in Alberta and Manitoba. After the war, most were "resettled" east of the Rocky Mountains, far away from their original homes. There were other victims of war: the nursing sisters serving in Hong Kong, who were raped, tortured, and confined to prisoner-of-war camps; and the thousands of Canadian women who lost sons, husbands, or lovers. When husbands did return from active duty, they were often virtual strangers, and the ensuing marital strains led to a dramatic increase in divorce. For aboriginal women, there was often a sense of loss as their traditional lifestyles were disrupted by the rapid economic and social changes brought about as a result of wartime activities.[23]

These negative experiences notwithstanding, a more optimistic assessment may be in order. For many Canadian women, the opportunity to expand their activities did have a positive impact. According to one woman,

> The war killed all this servant business, being a maid, and I think it did a lot to finish off the idea that a woman's place and her only place was in the home. . . . The war and working in plants so changed me I became an entirely different person. I wish I'd kept a diary.[24]

THE POST-WAR YEARS

Not surprisingly, once the war was successfully concluded, both governments and industry quickly adjusted their policies and practices to encourage women to stay

Community kitchen at Japanese-Canadian internment camp, Slocan City, British Columbia, 1943.

Source: William Lyon Mackenzie King Collection/National Archives of Canada/C-24452.

at home. In 1944 Dorise Nielsen, CCF member from Saskatchewan, gave Parliament a sardonic summary of men's attitudes toward women's appropriate role: "Well, girls, you have done a nice job; you looked very cute in your overalls and we appreciate what you have done for us; but just run along; go home; we can get along without you very easily."[25] The federal government withdrew its support for day nurseries, and amended its income tax regulations. After January 1, 1947, if a wife earned more than $250 — not even the pre-war $750 — her husband could no longer claim the full married status exemption.[26] Subsequently, there were reports that existing shortages of trained nurses and other types of women workers were exacerbated by this policy, since married women were quitting work once they had earned $250.[27] There was a deliberate effort as well to limit women's employment in the public service. The prime minister went so far as to request that his cabinet ministers not employ female secretaries. The minister of agriculture is reported to have responded, "To —— with him. I couldn't get along without her."[28] Within the public service, the married women who had been implored to help run the burgeoning wartime bureaucracy were now discharged, and married women continued to be barred from the federal civil service until 1955.

When the government disbanded the women's military services in 1946, postwar training programs for discharged members paid lipservice to the principle of equal opportunity for training for women and men, but in reality focussed on "suitable" occupations such as stenography, homemaking, dressmaking, and nursing. Moreover, women were to be redirected from manufacturing, where their continued presence might constitute a threat to male employment, into domestic service, where there was a dearth of workers. And once again, Canadian women workers responded by virtually ignoring the program.[29] Disillusioned by public failure to recognize women's contribution to the war effort adequately, one female reporter wondered whether married women would "go to war" again:

> We made munitions, served overseas or at home, whenever we were needed. And loved doing it. Then what happened when the war was over? We were patted on the head and told, "Good show, girls, but now back to kinder, küche and kirche. . . ." If married women are people in emergencies, why can't they be people when there isn't an emergency?[30]

By September 1945, nearly 80 000 women in war industry had been laid off and thousands of servicewomen discharged.[31] In 1944, at the peak of wartime employment, one-third of all women over the age of 15 had been in the paid labour force. Two years later, only one-quarter were working for pay. Only in 1967 did women's participation rate surpass the 1944 level. However, the decline in the period immediately after the war appears to have been caused less by the withdrawal of women already in the workforce than by the lower participation rate of younger women. Prolonged education, earlier age at marriage, and earlier age for starting a family together produced this result. In the United States, women's labour-force participation rate had reached even higher levels during the war, only to drop by 19 percent between 1945 and 1947.[32] The decline in Canada was much less pronounced — less than 9 percent during the same period. By the mid-1950s, women's labour-force participation was on the rise once again, and even the armed forces reversed their policy and started to accept women recruits back into all three services.

Despite the general absence of young mothers from the workforce in the post-war era, the proportion of married women among paid female workers continued to increase. In part, this was owing to the lower age at marriage and the growing acceptance of young married women working, providing that they did not have children; and in part, it stemmed from the presence in the labour force of older women with school-age or older children. In 1941, only slightly more than 10 percent of all employed women were married; during the war, the estimated proportion was from 25 to 35 percent. By 1951 the percentage had dropped slightly, but by 1961 nearly half of all female workers were married. This dramatic increase can also be measured by looking at the proportion of wives who were in the paid labour force: from only one in twenty-five in 1941, the figure had changed in twenty years to a remarkable one in five. These changes were already obvious by 1954, when the Dominion Chief Statistician declared, "The woman's place is no longer in the home, and the Canadian home is no longer what it used to be."[33]

The strong desire of Canadians to improve their material situations, frustrated by years of economic depression and war, was not to be denied. In the 1950s, television revolutionized mass advertising techniques, stimulating the demand for major consumer items such as cars, appliances, and furniture. To purchase these things, which most Canadians now considered essential, and to ensure access to higher education and better health care for their children, many married women had to augment family income by taking on paid employment. During the recession that lasted from 1957 to 1961, a *Financial Post* reporter noted that married women's wages were being used to supplement their husbands' unemployment benefits. He concluded that "this is a woman's world all right and getting more so. More and more married women are going to work and they are quickly being snapped into jobs. . . . Keep your eye on Mom."[34] In general, it was easier for women to find employment during this period than it was for men, because of the rapid expansion of the clerical and service sectors of the economy.

The increasing numbers of mothers working outside the home became the source of much controversy; possibly as a result, in 1955 the Department of Labour conducted a survey of employed married women in eight Canadian cities. More than 50 percent of those interviewed had dependent children, and some 80 percent worked full time. They had evidently taken jobs for economic reasons: only 15 percent of their husbands earned a relatively high income of $4000, but when the wives' wages were included, more than half the families reached this income level. The higher labour-force participation rate of married women in the late 1950s compared to the immediate post-war years was due in large part to the massive wave of immigration after the war. Indeed, one-third of the workers in the Department of Labour survey were born outside Canada.[35] For some immigrant groups, such as the southern Italians, married women's paid employment was central to the family's strategy for improving its financial situation.[36]

Women workers with pre-school children had to make their own childcare arrangements, and generally preferred family or friends. Marion Royce, director of the Women's Bureau created by the federal Department of Labour in 1954, persistently argued that there was a need for better daycare facilities and more part-time work for married women with children.[37] However, no level of government felt an obligation to provide such facilities, and most Canadians continued to believe that married women with young children should not be employed outside the home. It was still assumed that the vast majority of women could not successfully combine work and family. In 1955 one woman who tried but failed concluded vehemently,

> I don't care who you are or how well organized you are, you can't be a good wife and mother, hostess and housekeeper and also do a good job for your employer all at the same time. When you try, someone is bound to get cheated — your husband, your child or your boss — and in most cases, all three.[38]

Her solution: quit the job to save the marriage. But most married women in the paid labour force could not choose to quit their jobs. It was essential for them to work to maintain their families' standard of living in an increasingly consumer-oriented society.

The pronounced emphasis on consumption may also have increased the workload of most homemakers. As the standard of living rose, and the volume and diversity of consumer goods increased, the tasks associated with household management became more complex. The work entailed in managing the family budget and trying to balance family income against family needs was even more difficult in the new suburbs that mushroomed on the fringes of Canadian urban communities. Frequently isolated and without transportation, suburban housewives had little opportunity to engage in comparison shopping or to buy at the lowest prices. Shopping plazas, the first of which was constructed in Toronto in 1946, were somewhat helpful, but they provided only a limited choice of shops. Women were also responsible for dealing with the countless salesmen, repairmen, public officials, and community representatives who showed up on their doorsteps.[39] Cut off from traditional women's support systems, young suburban housewives found it difficult to gain access to the experience and advice of older women. Their response was to seek female companionship and support networks with women of their own age group through "coffee klatches," bridge clubs, home and school associations, and mixed volunteer groups.

For women in the paid workforce, there were some significant attempts at organization, as the labour militancy generated during World War II continued. During the war, as the demand for workers expanded, so did workers' bargaining power; union membership soared, especially with the expansion of industrial unionism.[40] Even the more conservative international unions became involved in organizing semi-skilled and unskilled workers, within whose ranks were to be found thousands of women. In the textile industry, Madeleine Parent and her future husband, Kent Rowley, made impressive inroads. Parent graduated from McGill in 1940 and became a labour activist while still a very young woman. In 1942 she and Rowley started to organize Quebec cottonmill workers in Valleyfield and Montreal. They faced formidable odds, for they had to confront not only the might of the textile cartel headed by Dominion Textile, but also the overt hostility of the Roman Catholic church, which denounced them as Communists. Because of the wartime ban on strikes, the workers had to wait until 1945 before they could walk off the job in an attempt to win union recognition, a shorter work week, and improved benefits.

In June 1946, some 3000 workers at Dominion Textile's Montreal mills and an additional 3000 workers at the Valleyfield mill staged a walkout. Approximately one-third of the workers were women. The blatantly pro-business government of Maurice Duplessis declared the Valleyfield strike illegal, since not all the bargaining procedures required by law had been followed. The authorities made a concerted effort to break the strike, using the provincial police to protect strikebreakers and intimidate the workers. The Valleyfield strike was long, bitter, punctuated by violence, and marked by the arrest of the union leaders, including both Parent and Rowley. However, it finally ended in September and resulted in a first contract, improved wages, and other benefits for the workers.

The importance of women's support for the trade union movement grew during and after World War II, as production workers saw many of their material gains threatened by the rising cost of living, and as women's consumer roles expanded. Some women's auxiliaries were also involved in the bitter internal struggles between local Communist union leaders and their international leadership that bedevilled many unions after the war. Such a situation occurred in Lake Cowichan, British Columbia, where the ladies' auxiliary supported the local "red" faction of the International Woodworkers of America. The political activities of this auxiliary also led it to support the "rolling pin brigade," a protest movement (largely composed of housewife consumers) that culminated in a march on Ottawa after the war to demand price and rent controls, low-cost housing, and the establishment of a peacetime agency to regulate prices.[41]

Middle-class women's organizations also·devoted considerable time and talent to improving economic opportunities for women in post-war Canada. In the late 1940s, the Canadian Federation of Business and Professional Women's Clubs (CFBPWC, or BPW for short) protested a federal government advertisement, which stated that the position of regional director of family allowances for New Brunswick was open only to male residents of the Maritimes. As a result of the BPW protest, the job went to its nominee, Muriel McQueen Fergusson, who subsequently became the first woman Speaker of the Senate. The group petitioned the federal government to open the competition for diplomatic appointments to women, and succeeded in having the federal Civil Service Commission drop the wording "for men only" from advertisements for many positions. Similarly, the BPW inundated the cabinet with requests to place women on the Civil Service Commission, the Unemployment Insurance Commission, the Board of the CBC, the Board of Broadcast Governors, and various royal commissions, as well as calling for the appointment of a woman senator from each province. Since these requests were invariably accompanied by an up-to-date list of qualified women candidates, the BPW was sometimes successful. Nor was the private sector neglected, for the Federation called for the appointment of women to the boards of corporations such as chartered banks.

Women's groups extended their campaigns well beyond the appointment to prominent positions of a few token women from their own class or from their own organizations. Concerted lobbying resulted in the creation within the federal Department of Labour of the vitally important Women's Bureau, which was devoted specifically to gathering and disseminating information on all facets of women's employment. Another significant achievement was the passage of "equal pay for equal work" legislation by the federal government and nearly all the provinces. The Women's Committee of the Ontario CCF was instrumental in having legislation introduced in 1949 that would have made "sex" a forbidden basis for employment discrimination, and that would have required equal pay, but the bill was defeated.[42] One year later, 21 YWCAs set up Public Affairs committees to promote anti-discrimination employment laws. It was against this background that Margaret Hyndman, the national president of the BPW, led a delegation in 1951 to meet with Ontario's provincial premier, Leslie Frost. She argued for inclusion of the principle of equal pay in the forthcoming Fair Employment Practices law. Despite the growing pressure from women's organizations, Frost expressed his reservations; but he invited the women to present a brief outlining what the likely impact would be. Since Hyndman was a lawyer, he also asked her to draft an equal pay bill. Within a week, not only had these submissions been delivered, but every member of the provincial legislature had been lobbied and supplied with a copy of the Universal Declaration of Human Rights, with the appropriate sections dealing with discrimination on the basis of sex and equal pay underlined. Co-sponsored by Agnes Macphail, who was now a member of the Ontario legislature, and Rae Lucock, another woman MLA, the Female Employees Fair Remuneration Act was introduced on the symbolically significant date of March 8 — International Women's Day — and on January 1, 1952, Ontario became the first province to put equal pay legislation into effect. The BPW subsequently lobbied other provincial governments to enact similar legislation; by 1960, with the exception of Quebec and Newfoundland, all had passed equal pay laws.[43]

In 1955 the BPW asked one of its own members, Ellen Fairclough, the Conservative labour critic, to introduce in the House of Commons a private member's bill requiring equal pay for equal work. Although the bill was defeated, the Liberal government took up the cause. According to the federal minister of labour, the government's 1956 decision to implement equal pay legislation to cover more than 70 000 women working under federal jurisdiction was taken largely because of the pressure exerted by the BPW and representatives of the National Council of Women, including his own wife.

WORK PATTERNS: 1960 TO THE PRESENT

After 1960, the percentage of women aged 15 and older who were in the labour force continued to climb, moving from 30 percent in 1961 to 39 percent in 1971. During the same period, the proportion of women workers who were married also rose dramatically, almost doubling. By the latter date, for the first time more than one-third of all married women were members of the labour force. These employment trends reflected the fact that increasing numbers of women now completed their families by age 30 and also had reduced childcare responsibilities once their children were in school. In previous decades, a woman's adult life had typically had two distinct phases: paid work before marriage, and then permanent withdrawal to the domestic realm. Now, for a relatively brief period lasting until the middle 1980s, a woman's life cycle had three distinct phases: paid employment until the birth of her first child, childrearing at home, and re-entry into the paid workforce once her children reached school age. By 1985, just over half of all Canadian women were gainfully employed, and a new pattern had emerged. For the majority of Canadian women, adult life was no longer divided into separate phases of employment and childrearing; rather, they typically combined the two. By 1993, 70 percent of women who had children under 16 years of age were in the labour force, compared to just 55 percent in 1976.[44]

FIGURE 12.1 *Composition of Female Workforce by Marital Status, 1941–1991*

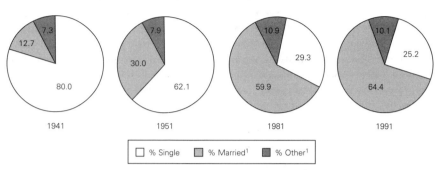

1941   1951   1981   1991

☐ % Single   ▨ % Married[1]   ■ % Other[1]

[1] FOR 1941 AND 1951, SEPARATED WOMEN ARE INCLUDED WITH MARRIED WOMEN, WHILE FOR 1961, 1971, AND 1981 THEY ARE INCLUDED IN THE "OTHER" CATEGORY—THAT IS, ALONG WITH WIDOWED AND DIVORCED WOMEN.

Source: Data for 1941, 1951, 1981: Pat Armstrong and Hugh Armstrong, *The Double Ghetto: Canadian Women and Their Segregated Work*, rev. ed. (Toronto: McClelland and Stewart, 1984), p. 169; Data for 1991: Statistics Canada, *Labour Force Annual Averages, 1991* (Ottawa: Minister of Industry, 1992), Table 3, p. B8.

Another distinctive feature by the early 1990s was that the labour-force participation rate of Canadian women actually declined slightly for the first time since the end of World War II—but so too did men's. The decline in both instances was attributable to the loss of employment brought on by the severe recession Canada experienced in the early 1990s. Women's labour-force activity continued to vary considerably not only according to age, but also according to region, race, ethnicity, and level of education. In 1993, when the national participation rate for women reached 58 percent, women in Alberta had the highest rate (60 percent), while women in Newfoundland had the lowest (46 percent). Visible-minority women were proportionately more attached to the labour force (64 percent); Indian women living on reserves were the least attached (36 percent).[45] The latter statistic reflected the few job opportunities available to most women in reserve communities, as well as the discrimination they routinely encountered off the reserve. All too common were situations such as that experienced by Irene Desjarlais when she entered nursing:

> My first day at Brandon General I was so scared I felt like turning around and running down the steps and home. This was the first time away from my people. I heard someone say that I'd be just like the rest of the Indians and quit, wasting the government's money.[46]

In Irene's case, these racist remarks only strengthened her resolve: she went on to establish a very successful career in nursing.

As in past generations, the majority of working mothers with young children had to fend for themselves to arrange childcare, which was often either prohibitively expensive or of dubious quality. In 1991, there were more than 3.1 million mothers with children under the age of 13 in the workforce, but there were only 333 082 licenced childcare spaces, and the number of new spaces was growing at the slowest rate since 1978.[47] This situation reflected the political realities of the 1990s. Governments, citing declining revenues during the prolonged recession, abandoned earlier commitments to make childcare a national priority. Brian Mulroney's federal government reneged on its 1984 election promise to implement a national childcare program, and provincial governments either cut or froze childcare spending.

The importance of married women's contribution to family income through paid employment increased substantially from the late 1950s on; it became the principal reason for women with young children continuing to participate in the labour force. After adjustment for inflation but without taking into account higher levels of taxation, the average family income in 1991 was roughly the equivalent of what it had been in 1980. In 1971, nearly 60 percent of all families derived income from a single-earner husband; twenty years later, only 19 percent did so. One of the effects of the recession and the decline in male earnings was that more wives earned either as much as or more than their husbands did. In 1992, nearly 25 percent of employed wives were in this category.[48] Wives' paid labour was especially crucial for low-income families: the lower the husband's earnings, the more likely it was that the wife would be in the labour force. A Portuguese textile worker married to a seasonally employed construction worker explained her role proudly: "That's life. I need money. I go to the factory. . . . The wife help, is good because I buy the house, need to pay . . . need the money." A farmer's wife in Saskatchewan gave a similar explanation:

> Sometimes we have bills that we can't meet. . . . That's why I started working in the first place. . . . Grain sales were so low that we couldn't make ends meet and I had to get a job.[49]

Greater female labour-force participation can also be related to the increase in "non-traditional" families. In 1991, only 48 percent of Canadian families consisted of a legally married couple with children; another 4 percent consisted of common-law spouses with children, 35 percent were couples with no children, and 13 percent were headed by a single parent — who, in four cases out of five, was a woman. According to a 1982 study of divorce cases, custody of dependent children was still awarded to the wife in more than 85 percent of the cases. Ten years later, another study reported that more than 80 percent of divorce settlements were defaulted on, despite the fact that some provinces had implemented mechanisms for garnisheeing the wages of individuals who were legally required to make spousal or child support payments and who were in arrears. The result was that divorced women usually ended up considerably poorer, while divorced men often improved their economic situation.[50]

From 1969 on, the jobless rate was usually slightly higher among Canadian women than among men. The new higher rates of female unemployment reflected the end of the rapid growth of clerical and service jobs, especially within the public sector. The likelihood of a woman being unemployed was influenced by her age, education, location, race, and ethnic origin. Young women from 15 to 24 years of age had the highest unemployment rate (15 percent) of any age group; regionally, unemployment rates for women were highest in the Atlantic provinces and in Quebec. Women who were members of visible minorities had a relatively higher rate of unemployment (13.4 percent); for aboriginal women, the rate of 21.6 percent was nearly double the national average of 11 percent.[51]

THE WORK ENVIRONMENT

Whatever her marital status, the female worker in post-war Canada experienced many problems similar to those encountered by her mother and grandmother. The most significant were the continued assignment of most work according to gender, and the lower rewards that accompanied work classified as female. From 1951 until the late 1980s, the massive influx of women into the paid workforce occurred primarily in clerical and retail jobs, the expanding areas where the demand for their services was highest. In 1991, more than 85 percent of all working women were in service industries, compared to 62 percent of all men, and five occupational groupings — clerical, sales, retail, teaching, and health-care occupations — accounted for seven out of every ten female workers. During the early 1990s, however, there was a decrease in the proportion of full-time women workers who were classified as clerical, as a result of widespread downsizing and restructuring programs in both the public and the private sectors. The recession, global competition, free trade with the United States, government deficits, and technological change all contributed to increased unemployment and underemployment. Since women continued to be concentrated in the clerical and service sectors, they were particularly vulnerable to the reduction in office personnel.

What, then, are we to make of the media accounts of women entering "male" areas of employment, and the attention given to such women as Roberta Bondar, the first Canadian woman astronaut; Maureen Kempston Darkes, the first woman president of General Motors of Canada; Dr. Wendy Clay, the first woman major-general in the Canadian armed forces; or Lenna Bradburn, whose appointment by the city of Guelph in 1994 made her the first woman chief of police in Canada? According to census data, there was a 27 percent increase in the proportion of women employed as managers and professionals between 1981 and 1991. However, this increase was primarily an artifact of changes in occupational definitions, such as reclassifying retail workers as managers even when there were no improvements in wages or working conditions. Certainly, women increased their representation in the "male" professions, but most were still in the less prestigious and lower-paying "women's" professions such as teaching or nursing. Moreover, when women did move into male-dominated professions, they were likely to be overrepresented in work areas characterized by lower status and lower salaries. In 1993, while approximately 30 percent of physicians and surgeons and 34 percent of lawyers were women, women doctors tended to be family physicians or specialists in treating women and children, and women lawyers were much more likely to practise family law rather than the more lucrative corporate law or criminal law. In the early 1990s, only 20 percent of women in teaching and related activities were employed at the postsecondary level, compared to nearly 30 percent of men in teaching; nearly 80 percent of women health or medical workers were nurses or therapists, compared to just over 30 percent of the men.[52]

While there was some movement of women into non-traditional occupations in the nation's mines, forests, steelworks, and railyards during the 1970s and 1980s, progress was slow. Companies like Stelco in Hamilton, Ontario, and Cominco in Trail, British Columbia, which had hired women as production workers during World War II, dismissed them when male workers became available after the war, and subsequently stopped offering production jobs to women. Faced with negative publicity from feminist coalitions such as "Women Back into Stelco," and court challenges under human rights legislation for their failure to hire female production workers, in the late 1970s companies began to accept female applicants for blue-collar jobs. However, the few women who did secure employment were often isolated; many became the objects of sexual harassment by male co-workers. One woman at Stelco, Joanne Santucci, told of the sexual harassment, which commonly took the form of pornographic pinups, but also told how it could be combatted:

> There was a really gross picture, eh? I saw it one day, and the next night I went in again and looked, and there was this little paper bikini taped to the girl's crotch . . . and up on her top. . . . Later BJ said she did it. The guys thought that was hilarious. Instead of ripping it down, she added to it. Turned it into something different.[53]

By the early 1990s, however, the newly hired women were among the first workers to be laid off when the economy slowed down. The upward trend in women's employment in primary and secondary industries reversed; the percentage of women involved in construction, transportation and materials handling, and manufacturing fell from 13 percent in 1981 to 10 percent ten years later.

Publicly owned enterprises were also slow to accept women into non-traditional occupations. It was 1981 before the Halifax Transit Commission hired its first permanent female bus driver, and only in 1987 did Air Canada hire a female cargo-handler in the Atlantic region.[54] In the case of Canadian National Railways, it took a ten-year legal battle initiated by a small Montreal women's group — Action travail des femmes, which was dedicated to finding jobs for women on welfare — to force the company to hire more women in non-traditional jobs. In June 1987, the Supreme Court ruled that the Human Rights Commission could require companies to hire a specified percentage of women. Many of the blue-collar positions that women were fighting for were dangerous jobs involving hard physical labour; however, the wages and benefits paid for such jobs were generally twice those paid for "women's work."[55]

Another development was the progress women made as entrepreneurs in the 1980s. In 1986 nearly one-quarter of the new businesses registered in Ontario were started by women, many of whom took advantage of the increasing trend toward franchises. Of the 145 Molly Maid franchises in Canada, for example, only one was owned by a man. This company, the largest maid service in the world, with franchises in the United States and Great Britain, was started in Canada by a woman in 1979. Aboriginal women entrepreneurs also developed innovative new businesses. In 1994, for example, the women of Ahousat Initiative and Nuu'chah'nulth Business Association developed an ecotourism project that provided visitors a unique opportunity to observe aboriginal culture on British Columbia's Flores Island.[56] Despite the lower bankruptcy rate among female owners of small businesses, however, women generally experienced more difficulty than men in securing the credit they needed to start up their enterprises. In one telling incident, Elizabeth Tower, who headed her own company, was asked to get her husband to co-sign a loan when, in fact, he was her employee.[57]

Few of the "success" stories of women's forays into previously prohibited occupational territory involved immigrant women, particularly those belonging to visible minorities. "It was so disappointing," said "Ziddah," a young Palestinian woman, "I

A woman engaged in non-traditional work as a heavy-equipment operator.

....

Source: *The Toronto Star*/Andrew Stawicki.

went around and made all these applications and no one called. I felt so badly because they hired Canadians after me, that I was too dark. Then K-Mart called me and I was so excited and so happy."[58] Women like "Ziddah" continued to be over-represented among low-status, low-paid employees such as domestic servants; hospital, restaurant, and laundry workers; and garment and textile workers. Moreover, as global competition undermined the Canadian garment and textile industries, there was a decrease in the better-paying unionized positions, and a greater tendency to contract work out to home workers. One source estimated that 26 000 of the 36 000 garment workers in Quebec in the early 1990s were "underground workers." In Montreal, Haitian, Greek, Portuguese, and other immigrant women were paid by the piece to sew clothes at home. Their wages were often below the legislated minimum, and they had to pay for their own sewing machines and thread. Unprotected by labour legislation, these workers expressed frustration over the constant tension they experienced as they struggled to meet their employers' strict deadlines while juggling childcare responsibilities and household duties.[59] Another remarkable example of the continuity of work patterns from pre-industrial times was the growing number of women working at home at computers — a modernized version of the cottage industry.

Immigrant women also continued to be overrepresented among domestic workers. Beginning in 1955, the federal government initiated a specialized service to recruit a fixed number of English-speaking domestic workers annually from the Caribbean countries. The vast majority of the women who entered Canada under this scheme were well-educated members of the West Indian urban middle class, for whom domestic labour offered the only opportunity to emigrate. At the same time, Haitian women were recruited to work in French-speaking households, and the number of Haitian women arriving in Montreal greatly increased in the 1960s.[60] By the 1990s, the largest numbers of domestic workers came from the Philippines and the Caribbean nations. Like their counterparts in previous generations, domestics were isolated and vulnerable to exploitation by unscrupulous employers.

Middle-class black women with professional training in education and nursing frequently encountered discrimination in employment. In 1964, for example, Gloria Baylis, a Barbadian who had trained in England and had two years' nursing experience in Montreal, responded to an advertisement for a part-time nurse placed by the Queen Elizabeth Hilton Hotel. When she arrived for the interview, she was told that the position was already filled. Subsequently, she discovered that this was not true; with the assistance of the Negro Citizenship Association, she laid charges against the Hilton management for discrimination in hiring practices. The company was found guilty and fined $25. But the case did not end there: the hotel chain appealed the decision through all levels of the Quebec court system, and it was only in 1977 that the case was finally decided (with the original verdict being upheld).[61]

Given the sexual division of labour, technological change — and the microelectronic revolution in particular — had a differential impact on women's and men's work. Just as employers during the Great Depression invested heavily in improved machinery to reduce labour costs, during the recession of the early 1980s many managers promoted the use of microtechnology to reduce the size of their staffs. For women who managed to retain their jobs, there were further threats: a dilution of skills required to perform the work, increased use of monitoring devices to record their rate of work, more shift work, alienation from other workers, and health problems such as backache, eye strain, and high levels of stress. The office worker hired to do word processing for other employees she did not even know, or the grocery store clerk pulling items over optical scanners while the electronic cash register at her counter monitored her speed and sales volume, illustrated the dehumanizing effects of microtechnology. Conditions like these led one researcher to coin the phrase "the electronic sweatshop."[62]

At first glance, working on computers at one's home could appear an improvement; after all, many women as well as men were taking advantage of the technological advances to set up their own small businesses at home. However, the prospect of the wholesale transfer of clerical work to the home was a serious issue for women. The clerical home worker employed by a company would be working under an entirely different set of conditions, for she would not be self-employed. It seemed likely that she would share many of the problems that women home workers in the past had experienced, such as isolation, as well as some new ones, such as being monitored by a machine.[63] Businesswomen of the 1980s and early 1990s, many of whom opted for working out of their homes, experienced a number of these disadvantages as well. Ironically, Norah Spinks, who established an agency to counsel other organizations and their employees about how to balance work and family, found it impossible to take any time off when her daughter was born. Because she was self-employed, she was not eligible for the maternity leave benefits provided for by unemployment insurance. Nor did she want to put her nine employees out of a job by suspending operations, although they could have collected unemployment benefits if she had done so.[64]

The trend for women to be overrepresented among part-time workers increased during the 1980s; by 1993, more than one of every four women in the labour force worked part-time, compared to only one in ten men, and women accounted for more than 70 percent of all part-time workers.[65] Most part-time workers were not covered by equal pay, unemployment, or maternity leave legislation, and this situation caused considerable concern among some labour-force analysts. A large number of major employers in the service sector, such as the multinational fast-food firms, successfully combined franchising, computerized work processes, and reliance on a predominantly part-time workforce to generate impressive profits. The high rate of turnover among most part-time workers made it extremely difficult for such workers to organize. A telling example of how difficult it was occurred in Orangeville, Ontario, in 1993, when 17-year-old Sarah Inglis attempted to organize a union at the local McDonald's. Had she succeeded, it would have been a landmark in North American labour history; however, the determined teenager and the Service Employees International Union proved no match for the giant McDonald's Restaurants of Canada organization.[66]

Women also continued to perform much of the taxing seasonal work in Canada in agriculture, in fish and fruit processing, and in retail establishments. Working conditions under these circumstances tended to be extremely trying, because of the long hours necessary during short-season employment, and the lack of job security. "You work for the season, however long it lasts," explained Gina Vance, who worked in a Nova Scotia seafood plant:

> This year it was only ten weeks; they didn't do any crab. But my first season was six months, six days a week, nine, ten hours a day. . . . During the season you only get Sunday off, but even Sunday is geared towards the factory because of washing uniforms, aprons and gloves.[67]

In that plant in the late 1970s, workers stood on concrete floors in rubber boots up to ten hours a day with their hands submerged in cold water for most of their shift, unable to talk with co-workers because of the noise of the machinery and

Women working at computers in an office.

Source: George Brown College, Mark Rubin.

the oppressive discipline imposed by management. Conditions for agricultural workers, many of whom were Native or immigrant women, were generally even worse. The backbreaking toil, long hours, very low wages, and deplorable living quarters provided on some farms ensured that people became agricultural labourers only as a last resort.

WAGES AND BENEFITS

The persistence of segregation by gender was a major cause of the continuing wage gap between women and men. After social class, gender had the biggest effect on differences in wages and salaries. There was a slow but steady improvement between 1970 and 1994 for full-time female workers, whose average annual income rose from approximately 60 percent to nearly 72 percent of the average annual income of full-time male workers. To some extent the narrowing of the gap in the early 1990s occurred because men's average earnings declined — by 1.1 percent in 1992 alone — as thousands of traditionally higher-paying male jobs in the automotive, construction, and resource industries disappeared. The wage differential was greater in Canada than in several industrialized European countries: in Sweden in 1986, a working woman made on average 80 cents for every dollar earned by a male worker, and her French and West German counterparts earned 75 cents. The reasons for the continuing gap were complex. In the retail sales sector and the food services industry, for example, women had lower average wages because they were often assigned work that earned them lower commissions. Selling lingerie did not carry the same financial rewards as selling refrigerators or automobiles. On the other hand, the smallest wage discrepancy occurred in teaching and nursing, occupations that were attracting growing numbers of men and that were strongly organized.[68] Jobs associated with women's work in the home remained woefully undervalued: in 1990, the lowest average salary — slightly over $13 000 — was that earned by childcare workers, many of whom were professionals with postsecondary training.

Women's earnings were also directly affected by the fact that they bore the children and still retained the primary responsibility for looking after them. As childcare alternatives became more limited in the 1980s, and many mothers wrestled with the dilemma of how to balance paid employment and childrearing, a growing percentage of those who could afford to do so stepped out of the labour force. Such pauses, however, were expensive: one federal study estimated that women who interrupted their employment for a decade or more, and then resumed employment, forfeited on average $80 000 of career earnings. In addition, they would also have significantly lower pensions at retirement. Men, by contrast, appeared to enjoy a 30 percent increase in their earning potential by being married.[69]

those w higher ed. earned more $

Education was an important influence on women's employment. Eight out of ten women with university education were gainfully employed in 1993, compared to one in five of those with only primary-school education. A smaller proportion of the female population held university degrees (9.3 percent in 1990, compared to 12.5 percent of the male population), although the same proportion (62 percent) of females and males had completed high school. When age and educational levels were held constant for full-time female and male workers, the wage gap persisted: in 1991, women with a university degree still earned on average only 72 percent of

FIGURE 12.2 *Women's and Men's Average Annual Earnings, 1971, 1981, 1992 (Thousands of Dollars)*

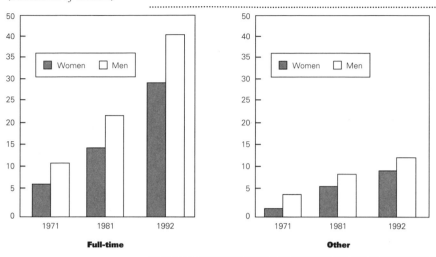

Source: Statistics Canada, *Women in Canada: A Statistical Report*, 2nd ed., Cat. No. 89-503 (Ottawa: Minister of Industry, 1990), Table 31, p. 100; Statistics Canada, *Earnings of Men and Women, 1992*, Cat. No. 13-217, Annual (Ottawa: Minister of Industry, 1994), Table 14, p. 44.

what men in the same educational category earned, and women in the ten highest-paying occupations earned only 61 percent of the average salary earned by men. Women of colour and aboriginal women earned less on average than did other Canadian women. In 1985, members of visible minorities who worked full-time had average earnings of $18 900, compared to $20 100 for other women. The full-time average wage for aboriginal women was even lower: $18 500.[70]

The wage differential continued to exist despite the enactment between 1951 and 1973 of "equal pay for equal work" legislation. The primary weakness of these laws was that they applied only when women performed work that was the same as or very similar to work done by men in the same establishment, a situation that the existence of female work ghettos precluded. Equal pay laws sometimes actually reinforced the sexual division of labour, since employers in industries highly reliant on female labour could benefit from employing only women and paying them low wages.[71] These flaws in the equal pay laws led women activists to demand legislation implementing equal pay for work of equal value. Under this approach, endorsed by the International Labour Organization in 1951 and ratified by Canada in 1972, women were not required to do jobs that were the same as or similar to men's jobs in order to receive equal monetary rewards. Jobs were to be evaluated according to a number of criteria (usually skill, effort, level of responsibility, and working conditions); similarly rated jobs were then to receive equal wages regardless of the gender of the worker.

In 1977 the federal government passed such legislation for all workers under its jurisdiction, which meant mainly those working in the federal public service, Crown corporations, and chartered banks. Although this legislation did not immediately

FIGURE 12.3 *Gender Gap in Full-time Earnings, 1977–1993*

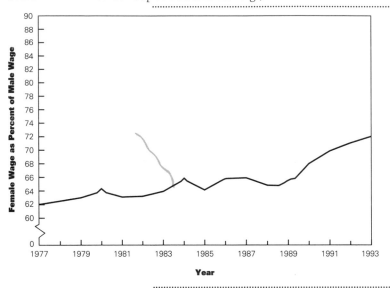

Source: *The Toronto Star* (February 8, 1995)/Statistics Canada.

have a major impact, its potential usefulness for female workers was demonstrated on a number of occasions: for example, in 1978, librarians working for the federal government, who were mostly female, had their salaries raised to the level of those of historical researchers, who were mostly male. Quebec passed similar legislation in 1976 covering both the private and the public sectors, as did Ontario in 1987.[72] Manitoba's legislation, passed in 1985, affected only the public sector. Even with the new legislation, old problems persisted and new ones arose. Women who worked for small employers were routinely excluded from coverage — for example, in Ontario, only women working for employers with more than ten employees were included in the legislation. The strict requirements that were established regarding which job classes could be compared, along with the difficulty of establishing gender-neutral job evaluation schemes, continued to hamper efforts to achieve equity.[73] Pay equity legislation was significant, for it formally recognized the systemic discrimination that women encountered in the paid labour force, and demonstrated that feminists — who had been instrumental in bringing about the legislation — could influence state policy.

In addition, pay equity was an essential part of the more comprehensive programs given the name of "employment equity" by Judge Rosalie Silberman Abella in 1984. Employment equity related to women, visible minorities, Natives, and persons with disabilities, all of whom were badly hampered by workplace rules and expectations that had been developed historically for white, male, able-bodied workers. For women in particular, positive or affirmative action was needed, not just to deal with pay disparities and workplace segregation, but also to provide the training and support services, such as daycare, necessary for them to participate as equals in the paid labour market. The federal government initiated modest equity programs for the public service and for institutions or businesses that had federal government contracts. In 1993, Ontario was the first province to approve legislation affecting all but very small workplaces. Such programs set goals or targets — not quotas — for hiring, promoting, and paying members of the four designated groups in the relevant workforce.[74]

Women's lower wages remained, however, a central fact of their working lives, affecting their standard of living and that of their children, and dooming many to an impoverished old age. Women's increasing life expectancy, together with low wages, produced a new class of poor people in Canada: widows and elderly single women. Existing pension plans, such as the Canada Pension Plan, were calculated on the basis of earnings accumulated through a continuous lifelong involvement in the labour force. The assumption was that approximately 70 percent of lifetime average earnings should be enough to support a retired worker. But what if she had a low income to start with, and no opportunity for savings? And what if she took years out of the labour force to raise children, as so many women had? Pensions for housewives became a major issue in the 1970s and 1980s, although some considered it a discriminatory measure, since by this time only the well-to-do could afford to have wives full-time in the home for their entire adult lives. Provincial governments gradually agreed to a "drop out provision," which meant that up to seven years could be dropped from Canada (or Quebec) Pension Plan calculations on account of absence from the workforce to care for children. There was at the same time a movement toward adapting pensions and other benefits to the pattern of women's working lives. By the end of the 1980s, there were just beginning to be legal require-ments that pro-rated benefits be provided to part-time workers, along with other provisions useful to women. Another hopeful sign was the employment lawsuit won by Edna Cronk in 1994. Cronk, a 29-year clerical employee of a Hamilton insurance company, was let go with a 9-month severance pay package when the company restructured. This was less than half the number of months' salary paid to managers who were dismissed at the same time. In a groundbreaking decision, she was awarded 20 months' severance pay, on the basis that her job had been as important to her as the managers' had been to them, and that she had suffered as much from the loss of her employment as they had from theirs.[75]

For most women workers, maternity leave was granted in the 1960s and 1970s under provincial legislation that entitled pregnant employees to leave and then resume their jobs without loss of position or seniority; payment replacing wages was given separately, under the federal unemployment insurance program. The initial legislation provided for a longer qualifying period than was required in cases of unemployment on other grounds, apparently on the assumption that women who were already pregnant might take jobs just to get support. Maternity leave, sometimes even with full replacement of pay, was also on occasion negotiated as part of union contracts. Most women workers, however, had to rely on the provisions of the com-bined federal and provincial legislation; and in the 1970s, those provisions had paradoxical implications, as Stella Bliss discovered.

In 1976 Bliss was unemployed, having been fired. She had at that point worked long enough to be eligible for normal benefits, but she did not apply for them because she was pregnant and did not intend to seek work until after the baby was born. Then, ready and eager to work but unable to find a job, she was refused benefits on the grounds that, having been pregnant when she became jobless, the only unemployment benefits she was entitled to were the pregnancy ones — for which she had not worked long enough to be eligible. This decision, she claimed, discriminated against women. The Supreme Court of Canada disagreed in 1978, arguing that Bliss was denied benefits not because she was a woman, but because she was pregnant. The discrimination was made not by law but by nature, which decreed that only women became pregnant. According to Mr. Justice Roland Ritchie, "If section 46 treats unemployed pregnant women differently from other unemployed persons, be they male or female, it is, it seems to me, because they are pregnant and not because they are women."[76] This situation got a certain amount of public attention. With the assistance of pressure from women's organizations, two legal changes occurred in 1983: an amendment to the Unemployment Insurance Act so that it was not necessary to be in the workforce longer for pregnancy than for other unemployment benefits, and an amendment to the Canadian Human Rights Act so that discrimination because of pregnancy was no longer allowed.

WORK IN THE FAMILY

Government legislation to improve wages and provide for paid maternity leave was of little benefit to the many women who continued to toil long hours at home, without the protection of labour laws. In 1981, more than 52 000 Canadian women laboured as unpaid workers in family enterprises. While nearly 60 percent worked on family farms, others staffed small retail establishments such as corner variety stores. Although amendments to the federal Income Tax Act in 1981 permitted the payment of salaries to spouses working in unincorporated family businesses, thereby entitling them to contribute to the Canada Pension Plan, many women were unable to take advantage of the change, since financially hard-pressed family businesses could not afford to pay them wages.[77]

For farm women, the 1980s were particularly difficult. Ownership of land by large agricultural enterprises increased, while the proportion of family-owned farms declined. Squeezed by rising interest rates and production costs, and by declining commodity prices, farmers' incomes plummeted and bankruptcies soared. While there were 623 000 farms in Canada in 1951, by 1981 there were only 318 361. In many instances, farm families survived precariously, thanks to the income wives obtained from paid employment off the farm. A 1982 survey of farm wives in Ontario's Grey and Bruce counties reported that 60 percent of them had had off-farm employment during the previous ten years. Many farm women were thus compelled to work not just a double day, but what could be termed a triple day. Not only did they hold down full-time jobs and perform the bulk of the household work, but they also did their share of the farm chores.[78]

Given the economic crisis confronting many farm families, rural women coped with high levels of stress, and with little access to support services such as daycare centres or health clinics. Contrary to the idyllic image of rural life, domestic violence, intergenerational conflict, and medical problems such as alcoholism, heart disease, and ulcers were increasingly frequent. "Jane's" story was typical. She was married to a full-time Ontario farmer, but in 1986, in order to pay the bills, the family of four depended on the $200 weekly salary she earned as an office worker. Her marriage was strained, and she was under medical care for stomach trouble.[79] Women in several provinces organized to save the family farm. These groups included Saskatchewan's Farm Women's Action, and Ontario's Women for the Survival of Agriculture (1975) and Concerned Farm Women (1981). The continued migration of the rural population to urban centres also resulted in a reduction in the community services and facilities that past generations of farm women had fought so hard to obtain. As rural post offices, stores, schools, and churches disappeared from the countryside, women were active in such groups as Rural Dignity for Canada, created to protest the closing of rural post offices.

Families working in the fishing industry experienced even greater economic and social crises. One widely publicized dispute between Newfoundland women and the federal bureaucracy occurred when "squidjigging" women were denied unemployment insurance benefits because government officials refused to believe that these women actually performed the heavy physical labour involved in the catching and preparation of squid. "Well, the men got their unemployment [benefits]," said Betty Burt, one of the leaders of the group, "and the women who had a man's name, such as Georgie, Frances, they got their money." When confronted by an angry deputation of "Squid Women," a Revenue Canada representative hastily declared that one of the women qualified for unemployment benefits — after he felt the muscles in her arm! In the end, about four-fifths of the women were deemed to qualify on the basis of their previous season's work, but the criteria for receiving unemployment benefits in subsequent years were made more restrictive.[80]

In many communities, it had been women's wage labour in fish-processing plants during the summer that had enabled them to claim the unemployment benefits needed to support their families during the rest of the year. When these plants — usually the only source of paid employment for women — closed, the workers were unable to qualify for unemployment benefits. The resulting anger and desperation of some workers in Newfoundland led, in November 1985, to a hunger strike in which more than 100 women and men protested the lack of job creation projects. Within two hours, the federal government pledged its support and the strike was called off. By the 1990s, the number of fish-processing plants and family fishing enterprises had declined dramatically because of the alarming drop in fish stocks. The failure of governments to provide alternative employment created enormous hardship and frustration for families displaced from the failing fishing industry.

Women of all regions, classes, and ethnic origins continued to perform the bulk of domestic labour. Such work, however, still went largely unrecognized and unrewarded. Nonetheless, government statisticians estimated that, if the unpaid services Canadian women provided in the home were assigned a value, they would account for one-third to one-half of the Gross Domestic Product. Further, they estimated that unpaid housework accounted for 25 billion hours of labour each year.[81] For housewives, there were none of the usual benefits of full-time employment — salary, vacation, sick leave, social security provisions — and, in spite of the introduction of labour-saving devices, the time women spent performing housework was not significantly reduced. While the work was not as physically taxing as it once was, the absence of full-time domestic help and the constantly rising standards of performance intensified the homemaker's responsibility for housework, and for consumption and family management.

In Inuit communities, as a result of government relocation schemes that forced people to move into larger permanent settlements, men who participated in hunting expeditions had to go farther away and be absent for extended periods in order to secure game. Childrearing, traditionally shared by parents, became predominantly women's work. Sewing machines and camp stoves made women's household tasks easier, but also represented increased work, as the women assumed responsibility for maintaining and repairing these items. In some cases, women stopped making traditional clothing altogether, and so lost touch with an important aspect of Inuit women's handicrafts and culture. Acculturation also seems to have exacted a physical price for Inuit women: according to a long-term study of one group of Inuit, the women were on average nearly 2.5 cm shorter in 1990 than they were in 1970. Scientists attributed this height loss to the fact that the women, who had traditionally carried children and other heavy loads on their backs (an activity that strengthens muscles and increases bone mass), no longer did so. Purchased food items, which were low in vitamin D and calcium, were also cited as likely causes of the problem.[82]

For many wives, housework continued to be rendered more difficult by the fact that their husbands worked shifts, so that they had to juggle different schedules in order to accommodate the conflicting needs of husband, children, and household. As one Flin Flon, Manitoba, wife explained:

> Those changing shifts are awful. It's a constant reminder that his work comes first over any other needs this family might have. We can never get ourselves organized into any regular pattern because our lives are always being turned upside down.[83]

Even when women took on paid employment, they continued to perform most of the domestic labour. A large survey conducted in 1990 found that in more than 50 percent of two-wage-earner families, women performed *all* the cooking and cleaning tasks: only in one out of ten households were the husbands said to assume responsibility for most or all domestic duties.[84]

The economic consequences of the undervaluation of women's work, both at home and in the workplace, were only too evident. In 1991, six out of every ten families headed by female single parents under the age of 65 lived below the poverty line, compared to two out of ten headed by male single parents. The daily physical and emotional toll that these families experience has been vividly described by a mother of three living on family benefits in Peterborough, Ontario. She did not become a single parent by choice, but was forced to leave an abusive husband; she resorted to public assistance only after she destroyed her own physical health working nights at the minimum wage.

> I get behind on bills and we eat a lot of cheap meals. My kids wear second-hand clothing and ride second-hand bikes. They take a lot of abuse from other kids because of it. . . . We don't go out to movies or dinner or even to the Dairy Queen, it's just not in our budget.[85]

UNION ACTIVITY

As awareness of their specific economic problems grew, so did the efforts of Canadian women to resolve them. In the workplace, women increasingly used their collective strength to improve wages and working conditions, and to address other issues such as daycare and sexual harassment. Between 1965 and 1981, union membership more than tripled among female workers. Most of the increase occurred among public-sector workers, a large proportion of whom were women. In 1990, nearly 62 percent of the female workers in public administration (which incorporated all levels of municipal, provincial, and federal government administration) were unionized. Women workers were also actively courted by large industrial unions such as the United Auto Workers (now the Canadian Auto Workers) and the United Steelworkers of America. These unions sought to maintain their numerical strength in the context of a shrinking manufacturing sector by organizing workers in the clerical and service sectors. But overall, only 30 percent of women workers were organized by 1990, compared to nearly 40 percent of male workers.[86]

In unions, special women's committees and women's caucuses were influential in defining issues and developing policies of importance to women in relation to maternity leave, childcare, equal pay, occupational health and safety, sexual harassment, and the elimination of discrimination against women workers. The success of these groups was especially noteworthy within the militant, nationalist trade union movement in Quebec.[87] In 1979, Quebec unions were the first to succeed in obtaining fully paid maternity leave for their female members in place of the partly paid leave available under the federal unemployment insurance plan. Trade union feminists have also been successful in making connections across union boundaries by means of such organizations as Saskatchewan Working Women, Union Sisters in Vancouver, Organized Working Women in Ontario, and the Women's Bureau of the Canadian Labour Congress, and have established ties to the broader-based contemporary women's movement.

Union women, both as leaders and as rank-and-file activists, assumed a more visible role during the 1970s and 1980s. Madeleine Parent and Kent Rowley worked to establish the nationalist Canadian Confederation of Unions in 1969. Grace Hartman, a mother of two who began work as a typist in 1954 to help supplement her husband's wages, rose through the ranks to become by 1985 the head of the largest national union, the Canadian Union of Public Employees. The links between the union movement and the women's movement were illustrated by Parent and Hartman, both of whom were actively involved with the National Action Committee on the Status of Women, the largest grouping of women's organizations in Canada (see Chapter Fourteen for a detailed discussion of NAC). In fact, Hartman served as the second president of this new organization, founded in 1972. In 1986, another historic moment occurred when Shirley Carr became the first woman president of the influential Canadian Labour Congress. One year later Gwen Wolfe, a laboratory technologist, became president of the Nova Scotia Federation of Labour, making her the first woman to head a provincial labour organization in Atlantic Canada.

On the picket lines, by their determination and courage, militant rank-and-file women won a grudging new respect from their employers, along with substantial public support. In a number of bitter strikes characterized by employer intransigence and marred by picket-line violence, working women fought to improve their situation. Among the most well-known of these disputes were the 1978 Fleck strike (in Exeter, Ontario), the 1979–80 Radio Shack strike (in Barrie, Ontario), the 1981 B.C. Telephone strike, and the 1984–85 Eaton's strike (in six Ontario locations).[88] In these disputes, workers were seeking union recognition, first contracts, equal pay, and improved wages and working conditions. Each dispute lasted for several months, and each constituted a remarkable demonstration of women's solidarity, not only among the workers themselves but also within the women's movement. Women of many different social and ethnic backgrounds walked the picket lines with the strikers and gave them financial support. Frances Lankin, later a cabinet member in the Ontario NDP government, underlined the importance of the "Women's Solidarity Picket" for the Fleck strike:

> As we climbed aboard the yellow and black schoolbus we could feel the excitement. There was an electric charge in the air — the kind of thing that occurs when you sense something important is happening. . . . The growing alliance between women's movement activists and trade union women activists was making an impression on the labour movement.

She noted with satisfaction that "Fleck was a woman's strike."[89] Women's solidarity pickets were also organized during the Radio Shack and Eaton's strikes, and additional support for the Eaton's workers was demonstrated on March 9, 1985, when the International Women's Day march made its way into Eaton's showplace store in downtown Toronto. During the Fleck and Radio Shack strikes, public support was also generated by managements' heavy-handed attempts to use strikebreakers and police to break the strikes. During the Fleck dispute, which lasted just over five months and involved 75 female strikers, 7000 police days were logged at a cost of more than $2 million.[90]

Less dramatic but of equal significance were the first partly successful attempts to organize clerical and retail workers into small independent unions operating along feminist principles. In 1972 the Service, Office, and Retail Workers' Union of Canada (SORWUC) was created to organize workers in banks, offices, and restaurants, and subsequently made news by setting up unions in some bank branches. Unfortunately, the SORWUC did not have the experience or financial resources necessary to wait out the lengthy periods involved in first-contract negotiation. In this instance, the interests of the women's movement and those of the trade union movement did not coalesce, since the Canadian Labour Congress opposed the independent union and was running its own organizational campaign among bank workers.[91] In the end, the SORWUC was no match either for the nation's most powerful financial institutions or for its largest labour federation, and by 1978 many of its locals had been decertified.

In contrast, unionization made major inroads among professional women, especially nurses and teachers. In several provinces, they exchanged their goal of developing traditional professional associations in favour of trade union affiliation and a more militant approach. An important change occurred for teachers when membership in teachers' associations became compulsory. In Ontario, this requirement came into effect in 1944, and greatly enhanced the prestige and power of the Federation of Women Teachers' Associations of Ontario, which became the official bargaining unit for all female elementary teachers in the public-school system. By the 1960s, the Federation was playing a leading role in addressing issues of importance to all women, such as sex-role stereotyping and affirmative action. On the other hand, female and male teachers in Quebec belonged to the same professional

British Columbia home support workers on strike to protest low wage rates and lack of recognition for their important services, March 1990.

....

Source: Courtesy of British Columbia Government and Service Employees' Union.

association, the *Centrale des enseignants du Québec* (CEQ), one of the most militant of all teachers' organizations and one that had co-operated closely with other trade unionists in that province. The CEQ leftist orientation enabled its women members to win support for a comprehensive and radical feminist agenda. Its call for equality extended well beyond the workplace and included such demands as the recognition of a woman's right to decide if and when to have children, and the reorganization of housework along egalitarian lines.[92]

Businesswomen also realized the benefits to be gained from mutual support; new organizations (such as the Canadian Association of Women Executives and Entrepreneurs) sprang up, and directories (such as Montreal's *Bottin des femmes*) emerged to facilitate networking among their members. Contacts between women in the corporate and business world were extremely important, because women often lacked the role models and mentors that male executives found so important. As one female vice-president commented, "There's still that old-boys' network when you're reaching above middle management."[93]

Finally, during the 1970s and 1980s — as earlier — working-class women played an important role in supporting the men in their families during the trying circumstances of prolonged strikes. When the workers at Inco in Sudbury went on strike in 1979, a group of local feminists and workers' wives set up a special committee to support the strikers by mobilizing community resources and promoting solidarity among the workers' families. Like the traditional union ladies' auxiliaries, "Women Supporting the Strike" organized clothing drives, community dinners, and Christmas parties for the strikers' families. They also raised money and travelled widely to win public support. However, unlike traditional trade union women's auxiliaries, the wives' committee sought to assert its financial and political autonomy from the union, an objective that led to frequent tension within the committee itself and with the striking local of the United Steelworkers of America. The wives' committee not only demonstrated the importance of mobilizing women's support for the strike, but also underlined the connections between wage work and domestic work by demonstrating the extent to which women were directly affected by the strike. Cathy Mulroy, a woman who worked in the Inco plant, reported with admiration the way "the wives of workers got together":

> I liked that these women were interested in what their husbands were doing. I went to a meeting about bargaining, and these women were at the door giving out pamphlets saying "come to the bean supper." . . . This man behind me says to one of the women, "What are you doing here? You have no business in the union hall." I turned around and said, "Of course they have. They're on strike just like their husbands are. They're going to have to go through a lot too."

Mulroy was invited to the wives' group and found that "it was exciting! All these women. Really huffing and puffing. Now *this* was a union meeting."[94] After the strike was successfully concluded, several of the women involved in the wives' committee became active in the local women's movement.

The experience of the Sudbury wives was very useful to the women who formed the United Miners' Wives Association during the 1981 miners' strike in Cape Breton. Once again it was striking workers' wives and local feminists who organized to represent women's interests. As in Sudbury, the activities of the wives' group had a transforming effect at both an individual and a collective level. As one participant pointed out, it "seemed like a new thing, women holding a bake sale to raise money to send themselves, not their husbands, to the Labour Day rally in Sydney."[95] During the lengthy and extremely bitter strike waged by the Canadian Association of Smelter and Allied Workers in Yellowknife, Northwest Territories, against Royal Oak mines in 1992–93, striking miners' wives also created their own organization to help families get through the strike. For most of these women, it was their first foray into political activism, as they travelled extensively on behalf of the strikers and promoted their "Adopt a Family" fundraising efforts.[96]

But such efforts were not new; they were merely part of the tradition of Canadian women helping themselves as well as others. Women of all classes now increasingly combined forces to pressure governments into moving in the direction of affirmative action and pay equity schemes, and employers into first contracts and the elimination of discriminatory practices. The resolution and creativity of individual working women, both in the home and at the workplace, the growing collective strength of women workers, and their involvement in the contemporary women's movement gave them a firmer base for the continuing struggle.

NOTES

1. Ruth Roach Pierson, *"They're Still Women after All": The Second World War and Canadian Womanhood* (Toronto: McClelland and Stewart, 1986), 36–37.

2. Geneviève Auger et Raymonde Lamothe, *De la poêle à frire à la ligne de feu* (Montréal: Boréal Express, 1981), frontispiece [our translation].

3. Auger et Lamothe, *De la poêle à frire*, 53.

4. Pierson, *"They're Still Women,"* 33.

5. Barry Broadfoot, *Six War Years, 1939–1945: Memories of Canadians at Home and Abroad* (Toronto: Paperjacks, 1974), 355–56.

6. Pierson, *"They're Still Women,"* 48.

7. Pierson, *"They're Still Women,"* 50.

8. Auger et Lamothe, *De la poêle à frire*, 128 [our translation].

9. Auger et Lamothe, *De la poêle à frire*, 128 [our translation].

10. Pierson, *"They're Still Women,"* 71.

11. Dorothy W. Williams, *Blacks in Montreal 1628–1986: An Urban Demography* (Cowansville, Que.: Éditions Yvon Blais, 1989); Beth Light and Ruth Roach Pierson, eds., *No Easy Road: Women in Canada, 1920s–1960s* (Toronto: New Hogtown Press, 1990), 297; Dionne Brand, " 'We Weren't Allowed to Go into Factory Work until Hitler Started the War': The 1920 to the 1940s," in Peggy Bristow, coord., et al., *"We're Rooted Here and They Can't Pull Us Up": Essays in African Canadian Women's History* (Toronto: University of Toronto Press, 1994), 171–91.

12. Sheila Kieran, *The Family Matters: Two Centuries of Family Law and Life in Ontario* (Toronto: Key Porter Books, 1986), 125.

13. This discussion of women in the armed forces relies extensively on Pierson, *"They're Still Women,"* chap. 3.

14. Carolyn M. Gossage, *Greatcoats and Glamour Boots: Canadian Women at War, 1939–1945* (Toronto: Dundurn Press, 1991), 40, 44–46.

15. Barbara Winters, "Canadian Servicewomen in the Second World War: A Revisionist Approach," paper presented to the Canadian Historical Association, Charlottetown, 1992, 16–17.

16. Gossage, *Greatcoats*, 94, 150–52.

17. Winters, "Canadian Servicewomen," 26.

18. Paul Ward, "Women in World War II: Focus on the Women's Royal Canadian Naval Service," unpublished paper, April 1987, 27.

19. The other members included Margaret Mackenzie (Fredericton), Thaïs Lacoste Frémont (Quebec City), Margaret Wherry (Montreal), Dr. A. Vibert Douglas (Kingston), Helen Smith Agnew and Marion Findlay (Toronto), Susan Gunn (Lloydminster), Grace MacInnis and Evelyn Lett (Vancouver); see Gail Cuthbert Brandt, " 'Pigeon-Holed and Forgotten': The Work of the Subcommittee on the Post-War Problems of Women, 1943," *Histoire sociale/Social History* 15, 29 (March/May 1982), 239–59; and Mary Kinnear, *Margaret McWilliams: An Interwar Feminist* (Montreal and Kingston: McGill-Queen's University Press, 1991).

20. *Saturday Night* (June 24, 1944), 6; *Halifax Herald* (February 2, 1944), 8.

21. Clare Boothe Luce, "Women Can Win the Peace," *Chatelaine* (February 1944), 3.

22. R.M. Farquharson, "Will Women Go Back to the Kitchen?" *Canadian Home Journal* 40, (January 1944), 3.

23. Jo-Anne Fiske, "Gender and Politics in a Carrier Indian Community," University of British Columbia, Ph.D. Thesis, 1989, 138.

24. Broadfoot, *Six War Years*, 358.

25. Canada, House of Commons, *Debates* (1944), 2629.

26. Pierson, *"They're Still Women,"* 49.

27. National Archives of Canada, MG 28, I–10, vol. 104, file 777, 1947.

28. Agnes Macphail, "Men Want to Hog Everything," *Maclean's* (September 15, 1949), 71–72.

29. Ruth Pierson, " 'Home Aide': A Solution to Women's Unemployment after World War II," *Atlantis* 2, 2 (Spring 1977), 85–96.

30. M.A.C. Francis, "Will Married Women Go to War Again?" *Saturday Night* 66, 17 (January 30, 1951), 21–22.

31. Pierson, *"They're Still Women,"* 215.

32. Alice Kessler-Harris, *Out to Work* (New York: Oxford University Press, 1985), 277.

33. Omer Leroux, "All This and Suffrage Too," *Financial Post* (September 4, 1954), 22.

34. Michael Barkway, "Save Your Tears: Watch the Girls," *Financial Post* (November 16, 1957), 1.

35. Canada, Department of Labour, *Married Women Working for Pay in Eight Canadian Cities* (Ottawa: 1958), 52.

36. Franca Iacovetta, "From *Contadina* to Worker: Southern Italian Immigrant Women Working in Toronto, 1947–62," in Jean Burnet, ed., *Looking into My Sister's Eyes: An Exploration in Women's History* (Toronto: Multicultural History Society of Ontario, 1986), 209–11; Iacovetta, *Such Hardworking People: Italian Immigrants in Postwar Toronto* (Montreal and Kingston: McGill-Queen's University Press, 1992).

37. Canada, Department of Labour, *Gazette* (1954), 1513.

38. Dorothy Manning, "I Quit My Job to Save My Marriage," *Chatelaine* (June 1955), 16.

39. John Kenneth Galbraith, *Economics and the Public Purpose* (New York: New American Library, 1973), 29–37.

40. See, for example, Julie Guard, "The 'Woman Question' in Canadian Unionism: Women in the UE, 1930s to 1960s," University of Toronto, Ph.D. Dissertation, 1994.

41. Sara Diamond, "A Union Man's Wife: The Ladies' Auxiliary Movement in the IWA — The Lake Cowichan Experience," in Barbara K. Latham and Roberta J. Pazdro, eds., *Not Just Pin Money: Selected Essays on the History of Women's Work in British Columbia* (Victoria: Camosun College, 1984), 287.

42. Dean Beeby, "Women in the Ontario CCF, 1940–1950," *Ontario History* 74, 4 (December 1982), 275–76.

43. Elizabeth Forbes, comp., *With Enthusiasm and Faith: History of the Canadian Federation of Business and Professional Women's Clubs . . . 1930–1972* (Ottawa: Canadian Federation of Business and Professional Women's Clubs, 1974), 56–111; David MacDonald, "The Most Powerful Woman's Lobby in Canada," *Chatelaine* (June 1957), 58.

44. Status of Women Canada, "Canada's National Report for the United Nations Secretariat of the Fourth World Conference on Women, September 1995 — Beijing, China" (May 12, 1994), 37, 41.

45. Punam Khosla, "Review of the Situation of Women in Canada," National Action Committee on the Status of Women (July 1993), 4.

46. "Irene Desjarlais," in *Speaking Together: Canada's Native Women* (Toronto: Hunter-Rose, 1975), 46.

47. Khosla, "Review," 18: Margaret Philp, "Money Crisis Blocks Ontario Child-Care Reform," *The Globe and Mail* (March 31, 1994), A8.

48. "Two-Earner Families Decline," *The Globe and Mail* (June 3, 1993), A6; Bruce Little, "In Recession, Women's Wages Pay the Way," *The Globe and Mail* (May 16, 1994), A11.

49. Pat Armstrong and Hugh Armstrong, *"A Working Majority": What Women Must Do for Pay* (Ottawa: Canadian Advisory Council on the Status of Women, 1983), 36.

50. Alanna Mitchell, "Divorce a Ticket to Poverty for Women, Figures Show," *The Globe and Mail* (June 4, 1992), A10; "Single Mothers Far below the Poverty Line," *The Globe and Mail* (December 1, 1992), A9.

51. Khosla, "Review," 5–6; Canadian Advisory Council on the Status of Women [CACSW], *Work in Progress: Tracking Women's Equality in Canada* (Ottawa: 1994), 89.

52. Khosla, "Review," 12–13; "Women Make Inroads into 'Male' Professions," *The Globe and Mail* (May 29, 1987), A1–A2; Bonnie J. Fox and John Fox, *Occupational Gender Segregation of the Canadian Labour Force, 1931–1981* (Toronto: Institute for Social Research, York University, 1987), 28–29: CACSW, *Work in Progress*, 65.

53. Jeanette Easson, Debbie Field, and Joanne Santucci, "Working Steel," in Jennifer Penney, *Hard Earned Wages: Women Fighting for Better Work* (Toronto: Women's Press, 1983), 200, 211; Khosla, "Review," 11.

54. *Today's Woman* [supplement to *The Halifax Chronicle–Herald* and *The Mail–Star*] (March 10, 1987), 8, 14.

55. Ann Rauhala, "Job Quota for Women Is Upheld," *The Globe and Mail* (June 26, 1987), A1, A2; Doris Anderson, "How a Tiny Women's Group Defeated a Corporate Giant," *The Toronto Star* (July 18, 1987), K1.

56. Status of Women, "Canada's National Report," 26; Judith Lavoie, "Women Combine Aboriginal Culture with Eco-tourism," *The Globe and Mail* (June 25, 1994).

57. Ellen Roseman, "More Women Entering the Business World, Determined to Overcome Cautious Attitudes," *The Globe and Mail* (May 29, 1987), C7.

58. Catharine W. Warren, *Vignettes of Life: Experiences and Self Perceptions of New Canadian Women* (Calgary: Detselig, 1986), 48; Charlene Gannagé, *Double Day, Double Bind: Women Garment Workers* (Toronto: Women's Press, 1986).

59. Khosla, "Review," 15; Micheline Labelle et al., *Histoire des immigrées: Itinéraires d'ouvrières colombiennes, grecques, haïtiennes et portugaises de Montréal* (Montréal: Boréal Express, 1987), 141, 197.

60. Williams, *Blacks in Montreal*, 63, 74.

61. "Queen Elizabeth Hotel Fined for Anti-Black Bias," *The Oracle* (February 3, 1977), 7.

62. Judith Gregory, "The Electronic Sweatshop," in Joan Turner and Lois Emery, eds., *Perspectives on Women in the 1980s* (Winnipeg: University of Manitoba Press, 1983), 99–112; Heather Menzies, *Women and the Chip: Case Studies of the Effects of Informatics on Employment in Canada* (Montreal: Institute for Research on Public Policy, 1981).

63. Pat Armstrong, *Labour Pains: Women's Work in Crisis* (Toronto: Women's Press, 1984), 167.

64. Alanna Mitchell, "Others Enjoy Benefits Unheard of in Canada," *The Globe and Mail* (January 24, 1994).

65. Status of Women, "Canada's National Report," 38, 43.

66. Kenneth Kidd, "Big Mac Meets the McUnion Kid," *Report on Business Magazine* 10, 12 (June 1994), 46–53.

67. Gina Vance and Anne Bishop, "No More Lobsters for Lizmore," in Penney, *Hard Earned Wages*, 42–43.

68. Fox and Fox, *Occupational Gender Segregation*, 1; CACSW, *Work in Progress*, 42, 50; Susannah J. Wilson, *Women, the Family, and the Economy* (Toronto: McGraw-Hill Ryerson, 1982), 106.

69. Jeff Sallot, "Career Pause Expensive for Wives," *The Globe and Mail* (July 7, 1992), A6.

70. Status of Women, "Canada's National Report," 41; Khosla, "Review," 9–10; CACSW, "Work in Progress," 50.

71. Hugh Armstrong and Pat Armstrong, *The Double Ghetto: The Segregation of Woman's Work in Canada*, rev. ed. (Toronto: McClelland and Stewart, 1984), 45.

72. Lorna R. Marsden, "The Role of the National Action Committee on the Status of Women in Facilitating Equal Pay Policy in Canada," in Ronnie Ratner Steinberg, ed., *Equal Employment Policy for Women: Strategies for Implementation in the United States, Canada, and Western Europe* (Philadelphia: Temple University Press, 1980), 242–60; Armstrong, *Labour Pains*, 59.

73. Pat Armstrong and Hugh Armstrong, "Lessons from Pay Equity," *Studies in Political Economy* 32 (Summer 1990), 29–54.

74. Rosalie Silberman Abella, *Equality in Employment: A Royal Commission Report* (Ottawa: Supply and Services Canada, 1984).

75. Michael Valpy, "The Wrong Way to Say Goodbye," *The Globe and Mail* (July 22, 1994).

76. Leslie A. Pal and F.L. Morton, "*Bliss v. Attorney General of Canada*: From Legal Defeat to Political Victory," *Osgoode Hall Law Journal* 24, 1 (Spring 1986), 141–60; Mary Eberts, "Sex-Based Discrimination and the Charter," in Anne F. Bayefsky and Mary Eberts, eds., *Equality Rights and the Canadian Charter of Rights and Freedoms* (Toronto: Carswell, 1985), 198.

77. Armstrong and Armstrong, *The Double Ghetto*, 45.

78. Gisele Ireland, *The Farmer Takes a Wife* (Chesley, Ont.: Concerned Farm Women, 1983), 14–15.

79. Muriel Lush, "The Family Farm Is Dying," *Women's Concerns*, Division of Mission in Canada of the United Church in Canada, 31 (Winter 1986), 8.

80. Betty Burt and Loretta Burt, "Squidjigging Women," in Penney, *Hard Earned Wages*, 228.

81. Alanna Mitchell, "Unpaid Housework Valued to $319 Billion, Statscan Says," *The Globe and Mail* (April 7, 1994), A7.

82. Stephen Strauss, "Inuit Shorter; Snowmobiles Blamed," *The Globe and Mail* (July 1, 1994), A1.

83. Meg Luxton, *More Than a Labour of Love: Three Generations of Women's Work in the Home* (Toronto: Women's Press, 1980), 48.

84. "Working Wives Toil at Home, Survey Finds," *The Globe and Mail* (September 4, 1993), A3.

85. "Living on Mother's Allowance No Bed of Roses: Single Mother," *Peterborough Examiner* (July 18, 1987), 8.

86. Linda Briskin, "Women and Unions in Canada: A Statistical Overview," in Linda Briskin and Lynda Yanz, eds., *Union Sisters: Women in the Labour Movement* (Toronto: Women's Press, 1983), 28–43; Heather Jon Maroney, "Feminism at Work," in Bryan D. Palmer, ed., *The Character of Class Struggle: Essays in Canadian Working-Class History, 1850–1985* (Toronto: McClelland and Stewart, 1986), 160–75.

87. Martine Lanctôt, "La genèse et l'évolution du mouvement de libération des femmes à Montréal, 1969–79," Université du Québec à Montréal, Thèse de maîtrise, 1982.

88. Lynda Yanz and David Smith, "Annotated List of Women's Strikes," *Resources for Feminist Research/Documentation sur la recherche féministe* 10, 2 (July 1981), 77–83; Linda Briskin and Patricia McDermott, eds., *Women Challenging Unions: Feminism, Democracy and Militancy* (Toronto: University of Toronto Press, 1993).

89. Frances Lankin, "Foreword," in Carole Conde and Karl Beveridge, *First Contract: Women and the Fight to Unionize* (Toronto: Between the Lines, 1986), 6–7.

90. Conde and Beveridge, *First Contract*, 72.

91. Laurell Ritchie, "Why Are So Many Women Unorganized?" in Briskin and Yanz, eds., *Union Sisters*, 208–9.

92. Maroney, "Feminism at Work," 162.

93. Rona Maynard, "Why Women Still Fail to Reach the Top," *Report on Business Magazine* 1, 5 (May 1985), 80–85.

94. Cathy Mulroy, "Miner's Daughter," in Penney, *Hard Earned Wages*, 182.

95. Luxton, "From Ladies' Auxiliaries to Wives' Committees: Housewives and the Unions," in Meg Luxton and Harriet Rosenberg, eds., *Through the Kitchen Window: The Politics of Home and Family* (Toronto: Garamond, 1986), 63–81.

96. Erin Mullen, "Women in the Strike," *Kinesis* (December 1992/January 1993), 8.

CHAPTER THIRTEEN

Changing Lives in a Changing Society: 1940–1995

By the late 1940s, women were beginning to shape and reshape their lives in the context of the dramatic demographic, economic, and social transformations that characterized post-war Canadian society. Throughout the remaining decades of the twentieth century, there were striking shifts in life course patterns. Individual women's actions coalesced to produce social changes in the timing of such events as leaving home, entering marriage, and starting a family. The experiences of most women surrounding childbearing, childrearing, and aging were also very different from those of previous generations of women. Moreover, in massive numbers, women of all ages and economic circumstances entered areas of activity previously defined as male. At first glance, they seemed to attain unprecedented levels of autonomy and equality. However, considerable tension persisted between the reality of women's personal experiences and the social constructions of what it was to be a woman. In the media, in sports and recreational activities, and in educational institutions, girls and women continued to encounter a deeply ingrained sexism—sometimes blatant, but more frequently subtle — that moulded and constrained their choices.

DEMOGRAPHIC PATTERNS

Demographic indicators are very useful for assessing the changes that occurred in women's lives as the hardships of the Great Depression gave way to the prosperity of the immediate post-war period. Increased marriage rates, lower average age of brides marrying for the first time, and larger completed families were some of the most important signs of the changes in the economic and social context in which

Arrival of a group of war brides and their children in Halifax, 1946. Some 40 000 brides and 20 000 children of Canadian servicemen were brought to Canada by the federal government.

Source: H.B. Jefferson Collection, 31.2.1 (N-082). Public Archives of Nova Scotia.

Canadians now found themselves. After World War II, marriage rates soared, especially among younger women. For those aged 15 to 19, the rate more than doubled, climbing from 30 per 1000 in 1937 to 62 per 1000 in 1954.[1] In addition, Canadian women were having more children, and having them earlier than had been the case for their mothers' generation. There was a sharp increase in the number of births per 1000 inhabitants, which rose from 20.1 in 1937 to 28.9 in 1947. It is important to note, however, that significant increases in the birth rate were recorded only among married women under 30, and most strikingly among those under 25. As one observer pithily commented, "Young girls are more interested in raising families than jobs; not-so-young girls like jobs better than children."[2] In the younger groups of married women, birth rates continued to climb until 1956; for women over 40, the rates continued to decline compared to those established by women in the same age category during previous generations.[3] Three of these trends — earlier age at first marriage, earlier births of first children, and larger completed families — combined to produce the renowned post-war "baby boom" of the late 1940s and early 1950s. In 1956, nearly half of all live births consisted of third or later children.[4] Nevertheless, after 1956, substantial declines in birth rates were recorded for women in all age groups. The surroundings in which Canadian infants were typically born also changed after the war as birthing moved from home to hospital. In 1941, just under 50 percent of babies were born in hospitals; twenty years later, the rate was 97 percent.[5]

One of the most striking changes that occurred in the lives of young women after the war involved the greater degree of independence they enjoyed. In the past, if a woman left her family before marriage, she usually went to live with another family, or with other young adults in a supervised setting such as a boarding house or boarding school. As a result, her life was still carefully monitored. By the end of the 1950s, it had become more common and more acceptable for a young woman to live on her own or independently with people her own age while working or completing her education. The boom in apartment construction, in particular between 1961 and 1970, facilitated this trend.[6] During the five-year period from 1966 to 1971, the total number of households in Canada grew by 17 percent, but there was an amazing 92 percent increase in households with single, never-married heads.[7] The growing tendency for young people to live on their own reflected the unprecedented freedom — economic, social, and sexual — enjoyed by the generation of Canadians that came of age in the 1960s.

The greater autonomy young people experienced in directing their lives apparently extended to decisions about when to marry, if we are to judge by the way in which the average age at first marriage continued to decline. For women, the average age dropped from 24.4 years in 1941 to only 22.6 years in 1971; for men, the average shifted from 27.6 to 24.9.[8] The decline in age at first marriage was related to the general prosperity of the post-war years, as well as the growing acceptability of married women without children working outside the home, the availability of social assistance programs, and easier access to credit. The growing affluence of Canadians may also have led many parents to give financial support to young people who, a generation earlier, would have been considered too dependent to marry.[9]

In both Inuit and Indian societies, young people increasingly chose their own marriage partners instead of entering into partnerships arranged by their parents. While not all older women felt they had been well served by arranged marriages, many associated the new, "white" custom with increased marital problems, domestic violence, and marriage breakdown. The declining role of the extended family and of communal mediation in women's lives was also exemplified by the erosion of the traditional practice of customary adoptions in Inuit society. In certain circumstances, birth parents might give over a child or children to members of their extended family or to friends. The children knew who their birth parents were, and frequently remained in close contact with them. This system had provided a mechanism for ensuring that all children were looked after and for helping to keep sex ratios within families in balance.[10]

The Canadian birth rate, which began its downward spiral after 1957, had fallen by 1971 to 16.8 per 1000 total population. In most segments of society, women were having fewer children, and they were compressing childbearing and childrearing into a shorter span of time. By 1970, fewer than one-third of all live births were third or later children. The average number of children per family declined from 1.9 in 1961 to 1.7 in 1971.[11] Overall, the size of the Canadian family was becoming more uniform. Between 1941 and 1966, the percentages of small families (0–1 child) and of large families (6 or more children) decreased.[12] Nonetheless, there remained considerable variation in fertility rates and family size that reflected regional, racial, religious, and ethnic differences. Rural families continued to be larger on average than urban families, and in the Northwest Territories, the Yukon Territory, and Newfoundland, fertility rates remained well above the national average from 1951 to 1970, while those of Ontario and British Columbia were slightly below.[13] The continued higher rates in the territories can be accounted for by the higher birth rate among Native women; in 1965, the birth rate for Indians was 43.5 per 1000, compared to 21.3 for all Canadians. Even within the Native population there were important regional variations: Indians living in the eastern provinces recorded birth rates similar to the provincial rates, while Indians in the prairie provinces and the territories had very high rates.[14]

In contrast to the Native populations, Quebeckers experienced a dramatic decline in their birth rate; in only one decade — 1959 to 1969 — the birth rate was cut in half, a change that in the rest of the country took place over the span of a century.[15] By 1970 Quebec had the lowest birth rate of any of the provinces (15 per 1000). This stunning change was an integral part of the "Quiet Revolution," the amalgam of demographic, economic, social, and political transformations that began in the 1940s and reached full impact in the 1960s. The rapid rate of urbanization and the modernization of Quebec agriculture during the 1950s rendered increasingly irrelevant the traditional arguments of French-Canadian nationalists in favour of a larger population. Mechanization of farms reduced the need for abundant labour; consequently, even in rural areas, the benefits of having a very large family evaporated.

In Quebec and elsewhere, the decline in fertility was in part the result of increased knowledge of and access to birth control methods. In the face of the unequivocal evidence that many of their parishioners were consciously limiting their family size, the Catholic clergy in Quebec were compelled to acknowledge publicly the "natural" forms of birth control, such as the "rhythm method" and the "thermometer method." By the 1940s, by organizing marriage preparation courses in which these methods were discussed, the clergy played a key role in the dissemination of information about at least some forms of birth control. The birth control pill was available by the early 1960s in the larger urban centres, but only by prescription; in most instances, physicians limited its use to married women. Indeed, legal penalties for displaying and selling contraceptive devices remained in force until 1969. It was in part the conviction and jailing of a Toronto pharmacist in 1960 for selling condoms that motivated Barbara and George Cadbury to organize the Planned Parenthood Association of Toronto one year later. By 1963 they had succeeded in establishing both the Planned Parenthood Federation of Canada and the Canadian Federation of Societies for Population Planning. In Quebec, the decline in the social power and moral authority of the Roman Catholic church translated into an increasing willingness on the part of Catholics to ignore church doctrine. Like other women throughout North America, *Quebecoises* adopted the birth control pill, and other methods of contraception officially condemned by the Vatican, as a means of asserting more effective control over their lives. When Pope Paul VI strongly condemned the use of artificial means of birth control in his 1968 encyclical, *Humanae Vitae*, Canadian Catholic bishops took a nuanced official position. In a collective statement, they declared that the use of birth control was a matter of individual conscience, which was to be informed by careful consideration of divine law and traditional church teachings.[16]

The widespread use of family limitation practices in Quebec, and the stand taken by the Catholic bishops in 1968, also made it politically possible the following year for the federal government to amend the provisions of the Criminal Code dealing with contraception and abortion. The urgent need for changes in the existing abortion laws was all too obvious: between 1954 and 1965, there were an estimated 50 000 to 100 000 illegal abortions. In British Columbia, abortion-related deaths accounted for one in every five maternal deaths occurring between 1946 and 1968.[17]

Like birth control and abortion, divorce was another controversial issue. Divorce rates in Canada almost tripled at the end of World War II, the result of the dissolution of unhappy wartime marriages and those weakened by long separations. The dramatic increase may also have reflected the economic independence acquired by some married women during the war. The divorce rate rose steadily from 1951 to 1968 (88.9 to 124.3 divorces per 100 000 married persons aged 15 and over), and then dramatically (to 311.5 in 1970) after the liberalization of the divorce laws in 1969.[18] The new legislation provided for a unified divorce law that permitted divorce on the grounds of marriage breakdown, as well as on the previously existing basis of matrimonial offence (for example, adultery). By the end of the 1960s, marital breakdown was becoming a familiar occurrence in Canadian society, and was a factor in the increased labour-force participation of women who had to support themselves —and in many cases their dependent children—after their marriages had ended.

Despite the increase in the incidence of divorce, the vast majority of Canadian marriages in the 1960s were still brought to an end by the death of one of the spouses. Canadians were living longer, however, owing to continued advancements in public health and medicine. The most significant advance was the reduction of infant mortality: the infant death rate was almost halved between 1946 and 1966. Furthermore, as a result of improved nutrition, and better pre-natal and post-partum care, fewer women died in childbirth. The likelihood of a Canadian woman dying during pregnancy fell from one in 150 in the 1930s to one in 3000 by the 1960s.[19]

It was also apparent that the difference in life expectancy for women and men was increasing. In the 1930s, women could expect to live about 62 years, and men to about 60 years; by 1971, women's life expectancy had increased to 76 years, but men's had risen to only 69 years, for a variety of reasons that are still not fully understood. For the Native peoples, however, life expectancy remained disturbingly short: in 1970 it was only 37 years for Indian women, and 34 years for Indian men. The principal reason for this was the continuing high infant mortality rate: at the end of the 1960s, eight times as many Indian children aged 2 years and under died as did white children in the same age category. An Indian woman who survived the first two years of life could expect a life span of 53 years, while her male counterpart was likely to survive only until the age of 50.[20] Other negative factors, such as a higher incidence of suicides and violent deaths in the Native population, also contributed to shortening the average life span.

For the 1970s, the demographic trends of the Canadian population in general can be summarized as follows: stable marriage rates, continued reductions in the average age at first marriage, declining fertility rates, and increased divorce rates.[21] By the end of the 1980s, however, another set of changes was occurring in the timing and the nature of the major demographic events in women's lives. For the first time in this century, the average age of women at first marriage increased, and it did so to a significant degree. In 1992, that age was 26.2 years, almost four years older than it had been at the beginning of the 1970s. And while the fertility rate declined throughout the early 1980s, dropping to 1.7 births per woman in 1985, it had risen again by 1990, when women gave birth to an average of 1.86 children. This slight increase was due to a number of factors, including the tendency of baby-boomers who had postponed having children to now start families. Consequently, the proportion of all babies born to mothers over the age of 30 increased from 1 in 5 in 1971 to 1 in 3 in 1990. The greatest increase in fertility took place in Quebec, where the government, in a move reminiscent of the pro-natalist government of New France, began to offer its citizens attractive "baby bonuses": $500 per year for each of the first two children, and $3000 for each subsequent child.[22] Fertility rates remained at very high levels for many First Nations peoples. One 1988 Saskatchewan study reported that approximately 50 percent of the entire Native population was under the age of 21. The majority of Indian women in that province were young, single mothers, and more than 90 percent of all Native single parents were living well below the poverty line.[23] By contrast, national demographic data suggest that a greater percentage of women were choosing not to have children. In 1991, 12 percent of women aged 35 to 44 who were or had been married did not have children, compared to less than 8 percent twenty years earlier. According to one expert, about half of such women were childless by choice.[24]

Finally, the age composition of the Canadian population changed. An increasing proportion was over the age of 65 (10.7 percent in 1986, compared to 6.7 percent in 1941), and women predominated in that group. The gap between female and male life expectancies remained: by 1986, women could anticipate living 80 years on average, while men might expect to live 73 years.[25] The majority of women would therefore outlive their spouses, and spend their last years as widows. As the numbers of solitary elderly women grew, so too did the problem of female poverty.

MARRIAGE AND MOTHERHOOD

The Canadian government's massive campaign to encourage women to enter the labour force and military service during World War II used newspapers, periodicals, radio, and the newly created National Film Board to modify the image of Canadian women. They were portrayed wearing coveralls and bandannas, swinging their lunch pails as they strode off to perform industrial war work. There were also many pictures and photographs of women in military and paramilitary uniforms, as they joined the armed forces, the Red Cross Corps, or Voluntary Aid Detachments.

At war's end, the image changed again: women's labour-force role was played down, and it was domestic duties that were the central feature of the idealized woman's life. For the most part, the Canadian media stereotyped women in the post-war years as happy homemakers who were dedicated stay-at-home mothers. Woman's role as consumer was also re-emphasized.[26] In *Maclean's* magazine between 1939 and 1950, the proportion of all advertisements that directly appealed to women as homemakers rose from about 40 percent in the period 1939–43 to more than 70 percent in 1950. And the emphasis shifted. No longer did the advertisements merely offer to free the housewife from the drudgery and boredom of her work; now they promised her a life of personal fulfilment — provided she wisely purchased the right products.[27] The francophone media followed a similar pattern, but adopted an even more traditional version: the ideal French-Canadian woman was a fervent Catholic, a devoted wife and mother, and still attached to the rural way of life.[28] During the 1950s in particular, articles dealing with women and the family thoroughly reflected the ideas of the Catholic church: that nature destined women to perform domestic work, and that women's paid employment outside the home was to be deplored.

In general, the media did not question whether or not the normal and desired fate of most women was marriage and motherhood. An advertisement for Weston's Bakery paid tribute to the Canadian mother as the "heart of her home," responsible for the moral and civic training of her children.[29] The message of this advertisement was remarkably similar to that delivered by Dr. Hilda Neatby, Canada's pre-eminent woman historian of the 1950s. A professor at the University of Saskatchewan and a member of the Massey Commission on cultural affairs, Dr. Neatby never married. However, she confidently assured other women that the establishment of "a moral tone and moral practices in her family is a woman's first obligation to society. . . . Women, gifted and otherwise, are the individuals who in the present state of society have a large, perhaps the largest share in determining the cultural atmosphere of the home."[30]

Spinsterhood was not a highly regarded state, although an occasional editorial in *Chatelaine* did champion a woman's right to remain single. Some articles in Canadian mass-circulation magazines such as *Saturday Night* also strongly advocated education for women that would enable them to pursue certain "women's careers." Moreover, increasing numbers of Canadian women did not conform to the powerful and pervasive image of women as stay-at-home mothers. Once again, it is important to underline the gap that existed between what women were told they should do and what women actually did. The very vigour with which the "happy homemaker" image was promoted by the media may well have been a reaction to women's growing involvement in activities outside the home and, in some cases, their resistance to conventional heterosexual roles.[31]

The belief that marriage and motherhood were the normal goals for women was reinforced by medical experts. As Freudian views about women and the psychosomatic approach to medicine became more widespread in the 1950s, doctors stressed the importance of women's reproductive and maternal responsibilities. The growing tendency for middle-class married women to work outside the home fuelled concern about the preservation of the family. Women suffering from gynecological disorders were considered to have rejected their traditional roles. According to one physician writing in the *Canadian Medical Association Journal* in 1958, women who experienced pre-menstrual tension tended to be those who resented their femininity and envied men. Another doctor asserted that women exaggerated the extent of their menstrual pain "in order to get revenge on men for their easy lot in life and to shirk their own work responsibilities." Specialists in obstetrics and gynecology were advised to determine the extent to which their patients accepted themselves as women.[32] Married working women were particularly suspect, for by forsaking their homes, they threatened to destabilize not only their own gender identity, but also that of their husbands. A significant number of commentators fretted over what they perceived as a loss of masculinity among the husbands of such women when they observed them performing "wifely" duties such as shopping and childcare.

By the early 1960s, however, sex-role stereotyping was already an important topic of discussion for some women journalists. The new editor of *Chatelaine*, Doris Anderson, was writing thought-provoking editorials that linked stereotyping to married women's domestic work and paid employment, and to the dearth of women in public life. June Callwood was also among those anglophone journalists who attacked the notions of femininity that constrained the activities of so many Canadian women. In Quebec as well, there was a subtle yet significant shift in the orientation of the women's press after 1960. With the appearance in 1960 of the French version of *Chatelaine*, and the appointment of Francine Montpetit as the new editor of Montreal's 50-year-old magazine *La revue populaire*, Quebec women were offered more realistic appraisals of their situation. However, an article on birth control published in *La revue* in September 1962 created a storm of controversy that resulted in the firing of Montpetit and the eventual demise of the magazine. *Châtelaine* remained as the sole commercial publication directed to Quebec women.[33] Although English-Canadian general-interest magazines contained a declining proportion of articles about women and work during the 1960s, *Chatelaine/Châtelaine* and the *Canadian Home Journal* continued to focus on women's changing roles.[34]

Feature articles and regular columns appearing in the women's magazines offered vast quantities of advice — frequently conflicting — about how to deal with the myriad problems inherent in raising a child. The expansion of the middle class in the prosperity of the post-war years created an enlarged audience of well-educated parents receptive to childrearing advice. Childcare experts emphasized the emotional bonds between mother and child, and as infant mortality rates for the general population continued to decline, most mothers could be increasingly confident that this emotional investment would not be destroyed by the untimely death of their children.

Many mothers were anxious about their abilities as parents, increasingly so with the popularization of the work of child psychologists such as Dr. John Bowlby. Bowlby was the British psychologist who coined the phrase "maternal deprivation," a notion central to his book *Child Care and the Growth of Love* and discussed widely in women's magazines in North America. On the basis of a study of orphaned children who had to be cared for in institutional settings or foster homes, Bowlby argued that irreparable damage was done to young children when they were separated from their mothers for a prolonged period. He counselled mothers not to leave children under 3 years of age in the care of others except for the most urgent reasons. Even "the holiday whilst granny looks after the baby" was "best kept to a week or ten days." Many mothers interpreted Bowlby's dictum about the "absolute need of infants and toddlers for the continuous care of their mothers" as meaning they should always be on call for their children.[35]

The conflicting advice received by mothers of infants further complicated their lives: should they feed the baby according to a strict time schedule, as their own mothers had done, or when the baby demanded it? Although infant-care experts pointed out the advantages of breast-feeding, and counselled mothers to try it, they assigned an inordinate amount of space in the literature to describing the procedures to be followed in bottle-feeding. Given the overwhelming importance accorded motherhood, and the confusion about how best to meet the demands of this role, it is small wonder that Canadian women relied on books such as the free government publication *The Canadian Mother and Child* (1940) and Dr. Benjamin Spock's *Baby and Child Care* (1945) for authoritative answers. By 1953 Canadian public health nurses had handed out to new mothers more than 2 million copies of the former book; by 1975 it was in its third edition.[36]

During the last quarter of the twentieth century, almost every aspect of mothering — pregnancy, delivery, and childrearing — was subject to radical change and was more complex than it had been a generation earlier. In some cases, there was increased medical intervention and control of women's bodies. One woman physician from the Maritimes recalled that in the early 1960s, "the two weeks before the beginning of the fishing or hunting season women estimated to be near term would be brought into the hospital to have labour induced — then, if that failed, a Cesarean section would be done."[37] The percentage of births by Cesarean section actually increased after 1970, rising from 6 percent to just under 20 percent in 1988. In one hospital, nearly one-third of all babies born in 1994 were delivered by C-section.[38] The cause for this high rate was probably in part the increased use and efficiency of new fetal monitoring devices, which could show when infants were in distress; many women were convinced that the causes also included doctors' convenience and their fear of malpractice suits. The large majority of births, like deaths, continued to take place in hospitals.

Furthermore, in a period when most women still completed their families before age 30, "older" pregnant women provoked increased medical supervision, and doctors warned about the risk of abnormalities such as Down's syndrome. Doctors tended to see age 30 as a cutoff for safe conception, though even women over 40 had only approximately one chance in 60 of bearing a chromosomally abnormal child.[39] Amniocentesis became routine for pregnant women over 30, along with ultrasound tests, internal and external fetal monitoring during birth, and an even higher incidence of Cesareans than for younger women. Women accordingly acquired a whole new range of anxieties and stresses, beginning with the feeling of a "biological clock" ticking away during childless years, and continuing through agonizing decisions about whether or not to abort an abnormal fetus. The biological impact of older fathers was overlooked in the discussions, which in effect put all the blame on women. Wendy Lill, who had a Down's syndrome child when she was 34, wrote angrily, "Instead of buying the theory about maternal age hook, line and sinker, I think we should be demanding more investigation on links between radiation, environmental pollutants, and all sorts of birth defects."[40]

By the 1980s, researchers had learned how to flush out human eggs, fertilize them outside the body (*in vitro* fertilization), and implant them, sometimes in a different woman's womb. Canada's hundredth test-tube baby was born in 1987; a year later, the nation's first test-tube quintuplets — only the third set in the world — appeared. This and other related processes were costly, and were subject to decisions by doctors on who was a "fit" subject for the procedures. The new reproductive technology alarmed feminists because it implied treatment of the female body as a "baby-making" machine. The complex health and ethical issues surrounding many of the scientific and medical innovations in the area of human reproduction became the focus of general public concern, and led the federal government to set up a Royal Commission on New Reproductive Technologies in 1989. After four years of exhaustive study, punctuated by serious internal rifts, the Commission released its controversial report in November 1993. It recommended that the government introduce legislation to ban some procedures, such as surrogate motherhood, and impose limits on the use of others. It also recommended the creation of a regulatory and licencing body to control the development and dissemination of new technologies.[41]

Artificial insemination was the one reproductive technology amenable to self-help.[42] By the 1980s, some lesbians had conceived in this way with the assistance of male friends. Such cases separated sexuality and reproduction in the most extreme way yet, and also seemed to reassert women's claim to define the identity of both children and families. As lesbianism became more public and dissociated itself from male homosexuality, key questions related to sexuality and to family composition were raised again from a different perspective. In 1985, Karen Andrews attempted to designate her female partner and her partner's children as dependents for the purposes of health insurance; although a human rights appeal and a court case were not successful, her workplace insurance company changed its rules, and the Ontario Health Insurance Plan shifted to insuring individuals without requiring definitions of family relationships.[43]

Women's increased autonomy was more widely expressed in demands for less mechanized childbearing and childrearing, and they had some success in their efforts. The use of forceps and total anesthesia were no longer seen as the ideals of "modern" childbirth. Experiments with less alienating forms of delivery were very influential, and were expounded by lay as well as medically trained practitioners. In the 1960s, women welcomed partial anesthesia such as spinal blocks, which left them conscious of the birthing process and able to apply some of the lessons of the widely attended pre-natal classes held for both mothers and fathers. By the next decade, fathers were encouraged to assist in labour and delivery; babies were allowed to be bigger and were considered less fragile; and babies "rooming in" with their mothers had become a routine practice in hospitals. Partly for financial reasons, medical administrators drastically reduced the hospitalization period for healthy mothers and their babies. And by the 1980s, a small but significant number of women were opting for home births or childbirth without medication. The ancient profession of midwifery, accepted in all industrialized areas except North America, began to be revived; in 1987 an Ontario task force headed by feminist lawyer Mary Eberts recommended a system of licencing.[44] By 1994, Ontario, British Columbia, Manitoba, and the Northwest Territories were well on the way to making midwifery services and, in some cases, home births available once more.[45] In Quebec, which had the longest recorded history of midwifery and where women's organizations were also calling for the re-establishment of midwives' services, progress was slower due to deep-seated opposition from the powerful medical establishment.

After they gave birth, conditions for most new mothers had also improved. The energetic efforts of La Leche League helped promote breast-feeding as the preferred form of infant feeding, at least for the first few months. Disposable diapers and bottle-liners, as well as better formulas and baby food, made childcare easier, and so did a relaxation of the insistence on either total permissiveness or complete regimentation in childcare. Dr. Spock issued a new, more flexible, and less sexist edition of his book. Nonetheless, the reasserting of traditional, woman-controlled patterns in medicine and family life should not be exaggerated.

For many Canadian women, the advice literature on mothering and many of the practices surrounding childbirth and childrearing were irrelevant, given the cultural and material contexts in which they found themselves. Poverty and isolation frequently impeded access to medical facilities and services. Aboriginal women in particular could not access services most Canadian women now routinely counted on for assistance in delivering and raising healthy children. In Inuit communities, for example, the practice of flying pregnant women out of their own communities to hospitals in larger centres remained widespread, and they often had to give birth far away from family and friends.

BODY IMAGE AND SEXUALITY

During the war, those responsible for recruiting women into the labour force and the armed forces felt compelled to reassure the public that the new tasks women were undertaking were short-term, and did not constitute any real threat to existing gender roles. Emphasizing the attractive uniforms and homey atmosphere of the women's barracks, military authorities undertook a massive educational and publicity campaign to reassure Canadians that the femininity of the women recruits was not being jeopardized. Female recruits were allowed to wear makeup, encouraged to be attractive and feminine, and reminded "at all times to act in a becoming and lady-like manner."[46] On the civilian side, print media advertisements stressed the importance for women of continuing to look feminine and glamorous even when they entered into masculine work environments. There was nonetheless some recognition that female roles were changing. Slacks were now considered to be an acceptable form of dress for women, and the shoulder pads that featured so prominently in women's wartime clothing gave women a stronger, more masculine appearance. In keeping with efforts to reduce the amount of material consumed by the civilian population, skirts and dresses were kept at knee length.

The fashion images of the immediate post-war period were markedly different. The 1950s were the decade of French designer Yves St. Laurent's "New Look," the sweater girl, and U.S. film star Marilyn Monroe. St. Laurent designed clothes, he said, "for flowerlike women, clothes with rounded shoulders, full feminine busts, and willowy waists above enormous spreading skirts."[47] For many women, achieving such an appearance required encasing themselves in padded bras, crinolines, and waist-cinchers. Hairstyles were also subject to the dictates of fashion, and some girls and women had to go to extraordinary lengths in order to conform to what was in style. Cheryl Foggo, a black Calgarian, has vividly recounted how hard her mother worked in the 1960s to straighten her daughters' hair:

> Hairday, as my sister and I referred to it, was a torment, a day of relentless brushing, pulling, plunging into the yellow tub of water and then at the end, the dreaded "hot comb." . . . We were stationed in a kitchen chair, eye-level with the blue flame that licked and scorched the heavy, iron pressing comb. Our mother divided our hair into tiny strands, coated each strand with Vaseline . . . then applied the teeth of the comb from our scalps to the ends of our hair. We felt the heat, heard the sizzle, smelled the burning protein and saw the smoke rise into the air around us.

Fortunately, in the following decade, "afros" were considered to be the latest fashion rage, and Foggo was able to vaunt her natural look.[48]

Another essential requirement for the proper feminine image was impeccable personal hygiene. Advertisements for soaps, deodorants, and sanitary napkins were numerous: one deodorant advertisement showed a tearful young woman under the caption "She lost her man because of *that*." It was not enough, however, to be clean and odour-free; a woman's chances of romantic success depended on improving her appearance by using the plethora of products the cosmetic industry had to offer her. Once she had used her beauty to effect the desired change in marital status, it was a woman's duty to continue to be sexually attractive to her husband. An advertisement for a disinfectant showed a distraught wife whose husband was walking out the door, suitcase in hand; if only she had used Lysol in her douche to keep herself fresh and dainty!

Views about dress and bodily adornment changed as "hippies" in the 1960s promoted a more natural and casual look. Young women typically opted for blue jeans and, gradually, older women who in earlier periods would never have considered wearing trousers adopted them at least for casual wear. In the late 1960s, many militant student feminists insisted on a sort of uniform of jeans or overalls and work boots, arguing that makeup or jewellery meant acceptance of sex-role stereotyping. But soon women began to work out notions about the relationship between self-respect and the esthetics of adornment. The goal should be to please oneself and those one cared for, an expression of autonomy. Businesswomen's clothes went through similar phases. Initially, "dressed for success," such women were steered into outfits that directed attention away from their sexual identity. By the 1970s, pantsuits were accepted as respectable clothing for the fashionable woman executive, as well as for secretaries and those in the service industries. By the following decade, however, women in the corporate world had largely abandoned bowed ties, mannish suits, and discreet black pumps for dresses and high fashion. More generally, the requirements of conformity in women's clothing relaxed to a degree that the permanent-waved, girdled, and nylon-stockinged women of a generation earlier would not have expected.

As skirt lengths fluctuated between mini and maxi, clothing was expected to display women's contours without assistance from the substantial foundation garments that had helped earlier generations of women conform to a womanly ideal. For many women, the quest for the perfect body became obsessive. Anorexia or self-starvation became a serious health hazard, especially for younger women, as did bulimia, characterized by binge eating between periods of compulsive dieting, with each binge followed by a purge (self-induced vomiting). Many people treated fat women as if they were diseased and made them feel like outcasts. In the 1970s, a movement for Fat Liberation announced that "fat is a feminist issue."[49] Fat was a cultural and generational issue for women, too, for the standards of some recent immigrant groups were being rejected in favour of a mainstream, commercial model. "In my time, fat women were honoured. . . . Truly, I don't understand present-day fashions at all. . . . Anywhere a man touches, he can feel bones," lamented "Hannah," an 89-year-old Morocco-born woman who lived in Montreal in the 1980s.[50]

If fashion and ideas about women's bodies underwent significant changes in the last half of the twentieth century, so too did attitudes about female sexuality. A major concern that emerged during the war involved the impact that the bending of gender roles was having on young women, particularly those in the armed forces. There was a widely held perception that servicewomen were promiscuous: rumours abounded that some were former prostitutes, that many were getting pregnant, and that a large proportion were suffering from venereal disease. Despite the fact that venereal disease was far more common among Canadian servicemen, who also accounted for nearly 90 percent of the fathers named by CWACs discharged for pregnancy, men's reputations were unaffected. Servicewomen who contracted venereal disease were much more likely to be discharged than servicemen with the same condition, and much greater effort was expended on setting up preventive programs for men. The latter were constantly reminded that it was predatory, unprincipled women who caused venereal disease.[51]

In the 1950s, pre-marital sex was still socially unacceptable for "respectable" young women. Sexual intimacy before marriage became more widespread by the late 1960s, however, as the student movements of the period adopted the slogan "make love, not war" and promoted both freer discussion and freer practice of sexuality. In October 1968, the McGill Student Society began to publish an illegal but widely distributed

Birth Control Handbook, and then became publicly involved in the even more controversial activity of abortion counselling. Despite the greater freedom, it seems likely that most single young women limited their sexual relationships to the men whom they intended to marry. At the same time, they were far more likely than in earlier periods to be living with their lovers, even having children, without immediate marriage plans.

As the 1970s turned into the 1980s, women became aware that "sexual liberation" had some major flaws for them. "Free love" represented greater freedom for men than for women, for it often provided men the possibility of greater access to sex with reduced responsibility. Specific, unexpected health hazards emerged as a result of the new sexual freedom. The number of sexually transmitted diseases increased, and they affected women particularly severely. The old curses of syphilis and gonorrhea were now more easily diagnosed and treated, but genital herpes, chlamydia, and pelvic inflammatory disease (PID) were increasingly common, likely to interfere with a woman's fertility, and likely also to be transmitted to children. By the middle of the 1980s, acquired immune deficiency syndrome (AIDS) had appeared, with no known cure. Women's vulnerability to AIDS was initially underestimated by public health authorities, who seemed aware of women mainly as potential carriers of the disease who could infect men and children; not until 1994 did the Canadian Society of Gynecologists and Obstetricians recognize that women are seriously at risk from infection via heterosexual intercourse. Condoms, now much improved, had a revived popularity as prophylactics, but the use of the pill had encouraged male aversion to them.

The established patterns of male initiative and domination in sexual matters were difficult to counter. Because men now often expected that women would take responsibility for contraception, women were under increased pressure. Coercive sexuality, including the newly identified phenomenon of "date rape," was alarmingly common, even among high-schoolers. But although oral contraception now entailed a smaller dose of hormones, many women distrusted such substantial chemical intervention into their bodies over a period of fertility that might span more than 30 years. The side effects ranged from depression and obesity to such potentially fatal conditions as blood clots and heart disease. The concentration of the more serious conditions among certain high-risk groups such as heavy smokers was little comfort: by 1992 Canadian women smokers outnumbered their male counterparts—the first group of women in the western world to do so.[52] The use of the intrauterine device (IUD) had also proved to be dangerous, sometimes producing ectopic pregnancy or sterility. Tubal ligation was still a surgical operation involving a hospital stay, whereas for men, a vasectomy was a simple procedure that could be carried out in a doctor's office. Despite this difference, female sterilization continued to be far more common than male sterilization: according to a 1984 study, of the 68 percent of women between 18 and 49 years of age who used contraception, 35 percent had been sterilized (compared to only 13 percent of their partners).[53] Progress on the development of a male contraceptive was unnoticeable. Some women returned to such earlier contraceptive devices as sponges, diaphragms, or douches; but, if safer in one sense, these approaches were still unreliable as contraceptives.

As the "baby boom" generation reached middle age, menopause became a much more widely studied and discussed phenomenon. Nonetheless, older ideas persisted about menopause as a crisis in a woman's life, and many doctors and their female

TABLE 13.1 *Therapeutic Abortions in Canada, 1971–1982*

	Abortions	Abortion Rate per 1000 Females Ages 15–44 Years[a]	Abortion Rate per 1000 Live Births
1971	30 949	6.6	8.5
1981	65 127	11.1	17.5
1991[b]	70 463	10.9	17.5

[a] PERFORMED IN HOSPITALS IN CANADA.
[b] FIGURES UNDERREPRESENTED FOR BRITISH COLUMBIA.

Source: Statistics Canada, *Therapeutic Abortions 1992*, Cat. No. 82-219
(Ottawa: Minister of Industry, 1994), Table 1, p. 2.

patients continued to consider it a medical and social problem. Writing in 1957, Dr. Marion Hilliard expressed a typical view of menopause and its treatment:

> Work is the wonderful antidote to the blues of menopause. This is a period when a woman's sense of uselessness is so acute that she can, literally, be driven to drink, dope, or mental illness. Her family is grown, her childbearing years are ending, her husband often could do just as well with a hired housekeeper. If she has some consuming occupation, . . . she isn't in as much danger of being shattered by what is happening to her physiology.[54]

In Canada as a whole, according to a 1991 figure, 15 percent of post-menopausal women were on hormone replacement therapy, 30 percent in Quebec.[55] Medical authorities who endorsed this therapy often cited new research on the significant incidence of osteoporosis and heart disease among post-menopausal women, and the efficacy of hormones in preventing these disorders.

If menopause had become a politicized issue, so too had breast cancer, which was estimated in 1992 to strike one in nine Canadian women. Feminists pointed to the thousands of Canadian women who died each year from this disease, and the relatively small amount of financial and human resources devoted by governments and the medical establishment to developing effective prevention and treatment strategies. Pat Kelly, who founded a self-help group for women with breast cancer, noted that in 1989, there were 333 AIDs-related deaths in Ontario, and 1814 attributable to breast cancer. That same year, the provincial Ministry of Health spent $37 million for AIDS research and community education programs, but nothing on breast cancer research or education. In response to pressure from women like Kelly, who flatly declared "No more daffodils, no more lunches. We want a cure," in 1992 the House of Commons Subcommittee on the Status of Women undertook a major review of breast cancer and its treatment.[56]

SPORTS

Old myths about women's biological weakness were still used to justify the many restrictions on what kinds of sports women could participate in, and with what intensity. During World War II, athletics for both women and men had a low priority. The cancellation of all international competition until the 1948 Summer Olympics also reduced top athletes' incentive and opportunity for participation. Even after the return to peace and the resumption of international competition, women's involvement in both competitive and recreational sport remained limited. Although a few women continued to win medals at international meets, they did so in individual events that were considered appropriate female activities, such as figure skating, swimming, skiing, and gymnastics. The association of female athletes with individual pursuits was reinforced by the lack of opportunity for women to compete in team events at the Olympic level: it was not until 1964 that the first such event for women, volleyball, was added to the Olympic roster.[57]

The development of professional sports, as big business, which had begun in the inter-war period, intensified after World War II. In the world of mass spectator athletics, there were few opportunities for women and significantly fewer material rewards. Even in recreational athletics and sports, girls and women encountered exclusion or discrimination; on the playground, in the schools and universities, and in community and privately owned recreational facilities, they were consistently denied equal facilities and financial resources. In contrast to the years when the Edmonton Grads made headlines, during the post-war period the media provided little coverage of women's athletics, and thus helped perpetuate the view that women's sports were of little importance.

Nevertheless, the Canadian public idolized a few outstanding female athletes who participated in individual sports, including Barbara Ann Scott, who won the Olympic, World, and European figure skating titles in 1948, and Marilyn Bell, who made history in 1954 at age 16 by being the first person to swim across Lake Ontario. They were admired, however, not just for what they did but also for the image they projected. The media were captivated by the petite blonde skater whom they saw as epitomizing feminine grace and beauty. Bell, on the other hand, was the wholesome "girl next door."[58] In track and field, the pre-eminence that Canadian women had achieved in the late 1920s was not regained; in fact, after 1948, not one Canadian woman reached a final track and field event in Olympic competition until the Tokyo games of 1964. Despite the relative lack of support, Canadian women athletes' overall performance at international events from the late 1920s to 1980 managed to remain on a par with that of Canadian men.[59] By the 1990s, such internationally acclaimed champions as Marnie McBean, Kathleen Heddle, and Silken Laumann (rowing), Kerrin Lee-Gartner (Alpine skiing), Miriam Bédard (biathlon), and Sylvie Frechette (synchronized swimming) had reinforced Canadian women's record of accomplishment in international sport. At the 1992 Summer Olympics in Barcelona, Spain, women athletes captured four of the seven gold medals won by the Canadian team.

At home, women's team sports had to contend with second-class status. Professional team sports, geared to men's interests and needs, syphoned off most of the financial support and public interest previously given to amateur athletics. As well, young girls had less opportunity than boys to play such team sports as hockey or baseball. Only occasionally could exceptional girls, such as future Olympic runner Abby Hoffman, register for a boys' hockey team; she was able to do so only by giving her name as A. Hoffman and because she had a slight and boyish frame. The few team sports that girls were encouraged to play were carefully designed to preserve their femininity; for instance, baseball was made less dangerous by the institution of

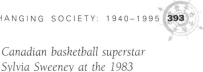

*Canadian basketball superstar
Sylvia Sweeney at the 1983
Pan-Am Games.*

....

Source: Courtesy of Sylvia Sweeney.

a "no sliding" rule. The view that active participation in sports was somehow incompatible with femininity was unwittingly reinforced in some cases by female physical educators themselves. One university instructor, writing in 1961, suggested drawing attention to "the most charming looking students through the election of baseball queens, field hockey queens and archery queens." The idea was to counteract the unattractive image of female athletes: the successful candidates were to be photographed in non-sports clothes, and to have their pictures prominently displayed.[60]

From the 1960s on, a growing number of Canadian girls and women were actively involved in recreational and competitive sports, challenging the stereotypes of what constituted "appropriate" female physical activity. Their increased participation can be attributed to a number of factors: the greater consciousness among most Canadians about the benefits of physical fitness, the increase in leisure time, and a renewed women's movement. In the 1990s, the Canadian women's national hockey team dominated world championships, and the University of Winnipeg women's basketball team equalled the North American university and college record for the largest number of consecutive victories by either a women's or men's team.

Nevertheless, despite these dazzling performances, media coverage remained discouragingly sparse.

Women's participation at all levels continued to be eclipsed by that of men, for reasons both structural and attitudinal. Working women with families found it difficult to take time from their hectic schedules to take part in sports, and few evening sports programs offered childcare. Participation levels are directly related to income, and on average women had less money than men; moreover, some girls and women continued to believe it was "unladylike" to sweat or to develop muscles. There were also proportionately fewer female coaches and physical education teachers than in the past, and women continued to be woefully underrepresented among sports administrators and executives.[61]

EDUCATION

At the end of World War II, many people believed that the sexes had equal educational opportunities. Full equality, however, remained an elusive goal. Even at the elementary-school level, the experiences and expectations of young girls and boys continued to differ, and sex-role stereotyping was pervasive in the materials used by the students. In the American *Fun with Dick and Jane* reading series, which was used well into the 1960s in some provincial school systems, Dick engaged in active play, running and jumping, while Jane played with her dolls. Their father was away at work all day, and drove home in his late-model automobile just in time to eat the dinner that had been prepared by his smiling, aproned, stay-at-home wife. In Quebec, *Guy et Yvette* gave the same message of female subordination. In the mid-1970s, seven of every ten people portrayed in Quebec school texts were male. Gone were the references to the outstanding women of the past that had been in the old manuals, especially those used by the teaching nuns in previous generations. The earlier images were not replaced: women simply disappeared.[62] Throughout Canada, parents often reinforced the messages implicit in the textbooks. An "Attitude Study" undertaken in 1966 by the Federation of Women Teachers' Associations of Ontario reported that parents considered nursing, teaching, and social work to be the best occupations for their daughters, but favoured medicine, engineering, science, architecture, the law, and business for their sons.[63]

Divergent expectations for girls and boys continued to influence both the extent and type of education they received at the secondary and postsecondary levels. The recognition during World War II that women had non-domestic responsibilities as well as their homemaking duties did have some impact. The teaching of home economics in Ontario schools in 1945, for example, had as one of its primary objectives the fostering of "a conception of homemaking as an undertaking in which all members of the family co-operate." Ten years later, home economics teachers were advised that their students would be pursuing "two future careers — wage-earning employment, and marriage with the establishment of families and homes of their own." Suggested class topics included "Fathers as wage-earners and homemakers," and "Mothers as homemakers and frequently wage-earners too." By 1964, however, guidelines stated unequivocally that it was the wife and mother who formed the nucleus of the family, and that she bore the principal responsibility for achieving either "an organized and artistic way of living or a chaotic and unattractive existence within the home."[64] Feminist educators' efforts to achieve gender equality in secondary schooling throughout the next three decades met with limited success. Curriculum materials continued to lack meaningful representation of girls and women; and in Ontario, for example, few schools were implementing the Ministry of Education's sex-equity policy. The words of one Grade 12 student summarized the experiences of many young women:

> I think to a certain extent, female students are expected to repress feelings of dissatisfaction — to ignore how they're feeling unappreciated or unrepresented. And to just accept it and think of it as normal and taken for granted.[65]

While sex-role stereotyping remained a substantial problem, poverty and racism posed additional problems. For girls growing up in Native communities, residential schools were often the only form of formal education available. Attending such schools caused irreparable damage for many of the children. Cut off from their families, they were prohibited from speaking their own language, and were all too often the victims of physical and sexual abuse. In black communities, educational opportunities were frequently limited. Women leaders, however, worked assiduously to open up career opportunities for young women, opportunities taken for granted by young white women. As a result of a campaign in Nova Scotia led by Dr. Pearleen Oliver, schools of nursing began to accept young black women. The first two black graduates from the Children's Hospital in Halifax received their diplomas in the fall

Domestic science class at Boulton Avenue School in Toronto.

Source: Domestic Science Class, Boulton Avenue Vocational School, Toronto. Archives and Museum, Toronto Board of Education.

of 1948. Four years later, Addie Aylestock was the first black Canadian woman to be ordained when she was named a pastor in the British Methodist Episcopal church. In 1958, she was appointed to the position of general secretary of the BME conference.[66]

At the university level, women's educational experience in English Canada immediately following the war closely resembled that of women in the labour force: female students constituted a "reserve army." During the war, they had represented a larger proportion of the student body than previously, in part because they were keeping places that would be occupied by men once the war was over.[67] A prime example of this trend occurred in the University of Toronto's Faculty of Medicine. During the war, women as young as 16 and 17 found it relatively easy to gain admission. The resulting increase in female students facilitated the Women's Medical Society's successful petition in 1948 to have the yearly quota for female interns at Toronto's largest hospital raised — from one to two.[68] Nonetheless, most women continued to enrol in traditionally female courses of study: arts, nursing, household science, and physical and occupational therapy.

Once the veterans returned, their educational needs were assigned top priority. Although ex-servicewomen such as future cabinet minister Judy LaMarsh used the veterans' programs to acquire a university degree, only 2600 of the approximately 50 000 servicewomen joined her. Although the actual numbers of women attending university increased, as a proportion of post-war university students, they dropped from 23 percent of all full-time undergraduates in 1940 to 21 percent in 1945.[69]

In post-war Quebec, where secondary and postsecondary education were under church control until 1964, the Catholic church continued to stress the necessity to educate women differently from men; indeed, papal instructions issued in 1957 rejected co-education as an acceptable principle for Catholic secondary education. While acknowledging the economic necessity of educating adolescent females with males in some instances, the guidelines set strict conditions for the mingling of the sexes. The preferred option for educating francophone Catholic women in Quebec was the *institut familial*. The emphasis on domestic education also prevailed in convent schools serving the francophone minority outside Quebec, such as the *Pensionnat Assomption* in northern Alberta. There is little evidence of adjustment to the changing times, even though French-Canadian women were experiencing demographic and economic transformations even more dramatic than those affecting other Canadian women. In Quebec, the building, maintenance, and staffing of the *instituts familiaux* were entrusted to the female religious orders, who were given financial assistance by the provincial government. An anglophone woman journalist who produced a detailed study of the *instituts* could not contain her enthusiasm for this particular type of education for women: it promised them "real freedom and happiness," whereas women's quest for equality with men gave them, in her view, only higher wages, more career choices, and dissatisfaction. More categorically, an Oblate priest reminded the graduates of one convent school in May 1956 that a woman achieved greatness through kneeling.[70]

While the church was promoting domestic science education for francophone women, the provincial government was providing other options. After the introduction of compulsory education by the Liberal government in 1943, the number of normal schools for francophone Catholic women grew rapidly. The implementation of compulsory education also resulted in the extension and reform of secondary schools, including the provision of free secondary education. By 1959, most young francophone women, regardless of class, could acquire some secondary schooling. Between 1954 and 1962, the possibility of continuing studies up to the university level was also increased by the establishment of an additional 15 classical colleges for women. The opening of the professions of lawyer (1941) and notary (1956) to women reflected a growing demand on the part of the francophone bourgeoisie that at least a few exceptional women be provided with the same educational and career opportunities as men.

However, *Québécoises* had to wait for additional reforms in the provincial educational system, undertaken in the wake of the comprehensive Parent Commission report (1964), before it became common for women to attend university. Among the results were the abolition of the domestic science schools and the creation of co-educational CEGEPs (*Collèges d'enseignement général et professionnel*). By 1970, women accounted for one-third of all full-time undergraduates in the province, and for nearly half of all part-time university students.[71] While the secularization of the Quebec educational system in the 1960s created many new opportunities, it also had negative consequences for those women who had overseen the education of girls and young women for three centuries — the nuns. With the closing of normal schools and the transfer of responsibility for teacher training to the universities, large numbers of them lost their teaching positions.[72]

Despite the myriad difficulties they encountered in all the provincial educational systems, growing numbers of women were attending Canadian universities. By 1970 they accounted for 37 percent of full-time undergraduates. However, women continued to be concentrated in certain areas considered appropriate to their sex. In 1969–70, they represented more than 95 percent of the students enrolled at Canadian universities in undergraduate programs in household science, nursing, secretarial science, and physical and occupational therapy, but only 1 percent of those enrolled in applied science and engineering.[73] By 1982–83, women students were in the majority both in community colleges (52 percent) and in university undergraduate faculties (56 percent); in 1988, 55 percent of all BAs or first professional degrees were awarded to women. By 1992, women constituted 69 percent of students in health-related programs and education, 63 percent of those pursuing studies in fine arts, and 61 percent of those in the humanities. However, they represented only 17 percent of students in engineering or applied sciences, and 28 percent of mathematics and physical sciences majors. Women's university participation rate was increasing most rapidly, however, among those pursuing studies on a part-time basis: in 1988, 65 percent of all part-time students were female. Overall, women still remained largely clustered in traditionally female fields that did not require scientific or mathematical training at the pre-university level.[74]

At the graduate level in Canadian universities, although there was also a steady increase in the number of female students after 1955, the proportion of students who were women (22 percent) was still lower in 1970 than it had been in 1921 (26 percent). Women earned only about one-fifth of the master's degrees and fewer than one-tenth of the doctorates awarded in 1969–70. By 1988, women received 45 percent of the master's degrees awarded and a third of the doctorates, and in 1992, they earned 44 percent of the medical degrees granted by Canadian universities.[75] One possible reason for the reluctance of women to pursue studies in non-traditional areas, especially at the graduate level, was the lack of positive female role models.

In the mid-1960s only slightly more than one in ten university teachers in Canada were women, and most were in the faculties of education, nursing, household science, and arts. Faculty women's second-class status was symbolized in some universities by a continuing exclusion from full Faculty Club privileges; at McGill, a few determined women faculty fought to eliminate the rules that prevented their use of the Faculty Club's dining room, a battle they finally won over the objections of one-third of the Club's members. Dr. Virginia Douglas, one of the principal organizers of the campaign, recalled meeting an elderly colleague at the Faculty Club a few weeks after the vote: "Placing a fatherly hand on her shoulder, he said, 'Dr. Douglas, it is such a pleasure to see you here, although I must admit I voted against having ladies in this dining room. But Dr. Douglas, I didn't mean you.' "[76]

In 1991, women still represented only 21 percent of university faculty; they had their highest representation (30 percent) in education, but only 4 percent of the faculty members in engineering and applied sciences were women.[77] In Canadian universities generally, proportionately more women than men were located in the lowest ranks and in non-permanent positions.

THE ARTS

In addition to attaining new levels of involvement in sports and education in the decades following World War II, women made outstanding contributions to the arts and to the development of Canadian culture. In 1950 the federally appointed Royal Commission on National Development in the Arts, Letters and Sciences (the Massey Commission) reported that the precarious state of cultural life in Canada might easily be further undermined by the all-pervasive American influence. American radio and television did not recognize the existence of the forty-ninth parallel and, for many Canadians, it was hard to distinguish between what was Canadian and what was American. It was in this difficult environment — before the establishment of the Canada Council in 1957 — that women initiated some of the most important projects in theatre, dance, and the visual arts. As artists, organizers, fundraisers, and administrators, they made a vital contribution to nearly all aspects of Canadian culture.

At art galleries throughout the country, women organized their own committees. Through their fundraising, pioneering of picture loan programs, encouragement of young artists, and pressure exerted on gallery boards to make new acquisitions, they had a major impact. As one noted art critic, Elizabeth Kilbourn, pointed out, "these women, perhaps more than any other group . . . consciously pioneered the public acceptance of contemporary art."[78] Women's committees also played a vital role in the development and support of the performing arts, especially opera, music, and ballet. Without their enthusiasm and extensive fundraising efforts, the nation's cultural life would have been greatly diminished.

In English Canada, Dora Mavor Moore played the role of "theatre's fiery godmother." Beginning in the 1920s, she organized amateur theatre productions and gave drama lessons in Toronto, but her most important contribution to the dramatic arts came in 1946 when she formed the New Play Society. Planned as a permanent, professional, non-profit company, it scored a number of theatrical "firsts," including the first performance of a Canadian play at the Royal Alexandra Theatre in Toronto. Moore's role in the success of the New Play Society was central:

> A classic diva, she begged, browbeat, improvised, scrimped, borrowed, wheedled and worked for years to keep theatre alive. . . . Moore used to put on classical productions costumed entirely in crepe paper and, when there was no money for crepe paper, presented Shakespeare in modern dress.[79]

Dora Mavor Moore was also one of the moving spirits behind the establishment of the Stratford Shakespeare Festival in 1952. A year later, her own company went into semi-retirement, largely as a result of Stratford's success.

In Montreal, Yvette Brind'amour developed *Le rideau vert*, a permanent professional theatre company that gave its first performance in 1949. It subsequently commissioned several new plays by French-Canadian playwrights — including Françoise Loranger's *Encore cinq minutes*, which won a Governor-General's award. In the same city, other women formed small theatres to present avant-garde drama, and by 1970, according to one critic, summer theatres in Quebec were "almost entirely the preserve of women."[80] Women also played a leading role in establishing children's theatre in Canada, as exemplified by the work of Joy Coghill and Jane Heyman in Vancouver, and Susan Rubes in Toronto. Many superb women actors such as Martha Henry, Kate Reid, Frances Hyland, Monique Mercure, Geneviève Bujold, Kate Nelligan, Sheila McCarthy, and Margot Kidder began their careers in Canadian theatre, and went on to win national and international acclaim both on stage and on screen.

Another innovative organizational project was the establishment of the Montreal Women's Symphony, founded by Ethel Stark in 1940. Stark, the first Canadian to hold a scholarship at the Curtis Institute of Music in Philadelphia, was a violinist and conductor. In 1947 this critically acclaimed group became the first Canadian orchestra to play in New York's Carnegie Hall. Despite its success, it was a shortlived venture, mainly because of the lack of financial resources: unlike many symphonies of the period, the Montreal Women's Symphony did not have a supporting women's committee to raise funds.[81]

Women also founded three major ballet companies in Canada in the post-war era. In 1949 Gweneth Lloyd and Betty Farrally organized the Royal Winnipeg Ballet, the country's first professional dance company; two years later, it received its royal charter. At about the same time, ballet enthusiasts in Toronto engaged Celia Franca, a principal dancer with the Sadler's Wells Company in Britain, to found a national company. The National Ballet of Canada gave its first performance in Toronto in 1951, but struggled throughout the decade to establish itself as a truly professional and permanent company. Funds were initially so scarce that its director, Celia Franca, had to work part-time in a department store.[82] One of the factors that contributed to the success of the National was the establishment of the National Ballet School in 1960 under the direction of Betty Oliphant. Nor was Montreal to be denied its own ballet company: thanks once again to the vision and energy of a determined woman, *Les grands ballets canadiens* became a reality in 1957. It was founded by Latvian-born Ludmilla Chiriaeff, who had trained with the Bolshoi Ballet and who had worked with a small group of dancers after her arrival in Canada in 1952.

As creative artists and performers in the 1950s, women faced special obstacles. Few artists, especially in the days before Canada Council grants, could support themselves on their artistic endeavours; and even when grants became more widely available, they were not always designed to meet the needs of women artists. In the visual arts, female applicants were not well served by the funding system established by the Canada Council after 1957. If their work borrowed techniques associated with women's traditional handicrafts, it was likely to be classified as craft rather than as art. The artificial distinction between art (male) and craft (female) served to devalue women's artistic endeavours and diminish their chances of securing financial assistance. Ironically, the agency established in the 1960s to promote greater support and recognition for the crafts was named the Canadian Craftsmen's Association. For most women in the performing arts, it was extremely difficult to combine motherhood with the demands of their careers. A notable exception was Maureen Forrester, the famous contralto, who later became the first woman head of the Canada Council. A mother of five, she delighted in telling people, "I can sing the morning I'm giving birth, and even during. It doesn't bother me. It's just the conductors who get nervous."[83]

Despite the obstacles they encountered, women played an activist role, both individually and collectively, in the development of the visual arts in the post-war period. In English Canada, Hamilton's Hortense Gordon was one of the first painters in Canada to experiment with abstraction and to promote non-representational art. Her work was displayed, along with that of more than seventy other women painters, in the Canadian Women Artists exhibition that opened to critical acclaim in New York in April 1947. The idea for the exhibition had come from Edna Breithaupt, chair of the National Council of Women's Art and Letters Committee, and funding was secured from the federal government to defray the shipping costs. This was the first example of the government co-operating with a voluntary organization to support the arts, and the exhibition "carved a niche for Canada's artists in one of the most important art centres of the western world."[84] In Montreal in 1948, the arts world was stunned by the publication of *Le refus global*, a ringing manifesto that called on all artists to reject the fetters of the past and to "break out of the walls of the common mould." Written by abstract painter Paul-Emile Borduas, it was signed by fifteen other *Québécois* painters, five of whom were women.[85] Quebec became a centre for abstract art, and with artists such as Rita Letendre, Suzanne Bergeron, Marcelle Ferron, and Lise Gervais, it had what one critic described as "more active women painters of the first rank than any other arts centre in the world."[86] These young artists were encouraged by such women as Agnes Lefort of Montreal, who, in 1950, opened the first Quebec art gallery committed to displaying contemporary work. Another important locus of artistic activity, Cape Dorset in the Northwest Territories, drew heavily on Inuit women's talents. Printmaker Pitseolak Ashoona was one of the best-known members of the artists' co-operative established there in 1959, and she enjoyed a high level of commercial success. Similarly, Jessie Oonark of the Baker Lake co-operative achieved international recognition by portraying Inuit themes in her cloth pictures.[87]

By the 1970s, Canadian women's contributions to the arts often explored simultaneously nationalist and feminist themes. A prime example was Joyce Wieland, whose 1971 show at the National Gallery was the first solo exhibition of the work of a living Canadian woman. An extraordinarily versatile artist, at home in a variety of media from collage to film, she drew inspiration from women's history and daily experiences, especially in her quilt works. Wieland's 1971 show, with its interwoven themes of nationalism, ecological concerns, and women's issues, was an important early statement of feminist esthetics.[88] Like Wieland, Newfoundland artist Mary Pratt

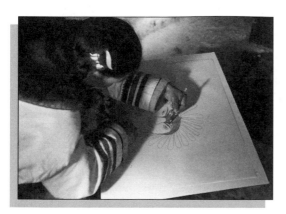

Kenojuak Ashevak, an Inuk print artist from Cape Dorset, Northwest Territories, working on a drawing.

Source: National Film Board of Canada/S-920.

turned to the world of women for much of her subject matter. Her best-known paintings had as their focus items from her own kitchen, such as cod fillets and aluminum foil.

Sculptors too drew from their own female experience. As she became involved in the feminist movement, Toronto sculptor Maryon Kantaroff began to question the male esthetics she had tried so hard to apply to her earlier sculptures. From strident, angular shapes she moved to rounder, softer, and more fluid ones. Characteristic of her attempt to reconnect her work with the female experience was the appearance of the egg in her works, a form she described as "a symbol of the beginnings of life, the essence of life, the seat of all potential, awareness."[89] Yet in spite of these individual success stories, the work of many women artists remained unknown. In 1984, a number of Ontario artists formed the Women's Art Resource Council, and as a tenth anniversary project, it undertook a national survey of publicly funded art galleries to determine the status of women in the arts. In general, the findings were disturbing: according to the author of the report, there had been little improvement since 1970 in the proportion of acquisitions budgets and gallery space devoted to women's art, and there was a "continuing effacement of Canadian women artists."[90]

It was in the area of literature that women made their best-known and most widely recognized contribution to Canadian cultural life; by the 1960s, issues related to women's lives and experiences were explicitly woven into women writers' work. Women writers were central to "Can Lit" in the 1960s and 1970s. Authors like Gabrielle Roy, Germaine Guèvremont, Marie-Claire Blais, Anne Hébert, and Antonine Maillet in French Canada, and Margaret Laurence, Margaret Atwood, Alice Munro, Mavis Gallant, and Marian Engel in English Canada, were international best-sellers. In poetry also, women's issues and imagery were incorporated in the work of such writers as Dorothy Livesay, Miriam Waddington, P.K. Page, Gwendolyn MacEwen, Phyllis Webb, Daphne Marlatt, Nicole Brossard, Madeleine Gagnon, France Théorêt, and Margaret Atwood. By the 1980s, a new generation of women writers was exploring issues surrounding ethnic, racial, and sexual identities. Victoria Kildaw Calihoo recorded stories relating to Métis pioneer life in Alberta, while Maria Campbell drew a disturbing picture of contemporary Métis women's experience in her autobiographical work *Halfbreed*. The poetry of Dionne Brand and that of Maxine Tynes, who was declared the People's Poet of Canada in 1987, represented and interpreted black women's experience in Canada, while Joy Kogawa's award-winning novel *Obasan* explored the world of a Japanese-Canadian family forcibly uprooted during World War II. Other outstanding examples of women whose works epitomized the country's regional and cultural diversity were Manitoba Mennonite writer di brandt and Native writer Beth Brant. In their presentation of a diversity of powerful central women characters, Canadian women's fictions, it has been suggested, have generally reflected resistance to any overriding national narrative and to their old status as a colonized gender.[91] In addition to winning many Canadian Governor-General's literary awards over the past two decades, several women writers distinguished themselves by garnering major international prizes. Two examples were Antonine Maillet, who was awarded France's prestigious Prix Goncourt in 1979, and Carol Shields, who won the Pulitzer Prize in 1995.

Explicitly feminist plays were also attracting considerable attention by the 1970s. The all-female *Théâtre des cuisines*, active from 1974 to 1976 and again from 1980, presented two plays, the pro-choice *Nous aurons les enfants que nous voulons* and *Môman travaille pas, a trop d'ouvrage*, about housework. In Toronto, Nightwood, an alternative women's theatre established in 1978, also created new opportunities for female playwrights to write women-centred works.

By the early 1980s, women dramatists had built up an impressive corpus of work. They included Marie Laberge, Elizabeth Bourget, Denise Boucher, Jovette Marchessault, and Pol Pelletier in Quebec, and Carol Bolt, Erika Ritter, Sharon Pollock, Judith Thompson, Margaret Hollingsworth, Anne Chislett, and Linda Griffiths in English Canada. Many of them explored explicitly feminist themes in their work, as did such playwrights as Wendy Lill and Joan McLeod. By the middle of the 1990s, women dramatists and their work powerfully reflected the regional, racial, and ethnic diversity of Canada. Native playwrights Margot Cane, Monique Mojica, and Susan Poteet, black playwright Djanet Sears, and Asian playwrights Betty Quan and Paula Wing represented this trend.[92]

In film as well, Canadian women won both national and international acclaim. In 1968 Anne Poirier became the first woman in Quebec to make a feature film. Entitled *De mère en fille*, it explored the physical and emotional experience of pregnancy. Five years later, she produced the NFB series *En tant que femmes*, which gave women film producers in Quebec their first opportunity to address issues of concern to women. "Studio D," the feminist filmmakers' group at the National Film Board, won several prestigious international awards for such documentary films as *Not a Love Story*, which investigated the pornography industry and its social and economic impact, and *If You Love This Planet*, which addressed global ecological issues from a feminist perspective. More recently, directors associated with Studio D have explored such varied issues as young women's identities (*Talk Sixteen*), lesbian relationships (*Forbidden Love*), and women's roles during World War I (*We Knew How to Dance*). Native women's lives and traditions have been captured by such filmmakers as Alanis Obomsawin, an Abenaki woman from Quebec, and Christine Welsh, a Métis whose *Keepers of the Fire* recorded the strength of Native women across Canada. For her part, Sylvia Hamilton explored the history and contribution of black women in Nova Scotia in her film *Black Mother, Black Daughter*. Yet other filmmakers, such as Sandy Wilson (*My American Cousin*), Patricia Roszema (*I've Heard the Mermaids Singing*), and Cynthia Scott (*Company of Strangers*), were successful in breaking into the commercial North American market.

In music, women achieved new standards of performance and contributed to the explosion of Canadian culture in the post-war era. Avant-garde composer and music educator Barbara Pentland, born in Winnipeg in 1912, explored new techniques of abstract structuring in her works, which were performed throughout the world. The text of her "Disasters in the Sun" (1976) was written by Dorothy Livesay; in this work, Pentland expressed her struggle against male domination. Like Pentland, Alberta's Violet Archer and Vancouver's Jean Coulthard combined composing with university teaching, and each produced a large and varied body of work that won international acclaim. Other innovative women composers, including Norma Beecroft from Ontario, Micheline Coulombe Saint-Marcoux from Quebec, and Alexina Louie in British Columbia, also influenced the development of contemporary Canadian music. The Canadian Music Council, which instituted a "composer of the year" award in 1977, bestowed that honour on Archer in 1984 and on Louie in 1986. In other music-related areas, opera singers Portia White, Teresa Stratas, Lois Marshall, and Maureen Forrester established themselves as international stars, while Melissa Hayden, Lynn Seymour, Veronica Tennant, Karen Kain, and Evelyn Hart accomplished the same in ballet. Cellist Ofra Harnoy, classical guitarist Liona Boyd, and pianist Angela Hewitt were similarly successful in developing strong international careers.

Female recording artists also helped develop a sense of Canadian achievement as two generations of women singers established highly successful careers in several different areas of popular music. They included Gisèle McKenzie, "Juliette," Marg Osborne, and Catherine MacKinnon in the 1950s and early 1960s, and Anne Murray, Sylvia Tyson, Joni Mitchell, Pauline Julien, Ginette Reno, Edith Butler, Angèle Arsenault, Kate and Anna McGarrigle, Rita McNeil, k.d. lang, Michelle Wright, Susan Aglukark, and Céline Dion in recent decades.

With the evolution of Canada into an increasingly diverse society in the post-war era, and the heightened awareness of the need to preserve and promote more than just mainstream culture, thousands of women contributed to the cultural mosaic that was closely associated with Canadian identity. Within their ethnic communities they organized language classes, choirs, theatre and dance groups, and cultural festivals. Among others, Jeni Le Gon in Vancouver, Anne Packwood in Montreal, and Grace Price Trotman in Toronto worked to preserve and reinforce black culture through drama, music, dancing, and fashion design.[93] Native women such as Anne Anderson, a Cree living in Edmonton, devoted many years of their lives to writing and teaching their ancestral language, and to passing on their customs to Native youth. Indeed, whatever their racial or ethnic community, women frequently assumed the leading role in preserving and transmitting their particular group's history and cultural heritage.

Many of the old patterns and rituals that had formerly dominated the lives of women disappeared in the post-war era. Women's roles were no longer ordered sequentially (work–marriage–family) but were increasingly intertwined. Marriage, once the great dividing line in women's lives, became a less significant event, since it no longer involved the end of employment and almost immediate initiation into motherhood. The role of wife became increasingly distinct from that of mother; it was now possible to be one but not the other. Moreover, there was less physical separation of the sexes. If home was still where many Canadian women's hearts were, they no longer spent most of their time in that female-oriented space. In the 1960s, women's efforts to achieve equality with men appeared to require a denial of a separate female identity.

By the end of the decade, however, awareness of the need for that identity had re-emerged. Increasingly, women recognized how necessary and desirable it was for women to draw upon their own experiences to bring about the changes they sought. Their contribution to Canadian culture either had a feminist bent, or was used by feminists to demonstrate the creativity of women and their essential role in making life more humane and enjoyable.

NOTES

1. Ruth Roach Pierson, *"They're Still Women after All": The Second World War and Canadian Womanhood* (Toronto: McClelland and Stewart, 1986), 216.
2. "You'll Hire Older Women, Miss Giggles Will Marry," *Financial Post* (May 4, 1957), 1.
3. Warren E. Kalbach and Wayne W. McVey, *The Demographic Bases of Canadian Society* (Toronto: McGraw-Hill, 1971), 61.
4. *Canada Yearbook, 1976–77, Special Edition* (Ottawa: Supply and Services Canada, 1977), Table 4.35.
5. F.H. Leacy, ed. *Historical Statistics of Canada*, 2nd ed. (Ottawa: Statistics Canada, 1983), B1–14.
6. John R. Miron, *Demographic Change, Household Formation and Housing Demand: Canada's Postwar Experience* (Toronto: Centre for Urban and Community Studies, University of Toronto, 1985), 7.18, Table 7.3.2.
7. *Canada Yearbook, 1976–77*, 169.
8. Monica Boyd, Margrit Eichler, and John R. Hofley, "Family: Functions, Formation, and Fertility," in Gail Cook, ed., *Opportunity for Choice: A Goal for Women in Canada* (Ottawa: Statistics Canada, 1976), 18.
9. Miron, *Demographic Change*, 3, 16–17.
10. Beth Light and Ruth Roach Pierson, eds., *No Easy Road: Women in Canada, 1920s–1960s* (Toronto: New Hogtown Press, 1990), 208; Lee Guemple, "Men and Women, Husbands and Wives: The Role of Gender in Traditional Inuit Society," *Études/Inuit/Studies* 10, 1–2 (1986), 13; Mary Crnkovich, *"Gossip": A Spoken History of Women in the North* (Ottawa: Canadian Arctic Resources Committee, 1990), 47–49; Julie Cruikshank, *Life Lived Like a Story: Life Stories of Three Yukon Native Elders* (Vancouver: University of British Columbia Press, 1992), 328; Cruikshank, "Becoming a Woman in Athapaskan Society: Changing Traditions on the Upper Yukon River," *Western Canadian Journal of Anthropology* 5, 2 (1975), 11.
11. *Canada Yearbook, 1976–77*, 171.
12. Kalbach and McVey, *The Demographic Bases*, 298, 293–95.
13. *Canada Yearbook, 1976–77*, 197–98.
14. James S. Frideres, *Canada's Indians: Contemporary Conflicts* (Scarborough: Prentice-Hall, 1974), 17.
15. Angus McLaren and Arlene Tigar McLaren, *The Bedroom and the State: The Changing Practices and Politics of Contraception and Abortion in Canada, 1880–1980* (Toronto: McClelland and Stewart, 1986), 125.
16. McLaren and McLaren, *The Bedroom and the State*, 132–33; Michael W. Higgins and Douglas R. Letson, *My Father's Business: A Biography of His Eminence G. Emmett Cardinal Carter* (Toronto: Macmillan, 1990), 101–13.

17. McLaren and McLaren, *The Bedroom and the State*, 136, 52–53.
18. Boyd, Eichler, and Hofley, "Family," 22–23.
19. McLaren and McLaren, *The Bedroom and the State*, 44.
20. Frideres, *Canada's Indians*, 19.
21. Boyd, Eichler, and Hofley, "Family," 13–52.
22. Stephen Strauss, "Baby Boomlet Continues, Statistics Canada Reports," *The Globe and Mail* (May 31, 1992), A6.
23. Roger Moody, ed., *The Indigenous Voice, Vol. 2: Visions and Realities* (London: Atlantic Highlands, 1988), 273–76.
24. Janice Turner, "Childless by Choice," *The Toronto Star* (January 25, 1994), B5.
25. John Robert Colombo, ed., *The 1995 Canadian Global Almanac* (Toronto: Macmillan, 1994), 61.
26. Yvonne Mathews-Klein, "How They Saw Us: Images of Women in National Film Board Films of the 1940s and 1950s," *Atlantis* 4, 2 (Spring 1979), 26.
27. M. Susan Bland, "Henrietta the Homemaker, and Rosie the Riveter: Images of Women in Advertising in *Maclean's* Magazine, 1939–50," *Atlantis* 8, 2 (Spring 1983), 70.
28. For one of the most consistent formulations of this nature, see *La terre et le foyer*, 1945–1962; see also Micheline Dumont-Johnson, "La parole des femmes: Les revues féminines, 1938–68," in Fernand Dumont, Jean Hamelin, et Jean-Paul Montminy, eds., *Idéologies au Canada français, 1940–1976* (Québec: Presses de l'Université Laval, 1981), vol. 2, 5–45.
29. *Maclean's* (June 15, 1951).
30. Hilda Neatby, "Are Women Fulfilling Their Obligations to Society?" *Food for Thought* 13 (November 1952), 20–21.
31. See, for example, Line Chamberland, "Remembering Lesbian Bars: Montreal, 1955–1975," in Wendy Mitchinson et al., eds., *Canadian Women: A Reader* (Toronto: Harcourt Brace, 1996), 352–79.
32. Deborah Findlay, "Professional Interests in Medicine's Construction of Women's Reproductive Health," paper presented to the Canadian Sociology and Anthropology Association, Winnipeg, 1986, 29, 10, 21.
33. Dumont-Johnson, "La parole des femmes," 5–45.
34. Gertrude Joch Robinson, "The Media and Social Change: Thirty Years of Magazine Coverage of Women and Work (1950–1977)," *Atlantis* 8, 2 (Spring 1983), 87–111.
35. Ruth Adam, *A Woman's Place, 1910–1975* (London: Chatto and Windus, 1975), 165–67.
36. For a full discussion of advice literature on childrearing during this period, see Katherine Arnup, *Education for Motherhood: Advice for Mothers in Twentieth Century Canada* (Toronto: University of Toronto Press, 1994).
37. Letter from Dr. B.R. to Wendy Mitchinson, August 9, 1993.
38. *Women in Canada: A Statistical Report* (Ottawa: Statistics Canada, 1985), 93, Table 14; Gene Allen, "MDs Urged to Reduce Cesarean Operations," *The Globe and Mail* (July 17, 1991), A5.
39. Rona Maynard, "Can We Avoid the Heartbreak of Birth Defects?" *Chatelaine* (September 1983), 215.
40. Wendy Lill, "Celebrating Sam's Birth," *Herizons* 4, 8 (December 1986), 20.
41. Royal Commission on New Reproductive Technologies, *Proceed with Care* (Ottawa: Government Services Canada, 1993).
42. "Women and Reproduction," *Canadian Journal of Women and the Law* 1, 2 (1986), 407–33.
43. "Same Sex Spousal Benefits," *Broadside* 8, 10 (August/September 1987), 6.

tauhala, "Task Force Calls for Training and Licencing of Midwives," *The Globe Mail* (October 16, 1987), A3.

dian Advisory Council on the Status of Women [CACSW], *Work in Progress: Tracking Women's Equality in Canada* (Ottawa: 1994), 35–6.

46. Carolyn Gossage, *Greatcoats and Glamour Boots: Canadian Women at War, 1939–1945* (Toronto: Dundurn Press, 1991), 123.

47. Susan M. Hartmann, *The Homefront and Beyond: American Women in the 1940s* (Boston: Twain, 1982), 203.

48. Cheryl Foggo, *Pourin' Down Rain* (Calgary: Detselig, 1990), 11, 51–52.

49. L. Schoenfielder and B. Wieser, eds., *Shadow on a Tightrope* (Iowa City, Iowa: Aunt Lute Book Company, 1983); C.M. Donald, *The Fat Woman Measures Up* (Charlotte-town: Ragweed, 1986).

50. Marie Berdugo-Cohen, Yolande Cohen, et Joseph Lévy, *Juifs marocains à Montréal: Témoignages d'une immigration moderne* (Montréal: VLB Éditeur, 1987), 109 [our translation].

51. Pierson, *"They're Still Women,"* chaps. 5 and 6.

52. "Women Smokers Outnumber Men," *The Globe and Mail* (June 5, 1992), A1.

53. *Women in Canada: A Statistical Report*, 2nd ed. (Ottawa: Statistics Canada, 1990), 139.

54. Marion Hilliard, *A Woman Doctor Looks at Love and Life* (Garden City, N.Y.: Doubleday, 1957), 112.

55. Pauline Couture, "Québécois Voices," *The Globe and Mail* (November 16, 1991).

56. Pat Kelly, "Breast Cancer Epidemic Is a Crime," *Kitchener-Waterloo Record* (March 13, 1992), A7.

57. Helen Lenskyj, *Out of Bounds: Women, Sport and Sexuality* (Toronto: Women's Press, 1986), 70.

58. Jean Cochrane, Abby Hoffman, and Pat Kincaid, *Women in Canadian Life: Sports* (Toronto: Fitzhenry and Whiteside, 1977), 54, 56.

59. M. Ann Hall and Dorothy A. Richardson, *Fair Ball: Towards Sex Equality in Canadian Sport* (Ottawa: Canadian Advisory Council on the Status of Women, 1982), 38–48.

60. Lenskyj, *Out of Bounds*, 84–85.

61. Cochrane, Hoffman, and Kincaid, *Women in Canadian Life: Sports*; and Hall and Richardson, *Fair Ball*.

62. Le Collectif Clio, *L'histoire des femmes au Québec depuis quatres siècles* (Montréal: Quinze, 1982), 439.

63. Shirley Stokes, *The Shortest Shadow: A Descriptive Study of the Members of the Federation of Women Teachers' Associations of Ontario* (Toronto: FWTAO, 1969), 3.

64. Ontario, Department of Education, *Courses of Study Grades IX, X, XI and XII, Home Economics, General and Commercial and Vocational Courses*, 1945; *Courses of Study in Grades XI and XII, The Home Economics Option of the General Course, the Commercial Course and the Art Course*, 1955; *Home Economics, Intermediate Division*, 1964.

65. Paula Bourne, Liza McCoy, and Dorothy Smith, "Girls and Schooling: Their Own Critique," unpublished paper, Centre for Women's Studies in Education, OISE, 1994, 1. See also Beth Light, Pat Staton, and Paula Bourne, "Sex Equity Content in History and Contemporary Studies Textbooks," *The History and Social Science Teacher* 25, 1 (Fall 1989), 18–20; Paula Bourne, "Women's Studies in Ontario High Schools: The Case of Women's History," in Debra Martens, ed., *Weaving Alliances: Selected Papers Presented for the Canadian Women's Studies Association at the 1991 and 1992 Learned Societies Conferences* (Ottawa: Canadian Women's Studies Association, 1993).

66. See Jean Barman, Yvonne Hébert, and Don McCaskill, eds., *Indian Education in Canada*, 2 vols. (Vancouver: University of British Columbia Press, 1986–87); Nova Scotian Black Women of Distinction, Past and Present *1990 — A Calendar* (Black Cultural Centre for Nova Scotia); Leo W. Bertley, *Canada and Its People of African Descent* (Pierrefonds, Que.: Bilongo, 1977), 158.

67. Nancy Kiefer, "The Impact of World War II on Female Students at the University of Toronto, 1939–49," University of Toronto, M.A. Thesis, 1984.

68. Interview with Dr. Marjorie Moore, Toronto, April 16, 1987.

69. Leacy, ed., *Historical Statistics*, 2nd ed., W340–57.

70. Basil Frison, *Coeducation in Catholic Schools: A Commentary on the Instruction on Coeducation* (Rome: Commentarium Pro Religiosis, 1959); Anne Gagnon, "The *Pensionnat Assomption*: Religious Nationalism in a Franco-Albertan Boarding School for Girls, 1926–1960," *Historical Studies in Education/Revue d'histoire de l'éducation* 1, 1 (Spring 1989), 95–117; Evelyn M. Brown, *Educating Eve* (Montreal: Palm, 1957), xiv–xv, 92–115.

71. Leacy, ed. *Historical Statistics*, 2nd ed., W389–94, W405–8, W436–42.

72. Thérèse Hamel, "L'enseignement d'hier à aujourd'hui: Les transformations d'un métier 'féminin' au Québec," in *Questions de culture 9: Identités féminines: Mémoire et création* (Quebec: Institut québécois de recherce sur la culture, 1986), 51–70.

73. Jill Vickers and June Adam, *But Can You Type? Canadian Universities and the Status of Women* (Ottawa: Canadian Association of University Teachers, 1977), 59, 32.

74. CACSW, *Work in Progress*, 32; "Women Still Choose Traditional Studies," *University Affairs* (October 1987), 10; *Census of Canada* (1991), Cat. No. 93-329, "Major Fields of Study of Post-Secondary Graduates."

75. *Women in Canada* (1985), 32, 33, 25; Canadian Congress for Learning Opportunities for Women, *Decade of Promise: An Assessment of Canadian Women's Status in Education, Training and Employment, 1976–1985* (Toronto: Avebury Research, 1986), 36–7; Vivian Smith, "Unwilling to Keep Taking It Like a Man," *The Globe and Mail* (April 24, 1993), A1, A4.

76. Margaret Gillett, *We Walked Very Warily: A History of Women at McGill* (Montreal: Eden Press, 1981), 404.

77. *Women in the Labour Force*, 1994 ed. (Ottawa: Statistics Canada, 1994), 37.

78. Sandra Gwyn, *Women in the Arts in Canada* (Ottawa: Information Canada, 1971), 21.

79. Barbara Moore, "Canadian Theatre's Fiery Godmother," *Maclean's* 71, 4 (February 15, 1958), 19.

80. Gwyn, *Women in the Arts*, 31.

81. Frances Rooney, "The Montreal Women's Symphony," *Atlantis* 5, 1 (Fall 1979), 70–82.

82. Gwyn, *Women in the Arts*, 36.

83. Gwyn, *Women in the Arts*, 13.

84. Maria Tippett, *By a Lady: Celebrating Three Centuries of Art by Canadian Women* (Toronto: Viking, 1992), 109–11.

85. Paul-Emile Borduas, "Refus global," in Ramsay Cook, ed., *French-Canadian Nationalism* (Toronto: Macmillan, 1969), 280.

86. Gwyn, *Women in the Arts*, 18.

87. Tippett, *By a Lady*, 150–51.

88. Marie Fleming, "A Tribute Whose Time Has Come," *Art Gallery of Ontario News* 9, 4 (April 1987), 1.

89. Maryon Kantaroff, "Breaking Out of the Female Mould," in Gwen Matheson, ed., *Women in the Canadian Mosaic* (Toronto: Peter Martin Associates, 1976), 287.

90. Linda Abrahams, "Who Counts? — and Who's Counting?" (Toronto: Women's Art Resource Centre, 1994).

91. Coral Ann Howells, *Private and Fictional Words: Canadian Women Novelists of the 1970s and 1980s* (London: Methuen, 1987). See also Janice Williamson, *Sounding Differences: Conversations with Seventeen Canadian Women Writers* (Toronto: University of Toronto Press, 1993).

92. Cynthia Zimmerman, ed., *Taking the Stage: Selections from Plays by Canadian Women* (Toronto: Playwrights Canada Press, 1994); Zimmerman, *Playwriting Women: Female Voices in English Canada* (Toronto: Simon and Pierre, 1994).

93. Rella Braithwaite and Tessa Benn-Ireland, *Some Black Women: Profiles of Black Women in Canada* (Toronto: Sister Vision, 1993), 37, 48.

CHAPTER 14

Reorganizing for Change: Post-War to Present

Women's organizations, like all others, were mobilized for the war so that their members could be available for public service. All the same, some continued, though at a reduced level, their efforts to influence social conditions and public policy. For example, in 1941 the Provincial Council of Women of Ontario started intensive efforts that ten years later produced women's eligibility for jury service.[1] After the war, women's voluntary organizations turned with renewed energy to their own social and political agendas. While they continued to engage in traditional service activities, they also paid sustained attention to issues ranging from economics, taxation, and the status of Native Canadians to urban planning, peace, and the arts. Unfortunately, contemporary comments were often patronizing and dismissive, iden-

tifying the groups as outlets for the idle rich. "Like most club women everywhere," read one typical account, members of the National Council of Women of Canada (NCWC) are "great hands for passing resolutions." Their "resounding outcries against strong drink, atomic warfare and the traffic in Chinese slave girls," the report went on, "come in for some gentle kidding." Such descriptions trivialized the important social issues — such as alcohol abuse, militarism, and the sex-trade in women and children — with which the members of the NCWC were grappling. Nor were contemporary commentators aware of the extraordinarily diverse membership of the Local Councils of Women, which in 1953 included several women's auxiliaries of the United Mineworkers of America and the Locomotive Engineers and Firemen. Along with its core of Protestant groups, the NCWC had both Jewish and Catholic members and member organizations.[2]

ORGANIZED WOMEN AFTER THE WAR

In the immediate post-war period the National Council of Women and the Canadian Federation of Business and Professional Women's clubs lobbied the federal cabinet annually, and played a significant role in advancing the social, political, and economic status of women. In Quebec it was in large part due to the concerted efforts of women's groups that the antiquated Family Code was finally reformed in 1964, under the sponsorship of Quebec's first elected woman provincial legislator, Claire Kirkland-Casgrain. Women's organizations with more specialized membership also continued to be active, though in most cases there is not yet much analysis of their activities, particularly at local levels. For example, the well-established organizations of Ukrainian women responded to the plight of compatriots in displaced-persons' camps in Europe, with particular attention to single mothers, widows, and orphans. As well as sending relief parcels of food, medicine, and clothing, the women's groups protested forced repatriations, lobbied for admission of refugees, and sponsored kindergartens in the camps. Many of the Ukrainian refugees who then made their way to Canada were strongly anti-Communist, and a new Women's Association emerged within the nationalistic Canadian League for the Liberation of the Ukraine.[3] Another example is the National Council of Jewish Women, which had a continuing commitment to promoting social legislation and creating social services, especially for the elderly. In addition to assisting Jewish refugees and to supporting many projects in the newly created state of Israel, the Council gave considerable financial support to the Canadian Mental Health Association, the Canadian Red Cross, and other volunteer groups. Like other federated women's organizations, the Council forwarded to federal and provincial politicians the resolutions passed at regular national meetings; in the post-war years, the topics of these resolutions included a Canadian bill of rights, family planning, and equal pay for equal work.[4]

The larger national groups are better documented. The Federated Women's Institutes of Canada (FWIC) continued to expand their activities and their membership, which was up to 95 000 by 1958. In conjunction with universities and provincial departments of agriculture, local Institutes offered evening courses specifically designed for married women in paid employment. At the national level, the FWIC lobbied for the introduction of equal pay for equal work. Stories abound of the extraordinary lengths to which rural women went to attend WI meetings, especially in wintertime. One devoted New Brunswick member, Mrs. J.D. Ross, found herself "snowbound at home atop a hill and unable to persuade her husband to shovel her out." Undaunted, she climbed aboard her son's "flying saucer" sled. "With a half-knitted afghan in one hand and a fresh pie in the other she sped downhill and thumbed a ride" to the Institute meeting; by the time she arrived home, the path had been shovelled. As noted by Gladys Manness, a woman from a small rural community in Manitoba, membership in the WI was important because it provided the opportunity to discuss national and international issues: "It's broadened our outlook."[5]

In Quebec the *Cercles de fermières* had, in 1940, organized their 645 clubs (with 28 000 members) into district federations independent of the Catholic church. In 1944, some 80 percent of the club's members resisted church attempts to incorporate them into a new, church-dominated auxiliary of the Catholic farmers' union. This assertion of autonomy was not easy for practising Catholic women, for the church went so far as to deny the sacraments in its attempts to control organizational affiliation; fifteen years later it was reported that some priests would still refuse to celebrate mass at conferences sponsored by the *Cercles*.[6] Despite clerical opposition, the *Cercles'* membership had grown to 50 000 by 1945. They developed a program that included a larger emphasis on public policy. In 1947 they drew attention to the economic value of work performed by women in the home, and in 1955 their annual congress urged committees working on the reform of the Quebec Civil Code to increase their efforts to improve the situation of married women in the province.

As the farming population decreased in size and social importance in Canada, members of rural women's groups were less likely to be women directly involved with farm production; their interests accordingly drew closer to those of urban women. In 1957 the church-controlled group of Quebec farm women changed its name to the *Union catholique des femmes rurales* (UCFR) so that it could recruit women who were not involved in farm production. The UCFR, which was about the same size as the *Cercles*, stressed its independence of state funding and discussed in its study groups such feminist issues as contraception.[7]

After experiencing a loss of membership during the war years, Protestant lay-women's groups also flourished during the early 1950s. In the United Church, the combined membership of the Women's Missionary Society and of the Women's Auxiliary almost doubled between 1942 and 1955, rising from 278 789 to 401 757, but membership then started to decline again. In 1962 the two organizations were amalgamated into the United Church Women, as the General Council, composed overwhelmingly of men, argued that the merger would prevent duplication of work. Unfortunately, the change also meant an end to the autonomy that the influential Women's Missionary Society had always exercised in relation to its missions; because the WMS was now subordinate to the national mission boards, men assumed control of what had previously been women's work and women's financial resources.[8]

Rooted in the first women's movement, the established women's groups formed the bridge to the resurgent feminism of the late 1960s. They helped effect tangible improvements in the lives of Canadians, especially children, women, and the elderly. Women's organizations were often ahead of governments. In Quebec, a number of analysts see them as having played a crucial role in the Quiet Revolution's transformation of women's lives.[9] On occasion they called for a thorough restructuring of government policies, and they established and maintained innovative programs until governments were ready to assume responsibility. As one exceptionally prescient journalist concluded, writing at the early date of 1952, "Every town and hamlet is jam-packed with worthwhile activities, all existing on woman-power. . . . Strawberry social thinking is dead."[10]

WOMEN AND PEACE IN THE ATOMIC AGE

The achievement of international peace, always a major concern of Canadian women's groups, assumed a new urgency in the light of Cold War anxieties about nuclear war. Although the Women's International League for Peace and Freedom never regained the membership it had before the war, post-war women's associations took a special interest in international affairs, and particularly in the work of the United Nations. The Women's Institutes and other women's voluntary associations mounted vigorous campaigns to have the federal government ratify the Declaration of Human Rights passed by the United Nations General Assembly in 1950; many of the national federations, such as the FWIC, the NCWC, the BPW, the WCTU, and the YWCA, were part of long-established international federations that acquired formal participatory status in the functional agencies of the United Nations. Women who were prominent in these associations served as Canadian representatives to the United Nations and its affiliated organizations, largely as a result of pressure from women's groups on the Canadian government to make such appointments. In addition, at various levels both the National Council of Women and the BPW included, belonged to, or actively supported the United Nations associations within Canada. The familiarity of the executive members of the BPW with events at the United Nations led them, in 1954, to petition the federal government for ratification of Convention 100 of the International Labour Organization, requiring equal pay for work of equal value, and of the United Nations Convention on Political Rights of Women.

It was directly around the issue of peace that the first significant new postwar national women's organization was born. This was Voice of Women (VOW). Its immediate forerunners were informal local discussion groups formed by women at the end of the 1950s, as they became aware of the dangerous fallout from nuclear tests. The earliest recorded is the Mothers' Committee on Radiation Hazards, founded in West Vancouver in 1958 by Marion Kellerman, who "just wanted safe milk for her children"; other small Radiation Hazards Committees soon appeared across the country.[11] When the Paris Summit Conference on disarmament broke up in May 1960, *Toronto Star* columnist Lotta Dempsey wrote despairingly about the failure and asked what women could do. The response to her article was overwhelming, and a hugely successful mass meeting led to the formation of Voice of Women in July. By the fall of 1961, membership had grown to 5000. Most members were politically inexperienced young women, but they were joined by former members of the socialist and peace movements and by women long active in traditional women's organizations. Thus Michèle Jean, age 22, became secretary of the Quebec branch after her aunt Mariana Jodoin, the first woman senator from Quebec, took her to an organizing meeting at the home of Thérèse Casgrain.[12]

The non-partisan organization initially won general acceptance from the Canadian public, and even the Canadian government listened politely to its representatives. However, when the Voice of Women aggressively criticized the decision of the newly elected Liberal government to accept nuclear weapons in Canada, it lost many early members who were active in the Liberal Party, including Maryon Pearson, the wife of the prime minister. VOW received enormous publicity in 1964, when two of its prominent leaders, Thérèse Casgrain and Kay Macpherson, to their delight, were arrested by the Paris police as a VOW delegation attempted to deliver a letter to the secretary-general of NATO.[13] However, the media increasingly insinuated that the organization was "soft on Communism." Such smears, reminiscent of the red-baiting of the inter-war period and very much part of the McCarthyism of the postwar years, were apparently encouraged by the fact that several of VOW's most active members, including Casgrain and Macpherson, had close connections with the NDP (the CCF's successor as of 1961).

Throughout the 1960s, Voice of Women actively pursued its goal of fostering peace through a wide variety of activities familiar to women's volunteer groups, such as writing briefs, sending delegations to international conferences, and sponsoring peace conferences within Canada. The activities undertaken by Voice of Women to gain peace led its members to question Canada's relationship with the United States, especially in the area of foreign policy. By so doing it placed itself at the forefront of the nationalist movement of the 1960s. Recalling the Cuban Missile Crisis of 1962, the external affairs minister of that period, Howard Green, stated that the vigorous lobbying led by VOW had contributed to the government's decision to delay putting the RCAF on the NORAD alert requested by the United States. Voice of Women also helped inspire the United Nations to declare 1965 International Co-operation Year, and played a significant role in organizing Canadian opposition to the war in Vietnam. Innovative and highly visible campaigns drew on women's specific experience. For example, Ursula Franklin, professor of metallurgy at the University of Toronto, organized the collection of thousands of children's baby teeth in order to demonstrate concretely how the radioactive fallout from bomb tests moved through the food chain into children's bones.

As it pursued its primary goal of the prevention of war, Voice of Women became involved in a number of other issues. For example, its early commitment to bilingualism and biculturalism was fuelled when its 1962 Peace Train delegation to Ottawa, led by Thérèse Casgrain and including hundreds of francophone women, was met by the unilingual Howard Green. Not only did the group gain media attention by

Toronto Voice of Women joins a Stop the Vietnam War march, Easter 1969. Note the rack of camouflage-coloured baby clothes and blankets; VOW members knitted thousands for the children of North Vietnam.

Source: Courtesy of Voice of Women.

demanding a government representative who spoke French, but two members of the delegation—Solange Chaput-Rolland and Gwethalyn Graham—were motivated by this incident to write *Dear Enemies*, an innovative contribution to the public discussion of French–English relations. Voice of Women activists were also prominent in many other progressive causes of the 1960s involving the environment, human rights, science policy, and the status of women. For example, Halifax Voice of Women supported the anti-discrimination movement by carrying out a study of bias against blacks in Nova Scotia. Muriel Duckworth, a long-time member, summed up the connections:

> Somehow we're always having to make these choices of how to separate what is strictly the Peace Movement and what is the Women's Movement, what is the Ecology movement and what is the Human Rights movement. I think these movements are alive and effective because more and more of us see these things as interrelated.

Although the continuing membership of Voice of Women soon declined to about 1000 activists, it did not cease to be a highly audible source of protest. It was of lasting importance because of the many women who moved from VOW to other areas of feminist activism and politics: these included support groups for women interested in mainstream politics, such as Newfoundland's 52% Solution and Toronto's Women for Political Action.[14]

TOWARD A NEW AGENDA FOR WOMEN

The 1960s and 1970s witnessed a resurgence of feminist activity all over the world. In Canada, old organizations supported and assisted newer ones in what has come to be identified as the "second wave" of feminism. The women's movement had worked its way through something like the trough between two waves, and the tide of change was ready to move further up the shore. There was a highly visible proliferation of women's organizations that mobilized an unprecedented range and number of women. Although their aims were recognizable, the groups often had new labels and even new ideologies. Moreover, millions of women who identified with no particular group or ideology became increasingly aware of their identity as women and their need for autonomy and recognition. Looking back over her experiences in the women's movement, one young woman writing in 1980 raised a fundamental issue: "How to measure the ripple effect generated when one person in transition touches another who touches another, the ripples colliding, intersecting, overlapping and causing further ripples?"[15]

The beginning of the public process of change can best be dated to 1966, when existing francophone and anglophone women's organizations began to regroup and reorganize in a way that they had not done for over a generation. In Quebec, after the celebration of the twenty-fifth anniversary of full enfranchisement, representatives of women's groups called together by Thérèse Casgrain agreed to found a new coalition of women's organizations. The result, the *Fédération des femmes du Québec* (FFQ), was the first substantial, enduring new organization of Quebec women since the formation of the suffrage leagues in the 1920s. An umbrella group apparently modelled on the

Councils of Women, the FFQ was, like them, limited by the need to reach consensus among its members. Unlike its predecessors earlier in the century, however, the organization had no religious ties. This important change reflected the reduced influence of the church in Quebec, and especially its decreasing importance for women. Becoming steadily more radical, in 1975 the FFQ took a public position in favour of removing abortion from the Criminal Code.[16]

The year 1966 also saw the founding of the *Association féminine d'éducation et d'action sociale* (AFEAS), which combined two old church-sponsored women's organizations that had been cautiously moving toward union for some years, the *Union catholique des femmes rurales* and the *Cercles d'économie domestique*. Although clerical interest in reasserting control over the Catholic laywomen's organizations had been the first impetus for the merger, the influence of church representatives steadily declined over the years; in 1975, the AFEAS overruled its chaplains and prepared a carefully worded statement that supported the current Canadian system of approval of abortions.[17] Focussing on housewives, the organization pointed out that all women worked, even though not all of them got paid. It developed a special interest in women who worked in family businesses and produced an important study of women's work in the home, *Pendant que les hommes travaillaient, les femmes elles . . .* , updated in 1984 by the AFEAS's daughter group, the *Association des femmes collaboratrices*.[18]

The first president of the AFEAS, Germaine Goudreault, was also a member of the FFQ's first executive, and the two organizations worked closely together. The new coalitions of Quebec women's groups produced a surge of reform activity, which by the end of the 1960s included major revisions of Quebec family law. The *Cercles de fermières* became increasingly interested in public policy, passing resolutions and initiating programs to deal with such widely divergent issues as ecology and sexually transmitted diseases. They remained unaffiliated, however, celebrating their fiftieth anniversary in 1965.[19]

A similar organizational process was also beginning in the rest of Canada. Native women were among the first to regroup, and in British Columbia an Indian Homemakers' Association was in place as early as 1960; the group was still active more than 30 years later. In 1968, Mary Two-Axe Early from the Kahnewake Reserve in Quebec drew together a group of Mohawk women who had lost entitlements under the Indian Act because of marriage to non-status husbands. Calling themselves "A Group of Women from a Canadian Indian Reserve," they made an influential submission to the Royal Commission on the Status of Women (RCSW).[20]

The RCSW itself came into being, in 1967, as a result of a co-ordinated campaign on the part of national women's organizations. There had always been communication and co-operation among the large national women's groups, if only because of the overlapping memberships of many of the women involved. In the 1960s, a loosely organized Canadian Committee on the Status of Women (CCSW) explicitly co-ordinated action, as when they testified before the Special Joint [Parliamentary] Committee on Divorce in 1966.[21] As vice-president of the Canadian Federation of University Women (CFUW), Laura Sabia was active with the CCSW; in 1966, as president of the CFUW, she formally called together representatives of some 30 national women's organizations to discuss their common concerns. The women present decided to call for a royal commission and to incorporate their request in a brief to the prime minister. Doris Anderson, editor of *Chatelaine*, attended the meeting, and in July 1966 she launched a public call for such an inquiry. Reluctant to suggest that "one more be added to the groaning shelfful of past Royal Commissions," she justified the request by referring to the rising level of women's participation in education and the workforce. "What we don't need in a commission," she concluded, "is an all-woman witch-hunt. We do need a forward-looking commission composed equally of impartial men and women prepared to take a cool twentieth-century approach to our problems."[22]

Laura Sabia, who spearheaded the push for the royal commission, was far less temperate. Educated in a Montreal convent school, she told an interviewer that the nuns' obsequious deference to the priests had been an early cause of her own "revulsion towards a male-dominated society." In later years, she attributed her independence to the strength of her parents, but also to having been an outsider in Canadian society: "As a child, I hated being 'Italian.' I resented the 'dirty-dago-wap syndrome' of the twenties and early thirties." When she graduated from McGill University, instead of following her plan to go to law school, she married, raised four children in St. Catharines, Ontario, and plunged into community activities, serving on the city council and hosting a radio hotline show.[23]

The 32-member Committee on Equality for Women (CEW) that Sabia drew together in 1966 consisted of leaders of the large continuing women's federations, including groups that had earlier been the most vocal and consistent campaigners for woman suffrage.[24] Their feminism can be inferred from their ready response to Sabia's appeal; in the same year, similar organizations in the United States had rebuffed suggestions that they become publicly involved in issues of women's equality. In addition, the 6-year-old Voice of Women was actively involved in the Committee. Although the *Fédération des femmes du Québec* did not take part in drawing up the presentation to the prime minister, its leaders shared the Committee's concern that the women of Canada should appear united by having representation from both francophone and anglophone women's groups; Thérèse Casgrain, along with lawyer Réjane Laberge-Colas, then president of the FFQ, joined the CEW's delegation to Ottawa. Women's groups from all three federal political parties also supported the brief calling for a royal commission, as did a considerable number of well-established women's professional and service groups.[25]

The Pearson government ignored this first decorous, mildly posed request from the Committee, provoking Laura Sabia into what *The Globe and Mail* described as an "ultimatum to the Government: establish a royal commission or face the consequences." Sabia's son, Michael, recalled the incident:

> Picture, if you will, a typical scene from our household in the 60s. Mother is preparing dinner. Father, a surgeon, and his 10-year-old son are waiting to be fed. The phone rings, and a brief discussion ensues, mother calmly saying: "Tell the Prime Minister that I will lead an uprising of Canadian women."[26]

She said that she would march three million women on Ottawa (the combined memberships of the groups that had supported the appeal to the government). Sabia has since noted repeatedly that she would have been lucky to mobilize *three* women for an actual march.

This gesture has become legendary, with Sabia and others convinced that it produced the Royal Commission on the Status of Women, which was formally established in February 1967. Certainly Sabia's bravado captured the headlines. And in terms of specific timing, it seems clear that the Committee's activities served as a catalyst for the commission that had been sought in vain by Judy LaMarsh; LaMarsh had followed Ellen Fairclough as the second solitary woman in the federal cabinet.[27] More generally, the explanation for the commission is probably to be found in the interrelated patterns of education and work that characterized women's lives in the 1960s, patterns that also explain women's renewed responsiveness to feminism. Strains had developed as a result of the combination of unchanged social attitudes with major changes in women's employment and education. The second-wave women's movement was to articulate the grievances that resulted.

In addition, an expanding economy required a vast infusion of labour. In Canada, the head of the federal Department of Labour's Women's Bureau, Sylva Gelber, was concerned that the failure "to utilize our human resources" (meaning women) to their full capability was "to deny to the nation the productivity essential for the maintenance of a high standard of living." Ten industrialized nations, including the United States, had already begun to look into the problems and economic possibilities represented by the status of women. In Parliament, where the Liberal government lacked an absolute majority, the New Democratic Party (which held the balance of power) used the issue of a women's commission as yet another handy weapon against the government; the NDP was urged on by its only woman MP, Grace MacInnis. By 1965 Canadian women were voting at the same rate as men, and participating in election campaign activities almost as frequently.[28] The CEW's specific request — for a royal commission — was ideally suited to the double purposes of getting the necessary information about fully integrating women into the workforce while also appeasing and, if necessary, defusing feminist complaints.

The general mandate of the commission, announced early in 1967, was "to inquire and report upon the status of women in Canada, and to recommend what steps might be taken by the Federal Government to ensure for women equal opportunities with men in all aspects of Canadian society."[29] The presidency of the commission was handed over to the first woman to head a royal commission in Canada: Florence Bird, then a broadcaster at the CBC specializing in the history of working women, was known to the prime minister through the Canadian Institute for International Affairs, for which she had written a pamphlet on the rights of women in 1950.[30] The usual regional and political concerns dictated the composition of the commission, which included two men, one of them from Quebec, as well as Quebec academic Jeanne Lapointe, who was selected because of her experience with the Parent Commission on education. All the same, the interests of women's groups were heeded, and members also included Lola Lange, active in the Alberta Farm Women's Union, and juvenile court judge Doris Ogilvie from New Brunswick. Elsie Gregory MacGill was effectively the vice-president; an informed and persuasive third-generation feminist, she was also a westerner, the first woman aviation engineer in Canada, past president of the Canadian Federation of Business and Professional Women's Clubs, and partly disabled from polio. The young research director, sociologist Monique Bégin, a protégée of Thérèse Casgrain, had been an activist in the Montreal Catholic school board, the University Women's Clubs, and the FFQ.

There were no minority, working-class, Native, or even young women on the commission itself, but the concerns of many such women were set out in the 469 briefs and approximately 1000 letters it received, and, above all, in the public hearings that were held in fourteen cities in all ten provinces and the Territories. The commission deliberately used its unprecedentedly wide-ranging public sessions as a device for public education, and also commissioned the first systematic studies of the situation of Canadian women. Initial media responses were sceptical if not frivolous. They provided "a field day for some cartoonists," Elsie MacGill recalled:

> These were so out of touch with reality about women's shapes and styles that they depicted women in the audience as simpering, large, bosomy, and wearing hats, although simpering had gone out with Queen Victoria, the popular fashion model was the very thin, very narrow, very flat-chested Twiggy, and hats had vanished from daily wear.[31]

But the media and public alike moved to a grudging interest and respect. "The petitioners weren't just strident suffragettes in garden-party hats," wrote one woman journalist who went to the commission's first Ottawa meeting as a self-described "lapsed feminist," nor were they merely women preoccupied with "female neuroses." Indeed, they included "the dispossessed of Canadian society . . . The Other Canada":

> In Yellowknife a Métis girl asked if the Chairman of the Commission could come to her prison cell; eighteen years old, pregnant and in despair, she'd been jailed for trying to kill herself by swallowing hairspray.[32]

The commission reported in 1970, having expanded its mandate to cover the many relevant areas of policy under provincial jurisdiction, such as health, education, and family law. Its report spelled out four principles: (1) women should be free to choose whether or not to take employment outside their homes; (2) the care of children is a responsibility to be shared by the mother, the father, and society; (3) society has an obligation to women because of pregnancy and childbirth, so that special treatment related to maternity will always be necessary; and (4) in certain areas women will, for an interim period, require special treatment to overcome the adverse effects of discriminatory practices.[33] In addition, it singled out for attention a number of particularly disadvantaged groups of women, such as those dispossessed of Indian status under the notorious Section 12(1)(b) of the Indian Act. "We were liberal, and pragmatic feminists," Monique Bégin reflected twenty years later, "yet parts of the report were, and still are, purely utopian in the eyes of the Canadian state, although these sections appeared to the commissioners as plain common sense."[34]

Deliberately published as a single, inexpensive volume, the report was a bestseller. In addition, the NCWC and the FFQ prepared shorter digests in English and French that were widely distributed through women's organizations. After a careful reading of the 167 recommendations it contained, a *Toronto Star* columnist told his readers that the report was nothing less than "a bomb already primed and ticking . . . packed with more explosive potential than any device manufactured by terrorists" and represented "a call to revolution."[35] In less inflammatory language, we can say that the second wave of feminism in Canada now had its agenda, an agenda that could transform Canadian society.

Feminists had produced the royal commission and its report through a familiar process of coalitions and pressures on government. Those who had been active in connection with the royal commission remained at the forefront during the follow-up period. Impatient when the government did not produce immediate responses to the commission's report, Laura Sabia led the Committee on Equality for Women as it evolved into the National Ad Hoc Committee on the Status of Women in Canada, which met during 1971 and early 1972 and then in turn became the ongoing National Action Committee on the Status of Women (NAC). This coalition now also incorporated representatives of new sorts of groups: women's liberation, radical feminism, and status of women. The Ad Hoc Committee presented a substantial brief to the government, incorporating three priority goals: expansion of daycare, insertion of "sex" as a prohibited basis of discrimination under Canadian human rights provisions, and decriminalization of abortion. The adoption of the third priority lost it the support of Catholic groups, but brought on board several groups that supported freedom of reproductive choice.[36]

The "Strategy for Change" conference that inaugurated NAC in the spring of 1972 set a pattern of co-operation among widely differing feminist groups, with Voice of Women president Helen Tucker in the chair, Elsie Gregory MacGill as keynote speaker, the radical-feminist Toronto New Feminists running the workshops, and more than 500 women from more than 40 groups present. A group including representatives of Toronto Women's Liberation and the seasoned union militant Madeleine Parent gave the organizing committee its first taste of disruption as they protested what they viewed as the excessively moderate approach of the conference. A "radical caucus" grabbed the microphone and called for, among other things, all-women media crews. In the end, the conference agreed to endorse all of the royal commission's recommendations except the proposal that status-of-women councils be appointed at all levels of government.[37] Laura Sabia then became NAC's first president.

NAC's initial program was, basically, the *Report of the Royal Commission on the Status of Women in Canada*. Its first move to extend that agenda to wider issues of national policy occurred in 1974. Under the leadership of its second president, trade unionist Grace Hartman, the group objected to wage and price controls because, among other things, they made it difficult to raise women's pay to make it equal to men's. A founder of the Manitoba Action Committee on the Status of Women, June Menzies was vice-chair of the board that imposed the controls. This was an early taste of the problems that would emerge for feminists as more women became participants in formal structures of power.[38]

After the publication of the RCSW's report, one of the central projects of many women's groups was to have governments set up official, state-funded advisory bodies on the status of women. The federal council (founded in 1973) was eventually joined by counterparts in each province. Laura Sabia left the first federal Advisory Council on the Status of Women to head the provincial one appointed shortly after in Ontario. Many of these groups did important, innovative work. For example, in New Brunswick *LES FAM* (*Liberté, Egalité, Sororité: Les Femmes acadiennes de Moncton*), the first explicitly feminist group in the province, pushed the government into appointing an advisory council in 1977; in 1979, that council produced the first Canadian publication on family violence.[39] In spite of such accomplishments, however, the advisory councils often encountered bureaucratic resistance, and they risked co-optation. Although the Ontario council was able to force action on family property law, Sabia finally resigned in response to a frustration shared by many women activists, exploding in her *Toronto Sun* column: "Today is the day of my liberation! Allelujia!

I have tossed the albatross of the 'Status of Women' from around my neck and resigned as chairman of Ontario's Status of Women Council." She felt that women had been outmanoeuvred:

> From "Royal Commission" to "Councils" we have been kept busy pushing paper. "Do advise us," say the astute politicians, "we're such numbskulls; tell us what to do." And we fell for it, God help us, hook, line and sinker.[40]

New non-governmental status-of-women organizations oriented specifically to the RCSW's report soon also appeared to press for provincial-level implementation of the Commission's recommendations. In Manitoba, a Volunteer Committee had co-ordinated women's groups in presenting a joint brief to the royal commission; four months after the report was issued, it became the Manitoba Action Committee on the Status of Women.[41] By the end of the decade, most provinces had similar voluntary groups. They varied so greatly that it is difficult to generalize about them, but status-of-women committees (or action committees) tended not to include men. They were usually small and informally structured, and sometimes completely unsubsidized. Concentrating on lobbying provincial cabinets and civil servants, they provided a policy-focussed form of feminist activism for young professional women who did not have explicit ideological commitments. Their members were actively involved in NAC. For example, the Manitoba Committee, which had been a member of NAC's ad hoc predecessor in 1971, continued uninterruptedly as a member from then on, and the Ontario Committee on the Status of Women provided many of the presidents of NAC. These volunteer groups were influential at the provincial level; in general, their professional competence and expertise seem to have given them access to governments, especially to bureaucracies.[42]

In Quebec, no voluntary status-of-women committee developed, in part because of the effectiveness of the exceptionally well-funded provincial *Conseil du statut de la femme*, which in 1978 published a comprehensive document entitled *Pour les Québécoises: Égalité et indépendance*. Volunteer pressure activism in Quebec was also in part pre-empted by the nationalist, social-democratic *Parti Québécois* (PQ), formed in 1968, which had an active women's committee and included influential, though not always feminist, women. When the PQ took office in 1976, Lise Payette, the first woman cabinet minister in Quebec and the first person to have responsibility for the status of women, pushed hard for change and helped to produce major improvements in areas like family law. It was in 1980, in the words of one analyst, that Quebec civil law finally broke with the old Napoleonic Code and recognized women "as complete human beings" equal to their spouses.[43]

WOMEN'S LIBERATION

Beginning in the last years of the 1960s, many women carried out a painstaking, sometimes painful reappraisal of their lives as women. Women's difficulties, they came to understand, were systemic rather than the result of individual bad luck or incompetence. The most routine and unlikely incidents could produce a "click" of understanding, a shared awareness of what women had in common. One woman recalls "checking neurotic hostess reflexes when a male dinner guest complains there are no serviettes on the table: knuckles white with the effort not to jump up when he could more easily reach them, we mystify him with roars of laughter at our shared struggle."[44] "Consciousness-raising," whether informal or based on the organized meetings of small discussion groups, was part of what defined the second wave of feminism; it motivated many women to work for public and political responses to their personal situation.

The women's liberation movement (WLM), initially a product of the international student movement of the mid-1960s, became public toward the end of the decade. Young women shared their dissatisfaction with the treatment of women in the militant student movement, and also with that movement's failure to take seriously the problems of women in the larger society. The events that unfolded at a conference held in Montreal in 1969 to protest U.S. involvement in Vietnam were typical. As participant Naomi Wall recalled:

> On the final day . . . all hell broke loose. Women refused to discuss the resolutions or the war until every woman present who had something to say about the conference was heard. The men went wild. How could these women insist on addressing their concerns as women when men were dying in Vietnam? . . . Who gave a damn whether they were listened to?[45]

Eventually the women's caucuses broke away from their mixed-sex origins. But they kept their vocabulary—the "liberation" of women echoed the liberation of colonized peoples, with Quebec included by Quebec theorists. They brought with them to the women's movement the views of the 1960s counterculture, including a preference for openness and self-expression and the rejection of customary standards of dress, behaviour, and sexuality. Furthermore, the members of women's liberation groups kept the analytic and organizational preferences of the student movement. Unlike the majority of women's groups, which inclined to relatively formal structures and to the conventional tactics of lobbies and pressure groups, women's liberation, whose goal was revolutionary change, relied on consciousness-raising through small, unstructured cells and through demonstrations. And whereas the older feminists had a perspective that combined women's maternal and family concerns with a liberal concern for equality, the beliefs of the younger feminists tended to be closely connected to Marxism or socialism. By the end of the 1960s, significant groupings of Canada's women activists were committed to socialist belief systems.

In 1967 a women's caucus at the University of Toronto rebelled against the male chauvinism in a student organization, the New Left Committee. As a result, Toronto's was one of the first five women's liberation groups existing in North America. In 1968 Toronto Women's Liberation (TWL) was followed by developments on the west coast, beginning with the Women's Caucus in Vancouver. At Simon Fraser University, two students rewrote the Communist Manifesto as the "Feminine" Manifesto (they thought the word "feminist" was too confrontational), ending "women of the world unite, you have nothing to lose but your apron strings." By September 1968 a Women's Caucus at Simon Fraser's Student Society was offering abortion counselling and referral, and by 1969 they had their own office and organization. Montreal Women's Liberation, made up of anglophone groups that started at Sir George Williams and Concordia Universities, followed much the same route and time frame.[46] The media were fascinated by the "libbers" and their more or less outrageous street demonstrations, often about such seemingly novel and certainly sensational issues as abortion and sexuality. The movement's members were happy to be described in the inflammatory language of "revolution," and they distrusted the co-operation with government in which the rest of the Canadian women's movement still had such confidence.

The first public action by Toronto Women's Liberation was a protest against a wintertime "outdoor bikini" contest in January 1969. In the words of one TWL member:

> A beautiful sister . . . stunned the organizers and onlookers by emerging fully clad under her borrowed furs, with a sign: "I Have A Mind." . . . The winner, a McMaster University philosophy student, was asked to comment on the incident. She was uncomprehending. Disgusted with being treated as a sex object? "That's what a girl wants most."[47]

In 1969, additional women's liberation groups started in Regina, Saskatoon, Winnipeg, Ottawa, Guelph, Hamilton, Halifax, Sudbury, Thunder Bay, and Edmonton.[48] Some apparently drew membership not just from students, but also from women who were members of other radical groups.

In Quebec, francophone women's liberation groups grew out of the Quebec student groups committed to Quebec nationhood. Montreal's *Front pour la libération des femmes du Québec* (FLF) dated its own start to a public protest in Montreal in 1969 by women calling themselves the *Front commun des Québécoises*. A response to the fact that the Montreal city administration had banned all demonstrations after a wave of trade union and other leftist activity, the street action used classic suffragist tactics: the women chained themselves together, and the fire department had to be called out to cut them free. The demonstration was initially an attempt to exploit possible police chivalry toward women, but it suggested to some of those involved that women could, and should, move out of a passive role in politics. The FLF's 1971 manifesto focussed on "colonization" rather than "oppression," on the experience of women in the Quebec independence movement, and on the absence of any mention of women in the earlier manifesto of the *Front pour la libération du Québec*. The FLF's first feminist action was a demonstration on Mothers' Day in 1970 in support of free access to abortion. The next year their *Cellule X: Action Choc!* demonstrated in protest against the continued exclusion of women from juries in Quebec. Francophone women's liberation supporters also arranged to have the McGill *Birth Control Handbook* translated into French and, along with members of the anglophone Montreal Women's Liberation, participated in the abortion referral service started at McGill. Before the end of the decade, however, the anglophone and francophone WLM groups in Quebec had permanently ceased to co-operate.[49]

Women's liberation was initially a continent-wide movement and also an international one. The trans-Canadian women's liberation movement made its first significant public appearance with the 1970 Abortion Caravan, probably the most innovative of a wide range of activities and organizations that responded to the failure of the 1969 legislation to remove abortion from the Criminal Code. The three-vehicle caravan took seventeen women across the country from Vancouver to Ottawa in two weeks, stopping along the way for street theatre and meetings. Hundreds more women joined en route and helped disrupt the House of Commons on the Monday after Mother's Day by chaining themselves to the Visitors' Galley. Two days earlier, they had left on the prime minister's doorstep a coffin symbolizing the victims of backstreet abortions. The Abortion Caravaners who disrupted Parliament recognized that they were using tactics militant suffragists had previously used in the United States and Britain. But the Canadian movement was at the same time significantly different, even though some of its early leaders were American immigrants to Canada. For one thing, the Abortion Caravan was modelled on the "On to Ottawa" Trek that took place during the Great Depression.[50] Acting explicitly in a tradition of women's activism in Canada, Winnipeg Women's Liberation successfully turned Nellie McClung's play *Votes for Women* into a musical. They presented it along with skits on current issues, including one that dramatized abortion with "coat hangers and bloody sheets as props."[51] Here, as in other ways, young women looked back to the roots of Canadian feminism, embracing leaders like Nellie McClung as heroes for the movement. Later, feminists would be critical of the race, class, and heterosexist biases of many first-wave leaders.[52]

In Quebec, local heroes were more difficult to find. When the *Front pour la libération des femmes* declined an invitation to join the Abortion Caravan, women's struggles were placed squarely in the centre of independentist politics in Quebec. The FLF, it said, was challenging the present Quebec government and the future Quebec nation to be more responsive to women than the federal government.[53] Such views made collaboration with anglophone women's liberation groups virtually impossible, even when linguistic barriers could be surmounted. Furthermore, relatively few young French-Canadian women were likely to join separate women's organizations that might divert energy away from a political struggle based on class as well as nationalist interests.[54]

Women's liberation in Quebec did produce a succession of small autonomous action groups and a series of feminist newspapers. Several of these were widely read and influential in spite of their short life spans. Best known were *Québécoises debouttel* and the radical-feminist *Les têtes de pioche*, a project of experimental writers that included Nicole Brossard. *Pluri-elles* was founded in 1976 by socialist feminists in an attempt to co-ordinate the many small autonomous groups; in October 1978 it was renamed *Des luttes et des rires des femmes*. None of these journals survived into the next decade. The successive names suggest the tendency toward pluralism,

Francine Volker, Marcella Lustig, Valerie Van Volz, and Diane Grant of Toronto's Redlight Theatre celebrate the suffragists in What Glorious Times They Had, *May 1974.*

Source: Courtesy of Francine Volker.

greater diversity, and mutual tolerance among Quebec's small autonomous feminist groups. By contrast, the more numerous Marxist and nationalist feminists soon came to concentrate, respectively, on action in the women's committees of the powerful trade union organizations and in the *Parti Québécois*.[55]

Outside Quebec, pan-Canadian nationalism was crucial to the women's movement, accounting to a large degree for the co-operation and even convergence between the supporters of women's liberation and other women activists. Anti-Americanism played a significant role, since the closest threat to Canadian national identity had always been American. Within the student movement, there was increasing hostility to the American war resisters who had come to Canada expecting to lead the left. Women's liberation groups shared the concerns of the student organizations. "The problem the Canadian left faces is not the draft," stated a 1969 Toronto Women's Liberation pamphlet; "it is American imperialism."[56] Those who founded Canadian women's liberation also shared with Voice of Women, as well as the surviving first-wave groups, the Canadian feminist conviction that women were better able than men to protect Canadian values. Central issues included both the equal treatment of women and active resistance to American influence.

In addition, many student- and community-based women's groups turned increasingly toward providing direct services for poor and needy women. The services they provided focussed on issues related to women's bodies and sexuality, which now meant abortion referral and counselling, rape crisis centres, and transition houses and other facilities for battered women. Most were deliberately organized according to a consensual model designed as a contrast to male-style hierarchy. By 1983, a national clearinghouse identified 146 facilities for abused women across Canada.[57] The motive was certainly new—a political attempt to sensitize women to the abuses of the patriarchal, capitalist state. The result, which some found dismaying, was similar — once again, women volunteers were providing social services the state neglected.

By the early 1970s, women's liberation groups were already experiencing breaks and schisms. The majority of Canadian women's liberation groups came to define themselves as "socialist feminists," to describe their focus on the ways in which capitalism and patriarchy were related so that both acted as systems of oppression for women. Independent socialist-feminist groups such as Saskatoon Women's Liberation, Bread and Roses of Vancouver, and the International Women's Day Committee in Toronto became a significant element of the women's movement in English Canada, sometimes participating in NAC but influential mainly on a local or provincial level. A key slogan was "A socialist who is not a feminist lacks breadth. A feminist who is not a socialist lacks strategy."[58] A major focus on women in the industrial labour force produced an emphasis on workplace activism, including attempts to found women's or feminist unions. Socialist feminists also devoted major attention to childcare, considered necessary to facilitate women's paid labour; co-operative daycare centres were among the earliest projects in both Vancouver and Toronto.[59]

Other women opted for a feminism that considered gender rather than class structures to be central to women's oppression. Those who identified themselves as "radical feminists" chose "to concentrate exclusively on the oppression of women as women and not as workers, students, etc."[60] Radical feminism did not grow out of any existing form of mainstream theory; its relationship to the other sorts of feminism became a major theoretical problem for second-wave feminists.[61] For radical feminists, feminism was related to asserting the uniqueness of women's situation; their earliest goal tended to be obliteration of gender roles as a basis of oppression. This logic produced efforts to get permission for girls to wear jeans instead of skirts to school, as well as major attention to sex-role stereotyping in literature and teaching materials. Over time, radical feminists tended to shift from the goal of abolishing sex roles to a focus on the importance of women's specific experience and values. If patriarchy was the oppressor, as embodied in men's attitudes and behaviour, it was reasonable to conclude that female values and practices were preferable. Bonnie Kreps, who had been active in New York radical feminism, appears to have started the first radical-feminist group in Canada in 1969 by walking out of a Toronto Women's Liberation meeting that refused to accept that "women were oppressed in the household."[62] She was followed or later joined by women somewhat older than the liberationists, young faculty or faculty wives, or sometimes career women, who felt uncomfortable with both the youth and the Marxist orthodoxy of women's liberation.[63]

Radical feminists tended to be unconventional, explicitly theoretical, insistent on consciousness-raising and on linking the personal and the political; it was out of radical feminism that some women moved to personal or political lesbianism and separatism. Such a style made them very different from non-liberationist women's groups, while their rejection of class analysis separated them from the original women's liberation movement. Toronto New Feminists voluntarily dissolved in 1973, agreeing that their raised consciousness ought now to be applied in their daily work, which tended to be in academic and artistic circles. Other radical-feminist groups seem to have existed in Sarnia, Oshawa, and Saskatchewan; as well, one anglophone group in Montreal, the Feminist Communication Collective, issued a newsletter aimed primarily at immigrant women.[64]

Nation-wide, the influence of radical feminism can, in general terms, be traced in second-wave groups organized around women's specific experience and values. Women Against Violence Against Women (WAVAW), which started in Canada in 1977 to carry out "spontaneous street action," had a clearly radical-feminist orientation. Such groups, including especially active ones in British Columbia, protested "snuff" movies, sadistic pornography for which the women being filmed were beaten, tortured, or even murdered. The activities of WAVAW groups included "Take Back the Night" marches, beginning in 1981, calling for streets safe from violence against women; Vancouver WAVAW started a rape crisis centre in 1982. Take Back the Night marches continued to be frequent, especially in large urban centres but also in small towns such as Prince Rupert, British Columbia, where in 1994 more than 150 women and children marched "to express the anger and frustration felt by women and children who are not safe in their own communities."[65]

Both socialist and radical feminism had a major impact on Women's Studies as the field developed in Canada, beginning in the late 1960s and early 1970s. A strong role was played in Canadian Women's Studies programs by socialist feminists and their analysis of women's paid and unpaid work. An important paper originating in the discussions of the socialist Vancouver Women's Caucus and written by Margaret Benston in 1969 identified housework as a significant category of labour; from this beginning, Canadian socialist-feminist analysts developed interpretations of "reproductive labour" as a parallel to "productive labour."[66] Sociologist Dorothy

Smith's critiques of conventional social science attracted international attention, especially her argument that the "everyday world" was the best starting point for theorizing about women's lives. Radical-feminist theorist Mary O'Brien, a former midwife who came to university late in life, coined the term "malestream" to highlight the androcentricity of mainstream political philosophy.[67] More widely, the radical-feminist emphasis on women's "difference" or "specificity" served as a major intellectual justification for study and research focussing on women. By the 1980s, Women's Studies were well established in a large number of Canadian universities, supported by three journals and by five regional Women's Studies chairs endowed by the Department of the Secretary of State. Many of the first generation of instructors were women's movement activists. But integrating women's experiences and perceptions into existing academic disciplines was a painfully slow process.

Finally, radical feminism was influential in the development of feminist separatism in Canada, both in its cultural dimensions and in the form of radical lesbianism or lesbian separatism. Radical-feminist attention to male dominance encouraged awareness of heterosexism and the analysis of lesbians' situation in a society dominated by heterosexual values. Some explicitly lesbian-feminist groups and lesbian service organizations were organized, but they tended to be shortlived. Under the auspices of the YWCA, the first national lesbian conference was held in Toronto in 1973 and, shortly afterward, *Long Time Coming*, the first lesbian newsletter in Canada, started in Montreal. When a Women's Place was founded in Vancouver, a small group of women took over the top floor for a Lesbian Resource Centre; the B.C. Federation of Women had a lesbian caucus in action at its organizing conference in 1974 and unanimously passed a formal policy on lesbianism two years later. The Lesbian Organization of Toronto (LOOT) survived for four years; the francophone *Coop-femmes* was started in Montreal in February 1977; and for some ten years, beginning in 1978, a national Lesbian Mothers' Defense Fund supported women threatened with loss of child custody because of their sexual orientation.[68]

The different sorts of women's organizations managed to co-operate on specific projects, even though they had different ideological perspectives. Voice of Women's orientation toward maternity—as reflected, for example, in its continuing campaigns against war toys—aligned VOW with radical feminists in the effort to eliminate sex-role stereotyping. Socialist-feminist interest in the economic dimension of domestic labour was an additional basis of possible agreement among women's groups, for the household, central for traditional women's organizations, was also crucial to the analyses made by radical feminists. The result was often joint action on specific issues, however much socialist-feminist theory condemned the concept of "sisterhood" as apolitical and inimical to class analysis.[69] In the 1970s, campaigns to include "sex," "sexual harassment," and "sexual preference" in human rights codes mobilized groups ranging from women's auxiliaries of the industrial unions to the most extreme radical feminists. A similar spectrum of groups protested sexism in advertising, in textbooks, and in the media more generally. Persistent coalitions responded to the violence and hostility to women expressed in widely distributed, increasingly sadistic, hard-core pornography, and carried on the long-drawn-out battles about reproductive freedom.

Abortion was a key issue that generated joint action among women in Canada, including many who had found the rhetoric of the women's liberation movement daunting. "Here was something I could support unequivocally," wrote Cerise Morris,

A pro-choice march in Montreal. The banner announces sponsorship by the national [Quebec] coalition for unrestricted abortion.

Source: Courtesy of Claudine Kurtzman.

a student at that time. "The right of a woman to legal abortion affects me personally —affects women of all classes and political beliefs."[70] Before the Royal Commission on the Status of Women reported, its relatively liberal recommendations were pre-empted by the 1969 revisions of the Criminal Code, which retained the criminality of abortions, permitting them only when performed by a doctor in an accredited hospital under specified conditions. Among these was certification by a three-doctor committee that continuation of the pregnancy would threaten the life or health of the mother; the pregnant woman was not allowed to appear before this therapeutic abortion committee (TAC) to present her own case. Geographic access was uneven, for hospitals were not required to establish TACs. The delays were often substantial and dangerous. The 1969 reforms accordingly disappointed many, and women and sympathetic men mobilized across Canada in a lengthy struggle to make abortion legal. Much of the activity focussed around the figure of Dr. Henry Morgentaler, a Holocaust survivor who defined himself as a humanist and became the chief symbol of the "pro-choice" movement. Morgentaler performed abortions in defiance of the law, announcing that he was carrying on legitimate acts of civil disobedience. Although he was repeatedly arrested and brought to trial, three Quebec juries and one in Ontario refused to find him guilty.[71]

Beginning in 1974, CARAL (initially the Canadian Association for the Repeal of the Abortion Laws and then the Canadian Abortion Rights Action League) led a coalition that also included more-radical groups such as the British Columbia and Ontario Coalitions for Abortion Clinics. In 1971 proactive anti-abortion groups became publicly visible, reacting to "pro-choice" activities with the first of what would become annual demonstrations in Ottawa calling for an end to all abortions. A pregnancy crisis service, Birthright, had been started in 1968 in Toronto by a Catholic laywoman, Louise Summerhill, to provide support for unmarried mothers. The world's first such service, it eventually comprised more than 600 centres in Canada, the United States, and Africa. But Birthright consistently refused to move toward any sort of active opposition to abortion.[72] Other "pro-life" activists, supported by the Catholic church as well as by fundamentalist and right-wing organizations, systematically picketed the abortion clinics that Morgentaler established, first in Ontario and Manitoba, harassing both the staff and the women who came to have abortions.

The *Canadian Charter of Rights and Freedoms* made it possible, on January 28, 1988, for the Supreme Court to strike down the federal law on abortion as unconstitutional. The judges found that the law, as enacted, interfered with women's security of person as guaranteed under the Charter. The Court's first woman justice, Bertha Wilson, took the argument one stage further: "forcing a woman, under threat of criminal sanction, to carry a foetus to term unless she meets certain criteria unrelated to her own priorities and aspirations, is a profound interference with a woman's body and thus a violation of security of the person." Even Madam Justice Wilson, however, found that it would be acceptable in constitutional terms for the state to limit abortions at an advanced stage of pregnancy. A compromise bill for recriminalization that satisfied no one was finally defeated by a tie vote in the Senate on January 31, 1991. Women senators voted as a bloc against the measure; Mira Spivak, a Conservative senator, was quoted as saying, "It's a step forward for women in being able to control their own destiny and choose what to do with their bodies."[73]

By 1992, according to a nation-wide poll, 79 percent of those surveyed agreed that "an abortion is a medical decision that should rest with the woman in consultation with her physician." Anti-abortion groups continued their attack, however. Morgentaler's Toronto clinic was bombed and partly destroyed in 1983 and then completely burned down in 1992; in November 1994 a Vancouver doctor who performed abortions was shot and seriously injured while he was eating breakfast in his kitchen; and early in 1995, after death threats, two of the four doctors who were targeted decided to cease performing abortions at the Victoria General Hospital.[74] After the 1988 Supreme Court decision, the issue of access became a provincial matter. Policies ranged from Ontario's, with establishment of freestanding clinics and full reimbursement of the costs of the procedure, to those in Prince Edward Island, which permitted abortions only in hospitals but had no hospital willing to perform them. In 1995, Dr. Morgentaler was still struggling with the government of New Brunswick, attempting to provide abortion services in a province that had none.[75]

THE WOMEN'S MOVEMENT: GENDER PLUS

In a variety of settings, women continued to organize to bring about fundamental change. Many of them rejected identification with feminism or with the women's movement, but their actions often belied their words. Women's caucuses or committees attached to mixed-sex institutions such as unions and churches represented one form of collective action. Such groups multiplied in the 1970s and 1980s, as did a new generation of separate women's organizations; the process continued into the 1990s, with more groups focussed on multiple identity, particularly women's various racial and ethnic affiliations. The newly mobilized members of these organizations were often newly militant, but they continued long-established traditions of women organizing within and for those communities marginalized by Canada's white, European, and Christian mainstream populations.

Iroquois women explained their right to participate in policymaking on the basis of "the matriarchal roots of the Six Nations Iroquois Confederacy." On occasion, they experienced serious internal conflicts as they attempted to assert their claims, fearing that it was a betrayal of cultural autonomy to appeal to white women, white women's organizations, and the white men's government over the heads of their own leaders. Nevertheless, aboriginal women developed acceptable rationales for organizing separately, initially in support of one another. A Maliseet of the Tobique Reserve in New Brunswick, Caroline Ennis, explained how it was that many Indian women got started in political activism:

> When I got involved in the demonstrations and lobbying, it wasn't for the non-status thing; it was purely a women's thing — because of the kinds of things they were doing to women like my mother — to women like Yvonne who used to get beat up by her husband all the time.[76]

Native women organized to deal concretely with problems including disease and alcohol and drug abuse, and began to challenge the assimilationist systems of education and public health that, respectively, shipped children off to residential schools and condemned tuberculosis patients to long hospital stays away from home. "Aboriginal women must provide the direction that encourages the Nation's warriors to respond as is appropriate to protect our children," stated the Ontario Native Women's Association, founded in 1971 in Thunder Bay.[77] In 1973, the Native Women's Association of Canada was formed with the goal of representing the women of all the varied aboriginal populations.

Some aboriginal women chose to act within the existing male-dominated Native organizations even in respect to women's issues. Concern about the identity and survival of their people led some to oppose not just inter-racial marriage but also birth control and abortion. An issue of both symbolic and practical importance was Section 12(1)(b) of the Indian Act, which gave Indian status to white wives and half-blood children of male Indians but took it away from Indian women and their children if the women married non-status men. Some Native women's organizations supported the men's groups that, unwilling to revise the Indian act, appealed a Federal Court of Appeal decision restoring Indian status to Jeannette Corbiere Lavell from the Wikwemikong Band in Ontario. Others argued persuasively that sexist components of the Indian Act came from white legislators who were attempting to assimilate the Native population, rather than from Native men. In 1973 the Supreme Court of Canada confirmed that Lavell had forfeited her status by marrying a white man; the same decision was given in the case of Yvonne Bedard of the Six Nations Reserve. The Court found that Indian women were entitled only to "equality in administration and enforcement of the law." The Bill of Rights enacted in 1960 did not forbid "inequality within a group or class by itself, by reason of sex."[78]

Métis Elder Edith McLeod and Jeanette Corbiere Lavell at a demonstration in support of Native women's rights.

....

Source: Canadian Women's Movement Archives.

With the court route blocked, Indian women who had lost their status turned to lobbying, sit-ins, and appeals to international organizations; they were supported in these endeavours by a number of women's groups, including NAC and VOW. The most widely publicized case was that of Sandra Lovelace, a Maliseet of the Tobique Reserve in New Brunswick, who finally took her case to the Human Rights Committee of the United Nations. Publicity and public pressure were generated when the Tobique women's group organized a 100-mile walk of women and children from the Oka Reserve, near Montreal, to Ottawa in July 1979. Lilly Enright was 62 when she participated in the walk:

> Oh, it was hot, but most people walked all the way. I think I was "the oldest walker." After we hadn't even walked very far, people came out from their homes with cakes and cold drinks for us. I thought that was very nice of them — they were French people.[79]

In 1981 the United Nations committee found Canada in breach of the International Covenant on Civil and Political Rights.[80] The federal government, reluctant to provoke the hostility of Indian leaders, professed itself helpless. Indian status had significant economic and political implications; along with the right to free medical treatment and free education, band membership entailed the right to a share in what were sometimes substantial resources, as well as a voice in Native self-government. It was not until 1985 that the discriminatory clauses of the Indian Act were revised. Even then, the reinstated women were not guaranteed the rights whose absence had originally triggered their protests, and their children could not pass on their status.[81]

For many women, the revival of feminism meant a movement toward nation-wide, co-ordinated action. In 1971, television actor and host Kay Livingstone drew together the many black women's groups across the country to form the Canadian Negro Women's Association. Two years later, members of the group were ready to organize the first national Conference of Black Women; after seven annual meetings, they formed the Canadian Congress of Black Women "to provide a network of solidarity for Black Women in Canada, and to be a united voice in the defence and extension of human rights and liberties for Blacks in Canada."[82] Projects carried on by the national and local sections of the Congress included research on health issues and the establishment of health support groups in relation to those diseases partic-ularly affecting black women and their families. In 1994, they were actively involved in overtly political activities such as the support of black women against police harassment.[83]

Some of the new groups represented the first attempts at collective action by particular groups of women. New areas of concern emerged, along with newly defined groups of women joining together for the first time. Prostitutes organized in their own defence: prostitution was not illegal, but provisions against soliciting were used to harass them. Wives of members of the Canadian military organized to claim the right simply to meet and discuss their needs, a right denied under the blanket prohibition of political activity on armed forces property.[84] The DisAbled Women's Network (DAWN—founded in 1985) developed a unique analysis that pointed out how all people are only temporarily able-bodied and liable to be disabled by disease, injury, old age, or simply an environment unresponsive to all but the young and healthy. Surveys of DAWN's membership reinforced the point that women with dis-abilities found it especially difficult to get education and jobs and that they were frequently victims of sexual or other abuse. Jill Summerhayes summed up the self-image of women with disabilities: "we all felt sexually inadequate, incapable, elderly, weak, dependent at various times, more so because we thought of ourselves as less than complete." Summerhayes's osteoarthritis, a common ailment that seriously limited mobility and stamina, forced her to give up a managerial job in newspaper advertising as well as community activities connected with the Family Crisis Centre, the Cancer Society, and the United Way. From her home in Cambridge, Ontario, she generated a very successful business, making and marketing fashion canes for women with disabilities like hers.[85]

As always, most new women's groups started with a small number of women who shared an identity and felt the need for joint action on immediate, local prob-lems. The India Mahila Association (IMA), founded by three women in Vancouver in 1973, shortly after South Asian women began to arrive on the west coast in large numbers, started with orientation services for new women immigrants. By the late 1970s, the group had become publicly visible around the issue of violence toward women. When an American doctor targeted South Asian community newspapers to advertise a service for determining the sex of fetuses, often the first step to abortion of a female, IMA led protests. In the 1980s, the group recruited a younger generation of South Asian women who had some involvement with the broader women's move-ment. IMA was still active some twenty years later, still on a volunteer basis, operating out of members' houses.[86]

Other groups were initiated by government action and funding but developed a momentum of their own. Such was the case with the National Organization of Immigrant and Visible Minority Women of Canada (NOIVM), founded in 1986 to co-ordinate and voice the concerns of the approximately 500 "world majority" women's groups that existed by that time. It succeeded in establishing links among a large number of groups, despite doubts about whether even Third World immigrant women really shared the perspectives of women of colour from long-established ethnic communities in Canada.[87]

The closest thing to a national voice for all this varied activity was NAC. Over the years, it grew into an effective lobbying group, a coalition that operated on a basis of consensus among its widely differing components. What was unusual and possibly typically Canadian about NAC was that the organization included, from the start, not just the new voluntary status-of-women groups, but also many of the surviving older women's organizations, along with representatives of a whole range of second-wave service and cultural groups such as rape crisis centres, transition houses, and women's centres. In 1984 NAC listed almost 500 member groups, and through them, indirectly, claimed to represent some 5 million Canadian women; by 1988 the Committee's figure for members was 576.[88]

Not all of the new groups joined NAC, the NCWC, or the FFQ, although many drew on these larger coalitions for support in times of need. Large or small, affiliated or independent, Canadian women's organizations now represented a multiple and diverse women's movement. As the century moved toward its close, their impact began to be felt in law, in public policy, and in the changed attitudes of many Canadians. In a 1992 Gallup poll, 60 percent of the respondents said that they supported "the goals of the feminist movement."[89]

NOTES

1. Vivien R. Kerr, *A Flame of Compassion: The History of the Provincial Council of Women of Ontario* (Toronto: T.H. Best, 1967), 37, 57.

2. David MacDonald, "Powerful Woman's Lobby in Canada," *Chatelaine* 29, 6 (June 1957), 57–58; N.E.S. Griffiths, *The Splendid Vision: Centennial History of the National Council of Women of Canada, 1893–1993* (Ottawa: Carleton University Press, 1993), 251–54.

3. Frances Swyripa, *Wedded to the Cause: Ukrainian-Canadian Women and Ethnic Identity 1891–1991* (Toronto: University of Toronto Press, 1993), 183–4.

4. Ethel Vineberg, *The History of the National Council of Jewish Women of Canada* (Montreal: National Council of Jewish Women of Canada, 1967), 58; Eliane Leslau Silverman, "Women in Women's Organizations: Power or *Pouvoir*" in Lorraine Radtke and Henrikus J. Stam, eds., *Power/Gender: Social Relations in Theory and Practice* (London: Sage, 1994), 270–86.

5. Robert Collins, "The Biggest Country Club in Canada," *Maclean's* 10, 7 (July 5, 1958), 48; Helen F. Morton, "Women on the Land," *Food for Thought* 10, 7 (April 1950), 7.

6. Yvonne Rialland Morrissette, *Le passé conjugé au présent: Cercles de fermières au Québec, Historique 1915–1989* (Montréal: Éditions Pénélope, 1989), 151; *La terre et le foyer* 12, 1 (janvier 1955), 25; Yolande Cohen et Suzanne Marchand, "Les relations entre les Cercles de fermières et l'État à travers leur correspondance (1920–1968)," unpublished paper, 18.

7. Le Collectif Clio, *L'histoire des femmes au Québec depuis quatre siècles* (Montréal: Quinze, 1982), 417–19; Jocelyne Lamoureux, Michèle Gélinas, et Katy Tari, *Femmes en mouvement: Trajectoires de l'Association féminine d'éducation et d'action sociale, 1966–1991* (Montréal: Boréal Express, 1993).

8. Shirley Davey, ed., *Women, Work and Worship in the United Church of Canada* (Toronto: United Church of Canada, 1983), 54.

9. Yolande Cohen, *Femmes de parole: L'histoire des Cercles de fermières du Québec 1915–1990* (Montréal: Éditions Le Jour, 1990); Lamoureux, Gélinas, et Tari, *Femmes en mouvement.*

10. Eileen Morris, "Canada . . . a Woman's World!" *Saturday Night* 67, 34 (May 31, 1952), 34.

11. Barbara Roberts, "Women's Peace Activism in Canada," in Linda Kealey and Joan Sangster, eds., *Beyond the Vote: Canadian Women and Politics* (Toronto: University of Toronto Press, 1989), 196.

12. Christine Ball, "The History of the Voice of Women/*La voix des femmes*: The Early Years," University of Toronto, Ph.D. Dissertation, 1994; Michèle Jean, "Idola Saint-Jean, féministe (1880–1945)" in Pol Pelletier, ed., *Mon héroïne* (Montréal: Éditions du remue-ménage, 1981), 119.

13. Thérèse F. Casgrain, *A Woman in a Man's World*, translated by Joyce Marshall (Toronto: McClelland and Stewart, 1972), 166–7; Kay Macpherson, *When in Doubt, Do Both: The Times of My Life* (Toronto: University of Toronto Press, 1994), 106–8.

14. Kay Macpherson and Meg Sears, "The Voice of Women: A History," in Gwen Matheson, ed., *Women in the Canadian Mosaic* (Toronto: Peter Martin Associates, 1976), 71–89; Muriel Duckworth, "Voice of Women Dialogue," *Atlantis* 6, 2 (Spring 1981), 172.

15. Patricia Carey, "The Personal Is Political," *Canadian Women's Studies/Les cahiers de la femme* 2, 2 (1980), 6.

16. Le Collectif Clio, *L'histoire des femmes*, 489.

17. Lamoureux, Gélinas, et Tari, *Femmes en mouvement*, 88–90.

18. Azilda Marchand, "Les femmes au foyer: Hier et demain," *Canadian Women's Studies/Les cahiers de la femme* 2, 2 (1980), 46–48; Yolande Bédard, "Quand le coeur et la tête des collaboratrices sont en affaires," in VOW Canada and Women for a Meaningful International Summit, *First World Summit: "Women and the Many Dimensions of Power,"* report of a conference to celebrate the 50th anniversary of women's right to vote in Quebec (held in Quebec, June 3–8, 1990), 34–37.

19. Cécile Coderre, "La fédération des femmes du Québec: Fille cadette de Thérèse Casgrain?" in Anita Caron et Lorraine Archambault, *Thérèse Casgrain: Une femme ténace et engagée* (Sainte-Foy: Presses de l'Université du Québec, 1993), 69.

20. "As *Kinesis* Goes to Press," *Kinesis* (December 1994/January 1995), 2.

21. Lorna R. Marsden and Joan E. Busby, "Feminist Influence through the Senate: The Case of Divorce, 1967," *Atlantis* 14, 1 (Spring 1989), espec. 79 n. 2.

22. *Chatelaine* 39, 7 (July 1966); Cerise Morris, " 'No More Than Simple Justice': The Royal Commission on the Status of Women and Social Change in Canada," McGill University, Ph.D. Thesis, 1982, 114.

23. Sylvia Fraser, "Laura Sabia: Not Exactly Mom and Apple Pie," *Chatelaine* 48, 11 (November 1975), 100; "How Laura Built a Lobby," *Saturday Night* 90, 6 (September 1978), 4; Laura Sabia, " 'You Are Not One of Us': The Roots of My Militant Feminism," *Canadian Woman Studies/Les cahiers de la femme* 8, 2 (Summer 1987), 36, 32.

24. Most important among the long-established national women's organizations represented on the CEW were the WCTU, the YWCA, the NCWC, the National

Council of Jewish Women of Canada, the IODE, the FWIC, and the CFBPWC. Cerise Morris, " 'Determination and Thoroughness': The Movement for the Royal Commission on the Status of Women in Canada," *Atlantis* 5, 2 (Spring 1980), 1–21; Penney Kome, *Women of Influence: Canadian Women and Politics* (Toronto: Doubleday, 1985), 76–87.

25. The brief was presented by Sabia, Laberge-Colas, Margaret Hyndman for the Canadian Federation of Business and Professional Women's Clubs, Julia Schwartz for the National Council of Jewish Women of Canada, and Margaret MacLellan for the National Council of Women of Canada. Morris, " 'Determination and Thoroughness,' " 121.

26. Barry Craig, "Women's March May Back Call for Rights Probe," *The Globe and Mail* (January 5, 1967), 1; Michael Sabia, "Growing Up Feminist," *Chatelaine* 59, 5 (May 1986), 44.

27. Judy LaMarsh, *Memoirs of a Bird in a Gilded Cage* (Toronto: McClelland and Stewart, 1969), 316.

28. News Release, "Text of an Address Prepared for Delivery by Miss Sylva M. Gelber, Director, Women's Bureau, Canada Department of Labour" (December 8, 1969); John Terry, *Male–Female Differences in Voting Turnout and Campaign Activities, Canada and Ontario* (Ottawa: Library of Parliament, Research Branch, Political and Social Affairs Division, 1982), 4.

29. *Report of the Royal Commission on the Status of Women in Canada [RCSW]* (Ottawa: Information Canada, 1970), vii.

30. Anne Francis, "The Rights of Women," *Behind the Headlines* 10, 4 (September 1950); Florence Bird, *Anne Francis: An Autobiography* (Toronto: Clarke, Irwin, 1974).

31. Elsie Gregory MacGill, "Legalist Feminism," presentation to a conference on the Canadian Women's Movement (held at York University, September 1977), 6–7.

32. Christine Newman, "What's So Funny about the Royal Commission on the Status of Women?" *Saturday Night* 84, 1 (January 1969), 22, 24.

33. *Report of the RCSW*, xii.

34. Monique Bégin, "The Royal Commission on the Status of Women," in Constance Backhouse and David H. Flaherty, eds., *Challenging Times: The Women's Movement in Canada and the United States* (Montreal and Kingston: McGill-Queen's Press, 1992), 29.

35. Anthony Westell, "Report Is More Explosive Than Any Terrorist's Time Tomb," *The Toronto Star* (December 8, 1970), 13.

36. Submission of the National Ad Hoc Committee on the Status of Women to the government of Canada, February 1972.

37. Susan Crean, "Introduction: Daring the Dance," in Susan Crean, ed., *Twist and Shout: A Decade of Feminist Writing in* This Magazine (Toronto: Second Story, 1992), xi–x.

38. Jill Vickers, Pauline Rankin, and Christine Appelle, *Politics As If Women Mattered: A Political Analysis of the National Action Committee on the Status of Women* (Toronto: University of Toronto Press, 1993); Leslie A. Pal, *Interests of State: The Politics of Language, Multiculturalism, and Feminism in Canada* (Montreal and Kingston: McGill-Queen's University Press, 1993), 226; Ustün Reinart, "Three Major Strands in the Women's Movement in Manitoba, 1965–1985," in James Silver and Jeremy Hull, eds., *The Political Economy of Manitoba* (Regina: Canadian Plains Research Center, University of Regina, 1990), 166 n. 2.

39. Micheline Piché, "Les acadiennes font entendre leur voix," *La gazette des femmes* 16, 1 (mai/juin 1994), 24.

40. Laura Sabia, "Liberation from the Women's Movement," *Toronto Sun* (July 7, 1976), 43.

41. Reinart, "Three Major Strands," 153.

42. Canadian Research Institute for the Advancement of Women, "Women's Involvement in Political Life: A Pilot Study," research report submitted to the United Nations Educational, Scientific, and Cultural Organization (April 1986), 24–29.

43. Diane Lamoureux, *Fragments et collages: essai sur le féminisme québécois des années 70* (Montréal: Éditions du remue-ménage, 1986), 73; Mariette Sineau and Evelyne Tardy, *Droits des femmes en France et au Québec 1940–1990* (Montreal: Les Éditions du remue-ménage, 1993).

44. Carey, "The Personal Is Political," 6.

45. Naomi Wall, "The Last Ten Years: A Personal/Political View," in Maureen Fitzgerald, Connie Guberman, and Margie Wolfe, eds., *Still Ain't Satisfied! Canadian Feminism Today* (Toronto: Women's Press, 1982), 16.

46. Frances Wasserlein, "A Twenty-Five-Year-Old Herstory: The Women's Caucus," *Kinesis* (December 1992/January 1993), 18–19.

47. Satu Repo, "Are Women Necessary?" *Saturday Night* 84, 8 (August 1969), 30.

48. *Women Unite! An Anthology of the Canadian Women's Movement* (Toronto: Canadian Women's Educational Press, 1972); Fitzgerald, Guberman, and Wolfe, eds., *Still Ain't Satisfied!*; Sara Evans, *Personal Politics: The Roots of Women's Liberation in the Civil Rights Movement and the New Left* (New York: Vintage, 1980), 208; Marylee Stephenson, "Being in Women's Liberation: A Case Study in Social Change," University of British Columbia, Ph.D. Dissertation, 1975; Daryl Webber, "The Women's Movement in Northern Ontario: Its History, Growth and Current Affairs," Glendon College, York University, Women's Studies Honours Thesis, 1986; Francie Ricks, George Matheson, and Sandra W. Pyke, "Women's Liberation: A Case Study of Organizations for Social Change," *The Canadian Psychologist* 13, 1 (January 1972), 31–40; Cheryl Lynne Malmo-Levine, "Behavior of Women in Consciousness-Raising Groups," University of Alberta, M.Ed. Thesis, 1972; correspondence in the New Feminists' files.

49. Véronique O'Leary et Louise Toupin, eds. *Québécoises deboutte! Vol. 1: Une anthologie de textes du Font de libération des femmes (1969–1971) et du Centre des femmes (1972–1975)* (Montréal: Éditions du remue-ménage, 1982), 1, 53; Un groupe de femmes de Montréal, *Manifeste des femmes québécoises* (Montréal: Éditions l'etincelle, 1971), 52; Martine Lanctôt, "La genèse et l'évolution du mouvement de libération des femmes à Montréal, 1969–79," Université du Québec à Montréal, Thèse de maîtrise, 1982; Michèle Lamont, "Les rapports politiques au sein du mouvement des femmes au Québec," *Politique* 5 (hiver 1984), 75–106.

50. Krista Maeots, "Abortion Caravan," *Canadian Forum* 50, 594–95 (July/August 1970), 15; Phyllis Waugh, "Movement Comment: Choice Description," *Broadside* 9, 2 (November 1987), 6; Wasserlein, "A Twenty-Five-Year-Old Herstory," 19.

51. Reinart, "Three Major Strands," 155.

52. Gwen Matheson and V.E. Lang, "Nellie McClung: 'Not a Nice Woman,'" in Matheson, ed., *Women in the Canadian Mosaic*, 1–22; Gloria Geller, "The Wartimes Elections Act of 1917 and the Canadian Women's Movement," *Atlantis* 2, 1 (Autumn 1976), 88–106; Linda Kealey, ed., *A Not Unreasonable Claim: Women and Reform in Canada, 1880s–1920s* (Toronto: Canadian Women's Educational Press, 1979).

53. Diane Lamoureux, "Nationalism and Feminism in Quebec: An Impossible Attraction," in Heather Jon Maroney and Meg Luxton, eds., *Feminism and Political Economy: Women's Work, Women's Struggles* (Toronto: Methuen, 1987), 51–68.

54. Pierrette Bouchard, "Féminisme et marxisme: Un dilemme pour la Ligue communiste," *Canadian Journal of Political Science* 20, 1 (March 1987), 57–78; Simonne Monet-Chartrand, *Pionnières québécoises et regroupements de femmes d'hier à aujourd'hui* (Montreal: Éditions du remue-ménage, 1990).

55. Micheline de Sève, *Pour un féminisme libertaire* (Montréal: Boréal Express, 1985); Ginette Legault, "L'institutionalisation du mouvement féministe," Université du Québec à Montréal, Thèse de maîtrise, 1982; Heather Jon Maroney, "Contemporary Quebec Feminism: The Interrelation of Politics and Ideological Development in Women's Organizations, Trade Unions, Political Parties and State Policy, 1960–1980," McMaster University, Ph.D. Dissertation, 1989; Madeleine Parent, "Fifty Years a Feminist Trade Unionist: An Interview," in M. Patricia Connelly and Pat Armstrong, eds., *Feminism in Action: Studies in Political Economy* (Toronto: Canadian Scholars' Press, 1992), 47–65.

56. Toronto Women's Liberation Group, "Is Feminism Necessary for Women's Liberation?" (Canadian Union of Students, 1969), 3.

57. National Clearing House on Family Violence, "Transition Houses and Shelters for Battered Women in Canada" (Ottawa: Health and Welfare Canada, February 1983).

58. Cited as an epigraph in Peggy Morton, "Women's Work Is Never Done," in *Women Unite!*, 46.

59. Danièle Fournier et Nancy Guberman, "Quelques défis pour le mouvement des femmes au Québec," *Revue internationale d'action communautaire* 20, 60 (automne 1988), 183–87; Linda Briskin, "Socialist Feminism: From the Standpoint of Practice," in Connelly and Armstrong, eds., *Feminism in Action*, 286.

60. Bonnie Kreps, "Radical Feminism," in *Women Unite!*, 74.

61. Naomi Black, *Social Feminism* (Ithaca, N.Y.: Cornell University Press, 1989).

62. Letter from Bonnie Kreps, November 1986.

63. Bonnie Kreps, *Guide to the Women's Movement in Canada: A Chatelaine Cope Kit* (Toronto: n.d.); Sherill Cheda, Johanna Stuckey, and Maryon Kantaroff, "New Feminists Now," *Canadian Women's Studies/Les cahiers de la femme* 2, 2 (1980), 27–31.

64. Lanctôt, "La genèse," 119.

65. "WAVAW Demands," *Broadside* 3, 2 (November 1981), 19; "Celebrating 20 Years 1974–1994," *Kinesis* (March 1994), 11, 20; "In Women's Interests: Feminist Activism and Institutional Change" (Vancouver: Women's Research Centre, 1988); "Take Back the Night," *Kinesis* (September 1994), 5; "Prince Rupert Women Take Back the Night," *Kinesis* (December 1994/January 1995), 9.

66. Margaret Benston, "The Political Economy of Women's Liberation," *Monthly Review* 21, 4 (September 1969), 13–29; Linda Briskin, "The Women's Movement: Where Is It Going?" *Our Generation* 10, 3 (Fall 1974), 23–34; Roberta Hamilton and Michèle Barrett, eds., *The Politics of Diversity: Feminism, Marxism and Nationalism* (Montreal: Book Center, 1986).

67. Dorothy Smith, *The Everyday World as Problematic* (Toronto: University of Toronto Press, 1987); Mary O'Brien, *The Politics of Reproduction* (London: Routledge and Kegan Paul, 1981).

68. M. Julia Creet, "A Test of Unity: Lesbian Visibility in the British Columbia Federation of Women," in Sharon Dale Stone, ed., *Lesbians in Canada* (Toronto: Between the Lines, 1990); Dorrie, "Creating Communities," in Nym Hughes, Yvonne Johnson, and Yvette Perreault, *Stepping Out of Line: A Workbook on Lesbianism and Feminism* (Vancouver: Press Gang, 1984), 161; Becki Ross, *The House That Jill Built: A Lesbian Nation in Formation* (Toronto: University of Toronto Press, 1995); "The LMDF is Three Years Old! An Interview with Francie Wyland," *Grapevine* (Spring

1981), 1–2; Katherine Arnup, "Lesbian Mothers and Child Custody," *Atkinson Review of Canadian Studies* 1, 2 (Spring 1984), 35–39; Arnup, ed., *Lesbian Parenting: Living with Pride and Prejudice* (Charlottetown: gynergy books, 1995).

69. Julie McLean, "Militantly Impotent: Has the Women's Movement Come to This?" *Branching Out* 3, 2 (April/June 1976), 9.

70. Cerise Morris, "Diary of a Feminist," in Margret Anderson, ed., *Mother Was Not a Person* (Montreal: Content Publishing/Black Rose, 1972), 182, 184.

71. Eleanor Wright Pelrine, *Abortion in Canada* (Toronto: New Press, 1972); Pelrine, *Morgentaler: The Case That Rocked Canada* (Toronto: Gage Educational Publishing/Signet–New American Library, 1976); Anne Collins, *The Big Evasion: Abortion, The Issue That Won't Go Away* (Toronto: Lester and Orpen Dennys, 1985).

72. "Louise Summerhill" [obituary], *The Globe and Mail* (August 14, 1991), D7.

73. Christine Overall, "Feminist Philosophical Reflections on Reproductive Rights in Canada," in Backhouse and Flaherty, eds., *Challenging Times*, 242; Shelley A.M. Gavigan, "Beyond *Morgentaler*: The Legal Regulation of Reproduction," in Janine Brodie, Shelley A.M. Gavigan, and Jane Jenson, eds., *The Politics of Abortion* (Toronto: Oxford University Press, 1992), 117–146; F.L. Morton, *Morgentaler vs. Borowski: Abortion, the Charter, and the Courts* (Toronto: McClelland and Stewart, 1992); "Federal Abortion Bill Defeated," *Pro-Choice News* (Spring 1991), 1.

74. Richard Mackie, "Public-Opinion Poll Results Fuel Fight for Abortion Pill," *The Globe and Mail* (July 22, 1992), A4; Robert Matas and Miro Cernetig, "B.C. Doctor Hit by Sniper," *The Globe and Mail* (November 9, 1994), A1; "Death Threats Aimed at Halifax Doctors," *The Globe and Mail* (February 3, 1995), A4.

75. "Prince Edward Island," *Pro-Choice News* (Fall 1994), 6; "Morgentaler Wins Fight to Reopen Clinic," *The Globe and Mail* (September 15, 1994), A4.

76. The Mohawk Women of Caughnawaga, " 'The Least Members of Our Society,' " *Canadian Women's Studies/Les cahiers de la femme* 2, 2 (1980); Marlene Pierre-Aggawamay, "Native Women and the State," in Joan Turner and Lois Emery, eds., *Perspectives on Women in the 1980s* (Winnipeg: University of Manitoba Press, 1983), 67; Janet Silman, *Enough Is Enough: Aboriginal Women Speak Out* (Toronto: Women's Press, 1987), 94.

77. Webber, "The Women's Movement in Northern Ontario," 16–22.

78. Judy Steed, " 'Mohawk Beauty' Paid High Price in Fight for Indian Status," *The Globe and Mail* (May 8, 1987); Kathleen Jamieson, *Citizens Minus: Indian Women and the Law* (Ottawa: Canadian Advisory Council on the Status of Women, 1978), 82; Paula Bourne, *Women in Canadian Society* (Toronto: OISE, 1976), 111–31; Elizabeth Atcheson, Mary Eberts, and Beth Symes, *Women and Legal Action: Precedents, Resources, and Strategies for the Future* (Ottawa: Canadian Advisory Council on the Status of Women, 1984), 14–15.

79. Silman, *Enough Is Enough*, 155.

80. Atcheson, Eberts, and Symes, *Women and Legal Action*, 17–18; Caroline Lachapelle, "Beyond Barriers: Native Women and the Women's Movement," in Fitzgerald, Guberman, and Wolfe, eds., *Still Ain't Satisfied!*, 257–64.

81. Sally Weaver, "First Nations Women and Government Policy, 1970–92: Discrimination and Conflict," in Sandra Burt, Lorraine Code, and Lindsay Dorney, eds., *Changing Patterns: Women in Canada*, 2nd ed. (Toronto: McClelland and Stewart, 1993), 92–150; Peter Sero, "Blood Lines Cross Mohawk Country," *NOW* magazine (October 6–12, 1994), 15.

82. Reports of the fifth and sixth conferences of the Congress of Black Women of Canada, 1982, 1984.

83. Status of Women Canada, Canada's National Report to the United Nations for the Fourth World Conference on Women, September 1995, Beijing, China (Ottawa: August 1994), 38; Linda Carvery, "Congress Has Ambitious Goals for Black Women," *Pandora* 4, 1 (September 1988), 27; Rosemary Sadlier, *Leading the Way: Black Women in Canada* (Toronto: Umbrella Press, 1994); Rudy Platiel, "Judge Halts Strip-Search Inquiry," *The Globe and Mail* (September 20, 1994), A6.

84. Frances M. Shaver, "Prostitution: A Critical Analysis of Three Policy Approaches," *Canadian Public Policy* 11, 3 (September 1985), 493–503; Janet Bagnall, "A New Attitude to the Oldest Profession," *The Montreal Gazette* (June 4, 1995), F6; Deborah Harrison and Lucie Laliberté, *There's No Life Like It! Military Wives in Canada* (Toronto: James Lorimer, 1994).

85. Pat Israel and Fran Odette, "The Disabled Women's Movement 1983 to 1993," *Canadian Woman Studies/Les cahiers de la femme* 13, 4 (summer 1993), 6–8; Jill Summerhayes, *Supporting Myself in Style: Confessions of the Cane Lady* (Cambridge, Ont.: Imp Press, 1990), 58.

86. Manisha Singh, "A 19-Year Old Herstory: India Mahila Association," *Kinesis* (March 1993); Sunera Thobani, "More Than Sexist . . . " *Healthsharing* 12, 1 (Spring 1991), 10, 11, 13; Aruna Papp, "A Matter of Gender," *Healthsharing* 12, 1 (Spring 1991), 12.

87. Carmencita R. Hernandez, "The Coalition of Visible Minority Women," in Frank Cunningham et al., eds. *Social Movements/Social Change: The Politics and Practice of Organizing* (Toronto: Between the Lines, 1988), 157–68; Roxana Ng, "Finding Our Voices: Reflections on Immigrant Women's Organizing," in Jeri Dawn Wine and Janice L. Ristock, ed., *Women and Social Change: Feminist Activism in Canada* (Toronto: James Lorimer, 1991), 184–97; Linda Carty and Dionne Brand, " 'Visible Minority' Women: A Creation of the Canadian State," in Himani Bannerji, ed., *Returning the Gaze: Essays on Racism, Feminism and Politics* (Toronto: Sister Vision, 1993), 169–81; Awha Al-Buasidy, "Generic Term More Accurate," *Quota Magazine* (February 1994), 5–6.

88. Jill Vickers, "The Intellectual Origins of the Women's Movements in Canada," in Backhouse and Flaherty, eds., *Challenging Times*, 43; Ann Rauhala, "Feminist Flagship Rocked by Feuding," *The Globe and Mail* (May 21, 1988), D1.

89. Lorne Bozinoff and Peter MacIntosh, "Feminist Movement Strongly Supported by Canadian Public," *The Gallup Report* (June 25, 1992).

CHAPTER FIFTEEN

The Personal
Becomes Political

Beginning in the last years of the 1960s, consciousness-raising taught women that

the political — law, state, and society — affected the personal lives of individuals.

Almost immediately, they moved, both as individuals and as members of groups, to

make the political respond to women's shared personal agendas. This meant sus-

tained efforts to alter public policy, social structures, and attitudes to take more

account of women. The 1970s saw major changes, and the 1980s even more. The

results were mixed. Along with significant successes, the increased number and

diversity of women's organizations generated serious tensions that were further

inflamed by the growing strength of anti-feminism and of more overt backlash. At

the same time, coalitions formed and reformed, and, as the century drew to a close,

it seemed clear that the energy of women's actions was not abating.

LAW, THE LEGAL SYSTEM, AND JUSTICE

One of the earliest second-wave examples of the impact of individual women's situations was the case of Irene Murdoch, whose private problems started a process that
produced major changes in family property law. Murdoch was an Alberta farm wife
who could represent the many wives who worked only "in the home." When her
jaw and her marriage were broken in 1968, she claimed a share of the family ranch
on the basis of her contributions to it. Urban feminists were stunned to learn that
Murdoch was regularly involved in "haying, raking, swathing, mowing, driving
trucks and tractors and teams, quietening horses, taking cattle back and forth to the

reserve, dehorning, vaccinating, branding," that she ran the ranch single-handed for about five months out of each year, and that she felt she did no more than what was expected of "any ranch wife." The Supreme Court shared Murdoch's assessment of what she did, but the justices did not believe that such labours "would give any farm or ranch wife a claim in partnership."[1]

In 1973 Murdoch was finally granted a lump-sum maintenance payment, but it implied no recognition of her role in the economic unit of the household. The assumptions of the law remained the same: women were entitled to support during marriage and to appropriate maintenance after its breakup, with return obligations of domestic duties and sexual availability on an exclusive basis for the duration of the marriage. The Murdoch case helped alter both law and attitudes about family property in the common-law provinces, for it mobilized women and women's groups to press for change. Beginning in 1977 with Manitoba, the provinces and territories approved legislation giving concrete recognition to the fact that domestic activities, usually carried on by women, were what made it possible for wage earners to acquire money and property for the family. Some fifteen years later, the Supreme Court completed the process of legal change when it established in the Beblow case that, under the new legislation, wives in common-law as well as formal marriages owned half the household assets when the relationship ended. In striking contrast to the Murdoch decision, the 1993 Supreme Court found that Catherine Peter was entitled to compensation for the twelve years during which she had lived with William Beblow, cared for his two children and her four, built a pigpen, tended and slaughtered chickens, and worked part-time as a cook.[2] The new legislation and court decisions concerning family property thus incorporated the feminist insistence that domestic work was as valuable as public work.

The law related to rape was another area in which attitudes and law changed, if slowly, as a result of individual action backed up by women's organizations. Rape crisis centres were among the services most energetically supported by the women's movement in the 1970s; despite modifications in the law in 1976, victims of rape were doubly victimized by their treatment in court. In 1977 Lorenne Clark and Debra Lewis published a groundbreaking book that showed the extent to which rape was underreported, underprosecuted, and unpunished in Canada — in part because of the very severe penalties that made juries reluctant to convict. Clark and Lewis also articulated an argument increasingly adopted by feminists: rape was a crime of violence against women, rather than one of sexuality. In response to persistent lobbying by women's groups, in 1983 the federal government enacted new legislation that redefined rape as assault. With less extreme jail sentences possible, successful prosecution would be more likely. This change was accompanied by the "rape shield" provision, intended to protect victims from having their sexual history put on trial; perhaps women would now be less reluctant to report rape or attempted rape. In the same legislation, marital rape was defined as a crime. These changes in law were regarded by feminists as among the most promising legal changes their activities had produced. But some women began to have doubts about whether rape was in fact merely assault as the new laws implied, since rape was routinely used as a way to control and punish women.

In any case, the law's protection turned out to be fragile, requiring continual scrutiny and action. In 1991 the Supreme Court found the rape shield provisions unconstitutional, so that new legislation was required. Feminist lawyers, along with representatives of prostitutes and other, diverse women's groups, participated in subsequent discussions that produced a law that stressed the importance of explicit consent on the part of those involved in sexual activity. The new law was popularly known as "No means no." Under it, signs of a struggle would no longer be required to establish that a woman had been sexually assaulted. Those involved in developing the new legislation encountered insistent opposition from some members of the legal profession and also from supporters of free speech, who were concerned about the rights of those accused of crimes. It was clear that the law implicitly required major changes in sexual behaviour and attitudes. However, those involved failed to get the new rape law to include recognition that certain groups of women — members of visible minorities, disabled women, lesbians, prostitutes — were at particular risk for forced sex.

In 1994, the Supreme Court appalled many by its decision in the Daviault case. They ruled that a new trial would be allowed to a 72-year-old man convicted of raping a 65-year-old woman he pulled from a wheelchair: his extreme drunkenness was allowed as a defence. Within weeks an Alberta man was acquitted of beating his wife, using the same defence. In July 1995, a bill limiting the use of such a defence was approved by Parliament, but assent was delayed because of concerns about its constitutionality.[3]

Feminist activity concerning legal matters relating to women was vigorous and much-praised. After the Charter of Rights and Freedoms was added to the Canadian constitution, feminist lawyers who had been active in the constitutional struggles beginning in 1981 organized an ambitious legal aid fund dedicated to fighting significant cases. The Legal Education and Action Fund (LEAF) was able from 1984 to 1992 and again from 1994 to take advantage of a federal program that funded Charter challenges in the courts; it raised the rest of the substantial amounts needed for proactive litigation from individual donors — including Nancy Ruth and her mother, Mary Rowell Jackman — as well as through women's groups such as the Federation of Women Teachers' Associations of Ontario. LEAF's initial cases were symbolic of all women's needs for autonomy and status. The first concerned married women's names; living in the Yukon, Suzanne Bertrand wanted to retain her birth name because it reflected her French-Canadian ancestry. The second case attacked the regulation that welfare recipients, most of whom were women, would lose assistance if there was a "spouse in the house" who might support them, or even a friend who carried out activities thought to be typical of a spouse. By 1993 LEAF was able to boast quietly about having supported "more than 100 legal test cases," singling out for mention the areas of "pregnancy discrimination, sexual harassment, violence against women, pension inequities and sex bias in welfare regulations."[4]

As women graduated from law schools in increasing numbers, some of them began to be appointed judges. First-wave magistrates Emily Murphy, Alice Jamieson, and Helen Gregory MacGill had lacked formal legal training, but Helen Kinnear, Canada's first woman barrister to be appointed a judge (in 1943), was also the first woman honoured as King's Counsel in the British Commonwealth. In 1969 Canada had its first woman Superior Court judge, when Réjane Laberge-Colas ascended to the bench in Quebec; in 1982 Bertha Wilson was appointed to the Supreme Court of Canada. She was joined there four years later by Quebec's Claire L'Heureux-Dubé and then, in 1989, by Albertan Beverly McLachlin. For a brief period, until Wilson retired in 1991, the Supreme Court had three women members. By 1985 women constituted about 13 percent of all judges and magistrates, and they were beginning to represent the diversity of Canadian women. When Maryka Omatsu was appointed to the Ontario Court (Provincial Division) in 1992, she was the first woman of East Asian descent to be made a judge. Active in the movement that obtained a small degree of financial redress for the survivors of the Japanese-Canadians who were interned during World War II, Omatsu found it difficult as a young woman, even though she was a fully qualified lawyer, to obtain respect in either her own ethnic community or the wider legal system.[5]

In February 1990, Madam Justice Bertha Wilson surprised her audience at Osgoode Hall Law School when she stated publicly her view that the law was a male and masculinist profession. After she retired from the Court, she was appointed to head a task force on sex equality set up by the Canadian Bar Association. Her report documented a high level of attrition of female lawyers—in part because firms would not accommodate childrearing obligations. It also reported widespread sexual harassment and discrimination against female judges and lawyers. These charges were confirmed by the 1993 Ontario inquiry into the conduct of the "kissing judge," who humiliated two young women Crown attorneys with deep kisses, groping, and sexual innuendo. Wilson's report recommended that law schools should adopt affirmative action programs, that the law societies should monitor law firms, and that judges should receive mandatory training programs concerning both racism and sexism. The public apparently shared Wilson's doubts about judges: a 1993 poll found that only 40 percent of Canadians felt that courts were fair to women.[6]

At the other end of the justice system, women emerged horrifyingly into public attention when, in a period of less than two years beginning in 1989, six aboriginal women killed themselves in the federal prison for women (P4W) in Kingston, Ontario. Echoing the 1938 findings of the Archambault Commission instigated by MP Agnes Macphail, every investigation of the federal penal system (16 between 1968 and 1981 alone) had recommended closing the women's prison and redistributing the very few federally convicted women to locations near their homes. In 1981 the Canadian Human Rights Commission found that women prisoners were discriminated against in terms of sex, since in virtually every dimension of program and facilities they were worse off than men. The disproportionate incarceration of aboriginal women was scandalous; they made up almost a quarter of the population of the federal prison, and even larger proportions of those incarcerated in the provinces and territories. In 1988, according to the Canadian Human Rights Commission, aboriginal women were more likely to be sent to prison than to attend university. Two years later, a unique federal task force consisting almost entirely of women, including representatives of the Native Women's Association of Canada (NWAC) and the Canadian Association of Elizabeth Fry Societies as well as two former prisoners, recommended replacing the single federal facility with five regional ones. In addition, a specially designed healing lodge was to be created for aboriginal women who preferred that alternative; it would be closely integrated with a Native community, have elders and other spiritual healers always available, and be staffed by aboriginal people. The other non-Native facilities were to be similarly linked in a holistic way to supportive networks of women's groups. However, although the healing lodge was undertaken as recommended, economy rather than principle seemed to dictate the placement of the other new facilities. In 1995 a spokesman for Correctional Service Canada promised that P4W would be closed in 1996.[7]

For the majority of women who were not personally involved with the formal machinery of law and justice, court decisions were of indirect but still substantial importance. The continuing issue of pornography was a particularly noteworthy example, because of everyday issues relating to freedom of speech and women's possibilities for self-expression. Pornography was also an issue about which women disagreed vehemently. In 1992 the Butler case established for Canada a new interpretation of pornography that attracted considerable international interest. Obscenity would no longer be interpreted to mean "offensive to conventional morality." Instead, material could be seized and its producers, importers, or distributors charged by either Customs or police if the material exploited sex in such a way that there was a tendency to promote harm to women or children. In particular, both child pornography and combinations of sex with violence were to be prohibited. Most women were uncomfortable with pornography that involved violent or degrading portrayals of women and still more uncomfortable with sexual material portraying children or models who looked like children. Indeed, radical-feminist groups, including WAVAW, had long opposed such publications and films. But the risks of censorship remained great, as many other feminists and feminist organizations pointed out. In particular, lesbians predicted that the new definitions would be used against homosexual erotic material rather than the widely distributed hard-core heterosexual pornography. Their fears were supported the first time the Butler case's decision was applied: in 1993 Customs officers seized copies of a lesbian erotic magazine, *Bad Attitude*, ordered by a gay and lesbian bookstore in Toronto. "It's our material — our books, our magazines, our voice — a voice that we're learning to speak with louder and louder," protested the manager of Little Sister's, a lesbian bookstore in Vancouver that, since 1986, had been regularly affected by delay and confiscation of material. In 1994 Little Sister's challenged Canada Customs in court about the legality of such action under the Charter of Rights; a judgement was expected in the fall of 1995.[8]

In other areas, it was easier for government to be responsive to women's needs. For example, Canada became the first nation in the world to allow women to achieve refugee status for gender-related reasons, on the basis of guidelines issued by the Immigration and Refugee Board in 1992. The guidelines provided shelter for a Zimbabwean forced against her will into a polygamous marriage, a Chinese woman resisting sterilization, and a Somali who did not want her daughter to suffer genital mutilation.[9] The mixed results of Canadian government initiatives were reflected in international statistics. In 1992 Canada was rated first in the world in a Human Development Index that the United Nations had developed to measure "quality of life." This ranking reflected the availability of the welfare measures, including education and health services, that women's groups had always supported. However, the country slipped down to number eight when the index was specifically adjusted to reflect the status of women, and in 1995 on that basis it was only ninth.[10]

POLITICS

The slowness and difficulty of changing public policy from the outside motivated activist women to seek more direct involvement in government. After Indian women gained the right to participate in band elections in 1951, there were no longer legal barriers to any woman's holding office. After 1964 nearly all women Members of Parliament held office on the basis of their own qualifications, with virtually none elected as political "widows." Yet attitudes and expectations were slow to change. A

1966 publication of the Department of Citizenship and Immigration stated flatly that "winter weather is a limiting factor" to Canadian women's political activity. As late as 1975, a national survey showed Canadians tending to believe that "the average man" would make a better politician than the "average woman."[11] The year 1972 was a turning point in terms of national electoral office, as Progressive Conservative Flora MacDonald and Liberals Jeanne Sauvé, Albanie Morin, and Monique Bégin were elected, joining the NDP's Grace MacInnis to multiply by five the number of women MPs. Bégin, MacDonald, and Sauvé all became cabinet ministers, holding some very powerful ministries that were not conventionally associated with women. Sauvé was later the first woman to be Speaker of the House and also the first to be governor-general, in 1980 and 1984, respectively. Along with other more conventional achievements as Speaker, she was responsible for the establishment of a day-care centre on Parliament Hill for children of civil servants.[12] Younger women began to be elected. Sheila Copps moved from the Ontario to the federal legislature in 1984 and provided two landmarks for women in Parliament, still not replicated by 1995: she was the first woman Member of Parliament to get married and the first to have a baby while in office.

Even though increasing numbers of women achieved notable political success, there was clearly still a "glass ceiling" for those attempting to acquire a real share in power. In 1975 Rosemary Brown was the first woman and also the first black to contest the leadership of a national party, the NDP; as a member of the B.C. legislature, she had been the first black woman to sit in any legislative body in Canada. She came in a strong second, but the delegates at the convention selected Ed Broadbent, the son of an Oshawa auto worker. Brown went on to head MATCH, a Canadian group that sponsored development projects for Third World women; in 1993 she became chair of the Ontario Human Rights Commission.[13] A year later, Flora MacDonald, the popular MP from Kingston and the Islands, former secretary of the Progressive Conservative Party, was overwhelmingly defeated in an attempt at the party's leadership. Although public-opinion polls had shown that 86 percent of the public would be willing to vote for a party with a woman leader, it was undeniable that MacDonald's sex had been a major element in her defeat.[14] The first woman to head a national party was finally selected by the NDP in 1989; Audrey McLaughlin, a former social worker who had represented the Yukon in Parliament for two years, was soft-spoken, a strong feminist, and inclined toward consensus-building. In the

Thérèse Casgrain, leader of the Quebec CCF, campaigning in the 1957 provincial election.

Source: Canapress Photo Service.

summer of 1993 Canada's first woman prime minister, Kim Campbell, came into office as the result of a Progressive Conservative Party leadership convention, where she was presented by Ellen Fairclough and endorsed by Flora MacDonald. However, many observers felt that both McLaughlin and Campbell, though qualified for the position, became party leader mainly because no male politician wished to take on the task at the time.[15] The 1993 federal election left the prime minister defeated in her own riding by Liberal Hedy Fry; another candidate in that riding, the NDP's Betty Baxter, was one of two avowed lesbians to run in this election. Although two major parties had women leaders, issues such as women's rights had been reduced in importance during the campaign.

In the last two decades of the century, women significantly increased their share of legislative seats both federally and provincially. Voters showed increasing hostility to incumbents, and the much-increased number of women candidates benefitted from the resultant dramatic changes of government. The 1993 Parliament included 53 women — 18 percent — a good percentage of women by international standards, second only to the Scandinavian countries.[16] However, the 1993 Parliament was noteworthy for women for reasons other than the increase in numbers. The Conservatives achieved gender parity: Elsie Wayne, who had been mayor of Saint John, New Brunswick, was the only new Progressive Conservative elected to Parliament, and constituted half of the Tory caucus of two. Newfoundland men lost their monopoly in Parliament, as two Liberal women from that province were seated. And among the new MPs were two women of colour, Jean Augustine and Hedy Fry. Augustine, who had been put into Toronto's Beaches–Woodbine riding as part of the Liberal Party's affirmative action for women candidates, had come from Grenada as a domestic at the age of 22 and then became a school principal, a leader in the Canadian Congress of Black Women, and head of the Metropolitan Toronto Housing Authority. She felt that she brought a special point of view to politics: "It's the perspective of an immigrant woman raising two daughters. . . . It's knowing something about, say, the issue of day care because you have had to take children on a bus to day care." Augustine was appointed parliamentary secretary to the prime minister, and identified as one of her constituencies "the community of black and ethnic women." The increased presence of women in Parliament also had a concrete impact on the Parliament building, which had been erected the year before Agnes Macphail set foot there. In 1994, after one rookie woman MP missed a vote because the women's washroom was so remote from the main chamber of the House of Commons, women MPs finally got a new washroom close to the legislative action.[17]

Although women were slower to increase their legislative representation provincially than federally, women did occasionally become leaders of provincial parties. The first of these, Alexa Stewart McDonough, led the Nova Scotia NDP from 1980 to 1994 and was then selected in 1995 to head the federal NDP. British Columbia's Rita Johnston was the first woman to serve as provincial premier, and two years later Catherine Callbeck became the first woman elected to that position, in Prince Edward Island. However, it was at the municipal level, so long a target of women's organizations, that women most rapidly increased their participation. From the end of the 1970s, women became more numerous as mayors of cities and towns, while also increasing their representation on city councils and school boards; they constituted 17 percent of city councillors by 1990 (25 percent in Montreal). Ottawa had several women mayors after 1951's pioneer, Charlotte Whitton, and in 1994 Barbara Hall followed June Rowlands as the second woman in a row to become mayor of Toronto, responsible for a budget larger than that of many nations. Small towns were most likely to have women at the helm — the first woman mayor in Canada, Barbara M. Hanley, presided from 1936 to 1944 over Webbwood, Ontario (population about 600). A more recent, typical example was Makkovik, Labrador, which had 395 citizens in 1987, when Ruth Flowers advanced from deputy mayor to mayor. "I got involved in municipal politics because I wanted to see things change around for us up here," said Flowers. "Things that the rest of Canada takes for granted like a safe home for women, daycare, more social services and police protection."[18]

THE CONSTITUTION

Constitutional battles dominated national politics in post-war Canada, as the modernization of Quebec politics fuelled separatism, economic and political change strengthened regional calls for devolution of powers, and the First Nations actively pursued land claims and self-government. Feminism and the action of women's groups became part of mainstream politics in the Parti Québécois's 1980 provincial referendum about a proposed new constitutional arrangement, sovereignty-association. Lise Payette, the first woman to serve in a Quebec cabinet, had responsibility for the status of women (along with consumer affairs, co-operatives, and financial institutions). A popular broadcaster, both a feminist and a committed sovereigntist, she caused a commotion by accusing federalist Québécoises of being "Yvettes." Yvette and Guy were the Dick and Jane of Quebec schoolbooks, and Payette used the name to stand for the traditional submissive wife-and-mother who does what her husband and father tell her. The Quebec Liberal Party responded vigorously, organizing first a "brunch" and then a series of public meetings, ending with a vast session in the Montreal Forum. There, more than 14 000 women cheered federalist feminists, including Monique Bégin and Thérèse Casgrain, who talked about the role of women in building Quebec and Canada and the way future generations in Quebec would benefit from federally provided opportunities and social services. Polls showed a significant shift in women's votes, and analysts agreed that women played a role in federalism's 10 percent victory in the referendum. Many journalists interpreted the whole episode as a rejection of feminism in favour of traditional values, while others saw it as manipulation by the Liberal Party. A third interpretation was that women had made a rational policy choice related to their own interests. Feminist political scientists pointed to the key role played by women members of the Liberal Party: one described the Yvettes' campaign as "a brilliant political strategy thought up by women."[19]

During the referendum, the federal government had promised redress of Quebec's persistent grievances about the structure of Confederation. After the defeat of sovereignty-association, it accordingly pressed for a reformulated and "patriated" constitution that would include a Charter of Rights and Freedoms entailing, for the first time, a formal judicial review of law in terms of basic principles. As many cases had shown — including those of Bliss, Lavell, Bedard, and Murdoch — the 1960 Bill of Rights was virtually useless for women. It was clear by the end of the 1970s that, generally speaking, unequal laws would be upheld by Canadian courts, the only remedy being the slow process of legislative change. Many women's organizations accordingly reacted with enthusiasm to the suggestion that women's rights to equality might be enshrined in fundamental law. Individual legislative or administrative acts could then be challenged directly and possibly ruled unacceptable.

For anglophone women, the 1980–81 campaign for the inclusion of women's rights in the constitution became a landmark similar to the Persons Case of 1929, an icon of feminist effectiveness. According to a feminist journalist, "a political earthquake occurred in Canada in 1981, dramatically changing the foundation for government policy making."[20] The reality was less clear-cut. In 1980 women's organizations lobbied intensively in connection with the proposed constitution, focussing particularly on getting adequate references to sexism into the Charter of Rights and Freedoms. It was partly in response to their efforts that, in January 1981, the justice minister announced a revision of the proposed Section 15 of the Charter, to read, "Every individual is equal before and under the law and has the right to equal protection of the law and equal benefit of the law." The experience of many women was behind that seemingly clumsy formulation, which attempted to ensure not just that laws were equally enforced, but also that they would have no discriminatory provisions and no discriminatory impact.[21]

That same January, a national conference on women and the constitution, scheduled for the next month by the federal Advisory Council on the Status of Women, was cancelled. The Council's chair, Doris Anderson, resigned dramatically with the charge that the cancellation had been ordered by the minister responsible for the status of women. A small, Toronto-centred group of feminists moved in as a self-appointed ad hoc committee to hold the conference as — and when — originally scheduled. They surprised themselves and many others by conducting in February 1981, without government funding, a successful three-day meeting of more than 1300 women from across Canada. Due in large part to the efforts of feminist journalists such as Penney Kome and Michele Landsberg, now well-placed in national media, Anderson's resignation and the bitter accusations and counteraccusations within and around the council attracted enormous publicity, as did the counterconference.[22] NAC, which had previously been unable to reach consensus about the Charter, now voted at its annual general meeting to support the entire patriated constitution. The *Fédération des femmes du Québec* left NAC: Quebec had not given approval to the patriation of the constitution.[23] Then, in April, after continued lobbying spearheaded by members of the ad hoc committee, the guarantees of equality in Section 15 were backed up by Section 28, which states that "notwithstanding anything in this Charter, the rights and freedoms referred to in it are guaranteed equally to male and female persons."

The drama was not over, however. That fall, a federal–provincial conference bypassed Quebec to work out an "over-ride" arrangement that would allow provinces to pass special limited-term legislation in any area, "notwithstanding" any guarantees in the Charter. It was several days before it was clear to the public and to politicians that the over-ride applied also to the hard-won Section 28. Edythe MacDonald, a federal civil servant present during the negotiations about the over-ride, recalls that she burst out in rage that "the women of Canada would not put up with this treachery." Nor did they. After an angry, intensive campaign of public meetings, letters, and telegrams, and private lobbying by women's groups and individual women, the provincial premiers agreed to exempt Section 28 from the over-ride.[24]

Many women were jubilant: thanks to their efforts, Canada now had the equal rights provisions that the United States had failed to acquire. But Marilou McPhedran, a well-known feminist lawyer who played an important role in the ad hoc committee, summed up the results as follows: "To make any lasting change you have to participate in the workings of the institution and that's not what the ad hoc committee did; we assaulted the institution and forced it to respond."[25] Many women felt pride for precisely that reason: the assault, the assumption and use of power, and the visible, if limited, success.

Both federally and in the provinces, governments now modified a considerable number of items of law and public policy in anticipation of obligations under the equality provisions of the Charter that came into effect in 1985. In particular, Bill C-31 removed the clause of the Indian Act that had deprived Indian women and their children of Indian status if the women married non-status men. However, it was not until October 1990 that the Canadian armed forces dropped limits on full integration of women into the services, in time for Canadian women to serve in the war zone of the 1991 Gulf War.

Constitutional negotiations continued, and the next round began in 1985, with the preparation of the so-called Meech Lake agreement, a renewed attempt to find some way of reconciling Quebec's nationalist demands with the maintenance of federalism. NAC presented the position of the many women who were alarmed at the possibility that the resulting constitutional changes would nullify Charter guarantees that were important for all women but especially for groups such as Native women, women of colour, refugee women, and women with disabilities. The proposal to give the provinces the financial control over programs such as childcare and second-language education was also troubling, because it threatened both funding and national standards. By contrast, speaking for most of Quebec's francophone women, both the *Conseil du statut de la femme* and the *Fédération des femmes du Québec* supported the Meech Lake agreement. They expressed confidence in the Quebec government and its institutions: "In the Province of Quebec, the respect of women's rights is more and more becoming part of political culture. . . . The progress we have made with regard to the status of women is linked to the concept of a distinct society." In 1990, when the Meech Lake agreement was discussed by national and provincial leaders in the unsuccessful attempt to complete its ratification, no women or representatives of women's groups were present at the negotiating table.[26]

It was in 1992 that women and women's organizations became, for the first time, publicly recognized players among those dealing with a possible constitutional settlement. In preparation for a nation-wide referendum on new constitutional arrangements, the federal government consulted widely with many citizens' forums and public action groups, including women's. Once again the main issue for many women activists was that the referendum document — the Charlottetown Accord — seemed likely to allow communal rights, particularly Quebec's and those of the Native peoples, to overrule the Charter of Rights and its protection for women and other "minority" groups. Critics also believed that the accord threatened national social programs. NAC got excellent media coverage for its outspoken opposition to the agreement.

By contrast, Audrey McLaughlin and other politically active women supported the accord, along with all three major parties, as did many other individual women, feminists or not. The media gave the title of "the new mothers of Confederation" to

Opponents to the Charlottetown Accord, during the pre-referendum debates in 1992. Judy Rebick of NAC knits on a raft tossing in the seas of the North American Free Trade Agreement, accompanied by Jacques Parizeau (Parti Québécois), Lucien Bouchard (Bloc Québécois), Preston Manning (Reform Party), and former prime minister Pierre Elliot Trudeau.

Source: *The Toronto Star* (September 30, 1992), p. 21. Reprinted with permission of the Toronto Star Syndicate.

three aboriginal women who were conspicuous among the representatives of the four national aboriginal organizations that helped develop the text for the referendum. Rosemarie Kuptana was the elected head of the Inuit Tapirisat of Canada (the national organization representing Canada's 35 000 Inuit), Nelly Curnoyea was government leader of the Northwest Territories, and Mary Simon was president of the Inuit Circumpolar Conference, which serves as a voice for the Inuit from Canada, Alaska, Greenland, and Siberia. Born in Kangiqsualujjaq in northern Quebec to an Inuk mother and a father who was a hunter and guide, Simon was described by an interviewer in terms that could have been applied to many of the leaders among the aboriginal women: "whatever she does, whether it's dining at Rideau Hall, or making tea in a fishing camp, she always retains the sense of herself and an enormous sense of her 'Inuitness.' "[27]

However, aboriginal women critical of the proposed agreement attracted even more public attention during the pre-referendum campaign. Although some Indian and Métis women had been consulted, many Indian women felt that their specific concerns were not fully served by the national association of chiefs. There were few women in this group, although by this time it had changed its name from the National Indian Brotherhood to the Assembly of First Nations. The Native Women's Association of Canada (NWAC) went to court to oblige the government to give direct funding and equal voice to their group as the representative of Native women in the constitutional discussions. NWAC's dissent was initially based on the possible loss of Charter protection for aboriginal women, but its continuing concern was the absence of spokespersons for women's concerns in the processes leading to Native self-government. In 1992, the Charlottetown Accord was rejected both in Quebec and in the rest of Canada. Perhaps because of their joint opposition to the proposal, by 1994 NAC and the FFQ were cautiously co-operating again, co-sponsoring a conference on social policy. The Supreme Court found against NWAC in 1994; however, by that time the federal government seemed to be accepting it as a legitimate participant — along with the four other national-level Native associations— in the ongoing talks about Native self-government.[28]

RELIGION

Within the established religions, women worked for change, but progress varied. Devoted Roman Catholic laywomen were essential to the everyday operations of a faith that, like all mainstream religions, was losing adherents. Questioning long-established practices, some began discussion groups and feminist activism designed to reform practices and doctrines so that they might remain within the communion.[29] But the appeal of the religious life declined for women. Entry into the orders dwindled, and many nuns broke their vows. As the trend increased, between 1968 and 1986, nearly 4000 nuns in Quebec left religious communities.[30] Many of those who remained were elderly, and communities dwindled. One example was the *Soeurs adoratrices du précieux sang*, a contemplative order that had been founded in 1861 and maintained a sequestered community life, requiring members to spend six hours in prayer each day. In 1991, the order closed its last French-speaking section outside Quebec when it sold its convent in Ottawa to the Royal Society of Physicians and Surgeons of Canada.[31] Official Catholic opposition to contraception and abortion continued, even though by the 1980s most Canadian Catholics were almost as permissive as the rest of the country on these issues.[32] There was still no possibility of ordaining women or even allowing laywomen a larger official role in the church. In Toronto in 1987, an 11-year-old girl, Sandra Bernier, who had regularly been serving at the altar, was barred from doing so during a special celebratory mass. The prohibition against female altar-servers was repeated in 1994 for the 150th anniversary of the diocese of Toronto. Later in 1994, the Vatican formally permitted such access, but in the same year the Pope himself repeatedly and categorically ruled out any possibility of women being accepted into the priesthood. Two thousand prominent Quebec women signed a statement of dissent, but shortly after his installation in November Jean-Claude Turcotte, Cardinal of Quebec, explicitly supported the Pope's position.[33]

The more conservative elements in Judaism were also resistant to change, despite the pressures exerted by feminists who wished to remain within the community. Although Reconstructionist and Reform Jewish congregations instituted bat mitzvah ceremonies for girls and hired women rabbis (or, more often, assistant rabbis), Orthodox women saw few changes. They continued to have to supplement legal divorce with their ex-husbands' permission (the *get*) if they wished to remarry inside their religion. However, as a result of pressure started by volunteer committees, Canadian divorce legislation was altered in 1990 so that the *get* could no longer be used as a bargaining chip in divorce settlements. Canadian Jewish women led an international campaign on the issue. "I feel that Judaism is at stake over this issue," said Norma Joseph, president of the Montreal-founded and -based International Coalition for Agunah Rights: "Judaism is a just religion and this is not justice."[34]

The Anglican Church of Canada made reforms more speedily than its counterparts in the United Kingdom. When it first ordained women ministers in 1976, church officials had to struggle with new issues: "I don't think when they first ordained women they thought about them getting pregnant," said one of the newest of the Anglican women priests in 1986 when she was within three months of needing maternity leave. Seventeen years after the first ordination of women, the Reverend Victoria Matthews was elected Canada's first female bishop, one of five women bishops in the world-wide Anglican communion. She described herself as a feminist, but "not a strident one": "I am a woman and have a woman's perspective, but I don't bring womanhood to the House of Bishops, I bring myself."[35]

The largest Protestant denomination in the country, the United Church of Canada, was also increasingly responsive to women, and in 1982 peace activist Lois Wilson was elected moderator. She later recalled that she "thrived on the demands of the job." She added, "Since as a woman I had no role models, I was free to innovate." Wilson went on to become the first woman president of the World Council of Churches and active with a wide range of groups including Amnesty International and the Canadian Civil Liberties Union; her memoirs, *Turning the World Upside Down*, ended with support of the Innu women who were campaigning against low-level NATO training flights in the area of Goose Bay. For Wilson, and for many other women, religion was still among the major motives for feminism and for activism.[36]

The mixed messages of religion continued to be powerful. Some Muslim women returned to observing the traditional *hijab*, the code of modesty and chastity prescribed for girls and women by Muslim religious law; it required wearing garments that concealed the hair and sometimes obscured the body. "Feeling that one has to meet the impossible male standards of beauty is tiring and often humiliating," wrote Naheed Mustafa, a young Canadian-born college graduate who described herself as having been "a borderline bulimic." For her, *hijab* was a way "to give women ultimate control of their own bodies." But for feminist Fauzia Rafiq, a member of the editorial committee of *Diva*, a magazine for South Asian women, the effort of some Canadian Muslim men to "enforce Islamic law pertaining to family life" amounted to "consolidating male power . . . in the name of religion, cultural diversity and hereditary rights." In 1994 some schools in Quebec attempted to forbid girls to wear the headscarf that was the commonest version of *hijab*, but the Quebec Human Rights Commission ruled that a school could intervene only if a student was wearing the scarf against her will.[37]

The search for a spirituality sympathetic to women led some women toward feminist religions, including groups that drew on ancient traditions of witchcraft. By the 1980s, Canadian women had available an eclectic range of Goddess cults made up of women only. Goddess-worshippers were the most extreme example of women who organized outside of mixed-sex religious groups. For such women, the problem of conflict between male standards and female autonomy was solved; their separate organization asserted their legitimate interests as women. It was estimated that some 60 to 70 percent of the participants in neo-paganism were women, apparently because of the prominent role of goddesses and the women who served them.[38]

OPPOSITION

Although many women responded enthusiastically to feminism and to the changes in women's lives, others reacted with suspicion, hostility, and organized opposition. The anti-feminist Federation of Women United for the Family was founded in Alberta in 1981, and in the mid-1980s a group headed by women formerly prominent in the "right to life" movement began to get media attention. Established in 1983, the organization called itself REAL Women, an acronym for Real, Equal, Active, for Life. It claimed that NAC represented only a small number of "radical feminists" and announced that it spoke for the "real" women of Canada. "What are we? plastic women?" responded Judy Erola, previously the federal minister responsible for the status of women. REAL Women opposed abortion, universality of social services, the equality clauses of the Charter of Rights, no-fault divorce, legislation on equal pay for work of equal value, publicly funded daycare, affirmative action in employment, and legal protection of the rights of homosexuals. Given the dependence of Canadian women's groups on public funding, REAL Women represented a genuine threat. They provoked a government review of the Women's Program in the Secretary of State. Although that review vindicated the program, its funding was cut substantially under the Progressive Conservative governments of the 1980s. Many members of the media were happy to counterpoise REAL Women with feminist organizations such as NAC and LEAF.[39]

Anti-feminist women's groups responded in part to the surviving inequities in the treatment of women. There could be no disagreement among feminists with the wish to adapt the workplace to the needs of the family. Even in their defence of an idealized traditional family, anti-feminist women were attempting to obtain recognition and reward for the distinctive abilities and activities of women. But such groups seemed unable to accept the alterations or diversity in values or lifestyles that the rest of a far-from-monolithic women's movement spoke for. Florence Bird summed up the problem:

> REAL Women wants to recreate the beautiful and happy society of the '50s ads — the happy mother, the beautiful, shining kitchen and the three happy children who never get sick. . . . It's nostalgia for the good old days that were never very good.[40]

Similar ideologies motivated parliamentarians who blocked national funding for daycare and formed a "family caucus" in 1989. The caucus, whose members had also supported the government's unsuccessful attempts to recriminalize abortion, blocked insertion of protection for lesbians and gay men into the federal Human Rights Act and generated legislation that would have excluded all same-sex couples from family-defined benefits, however long-lasting or well-established their relationship. The bill on same-sex couples died on the order paper before the 1993 election, but not before it had shown the strength of conservative forces in Canadian life.[41]

Some individual men also reacted with hostility to both the reality and the rhetoric of the second wave of women's activism. The most shocking example, the "Montreal Massacre" of December 6, 1989, became symbolic of opposition to feminism and also, more generally, of violence against women. The story of what happened is straightforward. Catherine Bergeron traced the events that led to the death of her sister, Geneviève, who had hoped to become an engineer like their father. Christmas break was near and Geneviève was in the cafeteria with her friend Marco, at a polytechnical institute that was part of the *Université de Montréal*. Afterward, Marco told Catherine what happened:

Geneviève Bergeron
Hélène Colgan
Nathalie Croteau
Barbara Daigneault
Anne-Marie Edward
Maud Haviernick
Barbara Maria Klueznick
Maryse Laganière
Maryse Leclair
Anne-Marie Lemay
Sonia Pelletier
Michèle Richard
Annie St-Arneault
Annie Turcotte

Murdered December 6, 1989,
Université de Montréal.

*We, their sisters and brothers, remember,
and work for a better world.*

*In memory and in grief for all the women
murdered by men, for women of all
countries, all classes, all ages,
all colours.*

Inscription for a memorial in British Columbia for women killed by men; the names are those of the victims of the Montreal Massacre (December 6, 1989).

Source: Women's Monument Project, Capilano College, Vancouver, B.C.

They were just sitting in the upper level of the cafeteria chatting about an essay which was nearly due. Geneviève heard noises and ran down the stairs to the main floor. She thought the man holding a gun was a joke, a carnival trick.

It was not a trick, or a robbery, as some of the young men thought when the man with the gun ordered them to leave. Geneviève tried to run and hide, but she was cornered behind the stereo speakers and shot twice, from so close that the spent cartridges from the bullets were found on her chest. She died instantly. Thirteen other young women students were also killed by Mark Lépine, who then shot and killed himself. He had failed to be admitted to an engineering program at the *École polytechnique*. "I hate feminists," he screamed at his victims, and he left a letter listing other targets, all of them successful women whom he identified as "feminists."[42]

Women's groups organized vigils and marches, and attempted with some success to focus the widespread feelings of grief and shock upon the more routine domestic violence committed by men against women. Some journalists helped to produce an improved understanding of the fear that constrained the lives of many women, while polls showed increasing public awareness that the courts failed to protect women from violent men. In one national survey four years after the massacre, 67 percent of respondents felt that violence against women had become worse in recent years; many blamed unemployment and economic hardship for the increased domestic tensions. By the 1990s, in contrast to the past, women were as likely as men to be victims of violent crime; for women, however, in four out of five cases, the attacker was someone they knew. A study released by Statistics Canada at the end of 1993 showed that more than half of a representative group of women had been physically or sexually assaulted by men at least once in their adult lives; another StatsCan study reported that more than 78 000 women and children had used battered women's shelters in 1991–92. Support for educational programs and resources to diminish violence against women increased, with both federal and provincial governments making some commitment. In 1991, December 6 was proclaimed a National Day of Remembrance and Action on Violence Against Women.[43]

However, some men objected to women-only ceremonies mourning the victims of the massacre, which they felt implied that all men were potentially violent. More generally, many men—and some women—became resentful of the continuing demand for changes in attitudes and policies relating to women. The resulting anti-feminism joined with a wave of anger about something labelled "political correctness," or PC for short. Apparently coined by socialists joking among themselves about the pressure to toe an orthodox party line, the phrase was widely adopted to describe those who rejected the assumption that European, white, male, heterosexual, and able-bodied added up to a norm to which all others should defer. Objections focussed on events like the cancellation of the Miss Canada pageant under feminist pressure (in 1992), policies barring sexual or racial slurs or other forms of harassment, insistence on gender-neutral language, and even the increasing disapproval and legal restriction of smoking. All of these changes related to what the majority of Canadians had, in the past, found acceptable, but that many now found sufficiently offensive to bar legally. In addition, during economic hard times, employment equity programs seemed threatening to white, able-bodied men already endangered by the constricting job market. They were made profoundly uneasy by targets for hiring and promoting women, visible minorities, Natives, and the disabled. Women were often treated as if they were simply some sort of narrow interest group. Critics raged about "the politicization of sex, race, class and language," labelling feminists "professional zealots" or "feminazis." Such reactions exaggerated the power of women, minorities, and their supporters.[44]

Ironically, in the 1990s attacks on an aggressive, powerful feminism co-existed with insistence that feminism was finished, so that this was a post-feminist era. There were also accusations that young women were repelled by feminism because it treated women as victims: "whining, poor-little-me feminists have turned women, especially young ones, off." Perhaps the successes of the second wave of feminism were overestimated by young women growing up in a formally equal but less prosperous world. Some feminists suggested, optimistically, that even the opposition to women's goals was evidence that women's concerns were now being taken more seriously. "I see the backlash as a sign of success," said Lorna Marsden, formerly president of NAC and then a senator, now president of Wilfrid Laurier University. "People are now paying more attention to gender issues. In the past, these issues were marginalized and trivialized."[45]

THE WOMEN'S MOVEMENT: DIVERSITY AND DISAGREEMENT

By the last two decades of the century, the structure of the women's movement had changed. "Identity politics" were now highlighted in Canadian politics, as various population groups mobilized to an unprecedented degree around shared characteristics such as race, ethnicity, or sexual orientation. The 1980s and 1990s saw the birth of many new organizations comprising women with multiple identities; such groups spoke for populations as specialized as Haitian women in Montreal (Neges Vanyan) or potentially as inclusive as immigrant domestic workers (Intercede). Women who were not part of Canada's historically white majority voiced anger at the way that government, media, and the established feminists felt entitled to define women's goals. As resources diminished because of recession and neo-conservatism, voluntary groups became increasingly competitive. Substituting the term "diversity" for the confrontational and relativist concept of "difference" did little to allay tensions.[46]

There were clearly issues that affected women of all kinds or persuasions. Foremost among these were those related to bodily conditions: abortion and contraception, incest and rape, birth and childrearing, sexuality and marriage. Paradoxically, these very issues provoked the most heated disputes among women and women's groups, for it was around such questions that loyalty to community and gender interest clashed most emphatically. One example was the question of domestic violence. In the early days of second-wave feminism, women involved with the shelter and transition house movement had recognized that police forces were reluctant to intervene in "family quarrels." In addition, battered women were often so dependent on their partners, both psychologically and economically, that they were reluctant to take legal action against them. Women's groups accordingly urged, with some success, that police practice be changed so that officers would automatically lay charges when called in because of family assault, whether or not the victim requested it. London, Ontario, was the first of many municipalities to adopt such a policy, in 1981. However, abused women in minority communities showed increasing reluctance to call on the police for help. Because their partners were likely to be treated in a discriminatory fashion, such women were under pressure from relatives and friends not to seek assistance from public authorities. The women "have to choose one kind of violence over another," said Shelley Das, executive director of the National Organization of Immigrant and Visible Minority Women of Canada (NOIVM), which in 1994 joined with the Elizabeth Fry Society and the National Association of Women and the Law to urge that ethnic communities should set up councils responsible for supporting the women in question and for disciplining and educating their partners. Both citizens and law enforcers had mixed responses to these suggestions.[47]

New issues of special concern to aboriginal women began to arise as Native organizations acquired power over social services, including areas such as adoption and foster care. Such agencies were, by and large, controlled by men. In 1991, Winnipeg aboriginal women's groups went to the media, against the orders of the Assembly of Manitoba Chiefs, to publicize cases like those of a young Ojibwa woman who brought her children to a Winnipeg shelter, saying they had been beaten by their father—who was on the board of the Native child welfare society that decided to return the children to his care. Marilyn Fontaine-Brightstar, a member of the

Aboriginal Women's Unity Coalition, presented such groups' views in *Weetamah*, Manitoba's aboriginal newspaper:

> Abuse and exploitation of women and children is a political issue of equal importance to achievement of our inherent right to govern ourselves. Given that our elected aboriginal leadership is reluctant to stand up for this part of our community, we have no other choice.[48]

For women activists, the racial and ethnic composition of women's groups sometimes seemed more important than their beliefs. An example that related to public policy was the Canadian Panel on Violence Against Women set up by the federal government in 1991 in collaboration with a diverse network of women's organizations. The panel's 1993 report, which comprised almost 500 recommendations, mostly targeted at the federal government, argued that violence against women would not end until women obtained fair and equal treatment in all areas of life: "a fundamental restructuring of society," in the words of panel chair Pat Marshall. Under other circumstances it might have been recognized that the report was a far-ranging successor to the *Report of the Royal Commission on the Status of Women in Canada*, highlighting problems and groups of women not given sufficient attention in the initial assessment. However, both NOIVM and NAC savaged the panel's report because of the virtual absence of women of colour from the panel and the relatively brief discussion of those women's particular problems. Indian women, by contrast, noted that the panel's research constituted the first major study of the violence they endured.[49]

In Quebec, the strains between Quebec nationalism and women's diversity continued. In 1990, Lise Payette, who had returned to broadcasting, was asked by the provincial government to head an official commemoration of the fiftieth anniversary of the emancipation of Quebec women. She now compounded her earlier remarks about "Yvettes" with what was heard as a statement that immigrant women, as newcomers, were not entitled to participate in the event. Some immigrant women's groups accordingly refused to take part in the celebration and exhibits. Outside the realm of public policy, the FFQ encountered related problems. In 1992, when the group set in motion extensive consultations for a project titled "Pour un Québec féminin pluriel," sovereigntist women blocked the formulation of what was intended to be a non-partisan feminist blueprint that would apply whether or not independence took place. However, the wide consultation and an epochmaking conference drew together representatives of many categories of women who had previously had little involvement with the umbrella group. The next year, the *Fédération* redefined its mandate to focus on those women who were economically disadvantaged and also those who suffered multiple discriminations, such as immigrants, aboriginal women, lesbians, those who had handicaps, or members of visible minorities.[50]

The confrontations occurring inside women's organizations also became an issue, and one that received much media attention. Disagreement around issues of women's diversity had been going on longer than most remembered, however. In a 1993 interview, well-known lesbian author Jane Rule recounted an episode in the "early 70s":

> I can remember sitting in one of the first women's movement consciousness raising groups when somebody brought in an article from a magazine about

lesbians and said she thought this would corrupt kids, and I said, you know, up to now, we've been talking about everything as *I* or *we*, and I think if you want to talk about lesbians, you have to do the same thing. You can't talk about *them*. And I am willing to start by saying that I am a lesbian and I am ready to talk about it. Dead silence.

Rule recounted that within two or three more years, everyone in the group was talking about "a range of sexuality." They developed a women's studies program and "saw to it that there was lesbian content in all the things we did."[51] But few women were as outspoken and brave as Rule, and few women's groups adapted as hers did. As a result, by the 1980s lesbians and women of colour had become increasingly resentful of what they perceived as the insensitivity of white, heterosexual women, including feminists, to other women's particular needs. In addition, women with disabilities and older women reacted to the failures of the young and able-bodied founders of the second wave to accommodate the contingencies of bodily condition. It also became clear that Jewish and Muslim women felt excluded by the pervasive Christian culture of Canada, with its anti-Semitism and its sense of superiority to all other religions.

Much of the friction among organized women resulted from the failure of long-hoped-for reforms to improve women's lives substantially, particularly for those whose disadvantages were multiple. Many groups split up or went out of existence. Service-providing groups and cultural media were the most vulnerable to the particularisms of identity politics, and the cross-pressures of race and sexual orientation were often excruciating for the women involved. The oldest feminist press in Canada went through a wrenching process of change after women of colour protested that they had been asked to participate in a lesbian fiction anthology only after the contents and procedure were set; Women's Press survived but many of the original members left to form a new feminist press, Second Story.[52] Some women's organizations adopted policies of affirmative action themselves. NAC chose a black movement activist, Beverly Bain, as executive director and acclaimed as president in 1992 a South Asian immigrant from Tanzania, Sunera Thobani. Thobani was from Vancouver, where she had been active with the India Mahila Association and the B.C. Coalition for Abortion Clinics. Her election represented the first time that NAC's leadership came from outside of Toronto, enhancing the organization's claim to be nationally representative.[53]

Such initiatives did little, however, to quell the increasing uncertainty about the role and scope of the large national women's organizations, especially NAC. In July 1993, following the publicity related to the constitutional battles, a national poll asked respondents to identify an organization that represented the interests of Canadian women; half of those polled said that there was no such thing, and only 14 percent mentioned NAC, although "dozens" of other groups were listed.[54] Contact and co-operation among women's groups of all kinds were in fact much increased, and NAC was best understood as one of the major intersection points. In 1993 NAC's list of member groups — more than 500 in number — included organizations as large as the women's committees of major trade unions and as small as radical action groups. CARAL and VOW remained members, as did a few first-wave organizations: BPW Clubs, YWCAs, the CFUW, and Anglican Church women. Although relatively few of the newer women's groups that were organized around ethnicity, race, religion, or bodily condition joined NAC, the Committee was in continuing contact with non-member federations, including the Canadian Congress of Black Women and NWAC, as well as with the other significant umbrella groups. Thus, links were maintained with the *Fédération des femmes du Québec*, the National Organization of Immigrant and Visible Minority Women, and the National Council of Women, whose national, provincial, and local groups still brought together many of the older ethnic women's groups and service organizations. Although the national groups varied in the degree to which they consulted their members—and there was no consultation at all with the large majority of women without institutional affiliations — most women apparently appreciated what activists were willing to do on their behalf. Canadians might not be very enthusiastic about feminism, but they seemed to think well of the women's movement. In March 1994, a poll reported that more than half of those who read newspapers thought that the women's movement had been a good influence.[55]

Many of the organizations that made up the web of women's groups were able to carry on their activities because of the funding they received from the Women's Program created in 1973 in the Department of the Secretary of State (now Human Resources Development). In 1986 this program disbursed some $12.4 million (about $1 per Canadian woman — not a vast sum). Citing the necessities of the recession and the need to reduce the national debt, the Progressive Conservative government of 1988 reduced the amount available and specified that it could be used only for projects and not for operating expenses. However, an attempt to stop funding women's centres altogether had to be rescinded after vigorous lobbying by women's groups. In 1994 the Program's funding stood at $10.7 million; NAC's budget was about $1 million in that year, with less than $300 000 of it provided by the government.[56]

As Canada moved into the 1990s, more information emerged about the many extraordinary women in Canada's diverse racial, ethnic, and religious traditions. History collectives and individual researchers started to uncover the rich inheritance of, for example, lesbians and women of colour. Publications and films made concrete the strength and coherence of ethnic and religious traditions, potentially freeing women to criticize their own communities with less defensiveness: even those disadvantaged because of ethnicity or religion or sexual orientation might have their own prejudices that needed combatting. Mixed-blood women pointed out the exclusionary effect of defining individuals by ethnicity or national origin. Few people in Canada were not of multiple ancestry, regardless of how they might identify themselves or be identified. For example, Elizabeth Goudie, who was born in Mud Lake, Labrador, in 1902, and who raised ten children as the wife of a Labrador trapper, began her memoirs with the following sentence: "In approximately the year 1806, our great-great-grand-mother, who was an Eskimo orphan, ran away from down Rigolet Eskimos." Marriages over the generations produced "quite a mixture — Eskimo, English, French, Scottish and Indian," she said, adding that her children "are proud of their Indian and Scotch blood." Ninety-one years after Goudie's birth, Anne Vespry, of even more complex ethnic background, reflected that

few of us identify as mixed race. It is easier to choose sides, identifying with one race over another, assimilating. Perhaps we are the heroes of the race wars, learning from the best that our ancestry has offered and disdaining the close-minded prejudice or xenophobia that lurks in our cultural closets.

When asked what her parents are, she replies, "librarians"; when pushed as to where they are *from*, she says "They're Canadians."[57]

As women learned more about one another, they found it easier to recognize some shared bases of disadvantage. Ageism, for example, became an issue at the end of the 1980s partly because feminist activists, youthful in the 1960s, were becoming aware of their own mortality. Although Canada's component cultures differed somewhat in their respect for the aged, most Canadians considered older women both sexually "over the hill" and unemployable. Elderly women of a variety of backgrounds were noteworthy, nevertheless, for their energy and imaginativeness. Some were able to resist ageism by insisting on maintaining their independence and physical activity. In 1992, Carrie Best, then aged 91, restarted the Nova Scotia *Clarion*, which had discontinued publication in 1956. Ivy Granstorm of Vancouver was a world record-holder in the "70 plus" category in track and field, with a repertoire ranging from 100 to 10 000 metres. Some followed American radical feminist Mary Daly in symbolic resistance, proudly proclaiming themselves "crones" or "amazing greys."[58] Other older women, beginning in 1978, mobilized themselves into street theatre groups under the name of the Raging Grannies. Decked out in pink running shoes and outrageous hats, singing satirical versions of popular songs, they soon had at least fourteen groups scattered from British Columbia to Newfoundland. Many were former members of VOW who had found a new way to oppose militarism and sexism. They continued to oppose nuclear submarines, war toys, environmental pollution, and pornography, but added new targets such as the Charlottetown Accord and the North American Free Trade Agreement. Typical of women activists in the last decade of the century, the Grannies explicitly saw themselves as feminists, and they also consciously valued the comradeship that came of women working together. Linda Siege, a former member of VOW, summed it up: "I want to live in a principled way but still have fun." Doran Doyle, who named the group, described herself as "Catholic and feminist" and commented, "We came together as older women at the peak of experience who would not be shunted aside. We're raging for peace. A wonderful paradox."[59]

The last years of the century were certainly not easy for activist women. The charges of "political correctness" were accompanied by the twin problems of "voice" and "appropriation." Many women who attempted to move beyond the perspective of their own situation found themselves accused of taking over the products and messages of those they attempted to help, while "help" itself was seen as condescension. One example was Anne Cameron, whose *Daughters of Copper Woman* had played a major role in making white women aware of the rich tradition of the aboriginal women of Canada. Cameron had lived for many years in Haida communities, where the old women had given her permission to publish the creation legends they controlled. Her children, whose father was a Métis, were accepted as Natives. She was nevertheless criticized for appropriating the voice of Indian women and for using her superior resources as a white woman to publish material that Native women could not get into print. "The guys in suits are hoping that we will divide so they can once again conquer," she responded. She pleaded for communication and co-operation among women for the sake of the tasks that still faced them, appealing eloquently to a tradition that she traced to diverse foremothers:

> We promised if ever the time came when The Grandmother, the Earth, needed us, the Children of her daughter First Woman, who became First Mother, would

Lavinia Crawley of East Preston, Nova Scotia, and her second husband, John Crawley. A descendant of a family that immigrated to Canada during the War of 1812, she was 88 when this photo was taken in 1982.

Source: Black Cultural Centre for Nova Scotia.

come together again and learn to live as a Rainbow Family, in love and in balance.

"I think that's what feminism is," she said. "The coming together of all the colours of sisters and cousins."[60]

NOTES

1. Linda Silver Dranoff, *Women in Canadian Life: Law* (Toronto: Fitzhenry and White-side, 1977), 52–53.
2. Lissa Geller, "Common Law Spouse Ruling," *Kinesis* (May 1993), 7; for information on rural women and feminism see Louise I. Carbert, *Agrarian Feminism: The Politics of Ontario Farm Women* (Toronto: University of Toronto Press, 1995).
3. Lorenne M.G. Clark and Debra Lewis, *Rape: The Price of Coercive Sexuality* (Toronto: Women's Press, 1977); Paula Bourne, "Women, Law and the Justice System," in Ruth Roach Pierson et al., eds., *Canadian Women's Issues, Vol. 1: Strong Voices* (Toronto: James Lorimer, 1993), 331–3; Sean Fine, "Different Styles on the Bench," *The Globe and Mail* (October 25, 1993), A9; Geoffrey York, "Lawyers Oppose Proposed Rape Law," *The Globe and Mail* (May 15, 1992), A3; Geoffrey York and Jeff Sallot, "Campbell Agrees to Amend Bill on Sexual Assault," *The Globe and Mail* (June 3, 1992), A8; Gay Abate and Tu Thanh Ha, "Drunkenness Defence

for Rape Worries Justice Department," *The Globe and Mail* (October 4, 1994), A7; Sean Fine, "Lose Mr. Justice Iacobucci and You Lose All," *The Globe and Mail* (November 11, 1994), A1; "Drinker Beats Assault Charge," *The Globe and Mail* (November 1, 1994), A1; "Drunkenness Defence May be Tested," *The Globe and Mail* (July 14, 1995), A4.

4. F.L. Morton, "The Political Impact of the Canadian Charter of Rights and Freedoms," *Canadian Journal of Political Science* 20, 1 (March 1987), 41–42; Doris Anderson, "Women Need Money to Test Charter," *The Toronto Star* (May 23, 1987), G1; Eleanor Wachtel, " 'The Day Daddy Died and Nancy Got Rich,' " *Financial Post Moneywise* (March 1989), 67; Michael Mandel, *The Charter of Rights and the Legalization of Politics in Canada* (Toronto: Thompson Educational Publishing, 1994); Sherene Razack, *Canadian Feminism and the Law: The Women's Legal Education and Action Fund and the Pursuit of Equality* (Toronto: Second Story, 1991), 48, 65, 128–30; advertisement on the back of *Herizons* 6, 4 (Winter 1993).

5. Dranoff, *Women in Canadian Life: Law*; Ann Rhodes, "Women Judges: A New Breed," *Chatelaine* 59, 5 (June 1985), 52, 87–90; Canadian Advisory Council on the Status of Women [CACSW], *Work in Progress: Tracking Women's Equality in Canada* (Ottawa: 1994), 108; "*Bittersweet Passage* Gets Award," *Kinesis* (February 1994), 8; Maryka Omatsu, *Bittersweet Passage: Redress and the Japanese Canadian Experience* (Toronto: Between the Lines, 1992).

6. Madam Justice Bertha Wilson, "Will Women Judges Really Make a Difference?" text of speech delivered at Osgoode Hall Law School, York University, February 8, 1990; Donn Downey, "Humiliated by Judge's Kiss, Crown Attorney Testifies," *The Globe and Mail* (September 14, 1993), A18; Downey, "The Strange Case of [the] Kissing Judge," *The Globe and Mail* (September 29, 1993), A17; Geoffrey York, "Most Feel Courts Unfair to Women," *The Globe and Mail* (July 29, 1993), A1.

7. Ellen Adelberg and the Native Women's Association of Canada, "Aboriginal Women and Prison Reform," 92 n. 19; Sheelagh Cooper, "The Evolution of the Federal Women's Prison"; Margaret Shaw, "Reforming Federal Women's Imprisonment"; Carol LaPrairie, "Aboriginal Women and Crime in Canada: Identifying the Issues"; all in Ellen Adelberg and Claudia Currie, eds., *In Conflict with the Law: Women and the Canadian Justice System* (Vancouver: Press Gang, 1993); John Edwards [Commissioner, Correctional Service Canada, Ottawa], "Women's Prisons," *The Globe and Mail* (February 14, 1995), A22.

8. Catherine Creede, "Lesbian Erotica in Porn Net," *Herizons* 6, 4 (Winter 1993), 4; Chris Dafoe, "Little Sister v. Big Brother," *The Globe and Mail* (October 8, 1994), C1; Brenda Cossman, "Little Sister's Shipments Routinely Detained," *Xtra!* (November 11, 1994), 24; Stuart Blackley, "Little Sister's on Trial," *Xtra!* 263 (November 25, 1994), 17; Nancy Pollak, "Business as Usual," *Ms.* (May/June, 1995), 11–15.

9. Shannon e. Ash and Theresa McCarthy, "Female Circumcision Refugee Accepted," *Kinesis* (September 1994), 6; Michael Valpy, "The Women Persecuted for Being Women," *The Globe and Mail* (March 11, 1993), A2; Valpy, "Many Answers Needed on Domestic Violence," *The Globe and Mail* (March 25, 1993), A2; "195 'Gender' Refugees in 1994," *The Globe and Mail* (March 10, 1995), A4.

10. Canadian Advisory Council on the Status of Women, "Work in Progress: Tracking Women's Equality in Canada," June 1994, 6–7; John Stackhouse, "Women Everywhere Still Trail in Wages, Power, UN Reports," *The Globe and Mail* (August 17, 1995), A12.

11. Rosamonde Ramsay Boyd, "Women and Politics in the United States and Canada," *Annals of the American Association of Political and Social Science* 375 (January 1968),

56; Decision Marketing Research, *Women in Canada* (Ottawa: Office of the Co-ordinator, Status of Women, 1976), 120.

12. Penney Kome, *Women of Influence: Canadian Women and Politics* (Toronto: Double-day, 1985), appendix I; Sherill MacLaren, *Invisible Power: The Women Who Run Canada* (Toronto: Seal Books, 1991), 213 n. 11, 226; Sydney Sharpe, *The Gilded Ghetto: Women and Political Power in Canada* (Toronto: HarperCollins, 1994).

13. Rosemary Brown, *Being Brown: A Very Public Life* (Toronto: Random House, 1989).

14. In this survey, 73 percent said it would make no difference, and 13 percent said they would be more likely to support such a party: Canadian Institute of Public Opinion, Poll No. 382; Val Ross, "The Honorable Flora," *Chatelaine* 53, 1 (January 1980), 36.

15. Edward Greenspoon, "Tories Ready — Finally — to Accept Woman Leader," *The Globe and Mail* (June 14, 1993), A9.

16. Richard Johnston, Neil Nevitte, and Henry E. Brady, "Campaign Dynamics in 1993: Liberals, Conservatives, and Reform," and Elizabeth Gidengil, "The NDP and Social Democracy in the 1990s," papers based on the 1993 Canadian National Election Study, presented to the Canadian Political Science Association, June 1994; Donley T. Studlar and Richard E. Matland, "The Growth of Women's Representation in the Canadian House of Commons and the Election of 1984: A Reappraisal," *Canadian Journal of Political Science* 17, 1 (March 1994), 53–80.

17. MacLaren, *Invisible Power*, 218–19; Rick Haliechuk, "Augustine First Black Woman in House," *The Toronto Star* (October 26, 1993), B6; Patricia Orwen, "Surge in Female MPs Raises Activists' Hopes," *The Toronto Star* (October 28, 1993), A11; Charlotte Gray, "House-Breaking," *Saturday Night* 109, 10 (December 1994), 130; "The March of Equality," *The Globe and Mail* (October 8, 1994), A4.

18. Donley T. Studlar and Richard E. Matland, "Representation of Women in the Canadian Provinces: A Preliminary Analysis," paper presented to the Canadian Political Science Association, June 1994; Chantal Maillé, *Primed for Power: Women in Canadian Politics* (Ottawa: Canadian Advisory Council on the Status of Women, 1990); Robert Sheppard, "Alexa McDonough Steps Down," *The Globe and Mail* (November 28, 1994), A15; James Doyle, "Barbara M. Hanley: First Woman Mayor in Canada," *Ontario History* 84, 2 (June 1992), 130–40; Interview by Marian Frances Wright in *A Woman's Almanac: Voices from Atlantic Canada* (St. John's, Nfld.: Creative Publishers), 78–81.

19. Evelyne Tardy, "Les femmes et la campagne référendaire," in *Québec: Un pays incertain* (Montréal: Éditions Québec-Amérique, 1980), 183–203; Michèle Jean et al., "Nationalism and Feminism in Quebec: The 'Yvettes' Phenomenon," in Roberta Hamilton and Michèle Barrett, eds., *The Politics of Diversity: Feminism, Marxism and Nationalism* (Montreal: Book Center, 1986), 322–38; "Les Yvettes douze ans après: Essais d'interprétation," in Anita Caron et Lorraine Archambault, eds., *Thérèse Casgrain: Une femme ténace et engagée* (Sainte-Foy: Presses de l'Université du Québec, 1993), 163–195; quote from Evelyne Tardy, "Le caractère paradoxal de l'engagement des Québécoises," in Caron et Archambault, eds., *Thérèse Casgrain*, 182.

20. Penney Kome, *The Taking of Twenty-Eight: Women Challenge the Constitution* (Toronto: Women's Press, 1983), 23.

21. Walter Tarnopolsky, "The Constitution and Human Rights," in Keith Banting and Richard Simeon, eds., *"And No One Cheered": Federalism, Democracy and the Constitution Act* (Toronto: Methuen, 1983), 272.

22. Beverly Baines, *Women, Human Rights and the Constitution* (Ottawa: Canadian Advisory Council on the Status of Women, 1980); Lynn McDonald, "The Charter

of Rights and the Subjection of Women," *Canadian Forum* 61, 710 (June/July 1981), 17–18; Chaviva Hosek, "How Women Fought for Equality," in Banting and Simeon, *"And No One Cheered,"* 280–300; Sandra Burt, "Women's Issues and the Women's Movement in Canada," in Alan Cairns and Cynthia Williams, eds., *The Politics of Gender, Ethnicity and Language* (Toronto: University of Toronto Press, 1986), 156–58.

23. Colette Beauchamp, "Anderson vs. Axworthy," *Féminin pluriel* 1, 1 (septembre 1981), espec. 17.

24. Sheila Copps, *Nobody's Baby: A Survival Guide to Politics* (Toronto: Deneau, 1986); in a 1988 speech cited by Donna Greschner, "Meech Lake: Constitution-Making as Patriarchal Practice," in Dawn H. Currie and Brian D. MacLean, eds., *Re Thinking the Administration of Justice* (Halifax: Fernwood, 1992), 59 n. 13.

25. Anne Collins, "Which Way to Ottawa?" *City Woman* (Holiday 1981), 30.

26. *Fédération des femmes du Québec*, "Are Women's Rights Threatened by the Distinct Society Clause?" in Michael D. Behiels, ed., *The Meech Lake Primer: Conflicting Views of the 1987 Constitutional Accord* (Ottawa: University of Ottawa Press, 1989), 296–7; Beverly Baines, "Gender and the Meech Lake Committee," in Clive Thompson, ed., *Navigating Meech Lake: The 1987 Constitutional Crisis* (Kingston: Institute of Intergovernmental Relations, Queen's University, 1988), 43–52; Ad Hoc Committee of Women on the Constitution, "We Can Afford a Better Accord: The Meech Lake Accord," *Resources for Feminist Research/Documentation sur la recherche féministe* 17, 3 (September 1988), 143–64.

27. Lawrence Leduc and Jon H. Pammett, "Referendum Voting: Attitudes and Behaviour in the 1992 Constitutional Referendum," *Canadian Journal of Political Science* 28, 1 (March 1995), 9, 15, 21; Marianne Stenbaek, "Mary Simon: Walking in Two Worlds but in One Spirit," in Mary Crnkovich, *"Gossip": A Spoken History of Women in the North* (Ottawa: Canadian Arctic Resources Committee, 1990), 261; Martha Greig, "Constitutional Notes," *Suvagunq* 7, 2 (1992), 7.

28. Miro Cernetig, "Resetting the Unity Table," *The Globe and Mail* (August 24, 1992), A1; Supreme Court of Canada, *R. v. Native Women's Association of Canada*, espec. Jeannette Corbiere Lavell, Affidavit, March 3, 1994.

29. Michael W. Higgins and Douglas R. Letson, *Women and the Church: A Sourcebook* (Toronto: Griffin House, 1986), espec. 142–208; Mary Jo Leddy, Bishop Remi de Roo, and Douglas Roche, "Women in the Church: The Unfinished Revolution," in Michael Creal, ed., *In the Eye of the Catholic Storm: The Church since Vatican II* (Toronto: HarperCollins, 1992), 44–54; Joanna Manning, "A Personal Challenge for the Empowering of the Laity," *Grail* 8, 3 (September 1992), 67–92.

30. Bernard Marotte, "Once Pervasive Quebec Nuns Seek Renewal," *The Globe and Mail* (October 1, 1987), A8.

31. Alan Freeman, "Another Chapter for Nuns' Home," *The Globe and Mail* (August 15, 1991), A6.

32. Reginald Bibby, "Religion à la Carte," *The Globe and Mail* (September 12, 1987), D2.

33. Linda Aisenberg, "Crusading Kids," *Chatelaine* 61, 3 (March 1988), 58, 135, 138–139; Jack Kapica, "Vatican to Allow Women at Altar," *The Globe and Mail* (April 13, 1994), A10; Kapica, "Altar Girl Has Forgiven, Not Forgotten," *The Globe and Mail* (April 27, 1994), A10; Richard Mackie, "Quebec Catholics Face Debate Over Women's Role," *The Globe and Mail* (January 3, 1995), 16.

34. Frances Kraft, "Vigil to Back Agunot Set," *Canadian Jewish News* (February 17, 1994); Lisa Rosenberg, "A Victory for Jewish Women? Revisions to the Provincial Family Law Act Pertaining to Jewish Divorce," York University, Major Research Paper, Graduate Program in Women's Studies, 1994.

35. Deborah Wilson, "Anglican Women Celebrate First Decade in Priesthood," *The Globe and Mail* (December 6, 1986), A18; Jack Kapica, "A Woman Joins the Men's Club," *The Globe and Mail* (December 7, 1993), A17.

36. Lois Wilson, *Turning the World Upside Down* (Toronto: Doubleday, 1989), 132.

37. Huda Khattab, *The Muslim Woman's Hand Book* (London: TA-HA Publishers, 1993); Naheed Mustafa, "My Body Is My Own Business," *The Globe and Mail* (June 29, 1993), A26; Sadia Zaman, "Canada's Muslim Women Set Gaze beyond the Veil," *NOW* magazine (May 21–27, 1992), 25; Zuhair Kashmeri, "Islamic Schism," *NOW* magazine (September 5–11, 1991), 22; Amber Nasrulla, "Educators outside Quebec Mystified by Hijab Ban," *The Globe and Mail* (December 13, 1994), A1, A4; André Picard, "Hijab in Schools Supported," *The Globe and Mail* (February 15, 1995), A4.

38. Naomi R. Goldenberg, *Changing of the Gods: Feminism and the End of Traditional Religions* (Toronto: Fitzhenry and Whiteside, 1979), 85–114; Bob Harvey, "Proud to Be Pagan," *Ottawa Citizen* (December 21, 1991), 16.

39. Ellen Long, "Traditionalist Women's Groups in the 1980s: A Case Study of the Alberta Federation of Women United for the Family," University of Alberta, Honours Thesis, 1986; Karen Dubinsky, *Lament for a "Patriarchy Lost"? Anti-Feminism, Anti-Abortion and REAL Women in Canada* (Ottawa: Canadian Research Institute for the Advancement of Women, 1985); Judy Erola speaking at York University, *The Second Decade/La deuxième décennie* 1, 2 (December 1986); REAL Women of Canada, "Presentation to the Standing Committee on the Secretary of State" (December 11, 1986); Danielle Crittenden, "REAL Women Don't Eat Crow," *Saturday Night* 103, 5 (May 1988), 27–36; Charlotte Gray, "Why Can't Women Get Their Act Together?" *Chatelaine* 61, 1 (November 1988), 83, 232, 234, 238, 240; Leslie A. Pal, *Interests of State: The Politics of Language, Multiculturalism, and Feminism in Canada* (Montreal and Kingston: McGill-Queen's University Press, 1993), 143–47.

40. Val Sears, "Will the Real Women Please Stand Up?" *The Toronto Star* (January 3, 1987), B4.

41. Katherine Teghtsoonian, "Neo-Conservative Ideology and Opposition to Regulation of Child Care Services in the United States and Canada," *Canadian Journal of Political Science* 26, 1 (March 1993), 97–121; Geoffrey York, "Tory Politicians Form Family Compact," *The Globe and Mail* (June 3, 1992), A1; Shannon e. Ash, "Human Rights and Lesbian Rights: Pissed Off, No Surprise," *Kinesis* (December 1992/January 1993), 5; Ash, "Canadian Human Rights Amendments: Not a Pleasant Package," *Kinesis* (March 1993), 5.

42. Colleen Turner, "Sister of Massacre Victim Remembers Music and Laughter," *The Gazette*, Montreal (December 6, 1993), 1, 6; "Text of Marc Lépine's Suicide Letter," in Louise Malette and Marie Chalouh, eds., *The Montreal Massacre*, translated by Marlene Wildeman (Charlottetown: gynergy books, 1991), unpaged appendix.

43. Gillian Walker, "The Conceptual Politics of Struggle: Wife Battering, the Women's Movement, and the State," *Studies in Political Economy* 33 (Autumn 1990), 63–90; Timothy Appleby, "Women As Likely As Men to Be Victims of Violence, Study Finds," *The Globe and Mail* (November 19, 1992), A11; Maria Crawford and Rosemary Gartner, *Woman Killing: Intimate Femicide in Ontario, 1974–1990* (Toronto: Women We Honour Action Committee, 1992); Alanna Mitchell, "50% of Women Report Assaults," *The Globe and Mail* (November 19, 1993), A1; Agnes Huang, "Beyond Surveying the Violence," *Kinesis* (December 1993/January 1994), A1, A6; Sange de Silva [Executive Director, Canadian Centre for Justice Statistics, Ottawa],

"Dimensions of Violence against Women," *The Globe and Mail* (December 3, 1994), D7.

44. Rick Salutin, "Loose Canons," *Saturday Night* 106, 10 (December 1991), 20, 22, 74, 76; Alanna Mitchell, "Sponsor Cancels Miss Canada Pageant," *The Globe and Mail* (January 4, 1992), A1; Barry Brown, "A Message to Feminist Fanatics: Get Real," *The Globe and Mail* (January 9, 1992), A16; Amy Friedman, *Nothing Sacred: A Conversation with Feminism* (Toronto: Oberon, 1992); Ray Conlogue, "Feminism: A Presumption of Guilt," *The Globe and Mail* (October 16, 1993), D5.

45. Kate Fillion, "Avoiding the Victim Syndrome," *The Globe and Mail* (March 16, 1994), C1; Deanne Rexe, "Feminism's Lost Generation," *The Globe and Mail* (May 17, 1993), A16; Geoffrey York, "Street Fighting Woman," *The Globe and Mail* (September 26, 1992), D4.

46. Carolle Charles, "Gender and Politics in Contemporary Haiti: The Duvalierist State, Transnationalism, and the Emergence of a New Feminism (1980–1990)," *Feminist Studies* 21, 1 (Spring 1995), 150; Brenda Thompson, "The Single Mother Movement," *Resources for Feminist Research/Documentation sur la recherche féministe* 17, 3 (September 1988), 124; Carol Camper, ed., *Miscegenation Blues: Voices of Mixed Race Women* (Toronto: Sister Vision, 1994).

47. Sean Fine, "End Sought to Mandatory Charges in Wife-Abuse Cases," *The Globe and Mail* (January 27, 1994), A1; Fine, "Black Policemen Support One Policy for All Wife Assault Cases," *The Globe and Mail* (February 1, 1994), A3; Dawn H. Currie and Brian D. MacLean, "Women, Men, and Police: Losing the Fight against Wife Battery in Canada," in Currie and MacLean, eds., *Re Thinking the Administration of Justice*, 251–75; Neil Bissoondath, *Selling Illusions: The Cult of Multiculturalism in Canada* (Toronto: Penguin, 1994), 135–44.

48. Stevie Cameron, "Chiefs to Speak Out on Family Violence," *The Globe and Mail* (December 16, 1991), A4.

49. Agnes Huang, "Canadian Panel on Violence against Women: Some Things Never Change," *Kinesis* (September 1992), 3; Vivian Smith, "Equality Called Key to Ending Violence," *The Globe and Mail* (July 30, 1993), A1; Lee Lakeman, "99 Federal Steps: Toward An End to Violence Against Women," (Toronto: National Action Committee on the Status of Women, December 1993), 38.

50. Sherene Razack, "Exploring the Omissions and Silences in Law around Race," in Joan Brockman and Dorothy Chunn, eds., *Investigating Gender Bias: Laws, Courts, and the Legal Profession* (Toronto: Thompson Educational Publishing, 1993), 40; Forum pour un Québec féminin pluriel, *Pour changer le monde* (Montreal: Les Editions Ecosociété, 1994), 119.

51. Keith Louise Fulton, "Bending the Rules: An Interview with Jane Rule," *Herizons* 6, 4 (Winter 1993), 30.

52. Chris Gabriel and Katherine Scott, "Women's Press at Twenty: The Politics of Feminist Publishing," in Linda Carty, ed., *And Still We Rise: Feminist Political Mobilizing in Contemporary Canada* (Toronto: Women's Press, 1993); Ayanna Black, "Working with Collectives," *Tiger Lily* 1, 2 (1987), 30–33, and 1, 3 (1987), 29–32.

53. Deborah Wilson, "Heir to NAC Stung by Attack," *The Globe and Mail* (May 10, 1993), A1; Angela Gogga, "From Rebick to Thobani: NAC Gets New Head," *Kinesis* (May 1993), 3; Patricia Elliott, "Feminism's New Face," *Canadian Living* 19, 8 (August 1994), 63–66.

54. York, "Most Feel Courts Unfair to Women," A1, A2.

55. NAC membership list, 1993; N.E.S. Griffiths, *The Splendid Vision: Centennial History of the National Council of Women of Canada, 1893–1993* (Ottawa: Carleton

University Press, 1993), 395–96; Susan Phillips, "Meaning and Structure in Social Movements: Mapping the Network of National Canadian Women's Organizations," *Canadian Journal of Political Science* 24, 4 (December 1991), 765–6; York, "Most Feel Courts Unfair to Women," A1; Murray Campbell, "Canadians Content, Survey Finds," *The Globe and Mail* (March 16, 1994), A1.

56. Sue Findlay, "Facing the State: The Politics of the Women's Movement Reconsidered," in Heather Jon Maroney and Meg Luxton, eds., *Feminism and Political Economy: Women's Work, Women's Struggles* (Toronto: Methuen, 1987), 31–50; Nancy Pollak, "SecState Funding Cuts: Death of a Thousand Cuts," *Kinesis* (March 1993), 3; Status of Women Canada, "Canada's National Report for the United Nations Secretariat of the Fourth World Conference on Women, September 1995 — Beijing, China" (May 12, 1994), 15; Pal, *Interests of State*, 232.

57. Elizabeth Goudie, *Woman of Labrador* (Toronto: Peter Martin Associates, 1973), 3, 4; Anne Vespry, "Coming Home: A One Act Play," *Xtra!* (August 20, 1993), 18.

58. Rosemary Sadlier, *Leading the Way: Black Women in Canada* (Toronto: Umbrella Press, 1994), 28, 32; Patricia Vertinsky, "Sport and Exercise for Old Women: Images of the Elderly in the Medical and Popular Literature at the Turn of the Century," *International Journal of the History of Sport* 9, 1 (April 1992), 83; Jane Taylor, "On Being Older and Wiser," cited in Pierson et al., eds., *Canadian Women's Issues*, vol. 1, 222; Wendy Putnam, "Amazing Greys: How Sweet the Years," *Kinesis* (December 1993/January 1994).

59. Toronto Raging Grannies flyer; Allison Gardner, "The Grannies Are Coming, Watch Out, Watch Out!" *Maturity* 13, 2 (March 1993); Karen Skowron, "Go, Granny, Go!" *Earthkeeper* (1993), 42, 44; Raging Grannies Songbook.

60. Christine St. Peter, " 'Woman's Truth' and the Native Tradition: Anne Cameron's *Daughters of Copper Woman*," *Feminist Studies* 15, 3 (Fall 1989), 499–523; Anne Cameron, "The Operative Principle Is Trust," in Libby Scheier, Sarah Sheard, and Eleanor Wachtel, eds., *Language in Her Eye: Views on Writing and Gender by Canadian Writers Writing in English* (Toronto: Coach House, 1990), 70, 71.

Appendix:
Tables and Figures

TABLE A.1 *Urban Population by Age, 1921–1991*

Year	Under 14		15–29		Over 30		Total	
	Total[a]	% Women	Total	% Women	Total	% Women	Total	% Women
1921	1 375	50.0	1 120	53.8	1 858	49.3	4 352	50.7
1931	1 599	49.8	1 505	52.6	2 470	49.2	5 574	50.3
1941	1 524	49.6	1 746	52.4	2 983	50.4	6 253	50.8
1951	2 350	49.2	2 077	53.0	4 201	51.2	8 628	51.1
1961	4 085	49.0	2 705	51.1	5 910	51.2	12 700	50.5
1971	4 648	48.9	4 357	50.3	7 406	51.9	16 411	50.6
1981	3 914	48.8	5 276	50.2	9 246	52.6	18 436	51.1
1991	4 157	48.8	4 890	50.0	11 860	52.8	20 907	51.3

[a] IN THOUSANDS.

Source: Calculated from F.H. Leacy, ed., *Historical Statistics of Canada* (Ottawa: Statistics Canada, 1983), p. A94–A109; Statistics Canada, *Profile of Urban and Rural Areas: Part A, Canada, Provinces and Territories*, Cat. No. 93-339 (Ottawa: Minister of Industry, 1993), Table 1, p. 6.

FIGURE A.1 *Life Expectancy at Birth by Sex, 1920–1992*

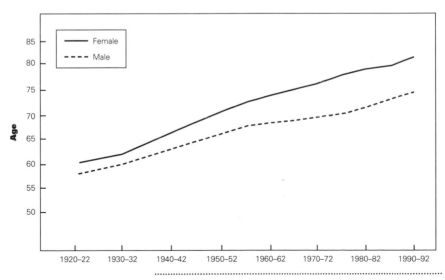

Source: Statistics Canada, *Deaths 1992*, Cat. No. 84-211 (Ottawa: Minister of Industry, 1995), Table 14, p. 32. Reproduced by authority of the Minister of Industry, 1995.

TABLE A.2 *Marital Status of Males and Females, Age 15 and Over,*
1911–1993 (Percent)

Census Year	Single[a]		Married[b]		Widowed		Divorced	
	M	F	M	F	M	F	M	F
1911	45.0	34.9	51.5	56.9	3.4	8.2	0.1	0.1
1921	39.2	32.0	56.7	59.2	4.0	8.6	0.1	0.1
1931	41.0	34.0	54.9	57.4	4.0	8.5	0.1	0.1
1941	39.8	33.0	56.1	58.0	4.0	8.8	0.2	0.2
1951	32.1	25.7	63.9	64.5	3.8	9.4	0.3	0.4
1961	29.9	23.7	66.4	66.8	3.6	9.7	0.4	0.5
1971	31.6	25.0	65.0	63.8	2.5	9.8	1.0	1.3
1981	31.3	24.5	64.3	62.4	2.2	10.0	2.2	3.1
1991	34.1	27.4	58.2	55.6	2.3	10.4	5.3	6.6
1993	22.8	19.6	67.9	55.5	5.6	19.8	3.9	4.8

[a] NEVER MARRIED.

[b] FOR 1971, 1981, AND 1991, FIGURES INCLUDE THOSE MARRIED, LIVING COMMON-LAW, OR MARRIED AND SEPARATED.

Source: Roy H. Rodgers and Gail Witney, "The Family Cycle in Twentieth Century Canada,"
Journal of Marriage and the Family 43, 3 (August 1981), p. 732; *Women in Canada: A Statistical Report*
(Ottawa: Statistics Canada, 1985); Statistics Canada, *Age, Sex and Marital Status*, Cat. No. 93-310
(Ottawa: Minister of Industry, 1992), Table 5, pp. 140–41; John Robert Colombo, ed., *The 1995*
Canadian Global Almanac (Toronto: MacMillan, 1994), p. 81.

FIGURE A.2 *Average Age at Marriage, Brides and Grooms, 1921–1990*

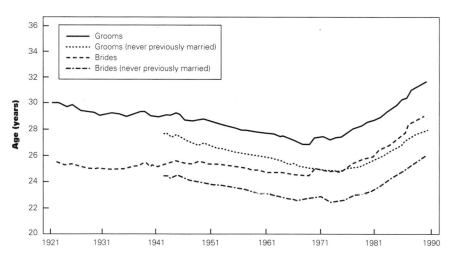

EXCLUDES DATA FROM NEWFOUNDLAND, YUKON TERRITORY, AND NORTHWEST TERRITORIES PRIOR TO 1950.

Source: Statistics Canada, *Health Reports 1992*, Cat. No. 82-003, Vol. 4, No. 4 (Ottawa: Minister of Industry,
1993), Chart 2, p. 409. Reproduced by authority of the Minister of Industry, 1995.

FIGURE A.3 *Divorce Rates, 1921–1991 (per 100 000 Population)*

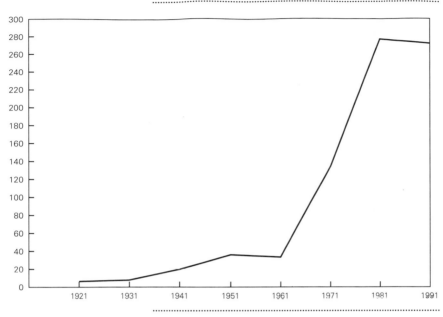

Source: Statistics Canada, *Vital Statistics, Vol. 2: Marriages and Divorces, 1973* (Ottawa: Minister of Industry, 1975), Table 15, p. 73; Statistics Canada, *Vital Statistics, Vol. 2: Marriages and Divorces, 1982* (Ottawa: Minister of Industry, 1983), Table 10, p. 16; Statistics Canada, *Divorces 1991*, Cat. No. 84-213 (Ottawa: Minister of Industry, 1994), Table 2, p. 371.

FIGURE A.4 *Fertility Rates per 1000 Women, 1851–1991*

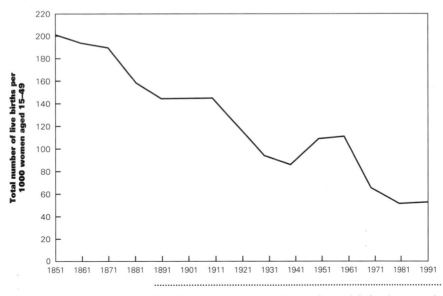

Source: Based on data from 1851–1961: Jacques Henripin, *Tendances et facteurs de la fécondité au Canada* (Ottawa: Bureau fédéral de la statistique, 1968), p. 21; data from 1971–1991: Statistics Canada, *Births 1991*, Cat. No. 84-210 (Ottawa: Minister of Industry, 1993), Table 17, p. 25.

TABLE A.3 *Average Number of Children Born to Ever-married Women, by Mother Tongue*

Period of Birth of Women (Approx.)	English	French	Other	All Languages
Before 1896	3.23	6.37	4.70	4.04
1896–1901	2.90	5.58	3.81	3.65
1901–1906	2.69	5.05	3.46	3.39
1906–1911	2.58	4.61	3.17	3.15
1911–1916	2.68	4.33	3.03	3.11
1916–1921	2.87	4.13	2.92	3.19
1921–1926	3.11	4.14	3.17	3.37
1926–1931	3.25	3.82	3.22	3.39
1931–1936	3.21	3.40	3.09	3.24
1936–1941	2.84	2.77	2.81	2.81
1941–1946	2.37	2.23	2.52	2.36
1946–51[a]	2.10	1.97	2.31	2.10
1951–56[a]	1.98	1.81	2.14	1.96

[a] THE FERTILITY OF THESE WOMEN WAS NOT COMPLETE IN 1991; WOMEN BORN BETWEEN 1946 AND 1951, FOR EXAMPLE, WOULD HAVE BEEN 40 TO 44 YEARS OLD IN 1991.

Source: A. Romaniuc, *Fertility in Canada: From Baby-Boom to Baby-Bust* (Ottawa: Statistics Canada, 1984), p. 16; Statistics Canada, *Fertility*, Cat. No. 93-321 (Ottawa: Minister of Industry, 1993), Table 4, pp. 113–16.

TABLE A.4 *Size of Completed Families (Percent)*

Period of Birth of Women (Approx.)	0	1	2	3	4	5	6+	Average Number of Children per Married Woman
Prior to 1876	12.83	9.23	11.08	10.86	9.99	8.65	36.89	4.818
1877–1886	13.20	11.16	13.46	12.31	10.38	8.16	31.01	4.398
1887–1896	12.31	12.36	15.44	13.32	10.55	7.96	27.77	4.167
1897–1901	12.62	14.11	17.31	13.85	10.30	7.52	24.04	3.795
1902–1906	15.48	14.99	19.04	14.40	9.90	6.81	19.38	3.385
1907–1911	15.25	15.76	21.32	14.92	9.76	6.56	16.43	3.154
1912–1916	13.12	15.12	22.48	16.82	10.85	6.75	14.87	3.110
1917–1921	11.77	13.14	22.41	17.96	12.24	7.66	14.83	3.189
1922–1926	9.59	11.26	22.00	19.62	13.96	8.45	15.12	3.315
1927–1931	8.35	9.43	21.23	20.80	15.43	9.47	15.29	3.407
1932–1936	7.20	8.98	22.8	22.89	16.53	9.30	12.22	3.260
1937–1941	8.03	10.02	28.89	25.36	14.39	6.81	6.50	2.814
1942–1946	9.38	12.56	38.08	24.08	9.90	3.43	2.58	2.356
1947–1951[a]	10.68	14.67	43.13	21.78	6.80	1.86	1.07	2.102
1952–1956[a]	12.99	16.43	42.89	20.19	5.52	1.28	.71	1.960

THIS TABLE SHOWS THE NUMBER OF CHILDREN BORN TO EVER-MARRIED WOMEN WHO HAVE REACHED THE END OF CHILDBEARING.

[a] THE FERTILITY OF THESE WOMEN WAS NOT COMPLETE IN 1991.

Source: A. Romaniuc, *Fertility in Canada: From Baby-Boom to Baby-Bust* (Ottawa: Statistics Canada, 1984), p. 31; Data for 1937–1956 calculated from Statistics Canada, *Fertility*, Cat. No. 93-321 (Ottawa: Minister of Industry, 1993), Table 1, p. 7.

FIGURE A.5 *Maternal Death Rates, 1921–1990*

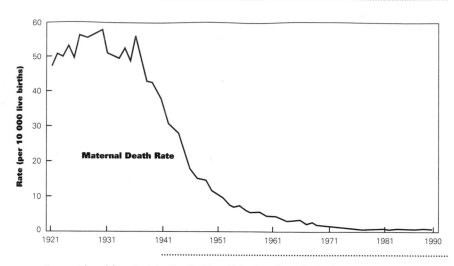

Source: Adapted from Statistics Canada, *Selected Infant Mortality and Related Statistics, Canada, 1921–1990*, Occasional, Cat. No. 82-549 (Ottawa: Minister of Industry, 1993), Chart 7, p. 21. Reproduced by authority of the Minister of Industry, 1995.

FIGURE A.6 *Births Occurring in Hospitals, 1931–1971 (Percent)*

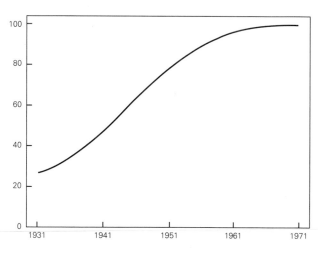

COMPARABLE FIGURES FOR 1981 AND 1991 ARE NOT AVAILABLE.

Source: Based on data from F.H. Leacy, ed, *Historical Statistics*, 2nd ed. (Ottawa: Statistics Canada, 1983), Table B1–14. Reproduced by authority of the Minister of Industry, 1995.

FIGURE A.7 *Labour-force Participation Rates of Women and Men, 1921–1993 (Percent)*

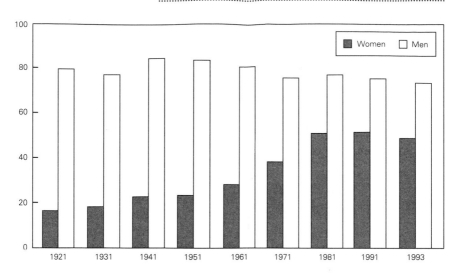

EXCLUDES NEWFOUNDLAND 1901–1961.

Source: 1921–1961: Based on data from F.H. Leacy, ed., *Historical Statistics of Canada*, 2nd ed. (Ottawa: Statistics Canada, 1983); 1971 and 1981: Statistics Canada, Cat. No. 71-201; 1991 and 1993: Statistics Canada, *Women in the Labour Force 1994*, Cat. No. 75-507E (Ottawa: Minister of Industry, 1994), Table 1.1, p. 10.

FIGURE A.8 *Women as a Percentage of the Labour Force, 1921–1993*

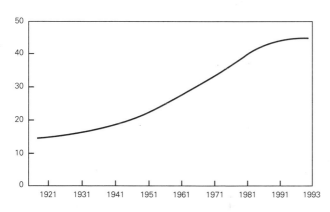

EXCLUDES NEWFOUNDLAND 1921–1961.

Source: 1921–1961: Based on data from F.H. Leacy, ed., *Historical Statistics of Canada*, 2nd ed. (Ottawa: Statistics Canada, 1983); 1971 and 1981: Statistics Canada, Cat. No. 71-201; 1991 and 1993: Statistics Canada, *Women in the Labour Force 1994*, Cat. No. 75-507E (Ottawa: Minister of Industry, 1994), Table 1.1, p. 10.

TABLE A.5 *Women's Participation in the Labour Force by Age, 1921–1991*

Year	1921	1931	1941	1951	1961	1971	1981	1985	1991
Age Category					Percentages				
15–24	29	33	41	42	41	49	61	71	65.1
25–34	17	24	25	24	30	44	66	69	77.2
35–44	11	13	16	22	31	44	64	69	78.4
45–54	11	13	13	20	33	44	56	60	69.9
55–64	10	13	10	14	24	34	42	34	35.7
Total %	18	20	21	24	30	39	52	55	58.2

Source: Canadian Congress for Learning Opportunities for Women, *Decade of Promise: An Assessment of Canadian Women's Status in Education, Training and Employment, 1976–1985* (Toronto: Avebury Research, 1986), p. 61; Statistics Canada, *Labour Force Annual Averages, 1991* (Ottawa: Minister of Industry, 1992), Table 1, p. B-2.

TABLE A.6 *Women as a Percentage of the Labour Force, by Occupation, 1901–1993*

Occupation	1901	1911	1921	1931	1941	1951	1961	1971	1981	1991	1993
Managerial	3.6	4.5	4.3	4.9	7.2	8.9	10.3	15.7	25.7	39.5	41.5
Professional	42.5	44.6	54.1	49.5	46.1	43.5	43.2	48.1	48.0	55.3	55.7
Clerical	22.1	32.6	41.8	45.1	50.1	56.7	61.5	68.4	77.3	81.7	81.2
Sales	10.4	20.2	25.6	26.0	32.1	38.3	40.3	30.4	36.9	44.4	43.4
Service	68.7	64.8	58.6	62.1	65.0	47.8	50.0	46.2	53.7	57.3	57.3
Primary	1.1	1.5	1.6	1.9	1.5	3.1	9.2	16.4	19.6	23.0	23.4
Blue Collar	12.6	10.2	10.1	8.5	11.0	11.5	10.6	12.0	–	–	–
All Occupations	13.4	13.2	15.4	17.0	19.9	22.0	27.3	34.3	38.3	44.5	44.8

FIGURES FOR 1901 ARE FOR WOMEN 10 YEARS OF AGE AND OLDER; FIGURES FOR 1911–1971 ARE FOR WOMEN 15 YEARS OF AGE AND OLDER; FIGURES FOR 1981, 1991, AND 1993 ARE FOR WOMEN 25 YEARS OF AGE AND OLDER.

Source: Liviana Calzavara, "Trends in the Employment Opportunities of Women in Canada, 1930–1980," in Rosalie Silberman Abella, *Research Studies of the Commission on Equality in Employment* (Ottawa: Supply and Services Canada, 1985), p. 525; data for 1981, 1991, and 1993 calculated from Statistics Canada, *Labour Force Annual Averages, 1993*, Cat. No. 71-220 (Ottawa: Minister of Industry, 1994), Table 1, p. A16–A17.

TABLE A.7 *Distribution of Women by Leading Occupational Groups,*
1901–1993 (Percent)

Occupational Group	1901[a]	1911	1921	1931	1941[b]	1951	1961	1971	1981	1993
Personal Service	42.0	37.1	25.8	33.8	34.2	21.0	22.1	22.3	18.3	17.2
Manufacturing and Mechanical[c]	29.6	26.3	17.8	12.7	15.4	14.6	9.9	11.2	9.9	6.3
Professional	14.7	12.7	19.1	17.8	15.7	14.4	15.5	17.5	19.8	23.3
Clerical	5.3	9.4	18.7	17.7	18.3	27.5	28.6	32.7	34.3	27.7
Commercial and Financial[d]	2.4	6.8	8.5	8.3	8.8	10.5	10.2	8.3	10.1	9.7
Managerial[e]	–	–	–	–	–	–	–	3.9	5.5	12.6
Other[f]	6.0	7.8	10.1	9.6	7.7	11.9	13.6	3.8	3.3	3.1
Total[f]	100.0	100.1	100.0	99.9	100.1	99.9	99.9	99.7	101.2	99.9

[a] 10 YEARS OF AGE AND OVER IN 1901; 15 YEARS OF AGE AND OVER IN 1911–1971.

[b] NOT INCLUDING ACTIVE SERVICE, 1941.

[c] INCLUDES STATIONARY ENGINEMEN AND OCCUPATIONS ASSOCIATED WITH ELECTRIC POWER PRODUCTION.

[d] INCLUDES SALESWOMEN.

[e] FIGURES FOR 1901 TO 1961 ARE UNAVAILABLE; BEFORE 1971, THIS CATEGORY WAS INCLUDED UNDER "OTHER."

[f] INCLUDES ARMED FORCES.

Source: Janice Acton, Penny Goldsmith, and Bonnie Shepard, *Women at Work: Ontario, 1850–1930* (Toronto: Canadian Women's Educational Press, 1974), p. 280; Labour Canada, Women's Bureau, *Women in the Labour Force, 1971: Facts and Figures*, Table 14, p. 29; Labour Canada, Women's Bureau, *Women in the Labour Force, Part 1: Participation* (Ottawa: Supply and Services Canada, 1983), Table 9b, p. 33; Labour Canada, Women's Bureau, *Women in the Labour Force, 1990–91* (Ottawa: Supply and Services Canada, 1990), Table 5, p. 19; Statistics Canada, *Women in the Labour Force 1994*, Cat. No. 75-507E (Ottawa: Minister of Industry, 1994), Table 2.8, p. 20.

TABLE A.8 *Female Enrollment as a Percentage of Full-time University Undergraduate Enrollment, Selected Fields of Specialization, 1891–1991*

Field of Specialization	1891	1920	1930	1945	1961	1971	1981	1991
Agriculture	–	1.3	1.1	4.0	4.2	13.1	36.6	45.5
Arts, Science, Letters	21.8	31.6	32.6	26.6	29.3	40.6	49.1	56.8
Commerce and Business Administration	–	3.0	14.3	8.9	7.0	13.9	38.7	45.9
Dentistry	0.0	1.8	1.3	1.2	4.5	7.5	22.7	40.3
Education	–	61.8	64.4	48.0	48.1	55.8	69.2	67.1
Engineering and Applied Sciences	0.0	0.1	0.2	0.6	0.7	2.4	10.6	17.6
Fine and Applied Arts	–	–	91.7	80.6	66.4	53.9	62.2	61.7
Health Professions (misc.)	–	–	–	100.0	82.6	72.7	82.8	61.4
Household Science	–	100.0	100.0	100.0	100.0	98.9	97.2	90.8
Law	0.4	3.7	3.4	4.4	5.3	14.9	39.9	51.2
Mathematics and Physical Sciences	–	–	–	–	–	–	28.1	29.7
Medicine	3.1	4.6	4.2	7.3	9.8	20.3	38.5	45.2
Nursing	–	100.0	100.0	100.0	99.8	97.9	97.4	93.4
Pharmacy	0.0	5.9	6.1	25.9	27.3	52.5	64.2	61.5
Religion and Theology	–	1.9	1.9	2.4	1.3	28.7	30.9	41.1
Veterinary Medicine	0.0	0.0	0.0	2.3	5.9	16.1	48.8	64.3
Unclassified	0.0	–	–	–	55.2	34.0	48.1	53.9
Female % of Total Undergraduate Enrollment	11.6	16.3	23.5	20.8	26.2	37.7	46.7	53.1

Source: Based on data from F.H. Leacy, ed., *Historical Statistics of Canada*, 2nd ed. (Ottawa: Statistics Canada, 1983), W439–455; Statistics Canada, *Universities: Enrolment and Degrees, 1981* (Ottawa: Minister of Industry, 1984), Table 8, pp. 22–23; Statistics Canada, *Universities: Enrolment and Degrees 1991*, Cat. No. 81-204 (Ottawa: Minister of Industry, 1994), Table 8, pp. 44–45.

TABLE A.9 *Degrees Granted by Canadian Universities, 1920–1991*

Academic Year	Bachelor and first professional degrees[a]		Master and licence[b]		Doctorates	
	Total	% Earned by Women	Total	% Earned by Women	Total	% Earned by Women
1920–21	3 627	18.3	218	22.0	24	1
1930–31	5 290	25.3	468	21.4	46	7
1940–41	6 576	24.1	673	10.6	75	5
1950–51	15 754	20.3	1 632	13.9	202	5.5
1960–61	20 240	25.8	2 447	19.0	305	8.5
1970–71	67 200	38.1	9 638	22.0	1 625	9.3
1980–81	86 243	49.5	12 432	37.4	1 738	23
1990–91	114 815	56.5	18 038	47.3	2 947	31.6

[a] INCLUDES EQUIVALENT DIPLOMAS (AS, FOR EXAMPLE, IN THEOLOGY) AND HONOURS DEGREES.

[b] THE LICENCE IN THE FRENCH-LANGUAGE UNIVERSITIES IS THE NEXT DEGREE AFTER THE BACHELOR, AS THE MASTER'S DEGREE IS IN THE ENGLISH-LANGUAGE UNIVERSITIES. THIS CATEGORY EXCLUDES MASTER'S AND LICENCE DEGREES (E.G., IN LAW, OPTOMETRY) THAT ARE IN REALITY THE FIRST PROFESSIONAL DEGREE; THOSE ARE INCLUDED UNDER THAT HEADING.

Source: Daniel Kubat and David Thornton, *A Statistical Profile of Canadian Society* (Toronto: McGraw-Hill Ryerson, 1974), p. 124; Statistics Canada, *Education in Canada: A Statistical Review for 1980–81*, Cat. No. 81-229 (Ottawa: Minister of Industry, 1981), Tables 31–33, pp. 150–54; Statistics Canada, *Education in Canada: A Statistical Review for 1992–93*, Cat. No. 81-229 (Ottawa: Minister of Industry, 1994), Tables 37, 39, 41, pp. 153–63, 167.

List of Acronyms

AFEAS	*Association féminine d'éducation et d'action sociale*
AWIs	Alberta Women's Institutes
BPW	Business and Professional Women's Clubs
CACSW	Canadian Advisory Council on the Status of Women
CARAL	Canadian Abortion Rights Action League (formerly the Canadian Association for the Repeal of the Abortion Laws)
CBC	Canadian Broadcasting Corporation
CCF	Co-operative Commonwealth Federation (later the New Democratic Party)
CCSW	Canadian Committee on the Status of Women
CEGEP	Collège d'enseignement général et professionel
CEQ	*Centrale des enseignants du Québec*
CEW	Committee on Equality for Women
CFBPWC	Canadian Federation of Business and Professional Women's Clubs
CFUW	Canadian Federation of University Women
CGIT	Canadian Girls in Training
CWAC	Canadian Women's Army Corps
DAWN	DisAbled Women's Network
FFQ	*Féderation des femmes du Québec*
FLF	*Front pour la libération des femmes du Québec*
FWIC	Federated Women's Institutes of Canada
FWTAO	Federation of Women Teachers' Associations of Ontario
IMA	India Mahila Association
IODE	Imperial Order Daughters of the Empire
IUD	intrauterine device
LCW	Local Council of Women
LEAF	Legal Education and Action Fund
LES FAM	*Liberté, egalité, sororité: Les femmes acadiennes de Moncton*
LOOT	Lesbian Organization of Toronto
NAC	National Action Committee on the Status of Women
NCWC	National Council of Women of Canada
NDP	New Democratic Party
NFB	National Film Board

NOIVM	National Organization of Immigrant and Visible Minority Women
NWAC	Native Women's Association of Canada
P4W	Prison for Women
PID	pelvic inflammatory disease
PQ	*Parti Québécois*
RCAF	Royal Canadian Air Force
RCMP	Royal Canadian Mounted Police
RCSW	Royal Commission on the Status of Women
REAL Women	Real, Equal, Active, for Life Women
RNAO	Registered Nurses' Association of Ontario
SCM	Student Christian Movement
SGGA	Saskatchewan Grain Growers' Association
SORWUC	Service, Office, and Retail Workers' Union of Canada
TAC	therapeutic abortion committee
TWL	Toronto Women's Liberation
UFWA	United Farm Women of Alberta
VON	Victorian Order of Nurses
VOW	Voice of Women
WAVAW	Women Against Violence Against Women
WCTU	Woman's Christian Temperance Union
WILPF	Women's International League for Peace and Freedom
WIs	Women's Institutes
WLM	women's liberation movement
WMS	Woman's Missionary Society/Women's Missionary Society
YWCA	Young Women's Christian Association

Selected Bibliography

1. BIBLIOGRAPHIES AND HISTORIOGRAPHICAL STUDIES

Andrews, Margaret. "Attitudes in Canadian Women's History 1945–1975." *Journal of Canadian Studies* 12, 4 (Summer 1977), 69–78.

Bradbury, Bettina. "Women's History and Working-Class History." *Labour/Le travail* 19 (Spring 1987), 23–43.

Bradbury, Bettina et al., eds. *Teaching Women's History: Challenges and Solutions.* Athabaska, Alta.: Athabaska University Educational Enterprises, 1995.

Brandt, Gail Cuthbert. "Postmodern Patchwork: Some Recent Trends in the Writing of Women's History in Canada." *Canadian Historical Review* 72, 4 (December 1991), 441–70.

Brouwer, Ruth Compton. "Transcending the 'Unacknowledged Quarantine': Putting Religion into English-Canadian Women's History." *Journal of Canadian Studies* 27, 3 (Fall 1992), 47–61.

Cohen, Yolande. "L'histoire des femmes au Québec 1900–1950." *Recherches sociographiques* 21, 3 (septembre/décembre 1980), 339–45.

Cohen, Yolande, ed. "La recherche universitaire sur les femmes au Québec 1929–1980: Répertoire de thèses de maîtrise et de doctorate déposées, dans les universités du Québec — Présentation thématique." *Resources for Feminist Research/Documentation sur la recherche féministe* 10, 4 (December 1981/January 1982), 5–24.

Conrad, Margaret. "The Re-Birth of Canada's Past: A Decade of Women's History." *Acadiensis* 12, 2 (Spring 1983), 140–62.

Diamond, Sara. *Women's Labour History in British Columbia: A Bibliography, 1930–1948.* Vancouver: Press Gang, 1982.

Fairbanks, Carol, and Sara Brooks Sundberg. *Farm Women on the Prairie Frontier: A Sourcebook for Canada and the United States.* London: Scarecrow, 1983.

Fulford, Margaret, ed. *The Canadian Women's Movement, 1960–1990: A Guide to Archival Resources.* Don Mills: General, 1992.

Gagan, Rosemary R. "Putting Humpty Together Again: The Challenge of Women's History." *British Journal of Canadian Studies* 4, 2 (1989), 276–95.

Gaskell, Jane. "Conception of Skill and Work of Women: Some Historical and Political Issues." *Atlantis* 8, 2 (Spring 1983), 11–26.

Hale, Linda, and Melanie Houlden. "The Study of B.C. Women: A Quarter-Century Review, 1960–1984." *Resources for Feminist Research/Documentation sur la recherche féministe* 15, 2 (July 1986), 58–68.

Jackel, Susan. *Canadian Prairie Women's History: A Bibliographic Survey*. Ottawa: Canadian Research Institute for the Advancement of Women, Paper No. 14 (April 1987), 1–22.

Kinnear, Mary, and Vera Fast. *Planting the Garden: An Archival Bibliography of the History of Women in Manitoba*. Winnipeg: University of Manitoba Press, 1987.

Lemieux, Denise, and Lucie Mercier. *La recherche sur les femmes au Québec: Bilan et bibliographie*. Québec: Institut québécois de recherche sur la culture, 1982.

Lévesque, Andrée. "Historiography: History of Women in Quebec since 1985." *Québec Studies* 12 (Spring/Summer 1991), 83–91.

Light, Beth, and Veronica Strong-Boag. *True Daughters of the North: Canadian Women's History — An Annotated Bibliography*. Toronto: OISE Press, 1980.

Mazur, Carol, and Sheila Pepper. *Women in Canada: A Bibliography, 1965–1982*. Toronto: OISE Press, 1984.

Mitchinson, Wendy. "Women's History." *In* Doug Owram, ed., *Canadian History: A Reader's Guide, Vol. 2: Confederation to the Present*. Toronto: University of Toronto Press, 1994, pp. 202–27.

Parr, Joy. "Nature and Hierarchy: Reflections in Writing in the History of Women and Children." *Atlantis* 11, 1 (Fall 1985), 39–44.

Pedersen, Diana. *Changing Women, Changing History: A Bibliography of the History of Women in Canada*. Toronto: Green Dragon, 1992.

Pierson, Ruth Roach. "Colonization and Canadian Women's History." *Journal of Women's History* 4, 2 (Fall 1992), 134–56.

———. "Experience, Difference, Dominance and Voice in the Writing of Canadian Women's History." *In* Karen Offen, Ruth Roach Pierson, and Jane Rendall, eds. *Writing Women's History: International Perspectives*. Bloomington: Indiana University Press, 1991, pp. 79–106.

———. "Women's History: The State of the Art in Atlantic Canada." *Acadiensis* 7, 1 (Autumn 1977), 121–31.

Pierson, Ruth, and Beth Light. "Women in the Teaching and Writing of Canadian History." *The History and Social Science Teacher* 17, 2 (Winter 1982), 83–95.

Pierson, Ruth, and Alison Prentice. "Feminism and the Writing and Teaching of History." *Atlantis* 7, 2 (Spring 1982), 37–46.

Prentice, Alison. "Writing Women into History: The History of Women's Work in Canada." *Atlantis* 3, 2, part 2 (Spring 1978), 72–83.

Silverman, Eliane Leslau. "Writing Canadian Women's History, 1970–82: An Historiographical Analysis." *Canadian Historical Review* 63, 4 (December 1982), 513–33.

Strong-Boag, Veronica. "Cousin Cinderella: A Guide to Historical Literature Pertaining to Canadian Women." *In* Marylee Stephenson, ed., *Women in Canada*. Toronto: New Press, 1973; rev. ed. Don Mills: General, 1977.

———. "Raising Clio's Consciousness: Women's History and Archives in Canada." *Archivaria* 6 (Summer 1978), 70–82.

———. "Writing about Women." *In* John Schultz, ed. *Writing about Canada: A Handbook for Modern Canadian History*. Scarborough: Prentice-Hall, 1990, pp. 175–200.

Van Kirk, Sylvia. "Toward a Feminist Perspective in Native History." Toronto: Centre for Women's Studies in Education, OISE, Occasional Paper No. 14, 1987.

———. "What Has the Feminist Perspective Done for Canadian History?" *In* Ursula M. Franklin et al., eds., *Knowledge Reconsidered: A Feminist Overview*. Ottawa: Canadian Research Institute for the Advancement of Women, 1984, pp. 43–58.

Van Kirk, Sylvia, ed. "Canadian Women's History: Teaching and Research." Special issue of *Resources for Feminist Research/Documentation sur la recherche féministe* 8, 2 (July 1979), 5–71.

2. COLLECTIONS OF ESSAYS

Acton, Janice, Penny Goldsmith, and Bonnie Shepard, eds. *Women at Work: Ontario 1850–1930.* Toronto: Canadian Women's Educational Press, 1974.

Adelberg, Ellen, and Claudia Currie, eds. *In Conflict with the Law: Women and the Canadian Justice System.* Vancouver: Press Gang, 1993.

Ainley, Marianne G., ed. *Despite the Odds: Essays on Canadian Women and Science.* Montréal: Vehicule, 1990.

Arnup, Katherine, Andrée Lévesque, and Ruth Roach Pierson, eds. *Delivering Motherhood: Maternal Ideologies and Practices in the 19th and 20th Centuries.* London: Routledge, 1990.

Backhouse, Constance, and David H. Flaherty, eds. *Challenging Times: The Women's Movement in Canada and the United States.* Montréal and Kingston: McGill-Queen's University Press, 1992.

Bourne, Paula, ed. *Women's Paid and Unpaid Work: Historical and Contemporary Perspectives.* Toronto: New Hogtown Press, 1985.

Briskin, Linda, and Lynda Yanz, eds. *Union Sisters: Women in the Labour Movement.* Toronto: Women's Press, 1983.

Briskin, Linda, and Patricia McDermott, eds. *Women Challenging Unions: Feminism, Democracy, and Militancy.* Toronto: University of Toronto Press, 1993.

Bristow, Peggy, co-ord., et al. *"We're Rooted Here and They Can't Pull Us Up": Essays in African Canadian Women's History.* Toronto: University of Toronto Press, 1994.

Burnet, Jean, ed. *Looking into My Sister's Eyes. An Exploration in Women's History.* Toronto: Multicultural History Society of Ontario, 1986.

Burt, Sandra, Lorraine Code, and Lindsay Dorney, eds. *Changing Patterns: Women in Canada*, 2nd ed. Toronto: McClelland and Stewart, 1993.

Carty, Linda, ed. *And Still We Rise: Feminist Political Mobilizing in Contemporary Canada.* Toronto: Women's Press, 1993.

Cavanaugh, Catherine A., and Randi R. Warne, eds. *Standing on New Ground: Women in Alberta.* Edmonton: University of Alberta Press, 1993.

Cook, Gail, ed. *Opportunity for Choice: A Goal for Women in Canada.* Ottawa: Statistics Canada, 1976.

Creese, Gillian, and Veronica Strong-Boag, eds. *British Columbia Reconsidered: Essays on Women.* Vancouver: Press Gang, 1992.

Demers, Jeanne, et Lijne McMurray, eds. *Femmes scandales 1965–1985.* Montréal: La nouvelle barre du jour, 1987.

Dodd, Diane, and Deborah Gorham, eds. *Caring and Curing: Historical Perspectives on Women and Healing in Canada.* Ottawa: University of Ottawa Press, 1994.

Dumont, Micheline, et Nadia Fahmy-Eid, eds. *Les couventines: L'éducation des filles au Québec dans les congrégations religieuses enseignantes 1840–1960.* Montréal: Boréal Express, 1986.

Fahmy-Eid, Nadia, and Micheline Dumont, eds. *Maîtresses de maison, maîtresses d'école: Femmes, famille et éducation dans l'histoire du Québec.* Montréal: Boréal Express, 1983.

Giles, Wenona, and Sedef Arat-Koc, eds. *Maid in the Market: Women's Paid Domestic Labour.* Halifax: Fernwood, 1994.

Guildford, Janet, and Suzanne Morton, eds. *Separate Spheres: Women's Worlds in the 19th-Century Maritimes.* Fredericton: Acadiensis Press, 1994.

Hamilton, Roberta, and Michèle Barrett, eds. *The Politics of Diversity: Feminism, Marxism and Nationalism.* Montréal: Book Center, 1986.

Heap, Ruby, and Alison Prentice, eds. *Gender and Education in Ontario: An Historical Reader*. Toronto: Canadian Scholars' Press, 1992.

Iacovetta, Franca, and Mariana Valverde, eds. *Gender Conflicts: New Essays in Women's History*. Toronto: University of Toronto Press, 1992.

Identités féminines: Mémoire et création. Questions de culture 9. Québec: Institut québécois de recherche sur la culture, 1986.

Innis, Mary Quayle, ed. *The Clear Spirit: Twenty Canadian Women and Their Times*. Toronto: University of Toronto Press, 1966.

Jean, Michèle. *Québécoises au XXe siècle*. Montréal: Éditions Le Jour, 1974.

Kealey, Linda, ed. *A Not Unreasonable Claim: Women and Reform in Canada, 1880s–1920s*. Toronto: Canadian Women's Educational Press, 1979.

———. *Pursuing Equality: Historical Perspectives on Women in Newfoundland and Labrador*. St. John's: Institute of Social and Economic Research, Memorial University, 1993.

Kealey, Linda, and Joan Sangster, eds. *Beyond the Vote: Canadian Women and Politics*. Toronto: University of Toronto Press, 1989.

Kinnear, Mary, ed. *First Days, Fighting Days: Women in Manitoba History*. Regina: Canadian Plains Research Centre, University of Regina, 1987.

Lacelle, Elizabeth J., ed. *La femme et la religion au Canada français*. Montréal: Bellarmin, 1979.

Latham, Barbara, and Cathy Kess, eds. *In Her Own Right: Selected Essays on Women's History in B.C.* Victoria: Camosun College, 1980.

Latham, Barbara K., and Roberta J. Pazdro, eds. *Not Just Pin Money: Selected Essays on the History of Women's Work in British Columbia*. Victoria: Camosun College, 1984.

Lavigne, Marie, et Yolande Pinard, eds. *Travailleuses et féministes: Les femmes dans la société québécoise*. Montréal: Boréal Express, 1983.

———. *Les femmes dans la société québécoise: Aspects historiques*. Montréal: Boréal Express, 1977.

Maroney, Heather Jon, and Meg Luxton, eds. *Feminism and Political Economy: Women's Work, Women's Struggles*. Toronto: Methuen, 1987.

Miles, Angela R., and Geraldine Finn, eds. *Feminism: From Pressure to Politics*. Montréal: Black Rose, 1988.

Muir, Elizabeth Gillan, and Marilyn Färdig Whitely, eds. *Changing Roles of Women within the Christian Church in Canada*. Toronto: University of Toronto Press, 1995.

Parr, Joy, ed. *A Diversity of Women: Women in Ontario since 1945*. Toronto: University of Toronto Press, 1995.

Prentice, Alison, and Susan Mann Trofimenkoff, eds. *The Neglected Majority: Essays in Canadian Women's History*. Toronto: McClelland and Stewart, 1985. Vol. 2.

Prentice, Alison, and Marjorie R. Theobald, eds. *Women Who Taught: Perspectives on the History of Women and Teaching*. Toronto: University of Toronto Press, 1991.

Spittal, W.G., ed. *Iroquois Women: An Anthology*. Ohsweken: Irografts, 1990.

Stone, Sharon Dale, ed. *Lesbians in Canada*. Toronto: Between the Lines, 1990.

Strong-Boag, Veronica, and Anita Clair Fellman, eds. *Rethinking Canada: The Promise of Women's History*. Toronto: Copp Clark Pitman, 1986; 2nd ed. 1991.

Trofimenkoff, Susan Mann, and Alison Prentice, eds. *The Neglected Majority: Essays in Canadian Women's History*. Toronto: McClelland and Stewart, 1977. Vol. 1.

Williamson, Janice, and Deborah Gorham, eds. *Up and Doing: Canadian Women and Peace*. Toronto: Women's Press, 1989.

Wine, Jeri Dawn, and Janice L. Ristock, eds. *Women and Social Change: Feminist Activism in Canada*. Toronto: James Lorimer, 1991.

3. DOCUMENTARY COLLECTIONS

Ahenakew, Freda, and H.C. Wolfart. *Kôhkominawak Otâcimowiniwâwa: Our Grandmothers' Lives, as Told in Their Own Words.* Saskatoon: Fifth House, 1992.

Atcheson, Elizabeth, Mary Eberts, and Beth Symes. *Women and Legal Action: Precedents, Resources, and Strategies for the Future.* Ottawa: Canadian Advisory Council on the Status of Women, 1984.

Braithwaite, Rella, and Tessa Benn-Ireland. *Some Black Women: Profiles of Black Women in Canada.* Toronto: Sister Vision, 1993.

Brand, Dionne. *No Burden to Carry: Narratives of Black Working Women in Ontario, 1920–1950s.* Toronto: Women's Press, 1991.

Conrad, Margaret, Toni Laidlaw, and Donna Smyth, eds. *No Place Like Home: Diaries and Letters of Nova Scotia Women, 1771–1938.* Halifax: Formac, 1988.

Cook, Ramsay, and Wendy Mitchinson, eds. *The Proper Sphere: Woman's Place in Canadian Society.* Toronto: Oxford University Press, 1976.

Crnkovich, Mary. *"Gossip": A Spoken History of Women in the North.* Ottawa: Canadian Arctic Resources Committee, 1990.

Fitzgerald, Maureen, Connie Guberman, and Margie Wolfe, eds. *Still Ain't Satisfied!: Canadian Feminism Today.* Toronto: Women's Press, 1982.

Jackel, Susan, ed. *A Flannel Shirt and Liberty: British Emigrant Gentlewomen in the Canadian West 1880–1914.* Vancouver: University of British Columbia Press, 1982.

Light, Beth, and Joy Parr, eds. *Canadian Women on the Move, 1867–1920.* Toronto: New Hogtown Press and OISE Press, 1983.

Light, Beth, and Alison Prentice, eds. *Pioneer and Gentlewomen of British North America, 1713–1867.* Toronto: New Hogtown Press, 1980.

Light, Beth, and Ruth Roach Pierson, eds. *No Easy Road: Women in Canada, 1920s–1960s.* Toronto: New Hogtown Press, 1990.

Monet-Chartrand, Simonne. *Pionnières québécoises et regroupements de femmes d'hier à aujourd'hui.* Montréal: Éditions du remu-ménage, 1990.

O'Leary, Véronique, et Louise Toupin, eds. *Québécoises deboutte! tome 1: Une anthologie de textes du Front de libération des femmes (1969–1971) et du Centre des femmes (1972–1975).* Montréal: Éditions du remue-ménage, 1982.

Pierson, Ruth Roach, et al., eds. *Canadian Women's Issues, Vol. 1: Strong Voices: Twenty-Five Years of Women's Activism in English Canada.* Toronto: James Lorimer, 1993.

————. *Canadian Women's Issues, Vol. 2: Bold Visions.* Toronto: James Lorimer, 1995.

Rasmussen, Linda, et al., eds. *A Harvest Yet to Reap: A History of Prairie Women.* Toronto: Women's Press, 1976.

Sadlier, Rosemary. *Leading the Way: Black Women in Canada.* Toronto: Umbrella Press, 1994.

Silman, Janet [as told to]. *Enough Is Enough: Aboriginal Women Speak Out.* Toronto: Women's Press, 1987.

Silverman, Eliane Leslau. *The Last Best West: Women on the Alberta Frontier, 1880–1930.* Montréal: Eden Press, 1984.

Staton, Pat, and Beth Light. *Speak with Their Own Voices: A Documentary History of the Federation of Women's Teachers' Associations of Ontario and the Women Elementary Public School Teachers of Ontario.* Toronto: FWTAO, 1987.

Women Unite! An Anthology of the Canadian Women's Movement. Toronto: Canadian Women's Educational Press, 1972.

Women's Book Committee, Chinese National Council. *Jin Guo: Voices of Chinese Canadian Women.* Toronto: Women's Press, 1992.

4. MONOGRAPHS

Adamson, Nancy, Linda Briskin, and Margaret McPhail. *Feminist Organizing for Change: The Contemporary Women's Movement in Canada*. Toronto: Oxford University Press, 1988.

Anderson, Grace, and Juanne Clark. *God Calls: Man Chooses: An Analysis of Women's Experience in Canadian Church History*. Burlington, Ont.: Trinity Press, 1990.

Anderson, Karen. *Chain Her by One Foot: The Subjugation of Women in Seventeenth-Century New France*. London: Routledge, 1991.

Armstrong, Pat, and Hugh Armstrong. *The Double Ghetto: Canadian Women and Their Segregated Work*, 3rd ed. Toronto: McClelland and Stewart, 1994.

Arnup, Katherine. *Education for Motherhood: Advice for Mothers in Twentieth-Century Canada*. Toronto: University of Toronto Press, 1994.

Bacchi, Carol. *Liberation Deferred? The Ideas of the English-Canadian Suffragists 1877–1918*. Toronto: University of Toronto Press, 1983.

Backhouse, Constance. *Petticoats and Prejudice: Women and Law in Nineteenth-Century Canada*. Toronto: Osgoode Society, 1991.

Baillargeon, Denyse. *Ménagères au temps de la crise*. Montréal: Éditions du remue-ménage, 1991.

Barry, Francine. *Le travail de la femme au Québec: L'évolution de 1940 à 1970*. Montréal: Université de Québec, 1977.

Bashevkin, Sylvia B. *Toeing the Lines: Women and Party Politics in English Canada*. Toronto: University of Toronto Press, 1985.

Benoit, Cecilia. *Midwives in Passage*. St. John's: Institute of Social and Economic Research, Memorial University, 1991.

Bochachevsky-Choniak, Martha. *Feminists despite Themselves: Women in Ukrainian Community Life, 1884–1929*. Edmonton: Canadian Institute of Ukrainian Studies, University of Alberta, 1988.

Bourne, Paula. *Women in Canadian Society*. Toronto: OISE, 1976.

Boyd, Monica. *Canadian Attitudes toward Women: Thirty Years of Change*. Ottawa: Women's Bureau, Labour Canada, 1984.

Bradbury, Bettina. *Working Families: Age, Gender, and Daily Survival in Industrializing Montréal*. Toronto: McClelland and Stewart, 1993.

Brodie, M. Janine. *Women and Politics in Canada*. Toronto: McGraw-Hill Ryerson, 1985.

Brouwer, Ruth Compton. *New Women for God: Canadian Presbyterian Women and India Missions, 1876–1914*. Toronto: University of Toronto Press, 1990.

Brown, Jennifer. *Strangers in Blood: Fur Trade Company Families in Indian Country*. Vancouver: University of British Columbia Press, 1980.

Burtch, Brian. *Trials of Labour: The Re-Emergence of Midwifery*. Montréal and Kingston: McGill-Queen's University Press, 1994.

Cleverdon, Catherine L. *The Woman Suffrage Movement in Canada*, 2nd ed. Toronto: University of Toronto Press, 1974.

The Clio Collective (trans. Roger Gannon and Rosalie Gill). *Quebec Women: A History*. Toronto: Women's Press, 1987.

Cochrane, Jean, Abby Hoffman, and Pat Kincaid. *Women in Canadian Life: Sports*. Toronto: Fitzhenry and Whiteside, 1977.

Cohen, Marjorie. *Women's Work, Markets, and Economic Development in Nineteenth-Century Ontario*. Toronto: University of Toronto Press, 1988.

Cohen, Yolande. *Femmes de parole: L'histoire des Cercles de fermières du Québec 1915–1990*. Montréal: Éditions Le Jour, 1990.

Le Collectif Clio. *L'histoire des femmes au Québec depuis quatre siècles*, 2e ed. Montréal: Éditions Le Jour, 1992.

Collins, Anne. *The Big Evasion: Abortion, The Issue That Won't Go Away*. Toronto: Lester and Orpen Dennys, 1985.

Comacchio, Cynthia R. *Nations Are Built of Babies: Saving Ontario's Mothers and Children*. Montréal and Kingston: McGill-Queen's University Press, 1993.

Crowley, Terry. *Agnes MacPhail and the Politics of Equality*. Toronto: James Lorimer, 1990.

Cruikshank, Julie. *Life Lived Like a Story: Life Stories of Three Yukon Native Elders*. Vancouver: University of British Columbia Press, 1992.

Daenzer, Patricia. *Regulating Class Privilege: Immigrant Servants in Canada, 1940s–1990s*. Toronto: Canadian Scholars' Press, 1993.

D'Allaire, Micheline. *Les dots des religieuses au Canada français, 1639–1800: Étude économique et sociale*. Montréal: Hurtubise HMH, 1986.

Danylewycz, Marta. *Taking the Veil: An Alternative to Marriage, Motherhood and Spinsterhood in Quebec, 1840–1920*. Toronto: McClelland and Stewart, 1987.

Diamond, Sara. *Chambermaids and Whistlepunks: An Oral History of Women in B.C. Labour 1930–1955*. Vancouver: Press Gang, 1983.

Dranoff, Linda Silver. *Women in Canadian Life: Law*. Toronto: Fitzhenry and Whiteside, 1977.

Dubinsky, Karen. *Improper Advances: Rape and Heterosexual Conflict in Ontario, 1880–1929*. Chicago: University of Chicago Press, 1993.

———. *Lament for a "Patriarchy Lost?" Anti-Feminism, Anti-Abortion, and REAL Women in Canada*. Ottawa: Canadian Research Institute for the Advancement of Women, 1985.

Duley, Margot I. *Where Once Our Mothers Stood We Stand: Women's Suffrage in Newfoundland 1890–1925*. Charlottetown: gynergy books, 1993.

Dumas, Silvio. *Les filles du roi en Nouvelle-France: Étude historique avec répertoire biographique*. Québec: Société d'histoire de Québec, 1972.

Ford, Anne Rochon. *A Path Not Strewn with Roses: One Hundred Years of Women at the University of Toronto, 1884–1984*. Toronto: Governing Council, University of Toronto, 1985.

Fowler, Marian. *The Embroidered Tent: Five Gentlewomen in Early Canada*. Toronto: Anansi, 1982.

Frager, Ruth A. *Sweatshop Strife: Class, Ethnicity, and Gender in the Jewish Labour Movement of Toronto, 1900–1939*. Toronto: University of Toronto Press, 1992.

Gagan, Rosemary R. *A Sensitive Independence: Canadian Methodist Women Missionaries in Canada and the Orient, 1881–1925*. Montréal and Kingston: McGill-Queen's University Press, 1992.

Gagnon, Mona-Josée. *Les femmes vues par le Québec des hommes: 30 ans d'histoire des idéologies, 1940–1970*. Montréal: Éditions Le Jour, 1974.

Gannagé, Charlene. *Double Day, Double Bind: Women Garment Workers*. Toronto: Women's Press, 1986.

Gee, Ellen, and Meredith Kimball. *Women and Aging*. Toronto: Butterworths, 1987.

Gillett, Margaret. *We Walked Very Warily: A History of Women at McGill*. Montréal: Eden Press, 1981.

Griffiths, N.E.S. *The Splendid Vision: Centennial History of the National Council of Women of Canada, 1893–1993*. Ottawa: Carleton University Press, 1993.

Hallett, Mary, and Marilyn Davis. *Firing the Heather: The Life and Times of Nellie McClung*. Saskatoon: Fifth House, 1993.

Harrison, Deborah, and Lucie Laliberté. *There's No Life Like It! Military Wives in Canada*. Toronto: James Lorimer, 1994.

Howard, Irene. *The Struggle for Social Justice in British Columbia: Helena Gutteridge, the Unknown Reformer*. Vancouver: University of British Columbia Press, 1993.

Jean, Marguerite. *Évolution des communautés religieuses de femmes au Canada de 1639 à nos jours*. Montréal: Fides, 1977.

Kinnear, Mary. *In Subordination: Professional Women, 1870–1970*. Montréal and Kingston: McGill-Queen's University Press, 1995.

———. *Margaret McWilliams: An Interwar Feminist*. Montréal and Kingston: McGill-Queen's University Press, 1991.

Kome, Penney. *The Taking of Twenty-Eight: Women Challenge the Constitution*. Toronto: Women's Press, 1983.

Lacelle, Claudette. *Urban Domestic Servants in 19th-Century Canada*. Ottawa: National Historic Parks and Sites, Supply and Services Canada, 1987.

Laforce, Hélène. *Histoire de la sage-femme dans la région de Québec*. Québec: Institut québécois de recherche sur la culture, 1985.

Lamoureux, Jocelyne, Michèle Gélinas, et Katy Tari. *Femmes en mouvement: Trajectoires de l'Association féminine d'éducation et d'action sociale, 1966–1991*. Montréal: Boréal Express, 1993.

Landry, Yves. *Les filles du roi au XVIIe siècle: Orphelines en France, pionnières au Canada*. Montréal: Leméac, 1992.

Lapointe-Roy, Huguette. *Charité bien ordonnée: Le premier réseau de lutte contre la pauvreté à Montréal au 19e siècle*. Montréal: Boréal Express, 1987.

Laurin, Nicole, Danielle Juteau, et Lorraine Duchesne. *À la recherche d'un monde oublié: Les communautés religieuses de femmes au Québec de 1900 à 1970*. Montréal: Le jôur, 1991.

Lemieux, Denise, et Lucie Mercier. *Les femmes au tournant du siècle, 1880–1940: Ages de la vie, maternité et quotidien*. Québec: Institut québécois de recherche sur la culture, 1989.

Lenskyj, Helen. *Out of Bounds: Women, Sport and Sexuality*. Toronto: Women's Press, 1986.

Létourneau, Jeanette. *Les écoles normales de filles au Québec*. Montréal: Fides, 1981.

Lévesque, Andrée. (trans. Yvonne M. Klein.) *Making and Breaking the Rules: Women in Quebec, 1919–1939*. Toronto: McClelland and Stewart, 1994.

Lindström-Best, Varpu. *Defiant Sisters: A Social History of Finnish Immigrant Women in Canada*. Toronto: Multicultural History Society of Ontario, 1988.

Lowe, Graham S. *Women in the Administrative Revolution*. Toronto: University of Toronto Press, 1987.

Luxton, Meg. *More Than a Labour of Love: Three Generations of Women's Work in the Home*. Toronto: Women's Press, 1981.

Luxton, Meg, Harriet Rosenberg, and Sedef Arat Koç. *Through the Kitchen Window: The Politics of Home and Family*, 2nd ed. Toronto: Garamond, 1990.

Martin, Michèle. *"Hello, Central?": Gender, Technology, and Culture in the Formation of Telephone Systems*. Montréal and Kingston: McGill-Queen's University Press, 1991.

McKenna, Katherine M.J. *A Life of Propriety: Anne Murray Powell and Her Family, 1755–1849*. Montréal and Kingston: McGill-Queen's University Press, 1994.

McLaren, Angus, and Arlene Tigar McLaren. *The Bedroom and the State: The Changing Practices and Politics of Contraception and Abortion in Canada, 1880–1980*. Toronto: McClelland and Stewart, 1986.

Mitchinson, Wendy L. *The Nature of Their Bodies: Women and Their Doctors in Victorian Canada*. Toronto: University of Toronto Press, 1991.

Morton, Suzanne. *Ideal Surroundings: Domestic Life in a Working-Class Suburb in the 1920s*. Toronto: University of Toronto Press, 1995.

Muir, Elizabeth Gillan. *Petticoats in the Pulpit: The Story of Early Nineteenth-Century Methodist Women Preachers in Upper Canada*. Toronto: United Church Publishing House, 1991.

Murray, Hilda. *More Than 50%: Women's Life in a Newfoundland Outport, 1900–1950.* St. John's: Breakwater Books, 1979.

Newton, Janice. *The Feminist Challenge to the Canadian Left, 1900–1918.* Montréal and Kingston: McGill-Queen's University Press, 1995.

Nicholson, G.W.L. *Canada's Nursing Sisters.* Toronto: Hakkert, 1975.

Parr, Joy. *The Gender of Breadwinners: Women, Men, and Change in Two Industrial Towns 1880–1950.* Toronto: University of Toronto Press, 1990.

Petitat, André. *Les infirmières: De la vocation à la profession.* Montréal: Boréal Express, 1989.

Pierson, Ruth Roach. *"They're Still Women after All": The Second World War and Canadian Womanhood.* Toronto: McClelland and Stewart, 1986.

Potter-MacKinnon, Janice. *While the Women Only Wept: Loyalist Refugee Women in Eastern Ontario.* Montréal and Kingston: McGill-Queen's University Press, 1993.

Prang, Margaret. *"A Heart at Leisure from Itself": Caroline Macdonald of Japan.* Vancouver: University of British Columbia Press, 1995.

Rayner-Canham, Marlene, and Geoffrey W. Rayner-Canham. *Harriet Brooks: Pioneer Nuclear Scientist.* Montréal and Kingston: McGill-Queen's University Press, 1992.

Razack, Sherene. *Canadian Feminism and the Law: The Women's Legal Education and Action Fund and the Pursuit of Equality.* Toronto: Second Story, 1991.

Rooke, P.T., and R.L. Schnell. *No Bleeding Heart: Charlotte Whitton, A Feminist on the Right.* Vancouver: University of British Columbia Press, 1987.

Ross, Becki. *The House That Jill Built: A Lesbian Nation in Formation.* Toronto: University of Toronto Press, 1995.

Royce, Marion. *Eunice Dyke, Health Care Pioneer.* Toronto: Dundurn Press, 1983.

Sangster, Joan. *Dreams of Equality: Women on the Canadian Left, 1920–1950.* Toronto: McClelland and Stewart, 1989.

———. *Earning Respect: The Lives of Working Women in Small Town Ontario, 1920–1960.* Toronto: University of Toronto Press, 1995.

Snell, James. *In the Shadow of the Law: Divorce in Canada, 1900–1939.* Toronto: University of Toronto Press, 1991.

Stewart, Lee. *"It's Up to You": Women at UBC in the Early Years.* Vancouver: University of British Columbia Press, 1990.

Strange, Carolyn. *Toronto's Girl Problem: The Perils and Pleasures of the City, 1880–1930.* Toronto: University of Toronto Press, 1995.

Strong-Boag, Veronica. *The New Day Recalled: Lives of Girls and Women in English Canada, 1919–1939.* Toronto: Copp Clark Pitman, 1988.

———. *The Parliament of Women: The National Council of Women of Canada 1893–1929.* Ottawa: National Museum's of Canada, 1976.

Sugiman, Pamela. *Labour's Dilemma: The Gender Politics of Auto Workers in Canada, 1937–79.* Toronto: University of Toronto Press, 1994.

Swyripa, Frances. *Wedded to the Cause: Ukrainian-Canadian Women and Ethnic Identity 1891–1991.* Toronto: University of Toronto Press, 1993.

Thivierge, Nicole. *Histoire de l'enseignement ménager-familial au Québec, 1882–1970.* Québec: Institut québécois de recherche sur la culture, 1982.

Thomas, Clara. *Love and Work Enough: The Life of Anna Jameson.* Toronto: University of Toronto Press, 1967.

Tippett, Maria. *Emily Carr: A Biography.* Toronto: Oxford University Press, 1979.

———. *By a Lady: Celebrating Three Centuries of Art by Canadian Women.* Toronto: Viking, 1992.

Tulloch, Elspeth. *We, the Undersigned: A Historical Overview of New Brunswick Women's Political and Legal Status, 1784–1984.* Moncton: New Brunswick Advisory Council on the Status of Women, 1985.

Valverde, Mariana. *The Age of Light, Soap, and Water: Moral Reform in English Canada, 1885–1925.* Toronto: McClelland and Stewart, 1991.

Vandelac, Louise, et Diane Bélisle. *Les dessous domestiques de l'histoire: Quelques aspects de l'évolution de la production domestique du Québec de 1850 à 1960 à la lumière des influences américaines, françaises et anglaises, et éléments d'analyse théorique.* Québec: Conseil du statut de la femme, 1983.

Van de Vorst, Charlotte. *Making Ends Meet: A History of Women's Economic Contributions to the Family Farm in Manitoba.* Winnipeg: University of Manitoba Press, 1992.

Van Kirk, Sylvia. *"Many Tender Ties": Women in Fur Trade Society, 1670–1870.* Winnipeg: Watson and Dwyer, 1980.

Vickers, Jill, Pauline Rankin, and Christine Appelle. *Politics As If Women Mattered: A Political Analysis of the National Action Committee on the Status of Women.* Toronto: University of Toronto Press, 1993.

Ward, Peter. *Courtship, Love, and Marriage in Nineteenth-Century English Canada.* Montréal and Kingston: McGill-Queen's University Press, 1990.

Warne, Randi R. *Literature as Pulpit: The Christian Social Activism of Nellie L. McClung.* Waterloo, Ont.: Wilfrid Laurier University Press, 1993.

White, Julie. *Sisters and Solidarity: Women and Unions in Canada.* Toronto: Thompson Educational Publishing, 1993.

Index

We are interested in your reaction to *Canadian Women: A History*, 2nd edition, by Alison Prentice et al. You can help us to improve this book in future editions by completing this questionnaire.

1. What was your reason for using this book?

   ❏ university course ❏ college course
   ❏ continuing education course ❏ professional development
   ❏ personal interest ❏ other _____

2. If you are a student, please identify your school and the course in which you used this book.

3. Which chapters or parts of this book did you use? Which did you omit?

4. What did you like best about this book?

5. What did you like least about this book?

6. Please identify any topics you think should be added to future editions.

7. Please add any comments or suggestions.

8. May we contact you for further information?

   Name: _____

   Address: _____

   _____

   Phone: _____

(fold here and tape shut)

MAIL POSTE

Canada Post Corporation / Société canadienne des postes

Postage paid
If mailed in Canada

Port payé
si posté au Canada

Business Reply

Réponse d'affaires

0116870399   01

0116870399-M8Z4X6-BR01

Heather McWhinney
Publisher, College Division
HARCOURT BRACE & COMPANY, CANADA
55 HORNER AVENUE
TORONTO, ONTARIO
M8Z 9Z9